AF352670

Canon Law in the Age of Reforms

(*ca.* 1000 to *ca.* 1150)

HISTORY OF MEDIEVAL CANON LAW

Edited by Wilfried Hartmann and Kenneth Pennington

---

*Canonical Collections of the Early Middle Ages (ca. 400–1140):
A Bibliographical Guide to the Manuscripts and Literature*

Papal Letters in the Early Middle Ages

The History of Western Canon Law to 1140

The History of Byzantine and Eastern Canon Law to 1500

*The History of Medieval Canon Law in the Classical Period,
1140–1234*

*The History of Medieval Canon Law in the Late Middle Ages,
1234–1500*

The History of Courts and Procedure in Medieval Canon Law

*A Guide to Medieval Canon Law Jurists and Collections,
1140–1500*

The History of Byzantine and Eastern Canon Law to 1500

Canon Law in the Age of Reforms (ca. 1000 to ca. 1150)

Canon Law in the Age of Reforms (*ca.* 1000 to *ca.* 1150)

Christof Rolker

With contributions by Robert Somerville

The Catholic University of America Press
Washington, D.C.

Copyright © 2023
The Catholic University of America Press

LIBRARY OF CONGRESS CATALOGING-IN-PUBLICATION DATA
Names: Rolker, Christof, 1979– author. | Somerville, Robert, other.
Title: Canon law in the age of reforms (ca. 1000 to ca. 1150) / Christof Rolker ; with contributions by Robert Somerville.
Description: Washington : The Catholic University of America, 2024. | Series: History of medieval canon law | Includes bibliographical references and index. | Summary: "This monograph addresses the history of canon law in Western Europe between ca. 1000 and ca. 1150, specifically the collections compiled and the councils held in that time. The main part consists of an analysis of all major collections, taking into account their formal and material sources, the social and political context of their origin, the manuscript transmission, and their reception more generally"— Provided by publisher.
Identifiers: LCCN 2023046484 (print) | LCCN 2023046485 (ebook) | ISBN 9780813237572 (hardcover) | ISBN 9780813237589 (epub)
Subjects: LCSH: Canon law—History. | Law reform—History.
Classification: LCC KBR160 .R65 2024 (print) | LCC KBR160 (ebook) | DDC 262.9/22—dc23/eng/20231010
LC record available at https://lccn.loc.gov/2023046484
LC ebook record available at https://lccn.loc.gov/2023046485

Contents

Preface

This book has been in the making for a very long time. It originally, in the 1990s, was planned as a multi-author edited volume, but in 2012 Wilfried Hartmann and Kenneth Pennington as the series editors invited me to write a monograph on the pre-Gratian collections of the eleventh and twelfth centuries. It was, and still is, a great honour to have been trusted with this task, and I am also very grateful that the series editors stood by their offer even when I indicated that I was unlikely to begin, let alone finish, the book very quickly as I was working on completely different topics at the time. Indeed, I only began to work on the book after the end of my first paternal leave, with most of its chapters being drafted between 2014 and 2016, when I was working with Andreas Thier at Zurich University on a research project *Changing Medieval Orders of Legal Knowledge*. My move to Bamberg University in 2017 and most pleasantly one more year of paternal leave interrupted my research routine, so that I only returned to writing the *History* in early 2020. Having submitted the manuscript to CUA Press just before Christmas 2020, the publication process was slowed down considerably, partly due to the global pandemic which is still not over as I write these lines.

In the ten years that I spent with this book, my ideas about the subject have changed in many respects. At the beginning I somewhat naively hoped to study all these collections from the manuscripts, and whatever would emerge from this would be interesting enough for my readers. This is not how I wrote the book in the end. To begin with, while the endeavour did provide me the opportunity to study a certain number of manuscripts in the original or at least from good reproductions, there evidently were limits to how many of them I could analyse in detail. There are several cases where this was particularly painful given the large number of unresolved questions on the genesis, development, and diffusion of the collections in question. Especially in the case of the *Collection in Two Books / Eight Parts*, the collections of Deusdedit and Anselm of Lucca, and the *Caesaraugustana* I expect (and hope) that my provisional findings will be checked, supplemented, and corrected by future scholarship. Also, as the footnotes and even the list of manuscripts in the appendix make painfully clear, pragmatic reasons played a much greater role than they should have when it came to selecting the manuscripts I studied. The collections at Bamberg, Cambridge, London, Munich, Paris, and (thanks to its digitization programme) the Vatican were much more easily accessible to me than other archives. I am thankful to the staff at all these places, and should add that my neglect to see comparable numbers of manuscripts kept in other libraries is almost exclusively due to my own laziness. This is particularly true for manuscripts today kept in archives on the Iberian Peninsula, in southern Italy, and in eastern Europe. On a brighter note, in some cases I could restrict myself to the rather modest task of double-checking particular readings, while others had done the real work of searching for, identifying, and collating large numbers of manuscripts in the preparation of critical editions. This is above all true for the Ivonian collections; while I was involved in the project to some degree, my contribution was minute compared to what Martin Brett over the past decades has achieved. His findings fundamentally have changed our understanding of the genesis, transmission, and mutual relation of the collections around Ivo of Chartres. Martin's acumen, his learning, and his generosity are well known to anyone working on canon law history, and I am more than happy to admit that in writing this book, I have profited enormously from his publications, his editions, and his unfailing support.

While I may have spent less time with collating manuscripts than I originally had hoped, rather more time and thinking than expected was needed to contemplate the selection of materials. Some choices were easy; as one can expect from a handbook, all 'major' collections of the period are covered. It would be strange indeed to write a history of pre-Gratian canon law without taking into account, for example, the *Liber decretorum* of Burchard of Worms, the *Collection in 74 Titles*, or the *Panormia*. Yet too narrow a focus on 'major' collections would be problematic. Clearly, the influence of 'minor' collections taken together was very considerable. This is not always evident from the secondary literature, not least because the collections in question are normally studied individually, if at all. The fact that they are not linked to known authors, that their place of origin often remains obscure, and that even their date can frequently be established only very approximately, does not help to attract the attention of many historians. In writing this book, I have tried to overcome the prejudice against these anonymous 'minor' collections, as I firmly believe that the diversity of canon law in the Middle Ages will never be understood properly if we focus on a small corpus of famous collections by known authors. Above all, it was the late Linda Fowler-Magerl (d. 2017) who made me aware of this problem in many discussions I enjoyed with her. It was also she who provided me—and the scholarly world at large—with the most important tool to study many of these collections, namely the invaluable *Clavis canonum* database. Indeed, I have used the *Clavis* database for every single chapter I wrote. Linda has supported my research ever since I began to study the pre-Gratian collections some twenty years ago, and I owe her an enormous debt of gratitude.

Highlighting the diversity of canon law which I have seen in the manuscripts was indeed one goal in writing this book. Another question, which I enjoyed discussing with Martin Brett, Kate Cushing, my dear *Doktorschwester* Danica Summerlin, and many others well before I started writing this book, was how best to organise the material to give a coherent, but not monolithic account of canon law history. A purely chronological arrangement of the individual chapters was out of the question, as was the division of the material into 'reform', 'anti-reform', and 'other' collections, a division which Paul Fournier famously had adopted for the *Histoire des collections canoniques*. My own solution, in the end, was to pay greater attention to the various groups within the Church—the episcopate, regular clergy, cardinals, and so on. In the end, four groups in particular seemed so relevant for the production and use of canonical collections in the period studied here that I devoted separate chapters (Chapters 2–5) to them and their contributions to canon law history: bishops, monks and canons, 'Gregorian' reformers, and the pre-university school masters in France and Italy. As for the reform papacy, I count myself lucky that Robert Somerville agreed to contribute a separate chapter on the papal councils *ca.* 1049 to *ca.* 1179, which demonstrates the importance of these assemblies for the development of canon law in masterly fashion. I have to thank him not only for providing these pages, and a very smooth cooperation at all stages of the work, but also for many discussions on all things canon law from which I have profited time and again.

It is my hope that this division of material will help us to better understand how canon law was an integral part of social change, and in particular how the collections assembled in the eleventh and twelfth centuries interacted with the changing fabric of the Church in Western Europe. The point is not that some of the collections examined here were partisan or even polemical; this is indeed the case, but the discussion will also make clear that the most important contributions to the history of canon law were not the collections compiled by the most zealous reformers, but rather those that could be used by different groups within the Church. As already indicated, there is still much for future scholars to do.

Any reader who wishes to use this book or one of its chapters as a starting point for the study of individual collections should have at hand Kéry's indispensable manual (the first volume in the *History of Medieval Canon Law* series), Fowler-Magerl's *Clavis canonum*, and her handbook of the same title. The next volume on such a reader's desk should probably be Fournier's *Histoire*; not only is it the most influential monograph on pre-Gratian canon law, but its condensed style and powerful arguments provide both clear guidance for the beginner and food for thought for the initiated. For more modern research, the other volumes of the *History of Medieval Canon Law* and various volumes in the *Great Christian Jurists* series provide an excellent starting point. Indeed, a number of very good books have appeared since the manuscript was completed in 2020, including a second edition of Brundage's *Medieval Canon Law*, revised by Melodie H. Eichbauer, the *Cambridge History of Medieval Canon Law* edited by Anders Winroth and John C. Wei, and David d'Avray's important study of *Papal Jurisprudence 385–1234*, a book I very much regret not having been able to take it into account.

Research evidently goes on, and if this book helps to bring some of the research findings of the last three or four decades to the attention of a wider readership, it will have achieved its goal. Reading all these wonderful studies and thankfully using the critical editions has been a pleasure in itself. Writing this book gave me the opportunity to reconsider many questions I have been pondering since I first became acquainted with medieval canon law as a graduate student. It was a great pleasure to discuss many questions with friends and colleagues around the world, whether they concerned the definition of 'canon law' or the punctuation of individual canons. In addition to those already mentioned, Evangelos Chrysos, Roy Flechner, Adriaan Gaastra, Michela Galli, Lotte Kéry, Rob Meens, Przemysław Nowak, John S. Ott, Steven Schoenig, Andreas Thier, and Anders Winroth kindly shared their thoughts, and often also research materials, with me; I want to thank them all for their generosity. Needless to say, all remaining errors are my own.

Bamberg, 7 September 2022
C.R.

Abbreviations

Canonical Collections

The titles and sigla by which medieval canonical collections are referenced can sometimes be confusing. Anonymous collections in particular are often given titles referring to their supposed place of origin, the current location of important manuscripts, or the division of the materials into books; this, however, has given rise to many homonymous collections (e.g. three *Collectiones Sangermanenses* and *Collections in Nine Books* each), and scholarly consensus about the place of origin and/or the division into books sometimes may change (e.g. in the case of the *Collection in 17 Books* / *Collection of Saint-Hilaire-le-Grand*, which is neither divided into seventeen books nor certainly from Saint-Hilaire). In addition, the use of both Latin and various modern languages for titles and abbreviations, and also diverging traditions concerning the use of Roman numbers, further multiply the ways any given collection may be referred to (*'Collection in Three Books'*, *'Drei-Bücher-Sammlung'*, *'3L'*, *'Coll. IIIL.'*).

In the present book, I have tried to use the most common titles consistently, preferring English titles where they exist. Titles referring to names of persons oder places are normally in Latin, especially in the footnotes and the register, where I use shorter forms (*'Dionysiana'* rather than *'Collectio Dionysiana'* or 'Collection of Dionysius Exiguus'). For the numerous collections only known by their division into books, parts, or titles, I often use sigla based on the Latin titles (*3L*, *10P*, *74T*, and so on), especially in the footnotes. In some cases, I have extended conventional sigla for the sake of disambiguation ('Berlin *13L*' and 'Vatican *13L*', for example). For the few collections attributed to known authors, I retain the traditional titles of the collections but in the footnotes simply cite them by the name of the compiler.

To cite specific canons, I quote the collection by author (or short title), book, and canon number ('Anselm 2.1', '*3L* 2.34'). For edited collections, the numbers are those of the editions unless otherwise stated; for other collections, I follow the division of canons in the *Clavis canonum* database unless otherwise stated. Small letters after the canon number indicate subdivisions within canons, often marked by an 'item' in the manuscripts (*'TC*

c. 129c'); additional canons found in some but not all manuscripts are designated by added capital letters ('Burchard 3.15A').

For quotations from printed editions the editors' names and page numbers are given; for full bibliographical details see the list below. If and only if texts are quoted from or checked against the manuscripts, shelf marks and folio numbers are provided. Where information on a specific canon is derived from the *Clavis canonum* database, an additional (hyperlinked) reference using the *Clavis* sigla is given (e.g. '<u>LP0146</u>'; for these sigla, see Fowler-Magerl's book or https://data.mgh.de/databases/clavis/db/).

The following list explains all sigla and short titles used for canonical collections. For all collections available in print, it also provides bibliographical details of the edition used in the present study.

2L/8P	The so-called *Collection in Two Books / Eight Parts*, partly ed. Jean Bernhard, 'La collection en deux livres (Cod. Vat. lat. 3832),' *Revue de Droit canonique* 12 (1962), 9–601. Commonly referred to simply as *Collection in Two Books*.
3L	*Collectio canonum trium librorum*, ed. Giuseppe Motta (2 vols. MIC Corpus collectionum 8; Vatican City 2005/08).
4L	The *Collection in Four Books* (unedited), a derivative of *74T*, sometimes referred to as *Collection in Three (Four) Books* in the pre-1983 literature.
5L	The Beneventan *Collection in Five Books*, partly edited in *Collectio canonum in v libris (lib. I–III)*, ed. Mario Fornasari (CCCM 6; Turnhout 1970).
7L (Turin)	The *Collection in Seven Books* in Torino, BNU, D.IV.33 (unedited).
7L (Vienna)	The *Collection in Seven Books* in Wien, Österreichische Nationalbibliothek, 2186, Vat. lat. 1346, and Cortona, BC, 43 (unedited).
9L (San Pietro)	The *Collection in Nine Books* in Città del Vaticano, Archivio del Capitolo di San Pietro, C. 118, a derivative of *3L* (unedited).
9L (Vatican)	The *Collection in Nine Books* in Vat. lat. 1349 (unedited).
9L (Wolfenbüttel)	The *Collection in Nine Books* in Wolfenbüttel, HAB, Cod. Guelf. 212 Gud. lat. and Ghent, BU, 235, also known as *Collection de Thérouanne* or *Collectio Sangermanensis IX voluminum* (unedited).

10P	The *Collection in Ten Parts*, or sometimes *Collectio X (IX) partium*, extant in several manuscripts; essentially an enlarged version of the *Panormia* (unedited).
10P (Cologne)	Another collection in ten parts, extant only in Köln, Historisches Archiv, 199 (unedited).
12P	The *Collection in Twelve Parts*, closely related to Burchard (unedited).
13L (Berlin)	The *Collection in Thirteen Books* in Berlin, SBPK, Savigny 3 (unedited).
13L (Vatican)	The *Collection in Thirteen Books* in Vat. lat. 1361 (unedited); it is sometimes referred to as a copy of Anselm's *Collectio*.
17L	The *Collection in Seventeen Books*, also known as *Collection of Saint-Hilaire-le-Grand* (unedited).
20L	The *Collection in Twenty Books* in Vat. lat. 1350 (unedited).
74T	*Diuersorum patrum sententie siue Collectio in LXXIV titulos digesta*, ed. John T. Gilchrist (MIC Corpus collectionum 1; Vatican City 1973); it also is translated as *The Collection in Seventy-Four Titles: A Canon Law Manual of the Gregorian Reform*, tr. John T. Gilchrist (Mediaeval Sources in Translation 22; Toronto 1980).
183T	The *Collection in 183 Titles*, also known as *Collection of Santa Maria Novella*, available in a critical edition: *Liber canonum diuersorum sanctorum patrum siue Collectio in CLXXXIII titulos digesta*, ed. Giuseppe Motta (MIC Corpus collectionum; Vatican City 1988).
Abbo	Abbo of Fleury, *Collectio canonum* (PL 139.473–508).
Alger of Liège	Alger's *Liber de misericordia et iustitia*, ed. Robert Kretzschmar in idem, *Alger von Lüttichs Traktat 'De misericordia et iustitia'. Ein kanonistischer Konkordanzversuch aus der Zeit des Investiturstreits: Untersuchungen und Edition* (Quellen und Forschungen zum Recht im Mittelalter 2; Sigmaringen 1985), 187–375.
Ambrosiana I / II / III	The three Milanese collections studied (and partly edited) by Giorgio G. Picasso, *Collezioni canoniche milanesi del secolo XII* (Pubblicazioni dell'Università cattolica del S. Cuore. Saggi e ricerche. Scienze storiche 2; Milan 1969).

Anselm	Unless indicated otherwise indicated, the *Collectio* of Anselm of Lucca is quoted in the 'A' version, almost completely edited in *Anselmi episcopi Lucensis collectio canonum una cum collectione minore*, ed. Friedrich Thaner (Innsbruck 1915). Other versions are quoted from the manuscripts.
Anselmo dedicata	The *Collectio Anselmo dedicata*, partly edited by Jean Claude Besse, *Histoire des textes du droit de l'Église au Moyen-Age de Denys à Gratien: Collectio Anselmo dedicata: étude et texte* (Paris 1960) and idem, 'Collectionis "Anselmo dedicata" liber primus' *Revue de Droit canonique* 9 (1959) 207–296; the Roman law parts are edited in Giuseppe Russo, *Tradizione manoscritta di Leges romanae nei codici dei secoli IX e X della Biblioteca capitolare di Modena* (Modena 1980).
Arsenal I/II	The two separate collections which must have been behind Paris, Bibliothèque de l'Arsenal, 713, fols. 117–192 (unedited).
Atto	The *Breviarium* (or *Capitulare*) of Atto of San Marco, edited as 'Attonis cardinalis presbyteri Capitulare seu Brevarium canonum: ex codice Vaticanum', *Scriptorum veterum nova collectio e Vaticanis codicibus edita*, ed. Angelo Mai (10 vols. Rome 1825–38) 6.2:60–100.
Barberiniana	The materials in Barb. lat. 538 labelled *Collectio canonum Barberiniana* and edited by Giuseppe Fornasari, 'Collectio canonum Barberiniana' *Apollinaris* 36 (1963) 127–141 (description) and 214–297 (edition).
Bonizo	Bonizo von Sutri, *Liber de vita christiana*, ed. Ernst Perels (Texte zur Geschichte des römischen und kanonischen Rechts im Mittelalter 1; Berlin 1930).
Britannica	The *Collectio Britannica* in London, BL, Add. MS 8873 (unedited).
Burchard	Unless otherwise stated, Burchard's *Liber decretorum* (also known as his *Decretum*) is quoted from the *editio princeps*, available online and as a reprint: *Decretorum libri XX* [...]. *Ergänzter Neudruck der editio princeps Köln 1548*, ed. Gérard Fransen and Theo Kölzer (Aalen 1992). The reprint also contains Burchard's preface not found in the *editio princeps*.
Burdegalensis	The *Burdegalensis*, occasionally also referred to as (Bordeaux) *Collection in Seven Books*. The collection is unedited, but see the analysis in Kriston R. Rennie, *The Collectio Burdegalensis: A Study and Register of an Eleventh-Century Canon Law Collection* (Medieval Law and Theology 6; Toronto 2013).

Caes. I/II/III	The three versions of the *Collectio Caesaraugustana* (all unedited).
Capitula Angilramni	Karl-Georg Schon, *Die Capitula Angilramni. Eine prozessrechtliche Fälschung Pseudoisidors* (MGH Studien und Texte 39; Hanover 2006).
Casinensis	*Collectio canonum Casinensis*, ed. Roger E. Reynolds in idem, *The Collectio canonum Casinensis duodecimi seculi (Codex terscriptus). . .: A Derivative of the South-Italian Collection in Five Books: An Implicit Edition with Introductory Study* (PIMS Studies and Texts 137 / Monumenta Liturgica Beneventana 3; Toronto 2001).
Catalaunensis I/II	The two versions of the *Collectio Catalaunensis* (unedited).
Collectio Lanfranci	The collection attributed to Lanfranc of Bec (unedited).
correctores Romani	See below s.v. Gratian.
Cresconius	Ed. in Klaus Zechiel-Eckes, *Die Concordia canonum des Cresconius. Studien und Edition* (2 vols. Freiburger Beiträge zur mittelalterlichen Geschichte 5; Frankfurt 1992).
Deusdedit	*Die Kanonessammlung des Kardinals Deusdedit, vol. 1: Die Kanonessammlung selbst*, ed. Victor Wolf von Glanvell (Paderborn 1905) [all published]. All quotations are by book number, canon number as found in the edition, and (in brackets) canon number as found in manuscript.
editio Romana	See below s.v. Gratian.
Farfensis	*Collectio canonum regesto Farfensi inserta*, ed. Theo Kölzer (MIC Corpus collectionum 5; Vatican City 1982).
Gratian	
editio Romana	The Ordinary Gloss and the comments of the *correctores Romani* to Gratian are quoted from *Decretum Gratiani emendatum et notationibus illustratum una cum glossis. Gregorii XIII pontificis maximi iussu editum, ad exemplar Romanum diligenter recognitum* (Rome 1582).
Gratian 1	The first recension of the *Decretum* as analysed by Anders Winroth; quoted from the provisional edition (5 October 2019 version) by Winroth et al. available at www.gratian.org.

Gratian 2	The second recension of the *Decretum*; quoted from *Decretum magistri Gratiani*, ed. Emil Friedberg (Corpus iuris canonici 1; Leipzig 1879).

Individual canons in Gratian

D.1 c.2	Distinctio 1, capitulum 2
C.2 q.3 c.4	Causa 2, questio 3, capitulum 4
d.a.c. / d.p.c. 5	dictum ante/post capitulum 5

Hibernensis	Edited and translated in Roy Flechner, *The Hibernensis* (2 vols. SMCL 17; Washington, D.C. 2019).
Hinschius	See below s.v. Pseudo-Isidore.
Hispana	*La colección canónica Hispana*, ed. Gonzalo Martínez Díez and Félix Rodríguez (6 in 7 vols. Monumenta Hispaniae sacra. Series canonica 1–6; Madrid 1966–2002).
Ivo	Ivo of Chartres, *Decretum*, ed. Martin Brett at https://ivo-of-chartres.github.io/ (date/revision stamp: 2015-09-23 / 898fb).
Ordinary Gloss	See above s.v. Gratian.
Panormia	The Pseudo-Ivonian *Panormia*, ed. Martin Brett and Bruce Brasington at https://ivo-of-chartres.github.io/ (date/revision stamp: 2015-09-23 / 898fb).
Polycarpus	The *Polycarpus* compiled Gregory of San Grisogono. A provisional edition by Carl Erdmann and Uwe Horst is available at https://www.mgh.de/de/mgh-digital/digitale-angebote-zu-mgh-abteilungen; the page numbers quoted are that of the pdf file.
Pragensis I	The canonical collection in Praha, Universitní Knihovna, VIII.H.7; siglum 'PR' in the *Clavis* database.
Pseudo-Isidore	For the sake of convenience, the Pseudo-Isidorian forgeries are normally quoted from *Decretales Pseudo-Isidorianae et Capitula Angilramni*, ed. Paul Hinschius (Leipzig 1863). A new edition is prepared by Eric Knibbs (MGH, Munich).
Quadripartitus	The ninth-century collection analysed in Franz Kerff, *Der Quadripartitus. Ein Handbuch der karolingischen Kirchenreform. Überlieferung, Quellen und Rezeption* (Quellen und Forschungen zum Recht im Mittelalter 1; Sigmaringen 1982).

Quadripartitus (saec. XII)	The Latin collection of English laws made early in the twelfth century, first edited by Felix Liebermann, *Quadripartitus. Ein englisches Rechtsbuch von 1114* (Halle 1892).
Regino	*Reginonis abbatis Prumiensis libri duo de synodalibus causis et disciplinis ecclesiasticis*, ed. Friedrich Wilhelm Hermann Wasserschleben (Leipzig 1840). An almost complete critical edition is found in *Das Sendhandbuch des Regino von Prüm*, ed. and tr. Wilfried Hartmann (FSGA 42; Darmstadt 2004).
Sandionysiana	An early version of *74T* from Saint-Denis extant only in Paris, BnF, nouv. acq. lat. 326 (unedited).
Sangermanensis	The early medieval collection edited by Michael Stadelmaier in idem, *Die Collectio Sangermanensis XXI titulorum. Eine systematische Kanonessammlung der frühen Karolingerzeit: Studien und Edition* (Frankfurt 2004) 121–351. Not to be confused with the Wolfenbüttel *Collection in Nine Books* (on which see above).
Sinemuriensis	The collection in Semur-en-Auxois, BM, M. 13 and a handful of other manuscripts (unedited); also referred to as as *Collection de Semur-en-Auxois* or, rarely, *Collectio Remensis* (unedited).
Tarraconenesis I/II	The two versions of the *Collectio Tarraconensis* (unedited). Sometimes referred to as *Liber Tarraconensis* or *Collection in Seven Books* in the older literature.
Taurinensis	The collection in Torino, BNU, E.V.44 (unedited).
TC	The collection found in Paris, BnF, lat. 13368 (siglum 'TC' in the *Clavis* database) and other manuscripts, analysed in Christof Rolker, 'Genesis and influence of the canon law collection in BN lat. 13368', ZRG Kan. Abt. 91 (2005) 74–105.
Toletana	*Collectio Toletana: A Canon Law Derivative of the South-Italian Collection in Five Books: An Implicit Edition with Introductory Study*, ed. Douglas Adamson and Roger E. Reynolds (PIMS Studies and Texts 159; Toronto 2008).
Tripartita	The *Collectio Tripartita* (or *Collectio trium partium*) sometimes attributed to Ivo of Chartres, ed. Martin Brett and Przemysław Nowak at https://ivo-of-chartres.github.io/ (date/revision stamp: 2015-09-23 / 898fb). The first two parts are referred to together as 'Tripartita A', the last part as 'Tripartita B'.

Other Abbreviations

Abh. Akad. […]	Abhandlungen der […] Akademie […] (see below)
ACA	Archivo General de la Corona de Aragón
ACO	Acta conciliorum oecumenicorum
AHC	*Annuarium Historiae Conciliorum*
AKKR	*Archiv für katholisches Kirchenrecht*
Barb. lat.	Città del Vaticano, Biblioteca Apostolica Vaticana, Codices Barberiniani latini
BC	Biblioteca comunale
BEC	*Bibliothèque de l'École des chartes*
BL	British Library
BM	Bibliothèque municipale (see below)
BMCL	*Bulletin of Medieval Canon Law, New series*
BML	Biblioteca Medicea Laurenziana
BN	Biblioteca Nacional / Biblioteca Nazionale
BNC	Biblioteca Nazionale Centrale
BnF	Bibliothèque nationale de France
BNU	Biblioteca Nazionale Universitaria

Böhmer, *Regesta imperii*

	Böhmer-Frech	*Papstregesten 1046–1058*, bearbeitet von Karl Augustin Frech (J. F. Böhmer, Regesta imperii Abt. III, Band 5, Teil 1; Vienna, Cologne, and Weimar 2011).
	Böhmer-Herbers	*Papstregesten 844–858*, bearbeitet von Klaus Herbers (J. F. Böhmer, Regesta imperii Abt. I, Band 4, Teil 2, Lieferungen 1–2; Vienna, Cologne, and Weimar 1999/2012).
	Böhmer-Unger	*Papstregesten 872–882 (Johannes VIII.)*, bearbeitet von Veronika Unger (J. F. Böhmer, Regesta imperii Abt. I, Band 4, Teil 3. Vienna, Cologne, and Weimar 2013).
	Böhmer-Zimmermann	*Papstregesten 911–1024*, bearbeitet von Harald Zimmermann (J. F. Böhmer, Regesta imperii Abt. II, Band 5; 2nd edition Cologne, Weimar, and Vienna 1998).

BP	Biblioteca Pública del Estado
BU	Bibliothèque Universitaire / Biblioteca Universitaria
C.Th.	*Theodosiani libri xvi cum constitutionibus Sirmondianis*, ed. Paul Krüger and Theodor Mommsen (Berlin 1905).
Catalogue général	*Catalogue général des manuscrits des Bibliothèques publiques de France* (116 vols. Paris 1849–1993).
CC	Corpus Christianorum
	CCCM Continuatio mediaevalis
	CCL Series latina
	COGD Conciliorum Oecumenicorum Generaliumque Decreta
CCC	Corpus Christi College, College Library
CFC	Church, Faith and Culture in the Medieval West
Cgm	München, Bayerische Staatsbibliothek, Codices germanici Monacenses
CHR	*Catholic History Review*
Clavis database	The database first published with Linda Fowler-Magerl, *Clavis canonum: Selected Canon Law Collections Before 1140: Access with Data Processing* (MGH Hilfsmittel 21; Hanover 2005). An updated version is now found online at https://data.mgh.de/databases/clavis/db/.
Clm	München, Bayerische Staatsbibliothek, Codices latini Monacenses
Cod.	*Codex Iustinianus*, ed. Paul Krüger (Corpus Iuris Civilis 2; 15th edition Berlin 1970).
COD	*Conciliorum Oecumenicorum Decreta*, ed. Giuseppe Alberigo, Péricles-Pierre Joannou, Claudio Leonardi, and Paulo Prodi (Freiburg 1962; 3rd edition Bologna 1973).
COGD	Conciliorum Oecumenicorum Generaliumque Decreta
CPL	Eligius Dekkers, *Clavis patrum latinorum* (CCL; 3rd edition Steenbrugge 1995).
CSEL	Corpus Scriptorum Ecclesiasticorum Latinorum
CSS	Variorum Collected Studies Series
DA	*Deutsches Archiv für die Erforschung des Mittelalters*
Dig. / Digest	*Digesta*, ed. Theodor Mommsen and Paul Krüger (Corpus Iuris Civilis 1; 22nd edition Berlin 1973).

Ep(p).	*Epistola(e)*
Epitome Juliani	*Epitome Latina novellarum Iustiniani*, ed. Gustav Hänel (Leipzig 1873).
Fournier, *Mélanges*	Paul Fournier, *Mélanges de droit canonique*, ed. Theo Kölzer (2 vols. Aalen 1983).
Fowler-Magerl, *Clavis*	Linda Fowler-Magerl, *Clavis canonum: Selected Canon Law Collections Before 1140: Access with Data Processing* (MGH Hilfsmittel 21; Hanover 2005).
FSGA	Freiherr-vom-Stein-Gedächtnisausgabe, Reihe A: Ausgewählte Quellen zur deutschen Geschichte des Mittelalters
Gallia pontificia 3	Beate Schilling, *Gallia pontificia. Répertoire des documents concernant les relations entre la papauté et les églises et monastères en France avant 1198, vol. 3: Province ecclésiastique de Vienne* (3 vols. Göttingen 2006–18).
Germania pontificia	*Germania pontificia sive repertorium privilegiorum et litterarum a Romanis pontificibus ante annum MCLXXXXVIII Germaniae ecclesiis monasteriis civitatibus singulisque personis concessorum* (Göttingen 1911–) [ongoing].
GW	*Gesamtkatalog der Wiegendrucke* (Berlin 1925–) and https://gesamtkatalogderwiegendrucke.de/ (especially for all 'M' numbers).
HAB	Herzog-August-Bibliothek
Hefele-Leclercq	Henri Leclercq's augmented translation of the second edition of the *Conciliengeschichte* by Karl Joseph von Hefele (and, for two volumes, Joseph Hergenröther) published as Charles Joseph Hefele, *Histoire des conciles d'après les documents originaux: nouvelle traduction française faite sur la deuxième édition allemande corrigée et augmentée* [...] (11 in 22 vols. Paris 1907–49).
Histoire	Paul Fournier and Gabriel Le Bras, *Histoire des collections canoniques en Occident, dépuis les Fausses Décrétales jusqu'au Décret de Gratien* (2 vols. Paris 1931/32).
HMCL	History of Medieval Canon Law
Inst. / Institutes	*Institutiones*, ed. Theodor Mommsen and Paul Krüger (Corpus Iuris Civilis 1; 22nd edition Berlin 1973).
Isidore, *Etym.*	The *Etymologies* of Isidore of Seville: *Isidori Hispalensis episcopi etymologiarum sive originum libri XX*, ed. Wallace M. Lindsay (2 vols. Oxford Classical Texts; Oxford 1911).

Italia pontificia	*Italia pontificia sive repertorium privilegiorum et litterarum a Romanis pontificibus ante annum MCLXXXXVIII Italiae ecclesiis monasteriis civitatibus singulisque personis concessorum*, ed. Paul Fridolin Kehr et al. (10 vols. Göttingen 1906–75).
Jaffé	The second and third editions of the *Regesta pontificum*; individual entries are quoted by Jaffé numbers:
	JK, JE, JL *Regesta pontificum romanorum ab condita ecclesia ad annum post Christum natum MCXCVIII*, ed. Philipp Jaffé, rev. second ed. by Samuel Löwenfeld, Friedrich Kaltenbrunner, and Paul Ewald (2 vols. Leipzig 1885/88).
	J³ *Regesta pontificum Romanorum: ab condita ecclesia ad annum post Christum natum MCXCVIII*, ed. Philipp Jaffé, rev. third ed. Klaus Herbers (4 vols. Göttingen 2016–19).
JEH	*Journal of Ecclesiastical History*
Kéry	Lotte Kéry, *Canonical Collections of the Early Middle Ages (ca. 400–1140): A Bibliographical Guide to the Manuscripts and Literature* (HMCL; Washington, D.C. 1999).
Liber pontificalis	*Le Liber pontificalis: texte, introduction et commentaire*, ed. Louis Duchesne (2 vols. Bibliothèque des Écoles françaises d'Athènes et de Rome, 2e série; Paris 1886/92).
Life and Thought	Cambridge Studies in Medieval Life and Thought
Maassen, *Quellen*	Friedrich Maassen, *Geschichte der Quellen und der Literatur des canonischen Rechts im Abendlande bis zum Ausgange des Mittelalters. Vol. 1: Die Rechtssammlungen bis zur Mitte des 9. Jahrhunderts* [all published] (Graz 1870).
Mansi	*Sacrorum conciliorum nova et amplissima collectio*, ed. Giovanni Domenico Mansi (31 vols. Venice 1758–78).
MGH	Monumenta Germaniae Historica
	Briefe dt. Kaiserzeit Briefe der deutschen Kaiserzeit
	Capit. Capitularia
	Capit. episc. Capitularia episcoporum
	Conc. Concilia
	Conc. suppl. Concilia. Supplementa
	Const. Constitutiones et acta publica imperatorum et regum

	DD	Diplomata
	Deutsches Mittelalter	Deutsches Mittelalter. Kritische Studientexte
	Epp.	Epistolae (in Quart)
	Epp. sel.	Epistolae selectae
	Fontes iuris	Fontes iuris Germanici antiqui in usum scholarum separatim editi
	Ldl	*Libelli de lite imperatorum et pontificum saeculis XI. et XII. conscripti*, ed. Ernst Dümmler, Lothar von Heinemann, Friedrich Thaner, and Ernst Sackur (3 vols. Hanover 1891–97).
	LL	Leges
	Necr.	Necrologia Germaniae
	Ordines	Ordines de celebrando concilio
	SS	Scriptores
	SS rer. Germ.	Scriptores rerum Germanicarum in usum scholarum separatim editi
	SS rer. Germ. N.S.	Scriptores rerum Germanicarum, Nova series
MIC		Monumenta Iuris Canonici
Miscellanea		Miscellanea del Centro di studi medioevali
MS		*Mediaeval Studies*
NA		*Neues Archiv der Gesellschaft für ältere deutsche Geschichtskunde*
Nachrichten Akad. […]		Nachrichten der […] Akademie […] (see below)
N.F.		Neue Folge
Nov. / Novels		*Novellae*, ed. Rudolf Schöll and Wilhelm Kroll (Corpus Iuris Civilis 3; 10th edition Berlin 1972).
NRHDFE		*Nouvelle revue historique de droit français et étranger*
Ottobon. lat.		Città del Vaticano, Biblioteca Apostolica Vaticana, Codices Ottoboniani latini
Pal. lat.		Città del Vaticano, Biblioteca Apostolica Vaticana, Codices Palatini latini
PG		*Patrologiae graecae cursus completus*, ed. Jacques-Paul Migne (161 vols.; Paris 1857–66).
PIMS		Pontifical Institute of Mediaeval Studies

PL	*Patrologiae latinae cursus completus*, ed. Jacques-Paul Migne (221 vols.; Paris 1844–64).
Potthast	*Regesta pontificum romanorum inde ab a. post Christum natum MCXVIII ad a. MCCCIV*, ed. August Potthast (2 vols. Berlin 1874/75).
Proceedings [...]	The proceedings of the International Congress of Medieval Canon Law published in the MIC Subsidia series since 1965 are quoted by the venue and year of the congress, the series volume number, and the page number (e.g. '*Proceedings Munich 1992* MIC Subsidia 10.149').
PS	The *Pauli Sententiae*, edited as 'Iulii Pauli libri quinque sententiarum ad filium' *Ulpiani liber singularis regularum / Pauli libri quinque sententiarum / Fragmenta minora*, ed. Paul Krüger (Collectio librorum iuris anteiustiniani in usum scholarum 2; Berlin 1878), 41–137.
QF	*Quellen und Forschungen aus italienischen Archiven und Bibliotheken*
Reg.	The registers of Gregory I and Gregory VII.
Reg. lat.	Città del Vaticano, Biblioteca Apostolica Vaticana, Codices Reginenses latini
Reg. Vat.	Città del Vaticano, Archivio Apostolico Vaticano, Registra Vaticana
Regesta Imperii	See above s.v. Böhmer.
Regesta pontificum	See above s.v. Jaffé.
SB	Staatsbibliothek
SBPK	Staatsbibliothek Preußischer Kulturbesitz
Sb. Akad. [...]	Sitzungsberichte der [...] Akademie [...] (see below)
Settimane	Settimane di studio del Centro italiano di studi sull'alto medioevo
SMCL	Studies in Medieval and Early Modern Canon Law
UB	Universitätsbibliothek
Vat. lat.	Città del Vaticano, Biblioteca Apostolica Vaticana, Codices Vaticani latini
WH	The Walther-Holtzmann-Kartei, available at https://www.kuttner-institute.jura.uni-muenchen.de/holtzmann_formular.htm

ZRG	*Zeitschrift der Savigny-Stiftung für Rechtsgeschichte*
	Kan. Abt. *Kanonistische Abteilung*
	Rom. Abt. *Romanistische Abteilung*

Abh., *Nachrichten*, and *Sb. Akad.* are used for the serial publications of the academies of Berlin, Göttingen, Munich, and Vienna; in each case, the abbreviations are understood to refer to the subseries for the humanities ('Historisch-philosophische Klasse' etc.).

The *Proceedings* of the International Congress of Medieval Canon Law are abbreviated in the notes and the bibliography (see above).

Library names are often abbreviated in the notes and the register, using conventional abbreviations (BAV, BM, BN, BnF, and so on) and traditional names; thus, some 'médiathèques' are quoted as 'BM', and university libraries are quoted as 'BU' or 'UB' only. The bibliography provides full names in all cases.

Canon Law in the Age of Reforms

(*ca.* 1000 to *ca.* 1150)

I

Canon Law and Canonical Collections

An Introduction

1.1 'Canon id est regula': A Medieval Definition

The present study is mainly about the canonical collections compiled in Latin Europe between the late tenth and the mid-twelfth century, before or at least independently of the *Decretum Gratiani*. They are commonly labelled 'pre-Gratian collections' in recognition of the importance of Gratian as 'the father of the science of canon law'.[1] Indeed, the compilation of the *Decretum Gratiani* around 1140 together with its wide reception in the course of the twelfth century was a turning point in legal history. For the period before, this also implies that one should not assume that 'canon law' meant the same as in the so-called classical period of canon law (*ca.* 1140 to 1234), let alone in modern times.

So what was 'canon law' in pre-Gratian times? This question is a difficult one, partly because before the twelfth century there was little if any legal theory.[2] In the following, three different approaches will be used

---

1. Stephan Kuttner, 'The Father of the Science of Canon Law' *The Jurist* 1 (1941) 2–19.

2. Charles Munier, *Les sources patristiques du droit de l'église du VIIIe au XIIIe siècle* (Mulhouse 1957), here at 210; Stephan Kuttner, *Harmony from Dissonance: An Interpretation of Medieval Canon Law* (The Wimmer Lecture 10; Latrobe, Penn. 1960), here at 7–8; Wilfried Hartmann, 'Autoritäten im Kirchenrecht und Autorität des Kirchenrechts in der Salierzeit', *Gesellschaftlicher und ideenge-*

to answer this question. First, and very briefly, the medieval semantics of 'canon' will be studied; second, an early medieval text addressing the question of 'canonical authority' will be analysed; and finally, the prefaces of canonical collections will be used to establish what the compilers chose to tell their readers about 'canon law'.

Let us therefore begin with the term 'canon'. It is a medieval, and indeed an ancient term to refer to texts claiming normative authority in the Church.[3] As in modern usage, it can designate both a set of canonical texts ('the biblical canon') and single texts or indeed portions of such texts ('Nicaea, canon 1'). In medieval usage, biblical books were canonical (or not), there was a 'canon' of councils which merited particular reverence, and later papal letters were attributed 'an authority not unlike that of the councils'.[4] The widely-quoted *Etymologies* of Isidore of Seville are a good example how broadly the term was understood.[5] Isidore explains the Greek κανών with the Latin term 'regula'; according to him, a canon is a rule, a ruler, or indeed a 'measuring rod' for the right (Christian) way of life.[6]

From this, one can deduce that a 'canon' was a text claiming normative validity—but as the use of 'canonical' for biblical books and councils implies, 'canonical authority' depended also on the reception of these

---

schichtlicher Wandel im Reich der Salier, ed. Stefan Weinfurter and Hubertus Seibert (Die Salier und das Reich 3; Sigmaringen 1991) 425–446; Christoph H. F. Meyer, *Die Distinktionstechnik in der Kanonistik des 12. Jahrhunderts. Ein Beitrag zur Wissenschaftsgeschichte des Hochmittelalters* (Mediaevalia Lovaniensia. Studia 29; Leuven 2000), esp. 12; Martin Brett, 'Finding the Law: The Sources of Canonical Authority Before Gratian', *Law Before Gratian: Law in Western Europe c. 500–1100: Proceedings of the Third Carlsberg Academy Conference on Medieval Legal History*, ed. Per Andersen et al. (Copenhagen 2007) 51–72; Christof Rolker, 'Kollisionen und Interferenzen in den Sammlungen des kanonischen Rechts (8.–12. Jahrhundert)', *Kollision und Interferenz normativer Ordnungen im frühen und hohen Mittelalter*, ed. Stefan Esders and Karl Ubl (Vorträge und Forschungen; Ostfildern) [forthcoming].

3. As Ohme established, κανών (and later 'canon') from early on referred not only to dogma but also to discipline: Heinz Ohme, *Kanon ekklesiastikos. Die Bedeutung des altkirchlichen Kanonbegriffs* (Berlin 1998).

4. On this important formula and its history up to and including the *Hispana*, see Dominic Moreau, 'Non impar conciliorum extat auctoritas: l'origine de l'introduction des lettres pontificales dans le droit canonique', *L'étude des correspondances dans le monde romain de l'Antiquité classique à l'Antiquité tardive: permanences et mutations*, ed. Janine Desmulliez et al. (Travaux et recherches 3; Lille 2010) 487–509. It is first found in JK 255; for an edition see Klaus Zechiel-Eckes, *Die erste Dekretale. Der Brief Papst Siricius' an Bischof Himerius von Tarragona vom Jahr 385 (JK 255). Aus dem Nachlass herausgegeben von Detlev Jasper* (MGH Studien und Texte 55; Hanover 2013).

5. See Isidore, *Etym.* 6.1–16 (ed. Lindsay) for a biblical canon (*Etym.* 6.1 and 2), the 'canon of the Gospels' (*Etym.* 6.15) and, immediately afterwards, the 'canon of councils' (*Etym.* 6.16). For a translation, see *The Etymologies of Isidore of Seville*, tr. Stephen A. Barney et al. (Cambridge 2006), here at 142–143.

6. Isidore, *Etym.* 6.16.1 (ed. Lindsay): '*Canon* autem Graece, Latine *regula* nuncupatur. Regula autem dicta quod recte ducit, nec aliquando aliorsum trahit. Alii dixerunt regulam dictam vel quod regat, vel quod normam recte vivendi praebeat, vel quod distortum pravumque quid corrigat.' The same definition is also found in the *Hispana* preface (ed. Martínez Díez and Rodriguez 1.46) and other prefaces to canonical collections.

materials. For this reason already, the body of canonical texts in principle could change over time,[7] and so it did. In the case of the 'canons' under discussion in this book, the most important aspect of their reception was their insertion into canonical collections. These works in turn were called 'canonical' because of the authority of the normative texts they contained, not because they derived their authority from any form of promulgation.[8] In other words, the authority of individual norms and the works that contained them was intertwined.

So 'canon law' in the Middle Ages was not a code of ecclesiastical laws, but a diverse body of normative texts the Church had come to accept as authoritative. Indeed, the sources of the collections studied in the following chapter included the Bible, conciliar canons, and papal decretals, but also material from very different backgrounds: exegetical literature, penitential books, pre-Christian and Christian Roman law, royal legislation, monastic rules, episcopal capitularies, hagiography, sermons, and liturgical books. These were the 'sacred scriptures and canons' priests administering penance and bishops acting as judges had to know.[9]

1.2 The Sources of the Law: The Case of a Not-So-Innocent Canon

In principle, therefore, 'canon law' in the Middle Ages was found in a large body of canonical texts of very diverse nature. For the compilers of the collections studied in the present volume, these were the sources of the law. Every collection was the result of selecting, omitting, rearranging, and sometimes reworking a large number of canons which itself was only a small selection from these sources. Making available canons in such collections on the one hand presented them as uniform, as far as all canons included were (implicitly at least) accorded canonical authority. On the other hand, such collections of canons coming from diverse backgrounds—divine scriptures, councils, papal letters, and so on—also made the differences between the canons evident to any diligent reader. Large collections in particular could, somewhat paradoxically perhaps, affirm the canonical authority of the normative texts they assembled while at the same time calling the authority of single texts into question simply because they also included other, and divergent, materials on the same issue

---

7. See already Isidore, *Etym.* 6.16.10 (ed. Lindsay).

8. Stephan Kuttner, '*Liber canonicus*: A Note on the "Dictatus papae" c. 17' *Studi Gregoriani* 2 (1947) 387–401, esp. at 387.

9. Toledo IV c. 24, as found in very many pre-Gratian collections (e.g. Burchard 1.100; *editio princeps*, fol. 15ra): 'Sciant igitur sacerdotes scripturas sacras et canones [. . .].'

from different sources. From early on, therefore, there were attempts to give some order to the texts that had to be consulted in order to help pastors and judges 'finding the law'.[10]

One such text, which will be taken as an example here, was a canon often attributed to Pope Innocent I.[11] It first surfaced in the eighth century, but only from the early eleventh century on was it received into many canon law collections, including those compiled by Burchard of Worms (d. 1025), Ivo of Chartres (d. 1115), and Gratian.[12] Its earliest version (that of the *Hibernensis*) reads as follows:[13]

> Innocent says concerning sources [*causae*] in which there is authority to loose and bind: These are the twenty-two books of the Old Testament and the four Gospels together with all the writings of the Apostles. Should an answer not present itself, turn to the divine texts that are called 'Hagiographa' in Greek. If you do not find the answer in them, reach for the catholic histories of the catholic Church, written by catholic doctors. If they do not have it, examine the canons of the apostolic see. If they do not have it, observe the examples of saints after having acutely searched for them. But if, after consulting all of these, the essence of the matter is not clearly revealed, convene the elders of the province and ask them. For something is more easily found if sought from many of one mind. For the true surety, the Lord, said: 'Should two of you come together upon the earth in my name, concerning anything whatsoever they shall ask, it shall be done for them'.[14]

10. See Gérard Fransen, *Les collections canoniques* (Typologie des sources du moyen âge occidental 10; Turnhout 1973), here at 8 and Brett, 'Finding'.

11. JK †320 (CPL 1641). See Fransen, *Collections canoniques* 8; idem, 'L'aspect religieux du droit', *Chiesa, diritto e ordinamento della «Societas Christiana» nei secoli XI e XII: atti Mendola 1983* (Miscellanea 11; Milan 1986) 159–170, here at 163–164; Bruce Clark Brasington, '"Congrega seniores provinciae": A Note on a Hiberno-Latin Canon Concerning the Sources of Authority in Ecclesiastical Law', *Plenitude of Power: The Doctrines and Exercise of Authority in the Middle Ages: Essays in Memory of Robert Louis Benson*, ed. Robert C. Figueira (CFC; Aldershot 2006) 1–10; Greta Austin, *Shaping Church Law Around the Year 1000: The Decretum of Burchard of Worms* (CFC; Farnham and Burlington 2009), here at 85–87; Brett, 'Finding' 55; Roy Flechner, *The Hibernensis* (2 vols. SMCL 17; Washington, D.C. 2019), here at 1.67*–68*.

12. *Hibernensis* 19.1 (ed. Flechner 1.111); Burchard 3.128 (*editio princeps*, fol. 68vb); Bonizo, *Liber* 4.131 (ed. Perels 174); Deusdedit 1.109 (90) (ed. Wolf von Glanvell 83); *Britannica* (London, BL, Add. MS 8873, fol. 184v); Ivo 4.70 (ed. Brett); *Tripartita* B6.3 (ed. Brett and Nowak); *Polycarpus* 7.2.4 (ed. Erdmann and Horst 747); Gratian 2, D.20 c.3 (ed. Friedberg 66). Note that it is not in Gratian 1. See below for details.

13. *Hibernensis* 19.1 (ed. Flechner 1.111): 'Innocentius dicit de causis in quibus solvendi ligandique auctoritas est: XXII librorum veteris testamenti, IIII quoque evangeliorum cum totis apostolorum scriptis. Si non appareat, ad divina recurrito scripta, que grece agiographa dicuntur. Si nec invenies in illis, ad catholice aeclesie historias catholicas doctoribus catholicis scriptas manum mitte. Si nec in his, canones apostolicae sedis intuere. Si nec in istis, sanctorum exempla perspicaciter explorata inspice. Quod si his omnibus inspectis huius questionis qualitas non lucide investigatur, seniores provinciae congrega et eos interroga. Facilius namque invenitur quod a plurimis in unum sentientibus queritur. Verus enim repromissor Dominus ait: "Si duo ex vobis conueniant super terram in nomine meo de omni re quamcumque petierint fiet illis" [Mt. 18.19].'

14. Translation largely adopted from Flechner, *Hibernensis* 2.556. For a translation based on Gratian 2 (D.20 c.3), see Gratian, *The Treatise on Laws (Decretum DD. 1–20): Translated by Augustine*

It is characteristic that many of the terms used here are difficult to trans-late[15]—and that the whole canon is found in several versions in various collections from the *Hibernensis* to the *Decretum Gratiani*. The two phe-nomena are related, as the textual vagrancy has to do with different inter-pretations of the passage; problems to make sense of the text were both cause and effect of its instability. From this it is evident that already in the Middle Ages the canon meant different things to different readers, and hence the textual history deserves closer attention.

Some of the textual variants are rather significant. The first sentence, for example, in later versions contains a 'non' or 'minime', and sometimes even a double negative.[16] Other changes are rather subtle, but do affect the meaning; in the case of *causae*, the meaning changes completely without any change to the letter of the text, as will be argued in the following.

Let us look at the textual history of Pseudo-Innocent sentence by sen-tence. The first difficult term (after *causae*) is *agiographa* as a designation of the third part of the Old Testament.[17] This meaning seems to have been obscure to some medieval readers, as it was changed and glossed already

Thompson with the Ordinary Gloss Translated by James Gordley and an Introduction by Katherine Chris-tensen (SMCL 2; Washington, D.C. 1993), here at 86. This translation is based on the 1582 Roman edition of Gratian and the *Glossa ordinaria* (quoted as *editio Romana* in the following); yet it omits the reference to the Old Testament as found in the *editio Romana*, col. 115 ('in libris Veteris Testa-menti'). For Gratian's text and its history, also see below (note 21).

15. See Flechner, *Hibernensis* 1.67* on *causae* (as 'sources'); for Gratian's version of the text, however, the best translation is 'cases' as in Fransen, 'Aspect religieux' 163 and Gratian, *Treatise on Laws* 86. See also Flechner, *Hibernensis* 1.68* on *seniores provinciae* (with the meaning 'presbyters' in some manuscripts) and 111 (apparatus) on *provincia* itself, which could also be translated as 'kingdom'.

16. Deusdedit 1.109 (90) (ed. Wolf von Glanvell 83): 'De causis, de quibus auctoritas minime in libris veteris testamenti et quattuor Evangeliorum cum scriptis totis Apostolorum apparet: ad divina recurrito scripta.' *Polycarpus* 7.2.4 (ed. Erdmann and Horst 475): 'De quibus nulla solvendi ligandique auctoritas in libris veteris testamenti et IIIIor evangeliorum cum scriptis totis apostol-orum non apparet, ad divina recurrito scripta Grece.'

17. Flechner, *Hibernensis* 2.556 n. 151 seems to be the first to have spelt out that 'agiographa' refers to the third division of the Old Testament books. However, the way the *Hibernensis* uses the term, it does not seem to refer to a subset of the Old Testament books as, for example, Saint Jerome had done. Maybe the confusion is with the *Hibernensis* compiler, or the main text of the *Hibernensis*; as Flechner (ibid.) further relates, the whole passage has a parallel to Cummian's Easter letter: 'For a whole year, Cummian says, he studied what various authorities had to say about the date of Easter: first he consulted the Old and the New Testaments, then he inquired into the practices of the Hebrews, Greeks, "Latins" and Egyptians, afterwards he sought advice from the writings of Greek and Latin Fathers (Origen, Jerome, Cyprian, Gregory) and only then he resorted to convening a synod.' The parallel to Cummian's letter is important, and extends to the quotation Dt. 32.7 (*Cummian's Letter*, ed. Walsh and Ó Cróinín 90), but does not explain the 'hagiographa'; if anything, Cummian seems to have consulted 'Greek holy writings' (specifically, Origen's *Homilia in Leviticum*). Cummian also mentions synodal legislation (*Cummian's Letter*, ed. Walsh and Ó Cróinín 68, 70, 72, 86, and 88) and 'canonical statutes of the fourfold apostolic see' (ibid. 71). The genuine letter by Innocent that may have served as a model for the forgery (JK 293) contains a biblical canon, but does not mention 'agiographa'.

in copies of the *Hibernensis*,[18] and the whole phrase was changed in later collections. In Burchard and many later collections, the phrase 'divine texts called "Hagiographa" in Greek' was changed into the more straightforward 'Greek holy scriptures'.[19] Deusdedit in his collection renders it as 'holy scripture'.[20] Both variants already alter the meaning significantly. In Gratian, the phrase was turned into a warning *not* to look up 'Greek divine writing'.[21] In all of these collections from Burchard to Gratian, the *Hibernensis*' reference to 'twenty-two' books of the Old Testament was dropped too; as a side effect of this, the '(Greek) holy scriptures' appear to be extra-biblical books.[22]

18. Flechner's manuscripts **A** ('agiographia') and **O** ('id est sancta scripta'), respectively: *Hibernensis* 19.1 (ed. Flechner 1.111), apparatus.

19. In Burchard 3.128 (*editio princeps*, fol. 68vb, here checked against Bamberg, SB, Msc.Can.6, fol. 92vb, Freiburg, UB, Hs. 7, fol. 94vb, and Frankfurt, UB, Ms. Barth. 50, fol. 91vb) the canon reads as follows: 'Ex decretis Innocentii pape, cap. XVIII. De causis de quibus nulla solvendi ligandique auctoritas in libris veteris testamenti, quatuor Evangeliorum, cum scriptis totis apostolorum non appareat, ad divina recurrito scripta Graece. Si nec in illis, ad catholicae Ecclesiae historias catholicas [catholicasque, ms Freiburg] a doctoribus catholicis scriptas manum mitte [Si nec in illis – mitte *om. sed add in marg.* ms Frankfurt]. Si nec in illis, canones apostolicae sedis intuere. Si nec in his, sanctorum exempla perspicaciter recordare. Quod si in [*om.* ms Bamberg] his omnibus inspectis huius questionis qualitas non lucide investigatur, seniores provinciae congrega et eos interroga. Facilius namque invenitur, quod a pluribus sentientibus quaeritur. Verus enim repromissor, Dominus, ait: Si duo ex vobis vel tres conveniant super terram in nomine meo, de omni re quancumque petierint, fiet illis a patre meo.' Burchard seems to have taken the canon directly from the *Hibernensis* accordning to Hartmut Hoffmann and Rudolf Pokorny, *Das Dekret des Bischofs Burchard von Worms. Textstufen – Frühe Verbreitung – Vorlagen* (MGH Hilfsmittel 12; Munich 1991), here at 195. The chapter number introduced by Burchard's spurious inscription ('cap. 18') may well have been inspired by the place of the canon in the *Hibernensis* (as the only canon in book 19).

20. Deusdedit 1.109 (90) (ed. Wolf von Glanvell 83): 'divina scripta'. The end of the canon is also different here; it seems to conflate the standard version as found in Burchard with a reading found in some *Hibernensis* manuscripts. In Flechner's manuscripts **H**, **V**, and (interlineally) **O**, the last sentence ('seniores provinciae congrega et eos interroga') is rendered as 'interroga patrem tuum et adnuntiabit [annuntiauit **V**] tibi presbiteros tuos et dicent tibi', a paraphrased citation of Dt. 32.7 (ed. Flechner 1.111). Deusdedit has 'seniores provinciae congrega et iusta illud interroga patrem tuum et annuntiabit tibi presbiteros tuos et dicent tibi' (ed. Wolf von Glanvell 83). Deusdedit's version is also found in *Caes.* 2.4.

21. Gratian 2, D.20 c.3 (ed. Friedberg 66): 'De quibus causis nulla solvendi ligandique auctoritas in libris Veteris Testamenti, quatuor Evangeliorum cum totis scriptis Apostolorum appareat, non ad divina recurratur scripta greca.' Friedberg does not report that any of his 'Gratian 2' manuscripts lacked the 'non'. Late medieval Gratian manuscripts and early prints seem to lack it, though. See Frankfurt, UB, Ms. Barth. 7, fol. 14vb ('ad divina recurrite scripta greca') and the Mainz 1472 printed edition [GW 11353], here at fol. 20r ('ad divina recurratur scripta greca'). The Roman edition of Gratian and the *Glossa ordinaria*, finally, gives a mixed version. It has 'divina scripta graeca' in the main text, with the variant reading 'grece'; the Gloss in this edition paraphrases this as referring to 'Graecorum scriptura', and quotes Huguccio, who inserts 'scriptura Greca' *after* papal decretals: *editio Romana*, col. 115. See Tatsushi Genka, 'Hierarchie der Texte, Hierarchie der Autoritäten. Zur Hierarchie der Rechtsquellen bei Gratian' ZRG Kan. Abt. 95 (2009) 101–127.

22. Both Burchard's and Gratian's version of the canon seem to juxtapose the biblical writings (the Old Testament, the Gospels, and the writings of the Apostles) to 'Greek holy scripture', while the *Hibernensis* in this order listed twenty-two books of the Old Testament, the Gospel, the writings of the Apostles, and *hagiographa* (i.e. the third division of the Old Testament).

The next authorities mentioned are the 'catholic histories of the catholic Church, written by catholic doctors'. Again, it may not have been clear to every reader which writings were referred to exactly. Many readers would have thought of the writings of patristic 'doctors' such as Saint Augustine, but it is difficult to determine this with any precision. Given that there was an intense debate in the eleventh and twelfth centuries over the respective authority of patristic sentences and (recent) papal legislation,[23] the fact that the 'catholic doctors' are mentioned before the popes is noteworthy. Whatever the precise meaning of the sentence, and the relevance of its position within the Pseudo-Innocentian text, the *Polycarpus* dropped the whole sentence.[24]

Only in the following sentence, decretal letters ('canons of the apostolic see') are mentioned. Like the preceding sentence, this sentence too is missing in an important branch of the transmission including the *Decretum Gratiani*. Given the discussions on the status of papal legislation just mentioned, such lacunae are potentially very significant. In the case of the *Decretum Gratiani*, the missing part of the Innocent canon can be explained by the formal source Gratian (Gratian 2, to be precise) relied on.[25] Later readers clearly felt something missing; anonymous glossators reintroduced papal decretals in the list of canonical authorities. Significantly, though, they achieved this not by changing the text of the *Decretum* but by way of a (rather stretched) comment.[26] Only in the sixteenth century, the *correctores Romani* indeed emended Gratian's text.[27]

Finally, Pseudo-Innocent advised, if searching all these books failed to provide an answer, to 'convene the elders of the province and ask them'. If the 'elders' are indeed bishops, and not priests,[28] and if gathering the 'elders of the province' meant 'celebrating a synod' (as one could infer), the

23. For an excellent analysis, see Genka, 'Hierarchie'.

24. *Polycarpus* 7.2.4 (ed. Erdmann and Horst 475). In at least one copy of Burchard (Frankfurt, UB, Ms. Barth. 50, fol. 91vb) the sentence was dropped too, but added at the lower margin and marked for insertion by the same scribe.

25. Gratian 1 did not yet contain D.20 c.3. Gratian 2 (ed. Friedberg 66) lacks the reference to the 'canones apostolicae sedis'. This is probably due to the use of the *Tripartita* B6.3 by Gratian 2, as some *Tripartita* manuscripts already have this gap. See Brett's edition for his manuscripts **RSWNBP**: https://ivo-of-chartres.github.io/tripartita/trip_b_a.pdf (date/revision stamp 2014-06-03 / b8a41).

26. As Fransen, 'Aspect religieux' 164 observed, the *Glossa ordinaria* 'reintroduced' papal decretals by glossing 'scriptis totis apostolorum' by 'Apostolorum id est Apostolicorum' (here checked against Frankfurt, UB, Ms. Barth. 7, fol. 14vb and the 1472 Mainz edition [GW 11353], fol. 20r).

27. The *correctores Romani* restored the phrase from the *Polycarpus*, see *editio Romana*, cols. 117/118 s.v. 'Canones'.

28. The *Glossa ordinaria* has 'seniores, id est sapientes' and cross-references to D.84 c.6 ('Presbiteri seniores dicuntur'): *editio Romana*, col. 115/116 n. i. Flechner's manuscripts **H**, **V**, and **O** replace the reference to 'seniores' by a biblical reference to priests, see Flechner, *Hibernensis* 1.67*. Note the parallel to Cummian (*Cummian's Letter*, ed. Walsh and Ó Cróinín 90).

question remained what the province in question was? The way the *Hibernensis* defined the term in the very next canons,[29] it could well mean 'kingdom',[30] but most later readers almost certainly understood the phrase as referring to a synod of a metropolitan and his suffragan bishops. (This in itself could mean very different things, given the different size of dioceses; the province of Mainz stretched from the Alps to the North Sea, while many Italian cathedral churches were less than a day's march aparat.) As for the reasons why convening the 'elders' helped to find a solution, readers were faced with slightly different explanations in different collections; some stressed unanimity, others placed hope on large numbers attending.[31]

To sum up, while the 'Innocent' canon was relatively widely spread, and indeed does address the issue of different levels of authority in canon law, one should not imagine that it expressed too uniform a consensus on how to deal with the different sources of the law. While it does offer a 'relatively straightforward formula for settling disputed issues',[32] the text itself called for interpretation, and is found in different versions in various collections. The canon may have helped some medieval readers to cope with the multiple sources of canon law, but it manifestly confused others; its textual instability up to the twelfth century (and beyond) adds to the impression that canon law, and even single canons, were understood differently by different readers in the Middle Ages.

1.3 'In uno volumine redigere': Prefaces to Canonical Collections

Another way to study what 'canon law' meant to the compilers of pre-Gratian collections is to study the prefaces that were written for, or at least travelled with, these collections.[33] Almost invariably, the compilers

---

29. According to *Hibernensis* 20.1–2 (ed. Flechner 1.112), a province is defined by having 'one law, one language, one rule' and 'ten *civitates* and one king and three lesser ones under him and one bishop and other lesser ones' (tr. Flechner 2.557).

30. Brasington, 'Congrega seniores' 3; Flechner, *Hibernensis* 2.557 n. 154.

31. *Hibernensis* 19.1 (ed. Flechner 1.111) stressed unanimity: 'Facilius namque invenitur quod a plurimis in unum sentientibus queritur.' In Burchard (and Bonizo), this has become 'quod a pluribus sentientibus queritur'. Ivo's *Decretum* 4.70 seems to be the first collection to have 'a pluribus senioribus'; *Tripartita* B6.3 and Gratian 2 have Ivo's version. This variant may be inspired by the 'seniores' mentioned in the sentence before (in the *Hibernensis* as well as in the other collections). Deusdedit 1.109 (90) (ed. Wolf von Glanvell 83) has 'a plurimis unum sentientibus', a change perhaps informed by the *Hibernensis*. In the *Polycarpus* and the *Britannica*, the canon is shorter and lacks this sentence completely.

32. Brett, 'Finding' 55.

33. See Robert Somerville and Bruce Clark Brasington, *Prefaces to Canon Law Books in Latin Christianity: Selected Translations, 500–1245* (New Haven and London 1998) for translations of all

stressed that they had benefited the reader by bringing together canons from a multitude of sources 'into one volume'; rarely, however, they engaged with the question of what 'canon law' was. Sometimes they quoted the Isidorian definition of 'canon' discussed earlier in this chapter; more frequently, they drew up a list of legal sources. At least indirectly, these lists give an idea of how 'canon law' was understood in the early and high Middle Ages. Starting with Dionysius Exiguus, these catalogues almost invariably mention decretal letters and conciliar legislation, and often also the so-called *Canones Apostolorum*. Pseudo-Isidore provided an important model for many high medieval collections in this respect.[34] Other sources, in contrast, are often used without being explicitly mentioned. The *Hibernensis*, for example, draws heavily on the Bible—mainly the Old Testament— for its canons, but does not mention it in the preface; Burchard of Worms, in contrast, only in one case took a canon directly from the Bible, but included the Old Testament in the (incomplete) list of sources in his preface.

Generally, the collections compiled from the tenth century on drew on more diverse sources than the earlier collections, but the prefaces often did not reflect this change. The *Anselmo dedicata*, for example, in eight of its twelve books has a separate section reserved for Roman law, but in the preface does not mention Roman law.[35] Other compilers went further by also disguising the origin of texts taken from secular legislation. Famously, Burchard of Worms did not mention secular legislation in his preface and in his collection changed the inscriptions of all excerpts taken from secular law so as to make them appear as coming from ecclesiastical sources.[36] In practice, this mainly concerned texts taken from royal capitularies. Excerpts from Charlemagne's *Admonitio generalis*, for example, appear as

---

prefaces mentioned here. See also Bruce Clark Brasington, 'Prologues to Canonical Collections as a Source for Jurisprudential Change to the Eve of the Investiture Contest' *Frühmittelalterliche Studien* 28 (1994) 226–242.

34. For the Latin text and its sources, see Emil Seckel, *Die erste Zeile Pseudoisidors, die Hadriana-Rezension In nomine domini incipit praefatio libri huius und die Geschichte der Invokationen in den Rechtsquellen. Aus dem Nachlaß mit Ergänzungen hrsg. von Horst Fuhrmann* (Sb. Akad. Berlin 1959.4; Berlin 1959) and Horst Fuhrmann, 'Pseudoisidor und die Bibel' DA 55 (1999) 183–191, here at 189–191.

35. The *Anselmo dedicata* in its preface (tr. Somerville and Brasington, *Prefaces* 93) mentions 'the teachings of the sacred canons, which from the earliest days of the Christian faith the masters of the holy, catholic Church, namely, the apostles and the popes, have set down in their writings.' While conciliar decisions are mentioned later on ('the canons, councils, and decretals of the Fathers'), Roman law is not.

36. Hoffmann and Pokorny, *Dekret* 159; Austin, *Shaping* esp. 122–126. See already Paul Fournier, 'Le Décret de Burchard de Worms: ses caractères, son influence' *Revue d'histoire ecclésiastique* 12 (1911) 451–473 and 670–701, here at 456.

canons from the councils of Orléans, Soissons, and Rouen.[37] Interestingly, Burchard did the same with texts coming from episcopal capitularies. Many compilers simply ignored capitularies as a source when compiling their collections; on the whole, Frankish capitularies did not provide many texts found in pre-Gratian canon law collections.[38] A third source that was treated with some reservations by many compilers of pre-Gratian canon law collections were penitentials. These books were certainly important for many compilers of canon law collections, and even more so for the ecclesiastical judges and pastors using any of these collections, but since Carolingian times their authenticity had also been subject to sometimes heated debate.[39] The polemic against a 'Roman penitential' in the preface to the *Breviarium* of Atto of San Marco belongs to this tradition,[40] and relatively few canon law collections in their prefaces mention penitential books, even if most of them contain at least some penitential canons. This all suggests that while normative texts taken from Roman law, Frankish capitularies, and penitential books were part of canon law collections, at least some compilers treated them differently from canon law in a more narrow sense.

37. Burchard 2.138 ('Orléans'), 2.82 ('apud S. Medardum'), 1.81, 2.59–61, and 11.42 (all 'Rouen'); the material source is *Admonitio generalis* cc. 3, 79, 41, 80, and 1 (ed. Mordek et. al., MGH Fontes iuris 16.184, 230/232, 200/202, 234, 186, and 184). On the transmission of these texts via Ansegis and Regino, see Hoffmann and Pokorny, *Dekret*.

38. Regino of Prüm was exceptional in using a large collection of capitulary canons (the *Collectio Senonica*). See Hubert Mordek, *Studien zur fränkischen Herrschergesetzgebung. Aufsätze über Kapitularien und Kapitulariensammlungen – ausgewählt zum 60. Geburtstag* (Frankfurt 2000), here at 49–53; Valeska Koal, *Studien zur Nachwirkung der Kapitularien in den Kanonessammlungen des Frühmittelalters* (Freiburger Beiträge zur mittelalterlichen Geschichte 13; Frankfurt 2001); Wilfried Hartmann, 'Capita incerta im Sendhandbuch Reginos von Prüm', *Scientia veritatis. Festschrift für Hubert Mordek zum 65. Geburtstag*, ed. Oliver Münsch and Thomas L. Zotz (Ostfildern 2004) 207–226. Most canon law collections of the eleventh and twelfth centuries, when they do contain more than a few capitulary canons, depend on Regino directly or indirectly for these materials.

39. Adriaan H. Gaastra, 'Penitentials and Canonical Authority', *Texts and Identities in the Early Middle Ages*, ed. Richard Corradini et al. (Forschungen zur Geschichte des Mittelalters 12; Vienna 2006) 191–204; Rob Meens, 'Die Bußbücher und das Recht im 9. und 10. Jahrhundert. Kontinuität und Wandel', *Recht und Gericht in Kirche und Welt um 900*, ed. Annette Grabowsky and Wilfried Hartmann (Schriften des Historischen Kollegs. Kolloquien 69; Munich 2007) 217–234; idem, *Penance in Medieval Europe, 600–1200* (Cambridge 2014). Famously, the councils of Paris 829 and Chalon 813 rallied against '[…] repudiatis ac penitus eliminatis libellis quos paenitentiales vocant, quorum sunt certi errores incerti auctores' (ed. Werminghoff, MGH Conc. 2.1:281). This passage is extremely well known, not least because it was included by Du Cange s.v. 'poenitentiale': Charles du Fresne Du Cange, *Editio novissima insigniter aucta, ubi non solum e Glossario Latinitatis, sed et Graecitatis addita cuique parti supplementa, suis quaeque locis inserta sunt* (4 vols. Frankfurt 1710), here at 3.367. Both Gaastra and Meens rightly point out that it is far from clear which penitentials were referred to at Chalon and Paris. It is indeed unlikely that criticism extended to *all* penitential books, and they certainly continued to be valued.

40. See Somerville and Brasington, *Prefaces* 118–119. On the so-called Roman penitential, see Rob Meens, 'The Historiography of Early Medieval Penance', *A New History of Penance*, ed. Abigail A. Firey (Brill's Companions to the Christian Tradition 14; Leiden and Boston 2008) 73–96, here at 73–89. It is, however, far from clear whether Atto had this penitential in mind.

Sometimes, then, the fact that specific sources are used but not highlighted in the prefaces is indicative of a lower authority accorded to them. Nonetheless, it would be rash to conclude that sources not mentioned in the prefaces generally were seen as less authoritative. The example of the *Hibernensis* and its 'silent' use of the Bible already warns against this. The other major counter-example are the writings of Augustine, Jerome, Ambrose, and other fathers from which many excerpts were taken into canon law. There can be little doubt that these saintly doctors enjoyed very high authority, but only rarely do the prefaces mention them by name. This is all the more striking as the integration of patristic doctrine into canon law is a major accomplishment of the century or so before Gratian; classical canon law on marriage, penance, and many other subjects would have been unthinkable without the introduction of many hundreds of excerpts from patristic sources. This process started already with the *Hibernensis*, but accelerated significantly in the second half of the eleventh century. The silence of the prefaces on patristic sources partly is indicative of the conservative nature of this genre, but partly also of the unsettled question whether the undisputed authority of these fathers also translated into an equally high *legal* authority of their opinions, a question that only Gratian would directly address.[41]

This brings us to another issue the prefaces, if imperfectly, address: the question of contradictions contained in canon law.[42] This question became ever more urgent in the eleventh century, if only because the collections drew on an increasingly diverse body of sources. Most compilers of collections largely ignored the problem, or claimed without discussion that their own collection at least was free from contradictions. Abbo of Fleury was exceptional in his blunt assertion that sometimes canons contradict each other, with one council prescribing what another one would prohibit.[43] Burchard of Worms applied the (traditional) complaint about the inconsistencies of penitential books to canon law (*iura canonum*) more generally;[44] while he claimed that his own collection was free from such conflicts, his preface may well have inspired some of the rather different approaches to the problem of contradictions in canon law. Some compilers in the later eleventh century tried, like Burchard, to minimize contradictions, but applied different techniques to achieve doctrinal unity.

---

41. Munier, *Sources patristiques*; Genka, 'Hierarchie'.

42. There is an abundant literature on this issue; see Rolker, 'Kollisionen'.

43. Abbo, *Collectio* c. 8 (PL 139.481): 'Et quid mirum? Cum nonnunquam inveniantur canones sibi contradicentes, et quod in altero concilio praecipitur, in altero prohibetur [...].'

44. Burchard, 'Praefacivncvla' (ed. Fransen and Kölzer 45; tr. Somerville and Brasington 99–100).

Specifically, some proposed that a hierarchy of sources were to be applied. Deusdedit was the first compiler to quote in his preface the Isidorian maxim that 'the lesser authority ought to yield to the more powerful' in case of conflicting canons; specifically, he argued that no one (not even the pope) could overturn the decisions of universal synods, whose authority 'only a lunatic' would doubt.[45] On the whole, however, the impact of such theories on the compilation of pre-Gratian collections was clearly limited. A different approach held that contradictions at the textual level did not affect the hidden unity of canon law. Most famously, Ivo of Chartres in his preface argued that seemingly conflicting canons were all expressions of God's 'mercy and justice'.[46] Bonizo of Sutri distinguished different meanings of the same terms to show that certain contradictions were only apparent ones.[47] These more positive attitudes to the diversity of canon law ultimately prevailed, as an increasingly developed hermeneutics allowed to see 'harmony from dissonance' (to use Kuttner's classical phrase).

All in all, the prefaces to canonical collections compiled between *ca.* 1000 and the time of Gratian reveal a broad consensus about the sources of the law, but are largely silent on related issues such as the status of Roman law in ecclesiastical affairs, the authority of patristic writers in legal contexts, or the general question of how to deal with contradictions in canon law. As far as they did develop a hierarchy of sources (like Deusdedit), such theories did not directly shape canonical collections, and even the widely-read *Prologue* of Ivo of Chartres was mainly concerned with the application of law, not the compilation of collections.

1.4 Reading, Copying, Reworking: The Reception of Canonical Collections

If there was a broad, though not uniform consensus concerning the sources of the law, where was this law found in the time before Gratian's

---

45. Deusdedit, *Praefatio* (ed. Wolf von Glanvell 3 lines 14–20); tr. Somerville and Brasington, *Prefaces* 125: 'But if it turns out that they patently are opposed, the lesser authority ought to yield to the more powerful. I excerpted, therefore, in the first place, the best things from certain universal synods, that is, Nicaea, first Ephesus, Chalcedon, and the sixth, seventh, and eighth synods, some of which by four or five patriarchs, some by their representatives, are known to have been convened as universal at different times. Concerning their authority, there is no one except a lunatic who would doubt.' Deusdedit is paraphrasing Isidore's letter to Masoda of Mérida (PL 83.901): '[...] illius concilii magis teneatur sententia, cuius antiquior aut potior extat auctoritas'.

46. Ivo, *Prologue* (ed. Brasington 116; tr. Somerville and Brasington, *Prefaces* 132–158).

47. For example, Bonizo 5.48 (ed. Perels 193 lines 2–13): 'De hac controversia, de reparatione scilicet lapsorum, multi non bene intelligentes putant sanctos patres sibi invicem in hac re esse diversos [...]. Quod ne videatur contrarium discutiamus [...] et inveniemus sanctos viros non diversa sensisse, sed unum.'

Decretum established itself as a standard textbook? Certainly 'the law' was not thought to be found in one specific collection alone. Nonetheless, for all practical purpose, 'the law' was found in a limited number of books, even though there was considerable variation what exactly this meant in different places. While the main focus of this book is on collections that were compiled in the eleventh and twelfth centuries, the story of canon law cannot be told by studying these works alone. The continuous use of 'old' collections was as important as the compilation of 'new' ones.[48] To begin with, there is no sharp distinction between the 'copying', 'improving', and 'reworking' of older collections on the one hand, and the production of new collections on the other hand. 'New' collections were never compiled from scratch, and sometimes seemingly minor changes to older collections made all the difference. Also, as will become clear in the course of the following chapters, the collections compiled in the eleventh and twelfth centuries in any case can only be understood properly if compared to the material available in this period.

So which collections were, generally speaking, available in Latin Europe between the turn of the millenium and the mid-twelfth century?[49] For the 'conciliar canons and decretals' the prefaces mention so often, the Pseudo-Isidorian collections (containing a mass of both forged and genuine materials) were the single most important source, either directly or indirectly. The early reception of this ninth-century work has been famously summarized as 'many manuscripts but little impact'.[50] So in Italy, France, and Germany (but not in England) in the later ninth and the tenth centuries, copies of the various forgeries were relatively widely available, and copied anew, but the number of new canon law collections drawing on this material was small. The *Anselmo dedicata*, compiled in the 880s,

48. See, for example, Adriaan H. Gaastra, *Between Liturgy and Canon Law: A Study of Books of Confession and Penance in Eleventh-and Twelfth-Century Italy* (PhD thesis; Universiteit Utrecht, Utrecht 2007), here at 205–215, and Martin Brett, 'Margin and Afterthought: The *Clavis* in Action', *Readers, Texts and Compilers in the Earlier Middle Ages: Studies in Medieval Canon Law in Honour of Linda Fowler-Magerl*, ed. Kathleen Grace Cushing and Martin Brett (CFC; Farnham and Aldershot 2009) 137–163 on the continuous importance of 'old' normative traditions well into the twelfth century.

49. The following is based on Kéry and Fowler-Magerl, *Clavis* in general, and on Wilfried Hartmann, *Kirche und Kirchenrecht um 900. Die Bedeutung der spätkarolingischen Zeit für Tradition und Innovation im kirchlichen Recht* (MGH Schriften 58; Hanover 2008) for the tenth century in particular.

50. Horst Fuhrmann, *Einfluß und Verbreitung der pseudoisidorischen Fälschungen. Von ihrem Auftauchen bis in die neuere Zeit* (3 vols. MGH Schriften 24; Stuttgart 1972–74), here at 1.232: 'Viele Handschriften, wenig Wirkung'; idem, 'The Pseudo-Isidorian Forgeries', *Papal Letters in the Early Middle Ages*, ed. Detlev Jasper and Horst Fuhrmann (HMCL; Washington, D.C. 2001) 135–195, here at 184. See Karl Georg Schon, 'Eine Redaktion der pseudoisidorischen Dekretalen aus der Zeit der Fälschung' DA 34 (1978) 500–511 as a case study for Pseudo-Isidorian derivative collections.

was the first collection divided into books devoted to specific topics that made ample (though also somewhat idiosyncratic) use of the forgeries; only in the eleventh century was Pseudo-Isidore regularly used for such enterprises.

The *Anselmo dedicata* in turn was copied on both sides of the Alps, and provided an important model of how to compile collections arranged by subject matter.[51] More specifically, in the Empire north of the Alps, Regino's *Libri duo* and the *Anselmo dedicata* together were the two most important collections arranged by subject matter for the tenth and early eleventh centuries. The two collections differed sharply in nature and, even more strikingly, in content. Regino is justly famous for having compiled a collection that suited the needs of a bishop as judge, and specifically the *Sendgericht*.[52] Accordingly, it contains much material on those issues that frequently came up in court, particularly marriage. The *Anselmo dedicata*, in contrast, is notoriously lacking in materials of this kind; while the *Anselmo dedicata* compiler evidently had much more Roman law at his disposal than Regino, he is remarkably brief on 'lay matters'. Above all, the *Anselmo dedicata* has rich materials on the ecclesiastical hierarchy, but little if anything on marriage or penance.

Other collections were available, too. The *Dionysio-Hadriana*, the *Dacheriana*, and various short versions of the False Decretals and Ansegisus had been copied frequently in the tenth century and were available in many places.[53] Some of the collections used in the eleventh century were even more ancient. Placidus of Nonantola, for example, in the early twelfth century was drawing on a ninth-century copy of the *Dionysiana*, compiled and translated by Dionysius Exiguus around the year 500.[54] Other compilers of the eleventh and twelfth centuries used Cresconius' *Concordia canonum*, the *Quesnelliana*, the *Herovalliana*, and the *Hibernensis*.[55] The latter

---

51. See the following chapter for further argument and references.

52. See Hartmann, *Kirche und Kirchenrecht* 149–162 (Regino) and 245–260 (*Sendgericht*). For an edition, see *Reginonis abbatis Prumiensis libri duo de synodalibus causis et disciplinis ecclesiasticis*, ed. Friedrich Wilhelm Hermann Wasserschleben (Leipzig 1840) and now *Das Sendhandbuch des Regino von Prüm*, ed. and tr. Wilfried Hartmann (FSGA 42; Darmstadt 2004).

53. See Kéry s.v. for an overview.

54. Jörg W. Busch, *Der Liber de honore ecclesiae des Placidus von Nonantola. Eine kanonistische Problemerörterung aus dem Jahre 1111. Die Arbeitsweise ihres Autors und seine Vorlagen* (Quellen und Forschungen zum Recht im Mittelalter 5; Sigmaringen 1990), here at 127–129.

55. See e.g. Klaus Zechiel-Eckes, *Die Concordia canonum des Cresconius. Studien und Edition* (2 vols. Freiburger Beiträge zur mittelalterlichen Geschichte 5; Frankfurt 1992), here at 2.268–290 (reception of Cresconius in the eleventh century); Johanne Autenrieth, 'Bernold von Konstanz und die erweiterte 74-Titelsammlung' DA 14 (1958) 375–394, here at 378–384 (Bernold working with *Quesnelliana*); Hubert Mordek, 'Die historische Wirkung der *Collectio Herovalliana*' *Zeitschrift für Kirchengeschichte* 81 (1970) 220–243. For a list of manuscripts, see Hartmann, *Kirche und Kirchenrecht* 321–338.

collection, compiled in early eighth-century Ireland,[56] is an example how distant in time and space the origin of a collection could be from its main impact on other canon law collections. While the collection is an important source for early medieval Irish history, in fact no extant (complete) manuscript was written in Ireland.[57] Complete copies and shorter versions were copied and preserved in English, Breton, French, German, and Italian libraries;[58] the richest evidence for canon law collections drawing on the *Hibernensis* comes from eleventh-century Italy.[59]

In addition to these rather bulky works, there were very many smaller collections—incomplete copies, florilegia, and dossiers drawing on various sources, and above all abbreviations of larger works like the Pseudo-Isidorian collections or the *Hibernensis*. These anonymous works are typically extant in single manuscripts. If there are more textual witnesses, it is sometimes impossible to distinguish between 'copies' and 'versions' of a given collection; to a large degree, they were 'living texts'.[60] This all can pose significant problems in studying any one of these short works; even if this work is undertaken, it is commonly impossible to link these collections to known authors or places, to date them with any precision, or to determine for what purpose they were compiled. Yet to omit them from the picture certainly would distort our understanding of canon law in the eleventh century. They illustrate much of the diversity of canon law in different areas, and modest as they seem, the laborious task of copying and reworking these minor collections reflects the growing demand for legal texts. Some of these amorphous collections travelled across much of Europe, making sometimes rare material available to their readers.[61] In addition, it would be misleading to imagine that the use of these sometimes unrefined collections was indicative of a low level of learning. An eminent scholar like Fulbert of Chartres (d. 1028), widely

56. On the date, see most recently Flechner, *Hibernensis* ch. 1.

57. Flechner, *Hibernensis* ch. 4; see also next note.

58. See Flechner, *Hibernensis* ch. 4 for the complete manuscripts. Kéry 74 lists three fragments as written in Ireland or under Irish influence; but Flechner, *Hibernensis* 1.48* n. 45 counts only one fragment as possibly of Irish origin: Trier, Stadtbibliothek, 137/50).

59. Roger E. Reynolds, 'The Transmission of the *Hibernensis* in Italy: Tenth to the Twelfth Century' *Peritia* 14 (2000) 20–50; idem, 'Further Evidence for the Influence of the *Hibernensis* in Southern Italy: An Early Eleventh-Century Canonistic Florilegium at Montecassino' *Peritia* 19 (2005) 119–135.

60. Linda Fowler-Magerl has provided a number of studies on these 'minor' collections. See, for example, her 'The Relationship Between Seemingly Unspectacular Pre-Gratian Collections in the Manuscripts Paris, Bibliothèque nationale, lat. 2858C and Florence, Biblioteca Medicea Laurenziana, Ashburnham 1554', *Scientia veritatis. Festschrift für Hubert Mordek zum 65. Geburtstag*, ed. Oliver Münsch and Thomas L. Zotz (Ostfildern 2004) 241–260.

61. Christof Rolker, 'Genesis and Influence of the Canon Law Collection in BN lat. 13368' ZRG Kan. Abt. 91 (2005) 74–105.

acclaimed for his learning and consulted by many, knew 'the law' from collections that around 1100 would be already regarded as 'minor', namely the *Breviarium Alarici*, an abbreviated collection of capitularies, and a short version of the *Hibernensis*.[62]

Much of what has been said so far is mainly true for the Carolingian heartlands, though even here there evidently was large variation between individual regions and indeed libraries. Of course, there were also marked differences between the Mediterranean and the northern Europe, between East and West, and between the British Isles and continental Europe. At least some of these characteristic differences have to be mentioned here.

As for Italy and the south of modern France, the most important difference to northern Europe certainly was the availability of Roman law texts and learning. Legal historians have often concentrated on the loss and, above all, the 'rediscovery' of the Digest, including the famous Digest excerpts found in the canon law collection known as the *Britannica* from the late eleventh century.[63] This should not obscure a continuity of Roman law learning especially in the cities of northern Italy. In general, there were many Roman law texts available in Italy, southern France, and Catalonia that were largely unknown further north. They were used for canon law collections like the *Lex Romana canonice compta* (also known as *Capitula legis Romanae*) or the *Anselmo dedicata*, to quote two important examples from the ninth century. Southern Italy is often neglected in studies on pre-Gratian canon law history, but as Chapter Three will make clear, it was the home of several important collections. The presence of Greek-speaking populations in the south of Italy, and exchange with Byzantium, may explain why these collections contain excerpts from the Greek fathers that are rarely found in other collections compiled in northern Europe.[64]

---

62. Christof Rolker, *Canon Law and the Letters of Ivo of Chartres* (Life and Thought: Fourth Series 76; Cambridge 2010) 54–59.

63. For the *Britannica*, see Chapter Five. On the 'rediscovery' of the Digest, which continues to attract divergent interpretations, see e.g. Charles M. Radding and Antonio Ciaralli, *The Corpus Iuris Civilis in the Middle Ages: Manuscripts and Transmission from the Sixth Century to the Juristic Revival* (Brill's Studies in Intellectual History 147; Turnhout 2007). For important criticism of Radding's arguments, see Wolfgang Kaiser, 'Verkürzt und wiederaufgefüllt?' *Rechtsgeschichte* 11 (2007) 182–185.

64. For an excellent overview, see Roger E. Reynolds, 'The Influence of Eastern Patristic Fathers on the Canonical Collections of South Italy in the Eleventh and Early Twelfth Centuries', *Canon Law, Religion and Politics: Liber amicorum Robert Somerville*, ed. Uta-Renate Blumenthal et al. (Washington, D.C. 2012) 75–106 (esp. on Vatican 9L and 5L). On the 'Greek' content of Roma, Vallicelliana, Tomus XVIII [not seen], see already Francis Dvornik, *The Photian Schism: History and Legend* (Cambridge 1948) esp. 290.

While Catalonia in many respects took a similar development as Aquitaine, the development of canon law elsewhere on the Iberian Peninsula was clearly different. The visigothic traditions (above all, the different versions of the *Hispana*, including an Arab translation) were still important in the eleventh century, and relatively little evidence is available that pre-Gratian canon law from northern Europe was read and used in Spain before *ca.* 1100. To judge from the extant manuscripts, collections such as Burchard, *74T*, *5L*, and Ivo's *Decretum* were available in the twelfth century, but many of these manuscripts were written in Italy or France, and it is largely unclear how early these collections were available at all on the Iberian Peninsula.[65] After *ca.* 1100, the picture relatively quickly changed, not least as a result of intensified contacts with Rome.

In England, the situation was different from that of the Continent, even if the exceptionalism claimed in the older literature cannot be maintained any longer.[66] On the whole, canon law collections from continental Europe played a less significant role in England in the tenth and eleventh centuries than they had done before. Only around 1100 did this change again;[67] and if we turn from pre-Gratian canon law collections to the early decretalists, it is striking to see that England in the twelfth century was indeed an important centre for the production of decretal collections.[68] Nonetheless, for most of the period under discussion here, there is a marked difference between English and continental approaches to canon

65. For a good overview, see Nicolás Álvarez de las Asturias, 'La difusión del derecho canónico "Gregoriano" en la Península Ibérica a través de las colecciones canónicas', *La reforma Gregoriana en España*, ed. José María Magaz and Nicolás Álvarez de las Asturias (Presencia y diálogo 31; Madrid 2011) 145–186.

66. Martin Brett, 'The *Collectio Lanfranci* and Its Competitors', *Intellectual Life in the Middle Ages: Essays Presented to Margaret Gibson*, ed. Lesley Janette Smith and Benedicta Ward (London 1992) 157–174, here at 165–169, correcting the position of Zachary Nugent Brooke, *The English Church and the Papacy: From the Conquest to the Reign of John* (Cambridge 1931). See also Michael D. Elliot, *Canon Law Collections in England ca 600–1066: The Manuscript Evidence* (PhD thesis; University of Toronto, Toronto 2013).

67. In addition to Brett, 'Collectio Lanfranci', see Peter J. Cramer, 'Ernulf of Rochester and Early Anglo-Norman Canon Law' JEH 40 (1989) 483–510, Michael Gullick, 'Lanfranc and the Oldest Manuscript of the *Collectio Lanfranci*', *Bishops, Texts and the Use of Canon Law Around 1100: Essays in Honour of Martin Brett*, ed. Bruce Clark Brasington and Kathleen Grace Cushing (CFC; Aldershot and Farnham 2008) 79–89, and Nicolás Álvarez de las Asturias, *La "Collectio Lanfranci": origine e influenza di una collezione della Chiesa anglo-normanna* (Monografie giuridiche 32; Milan 2008).

68. The classical study is Charles Duggan, *Twelfth-Century Decretal Collections and Their Importance in English History* (University of London Historical Studies 12; London 1963). See now Martin Brett, 'English Law and Centres of Law Studies in the Later Twelfth Century', *Archbishop Eystein as Legislator: The European Connection*, ed. Tore Iversen (Trondheim 2011) 87–102, and Danica Summerlin, 'Using the "Old Law" in Twelfth-Century Decretal Collections', *New Discourses in Medieval Canon Law Research: Challenging the Master Narrative*, ed. Christof Rolker (Medieval Law and Its Practice 28; Leiden and Boston 2019) 145–169.

law. Some of this may be called 'insular' tradition, in the sense that penitential books played a special role in Ireland and England; the reception of the *Hibernensis* in England—Worcester possessed three copied in the early eleventh century—may also be quoted in this context.[69] In contrast, between the ninth and the eleventh centuries, very few canonical collections were compiled in England. In a very careful study, Michael Elliot has recently confirmed that the number of pre-Gratian canon law collections produced in Anglo-Saxon England was small indeed; the collection known as *Excerptiones Ecgberhti* (Elliot's *Collectio Wigorniensis*), associated with Wulfstan of York (d. 1023), is an important exception. Yet while he on the whole confirmed that only very few collections were compiled anew in Anglo-Saxon England, Elliott at the same time has brought to attention considerable evidence for continental collections kept, copied, and used there.[70] An important difference to continental Europe concerns the reception of Pseudo-Isidore, as the forgeries apparently never attracted much interest in England before the Pseudo-Isidorian material became known via eleventh-century collections like the *Collectio Lanfranci*, the *74T*, and the *Tripartita*.[71]

1.5 Conclusion

In the period studied in this book, 'canon law' was still part of the 'canon' of sacred scripture and ecclesiastical writings. From Isidore of Seville and the *Decretum Gelasianum* to Hugh of Saint-Victor there are many examples how the sources of 'canon law' were treated as part and parcel of the 'canonical literature'.[72] Accordingly, the collections under discussion here contain 'canons' including, but not limited to, those canons that were most readily used in 'legal' contexts (including law courts). As is already

69. See Flechner, *Hibernensis* ch. 4 (*Hibernensis* manuscripts). For a strong case for mutual influence between Irish and English legal culture in the early Middle Ages, see Roy Flechner, 'An Insular Tradition of Ecclesiastical Law: Fifth to Eighth Century', *Anglo-Saxon/Irish Relations Before the Vikings*, ed. James Graham-Campbell and Michael Ryan (Proceedings of the British Academy 157; Oxford 2009) 23–46.

70. Elliot, *Canon Law*.

71. Brett, 'Collectio Lanfranci'; Fuhrmann, 'Forgeries' 184; see also Chapter 3.4.4 on the reception of *74T* in England.

72. For Isidore, see above; for Hugh of Saint-Victor, see the list in his *De scripturis* c. 6 (PL 175.15–16): 'Utrumque Testamentum tribus ordinibus distinguitur: Vetus Testamentum continet legem, prophetas, agiographos. Novum autem Evangelium, apostolos, patres. [...] In tertio ordine [scil. Novi Testamenti] primum locum habent decretalia, quos [*recte* quae, CR] canonicos id est regulares appellamus. Deinde sanctorum patrum scripta, id est: Hieronymi, Augustini, Ambrosii, Gregorii, Isidori, Origenis, Bedae et aliorum doctorum, quae infinita sunt. [...] Sicut post legem prophetae, et post prophetas agiographi, ita post Evangelium apostoli, et post apostolos doctores ordine successerunt.' While many terms are ambigious, 'decretalia' clearly means 'decretal letters'; on terminology, see in general Maassen, *Quellen* 230.

visible from the prefaces to these collections, in practice this particularly referred to conciliar canons and papal decretals. Nonetheless, many 'canons' were taken from other sources including the Bible, patristic writings, penitentials, secular law texts, monastic rules, hagiography, and sermons. Not every text found in a canonical collection was regarded as 'canonical', for some their status was disputed, and some were not even normative in nature.

In the period under discussion in this book, 'canon law' was known from various collections of different origin, content, and character. While new collections emerged, old collections remained in use, including some very ancient ones. Many collections were small, unsystematic, and difficult to use compared to certain 'great' collections that emerged since the early eleventh century, but still were seen as useful enough to be kept and copied. Likewise, the quality of the texts differed between individual collections and indeed from copy to copy; some normative texts circulated in profoundly different versions as a result of scribal negligence, deliberate manipulation, and more or less skilful attempts to correct perceived errors.

In short, there simply was no single textbook containing 'the law'. At the same time, the high Middle Ages were an 'age without jurists';[73] the compilers of canon law collections, judges, and other users were not university-trained specialists in law, as it became increasingly the case from the later twelfth century onwards. Rather, it was the figure of the bishop that was central to the production, dissemination, and use of the collections of the early and high Middle Ages.[74] With the church reforms of the eleventh century, other actors and institutions—legates, cardinals, popes—became important for legal development, too. All this, however, should not make one forget that all over Europe, religious communities were the places of highly regulated Christian life, where there was a constant demand (but also supply) for normative texts coming from the canonical tradition.

73. Manlio Bellomo, *The Common Legal Past of Europe, 1000–1800* (SMCL 4; Washington, D.C. 1995), ch. 2.

74. Timothy Reuter, 'A Europe of Bishops: The Age of Wulfstan of York and Burchard of Worms', *Strukturen bischöflicher Herrschaftsgewalt im westlichen Europa des 10. und 11. Jahrhunderts / Patterns of Episcopal Power: Bishops in Tenth and Eleventh Century Western Europe*, ed. Ludger Körntgen and Dominik Wassenhoven (Prinz-Albert-Forschungen 6; Berlin and Boston 2011) 17–38.

2

Burchard of Worms

Canon Law in a 'Europe of Bishops'

2.1 A 'Europe of Bishops'

Latin Europe during the times of Burchard of Worms has famously been called a 'Europe of bishops'.[1] Timothy Reuter made a powerful argument that dioceses were the most uniform, and in many respects also the most important administrative and political structures in medieval Europe; additionally, he argued that bishops around the year 1000 were, on the whole, in a rather strong position. Unlike at least some bishops of the ninth century, they were unlikely to face metropolitans intervening with their affairs.[2] At the same time, bishops were more independent from

---

1. Timothy Reuter, 'A Europe of Bishops: The Age of Wulfstan of York and Burchard of Worms', *Strukturen bischöflicher Herrschaftsgewalt im westlichen Europa des 10. und 11. Jahrhunderts / Patterns of Episcopal Power: Bishops in Tenth and Eleventh Century Western Europe*, ed. Ludger Körntgen and Dominik Wassenhoven (Prinz-Albert-Forschungen 6; Berlin and Boston 2011) 17–38. See also Susan Wood, *The Proprietary Church in the Medieval West* (Oxford 2006) and John Howe, *Before the Gregorian Reform: The Latin Church at the Turn of the First Millennium* (Ithaca, N.Y. and London 2016) ch. 8. Reuter's model mainly applies to north-western Europe; for southern Italy see, for example, Valerie Ramseyer, *The Transformation of a Religious Landscape: Medieval Southern Italy 850–1150* (Conjunctions of Religion and Power in the Medieval Past; Ithaca, N.Y. 2006), finding that 'large Benedictine abbeys rather than cathedral churches became the most influential elements in religious organization in most areas of southern Italy'.

2. Reuter, 'Europe' 33–34; for the early Middle Ages, see Matthias Schrör, *Metropolitangewalt und papstgeschichtliche Wende* (Historische Studien 494; Husum 2009) ch. 4.

Rome than they would be in the later Middle Ages. Concerning their temporal powers, the position of bishops vis-à-vis their cities was still largely uncontested in the tenth and eleventh centuries. Close cooperation between king, local nobility, and ecclesiastical parties in episcopal elections around the year 1000 was not yet seen as a problem, nor did the *Königsdienst* pose exaggerated burdens on most bishops; on the whole they received adequate compensation for their services. Many bishops were quite aware of this strong position; some of them were self-conscious to the point of unruliness, as popes, metropolitans but also emperors knew from experience.[3]

These bishops were pastors, administrators, lords, and judges who needed secular and canon law in their daily business. In addition, they were also legislators, both individually and collectively (in synods); at least some of them also dealt with canon law as teachers, as commentators, or as legal experts consulted sometimes well beyond their dioceses. All these functions were to a considerable degree still performed by the bishops themselves, rather than by university-trained specialists, as was increasingly the case in the later Middle Ages. This also extended to the compilation of canon law collections. A large part of high medieval canon law collections were indeed compiled by bishops and for bishops.

The wide diffusion of the Pseudo-Isidorian forgeries also meant that canon law around the year 1000 was episcopal in yet another sense.[4] The forgeries were not yet integrated into many systematic canon law collections, but in the course of the tenth century had been widely copied; both in Italy and in north-western (continental) Europe anyone systematically searching for synodal legislation and papal decretals would almost inevitably come across some version of the Pseudo-Isidorian forgeries. While these forgeries, like all canon law, could be (and were) employed to many ends, it is also true that the forgers' concern with episcopal rights had left a decisive impact on early medieval canon law. In the case of procedural law in particular, this worked in favour of bishops. If a bishop could successfully evoke these rules, he considerably strengthened his position in any legal conflict. To mention only the norms that most obviously worked in favour of bishops:[5] There were high procedural standards of

---

3. Ernst-Dieter Hehl, 'Der widerspenstige Bischof. Bischöfliche Zustimmung und bischöflicher Protest in der ottonischen Reichskirche', *Herrschaftsrepräsentation im ottonischen Sachsen*, ed. Gerd Althoff and Ernst Schubert (Vorträge und Forschungen 46; Sigmaringen 1998) 295–344, here at 306.

4. See Horst Fuhrmann, 'The Pseudo-Isidorian Forgeries', *Papal Letters in the Early Middle Ages*, ed. Detlev Jasper and Horst Fuhrmann (HMCL; Washington, D.C. 2001) 135–195.

5. See for the following still Seckel's 1905 article 'Pseudoisidor', *Real-Encyklopädie für protestantische Theologie und Kirche* (24 vols. Leipzig 1896–1913) 16.265–307, here at 279–280.

who could accuse a bishop or testify against him, while it was very easy
for an accused bishop to ignore an accusation brought against him; if
the accused bishop chose to appear, he had the right to nominate twelve
fellow bishops as his judges, and no less than seventy-two bishops were
needed as witnesses to sentence a bishop; finally, an accused bishop retained the right to appeal to Rome at any stage of the process. If followed
verbatim, these norms made it excessively unlikely that a bishop would be
sentenced.

These aspects of the forgeries are rightly famous, and many of the
procedural norms just quoted are found several times in the forgeries,
and are sometimes spelled out in great detail.[6] There can be little doubt
that (criminal) accusations against bishops, or rather strategies to counter them, were a special concern of the forgers. This said, it should not
be forgotten that the forgeries also contained various norms that effectively prevented metropolitans from exercising effective control over their
suffragan bishops. Specifically, metropolitans according to Pseudo-Isidore
needed the consent of all comprovincial bishops for many of their actions.
In this context, the forgers imagined provincial synods as rather powerful
when it came to control the metropolitan, but essentially powerless in
helping the metropolitan to control any of his suffragans. For example, a
provincial synod trying to bring a bishop to court needed papal approval
even for its summons, and could only act if all comprovincial bishops appeared; failing this, any verdict it might try to impose was void. In short,
the Pseudo-Isidorian forgeries went at considerable length 'to protect suffragan bishops from intervention by the metropolitans, the provincial synods, or the secular power', and specifically sought to make 'trial procedure
and the possibility of deposing bishops [...] immeasurably difficult'.[7]

However, Pseudo-Isidore was only slowly integrated into systematically ordered canon law collections. The first collection to do so was the
Anselmo dedicata, but as will be discussed below, the compiler of this collection used the Pseudo-Isidorian texts in a very unusual way that twisted
key concepts the forgers had sought to introduce into canon law. Thus,
it was only with Burchard of Worms that Pseudo-Isidorian material was

---

6. In addition to Seckel (see last note), see more recently Fuhrmann, 'Forgeries', Klaus
Zechiel-Eckes, 'Ein Blick in Pseudoisidors Werkstatt. Studien zum Entstehungsprozeß der
falschen Dekretalen. Mit einem exemplarischen editorischen Anhang (Pseudo-Julius an die orientalischen Bischöfe, JK †196)' *Francia* 28/1 (2001) 37–90, Karl Georg Schon, *Die Capitula Angilramni. Eine prozessrechtliche Fälschung Pseudoisidors* (MGH Studien und Texte 39; Hanover 2006),
and Clara Harder, *Pseudoisidor und das Papsttum. Funktion und Bedeutung des apostolischen Stuhls
in den pseudoisidorischen Fälschungen* (Papsttum im mittelalterlichen Europa 2; Cologne, Weimar,
and Vienna 2014).

7. Fuhrmann, 'Forgeries' 142.

fully integrated into a major canon law collection that arranged canon law according to subject matter.

2.2 Transalpine Contacts and Non-Contacts Around the Year 1000

In this context, it has often been stressed that for bishops in northern Europe the pope was a distant figure at least until the mid-eleventh century.[8] It is certainly true that the pope around the year 1000 was a more distant figure for most prelates than he would be in the twelfth century. Popes or even papal legates rarely crossed the Alps, for some regions it was even rare to exchange letters with the papal curia. Scholars have rightly stressed that contacts between the Roman church and the rest of Latin Christianity were greatly intensified in the second half of the eleventh century only.[9] Nonetheless, contacts between Rome and the churches outside Italy did exist; for example, Cluny's privileges or the foundation of new bishoprics in the first half of the century would have been 'utterly meaningless without papal validation'.[10] The key difference between the early and the late eleventh century was not so much the frequency, but the quality of papal intervention. During the eleventh century, the papacy partly revived old institutions, partly developed new forms of interaction with the Church at large, but above all it changed from reacting to request to acting on its own initiative. As Rudolf Schieffer put it, the papacy began to act *motu proprio*.[11]

So in the time of Burchard, popes *did* cross the Alps—at the invitation of the emperor. Likewise, papal legates at least occasionally *were* sent north well before the time of the reform papacy, but they were unlikely to challenge any bishop supported by the king. In Germany (or England, for that matter) it was unthinkable that the pope would convene a synod without the will of the king, as Leo IX famously did in France (Reims

---

8. E.g. Reuter, 'Europe' 34.

9. Gerd Tellenbach, *The Church in Western Europe from the Tenth to the Early Twelfth Century* (Cambridge Medieval Textbooks; Cambridge 1993), esp. 322–334; Rudolf Schieffer, 'Motu proprio. Über die papstgeschichtliche Wende im 11. Jahrhundert' *Historisches Jahrbuch* 122 (2002) 27–41; Kathleen Grace Cushing, *Reform and the Papacy in the Eleventh Century: Spirituality and Social Change* (Manchester Medieval Studies; Manchester and New York 2005); Claudia Zey, 'Die Augen des Papstes. Zu Eigenschaften und Vollmachten päpstlicher Legaten', *Römisches Zentrum und kirchliche Peripherie. Das universale Papsttum als Bezugspunkt der Kirchen von den Reformpäpsten bis zu Innozenz III.*, ed. Jochen Johrendt and Harald Müller (Abh. Akad. Göttingen N.F. 2; Berlin 2008) 77–108.

10. Cushing, *Reform* 23.

11. Schieffer, 'Motu proprio'.

1049).[12] It is also true that the papacy in the eleventh and twelfth centuries played an important role in major reorganisations of the fabric of the Latin Church. Namely, it was involved in the creation of new dioceses and archdioceses like Magdeburg, Gnesen, Bamberg, and in Southern Italy,[13] even if the exact role of the papacy sometimes remained obscure.[14] These and other important issues were at least sometimes decided upon by Roman synods presided over by the pope—that is, jointly with the emperor.[15]

'Ecclesiastical' and 'secular' affairs were closely intertwined, and in the Empire even more so than elsewhere. A dramatic case, well known to Burchard, may serve to highlight the possibilities, but also the limits of papal intervention in Germany around the year 1000.[16] Archbishop Willigis of Mainz (d. 1011), once Burchard's teacher and later his metropolitan, was perhaps the most powerful ecclesiastical lord of the Empire in the late tenth century.[17] His province stretched from the North Sea to the Alps, from the Rhine valley to Bohemia; he was archchancellor of the Empire, primate over 'Germania and Gallia', and papal *vicarius*, to name only some of his titles and functions. Already his predecessors were habitually called 'summus pontifex' by Widukind,[18] but Willigis further enhanced the position of his see when he obtained a papal privilege on his preeminence among the German bishops, making him 'second only to the pope' in the

12. Jochen Johrendt, 'Die Reisen der frühen Reformpäpste. Ihre Ursachen und Funktionen' *Römische Quartalschrift für christliche Altertumskunde und Kirchengeschichte* 96 (2001) 57–94, here at 92. On Reims 1049 see Böhmer-Frech 622–627 (with ample references).

13. Ernst-Dieter Hehl, 'Herrscher, Kirche und Kirchenrecht im spätottonischen Reich', *Otto III. – Heinrich II. Eine Wende*, ed. Bernd Schneidmüller and Stefan Weinfurter (Mittelalter-Forschungen 1; Sigmaringen 1997) 169–203 (Magdeburg); Ramseyer, *Transformation* ch. 4 (Salerno), esp. 127–135; Wolfgang Huschner, 'Benevent, Magdeburg, Salerno. Das Papsttum und die neuen Erzbistümer in ottonischer Zeit', *Das Papsttum und das vielgestaltige Italien. Hundert Jahre Italia Pontificia*, ed. Klaus Herbers and Jochen Johrendt (Abh. Akad. Göttingen N.F. 5; Berlin 2009) 87–108; Reuter, 'Europe' 34 (general); Przemysław Nowak, 'Das Papsttum und Ostmitteleuropa (Böhmen-Mähren, Polen, Ungarn) vom ausgehenden 10. bis zum Beginn des 13. Jahrhunderts. Mit einer Neuedition von JL 9067', *Rom und die Regionen. Studien zur Homogenisierung der lateinischen Kirche im Hochmittelalter*, ed. Jochen Johrendt and Harald Müller (Abh. Akad. Göttingen N.F. 19; Berlin and Boston 2012) 331–369.

14. Nowak, 'Papsttum' 345 (for Eastern Europe).

15. See e.g. Ernst-Dieter Hehl, 'Vorbemerkung zum zweiten Teil (962–1001)', *Die Konzilien Deutschlands und Reichsitaliens 916–1001, Teil 2: 962–1001*, ed. idem (MGH Conc. 6.2; Hanover 2007) XI–XIV, here at XI; Georg Gresser, *Die Synoden und Konzilien in der Zeit des Reformpapsttums in Deutschland und Italien von Leo IX. bis Calixt II. (1049–1123)* (Konziliengeschichte. Reihe A: Darstellungen; Paderborn, Munich, and Vienna 2006) (overview).

16. For the following, see Hehl, 'Kirche' 184–193, idem, 'Bischof' 316–329, and idem, 'Willigis von Mainz. Päpstlicher Vikar, Metropolit und Reichspolitiker', *Bischof Burchard von Worms, 1000–1025*, ed. Wilfried Hartmann (Quellen und Abhandlungen zur mittelrheinischen Kirchengeschichte 100; Mainz 2000) 51–77.

17. See Hehl, 'Willigis' 65–69 on the decline of Willigis' position, in particular after Otto III began to reign more independently in the second half of the 990s.

18. See the index to Widukind's *Res gestae saxonicae* (ed. Hirsch, MGH SS rer. Germ. 60) s.v. 'pontifex'.

Empire north of the Alps.[19] And yet, in the conflict over the *Reichsstift* of Gandersheim, he was seriously challenged by one of his suffragans, Bernward of Hildesheim, and at one point suspended from office by a legate of much lower rank.

The conflict started in 987 with the seemingly minor question whether Sophie, the sister of Otto III, could demand consecration as canoness at Gandersheim by the archbishop of Mainz rather than the bishop of Hildesheim. While the two prelates found a compromise concerning the consecration itself, the question on which grounds the archbishop could act as bishop in the diocese of one of his suffragans fuelled a prolonged dispute. In 1000, Willigis of Mainz was asked to consecrate Gandersheim abbey church, and when Bernward of Hildesheim tried to consecrate the church himself first, open conflict broke out. The dispute took a crucial turn when Bernward successfully appealed to Rome, resulting in the archbishop being severely censured by a Roman synod in 1001. Pope Silvester II and the synod declared void a synod Willigis had convened, and sent a papal legate to gather a synod that would hear the case anew. In the heated conflict over this synod, Willigis was suspended from office by the legate, a cardinal priest called Frederick.

This was unheard-of; in hindsight, one is reminded of the *causes célèbres* of the eleventh century. However, in contrast to the case of Archbishop Manasses I of Reims half a century later,[20] let alone the 'beheading of the French Church' in the time of Hugh of Lyon,[21] the papacy around the year 1000 did not have many means of enforcing its judgements. In Germany even more so than in France, such major cases inevitably involved the secular rulers.[22] Indeed, Willigis continued to act as archbishop, and the conflict was not, as the Roman synod had envisioned, ended by a legatine synod. Significantly, the whole process was put to a halt with

19. Hehl, 'Willigis' 60.

20. See John Stephens Ott, '"Reims and Rome Are Equals": Archbishop Manasses I (c. 1069–1080), Pope Gregory VII, and the Fortunes of Historical Exceptionalism', *Envisioning the Bishop: Images and the Episcopacy in the Middle Ages*, ed. Sigrid Danielson and Evan A. Gatti (Medieval Church Studies 29; Turnhout 2014) 275–302. The bold claim that 'Reims and Rome are equals' is found in a poem Fulconius of Beauvais wrote for Manasses (ibid. 286).

21. Rudolf Hiestand, 'Les légats pontificaux en France du milieu du XIᵉ à la fin du XIIᵉ siècle', *L'Église de France et la papauté (Xᵉ–XIIIᵉ siècle) / Die französische Kirche und das Papsttum (10.–13. Jahrhundert): actes du XXVIᵉ Colloque franco-allemand organisé en coopération avec l'École nationale des chartes par l'Institut historique allemand de Paris (Paris, 17–19 octobre 1990)*, ed. Rolf Große (Studien und Dokumente zur Gallia Pontificia 1; Bonn 1993) 54–80, here at 58 ('une véritable décapitation de l'Église de France').

22. As for France, the case of Arnulf of Reims may serve as an example. Arnulf's deposition in 991 was later declared void because it had taken place without papal approval, but evidently both the installation and the deposition of Arnulf would have been impossible without the consent of Hugh Capet.

the death of Emperor Otto III in 1002, and was only reopened years later, when Henry II intervened directly in 1007. While some questions remained, the main dispute was, in the end, resolved by the emperor.

Disputes like the Gandersheim conflict were closely watched by the German bishops, who very well understood the wider consequences for relations between metropolitans and suffragan bishops, between different kinds of synods, between Rome and local prelates, and between the secular and ecclesiastical sphere. It is this background against which 'the law' as contained in canonical collections old and new was understood. Therefore, major cases involving the pope and Italian bishops, already constituted a form of transalpine contact that shaped canon law around the year 1000. In addition, canon law texts crossed the Alps—in both directions. The *Anselmo dedicata*, compiled in northern Italy in the early 880s, was quickly known at Reims,[23] and in the tenth century was brought to and used on both sides of the Rhine. At the time of the Gandersheim conflict, Mainz certainly possessed a copy of *Anselmo dedicata*, and perhaps there also was one at Hildesheim. Freising possessed an older copy made in Italy.[24] The see of Bamberg is thought to have been provided with a copy at its foundation in 1007;[25] other episcopal libraries seemed to have acquired their copies at about the same time.[26] We only imperfectly understand the ways texts and manuscripts travelled, but several of these manuscripts were imported directly from Italy. There is also good reason to assume that the emperor played a role in the dissemination of canon law collections. It was Henry II who provided his foundation at Bamberg with canon law manuscripts, and he may also have helped to distribute Burchard's collections north and south of the Alps.[27] Henry's journey to Italy in 1013–14 for German prelates was an occasion to acquire canon law knowledge, and perhaps manuscripts; indeed, no less than three prelates linked with

23. Klaus Zechiel-Eckes, 'Quellenkritische Anmerkungen zur *Collectio Anselmo dedicata*', *Recht und Gericht in Kirche und Welt um 900*, ed. Annette Grabowsky and Wilfried Hartmann (Schriften des Historischen Kollegs. Kolloquien 69; Munich 2007) 49–65, here at 53–54.

24. See Jörg Müller, *Untersuchungen zur Collectio Duodecim Partium* (Abhandlungen zur rechtswissenschaftlichen Grundlagenforschung 73; Ebelsbach 1989), here at 355–356 on the acquisition of Italian manuscripts since the time of Abraham of Freising (952–993/994).

25. Bamberg, SB, Msc.Can.5. Gude Suckale-Redlefsen, *Die Handschriften des 8. bis 11. Jahrhunderts der Staatsbibliothek Bamberg* (2 vols. Katalog der illuminierten Handschriften der Staatsbibliothek Bamberg 1–2; Wiesbaden 2004) 1.57, pointed out that no cogent proof is known, but it remains an attractive assumption.

26. Rudolf Pokorny, 'Reichsbischof, Kirchenrecht und Diözesanverwaltung um das Jahr 1000', *Bernward von Hildesheim und das Zeitalter der Ottonen. Katalog der Ausstellung Hildesheim 1993*, ed. Michael Brandt and Arne Eggebrecht (2 vols. Hildesheim and Mainz 1993) 1.113–122; Kéry 124–128 (general).

27. For the *Liber decretorum* as a 'handbook' that specifically met the needs of Henry's anti-incest campaign, see Karl Ubl, *Inzestverbot und Gesetzgebung. Die Konstruktion eines Verbrechens (300–1100)* (Millenium-Studien 20; Berlin and New York 2008), here at 430–435.

the compilation of new canon law collections joined the emperor on this occasion.[28] The same journey led to the introduction of 'northern' material into Italian canon law collections. Not only were canons of Henry's Ravenna synod of 1014 integrated in the south-Italian *Collection in Five Books*, the latter also was the first Italian collection to contain substantial materials from older Frankish legislation.[29] Canon law materials travelled in both directions and the journeys of Henry II may well have helped to distribute texts and ideas on both sides of the Alps.

2.3 Burchard's *Liber decretorum*: Genesis, Structure, and Reception

The *Liber decretorum* (or *Decretum*) compiled by Burchard of Worms (d. 1025) and his collaborators was the single most important systematic canon law collection of eleventh-century Europe.[30] It is a large collection divided into twenty books according to subject matter, and was compiled between 1012 and 1022 at Worms.[31] Soon, it was known very widely, and

28. Müller, *Untersuchungen* 361–362 pointed out, the journey was one of many occasions where Egilbert of Freising (d. 1039), who might have played an important role in the making of *12P*, was in contact with Burchard of Worms and Walter of Speyer, one of Burchard's collaborators in the compilation of the *Liber decretorum*. The later one dates the *12P*, and the more one sees *12P* and Burchard's *Liber decretorum* as interrelated, the more likely is a participation of Egilbert in the compilation of *12P*.

29. Myron Wojtowytsch, 'Die Kanones *Henrici regis*. Bemerkungen zur römischen Synode vom Februar 1014', *Papsttum, Kirche und Recht im Mittelalter. Festschrift für Horst Fuhrmann zum 65. Geburtstag*, ed. Hubert Mordek (Tübingen 1991) 155–168; Koal, *Studien* 83. On *5L*, see the next chapter. 'Canons' of Henry II are also found in the collection extant in Montecassino, Archivio della Badia, MS 216, see Roger E. Reynolds, *The Collectio canonum Casinensis duodecimi seculi (Codex terscriptus)...: A Derivative of the South-Italian Collection in Five Books: An Implicit Edition with Introductory Study* (PIMS Studies and Texts 137 / Monumenta Liturgica Beneventana 3; Toronto 2001), here at 9.

30. For manuscripts, editions, and secondary literature, see Kéry 133–155, Fowler-Magerl, *Clavis* 85–90, and the literature mentioned below in notes 32–33 (manuscripts). For recent overviews, see Wilfried Hartmann, 'Burchards Dekret. Stand der Forschung und offene Fragen', *Bischof Burchard von Worms, 1000–1025*, ed. idem (Quellen und Abhandlungen zur mittelrheinischen Kirchengeschichte 100; Mainz 2000) 161–166 and most recently Kathleen Grace Cushing, 'Law and Reform: The Transmission of Burchard of Worms' *Liber decretorum*', *New Discourses in Medieval Canon Law Research: Challenging the Master Narrative*, ed. Christof Rolker (Medieval Law and Its Practice 28; Leiden and Boston 2019) 33–43. The best printed edition is still the *editio princeps* (also available online): *Burchardi Wormaciensis ecclesiae episcopi Decretorum libri XX ex consiliis et orthodoxorum patrum decretis, tum etiam diversarum nationum synodis seu loci communes congesti* (Cologne 1548). Its reprint contains an edition of Burchard's preface and a very useful introduction: Gérard Fransen, 'Le Décret de Burchard', *Burchard von Worms (Burchardus Wormaciensis ecclesiae episcopus), Decretorum libri XX [...]. Ergänzter Neudruck*, ed. idem and Theo Kölzer (Aalen 1992) 25–42. Migne's edition (PL 140; see below, note 38) should not be used, especially not the second edition of 1880. The fundamental study of the genesis of the *Liber decretorum* is Hoffmann and Pokorny, *Dekret*. A new long-term research project on Burchard ('Burchards Dekret Digital', based at the universities of Kassel, Mainz, and Erlangen) started when this book was mostly written.

31. See Burchard 2.217 for 1012 as *terminus post quem*; see Hoffmann and Pokorny, *Dekret* 111 (*terminus ante quem* 1022) and 160–161 (Worms manuscripts).

today there are still some eighty complete copies and dozens of fragments extant.[32] No other systematic collection before Gratian apart from the *Panormia* survives in so many manuscripts. The influence of Burchard's collection on canon law history was pervasive.[33]

The making of the *Liber decretorum* is known in much greater detail than that of most pre-Gratian canon law collections. This is due to the relatively large number of sources including the preface to the collection itself, the *Vita Burchardi*,[34] and generally the author's position as an influential bishop attested in many sources.[35] While there is no critical edition, research on the formal sources of the *Liber decretorum* has greatly elucidated Burchard's working method.[36] Fortunately for such research, the 1548 *editio princeps* relied on a very good copy.[37] (Less fortunately, the rather

32. See Pokorny's list in Kéry 134–144; for additions, see Mordek, *Kirchenrecht und Reform* 183 n. 402 (fragments), Reynolds, *Collectio Casinensis* 19–24 (overview), and idem, 'Penitentials in South and Central Italian Canon Law Manuscripts of the Tenth and Eleventh Centuries' *Early Medieval Europe* 14 (2006) 65–84, here at 82–83 (Beneventan manuscripts).

33. Otto Meyer, 'Überlieferung und Verbreitung des Dekrets des Bischofs Burchard von Worms' ZRG Kan. Abt. 24 (1935) 141–183 remains fundamental. See also Fournier, 'Décret' 695–701 (pre-Gratian collections); Peter Brommer, 'Kurzformen des Dekrets Bischof Burchards von Worms' *Jahrbuch für westdeutsche Landesgeschichte* 1 (1975) 19–45 (abbreviations); Peter Landau, 'Vorgratianische Kanonessammlungen bei den Dekretisten und in frühen Dekretalensammlungen', *Proceedings San Diego 1988* MIC Subsidia 9.93–116 (use after 1140); John Burden, *Between Crime and Sin: Penitential Justice in Medieval Germany, 900–1200* (Ph.D. thesis; Yale University, New Haven 2018) ch. 3 (abbreviations). For details, see below.

34. Stephanie Haarländer, 'Die Vita Burchardi im Rahmen der Bischofsviten seiner Zeit', *Bischof Burchard von Worms, 1000–1025*, ed. Wilfried Hartmann (Quellen und Abhandlungen zur mittelrheinischen Kirchengeschichte 100; Mainz 2000) 129–160.

35. Rudolf Schieffer, 'Burchard von Worms. Ein Reichsbischof und das Königtum', *Bischof Burchard von Worms, 1000–1025*, ed. Wilfried Hartmann (Quellen und Abhandlungen zur mittelrheinischen Kirchengeschichte 100; Mainz 2000) 29–49; see also Sita Steckel, *Kulturen des Lehrens im Früh- und Hochmittelalter. Autorität, Wissenskonzepte und Netzwerke von Gelehrten* (Norm und Struktur 39; Cologne, Weimar, and Vienna 2011), here at 730–741.

36. Paul Fournier, 'Études critiques sur le Décret de Burchard de Worms' NRHDFE 34 (1910) 41–112, 213–221, 289–331, and 564–584, esp. 41–112; Fuhrmann, *Einfluß und Verbreitung* 2.466–485; Max Kerner et al., 'Textidentifikation und Provenienzanalyse im Decretum Burchardi' SG 20 (1976) 19–63; Gérard Fransen, 'Le Décret de Burchard de Worms: valeur du texte de l'édition: essai de classement des manuscrits' ZRG Kan. Abt. 63 (1977) 1–19; Hoffmann and Pokorny, *Dekret* 165–276; Greta Austin, 'Secular Law in the *Collectio duodecim partium* and Burchard's *Decretum*', *Bishops, Texts and the Use of Canon Law Around 1100: Essays in Honour of Martin Brett*, ed. Bruce Clark Brasington and Kathleen Grace Cushing (CFC; Aldershot 2008) 28–44. See also Hubert Mordek, *Kirchenrecht und Reform im Frankenreich. Die Collectio Vetus Gallica, die älteste systematische Kanonessammlung des fränkischen Gallien: Studien und Edition* (Beiträge zur Geschichte und Quellenkunde des Mittelalters 1; Berlin and New York 1975), here at 177–178 and 182–183 for the indirect use of the *Vetus Gallica* (plausibly via the *Collection in 22 Chapters* in Paris, BnF, lat. 3841).

37. For the *editio princeps*, see above (note 30). See Gérard Fransen, 'La tradition manuscrite du Décret de Burchard de Worms: une première orientation', *Ius sacrum. Klaus Mörsdorf zum 60. Geburtstag*, ed. Audomar Scheuermann and Georg May (Munich 1969) 111–118, here at 117 on the text of the edition being very similar to Pal. lat. 585/586. As Fransen, 'Décret de Burchard' 34 pointed out, the 1548 edition shares variants with the copies today kept at Milan, Modena, and Cologne, with the latter possibly being the archetype of the others. The Cologne copy (Köln, Erzbischöfliche Diözesan- und Dombibliothek, Cod. 119), today fragmentary, was written at Worms in the 1020s according to Hoffmann and Pokorny, *Dekret* 20–21. For Pal. lat. 585/586, see ibid. 29–37.

unreliable Migne edition is still influential.[38]) In 1991, a palaeographical analysis of the early manuscripts provided scholars with exceptionally rich additional evidence for the making of this collection: Hartmut Hoffmann and Rudolf Pokorny traced several manuscripts of the *Liber decretorum* back to the scriptorium of Worms, and were able to show that some of them were written in Burchard's lifetime.[39] As they demonstrated, both the Vatican double codex and the Frankfurt copy contain traces of 'last minute' changes Burchard and his collaborators made to a mature version of the *Liber decretorum*.[40] The Frankfurt version (also known as 'Konstanzer Ordnung') became the vulgate version of Burchard, at least in Germany.[41] Together with the studies on the material and formal sources of the *Liber decretorum*, this discovery made it possible to study Burchard's working method in great detail. This is all the more important as Burchard is (in-)famous for having changed the texts he gathered in his collection, and this process can be analysed with much more confidence thanks to the identification of Burchard's 'working manuscripts'.

What was the library Burchard and his collaborators were working with like? Thanks to the continued work of many scholars,[42] the material sources of all but a handful of canons are known.[43] Yet despite this very considerable research, the exact transmission of the canons, in many cases, remains obscure. This has to do with Burchard's working method and the very independent nature of the *Liber decretorum*: Only very rarely did Burchard take over continuous series of canons from the collections he was working with.[44] Together with the absence of critical editions for

38. Migne's 1853 edition (PL 140.537–1058) was based on Fouchet's edition (Paris 1549), itself a reprint of the *editio princeps*; in 1880, a second edition of PL 140 was published. The textual quality decreased with every reprint. See already Emil Friedberg, *Eine neue kritische Ausgabe des Corpus iuris canonici: I. Das Decretum Gratiani. Herrn Gustav Friedrich Hänel zur Feier seines sechzigjährigen Doctorjubiläums am 18. April 1876 überreicht von der Juristenfacultät zu Leipzig* (Leipzig 1876), here at 25 ('überaus fehlerhaft'); more recently Kerner et al., 'Textidentifi kation' 23 and Fransen, 'Décret de Burchard' 27–28 came to similar conclusions.

39. Hoffmann and Pokorny, *Dekret* esp. 11–80.

40. Pal. lat. 585/586 (a Burchard copy in two volumes) and Frankfurt, UB, Ms. Barth. 50 (Hoffmann/Pokorny's **V** and **F**, respectively).

41. Meyer, 'Überlieferung' 180 (followed by other scholars) referred to the German vulgate version as 'Konstanzer Ordnung' because he assumed that Freiburg, UB, Hs. 7 (from Konstanz) was the oldest exemplar; but see Hoffmann and Pokorny, *Dekret* 12 (**F** produced 'unter Burchards Augen'). The version is sometimes referred to as 'Order of Worms, Type B' (Pokorny in Kéry 134); in the *Clavis* database, the relevant key is 'BV'.

42. For the older literature, see Kéry 145–155. The following is mainly based on Fournier, 'Études critiques' esp. 41–112, Kerner et al., 'Textidentifi kation', and Hoffmann and Pokorny, *Dekret* 165–276.

43. For the small number of unidentified canons, see Hoffmann and Pokorny, *Dekret* 168–169.

44. For example, Burchard 2.82–86 and 3.164–169 are among the longest series of canons taken *en bloc* from Regino. The short book twenty, which may have been added late, is slightly exceptional; here, there are series of up to a dozen canons or so taken from one work (Burchard 20.28–39, lifted from Ratramnus of Corbie, *De predestinatione*), and a very long series with only a few

many pre-Burchardian collections, this makes it difficult to establish the formal sources with certainty in many cases. However, plausible ways of transmission have been established for almost all canons.[45]

For a very large number of canons it is clear that they were taken from Burchard's main sources, the Italian *Anselmo dedicata* and the *Libri duo* of Regino of Prüm. While Regino provided more material (some 600 canons) than the *Anselmo dedicata* (some 300 canons),[46] the similarity of some book titles suggests that the latter may have been more important for the structure of the *Liber decretorum*. The other half of Burchard's canons came from a variety of sources. Burchard's collection draws on the *Dacheriana*, the *Hibernensis*, the collection of Pseudo-Remedius, two different versions of the Pseudo-Isidorian forgeries, and a small florilegium of excerpts taken from the letters of Gregory the Great ('C+P') that sometimes is transmitted together with Pseudo-Isidore.[47] Burchard further used a number of penitential books; the *Liber decretorum* contains excerpts from eight different penitentials, at least five of which were used directly.[48] Important sources, especially for German conciliar material, are intermediate collections used for both the *Liber decretorum* and 12P; some of them are extant, if in later copies, while others can only be reconstructed from the overlapping materials of subsequent compilers.[49] An especially interesting case is the collection in Clm 6241 (and the closely related Clm 3852), as it contains materials of relatively diverse origin (episcopal capitulary material, German councils, a short version of the *Hispana*, and penitential material) used for Burchard and the 12P.[50] No other manuscript is known that contains this combination of rare materials; some texts have no known circulation outside this collection. It seems to have been

interruption comes from the *Dialogues* and the *Moralia* of Gregory the Great (Burchard 20.44–53, 55–69, 70–90, and 94–99). See Hoffmann and Pokorny, *Dekret* 173–244 for all examples.

45. See Hoffmann and Pokorny, *Dekret* 165–171.

46. Hoffmann and Pokorny, *Dekret* 173–244 (general); Wilfried Hartmann, 'Einleitung. Regino von Prüm und sein Sendhandbuch', *Das Sendhandbuch des Regino von Prüm*, ed. and tr. idem (FSGA 42; Darmstadt 2004) 3–9, here at 7 (Regino); Kerner et al., 'Textidentifikation' 24 (*Anselmo dedicata*).

47. Fuhrmann, *Einfluß und Verbreitung* 2.466–479; Kerner et al., 'Textidentifikation' 36–39; Linda Fowler-Magerl, 'The Use of the Letters of Pope Gregory I in Northeastern France and Lorraine Before 1100', *"Ins Wasser geworfen und Ozeane durchquert". Festschrift für Knut Wolfgang Nörr*, ed. Mario Ascheri et al. (Cologne 2003) 237–260 (reception of 'C+P').

48. Hoffmann and Pokorny, *Dekret* 296–271 (eight different penitentials used for Burchard's *Liber decretorum*); Ludger Körntgen, 'Fortschreibung frühmittelalterlicher Bußpraxis. Burchards "Liber corrector" und seine Quellen', *Bischof Burchard von Worms, 1000–1025*, ed. Wilfried Hartmann (Quellen und Abhandlungen zur mittelrheinischen Kirchengeschichte 100; Mainz 2000) 199–226, esp. 213 (five penitentials used directly in book 19).

49. Müller, *Untersuchungen* 277–300; see below.

50. Hoffmann and Pokorny, *Dekret* 77–79.

compiled at Freising.[51] The canons Burchard took from this source characteristically are found at the end of single books of his *Liber decretorum*, and inserted as additions in the Vatican manuscripts, suggesting that the compilers learnt about them at a late stage of the work. This strongly suggests that Burchard, at a late stage, incorporated material that reached him from Freising.

As this short overview suggests, Burchard and his collaborators drew on a substantial set of sources, including several large collections. Often, these collections overlapped, containing the same or different versions of numerous canons. For example, Pseudo-Isidore's papal letters reached Burchard via the False Decretals themselves, but also via Pseudo-Remedius, Regino, and the *Anselmo dedicata*. Given that it was often very difficult to recognise this overlap, it is all the more impressive how coherent a collection the *Liber decretoum* is and how little internal overlap it contains. In addition, although the *Anselmo dedicata* partly served as a model for the division of material, the *Liber decretorum* in the end is a very independent collection. All this—internal coherence, absence of overlap, and independent structure—required not only considerable time, but a deep understanding of the materials and a clear plan. In addition to intellectual resources, the production of relatively many copies at Worms (as evident from the extant manuscripts) also required a well-equipped and well-trained scriptorium.

While Burchard's motives for this effort will be discussed later, the main result for his readers was that the scriptorium of Worms from the 1020s onwards, supplied many libraries with a well-structured collection of canon law. The *Liber decretorum* was a massive work, in some copies covering more than 300 folios, but the material is well organised; it is divided into twenty books according to subject matter, and a table of contents (a *capitulatio*) to every single book greatly helps to find what one is looking for. In addition to the canons themselves, the *Liber decretorum* contains other elements that various readers may have valued. Texts like the *formula* in Burchard 2.30 and the *epistola formata* in Burchard 2.227 may not be 'canon law', not even in the wide sense employed here, but were useful in the everyday business of church adminstration. The diagrams on the calculation of kinship are likewise 'user-friendly' elements of the collection.[52] After book three—or

---

51. The only known use of the material outside Burchard's *Liber decretorum* is the 12P; Clm 6241, and apparently Clm 3852 too, were written at Freising, and the episcopal capitulary just mentioned is from Freising (*Capitula Frisingensia tertia*). See the edition of the latter (ed. Pokorny, MGH Capit. episc. 3.216–230).

52. Hermann Schadt, *Die Darstellungen der Arbores consanguinitatis und der Arbores affinitatis. Bildschemata in juristischen Handschriften* (Tübingen 1982), esp. 109–135; as Schadt notes, Burchard's collection was the first major canon law collection to regularly contain such diagrams. This may

sometimes at the very beginning or end of the collection—a synodal order
is inserted.[53] This seems have met the needs of readers like Bishop Eber-
hard I of Konstanz (d. 1046) who highlighted the usefulness of the *Liber
decretorum* for the conduct of councils in particular, and similar praise
comes from Sigebert of Gembloux (d. 1112).[54] The large number of penitential canons and the considerable attention Burchard paid to lay matters
such as marriage made the *Liber decretorum* useful for pastors looking after
their flock.[55] For the secular clergy and indeed anyone dealing with confession, book 19 (also known as the *Corrector* or the *Medicus*) provided a good
overview of the Church's teaching in the form of a very long questionaire
which could easily be adopted for pastoral care (Burchard 19.5). One does
not imagine that parish priests would actually carry a complete copy of
Burchard with them when hearing confessions, and many would not have
been able to afford one. Still, the *Liber decretorum* and abbreviations thereof
could very well serve as teaching books for the 'simple priest', as Burchard
announced in the preface.[56] This is supported by a later source where the
Liber decretorum is mentioned among the penitential books a parish priest
could be expected to have access to and indeed to read frequently.[57] In any
case the *Corrector* had a wide circulation, as part of Burchard's collections,
in abbreviations thereof, and miscellany manuscripts.[58]

---

well have to do with the novelty of the rules Burchard presents, on which see Ubl, *Inzestverbot*.
For the Beneventan *Collection in Five Books*, which in some respects is similar to Burchard's *Liber
decretorum*, see Chapter 3.3.

53. Detlev Jasper, 'Burchards Dekret in der Sicht der Gregorianer', *Bischof Burchard von Worms,
1000–1025*, ed. Wilfried Hartmann (Quellen und Abhandlungen zur mittelrheinischen Kirchengeschichte 100; Mainz 2000) 167–198, here at 170. For the synodal order ('Ordo 5') itself and its transmission with Burchard, see Schneider (MGH Ordines 230–240).

54. Jasper, 'Burchards Dekret' 170.

55. Ludger Körntgen, 'Canon Law and the Practice of Penance: Burchard of Worms's Penitential' *Early Medieval Europe* 14 (2006) 103–117; Meens, *Penance* 148–157.

56. See also Meens, *Penance* 148–149 on this point.

57. The treatise *Homo quidam*, extant in two copies made around 1200, as quoted by Joseph
Goering, 'The Internal Forum and the Literature of Penance and Confession', *The History of
Medieval Canon Law in the Classical Period, 1140–1234: From Gratian to the Decretals of Pope Gregory
IX*, ed. Wilfried Hartmann and Kenneth Pennington (HMCL; Washington, D.C. 2008) 379–425,
here at 402 n. 78: 'Legat ergo sacerdos frequenter in abside ecclesiae poenitentiale Romanum vel
Theodori Cantuariensis vel Bedae vel Brocardi vel ex eis excerpta, quia, ut dicit Augustinus, poe-
nitentiae non sunt legitimae, quae secundum canones non assignantur.' See also Meens, *Penance*
211 (with discussion of the date).

58. Pokorny in Kéry 134–144 lists only three manuscripts for the *Corrector*, but see Hermann
Joseph Schmitz, *Die Bussbücher und die Bussdisciplin der Kirche. Nach handschriftlichen Quellen dargestellt* (2 vols; Mainz 1883 and Dusseldorf 1898) here at 2.764–772 and Brommer, 'Kurzformen'
24 n. 24. For important corrections of Schmitz and Brommer see Burden, *Crime and Sin* 81–84,
pointing out that contrary to what Schmitz suggested only few (mostly late) manuscripts contain
only the *Corrector*; most are abbreviations of Burchard or miscellaneous manuscripts. The Prague
manuscript Burden (ibid. 82 n. 13) refers to is Praha, Národní knihovna České republiky, X.A.11,
where the excerpts from Burchard 19 are found fols. 113va–119vb according to the catalogue: Josef

Of course, different readers used Burchard for different purposes. Generally speaking, the *Liber decretorum* seems to have met the needs of episcopal administration exceptionally well. Indeed the material contained in the *Liber decretorum* covers many of the diverse issues bishops were likely to deal with as pastors, judges, and administrators. On the whole, bishops seem to have valued these qualities of Burchard even more than abbots did, as most extant copies are from episcopal rather than monastic libraries.[59] This may also have to do with the special attention Burchard gave to episcopal rights, while monasteries are mainly treated in their relation to the diocesan bishop. Yet it is also true that abbots of great monastic houses had similar needs to those of many bishops, and would have found Burchard useful for the same reasons as bishops did. The twelfth-century library catalogue from Bec, for example, contains a handful of references to canon law collections. For most of these manuscripts, the modern reader is left to guess what was referred to specifically by terms like 'papal letters; canons; excerpts from decretals; a collection of canons', to quote the description of four volumes found in the library.[60] However, when the monk compiling the catalogue looked at Burchard, he seems to have become somewhat more enthusiastic: 'One manuscript with the collection of Bishop Burchard of Worms in twenty books, containing what is necessary to deal with both secular and ecclesiastic businesses'.[61] In addition to the praise for Burchard found here it is also worth noting that it is the only legal manuscript in the Bec catalogue that was linked to a named author. Burchard's name was not only attached to the collection (which is already rare for pre-Gratian collections), but the *Liber decretorum* was referred to by this name, a fact already commented upon by medieval authors like Sigebert of Gembloux.[62] Ivo of Chartres (d. 1115) in one of his letters to Fécamp quoted a canon 'as found in Burchard's collection'.[63] What is most striking, Ivo here in all likelihood was quoting from his *own* canon law collection,[64] but chose to tell where he himself had taken this material from. Apparently, Ivo assumed that this information was useful for the recipient of his letter.[65]

Truhlář, *Catalogus codicum manu scriptorum latinorum qui in C. R. Bibliotheca publica atque Universitatis pragensis asservantur* (2 vols. Prague 1905/06) 2.35–36 no. 1814.

59. Meyer, 'Überlieferung' 166.

60. The catalogue is printed in Gustav Becker, *Catalogi bibliothecarum antiqui* (Bonn 1885) 127. The four entries quoted above (Becker's nos. 120–123) are described as 'in alio [volumine] decreta pontificum; in alio canones; in alio excerpta decretorum; in alio corpus canonum'.

61. Becker, *Catalogi* no. 125: 'in uno volumine collectiones Burcardi Wormatiensis episcopi libri XX tam ad ecclesiastica quam secularia negotia pertractanda necessarie'.

62. See Jasper, 'Burchards Dekret' 170.

63. Ivo, *Ep.* 80 (PL 161.101): 'in collectionibus [...] Burchardi episcopi Wormacensis'.

64. Rolker, *Canon Law* 152.

65. Geneviève Nortier, *Les bibliothèques médiévales des abbayes bénédictines de Normandie: Fécamp,*

In short, the success of the *Liber decretorum* began very early and was directly linked to his name. Indeed, Burchard himself seems to have had his work distributed, and the scriptorium of Worms must have been brimming with activity during his pontificate.[66] Already in the 1020s the *Liber decretorum* was used on several occasions: It was quoted in Freising in 1022, at the Council of Seligenstadt in 1023, and by Conrad II in 1025.[67] Within two or three decades after its compilation it was known widely in Germany, Burgundy, and Italy. By the middle of the century, copies were held at Besançon, Bamberg, Eichstätt, Freising, Geneva, Hildesheim, Konstanz, Liège, Mainz, Modena, Montecassino, Nonantola, Novara, Parma, and certainly elsewhere too.[68] For the earliest reception, the scriptorium of Worms can be demonstrated to have played an active role, and it is plausible to assume that Henry II helped to have the collection distributed in the Empire. Nonetheless, the ultimate success of Burchard was driven by demand, not supply, and this demand clearly grew in the course of the eleventh century. This is particularly true for Italy, where most extant Burchard copies were produced. In the second half of the century, a large number of new collections were compiled in Italy, and an even larger number of polemic writings were produced; for both genres, the *Liber decretorum* was a valuable source.[69] Thus, a large number of so-called Gregorians, including Peter Damian, Humbert of Silva Candida, Bernold of Konstanz, Deusdedit, and Hugh of Lyon, all read and used Burchard, and so did very many compilers of canon law collections. In the rest of Europe, Burchard spread more slowly, but by 1100, the collection was known widely in the area of modern Germany, Italy, Belgium, Netherlands, and most of modern France. When Burchard reached Normandy, for example, is still subject to some speculation.[70] In England, Burchard was known before 1100, with Ernulf's *De incestis coniugiis* as the earliest securely datable work drawing on it.[71] Several manuscripts suggest that Burchard was

---

Le Bec, Le Mont Saint-Michel, Saint-Évroul, Lyre, Jumièges, Saint-Wandrille, Saint-Ouen (Bibliothèque d'histoire et d'archéologie chretiennes 9; Paris 1971) did not find any evidence that Fécamp possessed a copy of Burchard.

66. Hoffmann and Pokorny, *Dekret* 11–64 and 160–161.

67. Jasper, 'Burchards Dekret' 168–169 and MGH Conc. 8.16–32 (Seligenstadt); D Ko II 41 (ed. Bresslau, MGH DD 4.46–47); Müller, *Untersuchungen* 357. For Freising, see below.

68. Hoffmann and Pokorny, *Dekret* 160–161; Kéry 134–144; Jasper, 'Burchards Dekret' 168–170.

69. Jasper, 'Burchards Dekret' 168–170.

70. See most recently Fabrice Delivré, 'L'ombre de Lanfranc: l'espace canonique anglo-normand (XIᵉ–XIIᵉ siècle)', *Autour de Lanfranc (1010–2010): réforme et réformateurs dans l'Europe du Nord-Ouest (XIᵉ–XIIᵉ siècles)*, ed. Julia Barrow et al. (Caen 2015) 85–105, here at 89.

71. Cramer, 'Ernulf of Rochester' 498; Brett, 'Collectio Lanfranci' 167–168.

known either directly or indirectly in England around 1100.[72] By this time, the *Liber decretorum* had also reached eastern Europe.[73]

In the twelfth century, Burchard's collection continued to be copied, used, and quoted frequently. Gratian is exceptional in *not* having used the *Liber decretorum*, or at least not for more than a handful of texts.[74] Whatever the reason for this was, it was soon compensated by the first generation of Gratian's users: About half the *palea* are taken from Burchard.[75] The decretists still quoted from Burchard,[76] and new abbreviations of his *Liber decretorum* emerged in many places.[77] Burchard's collection had a massive influence from the time it was compiled, and well into the twelfth century; in the eleventh century, the *Liber decretorum* additionally was the most influential model of how to compile a canon law collection. As will become clear in the course of this (and the following) chapter, very many compilers took Burchard as the starting point for their own collections.

2.4 The *Collection in Twelve Parts*: Genesis, Structure, Versions

Canon law history of the early eleventh century has been dominated by studies on Burchard and his collection, and this is particularly true for research on the *Collection in Twelve Parts* (= 12P) from Freising.[78] From its compilation on, 12P was related to Burchard's *Liber decretorum*; soon after

72. A single Burchard canon was added early to Lanfranc's copy of the *Collectio Lanfranci* (Gullick, 'Lanfranc' 85). Durham, Cathedral Library, B.IV.17, a short version of Burchard, seems to have been written not long after 1100. The Hereford copy of the Burchard-derivative 17L is of a similar date, as Martin Brett kindly informed me (private communication); he also pointed out that is quite unclear when London, BL, Cotton MS Claudius C VI, probably written before 1100, reached Canterbury.

73. Nowak, 'Papsttum' 364–365.

74. Rudolf Weigand, 'Mittelalterliche Texte. Gregor I., Burchard und Gratian' ZRG Kan. Abt. 84 (1998) 330–344, here at 332–339; Peter Landau, 'Burchard de Worms et Gratien: à propos des sources immédiates de Gratien' *Revue de Droit canonique* 48 (1998) 233–245, followed by Anders Winroth, *The Making of Gratian's Decretum* (Life and Thought: Fourth Series 49; Cambridge 2000), here at 52 (all on 'Gratian 1').

75. Rudolf Weigand, 'Burchardauszüge in Dekrethandschriften und ihre Verwendung bei Rufin als Paleae im Dekret Gratians' AKKR 158 (1989) 429–451.

76. Weigand, 'Burchardauszüge'; Landau, 'Vorgratianische Kanonessammlungen'.

77. Brommer, 'Kurzformen' (almost all manuscripts listed here were copied in the twelfth century).

78. For manuscripts, editions, and secondary literature, see Kéry 155–157 and Fowler-Magerl, *Clavis* 91–93. The following is based on Müller, *Untersuchungen*; Hoffmann and Pokorny, *Dekret*; Jörg Müller, 'Die Überlieferung der Briefe Papst Gregors I. im Rahmen der CDP', *Licet preter solitum. Ludwig Falkenstein zum 65. Geburtstag*, ed. Lotte Kéry et al. (Aachen 1998) 17–31; Koal, *Studien* 138–197; Detlev Jasper, 'The Beginning of the Decretal Tradition: Papal Letters from the Origin of the Genre Through the Pontificate of Stephen V', *Papal Letters in the Early Middle Ages*, ed. idem and Horst Fuhrmann (HMCL; Washington, D.C. 2001) 3–133, here at 118–119; Greta Austin, 'Freising and Worms in the Early Eleventh Century: Revisiting the Relationship Between the *Collectio duodecim partium* and Burchard's *Decretum*' ZRG Kan. Abt. 93 (2007) 45–108; eadem, 'Secular Law'.

it was completed, the two collections were combined, and later readers of *12P* often confused it with the more famous collection from Worms.[79] From the time of the Ballerini brothers on, it was clear that Burchard's collection and *12P* were intimately related to each other.[80] The question of how exactly the two works were related had limited impact on Burchard studies, but it has dominated research on *12P*. This discussion has sometimes obscured the fact that *12P*—whatever its exact relation to Burchard— was an important collection in its own right that enjoyed considerable circulation. Compared to the *Liber decretorum*, the structure of *12P* is somewhat less refined, the number of extant manuscripts is modest, and the content of the collection is less stable. However, the same would be true for almost *any* pre-Gratian canon law collection if compared to Burchard; the comparison tells us something about the exceptionality of Burchard's collection but little about *12P*. If one compares *12P* not to Burchard but to other pre-Gratian collections, it is manifest that *12P* is a major collection by any standard. Even in its shorter version, *12P* contains more material than almost any pre-Gratian collection and was copied more widely than many earlier works (again including much smaller collections).

So what kind of collection is *12P*? It is a systematic canon law collection, taking its name from the twelve books (*partes*) into which it is divided. It was compiled in the early eleventh century at Freising; unlike Burchard, there was no tight control over any 'final' version. Rather, like so many pre-Gratian collections, the *12P* continued to be added to and revised with almost every copy made; this makes it difficult to analyse the collection, and in particular impairs a precise dating of the collection. Shared formal sources (which will be discussed below) indicate that *12P* and the *Liber decretorum* were the result of cooperation between Freising and Worms. While it is clear that the *12P* as found in the extant manuscripts cannot have been produced before the Frankfurt and the Vatican manuscripts of Burchard were available,[81] it is much more difficult to determine when *12P* was begun and at what date it became a collection in its own right. When one considers that the same sources (and perhaps even the same

---

79. See Müller, *Untersuchungen* 24 and 42–47 (*12P* manuscripts containing Burchard material) and ibid. 15 and 43 (*12P* manuscripts referred to as 'Burchard'). The Troyes manuscript, containing Burchard's preface, was described as containing 'Collectarium canonum Burchardi' by a late-medieval hand on fol. 1, an error repeated by the *Catalogue général* 21 (1885) 140 and, most recently, the description of the manuscript in the BVMM and Medium databases (https://bvmm .irht.cnrs.fr; http://medium-avance.irht.cnrs.fr/).

80. Pietro and Girolamo Ballerini, 'De antiquis tum editis tum ineditis collectionibus et collectoribus canonum ad Gratianum usque', *Sancti Leonis Magni Romani pontificis opera*, ed. iidem (Venice 1757) i–cccxx, reprinted in PL 56.11–354, here at 350–351.

81. On this point, I follow Hoffmann and Pokorny, *Dekret* 87–107.

manuscripts) were used both at Worms to produce the *Liber decretorum* and at Freising for *12P*, then it seems sound to assume that *12P* was compiled parallel to Burchard. This is supported by the fact that exchange between Worms and Freising is best attested for the time of Burchard of Worms and Egilbert of Freising—that is, the years between Egilbert's consecration in 1005 and Burchard's death in 1025.[82] In addition, the *12P* compilers seem to have exchanged manuscripts with Bamberg. The cathedral library early in the eleventh century acquired copies both of *12P* and collections that were used to produce *12P* (namely the *Anselmo dedicata* and the *Liber decretorum*); Bamberg may even have been a place where *12P* was reworked.[83] According to Hoffmann, scribes both from Bamberg and Freising produced the *12P* copy kept at Bamberg.[84] Evidence outside *12P* itself suggests that Burchard's collection was available at Freising as early as summer 1022,[85] while *12P* almost certainly was quoted at Freising in the life-time of Egilbert (d. 1039). His pontifical contains two passages, apparently written late in Egilbert's life, that seem to be taken from *12P*.[86] This suggests that *12P* was in existence in the 1030s, even if this does not tell us much what the version looked like. A much later completion of *12P* is

82. Müller, *Untersuchungen* 361–362 (Burchard and Egilbert); Hoffmann and Pokorny, *Dekret* 160 (manuscripts).

83. Bamberg, SB, Msc.Can.5 is a copy of the *Anselmo dedicata* from the late tenth century, written in northern Italy and commonly thought to have been given to Bamberg at its foundation in 1007. Bamberg, SB, Msc.Can.6 is a very early Burchard copy made in Worms; see Hoffmann and Pokorny, *Dekret* 16–18 (and passim) and Hartmut Hoffmann, *Bamberger Handschriften des 10. und des 11. Jahrhunderts* (MGH Schriften 39; Hanover 1995), esp. 122. Bamberg, SB, Msc.Can.7 contains the second version of *12P*; Müller, *Untersuchungen* 19 claimed that it was written saec. $XI^{1/3}$, but see Hoffmann, *Bamberger Handschriften* 418 (saec. $XI^{1/3}$ or saec. $XI^{2/3}$) and Suckale-Redlefsen, *Handschriften* 1.155 ('saec. $XI^{2/2}$', but quoting Hoffmann for saec. $XI^{2/4}$). Both Bamberg, SB, Msc. Can.8, fols. 1–182 and Msc.Can.9, fols. 2–101 contain 'excerpts' of the second version of *12P*; Msc. Can.9 was dated saec. $XI^{2/3}$ by Müller while Hoffmann thought an earlier date possible: Hartmut Hoffmann, *Buchkunst und Königtum im ottonischen und frühsalischen Reich* (2 vols. Stuttgart 1986), here at 418.

84. Bamberg, SB, Msc.Can.7; see Hoffmann, *Bamberger Handschriften* 122 (and passim).

85. Hoffmann and Pokorny, *Dekret* 110–113 demonstrate that a single leaf written at Freising (Cgm [*sic*] 5248,7) with a list of consecrations Egilbert conferred 16 June 1022 also contains a quote from the council of Chalcedon that could well have been taken from Burchard 2.6. The Freising fragment shares variant readings found in the Burchard copy at Bamberg (Bamberg, SB, Msc.Can.6) while *12P* has a version of the text also found in the Frankfurt copy of Burchard after correction (Frankfurt, UB, Ms. Barth. 50). Hoffmann and Pokorny conclude that the Freising scribe in 1022 had access to an earlier version of Burchard while *12P* depends on the version that incorporated the changes made to the Frankfurt manuscript.

86. Clm 6425, fols. 127r–129v and Clm 21587, fol. 138r, respectively, see Hoffmann and Pokorny, *Dekret* 113 n. 73. Clm 6425 was produced 'in the very last years of Egilbert's pontificate' according to Hoffmann, *Buchkunst* 211; Clm 21587 may have been written between 1025 and 1035 (but certainly before 1039) according to Elisabeth Klemm, *Die ottonischen und frühromanischen Handschriften der Bayerischen Staatsbibliothek* (Katalog der illuminierten Handschriften der Bayerischen Staatsbibliothek in München 2; Wiesbaden 2004), here at 96–97. Hoffmann has later argued that Clm 6425, fols. 127r–129v was written 'around 1040' (Hoffmann and Pokorny, *Dekret* 113 n. 73). Koal, *Studien* 154 assumed that Clm 6425 provided a *terminus ante quem* 1039 for *12P*.

unlikely in any case, as the earliest extant manuscripts may date from the middle of the eleventh century.[87] All in all, the evidence available strongly points to the pontificate of Egilbert for the compilation of *12P* including the production of the version found in the extant manuscripts, and perhaps even some of these very manuscripts.

For a better understanding of the genesis of *12P*, more systematic studies on the formal sources are needed.[88] For Burchard, decades of specialized scholarship have slowly reduced the number of canons from uncertain sources to a handful of texts; for *12P*, most of the work remains to be done. The key question here remains the exact relationship to Burchard, as it seems to have influenced the nascent *12P* at various stages, and all extant copies of *12P* are heavily influenced by a mature form of Burchard.[89] Some 90 per cent of the Burchard material is found in the larger *12P* too, and in the first version (Müller's 2CDP) in particular, long series of canons are found in the same order in both collections.[90] The texts in *12P* generally agree with the mature form of Burchard as found in Hoffmann/ Pokorny's manuscripts **V** and **F**, even where these two manuscripts contain changes made at a late stage of the work.[91] Yet Burchard's book twenty, possibly added to the *Liber decretorum* at the final stage, and the canons of the Council of Seligenstadt 1023, were not taken into the *12P*; this may be a clue to the Burchard version used at Freising, but alternatively it may also reflect the selection criteria of the *12P* compilers.

While *12P* in its extant form depends on a mature version of Burchard, it is also clear that Burchard used Freising materials and that *12P* cannot be simply a derivative of Burchard's collection.[92] Even if one assumes that

---

87. Müller, *Untersuchungen* 19 claimed that Bamberg, SB, Msc.Can.7 was written saec. XI$^{1/3}$, but see Hoffmann, *Bamberger Handschriften* 418 (saec. XI$^{1/3}$ or saec. XI$^{2/3}$) and Suckale-Redlefsen, *Handschriften* 1.155 (saec. XI$^{2/2}$, but quoting Hoffmann for saec. XI$^{2/4}$).

88. The most recent catalogue of sources is that by Jörg Müller, *Die Collectio duodecim partium und ihr Freisinger Umfeld* ([Munich] 1995), here at 13. In addition to the *Anselmo dedicata*, Müller lists 'die Konziliensammlung des Clm 27246, die Freisinger Materialsammlung, der Recueil Krause sowie die bereits oben erwähnten Werke Halitgars und Julians von Toledo, daneben einzelne Kapitel einer Collectio Novariensis, die nicht innerhalb einer Collectio Anselmo Dedicata der CDP vermittelt sein können. Weiterhin wurde Reginos Sammlung von den Redaktoren benutzt und zwar in der Wiener Version der interpolierten Fassung [...].' The following collections were used either directly or indirectly according to Müller (ibid.): 'eine Dacheriana in der Form B, die Hispana, die Dionysiana, mit vereinzelten Übernahmen aus dem Quadripartitus, außerdem Pseudo-Isidor sowohl in der "Cluny-Langversion" als auch in der "A2-Kurzversion".' This analysis is based on the assumption that similarities between Burchard and *12P* can be largely explained by a common source (ibid. 14). On the 'Cluny' version of Pseudo-Isidore, see Schon, 'Redaktion'.

89. Hoffmann and Pokorny, *Dekret* 87–107.

90. Müller, *Untersuchungen* 261–262.

91. Hoffmann and Pokorny, *Dekret* 87–107. The manuscripts are Pal. lat. 585/586 and Frankfurt, UB, Ms. Barth. 50, for which see above (notes 40 and 85).

92. This was claimed by Paul Fournier, 'La collection canonique dite "Collectio XII partium":

all texts *12P* and Burchard have in common were adopted from the latter, there remain texts in *12P* that show an independent use of the same sources Burchard had employed too.[93] The list of sources needed to compile *12P* includes every important collection required to produce Burchard.[94] Modern research has repeatedly stated that the two collections indeed seem to draw on a number of shared sources, but much research remains to be done. The case is clear for the important *Anselmo dedicata*;[95] it may have served the *12P* compilers as a model in dividing the material into twelve books (but not for the content of individual books).[96] Gregory I's letters not found in Burchard may have been taken into *12P* from the *Anselmo dedicata*, too.[97] The case of a direct use of Regino (independently from Burchard) is more difficult to decide. When Müller asserted a direct use of Regino, he assumed that *12P* predated Burchard's collection,[98] or that both collections drew on a common source.[99] In fact, a direct use of Regino is thought possible also by scholars who do not share this view. Both Greta Austin, who was sceptical vis-à-vis the assumption of an 'X' collection as explaining the similarities of Burchard and *12P*,[100] and Valeska Koal, who assumed that *12P* was largely derivative of Burchard, conceded that *12P* might have drawn on Regino independently of Burchard.[101] However, if one excludes Regino texts found in both Burchard and *12P*, the number

étude sur un recueil canonique allemand du XIe siècle' *Revue d'Histoire de l'Eglise de France* 17 (1921) 31–62 and 229–259.

93. On this, Hoffmann and Pokorny, *Dekret* 106 agree with Müller, *Untersuchungen*.

94. See already Fournier, 'Recueil canonique' esp. 229 on *Anselmo dedicata*, Regino, the *Hibernensis*, and the *Dacheriana*.

95. Müller, *Untersuchungen* 316–325. On the *Anselmo dedicata* version used for *12P*, see also Fowler-Magerl, *Clavis* 71: 'In both manuscripts [Bamberg, Msc.Can.7 and Paris, BnF, lat. 15392, CR] the texts of the last six canons in part 8 (all in the section containing excerpts from the register of Gregory) are missing although rubrics for these canons are found in the *capitulatio*. I supplied the missing texts from the Karlsruhe manuscript [Badische Landesbibliothek, Aug. perg. 142, CR]. Some of these missing canons are found in the 11th century Freising *Collectio XII partium* with exactly the same rubrics.'

96. Both versions are divided into twelve books, and the compiler of the second version seems to have made an effort to preserve this number: while the compiler essentially added a new book at the end, he reorganized the other material so that the total number was still twelve. For the preface of the second version, see below.

97. Müller, *Untersuchungen* 316–323; idem, 'Überlieferung'. See also Friedrich Wilhelm Hermann Wasserschleben, *Beiträge zur Geschichte der vorgratianischen Kirchenrechtsquellen* (Leipzig 1839), here at 37–38 (working with Berlin, SBPK, Savigny 2).

98. Müller, *Untersuchungen* 301–315, esp. 306–307 (as quoted below, note 73).

99. Müller, *Collectio* 13, referring to idem, *Untersuchungen* 301–315. See next note

100. Austin, 'Freising', using the term 'X collection' for a lost intermediary collection that already contained much of the shared material of Burchard and *12P*, as argued by Müller. As she put it (ibid. 102), 'most of the arguments for an X collection can be explained without an X collection. There does not seem to be compelling evidence for it.'

101. See Austin, 'Freising' 57–59 and Koal, *Studien* 185, respectively. Note that Koal's analysis of Burchard is based on the 1880 Migne edition.

of proof texts for an independent use of the *Libri duo* becomes very small indeed.[102] Here, further research is needed. This is also true for the *Dacheriana*; both Burchard and the *12P* contain texts from this collection, but it is difficult to distinguish between direct and indirect use in *12P* with certainty.[103] Likewise, a direct use of the *Hibernensis*, while repeatedly asserted in the secondary literature, in my opinion has still to be demonstrated.[104]

While these findings would not perhaps convince a sceptical reader of *12P* being an independent work, crucial evidence is available especially for the conciliar canons found in *12P* and the *Liber decretorum*. Fournier, Müller, and Hoffmann/Pokorny all agree that both *12P* and Burchard drew independently on common sources for these materials, and possibly even the same manuscripts. Collections similar to that extant in Clm 6241 and 6245 (both from Freising) were used by the *12P* compilers and Burchard for rare conciliar canons.[105] A collection similar to that in Clm 6245 seems also to have provided the *12P* compilers with excerpts from the letters of Nicholas I.[106] Likewise, a collection very similar to that in Clm 27246 seems to have been used by Burchard and *12P*.[107] The material taken from this source is extremely rare, it is not known to have been used in other collections, and the copies used at Worms and Freising must have been very similar.[108] The use of all these intermediate collections by

102. Müller, *Untersuchungen* 306–307, after having discussed a total of 48 canons in *12P* that have a parallel in Regino: 'Somit bleiben letztlich nur zehn Kapitel der CDP, die vermutlich ihre Vorlage in der Appendix 3 der Wiener Version [von Reginos *Sendhandbuch*, CR] haben. Nur zwei davon haben jedoch zu dem heutigen Textbestand, der allerdings nur aus seiner einzigen Handschrift bekannt ist, keinerlei Abweichungen.' As Müller further notes, the two canons in question are also found in Burchard (ibid. 307 n. 1343).

103. Müller, *Untersuchungen* 326–334.

104. Contrary to what Müller, 'Überlieferung' 21 suggests, Fournier, 'Recueil canonique' 249–250 was very cautious concerning a direct use of the *Hibernensis*. Müller, *Untersuchungen* 11 quotes Fournier's suggestion, but does not discuss it. Müller, *Collectio* 13 does *not* list the *Hibernensis* among the sources of *12P*. Müller, 'Überlieferung' 20–21 asserts the use of the *Hibernensis* for several excerpts from Gregory I, but quotes only two *Hibernensis* canons found in the first version of *12P* but not in Burchard. One of the two may also have been taken from a collection similar to Clm 6245, as Müller, *Collectio* 6 suggests. Both Fowler-Magerl, *Clavis* 91 and Austin, 'Freising' 45 assert a direct use of *Hibernensis* without discussion.

105. Müller, *Untersuchungen* 136–137; Hoffmann and Pokorny, *Dekret* 76 and 106.

106. Müller, *Untersuchungen* 166 and Jasper, 'Beginning' 118.

107. Müller, *Untersuchungen* 297–301; idem, *Collectio duodecim partium* 6–7. For the use of this collection at Seligenstadt 1023 see now Greta Austin, 'How the Local Council of Seligenstadt in 1023 Drew upon Books of Church Law', *The Use of Canon Law in Ecclesiastical Administration, 1000–1234*, ed. Danica Summerlin and Melodie Harris Eichbauer (Medieval Law and Its Practice 26; Leiden 2018) 159–182, here at 118–120.

108. See Fournier, 'Recueil canonique' esp. 27 and 36; Müller, *Untersuchungen* 297–301 (general) and 58–78 (on the Councils of Erfurt 932, Koblenz 922, and Hohenaltheim 916); Hoffmann and Pokorny, *Dekret* 106 (on Koblenz and Erfurt). See also Ernst-Dieter Hehl, 'Hohenaltheim', *Die Konzilien Deutschlands und Reichsitaliens 916–1001, Teil 1: 916–961*, ed. idem (MGH Conc. 6.1; Hanover 1987) 1–40, esp. 6–15.

Burchard and *12P* strongly suggests a close cooperation between Freising and Worms in the making of the two collections. As will be discussed later on, the exchange of texts must have included smaller working collections some of which can only have been assembled as a direct preparation for Burchard's *Liber decretorum*. Other materials were used for *12P* but not at Worms. Here, the most important source was the intermediate collection in München, Clm 3851 and 3853 (and other manuscripts), which Fournier called the 'receuil Krause'.[109]

The compilers of *12P* evidently drew on a large number of sources, including intermediate collections at least partly compiled at Freising (though not necessarily in preparation of the *12P*). A surprising number of these collections has survived. Even if much research is still needed, this allows one to study the working method of the *12P* compilers at close range. Above all, the compilers at Freising were far more reluctant to adapt their source texts than Burchard was, a further important argument for *12P* as an independent collection.

As some of the characteristic concerns of the *12P* compilers will be discussed later on, for the moment it suffices to say that the *12P* compilers produced a very substantial collection that covered all aspects of ecclesiastical life, and like Burchard may have been specifically useful for bishops. Two main versions of *12P* can be distinguished.[110] The earlier version (Müller's 2CDP) contains some 2,600 canons, the second one (Müller's 1CDP) some 2,900 canons in the extant manuscripts.[111] In addition, there are a number of 'excerpts', as they are known, shorter versions of *12P* which still contain between 1,000 and 2,000 canons; covering up to 180 folios, these 'short' versions are still much larger than most pre-Gratian collections.[112] In other words, *12P* is a massive collection by any standard, and both the original compilation and the later reworking must have required considerable effort.

The two main versions (Müller's 2CDP and 1CDP) contain much of the same material, and both divide their material into twelve books, essentially following the same plan. Within the individual books, however, there is wide variation, and the total number of canons is different too. The main difference contains the last book of the second version. All but

---

109. Fournier, 'Recueil canonique' 233–240, largely following the analysis of Victor Krause, 'Die Münchener Handschriften 3851 [und] 3853 mit einer Compilation von 181 Wormser Schlüssen' NA 19 (1893) 85–139. See Müller, *Untersuchungen* 277–284; idem, *Collectio duodecim partium* 2–5; Koal, *Studien* 158–184 (capitulary canons).

110. Fournier, 'Recueil canonique'; Müller, *Untersuchungen* 14.

111. Müller, *Untersuchungen* 23 and 37, respectively.

112. Bamberg, SB, Msc.Can.8, fols. 1–182 and Msc.Can.9, fols. 2–101.

three of the canons found here have no parallel in the earlier version, and can be considered as additions made by the compiler of Müller's 1CDP.

Both *12P* versions contain a preface, but only that to the second version was written from the outset to introduce what follows. Here, the collection is referred to as divided into twelve books 'for the love of the number of the Apostles', not unlike the *Anselmo dedicata*.[113] The two extant manuscripts of the first version, in contrast, contain the preface of Burchard's *Liber decretorum*.[114] In the Troyes manuscript this prologue is adapted to the structure of *12P* in announcing a collection in twelve books, while in the Saint-Claude manuscript the preface mentions twenty books (fitting the *Liber decretorum*). The preface is manifestly that of Burchard, who is mentioned by name in both manuscripts. This may seem odd to modern readers, but one should remember that prefaces to pre-Gratian canon law collections might circulate quite independently of the original work, and could be set at the beginning of other collections with or without much further reworking. Ivo's famous *Prologue*, for example, is found at the beginning of half a dozen canonical collections. Vice versa, some collections accumulated multiple introductions: *5L* has no less than eight prefaces (plus an epilogue), including three prefaces taken from other collections.[115] In contrast, the preface to Regino's *Libri duo* was not adopted by any other collection—in fact, it is found in only one copy of the *Libri duo* while most copies contains the collection but no preface.[116] The Burchard preface in the Troyes and the Saint-Claude manuscripts is additional evidence that these two copies of the first version of *12P*, or a common ancestor, were influenced by a mature version of the *Liber decretorum*;[117] but it is not proof that *12P* itself was only a reworked version of Burchard's collection. As for the content of the two *12P* versions, the book titles can give a first impression of the slightly different organisation of the two *12P* versions:[118]

---

113. *12P* preface, ed. Wasserschleben, *Beiträge* 35: 'Amore scilicet ductus apostolici numeri, duodenas in partes librum colligi'; *Anselmo dedicata* preface, ed. Jean Claude Besse, 'Collectionis "Anselmo dedicata" liber primus' *Revue de Droit canonique* 9 (1959) 207–296, here at 212: 'paginas in duodecim partes instar apostolici stemmatis censui distinguendas'.

114. Troyes, BM, 246; Saint-Claude, BM, 17. For these manuscripts, and two fragments of the first version, see Müller, *Untersuchungen* 34–42.

115. There are individual prefaces to books two to five, four prefaces introducing the whole collection, and an epilogue. See Fowler-Magerl, *Clavis* 83.

116. Hartmann, 'Einleitung' 5.

117. Émile van Balberghe, 'La Préface du Décret et la *Collectio XII Partium*' BMCL 3 (1973) 7–10. The preface may be assumed to have been written at a late stage in any case, and the reference to twenty books is further proof that the preface was adopted from a mature form of the *Decretum*, which originally contained only nineteen books according to Hoffmann and Pokorny, *Dekret* 40.

118. Adopted with minor corrections for the first version from Müller, *Untersuchungen* 16–18 and 35–36 (summarized in idem, *Collectio* 9). Where I did not find book titles in the Troyes manuscript (books 4–5, 7, 9, and 11), I follow Müller who supplemented them from the Saint-Claude

Table 1: Book Titles of the Two Versions of *12P*

First Version (Müller's 2CDP)	Second Version (Müller's 1CDP)
1. *De sacerdotali ordine*	1. *De episcopis*
2. *De ordinibus sacris* (Troyes, fol. 46r) or *De sacris ordinibus* (running title fols. 50–60) / *De ministerio episcoporum* (Saint-Claude)	2. *De sacris ordinibus*
3. *De communi vita*	3. *De communi vita*
4. *De synodo* (Saint-Claude)	4. *De ecclesiis et earum iustitiis*
5. *De universali ecclesia* (Saint-Claude)	5. *De sacramentis ecclesiae*
6. *De sacramentis ecclesiae* (Troyes) / *De sacramentis* (Saint-Claude)	6. *De festivitatibus et ieiuniis et crapula et ebrietate*
7. [No book title in either manuscript; content corresponds to book six of the second version.]	7. *De homicidiis et calumniis episcoporum et reliquorum ordinum*
8. *De incesto diversi generis et legitimis coniugiis* (Troyes) / *De incestis et diversis generis et legitimis coniugiis* or *De nuptiis* (Saint-Claude)	8. *De legitimis coniugiis et incesto diversi generis*
9. *De homicidiis* (Saint-Claude)	9. *De synodo celebranda*
10. *De periuriis et excommunicandis*	10. *De diversis conditionibus hominum et de excommunicatione reproborum*
11. *De rectoribus et iudicibus ecclesie, de furibus et sortilegiis* (Saint-Claude)	11. *De poenitentia et reconciliatione*
12. *De visitatione infirmorum, de penitentia et reconciliatione*	12. *De vita activa et contemplativa*

In the first version, the collection seems to be divided between four books on the ecclesiastical hierarchy, and another eight books treating those matters that were also relevant to the laity (baptism, marriage, penance, ecclesiastical jurisdiction); in the second version, the main difference is the addition of the last book, which has no equivalent in the first version. The titles of books ten and eleven are changed and, as a closer analysis confirms, this reflects the combination of material from both

manuscript (which I have not seen). See also Fowler-Magerl, *Clavis* 92 (partly erroneous). The table of contents found in *Histoire* 1.436–437 is based on the *capitulatio* of the second version (which is strongly influenced by that of Burchard) rather than the running titles in the manuscripts.

books in book eleven of the second version. Apparently, the compiler of the second version took seriously the 'love of the number of the Apostles' he expressed in the preface. Also, the book on the conduct of synods is moved, somewhat surprisingly, from fourth to ninth position. Finally, the title of the first book was changed between the two versions from 'On the priestly order' to 'On bishops'. The material is essentially the same, but the change to the title is indeed significant, as will be discussed later on.

What was the success of this voluminous collection? As indicated above, the number of extant copies may seem small if compared to Burchard—but with thirteen manuscripts, there are still considerably more *12P* copies extant than for most pre-Gratian canon law collections. All were produced in the eleventh and twelfth centuries, mainly in southern Germany. No less than five of the thirteen manuscripts were produced at Freising itself; three were and still are kept in Bamberg. While this points to a regionally restricted influence, the diffusion of *12P* should not be underestimated. A canonical collection sometimes associated with Bernold of Konstanz seems to draw on *12P*.[119] By the later twelfth century, an (earlier) copy had reached Troyes,[120] and the Saint-Claude one may have been made at Saint-Claude.[121] A twelfth-century manuscript from Olomouc contains substantial parts of *12P*.[122] In any case, the number of extant manuscripts is relatively high, and in the first century after it was produced, the collection seems to have considerable circulation and was met with enough interest to produce the rather different versions visible in the extant manuscripts.

2.5 Burchard and *12P*: A Comparative Analysis

In the following, Burchard's *Liber decretorum* and the *Collection in Twelve Parts* (= *12P*) will be analysed together. This is mainly because the two col-

---

119. The collection is found in a manuscript of Bernold's works (Sankt Paul im Lavanttal, Stiftsbibliothek, 24/1, fols. 25v–30v [not seen]) and has been printed in *Germaniae sacrae prodromus seu Collectio Monumentorum res alemannicas illustrantium*, ed. Emil Ussermann (2 vols. Sankt Blasien 1792). 2.414–426. The first section (ed. Ussermann 2.414–417) contains the canons also found in *12P* 1.180, 181, 182, 183, 184, and 188; I have not been able to find any meaningful parallels to other collections. Further research on this collection (not mentioned in Kéry) is needed.

120. Troyes, BM, 246 may have been written in Germany, but was at Troyes in the twelfth century; see Müller, *Untersuchungen* 34–37 (with further references).

121. van Balberghe, 'Préface' 8.

122. Olomouc, Zemský archiv v Opavě, pobočka Olomouc, Sbírka rukopisů Metropolitní kapituly u sv. Václava Olomouc, CO.202 (*olim* Státni vedecké knihovna, Universitni knihovna, 202), fols. 49v–225v, containing no less than 1618 canons from *12P* according to Müller, *Untersuchungen* 42–43. According to Kéry 156 perhaps from Mainz, but in fact made at Olomouc, see Nowak, 'Papsttum' 356–357 (also for the new signature).

lections are so closely interrelated. This comparative analysis is also meant to illustrate the choices the compiler of any pre-Gratian canon law collection might make, as the two collections (or three, if we count the *12P* versions as two separate works) made very different choices when working with the same materials. This is true, to different degrees, for all parts of the collections, certainly those parts of Burchard that have been studied in detail.[123] In the context of the present chapter, only two examples will be studied to demonstrate how distinct the working methods of the German compilers in handling their material were. The first example deals with the ecclesiology in Burchard and in the *12P* versions. Here, the comparison with the formal sources is of paramount importance, and necessitates a short glance at one of them, the *Anselmo dedicata*. As a second example, I have chosen the Burchard book that most clearly diverges from tradition, and one that arguably changed canon law more substantially than any other single book of any pre-Gratian collection (Burchard's book on incest) again compared to the two *12P* versions.

2.5.1 First Things First: The Ecclesiastical Hierarchy in the *Anselmo dedicata*, Burchard, and *12P*

Burchard and both *12P* versions begin, as earlier collections (e.g. the *Vetus Gallica*, *Hibernensis*, the *Sangermanensis*, and the *Anselmo dedicata*) had done, with an account of the ecclesiastical hierarchy. In the three German collections, the contents of the first books are more uniform than the different book titles (which will be discussed below) might suggest; they all begin with an account of the ecclesiastical hierarchy in general and the position of bishops in particular. Here, Regino provided little if any material, so it comes as little surprise that for the first books Burchard and the *12P* versions drew on the other main source they all relied on, the *Anselmo dedicata*. While this accounts for some similarities between the three German collections and their common source, there are important differences in detail which are, as I will argue, indicative of a different ecclesiology.

2.5.2 The *Anselmo dedicata*: Rome and Metropolitans

The *Anselmo dedicata* was an important model for Burchard and the *12P* compilers of how to arrange a large body of canons according to subject matter. For questions of the ecclesiastical hierarchy in particular, the

---

123. Gérard Fransen, 'Les sources de la Préface du Décret de Burchard de Worms' BMCL 3 (1973) 1–7 (preface); Austin, *Shaping* (books six, ten, and twelve); Patrick Corbet, *Autour de Burchard de Worms: l'église allemande et les interdits de parenté (IXème–XIIème siècle)* (Ius commune. Sonderhefte 142; Frankfurt 2001) and Ubl, *Inzestverbot* (book seven); Körntgen, 'Fortschreibung' (book nineteen).

Anselmo dedicata also provided much material for the German collections. While this is well known, and despite a number of studies on the collection,[124] there is no agreed interpretation about the character of *Anselmo dedicata*. Fournier's assertion that the compiler was especially interested in papal primacy has been treated with some scepticism in more recent research, but no alternative account of the main concerns of the collection has commanded general assent.[125] The absence of an edition,[126] the rather grim characterization of the collection by Horst Fuhrmann ('monstrous'),[127] and its sheer length may have deterred studies on the *Anselmo dedicata* that venture beyond its textual history.

So what was this collection like that furnished so much material for Burchard and the 12P alike? The *Anselmo dedicata* is an anonymous collection, taking its name from the dedicatee, Archbishop Anselm II of Milan (882–896), and in all likelihood was compiled early in his pontificate.[128] In contrast to the contemporary *Libri duo* by Regino of Prüm, the *Anselmo dedicata* is much more concerned with the ecclesiastical hierarchy, as both its content and structure show. All in all, the *Anselmo dedicata* is a massive work; it contains some 2,000 canons, and complete copies (typically in large format) normally have well above 200 folios. Contrary to what has been claimed,[129] the *Anselmo dedicata* manages to impose order on

124. For the older literature, see Kéry 124–128 and Fowler-Magerl, *Clavis* 70–74. Important recent studies are Wolfgang Kaiser, *Die Epitome Iuliani. Beiträge zum römischen Recht im frühen Mittelalter und zum byzantinischen Rechtsunterricht* (Ius commune Sonderhefte 175; Frankfurt 2004) 550–561, Zechiel-Eckes, 'Anmerkungen', and Hartmann, *Kirche und Kirchenrecht* 143–149. For quotations from the *Anselmo dedicata*, I have used Bamberg, SB, Msc.Can.5 (= **Ba**). More details on the manuscripts are found in my chapter in the forthcoming HMCL volume *The History of Western Canon Law to 1000*, of which the following pages are a summary.

125. Fournier saw the collection as a pro-papal work: Paul Fournier, 'L'origine de la collection "Anselmo dedicata"', *Mélanges P. F. Girard: études de droit romain dédiées à Paul Frédéric Girard à l'occasion du 60e anniversaire de sa naissance (26 octobre 1912)* (Paris 1912) 475–492, here at 496. Most scholars more or less followed this interpretation repeated in *Histoire* 1.239–240 (e.g. Dvornik, *Photian Schism* 284, Besse, 'Anselmo dedicata' esp. 207–208, and Fuhrmann, *Einfluß und Verbreitung* 2.431–432). Fowler-Magerl, *Clavis* 73 tentatively suggested that *Anselmo dedicata* could have a monastic background.

126. Partial editions are Besse, 'Anselmo dedicata' for book one and Giuseppe Russo, *Tradizione manoscritta di Leges romanae nei codici dei secoli IX e X della Biblioteca capitolare di Modena* (Deputazione di storia patria per le antiche provincie Modenesi: Biblioteca Nova Series 56; Modena 1980) for the Roman law content. The incipit/explicit list of Jean Claude Besse, *Histoire des textes du droit de l'Église au Moyen-Age de Denys à Gratien: Collectio Anselmo dedicata: étude et texte (extraits)* (Paris 1960) has been superseded by the *Clavis* database. New editions have been announced several times, most recently by Irene Scaravelli, 'La collezione canonica "Anselmo dedicata": lo status quaestionis nella prospettiva di un edizione critica', *Le storie e la memoria: in onore di Arnold Esch*, ed. Roberto delle Donne and Andrea Zorzi (Florence 2002) 33–52.

127. Fuhrmann, *Einfluß und Verbreitung* esp. 2.433 ('geschwätzig[]') and 434 ('monströs', 'unbeholfen[], weitschweifig[] und sachlich lückenhaft[]').

128. Zechiel-Eckes, 'Anmerkungen' 64.

129. Fuhrmann, *Einfluß und Verbreitung* esp. 2.425, 428, 429, 433, 434 (for quotes, see above, note 127). For a different view, see Fowler-Magerl, *Clavis* 70 ('extraordinarily rich and well organized').

this very considerable body of normative texts. It does so by a division of the material into twelve books (*partes*), each devoted to specific groups within the Church (e.g. bishops, lower clergy, laypeople) or subject matter (e.g. baptism). The books are divided into three subsections each, with the first containing papal decretals (and some conciliar material), the second excerpts from the works of Gregory the Great, and the third secular (Roman) law. At least sometimes a third level of subdivision is found in form of shorter sections with their own headings. For example, within the first subsection of book four, there are series of canons on witnesses, on the alienation of church property, and on judges which all are singled out by appropriate headings.[130] Every book has its own *capitulatio*, which mirrows the division of the books into subsections by repeating the respective headings. Internal overlap resulting from individual canons being relevant for more than one topic is dealt with by cross-references both within and between individual books.

For our context, the material sources of the *Anselmo dedicata* are important for two reasons.[131] First, by introducing more than 500 excerpts from the Pseudo-Isidorian forgeries into canon law, the *Anselmo dedicata* made this important legal and ecclesiological source more widely available. Second, and more importantly in the context of the present chapter, both Burchard and the *12P* compilers used the *Anselmo dedicata* for their books on the ecclesiastical hierarchy. However, the close textual relation between the collections does not mean that they are similar in nature; rather, the different way they used the same materials only highlights the stark contrast between the collections.

The *Anselmo dedicata* begins with a book on the 'primacy and dignity of the Roman see and that of other primates, patriarchs, archbishops, and metropolitans'. It contains unusually rich material on the special rights of churches above the rank of 'normal' bishoprics, including special cases like the rank of Constantinople ('second only to Rome'),[132] the numerous privileges bestowed on Justiniana Prima,[133] the eminence of Antioch

---

130. **Ba**, fol. 73r: 'De testibus', 'De […] ecclesiasticis viris rebus expoliatis', 'De iudicibus atque iudiciis'.

131. Kaiser, *Epitome Iuliani* 553–561; Zechiel-Eckes, 'Anmerkungen'.

132. *Anselmo dedicata* 1.117–118 (**Ba**, fol. 19va) and 129 (**Ba**, fol. 22rb): 'Papa romanus prior omnibus episcopis et patriarchis sedeat, et post illum Constantinopolitanae civitatis archiepiscopus.' The former two canons are from the Council of Constantinople 381, the latter canon was taken from the *Epitome Juliani*, const. 109, cap. 507 (ed. Hänel 165).

133. *Anselmo dedicata* 1.130, taken from the *Epitome Juliani*, const. 109, cap. 508 (ed. Hänel 165). On the ecclesiastical history of Justiniana prima, see R. A. Markus, 'Carthage-Prima Justiniana-Ravenna: An Aspect of Justinian's Kirchenpolitik' *Byzantion* 49 (1979) 277–302, here at 289–292.

and Alexandria,[134] and the importance of the pallium.[135] More generally, the *Anselmo dedicata* stresses the special dignity of metropolitans and patriarchs. This already marks a contrast to Pseudo-Isidore who had specifically sought to curtail the rights of metropolitans and instead strenghthened the position of local bishops.[136]

Further evidence on the ecclesiology of the *Anselmo dedicata* comes from the second book which is dedicated to bishops (including *chorepiscopi*). Perhaps surprisingly, of all twelve books this is the one with the *lowest* share of Pseudo-Isidorian material.[137] Given that Pseudo-Isidore at great length dealt with the rights of this group in particular, this is already indicates that book two of the *Anselmo dedicata* takes a different view. Indeed, while the *Anselmo dedicata* in book two retains many important False Decretals on the rights of local bishops, many other canons are omitted and some are manipulated, if only in subtle ways. For example, book two contains canons against the use of pompous titles, including an ancient canon from the African Church.[138] Originally, the provision was coined against the bishop of Carthage, who tried to take advantage of his position as 'bishop of the first see'; in the *Anselmo dedicata*, in contrast, it is presented as a general rule: no bishop ought to be called *princeps sacerdotum*.[139] If the compiler knew that the canon originally was directed against bishops of the 'first see', as he may well have,[140] it is even more striking that he chose to insert it in his second book on suffragan bishops rather than book one which specifically dealt with bishops above the rank of diocesan bishops including, one would think, 'bishops of the first see'.

Stronger evidence is available if we turn again to the Pseudo-Isidorian texts which the *Anselmo dedicata* contains, and specifically those that were manipulated.[141] Their number is small enough to discuss them in some detail here. The first manipulation (in the order of the collection) is a

134. *Anselmo dedicata* 1.110–114. Antioch is praised as the 'first see of the first of the Apostles' (*Anselmo dedicata* 1.114; **Ba**, fol. 18va), and Alexandria is described as having been founded by Saint Marc 'on behalf of Saint Peter' (*Anselmo dedicata* 1.109).

135. On the *pallium*, see Steven A. Schoenig, *Bonds of Wool: The Pallium and Papal Power in the Middle Ages* (SMCL 15; Washington, D.C. 2016).

136. Fuhrmann, 'Forgeries' 140–144; Schrör, *Metropolitangewalt* ch. 4.

137. Fuhrmann, *Einfluß und Verbreitung* 2.430.

138. *Anselmo dedicata* 2.50 (see next note) and 266–267 (from Gregory the Great).

139. Rubric to *Anselmo dedicata* 2.50 (**Ba**, fol. 33ra): 'Ut princeps sacerdotum non appeletur episcopus.' This form of the rubric is not unique, but most collections up to and including Gratian (D. 99 c.3) have a more specific form of the rubric (often on 'bishops of the first see') according to the *Clavis* database. The material source is Carthage 397 c. 25 (ed. Munier, CCL 149.40).

140. Fulgentius Ferrandus, for one, made this clear; see his *Breviatio canonum* c.81 (ed. Munier, CCL 149.294). On the *Anselmo dedicata* compiler being familiar with the *Breviatio*, see Zechiel-Eckes, 'Anmerkungen' 56.

141. The changes in *Anselmo dedicata* 3.126 were noted by Fuhrmann, *Einfluß und Verbreitung* 2.434.

modification without any change to the text of the formal source. Both the rubric and the text of the canon state that 'everyone could appeal to Rome'.[142] This is familiar enough, but in the 'original' (i.e. the False Decretals), the context made clear that this referred to all *bishops*.[143] In the *Anselmo dedicata*, in contrast, the excerpt from Pseudo-Damasus is presented in such a way that it seems to give *everyone* the right to appeal to Rome. Neither the rubric nor the text mention bishops, and the canon is placed in a book which does not deal with diocesan bishops. This was certainly no mere coincidence; if further proof were needed, it is found a few pages later. The same excerpt from Pseudo-Damasus here appears a second time, and again the rubric fails to mention that the right to appeal to Rome was a specifically episcopal privilege.[144] So while Pseudo-Isidore had invented this privilege specifically to protect bishops, in the *Anselmo dedicata* it has become a rather general rule placed not in the relevant (second) book on bishops, but in the first one on supra-diocesan institutions. As a result, the stress is on the right of appeal as part of papal primacy. This fits the tendency of *Anselmo dedicata* to highlight papal privileges, as Fournier had argued,[145] but at the same time it is an interesting example of how a Pseudo-Isidorian text is used in a way contrary to Pseudo-Isidore's intentions.

A similar, if more harmless, case is an excerpt taken from Pseudo-Zephyrinus. It is the famous concept that 72 witnesses were needed to convict an accused bishop.[146] It is faithfully preserved in *Anselmo dedicata*—but again in book one on the rights of the prelates above the rank of diocesan bishops and not in book two on episcopal rights. So while the *Anselmo dedicata* does not change the letter of the law, and does not even distort the interpretation of the excerpt in question, the canon is simply not found where one would expect it. For Pseudo-Isidore, this canon clearly belonged to the privileges of bishops, but the compiler of the *Anselmo dedicata* begged to differ.

A much more straightforward case of manipulation is found in book three. It is ultimately taken from the same forged decretal attributed to

---

142. *Anselmo dedicata* 1.39 (**Ba**, fol. 8vb): 'Quod omnes possint appellare Romanam sedem. Quam omnes appellare, si necesse fuerit, et eius fulciri auxilio oportet. Nam, ut nostis, synodum sine eius auctoritate fieri non est canonicum, nec episcopus, nisi in legitima synodo et suo tempore apostolica vocatione congregata, definite damnari potest, neque ulla unquam concilia rata leguntur, quae non sunt fulta apostolica auctoritate.'

143. Ps.-Damasus I, JK †243 (ed. Hinschius 503).

144. *Anselmo dedicata* 1.39 (**Ba**, fol. 8vb) and 59 (**Ba**, fols. 11vb–12ra).

145. See Fournier, 'Anselmo dedicata' (who did not deal with this canon).

146. *Anselmo dedicata* 1.54 (**Ba**, fol. 11r), taken from Ps.-Zephyrinus, JK †80 c. 2 (ed. Hinschius 131).

Zephyrinus, and again, a key concept of Pseudo-Isidore was at issue. According to Pseudo-Zephyrinus, an accused bishop was allowed to choose no less than twelve judges from among his fellow bishops.[147] This was one of many procedural norms in the Pseudo-Isidorian forgeries that, if applied verbatim, made it extremely unlikely that bishops could be convicted. In the *Anselmo dedicata*, however, this privilege is severely reduced by simply omitting the number twelve. What remains is the uncontroversial principle that prelates could only be judged by those of at least equal rank.[148] Thus, the pro-episcopal provisions the Pseudo-Isidorian forgeries had introduced by fabricating the Pseudo-Zephyrinus letter were undone by the compiler. Again, the textual change is slight, but significantly reduces the force of a key concept of the Pseudo-Isidorian forgeries.

Another case in point is the use of a letter attributed to Pope Miltiades (Melchiades), yet another forgery specifically concerned with the protection of bishops from unjust prosecution. According to this decretal, the right to judge bishops (referred to as those 'whom the Lord elected as his eyes and whom he wanted to be pillars of the Church') was first reserved to the Lord himself and later descended to Saint Peter and his successors.[149] In this context, the biblical admonition 'Judge not, that you be not judged' is applied to the accusation of bishops: 'Do not judge or condemn bishops without the authority of this see.'[150] The pro-episcopal character of the forgery is manifest; in the *Anselmo dedicata*, however, it is largely lost. To begin with, the decretal is *not* quoted in book two on suffragane bishops; instead, overlapping excerpts are found in *Anselmo dedicata* 3.169 and 12.54. The excerpt in book three is presented as a general procedural norm, with no references to bishops in particular.[151] In book twelve, no such such hint is given, and indeed the word 'bishops' is left out from the passage just quoted.[152] This seemingly minor change has an import-

---

147. Ps.-Zephyrinus, JK †80 (ed. Hinschius 131–133).

148. *Anselmo dedicata* 3.126 (**Ba**, fol. 87v): 'Episcopos enim iudices quilibet episcopus accusatus, si necesse fuerit, eligat, a quibus eius causa iuste iudicetur.' This manipulation was first brought to attention by Fuhrmann, *Einfluß und Verbreitung* 2.434.

149. Ps.-Miltiades, JK †171 (ed. Hinschius 243): 'Episcopos ergo, quos sibi dominus oculos elegit et columnas ecclesiae esse voluit, quibus etiam ligandi et solvendi potestatem dedit, suo iudicio reservavit atque hoc privilegium beato clavigero Petro sua vice solummodo commisit.' (I assume that 'claviero' in the edition is a typo.)

150. Ps.-Miltiades, JK †171 (ed. Hinschius 243): 'Mementote semper sermonis domini, qui ait: "Nolite iudicare, ut non iudicemini, nolite condemnare, ut non condemnemini. In quo enim iudicio iudicaveritis, iudicabimini." Episcopos nolite iudicare, nolite condemnare absque sedis huius auctoritate.' The quote is from Mt. 7.1–2.

151. *Anselmo dedicata* 3.169 (**Ba**, fol. 91vb; **Pa**, p. 143; **P2**, fol. 96va).

152. *Anselmo dedicata* 12.54 (**Pa**, p. 420; **Ba** lacks a folio here): '[…] In quo enim iudicio iudicaveritis, iudicabimini. Nolite iudicare, nolite condempnare sine absque sedis huius auctoritate.' The change was first noted by Fuhrmann, *Einfluß und Verbreitung* 3.924.

ant effect: the canon no longer specifically protects bishops but becomes a general principle. Again, both the context of the canon (books three and twelve), the rubrics (not referring to bishops), and small textual changes together render a resolutely pro-episcopal forgery largely meaningless in our collection.

The Pseudo-Isidorian canons discussed here constitute only a tiny part of either the False Decretals or the *Anselmo dedicata*, and the textual manipulations are sometimes subtle. Nonetheless, the manipulations do follow a common pattern: in all cases the privileges specifically coined for bishops in the *Anselmo dedicata* were either reduced severely (as in the case of electing one's judges) or extended to other groups (as in the case of the appeal to Rome). Further, they are not found where their original concerns would lead one to expect, and combined with the appropriate rubrics could be enough to change the meaning of the texts. This all strongly suggests that the *Anselmo dedicata* compiler, while using the False Decretals extensively, yet had interests quite different from those of Pseudo-Isidore; consistently, he selected canons that strengthened the position of metropolitans and archbishops, while in several cases reducing the rights Pseudo-Isidore had accorded to diocesan bishops. This effort was far from systematic; yet it is evident that the *Anselmo dedicata* compiler felt uneasy with Pseudo-Isidore's pro-episcopal tendencies and cunningly reversed them at least in some cases. Although he was otherwise very conservative, in this case the *Anselmo dedicata* compiler chose to make a number of changes that were small (on the textual level) but significantly changed the meaning of the canons in question.

These findings are relevant for the reception of Pseudo-Isidore, for the understanding of the *Anselmo dedicata*, and for our analysis of the German collections using the *Anselmo dedicata*. As for the early reception of Pseudo-Isidore, the treatment of Pseudo-Zephyrinus and other forgeries in the *Anselmo dedicata* shows that some readers of the False Decretals at least were aware how radical Pseudo-Isidore was, and that they sought to counter what they preceived as excessive protection of diocesan bishops. As for the *Anselmo dedicata*, the manipulations discussed above confirm that the collection was made by someone with special interest in the ecclesiastical hierarchy, and above all the supra-episcopal institutions like the metropolitan office which in the late ninth century were in a flux.[153] As for

153. See Schrör, *Metropolitangewalt* ch. 4 (metropolitans) and Horst Fuhrmann, 'Studien zur Geschichte mittelalterlicher Patriarchate' ZGR Kan. Abt. 39 (1953) 112–176, 40 (1954) 1–84, and 41 (1955) 95–183 (patriarchs); for a general overview, see Roger E. Reynolds 'The Organisation, Law and Liturgy of the Western Church, 700–900', *The New Cambridge Medieval History* (7 vols. Cambridge 1995–2005) 2.587–621.

Burchard's *Liber decretorum* and the two *12P* versions, finally, the treatment of key Pseudo-Isidorian concepts in the *Anselmo dedicata* is mainly interesting because none of the three German collections retained the changes the Milanese collections introduced into canon law. None of the manipulated and diplaced canons from Pseudo-Isidore is found in this form in Burchard or either *12P* version. Negative evidence alone is, of course, not very reliable; there may be many reasons why the relevant *Anselmo dedicata* canons are not found in the German collections. However, at least for Burchard of Worms there is some evidence that he had sensed what the *Anselmo dedicata* compiler was doing, and chose to undo it. As mentioned above, the *Anselmo dedicata* presented an African conciliar canon coined against 'bishops of the first see' in a way that it mainly targed diocesan bishops. Burchard, who may have known this widely-known canon from other sources, gave it a new meaning when he placed the same texts, with the very same wording, in the opening section of his book. This time, however, the canon no longer refers to local bishops, nor does Burchard restore the reference to 'bishops of the first see'. Instead, the contexts in the first book of the *Liber decretorum* makes this African canon appear to refer to the pope. While Burchard left the main text of the canon unchanged, he placed in a short series of canons of the papacy, and to remove all ambiguity, he coined a new rubric that the pope was not to be called *summus sacerdos*![154] This in itself is interesting enough (and I will return to the question of Burchard's view of the papacy in the next section), but if my impression is right that Burchard manipulated this proof texts knowing that the *Anselmo dedicata* had manipulated it in the first place, we may have a glimpse into the way compilers of canonical collections learned their trade: comparing the same canons found in different collections they might have learned from each other how to change the meaning of a text cimply by placing it in a new context

2.5.3 Burchard and *12P*: Canon Law by Bishops and for Bishops

These traits of the *Anselmo dedicata* have been given some room here as this was precisely the model the German compilers chose *not* to follow. Virtually all characteristics of *Anselmo dedicata* mentioned above were undone when the collection was reworked at Worms and Freising.

Let us begin with the division of the material into books. In Burchard and *12P*, the opening material which the *Anselmo dedicata* had divided into two books is gathered into one. In addition, the German collections left

---

154. Rubric to Burchard 1.3 (*editio princeps*, fol. 1v): 'Ut summus sacerdos non vocetur Romanus pontifex sed prime sedis episcopus.' For details, see the next section.

aside most *Anselmo dedicata* materials on patriarchs and archbishops, and added much more on bishops. So the first book in Burchard and in both *12P* versions contains less on metropolitans and more on bishops than the first two books of *Anselmo dedicata*, and at the same time removes the division between diocesan bishops on the one hand and the higher ranks of the ecclesiastical hierarchy on the other. In doing so, the compilers of the German collections reversed the characteristic choices the *Anselmo dedicata* compiler had made, and returned to a model that put bishops first.

These changes at least partly are reflected by the title given to the first book, but in different ways. While Burchard chose the most conservative solution, basically combining the titles to the first two *Anselmo dedicata* books,[155] the *12P* compilers presented a new title for essentially the same material. In the first version of *12P*, the first book has the title 'On the priestly order'; in the second version, the title is 'On bishops'.[156] These titles seem innocent enough, but as will become clear in the following, they do prepare the reader for a specific reading of the material that is characteristic of the German collections in contrast to their shared Italian source.

To elucidate this, let us turn from the titles to the opening canons of the first book. In *Anselmo dedicata*, the very first canon was taken from the first Pseudo-Clementine letter on Saint Peter as the first of the Apostles.[157] Both Burchard and the first version of *12P* begin with an excerpt taken from the second letter of Pseudo-Anaclete on the institution of the priestly order with Saint Peter.[158] The second version of *12P* opens with the institution of priesthood in Aaron as found in the third Pseudo-Clementine letter.[159]

As so often with pre-Gratian canon law collections, the choices of the opening texts are revealing. The contrast between *Anselmo dedicata* and the second version of *12P* seems clear enough; while the former opens with a classic proof text of Roman primacy, the latter equally clearly chose a text stressing the unity of all ordained clergy. The Pseudo-Anacletian text found at the beginning of the other two collections is more ambiguous

---

155. 'Primus liber de potestate et primatu apostolice sedis, patriarcharum ceterorumque primatuum metropolitanorum et de sinodo celebranda et vocatione ad sinodum, de accusatis et accusatoribus et testibus, de expoliatis iniuste, de iudicibus ac de omni honore competenti ac dignitate et diverso negotio et ministerio episcoporum.'

156. See Müller, *Collectio 9* and Fowler-Magerl, *Clavis* 92. In Troyes, BM, 246 the title is found in the upper margin from fol. 38v on. According to Müller, *Collectio 9*, the Saint-Claude copy instead has 'De ministerio episcoporum'.

157. *Anselmo dedicata* 1.1, taken from Pseudo-Clement, JK †10 (ed. Hinschius 30).

158. Ps.-Anaclete, JK †3 (ed. Hinschius 83).

159. *12P* 1.1, taken from Pseudo-Clement, JK †12 (ed. Hinschius 58).

and deserves a closer look. According to the excerpt introducing both Burchard and the first version of *12P*, it was Saint Peter as the first priest who was given the power to bind and to loose.[160] At first sight, this may seem to be a relatively conventional choice; but this is mainly so because Burchard was followed by so many compilers of later collections who gave the Pseudo-Anacletian canon a prominent place.[161] Burchard and the second version of *12P* were the first collections to place this passage at the beginning of their text, and later collections would follow them in this; Anselm of Lucca, the compiler of the *Gaddiana,* and other compilers of pre-Gratian collections all chose the same passage as their opening canon.[162] It is found in *Anselmo dedicata* too, but as the second canon of the first book.

So Burchard and *12P* were the first collections to place this excerpt at the very beginning. In fact, it is found in *Anselmo dedicata* too, but as the second canon of the first book. Placing a text first or second may seem like a minor difference, and sometimes it is a mere detail, but here it is indeed significant. After all, the passage from Pseudo-Anaclete is fundamentally ambivalent:[163]

> In the New Testament, however, after Christ our Lord the order of priesthood began with Peter, as to him the pontificate in the Church of Christ was first given when the Lord said to him: 'You are Peter, and it is on this rock that I will build my congregation, and the gates of hell will not conquer it. I will give you the keys of the kingdom of heaven.' He was therefore the first to receive the authority of binding and loosing from the Lord, and the first to bring people to the faith by the grace of God and the power of his preaching.

This can be read to stress that Saint Peter was the *first* priest—or to highlight that it was Saint Peter as the first *priest* (rather than as Prince of the

---

160. Burchard 1.1 (*editio princeps,* fol. 1ra) = *12P* 1.1 (Troyes, BM, 246, fol. 17rb) as quoted below. The canon is taken from Pseudo-Anaclete, JK †3 (ed. Hinschius 79).

161. The letter, containing much of Pseudo-Isidore's ecclesiology, provided several pre-Gratian canon law collections (and Gratian) with important proof texts on ecclesiastical hierarchy, procedural law, and episcopal elections in particular. See Fuhrmann, *Einfluß und Verbreitung* 3.1058 s.v. 'JK †3' and now Schon, *Rezeptionstabelle.*

162. In Anselm A, the *Collection of Saint-Victor* (in Arsenal 721), the Vienna *7L,* and the San Pietro *9L,* the canon is the first canon of the first book; in Ivo's *Decretum,* the collection in Paris, Bibliothèque Sainte-Geneviève, 166, and *183T,* it is the first canon of the respective book or section on ecclesiastical hierarchy. For all these collections, see the *Clavis canonum* database and manual.

163. Burchard 1.1 (*editio princeps,* fol. 1ra) = *12P* 1.1 (Troyes, BM, 246, fol. 17rb): 'In Novo autem Testamento post Christum dominum nostrum, a Petro sacerdotalis coepit ordo, quia ipsi primo pontificatus in ecclesia Christi datus est dicente Dominus ad eum: "Tu es, inquit, Petrus, et super hanc petram edificabo ecclesiam meam, et portae inferi non praevalebunt adversus eam, et tibi dabo claves regni coelorum." [Mt. 16.18–19] Hic ergo ligandi solvendique potestatem primus accepit a Domino, primusque ad fidem populum Dei gratia et virtute sue predicationis adduxit.' The translation is largely adopted from Isidore of Seville, *De ecclesiasticis officiis,* tr. Thomas Louis Knoebel (Ancient Christian Writers 61; New York 2008) 72.

Apostles) who was given the power to bind and to loose. While the first reading could be, and has been, used to support claims to papal primacy, the second stresses instead the fundamental equality within the priestly order.[164]

Given this ambivalence, the context in which the text is read is decisive. In the absence of other forms of comment,[165] the actual *mis-en-page* of the collections comes into play. The natural reading the Pseudo-Anacletian text in the *Anselmo dedicata* is that it simply adds to papal supremacy, if only because the preceding canon relates that Saint Peter was the first of the Apostles and the 'foundation of the Church', and that he chose to end his life in Rome.[166] Further, in the *Anselmo dedicata* the canon is an integral part of a long series of canons all stressing the special role of Saint Peter among the Apostles, of the Roman church among all other churches, and of the pope among all other bishops. After the first canon had already stressed this, the following canons affirm that in Saint Peter, the priestly order was founded as well as the episcopate (cc. 2–3), that archbishops exercise their rights only within the limits of papal prerogatives (c. 4), that Saint Peter himself ordained Pope Clement (cc. 5–6), that Saint Peter was Prince of the Apostles (c. 7), that all 'major cases' should be decided by the apostolic see (cc. 7–8, 10), and that synods conducted without papal approval are null and void (c. 9). In this context, there is little to doubt that c. 2 too was meant to be a proof text of the special role of Saint Peter and his successors. The opening canons of *Anselmo dedicata* do indeed, as Fournier argued long ago, display a strong interest in papal primacy, and contain a careful selection of proof texts on different aspects of this primacy. In this, *Anselmo dedicata* resembles a group of eleventh-century collections that, under rather different circumstances, also gathered these and similar canons at the very beginning to put an emphasis on papal prerogatives.[167]

164. See Pierre Batiffol, *Cathedra Petri: études d'histoire ancienne de l'Église* (Unam Sanctam 4; Paris 1938) ch. 2 on older traditions of the maxim 'Petrus initium episcopatus'.

165. Burchard's rubric preserves the ambivalence of the canon; it reads (*editio princeps*, fol. 1ra): 'Quod in Novo Testamento post Christum dominum nostrum a Petro sacerdotalis coepit ordo'. Indeed, the rubric is the same in all four collections under discussion here, and already found in the False Decretals: JK †3 (ed. Hinschius 79).

166. 'Quod Simon Petrus vere fidei merito primus fuerit primitie electionis Domini Apostolorum et quod Rome pro pietate patiendo volens vitam finivit', the rubric summarizes this famous passage from Ps.-Clement.

167. Anselm of Lucca, for one, followed a similar strategy in his collection by placing Pseudo-Anaclete first, but followed suit by a plethora of canons asserting the unique position of Saint Peter and his successors. On the contrast to Burchard, see Yves Congar 'Der Platz des Papsttums in der Kirchenfrömmigkeit der Reformer des 11. Jahrhunderts', *Sentire Ecclesiam. Das Bewusstsein von der Kirche als gestaltende Kraft der Frömmigkeit*, ed. Jean Daniélou and Herbert Vorgrimler (Freiburg 1961) 196–217, here at 207 and Kathleen Grace Cushing, *Papacy and Law in the*

Burchard and the *12P*, however, do not belong to this group. While the Anacletian text is the same as in *Anselmo dedicata*, the context that turned it into a proof text of Roman primacy is notably lacking in these collections. Where the *Anselmo dedicata* compiler inserted the Anacletian canon into a long series of texts on Saint Peter, his successors, and the apostolic see, the context in the German collections is quite different; here, only two of the following texts even mention the pope. Both in Burchard and in the first version of *12P*, Pseudo-Anaclete is immediately followed by the privilege of the apostolic see to decide 'major cases'. In itself, this could still be made fit into a series of proof texts on papal primacy;[168] yet Burchard's following canon excludes all such readings. Rather than extolling the privileges of the papacy, this canon forbids the use of a fairly conventional papal title. In the words of Burchard's rubric, the Council of Carthage had allegedly ruled 'that the Roman pontiff ought not be called "high priest", but "bishop of the first see"'.[169] The canon is actually taken from *Anselmo dedicata*, but comparing the collections only adds to the impression that Burchard here is highly unconventional. For in the *Anselmo dedicata* the same canon is placed in a very different context and given a different rubric—and thus a very different meaning. It is found in book two on bishops, and to remove all doubt, the rubric reads 'That a bishop should not be called "prince of priests"'.[170]

Here, the differences between Burchard and *12P*, on the one hand, and *Anselmo dedicata*, on the other, become manifest, with Burchard being the most radical.[171] Strikingly, the main text (as opposed to the rubric) is the same in all collections under discussion here; it stresses that 'bishops of

---

Gregorian Revolution: The Canonistic Work of Anselm of Lucca (Oxford Historical Monographs; Oxford 1998), esp. 112–113.

168. This is indeed the case in *Anselmo dedicata*, where it is found as *Anselmo dedicata* 1.7. Anselm of Lucca, too, integrated similar texts in the opening section of his first book.

169. Rubric to Burchard 1.3 (*editio princeps*, fol. 1v; here checked against Bamberg, SB, Msc. Can.6, fol. 10v and Frankfurt, UB, Ms. Barth. 50, fol. 6v): 'Ut summus sacerdos non vocetur Romanus pontifex sed prime sedis episcopus.' Given that no earlier collection has this rubric and that Burchard places it so prominently, I have no doubt that the rubric was indeed coined at Worms. In Burchard (but not *12P*), the radical content of the rubric is supported by the arrangement of the canons. As far as I can see, the rubric was first commented upon by Julius Harttung, 'Beiträge zur Geschichte Heinrichs II. Die Synode von Seligenstadt und Burchards Decretum' *Forschungen zur deutschen Geschichte* 16 (1876) 587–598, here at 590 n. 1.

170. *Anselmo dedicata* 2.50: 'Ut princeps sacerdotum non appelletur episcopus.'

171. Both *12P* versions have the same rubric as Burchard but differ in the arrangement. In the first version *12P*, the canon is somewhat hidden (*12P* 1.280; Troyes, BM, 246, fol. 41vb), and not among other proof texts on the papacy. The canons before and after 1.280 deal with diocesan bishops in general. In the second version of *12P*, the canon is again placed relatively early in the first book (*12P* 1.11) and after texts dealing with apostolic see, so the effect is much closer to that in Burchard, which nonetheless is more radical in placing this canon third, and also as one of only two canons in the beginning of his collection that even mention the apostolic see.

the first see' should be called thus, and not referred to by any grand titles.[172] Originally, it is a very ancient text from the African Church and was coined against those bishops that normally are called primates.[173] It was widely diffused in the Latin West, where the specific background of the canon must have become more and more obscure. As it seems, a generalizing reading established itself early on; already in ancient collections like the *Dionysiana* and Cresconius's *Concordia* one finds the rubric also found in the *Anselmo dedicata*, making the canon a warning for *all* bishops not to adopt grand titles.[174] Along the same lines, in *Anselmo dedicata* and some other collections arranged by subject matter, the text was placed together with other canons against the sin of ambition from which all bishops should be free, thus further adding to the generalizing tendency that can still be found in Gratian.[175]

Reading the canon in any of these collections, one would thus not think that it referred to the Roman pontiff in particular—if at all. This, however, is precisely the reading that Burchard makes extremely likely by the arrangement (inserting this canon after one on the apostolic see) and the rubric, which can be assumed to be his own work.[176] This may sound gross, but how else should one understand Burchard's rubric 'That the Roman pontiff ought not be called "highest priest" [*summus sacerdos*], but "bishop of the first see"'?[177] As in the *Anselmo dedicata*, the rubric guides the reader, but in a different direction; the warning is here addressed to the pope and the pope alone. In this, Burchard was strikingly innovative; his rubric is unprecedented in earlier canon law, and only very few later collections retained it.[178] Given that the texts of the *Liber decretorum* were

---

172. Burchard 1.3 (*editio princeps*, fol. 1v): 'Ut primae sedis episcopus non appelletur princeps sacerdotum, aut summus sacerdos, aut aliquid huiusmodi, sed tantum primae sedis episcopus.'

173. Carthage 397 c. 25 (ed. Munier, CCCM 149.40).

174. See *Clavis* entries DY05.039, SD256, and also FY02.176.

Both *Anselmo dedicata* and the Vatican *9L* mention bishops in the rubric (DE02.050 and FY02.176 in the *Clavis* database). In *3L* (DR02.07.004) and the San Pietro *9L* (DS02.07.004), the African council is part of a series of canons on 'ne quis universalis appelletur'. Gratian 2 is closer to the original meaning by quoting it in D.99 c.3 (ed. Friedberg 350–351) in the context of primates and patriarchs, but as in *3L* it is generalized, and it is followed by a canon that no patriarch and 'not even the pope was to be called universal'.

176. See above (note 171).

177. Rubric to Burchard 1.3 (as quoted above, note 169).

178. On *12P*, see above (note 170). Ivo of Chartres, as he usually does, retains Burchard's rubric, but puts the canon in context of the rather limited rights of primates and archbishops: Ivo 5.54.1b and 56. The *Gaddiana*, an Italian collection from the early twelfth century, takes its opening canons from Burchard's book one (*Gaddiana* cc. 1–37 are all taken from Burchard 1.1–96, with omissions but no rearrangement, and the first seven canons are identical; see *Histoire* 2.209 and Fowler-Magerl, *Clavis* 214–215). This also extends to the rubrics, with the notable exception of this canon, which is left without a rubric in the *Gaddiana*. (My knowledge of the *Gaddiana* is entirely dependent on the *Clavis canonum* database.)

commonly preserved so faithfully in later collections, this may indicate
that some of his readers felt uneasy with the choice Burchard had made.
This said, there undoubtedly was a sound canon law tradition against 'universal' titles. Apart from the African councils, the False Decretals and the
letters of Gregory the Great could be quoted to this end.[179] Whether Saint
Peter indeed was 'prince of the Apostles' and if so, what this meant, was a
matter of dispute around 1100.[180] Calling the pope 'bishop of the first see'
(only) was unusual, and sometimes may have had anti-papal undertones.[181]
In this context, all these texts were gaining renewed attention around 1100,
and still figured prominently in Gratian's collection.[182] Burchard could not
possibly have foreseen these developments, but his unusual rubric may
well have contributed to later debates on papal primacy.

Back to the comparison of Burchard and the *Anselmo dedicata*. While
the latter had opened with a long series of canons on Saint Peter, Rome,
and the papacy, in Burchard the two texts (from Ps.-Anaclete and Carthage) are in fact the *only* texts on the papacy that are found at the very
beginning of the collection. Instead, Burchard and *12P* quickly turn to
bishops, characteristically using texts not found in *Anselmo dedicata*. The
material source is, once more, Ps.-Anaclete, here on the 'bipartite' order
of priest, that is, the difference between priests and bishops. According to
Ps.-Anaclete, the order of bishops began with the Apostles, while priests
(and lower clergy) were instituted with the seventy-two disciples. Again,
the stress is on the equality of all Apostles—there is no mention of the

179. Ps.-Pelagius II, JK †1051; Gregory I, JE 1352, 1354, and 1518.

180. This was at least the position of the Norman Anonymous (ed. Pellens 13): Even if Peter
was called 'princeps apostolorum', this had nothing to do with his capacity to judge other Apostles as he was not made their judge; but in any case according to the Norman Anonymous he was
never called by this title by Christ or the Apostles: 'Sed neque legitur, quod a Christo vel ab eius
apostolis "Petrus, apostolorum princeps" sit nuncupatus. Neque legitur, ut huius principis cęteri
apostoli satellites vel ministri sint apellati vel a Petro iudicati.'

181. Ernst Hartwig Kantorowicz, *Laudes regiae: A Study in Liturgical Acclamations and Mediaeval
Ruler Worship* (Berkeley and Los Angeles 1958), here at 243, claimed that the Laudes of Ivrea could
be read as anti-papal on ground of the reference to the pope as bishop of the first see (only):
'The Laudes of Ivrea sung to Emperor Henry IV and his antipope Clement (III) display certain
peculiarities [. . .]. The most striking feature is the acclamation to the pope as *prime sedis episcopus*.
It discloses Henry's political program according to which the pope was to be merely the first
among the imperial bishops.'

182. Ps.-Pelagius (JK †1051) circulated widely, but only with *74T* the section against universal
titles was made a separate canon, and given an appropriate rubric ('Ne universalis quisquam vocetur'). From *74T*, both canon and rubric were taken in to many collections including Anselm of
Lucca, the *Tarraconensis*, Polycarp, and *3L*, to mention only the most prominent ones. Likewise,
Gregory's letters were well known, but only in the twelfth century the relevant passages gained
special attention. The canon law collection in Vat. lat. 3829, for example, gathered no less than
five excerpts from Gregory I, and in the rubric highlighted in all cases that no-one should be
called 'universal' (see the entries in the *Clavis canonum* database with the key PG63.046, PG63.059–
61, and PG63.075). Gratian gathered his proof texts in D.99.

Prince of the Apostles—and hence all bishops, including metropolitans and, for that matter, the Roman pontiff.[183]

12P, while essentially using the same materials, in some aspects differed from Burchard. Like the *Liber decretorum*, the two *12P* versions are 'episcopalist', but some of Burchard's radical points are slightly tempered in *12P*. For example, both versions of *12P* have simply more canons on the papacy in their opening sections, in contrast to Burchard, who chose to mention the pope only twice in the openings section of his first book. Burchard's provocative claim that the pope should be called 'bishop of the first see' only (Burchard 1.3) is treated differently by the two *12P* versions. Both versions retain Burchard's canon (including the rubric), but the first version presents it less prominently than Burchard had done by inserting it into a series of canons on bishops towards the end of the first book (*12P* 1.280). The second version of *12P*, however, retains Burchard's canon and its rubric as part of the opening section (*12P* 1.11).[184]

2.5.4 Secular Rulers and Synods

Another aspect that calls for a comparison of the *Anselmo dedicata*, Burchard, and *12P* is the role of secular rulers, and in particular their role in ecclesiastical affairs. This in turn brings up the question of the role of secular rulers in synods. Let us begin with the question of the presence and presentation of secular legislation in the four collections in question here. At the surface, secular legislation plays the most important role in the *Anselmo dedicata* which includes very considerable shares of Roman law (mainly Justinian legislation) and prominently highlights the source of these materials by gathering them in separate subsections with appropriate titles; for every single canon, the source is given with precision in the inscription. In contrast, Burchard contains little secular legislation and famously chose to conceal the origin of these materials by inventing new inscriptions, passing them as conciliar legislation.[185] *12P*, finally, largely has the same secular legislation as Burchard but does not make any effort to conceal the origins of these texts.[186] However, if we turn from mere

183. Burchard 1.4; *12P* 1.7 (first version) and 13 (second version), respectively.

184. All in all, the opening section of the second version of *12P* is closer to the first version of *12P* than to Burchard. Only the first four canons found at the beginning of Burchard are also found at the beginning of the second version of *12P* (*12P* 1.3, 4, 11, and 13, respectively); the other canons are dispersed all over the first book of *12P*.

185. Scholars from early on commented on the unreliability of Burchard's inscriptions; see, for example, PL 132.181 (Baluze), PL 56.325 (Ballerini brothers), and Fournier, 'Décret' esp. 455. For an overview, see Peter Landau, 'Gefälschtes Recht in den Rechtssammlungen bis Gratian', *Fälschungen im Mittelalter* (6 vols. MGH Schriften 33; Hanover 1988) 2.11–49, esp. 30 and Austin, 'Secular Law'.

186. Müller, *Collectio* 15.

statistics and the accuracy of rubrics to the material law, a different picture emerges. In fact, while the collections have very different positions on the role of metropolitans and diocesan bishops, they (for very different reasons) largely agree concerning the important role of secular rulers in ecclesiastical affairs.

In the *Anselmo dedicata*, this is largely due to the high share of Justinian legislation just mentioned. Given the active role of this Christian emperor in church affairs, this is not very surprising, but it is noteworthy that some texts could be read as asserting imperial rights, and may even have been selected for this reason. For example, as mentioned above,[187] the *Anselmo dedicata* contains excerpts from the *Epitome Juliani* that assert that the patriarch of Constantinople was second only to Rome.[188] The selection of these texts may very well reflect his attitudes towards the patriarch of Constantinople,[189] but it can also be read as evidence for far-reaching imperial competences in ecclesiastical affairs. A clearer case are the generous privileges for Justiniana prima, rarely taken into account by scholarship.[190] This may be due to the fact that Justiniana prima is not a familiar subject, but as I will argue, this is precisely the point in understanding why this canon was taken into the *Anselmo dedicata*. Justiniana prima is, or rather was, an episcopal see in Illyricum; modern scholarship was long divided where to locate it exactly. What is certain is that Justinian had founded this city in 530 near his birth-place, and conferred on it high civil and ecclesiastical status by formal enactment. This material, taken into the *Anselmo dedicata* from the *Epitome*, is otherwise very rare in the West. Even if we allow for some knowledge of the Greek Christian world in ninth-century Milan, one wonders how much the compiler really knew about this Illyrian see, or why he thought this material relevant. After all, Justiniana prima was destroyed in 615, more than 250 years before the *Anselmo dedicata* was compiled. It is therefore unlikely that the *Anselmo dedicata* compiler was genuinely interested in the rights of this Illyrian see. However, like the Novel on Constantinople, Justinian's unusual move to bestow very generous privileges by law onto a church may have been of interest in the

187. See above, note 132.

188. *Anselmo dedicata* 1.117–118 and 129 (ed. Besse 293); the latter canon reads: 'Papa romanus prior omnibus episcopis et patriarchis sedeat, et post illum Constantinopolitanae civitatis archiepiscopus.' The first two canons are from the Council of Constantinople (381), the third one was taken from the *Epitome Juliani*, const. 109, cap. 507 (ed. Hänel 165). On the see of Constantinople, see also *Anselmo dedicata* 1.96–97.

189. This was already proposed by Fournier, 'Anselmo dedicata' 497 and followed e.g. by Dvornik, *Photian Schism* 284–286.

190. *Anselmo dedicata* 1.130, taken from the *Epitome Juliani*, const. 109, cap. 508 (ed. Hänel 165). On the ecclesiastical history of Justiniana prima, see Markus, 'Carthage' 289–292.

context of imperial rights in general. Even if the *Anselmo dedicata* compiler and the later readers of this collection may not have been aware that Justinian's privileges for 'his' see were a way to curtail the influence of the Roman pontiff (as in fact they were[191]), they might have learnt from this that an emperor could interfere very directly with the ecclesiastical hierarchy. This may indeed have made the canon interesting also for the compilers in Germany around the year 1000, when imperial foundations of bishoprics were anything but a theoretical issue.[192]

Less speculatively, Burchard and the *12P* compilers generally assumed that secular rulers cooperated closely with synods. For example, a series of conciliar canons in Burchard's book fifteen asserts that 'enemies of the king' were to be excommunicated and detail the obedience owed to secular rulers.[193] Unlike the *Anselmo dedicata* compiler, Burchard and the *12P* compilers did so not because of the laws of venerable Christian emperors of a distant past, but because this was how synods functioned in their experience. Burchard for good reasons has been quoted as the archetypical *Reichsbischof*,[194] and the bishops of Freising likewise had close relations to the emperor.[195]

The most direct expression of this is found in Burchard 15.20. Burchard inserted a text that approved the king's right to call synods,[196] and a large number of Carolingian and post-Carolingian conciliar canons leave no doubt that Burchard thought this legislation valid. At the same time, Burchard (quite in tune with the general tendency of his collection) restricted the role of the papacy in the convocation of synods. The decisive evidence comes from Burchard 1.42, a canon that has attracted considerable scholarly attention since the mid-nineteenth century.[197] The canon

191. Markus, 'Carthage' 290.

192. Hehl, 'Bischof'; Huschner, 'Neue Erzbistümer'; Bernd Schneidmüller, '"Tausend Jahre sind für dich wie der Tag, der gestern vergangen ist". Die Gründung des Bistums Bamberg 1007', *Das Bistum Bamberg in der Welt des Mittelalters. Vorträge der Ringvorlesung des Zentrums für Mittelalterstudien der Otto-Friedrich-Universität Bamberg im Sommersemester 2007*, ed. Christine van Eickels and Klaus van Eickels (Bamberger interdisziplinäre Mittelalterstudien. Vorträge und Vorlesungen 1; Bamberg 2007) 15–32.

193. Burchard 15.22–29.

194. E.g. Theo Kölzer, 'Burchard I., Bischof von Worms (1000–1025)', *Burchard von Worms (Burchardus Wormaciensis ecclesiae episcopus), Decretorum libri XX [...]. Ergänzter Neudruck*, ed. Gérard Fransen and Theo Kölzer (Aalen 1992) 7–23, Reuter, 'Europe', and Schieffer, 'Burchard von Worms'.

195. Müller, *Untersuchungen*; idem, *Collectio* 16–17.

196. This was first observed by Albert Hauck, 'Ueber den liber decretorum Burchard's von Worms' *Sb. Akad. Leipzig* 46 (1894) 65–86, here at 84.

197. Burchard 1.42 (*editio princeps*, fol. 6r). See August-Friedrich Gfrörer, *Allgemeine Kirchengeschichte* (4 in 7 vols. Stuttgart 1846), here at 4.1:177–178; Hauck, 'Burchard' 84; idem, *Kirchengeschichte Deutschlands* (5 in 6 vols. Berlin 1887–1920), here at 3.435–440 (context); Albert Michael Koeniger, *Burchard I. von Worms und die deutsche Kirche seiner Zeit (1000–1025). Ein kirchen- und sittengeschicht-*

largely is taken from the preface to the Pseudo-Isidorian forgeries. There, one could read that synods without papal approval were not valid. Yet Burchard restricts this provision to 'general' synods.[198] This brings the canon in line with long-standing custom, but evidently distorts a concept that was dear to the Pseudo-Isidorian forgers. Ironically, Burchard's manipulation may even be inspired by Pseudo-Isidore.[199] Yet more importantly, and evidently, Burchard agreed with the general idea of the Pseudo-Isidorian forgers; in the False Decretals, the necessity of papal approval is linked to synods hearing cases against bishops, and this is an idea that Burchard clearly valued and retained.[200]

2.5.5 Marriage and Incest in Burchard and *12P*

Marriage and Incest in Burchard

Another way to study the preoccupations of a compiler, and his impact on the law, is to look for those matters where he diverged from tradition. In the case of Burchard's *Liber decretorum*, this is most clearly the case with his account of marriage law and, more specifically, his book seven on incest. Scholars have long studied Burchard's views on marriage and sexuality. In the older literature, the *Liber decretorum* was sometimes described as expressing a lax position on marriage and sexuality.[201] In the case of incest,

---

liches Zeitbild (Veröffentlichungen aus dem kirchenhistorischen Seminar München 2.6; Munich 1905), here at 60; Fournier, 'Décret' 468 (maintaining that Burchard 1.179 effectively countered Burchard 1.42); Fuhrmann, 'Studien' ZRG Kan. Abt. 40.46–47; idem, 'Das Ökumenische Konzil und seine historischen Grundlagen' *Geschichte in Wissenschaft und Unterricht* 12 (1961) 672–695, here at 683–684.

198. Burchard 1.42 (*editio princeps*, fol. 6ra–b): '[…] Nec ullam synodum generalem ratam esse legimus, quae eius non fuerit auctoriate congregate vel fulta.' As already Hauck, 'Burchard' 84 pointed out, the 'generalem' was Burchard's addition to Pseudo-Isidore's *Praefatio* c. 8 (ed. Hinschius 19). Robert Somerville (private communication) drew to attention JK †1051 (ed. Hinschius 721) as a possible source for Burchard's interpolation.

199. See Ps.-Julius, JK †195 c. 5 (ed. Hinschius 459), where 'convocandarum generalium synodorum iura' are attributed to the pope.

200. Burchard 1.179 (*editio princeps*, fol. 25ra): 'Quod omnes possint appellare Romanam sedem. Quam omnes appellare, si necesse fuerit, et eius fulciri auxilio oportet. Nam, ut nostis, synodum sine eius auctoritate fieri non est canonicum, nec episcopus, nisi in legitima synodo et suo tempore apostolica vocatione congregata, definite damnari potest, neque ulla unquam concilia rata leguntur, quae non sunt fulta apostolica auctoritate.'

201. E.g. Ignaz Fahrner, *Geschichte der Ehescheidung im kanonischen Recht. Teil 1: Geschichte des Unauflöslichkeitsprinzips und der vollkommenen Scheidung im kanonischen Recht* (Freiburg 1903), here at 110 (divorce), Fournier, 'Décret' 690 (celibacy) and 682 (divorce). See also *Histoire* 1.409 and Jean Gaudemet, *Le mariage en Occident: les mœurs et le droit* (Paris 1987), here at 240–241. An extreme version was presented by Georges Duby, *The Knight, the Lady and the Priest: The Making of Modern Marriage in Medieval France* (London 1984), esp. 70. Duby's interpretation of Burchard is untenable, see Wilfried Hartmann, 'Bemerkungen zum Eherecht nach Burchard von Worms', *Bischof Burchard von Worms, 1000–1025*, ed. idem (Quellen und Abhandlungen zur mittelrheinischen Kirchengeschichte 100; Mainz 2000) 227–250. The same is true for his account of the marriage affair of Philip I (Duby, *Knight* ch. 3) which he quotes as a contrasting example; on this issue, see Rolker, *Canon Law* 230–242.

however, Fournier had already observed the opposite. While greatly un-
derestimating the changes Burchard introduced in the area of impediments to marriage, Fournier keenly observed that Burchard's computation
of kinship effectively extended the prohibited degrees.[202] More generally,
Fournier pointed out that the *Liber decretorum* could only be understood
in the context of contemporary marriage cases like the Hammerstein
case.[203] Patrick Corbet was the first to systematically study Burchard's contribution to the law of marriage in the context of contemporary marriage
cases and the politics of Henry II.[204] He concluded that Burchard's rigorist
position demonstrated that the reformers of the second half of the century including Gregory VII owed much more to Burchard and, ultimately,
Henry II than had been assumed for a long time.[205] Yet it was left to Karl
Ubl to demonstrate how radically Burchard changed the canon law on the
prohibited degrees of kinship. As he argued convincingly, it was only with
Burchard that marriage was forbidden with kin in the seventh degree in
canonical computation.[206] As for the background of the new prohibitions,
he argued that Burchard compiled his collection as a 'handbook for the
anti-incest campaign of King Henry II',[207] and more generally argued that
the kings had an interest in preventing the high nobility from endoga-
mous marriages.

As this suggests, Burchard was not alone in making these far-reaching
changes, but his *Liber decretorum* was the single most important canon law
collection to establish the new prohibitions. How did Burchard manage
to introduce such a massive change in an area that manifestly touched
the lives of so many people? To begin with, Burchard divided his material
on marriage in an unusual way—strikingly different from all earlier and
most later collections. While marriage law clearly plays a prominent role
in the *Liber decretorum*, it is dispersed over several books. The most unusual of these is book seven 'On incest'. Given that by the time of Burchard
there already was a century-old, complex tradition of Christian legislation on marriage, and not least on incest, it may surprising that the *Liber
decretorum* should be the first canon law collection to contain a separate
book 'On incest'.[208] It is yet more striking that the book is anything but

---

202. Fournier, 'Décret' 681–682; *Histoire* 1.408.

203. Fournier, 'Décret' 466–468. In his characteristic fashion, Fournier after pointing out the
importance of the Hammerstein case for Burchard and his collaborators quickly turned to the
question of papal primacy, suggesting that this was the most important (legal) aspect of the case.

204. Corbet, *Burchard*.

205. E.g. Corbet, *Burchard*.

206. Ubl, *Inzestverbot*.

207. Ubl, *Inzestverbot* 435.

208. Apart from Burchard and 12P, there is no early canon law collection having a separate

a comprehensive treatment of the issue. Famously, incest in the Middle
Ages was commonly defined as sexual relations with kin or consecrated
women,[209] and equally famously, 'kin' in the course of time was defined as
covering blood-relatives, in-laws and spiritual kin alike.[210] Burchard's book
seven, in contrast, is only concerned with the prohibition of marriage between blood-relatives; the other kinds of forbidden marriage are treated
separately in books eight, nine, and seventeen. Only relations by blood are
treated in a separate book, and only the title of that book calls the violation of these prohibitions 'incest'. Compared to the current tradition of
his time, quoted above, this is a narrow definition.

Another unusual aspect is the brevity of book seven, containing a
mere thirty canons or about a third of the average number of canons
found in individual books of Burchard. This again indicates the special
importance given to these texts, which otherwise could easily (and conventionally) have been integrated into a book on marriage, for example.
The main evidence, however, are the texts themselves. While they are
not very numerous, they were clearly very carefully selected, arranged,
and relatively frequently even manipulated to produce a radical polemic
against consanguineous marriages. The most important novelty Burchard
introduced was the combination of two traditions.[211] As is evident from
his skilful tampering with his proof texts, Burchard was well aware of the
long and sometimes contradictory history of prohibitions on various kin
marriages. From these texts, he selected the most radical prohibitions to
establish the seventh degree as prohibited. Secondly, concerning the difficult question of how these degrees were counted, he chose (and carefully
explained) the method later known as the canonical computation.

Burchard invented neither the seventh degree nor the canonical computation, even if he partly manipulated the proof texts on these matters.
However, as Ubl established, the two traditions before Burchard had not
been combined. Isidore of Seville, to take a prominent example, had
defined kinship as extending to the sixth (not the seventh) degree, but

book on incest and/or a book that mentions 'incest' in the title. Only occasionally, the term is
used at least for smaller subsections, e.g. in the *Vetus Gallica* that groups seven canons under the
heading 'De incestis et adulteris et qui uxores suas demittunt'.

209. E.g. Isidore, *Etym.* 5.27.24 (on which see below).

210. The treatment of these rather different social relations as impediments to marriage (to
use the language of classical canon law) has often been stressed as one of the most striking developments of medieval canon law: Anita Guerreau-Jalabert, 'Sur la structure de parenté dans l'Europe médiévale' *Annales ESC* 36 (1981) 1028–1049, esp. 1035–1042; Jack Goody, *The Development of
the Family and Marriage in Europe* (Cambridge and New York 1983), esp. 194–221; Bernhard Jussen,
Patenschaft und Adoption im frühen Mittelalter. Künstliche Verwandtschaft als soziale Praxis (Veröffentlichungen des MPI für Geschichte 98; Göttingen 1991).

211. The following is based on Ubl, *Inzestverbot*.

counted the degrees according to Roman custom.[212] Both this definition of 'blood relatives' and the diagram that illustrates it are clearly about inheritance law, not marriage or 'incest'.[213] Isidore's definition of 'incest' in turn does not suggest that all prohibited marriages (e.g. between second cousins) were 'incestuous'.[214] By the time Burchard was compiling his collection, Isidore's *Etymologies* had long been widely known and held in high esteem. It was then natural for Burchard to turn to Isidore's definition of kinship when forging his version of the prohibitions of marriage. Surprisingly perhaps, Isidore's text including the reference to six (not seven) degrees is retained,[215] and the diagram found in the *Etymologies* are only lightly modified in Burchard's *Liber decretorum*. The real change is the context; Burchard quotes Isidore's definition of 'kinship' not in the original context (inheritance law) but in his book 'On incest', preceded by canons on 'incest', and followed by an explanation of the canonical computation of kinship. As a result, Isidore's text reads quite naturally as a proof text for a doctrine utterly unknown in the time it was written. Isidore may have considered cousin marriage as forbidden, but certainly not marriages in the seventh degree in canonical computation (this would have been the fourteenth in the Roman computation he was familiar with). He certainly would have been astonished to learn that his own definition of kinship was employed to declare such marriages not only forbidden but 'incestuous'.

It is well worth remembering that the normative texts Burchard's contemporaries were likely to come across could be thoroughly confusing. Some of the inconsistencies between (and within) the collections were simply the result of the changing ecclesiastical legislation of five centuries. Further confusion came from the fact that this legislation also quoted incest prohibitions from the Old Testament and Roman marriage law. In

---

212. Isidore, *Etym.* 9.6.29: 'Consanguinity is established up to the sixth degree of kinship, so that just as the generation of the world and the status of humankind comes to an end through six ages, so kinship in a family is terminated by the same number of degrees.' The translation is taken from *Etymologies*, tr. Barney et al. 210. On Isidore's counting of the degrees of kinship, see Ubl, *Inzestverbot* 242–243. Isidore largely follows Saint Augustine's definition of kinship as found in *De civitate Dei* 15.16 (ed. Dombart and Kalb, CCL 48.476).

213. Isidore, *Etym.* 9.6.28 is about the Roman law diagram known as 'stemma', and illustrated by such a family tree. In Roman law, such diagrams were used in inheritance cases but not in the context of marriage prohibitions, and the whole passage is indeed lifted from a discussion of inheritance in the *Pauli Sententiae* 4.11, see Schadt, *Darstellungen* 22 and 110.

214. Isidore, *Etym.* 5.27.24: 'The judgement of incest (*incestum*) is made with regard to consecrated virgins or those who are closely related by blood.' Note that this definition is found in a completely different context; in Isidore's discussion of kinship and marriage (Isidore, *Etym.* 9.6), the term 'incest' does not even figure. The translation is taken from *Etymologies*, tr. Barney et al. 123.

215. Burchard 7.10 (*editio princeps*, fol. 208v), taking up some of *Etym.* 9.6.29.

Leviticus, incest was condemned very clearly but, embarrassingly for medieval Christian readers, marriages, for instance, between uncle and niece were allowed. Roman law authorities that allowed cousin marriage were not completely forgotten in the Middle Ages.[216] It must have been difficult to establish a clear reading of all these texts, especially when reading them side by side. Sometimes however, the texts themselves were fundamentally ambiguous. A key document was Gregory's *Libellus responsionum*.[217] Crucially, concerning kin marriage it stated:[218]

> Whence it is necessary that the third and fourth generations of the faithful may freely join together, but the second generation, as we have said, ought wholly to abstain [from marrying each other].

This passage was widely read and copied, but again depending on which manuscript or which collection one was reading, the crucial terms refer to the 'third or fourth',[219] 'fourth',[220] 'fourth or fifth',[221] 'fourth or sixth',[222] or 'third, fourth, or sixth' generations;[223] yet another tradition turned this passage in a prohibition for the 'third, fourth, fifth, sixth, and seventh genera-

216. Augustine, *De civitate Dei* 15.16 (ed. Dombart and Kalb, CCL 48.478) mentions that cousin marriage had been legal in his lifetime. Gregory I, JE 1843 (ed. Ewald and Hartmann, MGH Epp. 2.335) refers to 'quidem terrena lex in romana republica' which allowed 'ut sibi fratris aut sororis seu duorum fratrum germanorum vel duarum sororum filii et filiae misceantur'. A passage lifted from the *Codex Justiniani* (Cod. 1.10.2.4) was faithfully preserved in the *Britannica* (London, BL, Add. MS 8873, fol. 57v) and the first Arsenal collection (Paris, Bibliothèque de l'Arsenal 713, fol. 158r): 'Duorum autem fratrum sororumve liberi, vel fratris et sororis iungi possunt.' Ivo of Chartres in his *Decretum* 9.1 presents a version containing a 'non' inserted before 'iungi'.

217. Gregory I, JE 1843 (ed. Ewald and Hartmann, MGH Epp. 2.332–343). See Paul Meyvaert, 'Le *Libellus responsionum* à Augustin de Cantorbéry: une œuvre authentique de Saint Grégoire le Grand', *Grégoire le Grand*, ed. Jacques Fontaine et al. (Colloques internationaux de Centre national de la recherche scientifique; Paris 1986) 543–550, Ubl, *Inzestverbot* 221–233, and Michael D. Elliot, 'Boniface, Incest, and the Earliest Extant Version of Pope Gregory I's *Libellus responsionum* (JE 1843)' ZRG Kan. Abt. 100 (2014) 62–111 (with ample references to the abundant literature). Some 200 manuscripts of the *Libellus* are known. I agree with Ubl and Elliot (against Meyvaert) concerning the authenticity of the incest prohibitions in JE 1843.

218. Gregory I, JE 1843 (ed. Ewald and Hartmann, MGH Epp. 2.335): 'Unde necesse est, ut iam tertia vel quarta generatio fidelium licenter sibi iungi debeat. Nam secunda quam praediximus a se omni modo debet abstinere.' For a slightly different translation, see Elliot, 'Boniface' 88: 'Whence it is lawful that now, among the faithful, the third and fourth degrees [*generatio*] may freely join together, but from [a relation in] the second degree, as we have said, one ought wholly to abstain.'

219. See last note. This version is found for example in *12P* 8.7 (Troyes, BM, 246, fol. 152va) and *Polycarpus* 6.4.21.

220. Gregory I, JE 1843 according to the Capitula version (Ewald's 'A'), where some words are erased before 'quarta' (Elliot, 'Boniface' 88 n. 62). I follow Elliot's argument that the Capitula version is more likely to be closest to the original than the Letter version (*pace* Meyvaert, 'Libellus').

221. Burchard 7.19, taken up by very many later collections (Ivo 9.55; *Panormia* 7.71; Gratian C.35 q.2/3 c.20).

222. Regino, *Libri duo*, Appendix 2.2 (ed. Wasserschleben 424).

223. Wolfenbüttel, HAB, Cod. Guelf. 454 Helmst., fol. 13v as quoted by Corbet, *Burchard* 323: 'Unde necesse est ut iam III vel IIII vel VI generatio fidelium licenter sibi iungi debeat. Nam in secundo quam praediximus omnino debeat abstineri.'

tions'.[224] Burchard integrated this prominent text in his collection and only slightly changed the text.[225] More importantly, in the following canon and its rubric Burchard made clear that Gregory had allowed these marriages by a 'special' dispensation, one only offered for a people newly converted to Christianity.[226] By this, he found a way to integrate Gregory's well-known text into his own account, effectively neutralizing an important authority that was quoted by those sceptical of the excessive prohibitions.[227]

Burchard's book seven is one of the most cleverly composed books in medieval canon law history.[228] In the present context, the above examples must suffice to show that by relatively small changes (as far as the actual texts are concerned) Burchard massively changed the meaning of his proof texts and thus ultimately the law itself. The textual manipulations are only one part of his strategy; the crucial effect is achieved by the selection, arrangement, and comment (in form of book title and rubrics). As a result, Burchard's proof texts looked familiar to any learned contemporary, as almost every element could be found elsewhere. By these means, Burchard unambiguously established the seventh degree in canonical computation as prohibited, as Ubl demonstrated. With this extension of the marriage prohibition, Burchard also greatly extended the use of highly charged terms like 'incest' to very distant kin marriages, in stark contrast to earlier (and many later) collections which prohibited certain kin

---

224. Vatican *9L* 7.65 (Vat. lat. 1349, fol. 153vb) and also *5L* 5.215 (Vat. lat. 1339, fols. 306v–307r): 'Unde necesse est, ut iam tertia, quarta, quinta, sexta, septima generatio fidelium licenter sibi iungi nequaquam [!] debeat.'

225. Burchard's version is largely identical to that of John the Deacon in his *Vita Gregorii* (PL 75.101) and Regino, *Libri duo*, Appendix 2.2 (ed. Wasserschleben 424), with minor differences to both versions. In Burchard, John the Deacon is presented as 'John of Constantinople' writing to a Bishop Felix of Sicily (Burchard 7.19–20). Felix of Sicily in turn was also the addressee of the Ps.-Gregorian JE †1334 (ed. Hinschius 749–753), which normally is seen as a Pseudo-Isidorian forgery. Fuhrmann, *Einfluß und Verbreitung* 1.190 was not convinced, but Corbet, *Burchard* 88–89, Ubl, *Inzestverbot* 336–340, and Elliot, 'Boniface' 69 accept it as Pseudo-Isidorian.

226. The argument that Gregory in JE 1843 had granted dispensation to the English 'specialiter, non generaliter' is already found in Ps.-Gregory, JE †1334 (ed. Hinschius 749), and similar arguments are even older (Ubl, *Inzestverbot* 338–339). Burchard is the first to quote from JE †1334 immediately after JE 1843 (*Liber decretorum* 7.19–20) and to highlight this in the rubric to 7.20 (*editio princeps*, fol. 109ra): 'Quod sanctus Gregorius hoc Anglorum genti specialiter, non generaliter permisit'. The rubric to 7.19 likewise highlights that JE 1834 was granted as a dispensation: 'Gregorius papa requisitus ab Augustino Anglorum gentis episcopo, quota generatione fideles debeant copulari, dispensatorie sic rescribit'. For *12P*, see below.

227. For attempts to restrict the application of the *Libellus responsionum* (e.g. by Pope Zachary, the Roman council of 721 under Gregory II, Jonas of Orléans, and Pseudo-Isidore) see Ubl, *Inzestverbot* 225, 304–307, 336–340 and 342–344, and Elliot, 'Boniface' 68–70.

228. For details, see Ubl, *Inzestverbot* and Christof Rolker, 'Two Models of Incest: Conflict and Confusion in High Medieval Discourse on Kinship and Marriage', *Law and Marriage in Medieval and Early Modern Times: Proceedings of the Eighth Carlsberg Academy Conference on Medieval Legal History*, ed. Peer Andersen et al. (Copenhagen 2012) 139–159.

marriages without calling them 'incestuous'.[229] This may seem like mere rhetoric, but depending on context, it was indeed significant whether a canon law collection called a union of two distant cousins 'prohibited' or 'incestuous'. Prohibitions could be changed, but the vocabulary of 'incest' came with religious overtones that may have made it difficult to even discuss such a change. While I believe Burchard's position on incest cannot be explained by 'pollution fears', the reluctance to correct the extreme changes he had introduced may well have to do with the rhetoric of 'incest' and taboo he was using.[230] In any case, it was many years before the western Church dared to reduce the marriage prohibitions that Burchard had established: it was not until the Fourth Lateran Council of 1215 that his seven prohibited degrees were reduced to four.[231]

Marriage and Incest in *12P*

Since the incest prohibitions are the part of canon law where Burchard introduced the greatest changes and where he seems to have taken most care in manipulating his proof texts, a comparison of these passages with the corresponding section of *12P* should be particularly enlightening. On the one hand, *12P* emerged essentially under the same circumstances as Burchard. On the other hand, *12P* is known to be 'conservative' in the sense of preserving the text of the canons very faithfully; in particular, the *12P* compilers are not known to have changed their texts as Burchard often did, most strikingly in his book seven. It is therefore unfortunate that the marriage legislation in *12P* has not been given much attention in modern scholarship.[232] Partly this is due to the perception of *12P* as a mere derivative of Burchard.[233] The fullest account is that of Patrick Corbet; unfortunately it is flawed in its treatment of both *12P* and Burchard.[234]

---

229. Rolker, 'Two Models'.

230. See Cushing, *Reform* ch. 6 on the 'rhetoric of reform' (including purity and pollution). For arguments that anti-incest legislation was the product of pollution fears, see Mayke de Jong, 'To the Limits of Kinship: Anti-Incest Legislation in the Early Medieval West (500–900)', *From Sappho to De Sade: Moments in the History of Sexuality*, ed. Jan N. Bremmer (London 1989) 36–59 and Amy G. Remensnyder, 'Pollution, Purity and Peace: An Aspect of Social Reform Between the Late Tenth Century and 1076', *The Peace of God: Social Violence and Religious Response in France Around the Year 1000*, ed. Thomas Head and Richard Landes (Ithaca, N.Y. 1992) 280–307.

231. See Norman P. Tanner, *Decrees of the Ecumenical Councils* (2 vols. London 1990), here at 1.257–258. On Burchard's success in this area in particular, see Corbet, *Burchard*. On Lateran IV and incest, see David L. d'Avray, 'Lay Kinship Solidarity and Papal Law', *Law, Laity and Solidarities: Essays in Honour of Susan Reynolds*, ed. Pauline A. Stafford et al. (Manchester and New York 2001) 188–199. See also Chapter 5.7.5 on the *Panormia* preparing the 1215 provisions.

232. Müller, *Untersuchungen* does not treat marriage law separately; Ubl, *Inzestverbot* does not treat *12P*. See Fournier, 'Recueil canonique' 55–60 and Hartmann, 'Bemerkungen' 237–239.

233. This is mainly true for Fournier, 'Recueil canonique' 55–60 and those scholars following his account of *12P*.

234. Corbet, *Burchard* 106–113. To follow Corbet's account, it is important to understand

So how do the two *12P* versions present marriage legislation and in particular the incest prohibitions Burchard was so interested in?[235] At first sight, all three collections are similar, as the textual overlap of *12P* and Burchard is considerable.[236] Both *12P* versions, while arranging the canons somewhat differently, have identical series of canons in the same sequence as Burchard has them, including many (but not all) the texts he altered.[237] Interestingly, these series are rather short;[238] this may already indicate an independent reworking of the material even where the texts are taken from Burchard (or, for that matter, a shared source used by both collections). A closer look reveals important differences. In particular, the extreme concern with consanguineous marriage that shaped Burchard is not found in the first version of *12P*, and even less so in the second version.

The difference begins with the organisation of the collections into books. While the canons of Burchard's incest book all re-appear in *12P*, they do not form a separate book, but are combined with other marriage legislation in one book (book eight). This decision made good sense, as the marriage prohibitions on ground of blood relations were clearly part of marriage law, and in the end only a small part; however, it also reduced the emphasis on consanguinity that marked Burchard. In the first version of *12P*, consanguinity is still given some prominence in that the opening canons of the book on marriage deal with consanguinity, and the title reads 'On incest and legitimate marriage'. In the second version, the order is reversed both in the book and in the title;[239] consanguinity is treated towards the middle of the book (*12P* 8.79–121), together with other forms of kinship that impede marriage, i.e. affinity and spiritual kinship.

Nonetheless, the material contained in Burchard's books seven is found in both *12P* versions; even if *12P* emphasized it slightly less by presenting it as part of marriage law, these texts still assert, as they did in the *Liber decretorum*, that marriages in the seventh degree of canonical computation

---

that he apparently was confused by Müller's sigla, treating Müller's 'CDP1' as the earlier of the two versions. In fact, the version extant in Troyes, BM, 246 (Fournier's **T**; 'TX' in *Clavis*) and Saint-Claude, BM, 17 (unknown to Fournier; not used for *Clavis*) represents the earlier version of *12P*, referred to as '2CDP' [*sic*] by Müller, *Untersuchungen*. For important corrections of Corbet's reconstruction of Burchard's views on marriage, see also Ubl, *Inzestverbot* s.v. 'Corbet'.

235. The following analysis is based on the *Clavis canonum* database; for this reason, I have consulted the manuscript also chosen by Dr Fowler-Magerl, Troyes, BM, 246 (her 'TX'), for the earlier version.

236. Fournier, 'Recueil canonique' 55–60; Hartmann, 'Bemerkungen' 237–239.

237. Hartmann, 'Bemerkungen' 238.

238. The longest series from book seven is Burchard 7.11–16 reappearing in the same order in *12P* (TX08.014–19, TW08.095–100). The canons immediately before and after (all dealing with the seventh degree) are also found in Burchard, but not in the same sequence as in *12P*.

239. This was observed by Corbet, *Burchard* 108; if he claims a different direction of reworking, this is due to his confusion of 'CDP1' and 'CDP2' (see above, note 234).

are prohibited. If one turns to *12P* material not found in Burchard, a more complex picture emerges. Compared to Burchard's highly selective account, *12P* preserves the text and the sequence of the formal sources and often that of the material sources much more faithfully than Burchard and almost always has fuller texts.

An example of the different treatment of the same material are the canons of the Roman synod of 721 presided over by Gregory II.[240] Both the *Anselmo dedicata* and Burchard had used this important source, but *12P* did so independently from both. In *12P*, the *praefatio* and the first twelve of the seventeen canons from this synod are found in one series, in the order of the material source.[241] Burchard, in contrast, included only three canons in book seven, and two more in book nine.[242] Characteristically, *12P* is more complete and follows its source, even where this does not fit its own division of the books. Indeed, both *12P* versions retain one text that has nothing to do with marriage, apparently for the sole reason that it was promulgated in the same synod.[243] For Burchard, it is equally characteristic that he ignored most material, especially so if it suggested a much more narrow definition of 'incest' than his own *Liber decretorum* did,[244] or where other forms of incest than consanguineous marriages were at issue.[245]

Another interesting case concerns the famous letter of Rabanus Maurus on the prohibited degrees of kinship.[246] As Corbet noticed, the inclusion of this letter in *12P* could be seen as contradicting Burchard's insistence on the seventh degree.[247] Certainly Rabanus held very different views from Burchard. In his letter, he criticised papal legislation on the seventh degree severely in a passage included among the excerpts taken into *12P*.[248] Although Burchard omitted this part of the letter in his *Liber*

---

240. Mansi 12.262–268. On the council, see Ubl, *Inzestverbot* 235–240.

241. In *Clavis*, the series of canons taken from this council is counted as one canon (*12P* 8.29 in the first version, *12P* 8.121 in the second version).

242. Burchard 7.22–24 and 9.11–12.

243. *12P* 8.29n and 8.121n, respectively. (For the subdivision of the *12P* canons, I follow the *Clavis* database.)

244. Concerning relatives by blood, the Roman synod mentioned none beyond the *consobrina*.

245. This was in fact the case with most canons at issue here, as the Roman synod dealt with marriages to women consecrated to God (the *presbytera*, the *diacona*, and the *monacha* are mentioned), in-laws and spiritual kin.

246. Rabanus, *Ep.* 29 (ed. Dümmler, MGH Epp. 5.445–448). See Ubl, *Inzestverbot* 308–322 on the letter (though not *12P*).

247. Corbet, *Burchard* 112.

248. Rabanus, *Ep.* 29 (ed. Dümmler, MGH Epp. 5.446): 'Quod autem proxima temporibus Romanorum pontificum scripta continent usque ad sextam vel septimam generationem coniugii usum esse differendum magis ex consuetudine humana quam ex lege divina hoc eos praecepisse credendum est.'

decretorum, he clearly knew it very well. In fact, he even used it in his book on incest: it was the source from which Burchard lifted the material for a forged letter, which is attributed there to Isidore and asserts rather than challenges the seventh degree (Burchard 7.9). So Burchard of Worms knew, but did not retain, the original version of Rabanus's letters as found in *12P*. Yet much more interestingly, the *12P* compilers in turn knew and retained Burchard's forged version of the letter. In the first version of *12P*, this 'Isidore' canon even follows immediately after the Rabanus Maurus excerpt; in other words, both the genuine Rabanus letter and the forgery based on it are found side by side.[249] Given their rather contradictory content, this could seriously confuse a diligent reader. This was probably not intentional. Given that *12P* on the whole agrees with Burchard on the seventh degree, it seems unlikely that the compilers at this instance chose to criticize Burchard's position (as Corbet held) or intentionally wanted to draw attention to the manipulations (as in effect they do). Nonetheless, the juxtaposition is striking and calls for an explanation. If one assumes that it was indeed Burchard who forged the 'Isidorian' canon (and this does fit the general pattern), than he must have used the Rabanus letter, and at some point, both the original and the nascent forgery were on someone's desk—and perhaps even copied together. It seems natural for Burchard (whose desk might be the one under discussion here) to avoid giving the genuine letter of Rabanus when he inserted his altered version into the *Liber decretorum*. What really needs explanation is how the materials made it from the forger's workshop into the first version of *12P* (and thence into the second version too). If we exclude the possibility that the *12P* compilers wanted to confuse their readers and/or criticize Burchard, the most likely explanation seems to be that they had access to Burchard's working materials and treated it more or less in the same way as their other formal sources: carefully retaining all that seemed useful, even if they knew that Burchard had in many cases opted for brevity rather than completeness. If the compilers of the first version of *12P* were aware of the difference between the texts, they were apparently not much concerned. A similar argument can be made for the compilers of the second version of *12P*; here, both canons are retained, but instead of presenting them together and at the beginning of the incest book, they are moved elsewhere.[250] That the two canons were retained in the second version of *12P* may still

249. See Burchard 7.9 = *12P* 8.10 (first version) = *12P* 8.101 (second version) for the 'Isidore' forgery and *12P* 8.9 (first version) and 8.120 (second version) for Rabanus' original letter. For the first version of *12P*, I have used Troyes, BM, 246, fol. 153r.

250. *12P* 8.101 and 120 (see last note).

be explained by scribal inertia, but the fact that they were moved at least suggests that some decision was made concerning these canons.

Incest Prohibitions in Burchard and *12P*: Conclusions

While *12P* in effect dilutes Burchard's carefully composed polemic, the arrangement here has its own merits. For example, *12P* groups all canons on the seventh degree of kinship together, while in Burchard they were slightly more dispersed;[251] it also treated consanguinity, affinity, and spiritual kinship together, as canon law more generally treated these three relations as fundamentally similar, while Burchard paid special attention to consanguinity but less to other forms of kinship.

The *12P* compiler evidently had materials at hand also used by Burchard, and treated these materials differently. In the case of the two versions of Rabanus's letter at least, *12P* seems to preserve materials which must have been at Burchard's desk at some point but very plausibly were never intended for circulation by Burchard. Including the original version next to the forgery would have contradicted the doctrine Burchard presented in his book seven, and more specifically could have called into question the authenticity of a canon which was part of Burchard's overall argument. The *12P* compilers, generally much less concerned with doctrinal coherence, seem to have preserved both texts simply because both were relevant—not because they fit a particular doctrine. Quite independently of the differences in doctrine between Burchard and *12P* this was the main difference between the compilers: compared to most compilers of pre-Gratian collections, Burchard of Worms was unusually concerned with doctrinal unity, and successfully implemented this—often at the expense of completeness or accuracy, but with lasting effect.

2.6 The Italian Burchard(s)

As mentioned above, Burchard's collection soon after it was compiled was known outside Worms, and by the middle of the century had spread widely in Latin Europe. In particular, it travelled south very quickly and reached several places in northern Italy before the middle of the eleventh century. Imperial monasteries like Nonantola may have played a special role in the early dissemination of the new collection,[252] but above all there was a demand for canon law in Italy which the *Liber decretorum* was able to satisfy better than many other collections available.

251. Burchard 7.11–16, 28, and 30.
252. Nonantola had a *Liber decretorum* by 1035, and had at least three Burchard copies at times; see Busch, *Liber de honore* 76–100.

The Italian transmission of Burchard's *Liber decretorum* is particularly important for two reasons. First, as already the number of manuscripts makes clear, Burchard was very frequently copied in eleventh- and twelfth-century Italy. At least half of the extant copies of Burchard come from Italian scriptoria. Second, in this context a number of distinct versions emerged which in turn became influential well beyond Italy. Many Burchard copies produced or held in medieval Aquitaine, Spain, and northern France ultimately depend on Italian versions of the *Liber decretorum*. The same is true for canonical collections compiled in Italy, Spain, Aquitaine, or northern France; if they use Burchard, they almost invariably employed a version going back to Italian exemplars. Unlike the canonical collections compiled in Italy in the eleventh century the Italian Burchard versions were read, copied, and used on a considerable scale across much of western Europe. For the same reason, it was almost exclusively via the Italian branch of the tradition that the materials Burchard had selected were received into major canonical collections in the long run. Gratian, for example, while not directly using Burchard (or if so, only marginally), contains many canons Burchard had gathered in his *Liber decretorum*, which he took from collections like the *Panormia*, the *Tripartita*, Anselm's *Collectio canonum*, and the *Collection in Three Books*. Yet all these collections, whether they were compiled in northern France or Italy, ultimately depend on Italian versions of Burchard.

2.6.1 The *Deteriores* Gaps

The reception and gradual reworking of Burchard in eleventh-century Italy remains to be studied. Nonetheless, it is generally recognized that the *Liber decretorum* was copied, used, and reworked in many places, above all in Lombardy and Tuscany. It is also clear that almost all Italian manuscripts of Burchard belong to the so-called *deteriores* group of manuscripts. This label was introduced by Gérard Fransen who established that many copies of Burchard either have a number of distinctive omissions, or show signs that they ultimately depend on an exemplar having these gaps.[253] Fransen argued that these gaps first occurred early in the Italian transmission of the *Liber decretorum*, and indeed almost all copies of Burchard's collection written in Italy or made from an Italian exemplar I have seen either have these gaps or 'scars' going back to these gaps having been mended.

---

253. Fransen, 'Tradition manuscrite'; idem, 'Le manuscrit de Burchard de Worms conservé à la Bibliothèque municipale de Montpellier', *Mélanges Roger Aubenas* (Société d'histoire du droit et des institutions des anciens pays de droit écrit. Recueil de mémoires et travaux 9; Montpellier 1974) 301–311; idem, 'Essai de classement'; idem, 'Décret de Burchard'.

These gaps typical of the *deteriores* tradition are found in books eight, twelve, nineteen, and twenty of the *Liber decretorum*. It is not clear whether all these gaps go back to a single event (Fransen's 'accident majeur'), but in any case, the canons in question seem to have been lost very early in the reception of Burchard in northern Italy. The first gap begins in Burchard 8.38 which in *deteriores* copies breaks off mid-sentence; the rest of the canon is missing, and so are the next canons (Burchard 8.39–48 and the first half of canon 49). The result is a canon that begins as canon 38 but in mid-canon and indeed in mid-sentence continues with the second half of Burchard 8.49. As both canons deal with related matters, one can still somehow make sense of the text, but the grammar is badly disturbed. As Fransen pointed out, the missing ten canons would have filled precisely one folio, and in a two-volume copy this folio could well have been the last folio of the first volume, as Burchard 8.38 is found almost exactly in the middle of the *Liber decretorum*.[254] The second gap in book twelve almost certainly is the result of the loss of one folio, too. Indeed, a manuscript today at Milan seems to preserve the *mis-en-page* of the exemplar from which the folio went missing. Here, Burchard 12.9 breaks off in mid-sentence at the end of the verso of the last folio of a quire; the next quire begins with Burchard 12.21; most of c. 9, cc. 10–19, and the rubric to c. 21 are missing.[255] The Milan manuscript itself is physically complete, but it seems to have been copied very faithfully—perhaps even line by line— from an exemplar where one folio in book twelve was missing. Finally, the last third of book nineteen and the second half of book twenty (Burchard 19.109–159 and 20.58–110) are missing in the *deteriores* copies. These larger lacunae may well have been the result of an accident, too. This is suggested by the Cologne manuscript of Burchard which is incomplete due to the loss of nine quires at the beginning and two more at the end; in its current state, it begins only with Burchard 2.196 (mid-canon) and towards the end lacks almost exactly the same canons as the *deteriores* (Burchard 19.102–159 and 20.58–110).[256] Perhaps, therefore, the notional exemplar at the beginning of the *deteriores* tradition was an Italian Burchard with a layout similar to the Milan manuscript, losses of quires similar to the Cologne manuscript at the end, but also damaged by the loss of two more folios at the end of two quires.

254. Fransen, 'Essai de classement' 9–11.

255. Milano, Ambrosiana, E.144.sup.; see Fransen, 'Essai de classement' 8.

256. See Fransen, 'Essai de classement' 11–12 and idem, 'Décret de Burchard' 34, who suggested Milano, Ambrosiana, E.144.sup. was copied from Köln, Erzbischöfliche Diözesan- und Dombibliothek, Cod. 119. This, however, partly contradicts his own assertion (Fransen, 'Décret de Burchard' 34) that the smaller gaps (not found in the Cologne manuscript) must be older than the larger ones.

Whatever the genesis of the four gaps just described, they had a marked impact on the textual history of Burchard, and in particular the Italian branch of the transmission. According to Fransen, almost all complete copies were written in Germany. In particular, almost all Burchard manuscripts known to have been written in medieval Italy or copied from Italian exemplars either have these gaps, or show signs that these gaps had been mended more or less ingeniously.[257] Indeed, as the *Liber decretorum* was copied, scribes reacted very differently to the gaps they encountered. Some simply left out the incomplete sentences caused by the textual loss in Burchard 8.38/49 and 12.9, resulting in abbreviated but grammatically correct canons. Other scribes noted that something was missing, highlighted the gaps,[258] and sometimes left space for additions. This space in turn later was filled with some or all of the missing canons or indeed with other material, for example privileges relevant for the local community, or widely-read texts like the *Epistola Widonis* (JL †6613a).[259] Even if based on more complete exemplars of Burchard, these corrections tended to leave traces in the manuscripts. In the Bologna manuscript, for example, Burchard 8.38 is found in the defective form typical for the *deteriores*, and with a note 'hic minus habetur'; after this comment follow both the second half of Burchard 8.49 (as one would expect in the *deteriores* manuscripts) and a fairly long paraphrase of the missing parts of Burchard 8.38 (based evidently on a complete version of Burchard). This unusual version of the canon is followed in turn by a Burchard 8.49 in its complete form, resulting in considerable overlap between the two canons.[260] In a similar way, adding the missing parts of books nineteen and twenty from a complete exemplar in principle was a straightforward operation, but frequently left hints in the manuscripts. Sometimes, the missing canons from books nineteen and twenty were inserted not where they belonged, but as one section at the end of the collection, or (for unknown reasons) between Burchard 19.152 and 153. This in turn led later scribes to transfer the canons once more, but again this operation could result in single canons

---

257. Fransen, 'Essai de classement' 9 claimed Parma, Biblioteca Palatina, 3777 and 'maybe' Vat. lat. 3809 as the only 'complete' Burchard copies written in Italy. In my PhD thesis, I claimed that latter was actually from Chur (Rolker, *Canon Law* iii n. 136); in fact, it is closely related to Clm 4570 from Chur, but not itself from there.

258. Fransen, 'Manuscrit de Montpellier' 304 reports the same phrase 'hic minus habetur' for Burchard copies in Bologna, Modena, and Pistoia. Annamaria C. Ambrosioni, 'Il più antico elenco di chierici della diocesi ambrosiana ed altre aggiunte al Decretum di Burcardo in un codice della Biblioteca Ambrosiana (E 144 sup.): una voce della polemica antipatarinica?' *Aevum* 50 (1976) 274–320, here at 289, reports a longer note in Milano, Ambrosiana, E.144.sup. [not seen] concerning the missing second half of book 20.

259. Fransen, 'Essai de classement' 10; see also below.

260. Bologna, BU, 2239 (1107), fol. 167va.

'forgotten'; Fransen found several manuscripts in which Burchard 20.95 alone is found after Burchard 19.152.[261] All in all, if the four gaps were so to speak 'wounds' inflicted on the *Liber decretorum*, many scribes did their best to heal them, but scars remained visible for a very long time.

2.6.2 Added Materials and Augmented Texts

Apart from these gaps, Fransen highlighted five more features found in *deteriores* manuscripts:[262] augmented versions of Burchard 1.21 and 112, added canons after Burchard 1.23 and 3.15, and Burchard 2.23 being displaced (for no apparent reason) between canons 18 and 19. Fransen stressed the importance of the two augmented canons in book one and labelled *Liber decretorum* manuscripts containing both of them 'Gregorian Burchard'.[263] Fowler-Magerl identified a sub-group of *deteriores* manuscripts ('Milan Burchard'), originating perhaps from Lombardy or Tuscany and extant in some twenty copies.[264] This version contained the augmented version of Burchard 1.21, an additional canon after Burchard 1.112 (two excerpts from JL 4432), and the *Epistola Widonis* (JL †6613a) at the end of book sixteen. She also argued that the augmented form of Burchard 1.21 as found in the *deteriores* may have originated in Milan; at least the first collection to contain the text—the *Ambrosiana II*—seems to be Milanese, and the earliest known copy of the *Liber decretorum* to contain this augmented form of Burchard 1.21 is also from Milan (Ambrosiana, E.144.sup.).[265]

At present, there is no survey of Burchard manuscripts that would allow to map the genesis and reception of the various features of the Italian manuscripts with precision. The distinctive *deteriores* gaps seem to go back to an accident early in the Italian transmission, in my opinion clearly predating the various additions. This at least is suggested by the existence of *deteriores* copies which still have the version of Burchard 1.21 found in German copies, not the 'Milan' version typical of the *deteriores* manuscripts.[266]

261. Fransen, 'Décret de Burchard' 38–39.

262. Fransen, 'Manuscrit de Montpellier' esp. 306–307 and idem, 'Décret de Burchard' 38–39. For the manuscripts, see Pokorny in Kéry 134–144; for discussion, see Linda Fowler-Magerl, 'Fine Distinctions and the Transmission of Texts' ZRG Kan. Abt. 83 (1997) 146–186, here at 147–149, and most recently Stephan Dusil, *Wissensordnungen des Rechts im Wandel. Päpstlicher Jurisdiktionsprimat und Zölibat zwischen 1000 und 1215* (Mediaevalia Lovaniensia 47; Leuven 2018), here at 249–256.

263. Fransen, 'Décret de Burchard' 38–39. See also his comment quoted by Fowler-Magerl, 'Fine Distinctions' 149 n. 18: 'Pour moi: 1. 21 augmenté + 1. 112 augmenté … = Burchard grégorien !'.

264. Fowler-Magerl, 'Fine Distinctions' 147–148 and eadem, *Clavis* 89, based on Paris, BnF, lat. 4283 and Troyes, BM, 1386. The canons in question are found in the database as 'BW'.

265. Fowler-Magerl, 'Fine Distinctions' 147–148. The 'Milan' version of Burchard 1.21 is found, for example, in Vat. lat. 1355, fol. 11r.

266. E.g. Paris, Bibliothèque de l'Arsenal, 678. The manuscript, clearly written in Italy, has the typical gaps in books 8 and 12, and also some of the additional canons found in many *deteriores* manuscripts (Burchard 3.15A on fol. 46v. Nonetheless, it has (on fol. 5ra) Burchard 1.21 in the form found in Pal. lat. 585/586 and other German Burchard manuscripts.

The addition of the *Epistola Widonis* after Burchard 19.108 also is a clear sign that this gap predates the addition.[267] Whether all additions in the *deteriores* were made at a single centre is difficult to establish. Given that they normally are found together and that almost all of them deal with simony, it may well be that they are the result of a conscious effort to produce a Burchard version addressing this issue in particular. On the other hand, there also is evidence that Burchard readers in different places made similar observations how the *Liber decretorum* could be improved. For example, Bernold of Konstanz in his copy of Burchard noted that Burchard 1.112 was rather shorter than the *fons materialis* ('Hic deest multum');[268] he presumably was not aware that Italian scribes at about the same time augmented this very canon by going back to more complete transmissions of the canon coming from the council of Chalcedon. In the case of the *Epistola Widonis*, it is very likely that it was added to Burchard copies at more than one occasion. This would at least explain why it is found as an addition to at least four different books.[269]

More generally, the additions had a certain life of their own. Manuscripts copied from exemplars without any gaps could still contain augmented and added materials typically found in *deteriores* manuscripts, either in the margin or in the main text. A fragmentary Milan copy, for example, does not have the *deteriores* gaps, nor most additions typical of this branch of the tradition, but contains Burchard 3.15A.[270] Likewise, the *Epistola Widonis* is not only found with *deteriores* manuscripts, but also in a sub-group of the (complete) German Burchard tradition.[271] All in all, it seems that there was considerable cross-contamination between the different branches of the transmission, so that additions (including additions in mid-canon) typical for one group of manuscripts could also be inserted into copies made from altogether different exemplars.

Another addition found in almost all *deteriores* manuscripts is a distinct

267. Fransen, 'Décret de Burchard' 36.

268. Freiburg, UB, Hs. 7, fol. 27ra as quoted by Johanne Autenrieth, *Die Domschule zu Konstanz zur Zeit des Investiturstreits. Die wissenschaftliche Arbeitsweise Bernolds von Konstanz und zweier Kleriker dargestellt auf Grund von Handschriftenstudien* (Forschungen zur Kirchen- und Geistesgeschichte N.F. 3; Stuttgart 1956), here at 95 and Dusil, *Wissensordnungen* 250.

269. It is found at the end of book one, the end of book sixteen, after Burchard 19.108, or after book 20; see John T. Gilchrist, 'Die Epistola Widonis oder Pseudo-Paschalis. Der erweiterte Text' DA 37 (1981) 576–604, esp. 583 n. 22.

270. Milano, Biblioteca Trivulziana, 601, fol. 41rb.

271. Clm 4570, fols. 34r–35r and Vat. lat. 3809, fols. 28vb–29rb. Both manuscripts are closely related to each other (and to Lambach, Stiftsbibliothek, XVI [not seen]). See Friedrich Pelster, 'Das Dekret Burkhards von Worms in einer Redaktion aus dem Beginn der gregorianischen Reform (Cod. Vat. Lat. 3809 und Cod. Monacen. Lat. 4570)' *Studi Gregoriani* 1 (1947) 321–351 and Gilchrist, 'Epistola Widonis' 587; on all three manuscripts see also Pokorny in Kéry 135 and 137, where JL †6613a is mentioned only for Clm 4570.

synodal ordo (Schneider's *Ordo 5*) which seems to have been compiled in northern or middle Italy not long before it was added to Burchard's collection around the middle of the eleventh century.[272] To judge from the large number of *deteriores* manuscripts to contain this ordo, it became part and parcel of this Burchard version at an early stage; significantly perhaps, the Milan manuscript which Fransen thought to be the earliest representative of the *deteriores* (Ambrosiana, E.144.sup.) is one of the very few Italian manuscripts not to contain this ordo. The fact that *Ordo 5* is found in almost all Italian manuscripts of the *Liber decretorum* but not in Parma, Biblioteca Palatina, 3777 and Vat. lat. 3809 (the only complete copies of Burchard from medieval Italy) also supports the argument to see *Ordo 5* as a part of the *deteriores* tradition.

The canons of Seligenstadt 1023, in contrast, are not specifically linked to the *deteriores* manuscripts.[273] While the Italian Burchard manuscripts containing Seligenstadt are a distinct branch of the tradition of these conciliar canons, these manuscripts do not form a sub-group of the *deteriores*. Most *deteriores* copies of Burchard do not contain the Seligenstadt canons, only seven do; and not only *deteriores* but also one of the two complete Italian Burchard copies (Parma 3777) contains them.

2.6.3 Complete Burchard Copies in Italy

Complete Burchard copies must have circulated more widely in Italy than the extant manuscripts reveal. As already mentioned, only two of the many Italian Burchard manuscripts are 'complete' copies which neither have the *deteriores* gaps nor display any signs of being derived from an exemplar that did have these lacunae. However, some originally complete copies have survived as fragments,[274] and several more can be inferred. In general, the Burchard manuscripts brought to Italy from Germany must have been complete copies. The earliest evidence for Burchard in Italy comes from the abbey of Nonantola which acquired a Burchard copy before 1035, long before the *deteriores* are thought to have emerged.[275] Complete ('German') versions of the *Liber decretorum* were manifestly used for Italian canon law collections of the eleventh century, namely *183T*, Bonizo, and perhaps the *Farfensis*.[276] There are complete Burchard codices which

272. See Herbert Schneider, 'Einleitung', *Die Konzilsordines des Früh- und Hochmittelalters*, ed. idem (MGH Ordines; Hanover 1996) 1–124, here at 31–37 (comment) and the edition (ibid. 230–244).

273. Jasper (MGH Conc. 8.16–32).

274. E.g. Milano, Biblioteca Trivulziana, 601, which has several physical gaps and omits single canons but does not display the *deteriores* gaps.

275. Busch, *Liber de honore* 83.

276. For *183T*, see the concordance in Motta's edition (at 350–357); for Bonizo of Sutri see

were copied in Spain but presumably from Italian exemplars.[277] All in all, there must have been several and perhaps even many 'complete' copies of Burchard circulating in medieval Italy, including manuscripts produced in Italy. If the extant manuscripts almost all belong to the *deteriores* tradition, this may reflect the sudden success of this more recent version of Burchard; this is all the more remarkable given the manifest incompleteness of these Burchard copies. Perhaps the 'accident majeur' that produced the *deteriores* gaps occurred in a very busy scriptorium which provided other places with their Burchard copies before the error was spotted.

2.6.4 Burchard and the Gregorians

The reception of Burchard's collection in Italy and beyond intensified in the last quarter of the eleventh century, and this included the use of the *Liber decretorum* by many Gregorian prelates. Indeed, contrary to what has been thought, the Gregorian reaction towards Burchard was on the whole positive.[278] Only very few compilers of canon law collections deliberately chose not to use the *Liber decretorum*, as Atto of San Marco seems to have done for his collection.[279] In contrast, Bernold of Konstanz, Deusdedit, Anselm of Lucca, Bonizo of Sutri, and Gregory of San Grisogono knew and used Burchard, as did other prominent Gregorians.[280] Bernold knew the *Liber decretorum* very well and augmented the so-called Swabian version of the *Collection in Seventy-Four Titles* from it.[281] While Deusdedit made but little use of the *Liber decretorum* for his collection,[282] for Bonizo of Sutri it was his single most important formal source.[283] Anselm of Lucca clearly used the *Liber decretorum* and even preferred Burchard's

Chapter 4.5.4. Whether the *Farfensis* employed a complete Burchard, an incomplete one, or a copy where the *deteriores* gaps were supplemented from other sources, is hard to tell; see Theo Kölzer, 'Prolegomena', *Collectio canonum Regesto Farfensi inserta*, ed. idem (MIC Corpus collectionum 5; Vatican City 1982) 1–123, here at 59–62.

277. E.g. Burgo de Osma, Biblioteca de la Catedral, 157, which contains *Ordo 5* (fols. 62rb–63vb), an augmented form of Burchard 1.21 (fol. 6rb–va) and other 'Italian' features but also the complete books 8, 12, 19, and 20; there is no evidence that these books were originally incomplete.

278. Jasper, 'Burchards Dekret' 173–193 against Fournier, 'Décret' 689–690.

279. On Atto, see Chapter 4.2.

280. See Rolker, *Canon Law* 64 (esp. n. 86) on Humbert of Silva Candida, Manegold of Lautenbach, Peter Damian, Hugh of Lyon, and Gebhard of Salzburg.

281. Autenrieth, *Domschule* 122 (glosses); eadem, 'Bernold von Konstanz' ('Swabian appendix').

282. Jasper, 'Burchards Dekret' 180.

283. Paul Fournier, 'Les sources canonique du *Liber de vita christiana* de Bonizo' BEC 78 (1917) 117–134, briefly summarized in Walter Berschin, *Bonizo von Sutri. Leben und Werk* (Beiträge zur Geschichte und Quellenkunde des Mittelalters 2; Berlin and New York 1972), here at 7.

version of several canons to that found in Pseudo-Isidore.[284] In addition, Anselm's collection was soon added to from the *Liber decretorum* ('Anselm Bb'). Cardinal Gregory for his *Polycarpus* took about one in five canons from Burchard, and a large portion of more or less prominent Italian collections likewise drew on the *Liber decretorum*.[285] As these short remarks should make clear, there is ample evidence that Burchard's collection was used extremely widely for a long time; evidence for opposition to his collection, while not completely lacking, is very scarce. Not only are ideas about the rejection of Burchard's collection by Gregorians (Fournier) unfounded; in fact, the whole idea that the reception of canon law collections followed lines of political allegiance should be given up.

2.7 A Forgery to End All Forgeries: 'Forgery' and Legal Change

Burchard's *Liber decretorum* has been given special attention in this chapter, and some of the reasons for this have been mentioned already. No systematic collection of the eleventh century had a comparable influence on medieval canon law: Among the pre-Gratian collections, only the twelfth-century *Panormia* survives in more copies. It was Burchard who provided so many compilers of the eleventh century with a model of how to structure their own work. This success certainly has to do with the exceptional skill Burchard and his collaborators display in their handling of the vast materials they were working with. It is striking to see how Burchard gave new meanings to old texts by making small, sometimes subtle changes. The opening canons of the *Liber decretorum* are a spectacular example; Burchard made a provocative statement in the form of a seemingly innocent 'quotation' of a traditional text ('That the pope is only bishop of the first see'). The inscriptions he changed to pass secular legislation as conciliar decisions, or penitential material as coming from papal letters,[286] are comparatively clumsy manipulations. As the analysis

---

284. Fuhrmann, *Einfluß und Verbreitung* 2.516; Kathleen Grace Cushing, 'Anselm of Lucca and Burchard of Worms: Re-Thinking the Sources of Anselm 11, De penitentia', *Ritual, Text and Law: Studies in Medieval Canon Law and Liturgy Presented to Roger E. Reynolds*, ed. Richard F. Gyug and Kathleen Grace Cushing (CFC; Aldershot 2004) 225–239.

285. See Rolker, *Canon Law* 66 n. 96 on the *Farfensis*, 20L, the *Ambrosiana I*, 2L/8P, 183T, Placidus of Nonantola, and the Vienna 7L. Another example from the twelfth century is the collection analysed by Uta-Renate Blumenthal, 'An Episcopal Handbook from Twelfth-Century Southern Italy: Codex Rome, Bibl. Vallicelliana F. 54/III', *Studia in honorem eminentissimi Cardinalis Alphonsi M. Stickler*, ed. Rosalio J. Castillo Lara (Studia e textus historiae iuris canonici 7; Rome 1992) 13–24 which used Burchard as its 'basic formal source'. On the *Polycarpus*, see Uwe Horst, *Die Kanonessammlung Polycarpus des Gregor von S. Grisogono. Quellen und Tendenzen* (MGH Hilfsmittel 5; Munich 1980), here at 21–24.

286. On secular law, see above (note 185). For penitential canons, see in particular Burchard

of Burchard's presentation of episcopal rights and the marriage prohibitions on grounds of kinship should have made clear, Burchard was willing and able to apply his skill to adopt whole areas of ecclesiastical legislation to the needs of his time. Needless to say, these 'needs' were those of specific groups; Burchard's book seven was very welcome to Henry II, and book fifteen could only have been compiled by an imperial bishop of the tenth or eleventh century. (Indeed, French and Italian compilers working with Burchard at the end of the eleventh century show a marked reserve towards this book in particular.[287])

In the late nineteenth and early twentieth centuries, there was a considerable debate whether Burchard was a 'forger'.[288] Manifestly, many of these scholars applied a very modern concept of 'forgery', often using it in a morally charged sense. More importantly, these discussions were fuelled by the fact that the *Liber decretorum* was seen as a key document of the relation of 'Church and state' in eleventh-century Germany;[289] accordingly, Burchard was depicted very differently in different denominational and national traditions—on the whole, catholic scholars, and especially French legal historians, accused Burchard of forgery to make clear that his *Liber decretorum* was the result either of Burchard's partisan interests, or his deplorable submission to royal power;[290] German scholars, and most forcefully protestant church historians, in turn were quick to defend Burchard against all charges of forgery, or—where textual manipulations were evident—to declare them as genuine expressions of eleventh-century Church law.[291] Many of the morally charged labels attached to Burchard (e.g. 'lax sexual morals') are best understood as results of these nineteenth-century debates,[292] but were repeated well into the twentieth century. Georges

12.3–6, 9, and 11 as discussed by Hoffmann and Pokorny, *Dekret* 222–223 and Christof Rolker 'Die Briefe Papst Pelagius' I.: Handschriften, Editionen und Regesten. Kritische Notiz zur dritten Auflage der Regesta pontificum' DA 75 (2019) 415, here at 439–442 (Pseudo-Pelagius, JK 967).

287. See Chapter Three on the French *Burdegalensis* (Chapter 3.52) and the Italian *2oL* (Chapter 3.7.2) which both rely heavily on Burchard but omit his book fifteen completely.

288. Hauck, *Kirchengeschichte* esp. 3.439; Emil Seckel, 'Zu den Acten der Triburer Synode von 895' NA 18 (1893) 367–408 esp. 380 (on Burchard 'so oft fröhlich fälschend[]'); Hauck, 'Burchard'; Fournier, 'Études critiques' esp. 99–111; idem, 'Décret'. Among the more recent literature, see Fuhrmann, *Einfluß und Verbreitung* 2.447–450 and 479–484; Landau, 'Gefälschtes Recht' 29–32; Hoffmann and Pokorny, *Dekret* 158–169; Hartmann, 'Burchards Dekret' 165–166; Austin, *Shaping* ch. 11.

289. Karl Wilhelm Nitzsch, *Ministerialität und Bürgerthum im 11. und 12. Jahrhundert* (Leipzig 1859), here at 132 (Burchard striving for 'möglichste Trennung der kirchlichen von der weltlichen Gewalt').

290. Fournier, 'Décret' 688 ('partisan convaincu du pouvoir épiscopal') and 691 ('Burchard, qui représente l'Église soumise au pouvoir impérial').

291. Hauck, 'Burchard'. See also Gfrörer, *Kirchengeschichte* 4.1:177–180 for a stern critique of Burchard being 'too papalist'.

292. E.g. Fahrner, *Geschichte* 110 (divorce), Fournier, 'Décret' 690 (celibacy) and 682 (divorce). See also *Histoire* 1.409.

Duby, for one, uncritically followed this tradition and helped to disseminate the image of Burchard's 'lax' position on marriage and sexuality.[293]

These debates will be neither analysed nor further commented on here, as they rely on assumptions and interests modern scholarship no longer shares. The only result of these debates that is relevant in our present context is that although Burchard has been scrutinized with unusual zeal—Deusdedit and Ivo of Chartres, for example, have largely escaped similar suspicion—only very few forgeries were identified.[294] Most manipulations are changed inscriptions, apparently all motivated by Burchard's desire to lend higher authority to certain materials coming from less reputable sources and/or issued in relatively recent times.[295] Changes to the material content of canons almost exclusively concern penitential tariffs, which Burchard changed to make the provisions more consistent.[296] Otherwise, 'major' manipulations are small in number—in fact, they all have been discussed in the present chapter. Fournier's suspicion that Burchard had forged complete canons has not been confirmed, not even in single cases.[297]

Rather than discussing whether Burchard was a forger, the important point to me is what Burchard did *instead* of introducing forged texts. As has been argued above, Burchard very skilfully selected, arranged, and abridged the canons he found in older collections, and additionally used inscriptions and rubrics to guide the reader. Crucially, Burchard mainly relied on these techniques even where he made profound changes, as in the case of the marriage prohibitions (as discussed in detail above). There can be no doubt that Burchard deliberately presented these prohibitions in a very different way than earlier collections had done, and that he was ready to manipulate some of his texts dramatically. Nonetheless, even in this area of the law, Burchard only exceptionally (in the case of the 'Isidore' canon produced from Rabanus's letter) came close to forgery in the ususal sense of the word. Mainly he relied on selecting the 'right' canons (and suppressing many others), on finding the appropriate labels (using the highly charged vocabulary of 'incest' in the rubrics), taking proof texts out of context and, crucially, creating a new context by skilful-

---

293. See Duby, *Knight* esp. 70; his interpretation is unsound, see above (note 201). See also Gaudemet, *Mariage* 240–241.

294. Landau, 'Gefälschtes Recht' 29–32, followed by Hoffmann and Pokorny, *Dekret* 159–161 and Austin, *Shaping* 212–213.

295. See the literature quoted above (note 36).

296. Austin, *Shaping* ch. 11.

297. Hoffmann and Pokorny, *Dekret* 158. For Fournier's suspicions, see his 'Études critiques' 99–111; already the title to this chapter is highly suggestive: 'Chapitre III: Les textes composés par Burchard ou [*sic*] d'origine inconnue'.

ly rearranging his materials in a newly created book. This was 'secondary norm-creation' at its best.[298]

The implications of these findings go well beyond the impact Burchard had on ecclesiastical marriage legislation or, for that matter, any other part of canon law. In the light of the reception of Burchard's *opus magnum*, it is plausible to assume that many of his readers learnt much more from the *Liber decretorum* than simply the material law it contained. This is particularly true for those readers who turned to Burchard as a model for their own collections. After all, compiling a major collection arranged by subject-matter was a difficult task that normally required a thorough reading of many older collections which often presented similar or even the same materials in very different ways, as has been argued above in the comparative analysis of *Anselmo dedicata*, Burchard, and the two *12P* versions. It is therefore plausible to assume that a close study of such collections was also a way to learn the very techniques by which the earlier collections had been produced. In the case of the *Liber decretorum*, there was a great deal to learn. Indeed, one can assume that for the whole eleventh century, Burchard was the most important source helping to disseminate the techniques just mentioned. From Burchard, one could learn that the vast body of traditional canon law may be confusingly diverse, but by careful selection, interpretation, labelling, and re-contextualisation could be used to produce remarkably coherent doctrine. As will be discussed in detail in the following chapters, many compilers of the eleventh century employed similar techniques in compiling their collections; many can be assumed to have learned their trade by comparing the large, but neat *Liber decretorum* to the often confused masses of canons they encountered in other contexts. The closer they compared the presentation of the material and perhaps even the wording of individual canons, the more likely they were to understand how Burchard had achieved the doctrinal unity of the *Liber decretorum* which no doubt contributed to its lasting popularity. In this way, studying Burchard could teach one how to achieve similar goals without taking refuge in the outright fabrication of canons. The *Liber decretorum* may contain striking manipulations at the verge of forgery; but in effect the success of Burchard reduced the role of forgery in canon law history.

---

298. On 'sekundäre Normbildung', see Andreas Thier, *Hierarchie und Autonomie. Regelungstraditionen der Bischofsbestellung in der Geschichte des kirchlichen Wahlrechts bis 1140* (Recht im ersten Jahrtausend 1; Frankfurt 2011), here at 343–421.

3

Monastic Canon Law

3.1 Introduction: Monks, Canon Law, and Monastic Collections

Monks have played an important role in canon law history from early on. It was a Scythian monk, Dionysius Exiguus (d. around 540), who translated important canons from Greek into Latin and compiled the influential *Collectio Dionysiana*. The Pseudo-Isidorian forgeries may have been compiled at the monastery of Corbie; Regino of Prüm (d. 915) compiled his collection after he had entered Sankt Maximin at Trier; the monk Olbert helped Burchard of Worms (d. 1025) to compile his great *Liber decretorum*. Most famously, the compiler of the *Decretum Gratiani* was long believed to have been a monk, and even if there is no cogent evidence to confirm this, it is not impossible that he indeed was.[1] Yet all these examples also show that collections compiled by monks are not necessarily monastic in character. The *Dionysiana* is above all Roman in nature, and the Pseudo-Isidorian forgeries are rightly famous for their pro-episcopal agenda. The collections compiled by Regino and Burchard specifically fit the needs of episcopal readers, even if abbots of great houses found them equally useful. An analysis of the *Decretum Gratiani*, finally, would make plausible that the compiler was a teacher, an exegete, a theologian, and

---

1. Anders Winroth, 'Where Gratian Slept: The Life and Death of the Father of Canon Law' ZRG Kan. Abt. 99 (2013) 105–128, here at 114 (sceptical).

a legal scholar; but internal evidence supporting the idea that he was a monk is meagre.

In this chapter, the focus will be on monastic canon law collections compiled between the late tenth and the mid-twelfth centuries.[2] Following scholarly convention, collections of rights and privileges of individual churches (chartularies) or local customs (*consuetudines*) are not considered 'canon law' for the purpose of this chapter. Otherwise, 'canon law' is understood in the rather wide sense as discussed in the first chapter; canonical collections are considered as 'monastic' here if they were specifically concerned with religious communities, the rights and duties of their members, and their place in the Church at large. As monks (rather than canons or nuns) are normally at the centre of attention, I use 'monastic canon law' as a short form. As will be discussed in detail, these collections not only shared a certain concern for the needs of religious communities, but also are linked to each other by shared materials, sometimes suggesting that the works were the result of cooperation. Special attention will be given to the actual use of these collections. Like other canonical collections, some monastic collections were clearly partisan in nature. Yet it is not so much the pro-monastic content that is most relevant here; it is the monastic readership and the use by religious houses that is central for the argument to study monastic canon law collections as a separate group.

Given the limited evidence available for the actual use of pre-Gratian collections, internal evidence is nonetheless important to argue the needs of which groups of readers a given collection may plausibly have met. It goes without saying that no collection was compiled for one use only, and even if that had been the case, no compiler could control the multiple uses his readers found for his work. Monastic canon law collections

---

2. See in general Giles Constable, 'Monastic Legislation at Cluny in the Eleventh and Twelfth Centuries', *Proceedings Toronto 1972* MIC Subsidia 5.151–161; Theo Kölzer, 'Mönchtum und Kirchenrecht. Bemerkungen zu monastischen Kanonessammlungen der vorgratianischen Zeit' ZRG Kan. Abt. 69 (1983) 121–142; Hubertus Seibert, *Abtserhebungen zwischen Rechtsnorm und Rechtswirklichkeit. Formen der Nachfolgeregelung in lothringischen und schwäbischen Klöstern der Salierzeit (1024–1125)* (Quellen und Abhandlungen zur mittelrheinischen Kirchengeschichte 78; Mainz 1995); Klaus Schreiner, 'Observantia regularis. Normbildung, Normkontrolle und Normwandel im Mönchtum des hohen und späten Mittelalters', *Prozesse der Normbildung und Normveränderung im mittelalterlichen Europa*, ed. Doris Ruhe et al. (Stuttgart 2000) 275–313; Gert Melville, 'Regeln – Consuetudines-Texte – Statuten. Positionen für eine Typologie des normativen Schrifttums religiöser Gemeinschaften im Mittelalter', *Regulae – Consuetudines – Statuta: studi sulle fonti normative degli ordini religioni nei secoli centrali del Medioevo: atti del I e del II Seminario internazionale di studio del Centro italo-tedesco di storia comparata degli ordini religiosi (Bari/Noci/Lecce, 26–27 ottobre 2002 / Castiglione delle Stiviere, 23–24 maggio 2003)*, ed. Cristina Andenna and Gert Melville (Vita regularis 25; Münster 2005) 5–37; Adriaan H. Gaastra, *Between Liturgy and Canon Law: A Study of Books of Confession and Penance in Eleventh- and Twelfth-Century Italy* (PhD thesis; Universiteit Utrecht, Utrecht 2007), esp. 205–215; for the studies of Roger E. Reynolds, see below (notes 75, 80, and 89).

therefore are collections for which it is plausible that they were used by monastic communities because they were more concerned with specifically monastic needs than other collections, without assuming that these collections were useful for monks only.

There are a number of features that distinguish monastic canon law collections of the high Middle Ages from other collections. One of the reasons is the 'episcopal' character of traditional canon law. Above all, the Pseudo-Isidorian forgeries and later Burchard's *Liber decretorum* (two collections disseminated very widely) contained procedural norms that worked mainly in favour of bishops, and also contained material law strengthening episcopal rights; in contrast, they contained little if any canons specifically protecting the rights of religious communities.[3] If Europe in the time of Burchard was a 'Europe of bishops' (Reuter), contemporary collections often represented a 'canon law of bishops'.

Compilers of monastic canon law collections in the high Middle Ages must have been aware of this situation. To begin with, monks and their rights were not a prominent issue in canon law. Also, from the perspective of the high Middle Ages, the ancient canons did not provide much guidance for many of the urgent issues the compilers may have had in mind. To take only one example, the synodal fathers legislating on church property in the fourth, fifth, and sixth centuries could not possible have foreseen the military role of institutionalised monasticism in feudal societies of the high Middle Ages. Yet in the tenth and eleventh centuries, monasteries indeed controlled sizeable lands. In the Empire, as can be seen from sources such as the 981 *indiculus*,[4] the king expected great abbeys like Fulda, St Gall, and Reichenau to muster more troops than many bishops, let alone secular lords. In Francia not much later, Abbo of Fleury (d. 1004) is reported to have declared himself 'more powerful than the king' at least in Gascony, and even if this mainly was a statement on royal power (or weakness), it is also true that Fleury controlled formidable military assets.[5] As for Normandy and England, there were 'warrior abbots' as well as the more famous 'warrior bishops' both before and after 1066.[6] Or, to

---

3. Fuhrmann, for one, commented on the striking absence of monastic issues in the forgeries: Horst Fuhrmann, 'Stand, Aufgaben und Perspektiven der Pseudoisidorforschung', *Fortschritt durch Fälschungen? Ursprung, Gestalt und Wirkungen der pseudoisidorischen Fälschungen. Beiträge zum gleichnamigen Symposium an der Universität Tübingen vom 27. und 28. Juli 2001*, ed. Wilfried Hartmann and Gerhard Schmitz (MGH Studien und Texte 31; Hanover 2002) 227–262, esp. 257.

4. *Indiculus loricatorum* (ed. Weiland, MGH Const. 1.632–633, no. 436). See Tellenbach, *Church* 86.

5. Aimoin, *Vita S. Abbonis* c. 20 (PL 139.410).

6. Martin Brett, 'The English Abbeys, Their Tenants and the King (950–1150)', *Chiesa e mondo feudale nei secoli X–XII: atti Mendola 1992* (Miscellanea 40; Milan 1995) 277–302, here at 293–294.

take a last example from Italy, the famous *incastellmento* was of direct relevance for monastic houses like Farfa that owned very many of the castles which became the kernel of these new structures.[7]

The military role of the great monasteries was quoted here as an example as it manifestly gave rise to many questions that could not possibly have been addressed by traditional canon law. Similar arguments can be made for many aspects of monastic life in the eleventh and twelfth centuries. For example, monastic tithes and parochial revenues were disputed both between 'monks and their enemies' and within the monastic sphere;[8] needless to say that ancient synodal legislation and, for that matter, the Rule of Benedict was silent on tithes. As far as canon law did mention monastic property, it mainly stressed episcopal control.[9] In practice, however, churches and abbeys were largely independent, and many great houses owned larger estates than the local bishop. Or to take another example, there were a number of canon law authorities that monks should not preach; but what exactly did this mean for a monastery that owned a parish church—or indeed more than one-hundred churches?[10] Many provisions found in canon law collections went back to times well before Benedictine monasticism; as a consequence, they were silent on many issues of institutionalised monasticism, let alone the complexities of monastic networks that slowly grew into separate 'orders' or, for that matter, regular canons. Monks interested in canon law, therefore, with all due reverence for ancient canon law, had reason to welcome legal change.[11]

7. On the *incastellmento* and on monastic property, see the classical study by Pierre Toubert, *Les structures du Latium médiéval: le Latium méridional et la Sabine du IXe siècle à la fin du XIIe siècle* (2 vols. Bibliothèque des Écoles françaises d'Athènes et de Rome 221; Rome 1973) and more recently Susan Wood, *The Proprietary Church in the Medieval West* (Oxford 2006) 681–689. For individual abbeys, see e.g. Toubert, *Latium médiéval* 2.900–912 (Farfa), Heinrich Dormeier, *Montecassino und die Laien im 11. und 12. Jahrhundert* (MGH Schriften 27; Stuttgart 1979), and Valerie Ramseyer, *The Transformation of a Religious Landscape: Medieval Southern Italy 850–1150* (Conjunctions of Religion and Power in the Medieval Past; Ithaca, N.Y. 2006) ch. 5 (Cava dei Tirreni).

8. Giles Constable, *Monastic Tithes: From Their Origins to the Twelfth Century* (Life and Thought: New Series 10; Cambridge 1964); Barbara H. Rosenwein et al., 'Monks and Their Enemies: A Comparative Approach' *Speculum* 66 (1991) 764–796.

9. Most prominently, Chalcedon 451 c. 4; see *The Acts of the Council of Chalcedon*, tr. Richard Price and Michael Gaddis (3 vols. Translated Texts for Historians 45; Liverpool 2007), here at 3.95–96: 'Those who practise monasticism in each city and territory are to be subject to the bishop, and are to embrace silence and devote themselves to fasting and prayer alone, persevering in the places where they renounced the world; they are not to cause annoyance in either ecclesiastical or secular affairs, or take part in them, leaving their own monasteries, unless indeed for some compelling need they be permitted to do so by the bishop of the city. [...] The due care of the monasteries must be exercised by the bishop of the city.'

10. See Wood, *Proprietary Church* 681–683 (general); Toubert, *Latium médiéval* 2.900–912 (Farfa's 132 churches in the Duchy of Spoleto).

11. See Abbo, *Collectio* c. 8 (PL 139.481): '[...] considerandus est terrarium situs, qualitas temporum, infirmitas hominum, et aliae necessitates rerum, quae solent mutare regulas diversarum

For monks and canons interested in written norms, many canonical collections available around the year 1000 were therefore not very useful. Therefore, monks often turned to other sources—above all the Rule of Benedict, comments on this formidable lawbook, local *consuetudines*, but also patristic literature, penitential books, and of course the Bible. As far as the relations to the world outside the monastery were concerned, privileges were the most important group of normative texts. However, if only because of the increasing importance of written law and juridical procedure in the Church at large, many monks may have felt the need to read and finally to compile themselves the kind of canon law collections bishops, papal legates, synodal fathers, and the papal curia increasingly turned to in case of conflict. Many of these conflicts were related to the question of monastic property, which already in the earlier Middle Ages was often considerable but grew even more between the late tenth and the twelfth century. On this issue, traditional canon law collections were from a monastic perspective were particularly disappointing, partly because of the anachronisms they contained, partly because of their 'episcopal' character, but mainly because they were silent on so many urgent issues abbots and priors were confronted with. For this reason perhaps, the issue of monastic property and disputes over monastic 'liberty' (*libertas*) became increasingly prominent in pre-Gratian canonical collections.

For all these reasons, monks had good reasons not only to engage with canon law, but to develop a specifically monastic approach to deal with the law. The collections studied in this chapter are the result of this engament. Of course, they greatly vary among themselves, and often touch also on topcis which are not specifically monastic. Nonetheless, the monastic background and the specifically monastic perspective of these collections in my opinion justifies treating them as a group. Such a view has sometimes been proposed, in particular by Theo Kölzer.[12] However, scholarship on the whole has retained the traditional division of pre-Gratian col-

---

provinciarum. Potestate etiam multa mutatae sunt pro communi utilitate ecclesiarum, quae nemo reprehendit fidelium.'

12. Theo Kölzer, 'Prolegomena', *Collectio canonum Regesto Farfensi inserta*, ed. idem (MIC Corpus collectionum 5; Vatican City 1982) 1–123, here at 96–100; idem, 'Mönchtum und Kirchenrecht'; idem, 'Mönchtum und Außenwelt – Norm und Realität', *Proceedings San Diego 1988* MIC Subsidia 9.265–283. See also Kathleen Grace Cushing, 'Monastic "Centres" of Law? Some Evidence from Eleventh-Century Italy', *From Learning to Love: Schools, Law and Pastoral Care in the Middle Ages: Essays in Honour of Joseph W. Goering*, ed. Tristan Sharp et al. (Papers in Mediaeval Studies 29; Toronto 2017) 315–326 and Christof Rolker, 'Monastic Canon Law in the Tenth, Eleventh, and Twelfth Centuries', *The Cambridge History of Medieval Monasticism in the Latin West, Volume 1: Origins to the Eleventh Century*, ed. Alison I. Beach and Isabelle Cochelin (Cambridge 2020) 618–630. My thanks are to Dr Cushing for many discussions on monks and manuscripts in general, and the complexities of the Italian collections in particular.

lections into 'reform collections', 'anti-reform collections', plus a residual category of other (sometimes dubbed 'local') collections.[13] This division is problematic for many reasons, but was particulalry inapt to describe monastic collections.[14] Vice versa, scholarship on monasticism has often ignored legal aspects of religious life. The study of monastic canon law collections as a group will, as I hope, support a better understanding of the relation between canon law and monasticism.

3.2 Abbo of Fleury: Monastic Canon Law Around the Year 1000

3.2.1 Abbo and His Canon Law Works

Abbo of Fleury (d. 1004) is best known as a monastic reformer and scholar deeply involved in the politics of early Capetian France.[15] He spent most of his life in Fleury, or Saint-Benoît-sur-Loire, as this monastery not far from Orléans was called since it housed the relics of Benedict of Nursia. Abbo had entered this house as an oblate, and after a stay in England (where he was abbot of Ramsey) in 987 he returned to become abbot of Fleury. This made him one of the most important prelates in Francia; in the words of the papal privilege he obtained in 997, he was 'first among all abbots in Gaul'.[16] At the same time, Abbo was an eminent scholar who

13. This division was canonized by the *Histoire*; it was repeated by almost all textbooks and other *Hilfsmittel*. See Christof Rolker, 'Fournier's Model and Its Merits', *New Discourses in Medieval Canon Law Research: Challenging the Master Narrative*, ed. idem (Medieval Law and Its Practice 28; Leiden and Boston 2019) 4–32, here at 4 n. 1 (handbooks), 19–22 and 29–30.

14. Kölzer, 'Prolegomena' 96–100 (critique); Rolker, 'Fournier's Model' (background).

15. Marco Mostert, *The Political Theology of Abbo of Fleury: A Study of the Ideas About Society and Law of the 10th-Century Monastic Reform Movement* (Middeleeuwse studies en bronnen 2; Hilversum 1987); idem, 'Die Urkundenfälschungen Abbos von Fleury', *Fälschungen im Mittelalter* (6 vols. MGH Schriften 33; Munich 1988) 4.287–318; Pierre Riché, *Abbon de Fleury: un moine savant et combatif (vers 950–1004)* (Turnhout 2004); Franck Roumy, 'Remarques sur l'œuvre canonique d'Abbon de Fleury', *Abbon, un abbé de l'an mil*, ed. Anne Dufour and Gilette Labory (Bibliothèque d'histoire culturelle du Moyen Âge 6; Leuven 2008) 311–342. For Abbo's life, see Frederick S. Paxton, 'Abbas and Rex: Power and Authority in the Literature of Fleury, 987–1044', *The Experience of Power in Medieval Europe, 950–1350: Essays in Honor of Thomas N. Bisson*, ed. Robert F. Berkhofer et al. (London 2005) 197–212 and Elizabeth Eileen Dachowski, *First Among Abbots: The Career of Abbo of Fleury* (Washington, D.C. 2008).

16. Gregory V, JL 3872, ed. in *Papsturkunden 896–1046*, ed. Harald Zimmermann (3 vols. Veröffentlichungen der historischen Kommission III 174, 177, and 178; 2nd edition Vienna 1989), here at 2.656 (no. †335): 'primus inter abbates Galliae'. The authenticity of the letter, including the primacy claims it contains, is disputed. Doubts on the authenticity were mainly raised by Mogens Rathsack in his 1980 monograph translated as *Die Fuldaer Fälschungen. Eine rechtshistorische Analyse der päpstlichen Privilegien des Klosters Fulda von 751 bis ca. 1158* (2 vols. Päpste und Papsttum 24; Stuttgart 1989) at 313–331, but Mostert, 'Urkundenfälschungen' 305 and 312 argued that the letter was genuine, even if based on Abbo's draft (ibid. 305: 'validierte Empfängerausfertigung'). Zimmermann in the first (1985) edition of his *Papsturkunden* partly followed Rathsack and with some qualifications described the letter as interpolated: *Papsturkunden 896–1046*, here at 2.656–657 (no. †335) but later retracted. In 1998, Zimmermann was positive that the letter was genuine

wrote on diverse matters from arithmetic to grammar and from hagiography to astronomy.[17] As for his canon law, he compiled a small legal collection simply known as *Collectio canonum*.[18] In addition, Abbo in his letters often addresses canon law issues. One letter (known as *Letter 14* after its place in the edition) contains a particularly large number of canon law authorities, which will be discussed briefly below. Abbo's famous *Apologeticus*, written in the context of the tumultuous synod of Saint-Denis in 994, will also be taken into account. In addition to these extant writings, it can plausibly be assumed that Abbo compiled smaller florilegia of canon law.[19] They must have been similar the numerous florilegia extant in the Fleury manuscripts, and together may have constituted a kind of working library or a raw form of a larger collection.[20] Apart from collecting old and obtaining new decretals, Abbo is known to have forged some papal letters, not least to have them confirmed by the present pope;[21] they too are part of his contribution to canon law.

3.2.2 Date and Content of Abbo's *Collectio canonum*

Abbo dedicated his *Collectio canonum* to King Hugh Capet and his son, King Robert. This implies a date before the death of the former in 996 but

---

(Böhmer-Zimmermann 777). Dachowski, *First Among Abbots* 180–184 follows Mostert on JE 3872. The third edition of Jaffé's *Regesta* seems to return to Zimmermann's 1985 position, treating the letter as a forgery (J³ †8290); note that no mention is made in J³ †8290 of the confirmation of Fleury's privileges by Alexander II (JL 4708). On Rathsack's monograph, see below (note 21).

17. The only edition of his letters and his *Collectio* is found in PL 139. The preface to his *Collectio* is translated in Somerville and Brasington, *Prefaces* 97–98. For Abbo's other works, see Dachowski, *First Among Abbots* 13–16 and Aimoin de Fleury, 'Vie d'Abbon, abbé de Fleury; Vita et passio sancti Abbonis et pièces annexes', *L'abbaye de Fleury en l'an mil*, ed. and tr. by Robert-Henri Bautier and Gilette Labory (Sources d'histoire médiévale 32; Paris 2004) 34–162.

18. The most widely used edition (a reprint of Mabillon's 1676 edition) is found in PL 139.473–508. Roumy, 'Abbon' 331–340 provides an 'implicit edition' based on the only extant manuscript (Paris, BnF, lat. 2400).

19. It is plausible that he did so in preparation of the synod of Saint-Basle, for which see below. Aimon reports that Abbo had compiled a work specifically to protect monastic property which was 'at the moment not found' (PL 139.393). Unless this was a reference to *Letter 14* (as suggested by Ernst Sackur, *Die Cluniacenser in ihrer kirchlichen und allgemeingeschichtlichen Wirksamkeit: bis zur Mitte des elften Jahrhunderts* [2 vols. Halle 1892/94] 1.288 n. 3) or, even less likely, the *Collectio canonum*, Aimon here refers to a lost work. It may be identical to the lost appendix to the *Apologeticus*, the existence of which may be deduced from a reference in the work itself ('nec tamen haec verbis meis, sed authenticis sanctorum dictis', PL 139.470) as well as one in the dedicatory letter to the *Collectio canonum* (PL 139.473).

20. Mostert, *Abbo of Fleury* 65–75. On the library, see idem, *The Library of Fleury: A Provisional List of Manuscripts* (Middeleeuwse studies en bronnen 3; Hilversum 1989).

21. The fundamental study is Mostert, 'Urkundenfälschungen'. See also the controversial account of Rathsack, *Fuldaer Fälschungen* 313–331; for discussion and important corrections, see e.g. Hermann Jakobs, 'Spätottonische Klosterfreiheit. Die Privilegien "Creditae speculationis" Johannes' XIII. und Benedikts VII. für Thankmarsfelde/Nienburg, Aisleben und Arneburg', *Papsturkundenforschung und Historie: Aus der Germania Pontificia Halberstadt und Lüttich*, ed. idem and Wolfgang Petke (Studien und Vorarbeiten zur Germania Pontificia 9; Cologne, Weimar, and Vienna 2008) 1–128, esp. at 9–19.

after the coronation of the latter in late 987. As Abbo seems to refer back to and quote from his *Apologeticus* of 994, the collection in all likelihood was compiled in or around 995. It is a short work, but not a minor one, as it deals with fundamental questions of canon law.

Abbo's *Collectio canonum* contains a total of 89 canons, divided across 51 chapters (*capitula*); every chapter is composed of one or more excerpts taken from canon law and, in some cases, Abbo's comment.[22] The dedicatory letter contains a list of all chapters that serves as a *capitulatio*. The collection itself begins with a long section 'on the honour of churches and monasteries', that is, the special status of all places dedicated to God. Three chapters on the 'defenders of churches', the duties of the king, and the loyalty owed to the king provide an outlook of Abbo's view of royal office including the duty to protect churches—in particular monasteries, as Abbo was quick to add. The fifth chapter on privileges is the first to mention the papacy, and also the first to quote one of Abbo's favourite sources, the letters of Gregory the Great. The chapter emphatically stresses the inviolability of papal privileges, and once more, the *Collectio canonum* does not fail to mention monasteries in this context. The following chapter six in a similar fashion, though backed with fewer canonical authorities, stresses the inviolability of royal precepts. Chapter seven on testaments in fact deals with donations—especially to churches—as confirmed by papal or royal authority, and in this sense belongs to the preceding two chapters. The next chapters deal with the nature of the law, containing substantial legal argument. Abbo discusses legal change and contradictions in canon law (c. 8); in this context, he distinguishes between divine and human, ecclesiastical and secular, written and unwritten law (cc. 8–9).

The rest of the collection (cc. 10–51) deals with the secular clergy and, at much greater length, monastic communities. These chapters do not contain any comment by Abbo, and are mainly drawn from papal decretals and synodal legislation. Monastic rights are dealt with at great length, including one chapter specifically on the abbot of Fleury (c. 20). The secular clergy is mainly dealt with in the relation to the monastic sphere, e.g. monks receiving holy orders (cc. 16, 21), priests taking monastic vows (cc. 23–24) and 'episcopal arrogance against monks' (c. 23). Ecclesiastical property plays a significant role, and so does procedural law; once more, both areas of the law are dealt with a special view to monastic communities. As will be discussed below, much of the material had particular significance in the conflicts Abbo was involved in at the time the *Collectio canonum* was compiled.

22. For the numbers, I here follow Roumy, 'Abbon' 317.

Much of the same is true for Abbo's *Letter 14*, for which no precise date can be established, although a composition in the mid-990s seems plausible.[23] Abbo wrote it to a certain 'G.', apparently an abbot involved in conflict with his local bishop (Gausbert of Saint-Julien?). It mainly consists of quotations taken from the Fathers; in fact, it is best described as a canon law dossier preceded by a short letter. Many topics overlap with the *Collectio canonum*, and it is evident that the dossier draws on materials which Abbo used for various other works.[24] *Letter 14* deals with episcopal authority and monastic liberty, and in particular with the defence of monastic property against episcopal intrusion. Interestingly, Abbo here borrows from a letter attributed to Gregory I and transmitted with the Pseudo-Isidorian forgeries to support this idea; given that the *Collectio* contains no direct quotations from the False Decretals, this passage has rightly attracted scholarly attention.[25] The dossier also deals with the secular clergy, and in particular the requirement of chastity, a topic it has in common with Abbo's *Collectio canonum* and his *Apologeticus*.

3.2.3 Material and Formal Sources of Abbo's *Collectio*

An analysis of the formal and material sources of the *Collectio canonum* can help to understand what 'canon law' was for a learned abbot around the year 1000, and also to establish Abbo's contribution to the development of (monastic) canon law. Fortunately for such an enterprise, the library of Fleury in Abbo's time can be reconstructed from a wide range of sources, and scholars have been able to identify many of Abbo's sources.[26]

To begin with, what kind of material did Abbo gather in the *Collectio canonum*? By all standards, the *fontes materiales* are mixed.[27] Not counting numerous allusions, the collection contains 35 conciliar canons, 21 excerpts from papal letters, seventeen Roman law texts, eleven patristic and literary texts (above all, from Saint Augustine); three canons were taken from capitularies, two canons each ultimately are taken from the Rule of Benedict and from Martin of Braga.[28]

---

23. Mostert, *Abbo of Fleury* 63–64.

24. Mostert, *Abbo of Fleury* 64.

25. Mostert, *Abbo of Fleury* 64. The letter in question is JE †2579, attributed to Gregory I here but to Gregory IV elsewhere. On the vexed question of the authenticity of JE †2579 see Eric Knibbs, 'Pseudo-Isidore at the Field of Lies: *Divinis praeceptis* (JE †2579) as an Authentic Decretal' BMCL 29 (2012) 1–34. On the reception of JE †2579 see Lotte Kéry, *Die Errichtung des Bistums Arras 1093/1094* (Francia. Beihefte 33; Sigmaringen 1994), here at 129–134.

26. Mostert, *Abbo of Fleury* ch. 4; idem, *Library* passim; Kéry 199–201; Riché, *Abbon* esp. 166–170; Fowler-Magerl, *Clavis* 75–77; Roumy, 'Abbon'.

27. The following is based on Roumy, 'Abbon' 321–330 unless otherwise noted.

28. Roumy counts the two canons from the synod of Ver 755 (Abbo, *Collectio* cc. 18–19; PL 139.487) as conciliar canons rather than capitulary canons; therefore, in his count there are 37

Where did Abbo take these materials from? The *Collectio* quotes (genuine) conciliar texts and a number of papal decretals from the *Hispana* and the *Dionysiana*.[29] For the letters of Gregory the Great, which provided Abbo with the overwhelming majority of his excerpts from papal letters (17 of 21 canons), Abbo may have used the so-called 'R' version of the register extant in two Fleury manuscripts (see below), but also used the 'C' version.[30] However, the brevity of Abbo's excerpts in many cases makes it difficult to determine his exact source,[31] and a combined use of different collections of Gregory's letters is possible. As for the Roman law, the sole excerpt from the *Codex Theodosianus* was taken from Breviary of Alaric, while the rest came from the Novels via the *Epitome Juliani*.[32] The three capitulary canons, including the one also found in Ansegisus, were taken from the ninth-century *Collectio capitularium Senonensis*.[33] The use of the Pseudo-Isidorian forgeries poses a special problem. Fuhrmann claimed that Abbo in his *Collectio canonum* did not use, and indeed 'avoided', Pseudo-Isidore.[34] However, Mostert was able to show that Abbo's *Letter 14* (not considered by Fuhrmann) had numerous parallels to the Pseudo-Isidorian forgeries, and concluded that the absence of such material in the *Collectio* was more likely to be accidental.[35] Roumy asserted that Abbo's *Collectio* too contained allusions to Pseudo-Isidore.[36] The acts of the council of Saint-Basle make it clear that Abbo knew Pseudo-Isidore in some form.[37]

All in all, the collection was compiled from a large number of earlier works, indicating that Abbo took considerable effort to search materials

---

conciliar canons and only one capitulary canon. See Hubert Mordek, *Bibliotheca capitularium regum Francorum manuscripta. Überlieferung und Traditionszusammenhang der fränkischen Herrschererlasse* (MGH Hilfsmittel 15; Munich 1995), here at 780–781.

29. Fowler-Magerl, *Clavis* 76.

30. Fowler-Magerl, 'Fine Distinctions' 158–159. Roumy, 'Abbon' 322–323 argued that Abbo probably used the version known as 'R+C+P'.

31. Fowler-Magerl, 'Use of Gregory' 243.

32. See already Max Conrat (Cohn), *Geschichte der Quellen und Literatur des römischen Rechts im frühen Mittelalter* (Leipzig 1891), here at 260.

33. Abbo, *Collectio* cc. 6, 18, and 19 as established by Koal, *Studien* 62; see also Mordek, *Bibliotheca capitularium* 780–781.

34. Fuhrmann, *Einfluß und Verbreitung* 1.231. Sackur, *Cluniacenser* 1.281 had asserted the use of Pseudo-Isidore, but later retracted (ibid. 2.488). Fowler-Magerl, *Clavis* 76 claimed that Abbo did not use Pseudo-Isidore.

35. Mostert, *Abbo of Fleury* 74 n. 42.

36. Roumy, 'Abbon' 318 and 329 on *Collectio* c. 8 (PL 139.481), claiming that Abbo's reference to a prohibition of episcopal translations by the council of Antioch was in reality an allusion to Anterus, JK †90 (ed. Hinschius 152). Roumy, 'Abbon' 321–322 further claimed that Abbo knew Gregory's *Libellus responsionum* (JE 1843) via Pseudo-Isidore.

37. See Gerbert, *Acta* (ed. Pertz, MGH SS 3.666–667) for evidence that Pseudo-Isidore was quoted by both sides at the synod of Saint-Basle in 991 (see below).

he was looking for—and, of course, that he was a trained scholar working in one of the best libraries of northern France. For a number of these sources, the very manuscripts used by Abbo have been identified. Guillot has argued that Abbo used two extant manuscripts from Fleury for his Gregory I excerpts, and Mostert pointed out that the annotation found in these manuscripts fits Abbo's interests well.[38] Giordanengo and Roumy have argued for the use of Paris, BnF, nouv. acq. lat. 1632 which may have provided Abbo with conciliar material.[39] Roumy also asserted the use of the *Epitome Juliani* extant in Paris, BnF, lat. 4568.[40] Abbo's Breviary copy may be extant in Bern, Burgerbibliothek, 263.[41] Hartmann has drawn attention to the *Dacheriana* copy at Wolfenbüttel as containing a combination of materials also used by Abbo and also a variant inscription that may indicate that Abbo used this manuscript or a very similar one.[42]

3.2.4 Context

Abbo compiled his *Collectio canonum* in the 990s in the midst of the turmoil following the recent ascension of Hugh Capet as king of Francia.[43] As Abbo was deeply involved in these conflicts, and this visibly shaped his writings including his canon law work, some of these events will have to be briefly sketched here. Abbo was elected abbot in 988, less than a year after Hugh Capet had become king. The balance of power between the Carolingians and the new rulers was delicate, and Ottonian intervention in Francia was not unlikely. Under these conditions the single most important political conflict Abbo was involved in from the very beginning of his pontificate broke out: the dispute over the see of Reims. Archbishop Adalbero of Reims, who had been an important player in the transition from

---

38. Olivier Guillot, 'Un exemple de la méthode suivie par Abbon de Fleury pour recueillir et ordonner les textes à partir des lettres de Grégoire le Grand incluses dans l'*Epistola XIV*', *Le istituzioni ecclesiastiche della «Societas Christiana» dei secoli XI–XII: diocesi, pievi e parrocchie: atti della sesta Settimana internazionale di studio, Milano, 1–7 settembre 1974* (Miscellanea 8; Milan 1977) 399–405, here at 400; Mostert, *Abbo of Fleury* 71–75; see Bruno Judic, 'La production et la diffusion du registre des lettres de Grégoire le Grand', *Les échanges culturels au moyen âge: XXXIIe congrès de la SHMES (Université du Littoral Côte d'Opale, juin 2001)*, ed. Patrick Boucheron (Publications de la Sorbonne. Série Histoire ancienne et médiévale 70; Paris 2002) 71–87, here at 81.

39. Gérard Giordanengo, 'La Collectio canonum d'Abbon de Fleury', *Autour de Gerbert d'Aurillac, le pape de l'an Mil: album de documents commentés*, ed. Olivier Guyotjeannin and Emmanuel Poulle (Matériaux pour l'histoire publiés par l'École des chartes 1; Paris 1996) 157–163, here at 162–163; Roumy, 'Abbon' 323–324. Giordanengo further claimed that Abbo quoted Ansegisus from this manuscript, but as Koal, *Studien* 63 pointed out, the evidence is unconvincing.

40. Roumy, 'Abbon' 326.

41. Mostert, *Abbo of Fleury* 67 n. 68.

42. MGH Conc. 3.456. The manuscript is Wolfenbüttel, HAB, Cod. Guelf. 1062 Helmst. [not seen].

43. For a recent account, see Jason Glenn, *Politics and History in the Tenth Century: The Work and World of Richer of Reims* (Life and Thought: Fourth Series 60; Cambridge 2004) ch. 5–7.

Carolingian to Capetian rule, died in early 989. He was succeeded by Arnulf, the illegitimate son of Lothar of France (hence half-brother of Louis V and nephew of Charles of Lorraine), seen by many as the representative of the old dynasty. His election was contested by Gerbert of Aurillac who as a protégé of Adalbero had hoped to become archbishop of Reims himself. After Arnulf supported his uncle Charles of Lorraine in his claims to royal power, or appeared to do so, his opponents managed to have him tried for treason at a synod held in the monastery Saint-Basle-de-Verzy near Reims in 991. The synod was convinced that Arnulf was guilty; but three monks including Abbo opposed his deposition. They did not claim Arnulf was innocent, but vehemently argued for the case to be heard by the pope. This in turn was rejected in strong terms by the majority of the synod. Crucially for Abbo, this course of events brought him in conflict not only with Gerbert of Aurillac but also his own diocesan bishop, Arnulf of Orléans. The synod in the end deposed Arnulf, and Gerbert succeeded him as archbishop of Reims, but this was not the end of the story. A papal legate, and soon after the pope himself too, denounced the deposition as void, and while Gerbert spent considerable effort to argue his case, he lost royal support with the death of Hugh Capet in November 996. In May 997, Gerbert left Reims for the court of Otto III (who in 998 made him archbishop of Ravenna), and Arnulf returned to office. In 997, it was Abbo who was sent to Reims with the pallium for Arnulf. This was only fitting, as it was above all Abbo who had secured papal intervention in this affair. The affair only ended when Gerbert immediately after he had become pope in 999 (as Silvester II) confirmed the reinstallation of his opponent, who remained archbishop of Reims until his death in 1021.

In the 990s, the case divided the magnates of Francia, and, both for the king and for the pope, more was at issue than 'only' the question of who was archbishop of Reims, an office that traditionally went with the right to crown the kings of Francia. For Hugh Capet, the affair was an important test case for royal control over the appointment and deposition of bishops. For the papacy, it was an unexpected (and perhaps not entirely welcome) test case for the papal right to decide 'major cases'. The prolonged conflict therefore involved the new and the old ruling dynasty, it touched upon the relations of the papacy and the French Church as well as the relations between the king, the episcopate and the great monastic houses of Francia. Loyalties were shifting, and sometimes as opaque to contemporaries as to modern historians, but there was little doubt that Abbo of Fleury and Arnulf of Orléans represented two very different positions, and, from 991 at the latest, this conflict dominated their relations.

In fact, the two had already clashed for the first time in 988 when Arnulf demanded an oath of fealty from the newly elected Abbo, which the latter refused to take. In the following years, dissent over Fleury's property led to conflict, sometimes escalating to violence. The synod of Saint-Denis in 994 reveals something of the structural element of the conflict here, as the bishops expressed general concern about monastic possession of tithes. Both the monks at Saint-Denis and local laypeople were offended, and the synod ended in uproar and chaos. Abbo was made responsible for the violence, and in this context wrote his *Apologeticus* to justify his position. Apparently, he convinced the king, who later pointed to Gerbert and Arnulf of Orléans as culprits.

These events, and most visibly the two synods mentioned above, had a very direct impact on Abbo's canon law work. Synods generally were occasions to read, copy, learn and indeed make canon law. At the synod of Saint-Basle, for example, both sides were well equipped with legal collections; Abbo and the two other monks are said to have consulted 'many books of canon law'.[44] The account of Gerbert of Aurillac makes clear that both sides quoted Pseudo-Isidorian material.[45] Even if Abbo had not brought some dossiers of canon law compiled for the occasion, he may well have left the synod with such materials. By the time of the synod of Saint-Denis, he must have had considerable materials at his disposal to bolster his claims concerning monastic liberty articulated in his *Apologeticus*, and also to draft a to-do list for a national synod.[46] Both the *Collectio canonum* and *Letter 14* drew on the same materials again, and reveal considerable legal learning. The recurrent theme of these works is monastic liberty in general, and the defence against episcopal encroachment in particular.

Older scholarship has often seen the struggle between Abbo of Fleury and Arnulf of Orléans as a conflict over monastic exemption, and depicted Abbo as a champion of Cluniac reform supported by the papacy but directed against local bishop and indeed royal power.[47] Accordingly,

---

44. Richer, *Historia* 4.67 (ed. Hoffmann, MGH SS 38.278): '[...] librorum multa volumina aperta sunt, multa quoque ex patrum decretis prolata.' See also Gerbert, *Acta* cc. 19–26 (ed. Pertz, MGH SS 3.666–671).

45. Gerbert, *Acta* (ed. Pertz, MGH SS 3.666–667) preserves some of the material the three quoted, namely from the forged Damasus correspondence (JK †243; ed. Hinschius 501–508). Likewise, Bishop Ratbold of Noyon had a canon law collection at hand, too (a *tomus*, writes Gerbert) which contained some Pseudo-Isidore (ed. Pertz, MGH SS 3.668). Ratbold was quoting Clement as found in Ps.-Anaclete, JK †2 (ed. Hinschius 68).

46. Abbo, *Apologeticus* (PL 139.470): '[...] capitulatim subtexam huic indiculo quae maxime sunt corrigenda in vestro imperio, nec tamen haec verbis meis, sed authenticis sanctorum dictis, ut postmodum episcopos moveatis haec canonice emendare in suis conciliis.'

47. For the latter point, see esp. Sackur, *Cluniacenser* ch. 6. See also Georg Schreiber, *Kurie und*

Abbo's final success over Arnulf of Orléans was seen as pre-shadowing the reform movements of the late eleventh century.[48] Modern scholarship in contrast has stressed that most monasteries sought protection of their property but not 'exemption', and that open conflict between monks and bishops was the exception, not the rule.[49] In the case of Fleury, the struggle indeed was about exemption, and the conflict with the diocesan bishop was open, violent, and persistent. Also, the right to appeal to Rome was indeed important in Fleury's dealing with Arnulf and other bishops. That said, it would be misleading see Fleury's papal privileges as directed against royal control. As Abbo knew very well, Merovingian, Carolingian, and Robertine donations and privileges were as important for Fleury's liberty as papal privileges. The very considerable number of royal immunities and papal exemptions, not to mention relics, miracles, and historiography, can be seen as resources Fleury had accumulated well before the time of Abbo, and they all played a role for the exemption it finally achieved. This all may strengthen the case for Fleury as an impressive model for other communities seeking greater independence from their local bishops and closer contact with Rome, but at the same time, it makes abundantly clear that Fleury was atypical in almost every aspect. The resources Fleury had at its disposal were already unusual, and the combination of royal immunities and papal exemptions almost unique; the fact that Fleury had obtained the right to appeal to Rome in the eighth

---

Kloster im 12. Jahrhundert. Studien zur Privilegierung, Verfassung und besonders zum Eigenkirchenwesen der Vorfranziskanischen Orden vornehmlich auf Grund der Papsturkunden von Paschalis II. bis auf Lucius III. (1099–1181) (2 vols. Kirchenrechtliche Abhandlungen 65–68; Stuttgart 1910), passim on exemption and 1.99 n. 1 on Abbo.

48. See in particular Jean-François Lemarignier, 'L'exemption monastique et les origines de la réforme grégorienne', *À Cluny: congrès scientifique: fêtes et cérémonies liturgiques en l'honneur des saints Abbés Odon et Odilon, 9–11 juillet 1949* (Dijon 1950) 288–340, here at 303–313 and Jean-François Lemarignier, 'Political and Monastic Structures in France at the End of the Tenth and the Beginning of the Eleventh Century', *Lordship and Community in Medieval Europe: Selected Readings*, ed. F. L. Cheyette (New York 1968) 100–127. For an analysis of Lemarignier, see John Stephens Ott and Anna Trumbore Jones, 'Introduction: The Bishop Reformed', *The Bishop Reformed: Studies of Episcopal Power and Culture in the Central Middle Ages*, ed. iidem (CFC; Aldershot 2007) 1–20, here at 12–18.

49. Rosenwein et al., 'Monks'; Ludwig Falkenstein, *La papauté et les abbayes françaises aux XIe et XIIe siècles: exemption et protection apostolique* (Bibliothèque de l'École des hautes études. Sciences historiques et philologiques 336; Paris 1997); Jörg Oberste, '*Contra prelatos qui gravant loca et personas ordinis*: Bischöfe und Cluniazenser im Zeitalter von Krisen und Reformen (12./13. Jahrhundert)', *Die Cluniazenser in ihrem politisch-sozialen Umfeld*, ed. Giles Constable et al. (Vita regularis 7; Münster 1998) 349–392; Jakobs, 'Klosterfreiheit' esp. 89–90. See already Herbert Edward John Cowdrey, *The Cluniacs and the Gregorian Reform* (Oxford 1970), here at 70. On exemption in the legal sense and the rarity of the concept even in twelfth-century sources, see Lotte Kéry, 'Klosterfreiheit und päpstliche Organisationsgewalt. Exemtion als Herrschaftsinstrument des Papsttums?', *Rom und die Regionen. Studien zur Homogenisierung der lateinischen Kirche im Hochmittelalter*, ed. Jochen Johrendt and Harald Müller (Abh. Akad. Göttingen N.F. 19; Berlin and Boston 2012) 83–144.

century was particularly exceptional. So, while Fleury-style exemption may have been attractive for some (but not all) French monasteries, only few of these houses could hope to obtain even a fraction of the privileges Fleury had accumulated over the centuries.

3.2.5 Analysis

With this background, let us return to Abbo's collection itself. The *Collectio canonum* is clearly a monastic collection in the sense that it deals in unusual detail with the relations between monasteries and the Church at large. In the dedicatory letter, Abbo claims to have compiled it in 'defence of the monastic order', which he also refers to as the 'senate of monks', an instructive metaphor that clearly hints to Abbo's contention that his order should be heard in the realm.[50] The superior spiritual rank Abbo accorded to monks and the greater political influence he hoped for cannot be separated. In the *Apologeticus*, for example, he had divided Christian society in three orders: laypeople, secular clergy, and monks. While this may be read as a variant of the 'three estates' model, it also was a self-conscious reminder of the importance of the great houses for the new kings. Abbo's comment on elections in his *Collectio* likewise seems to express such a perception; there are, Abbo affirms, three kinds of elections 'that of a king or emperor, the second that of a bishop, the third that of an abbot'.[51] As in the *Apologeticus*, Abbo supposes a tripartite model of Christian society, with the monastic order as the highest estate. At the same time, the stress on royal elections together with Abbo's claim that royal descent was not enough to claim kingship, to any contemporary reader must have echoed the debates over Hugh Capet being elected king in 987, which resurfaced in the civil war of 991.[52]

In this sense, the whole *Collectio canonum* was at the same time part of Abbo's attempts to assert Fleury's position in early Capetian France and a discussion of the place of the monastic order in Christian society. The former aspect is evident; while the collection deals with many topics, Abbo almost invariably returns to the question of monastic liberty, with special attention to Fleury's situation. The *Collectio canonum* contains

---

50. Abbo, *Praefatio* (PL 139.474): 'Ad defensionem quoque monastici ordinis plura congessi: qui monachorum senatum semper salvum esse et volo et volui, quorum etiam vos piissimi defensores et advocati estis.' See also the parallel in *Apologeticus* (PL 139.641), a passage is taken up by Aimon, *Vita* (PL 139.395).

51. Abbo, *Collectio* c. 4 (PL 139.478): 'Tres namque electiones generales novimus, quarum una est regis vel imperatoris, altera pontificis, tertia abbati.'

52. Mostert, *Abbo of Fleury* 142–143. Abbo seems to have deliberately blurred the distinction between imperial and royal office, presumably as part of his depiction of Carolingian rule as a direct model for the new rulers.

an unusually high number of authorities on ecclesiastical property (cc. 2, 5–17, 11, 25, 27–35), and specifically deals with monastic tithes which were so violently debated at Saint-Denis in 994 (cc. 31, 25, 41). It also includes a chapter on the abbot of Fleury (c. 20). Significantly, the chapter on abbatial ordination and the right of the bishop to enter a monastery in his diocese is the longest chapter of the whole collection (c. 15); this question was repeatedly at issue between the abbots of Fleury and the bishop of Orléans. The canon on the excommunication of an abbot may also have had very real importance for Abbo in the early 990s.[53]

If Abbo's desire to defend monastic freedom is 'apparent on every page',[54] how did he envision it in practice? Above all, it was joint royal and papal protection he hoped for, and his collection depicts the Carolingian past as an ideal time where these two powers harmoniously cooperated to the benefit of the monastic order as well as the whole Church. This view may also explain his stress on 'books of canon and secular law'[55] in the dedicatory letter even if quantitatively secular law clearly played a minor role. From the beginning of his work, Abbo addressed the king and his son as protectors not so much of Fleury but all monasteries in their realm, praising Hugh (and Robert) for their support but also reminding them of their duty to do so.[56] In a similar way, Abbo can be said to introduce the papacy with a special view to its role in protecting monastic rights. While it is striking to see how much emphasis Abbo placed on papal primacy (many scholars have drawn parallels to late eleventh-century events in this context[57]) it is also true that he quickly returned to the issue of monastic rights. The beginning of chapter five from his *Collectio canonum*, the first to mention the papacy, is instructive here:[58]

> The authority of the Roman and apostolic see shines over the universal Church of the whole world with the favour of Christ our Lord. And no wonder, when the pontiffs of the same see are seen to fill the place of Saint Peter, who is the prince of the whole Church. From the Christian emperors they have also obtained this same singular excellence that, episcopal churches or monasteries of men or nuns having been founded, they would never lose the law which they [the popes] once imposed on them under the anathema of excommunication, unless necessity intervened.

The protection of monastic property by both imperial (or royal) and papal authority is indeed a recurring theme of the *Collectio canonum*; it fits well

<hr>

53. Mostert, 'Urkundenfälschungen' 303.
54. Mostert, *Abbo of Fleury* 54.
55. Abbo, *Praefatio* (PL 139.473): 'capitula inferius scripta ex canonum legumve libris'.
56. Abbo, *Praefatio* (PL 139.474).
57. Lemarignier, 'Structures' 113; Falkenstein, *Papauté* 5–6.
58. The translation is taken from Mostert, *Abbo of Fleury* 112.

the privileges Fleury had obtained over the centuries, the privileges Abbo obtained himself, and the forgeries he produced. The forgery attributed to Gregory IV (JE †2570) may serve as an example here. It was forged by Abbo using materials also employed for his *Collectio canonum*, it confirmed precisely the claims Abbo made vis-à-vis Arnulf of Orléans, and it provided an apparently ancient authority for the abbot of Fleury as 'first among all abbots in Gaul'.[59] It also mentioned how Charlemagne had provided Fleury with many donations—and how he had confirmed the 'testaments' of other magnates doing the same, a topic also expounded in the *Collectio canonum*.[60] Both passages—those on Fleury's primacy and that on Charlemagne—were later copied verbatim into the (genuine) privilege Abbo obtained from Gregory V.[61] There can be little doubt about the source of inspiration for the young pope. Indeed, Abbo himself described the way he proceeded with great clarity. In 998, he wrote to Abbot Gausbert of Saint-Julien in Tours how he had made sure that an important passage from Gregory the Great had been inserted in the privilege he obtained for Fleury. Abbo also inserted this excerpt in his *Collectio* (c. 17).[62] This strongly suggests that the Fleury privileges were written partly at Fleury (*Empfängerausfertigung*); it also supports the idea that Abbo provided the pope with a canon law dossier, perhaps even his own *Collectio canonum*.

All in all, Abbo of Fleury in his *Collectio* as well as in his other works, and in particular in the privileges he secured for Fleury, can be seen to return to the same topics and the same texts. The collection gathers ancient authorities, and by this also presents a historical narrative; Merovingian and Carolingian times appear as an ideal past when kings and popes jointly protected monasteries. Charlemagne is presented as a model for Hugh Capet and Robert, and Gregory V is praised as the 'Gregory of our time' by Abbo.[63]

In this way, Abbo's collection stressed the responsibility of kings and popes to protect monasteries. It is also transparent from which side monastic liberty is in danger according to the *Collectio canonum*; in the words of the rubric of one of the chapters, it is 'episcopal arrogance against monks' (c. 23). Mabillon was right that this 'may sound harsh', but there

---

59. Mostert, *Abbo of Fleury* 58; idem, 'Urkundenfälschungen' 298–302 and 312. On the formula and its source see above (note 16).

60. Abbo, *Collectio* c. 7.

61. Gregory V, JE 3872.

62. Gregory I, JE 1877; Abbo, *Ep.* 8 (PL 143.429); Abbo, *Collectio* c. 17. See Mostert, 'Urkundenfälschungen' 294–295, who assumed that it was possible (though not proven) that Abbo took his collection to Rome.

63. Abbo, *Ep.* 8 (PL 139.429) as quoted by Mostert, *Abbo of Fleury* 58.

can be little doubt that this was precisely what Abbo wanted to say.[64] Indeed, throughout the collection the secular clergy is mainly talked about in the context of moral standards they fail to meet (c. 35 'On the avarice of priests', c. 40 'On the offspring of secular clergy'), while monks and abbots are mainly mentioned in the context of the privileges they enjoy. Or, to take a seemingly innocent example, a subseries of canons deals in this sequence with the ordination of priests, episcopal elections, and the election of abbots (cc. 12–14); in the light of the general tendency of the *Collectio* (and the *Apologeticus*), it seems natural to read this as an ascending order. It may also be significant that for priests and bishops, but not for abbots, the danger of simony is mentioned.

While much of this may be informed by Abbo's experience with episcopal authority in the 990s, it is plausible to assume that the affair over Arnulf of Reims also had a more direct impact on his collection. For example, the *Collectio canonum* contains a number of authorities on episcopal elections including (as c. 42) the prohibition for a bishop to designate his successor. These canons may have had particular resonance in the dispute over the see of Reims, as Adalbero of Reims allegedly had named Gerbert of Aurillac as his successor before he died. Abbo's quotation of the relevant prohibition may well be understood as a comment on this. The chapter on fealty owed to the king, and on those who break their oath of fealty to conjure with the enemy likewise can be read as a comment on bishops changing sides in the civil war of 991—and above all on the oath Arnulf of Reims had taken at his election.[65]

Another chapter in Abbo's *Collectio canonum* is best understood if read in the context on the synod of Saint-Basle in 991. What reads as a rather abstract discussion of legal change in chapter eight of Abbo's collection was a matter of very practical relevance at the synod. Gerbert of Aurillac had vehemently argued that traditional canon law could not be altered by the pope, as this would open the door to arbitrary change and violate the

---

64. Abbo, *Collectio canonum*, rubric to c. 23 (PL 139.488): 'De clericis qui monachi volunt fieri et de insolentia episcoporum in monachos.' Mabillon thought the comment harsh ('Durior videri posset haec inscriptio [...]'), and suggested a more moderate version: 'titulum rectius temperasset hoc modo: De insolentia quorumdam Episcoporum in Monachos' (PL 139.488). – The canon, taken from Toledo IV, is extremely common; but no other canon law collection in the *Clavis* database has a rubric that mentions 'episcopal arrogance' as Abbo does. On the transmission, see Giorgio G. Picasso, 'Monachesimo e canoniche nelle sillogi canonistiche e nei concili particolari', *Istituzioni monastiche e istituzioni canonicali in Occidente (1123–1215): atti Mendola 1977* (Miscellanea 9; Milan 1980) 133–158, here at 145–146.

65. When Hugh Capet accepted Arnulf as archbishop, he had demanded an oath of loyalty and, famoulsy, also a written contract (in form of a chirograph); the treason Arnulf was condemned for was also a direct violation of this oath. Bishop Adalberon of Laon was likewise notorious for his betrayal of Arnulf.

authority of ancient principles.[66] Abbo, in contrast, in his *Collectio canonum* articulated a theory of legal change that accorded the papacy the right to make new law. More clearly than any earlier 'canonist' Abbo pointed out that canon law contained many provisions that fit the time and place of origin but not necessarily could be applied in different circumstances.[67] Like later authors writing on the subject, Abbo quoted the rules on the transmigration of bishops as a prime examples for the historicity of canon law.[68] Crucially, he held that the papacy (and not, for example, a synod) was allowed to make new law because of necessity ('necessitas temporum').

3.2.6 Reception

While the monastic background, and specifically Abbo's situation when compiling the *Collectio canonum*, left a marked impact on his work, it is a separate question how it was understood by the later readers. Many parallels between the collection and the political situation of the 990s must have been evident to any contemporary reader (e.g. the question of royal elections), while others may have been transparent only to those also familiar with Fleury's privileges (e.g. the parallel between Gregory the Great's letters, Abbo's collection, and the privilege of 997).

Yet the first question of course is not how, but whether the collection was read at all. The fact that Abbo's *Collectio canonum* is extant in one manuscript only tells against the idea that other monasteries equipped themselves with this collection when they sought protection from the

66. Gerbert, *Acta* (ed. Pertz, MGH SS 3.672): 'Duo autem sunt quae magnopere a nobis praevideri debent, id est, si Romani pontificis silentium aut nova constitutio promulgatis legibus canonum vel decretis priorum decreta, eo silente, silere necesse est. Si enim silentium praeiudicat, omnes leges, omnia priorum decreta, eo silente, silere necesse est. Si autem nova constitutio, quid prosunt leges conditae, cum ad unius arbitrium omnia dirigantur? Videtis, quia his duabus causis admissis, ecclesiarum Dei status periclitatur, et dum legibus leges quaerimus, nullas omnino leges habemus.'

67. Mostert, *Abbo of Fleury* 109–118; Hans-Henning Kortüm, 'Necessitas temporis. Zur historischen Bedingtheit des Rechts im früheren Mittelalter' ZRG Kan. Abt. 79 (1993) 34–55, here at 41–42. See also Brett, 'Finding' 54 n. 9, 61–62, 64 n. 38, and 69–70 for later discussions of the same issue.

68. Abbo, *Collectio* c. 8 (PL 139.481–482); Mostert, *Abbo of Fleury* 117–118. The same example was used by many other prelates including Hincmar, Bernold of Konstanz, and Ivo of Chartres; see Hincmar, *Opusculum LV capitulorum* (ed. Schieffer, MGH Conc. 4 supp. 2.216); idem, *De translatione episcoporum* (ed. Schieffer, MGH Epp 8.2:440–459); Bernold, *De fontibus* cc. 53–54 (ed. Stöckly and Jasper, MGH Fontes iuris 15.172–174); Ivo, *Epp.* 146 and 241; idem *Prologue* (ed. Brasington 133–140). Significantly perhaps, two canons on episcopal translation in 74T are manipulated (74T cc. 91 and 188), see Fuhrmann, *Einfluß und Verbreitung* 2.505. On the issue in general (though not Abbo), see Sebastian Scholz, *Transmigration und Translation. Studien zum Bistumswechsel der Bischöfe von der Spätantike bis zum Hohen Mittelalter* (Kölner historische Abhandlungen 37; Cologne, Weimar, and Vienna 1992). My thanks are to Dr Claudia Esch (Bamberg) for stimulating discussions on the canon law and practice of episcopal translations.

local bishop. On the other hand, the important role of the forged version of *Quam sit necessarium* in later monastic collections—namely 74T and its derivatives—makes one wonder whether this may not have to do with the fact that Abbo was the first to introduce the genuine version of this canon into a canon law collection. Also, Abbo's *Letter 14* reminds us that both ideas and canon law texts travelled in many ways.[69] More specifically, Abbo was in close contact with many abbots, and already the privileges he obtained did have consequences well beyond Fleury.

This can be observed on several levels. Abbo's biographer Aimon (d. 1010), for example, felt the need to defend him against the claim that Fleury's privileges contradicted canon law, and added further excerpts from Gregory the Great, apparently taken from Abbo's working materials.[70] Aimon's *Vita Abbonis* in this sense was a continuation of Abbo's canon law activities. It was written in a time when Fleury's privileges were indeed fiercely disputed. In 1007, Abbot Gauslin of Fleury was excommunicated by Bishop Fulk of Orléans after the latter had entered Fleury without the abbot's permission, thus violating the privilege of 997. This new conflict was watched well beyond the Orléanais and also involved Fulbert of Chartres, who openly sided with Fulk.[71] Allegedly, the latter at a synod declared that one should burn Fleury's privilege.[72] Pope John XVIII, who was informed by his legate, intervened quickly and sent furious letters to both bishops (and the king). The excommunication of Gauslin was lifted, the litigants were summoned to Rome, and the bishops were threatened with excommunication. This not only strengthened Gauslin, but also the authority of all similar privileges which more and more monasteries obtained in the course of the eleventh century. The process by which such papal intervention in favour of (mainly French) monastic communities

69. Excerpts from Gregory I, JE 1362 found in Abbo's letter were also used in a privilege for Saint-Bertin, see Laurent Morelle, 'Par delà le vrai et le faux: trois études critiques sur les premiers privilèges pontificaux reçus par l'abbaye de Saint-Bertin (1057–1107)', *L'acte pontifical et sa critique*, ed. Rolf Große (Studien und Dokumente zur Gallia Pontificia 5; Bonn 2007) 51–86.

70. Aimon, *Vita Abbonis* (PL 139.492) as quoted by Mostert, 'Urkundenfälschungen' 307: 'Sed ne quis eos, domnum dico apostolicum et Abbonem sanctum, existimet in hoc facto contraria regulis sanctorum sensisse Patrum, necessarium nobis visum est, ex epistolis Magni papae Gregorii pauca de pluribus hic exempla inserere, in quibus exquirendis pia huic beato viro semper fuit intentio.'

71. Fulbert of Chartres, *Ep.* 16. For an edition, see *The Letters and Poems of Fulbert of Chartres*, ed. and tr. by Frederick Behrends (Oxford Medieval Texts; Oxford 1976), here at 32. See Lemarignier, 'Structures' 114 and Mostert, 'Urkundenfälschungen' 307–308.

72. JL –; Böhmer-Zimmermann 1026. The only source for this story is the partisan account of Andrew of Fleury; see *Vie de Gauzlin, abbé de Fleury / Vita Gauzlini, abbatis Floriacensis monasterii*, ed. and tr. Robert-Henri Bautier and Gilette Labory (Sources d'histoire médiévale 2; Paris 1969), here at 50–58. See also Thomas Head, *Hagiography and the Cult of Saints: The Diocese of Orléans, 800–1200* (Life and Thought: Fourth Series 14; Cambridge 1990), here at 255–257.

gradually changed the relations between monasteries, bishops, and the papacy has often been analysed.[73] In the context of the present study, the important point is Abbo's contribution to this development which indeed changed the law of the Church. The clearest example concerns Cluny which between 998 and 1024 received several privileges that were modelled on those for Fleury. Important clauses were directly lifted from forged decretals Abbo had fabricated, and thus ultimately on Abbo's canon law work that is extant, in part, in his *Collectio canonum*.[74] So while the evidence for a direct use of the collection is lacking, the long-term influence of Abbo's efforts to gather and to interpret ancient canon law, to forge and to have confirmed old privileges, and to obtain new ones was no doubt significant.

3.3 The *Collection in Five Books*: A Voice from Southern Italy

The *Collection in Five Books* (= *5L*) is an influential monastic canon law collection of the early eleventh century from southern Italy.[75] Only three manuscripts, all from the eleventh century, are known.[76] None of these three manuscripts is a copy of any of the other two, and none is the original of the collection,[77] although the Vallicelliana copy stands out

73. Falkenstein, *Papauté* esp. 5–6; see also Mostert, *Abbo of Fleury* 127–130 and more recently Anna Trumbore Jones, *Noble Lord, Good Shepherd: Episcopal Power and Piety in Aquitaine, 877–1050* (Brill's Series on the Early Middle Ages 17; Leiden and Boston, Ma. 2009), here at 107–108 and Kéry, 'Klosterfreiheit'. For further literature, see nn. 47–49 above.

74. Mostert, 'Urkundenfälschungen' esp. 303–304; Cushing, *Reform* 60.

75. For bibliogaphy, see Kéry 157–161 and Fowler-Magerl, *Clavis* 82–85. The following is based on Paul Fournier, 'Un groupe de recueils canoniques italiens des Xe et XIe siècles' *Mémoires de l'Institut National de France, Académie des Inscriptions et Belles-Lettres* 40 (1916) 95–213, here at 159–212; Mario Fornasari, 'Introduzione', *Collectio canonum in v libris* (lib. I–III), ed. idem (CCCM 6; Turnhout 1970) VII–XIX; Fowler-Magerl, *Clavis* 82–85; Roger E. Reynolds, 'The South-Italian Canon Law Collection in Five Books and Its Derivates: New Evidence on Its Origins, Diffusion and Use' *MS* 52 (1990) 278–295; idem, 'The South-Italian Collection in Five Books and Its Derivates: The Collection of Vallicelliana Tome XXI', *Proceedings San Diego 1988* MIC Subsidia 9.77–91; Zechiel-Eckes, *Concordia* 1.269–277; Reynolds, 'Canonistica Beneventana', *Proceedings Munich 1992* MIC Subsidia 10.21–40; Valeska Koal, 'Zur Überlieferungsgeschichte der Fünf-Bücher-Sammlung', *Quellen, Kritik, Interpretation. Festgabe zum 60. Geburtstag von Hubert Mordek*, ed. Thomas Martin Buck and Julia Herrmann (Frankfurt 1999) 127–134; eadem, *Studien* 67–135; Reynolds, *Collectio Casinensis*; idem, 'The South Italian Collection in Five Books and Its Derivatives: A South Italian Appendix to the Collection in Seventy-Four Titles' *MS* 63 (2001) 353–365; Kaiser, *Epitome Iuliani* 630–637; Gaastra, *Liturgy*. For the sake of disambiguition, Reynolds' articles on *5L* are quoted with the publication year in brackets in addition to the short titles ('Five Books [1990]' etc.).

76. Montecassino, Archivio della Badia, MS 125 (written at Montecassino in the first half of the eleventh century), Vat. lat. 1339 (mid-eleventh century, probably from Narni), and Roma, Vallicelliana, B.II (San Eutizio, before 1087) on which see Reynolds, 'Five Books [1990]' 281–286. In addition, see Fowler-Magerl, *Clavis* 82; Zechiel-Eckes, *Concordia* 1.270; Koal, *Studien* 69–71. For the dates, I follow Reynolds.

77. See Gérard Fransen, 'Principes d'édition des collections canoniques' *Revue d'histoire ecclési-

by preserving certain texts in better quality than the other two.[78] Another eleventh-century copy survives as a fragment.[79] The number of extant manuscripts therefore is small, but there is ample evidence for other, lost manuscripts, and crucially, *5L* 'spawned a mass of derivatives'.[80] Already Fournier knew more than a dozen collections influenced by *5L*, and by 1990, Reynolds had identified at least twenty-five such collections.[81] Compared to the scope and the influence of the collection, it has played a relatively modest role in historiography. It was known to canon law scholars from the time of the Ballerini brothers, not least for its rich Lombard law content. In the 1950s, it was one of the first pre-Gratian collections to be discussed as a specifically monastic contribution to canon law.[82] Fornasari attempted to edit the collection, but the result was severely criticized and he never finished this work.[83] Reynolds later devoted a series of very substantial studies to *5L* and its derivatives.[84] Otherwise, however, the collection was rarely studied in detail. This may well have to do with the absence of an authoritative 'original', the complicated textual history, and the lack of an edition that would meet modern standards—although this is all quite typical for any pre-Gratian collection. In the case of *5L*, one has also to take into account that it is one of the collections that were not given much attention by scholars following Fournier's division of 'papal' and 'anti-papal' collections.[85]

---

astique 66 (1971) 125–136, here at 131–132 against the idea of Vat. lat. 1339 as the 'original' and/or the model of the other two copies, and Reynolds, 'Five Books [1990]' esp. 282.

78. Zechiel-Eckes showed that the Vallicelliana copy of *5L* in several cases preserved Cresconius' text better than the other two extant manuscripts, and Koal made a similar argument for the capitulary canons: Zechiel-Eckes, *Concordia* 1.276 n. 30; Koal, 'Überlieferungsgeschichte'; eadem, *Studien* 135. Both took up the arguments first articulated by Fransen, 'Principes' 131–132.

79. Reynolds, 'Five Books [1990]' 285.

80. Roger E. Reynolds, 'The *Collectio Angelica*: A Canon Law Derivative of the South Italian *Collection in Five Books*', *Bishops, Texts and the Use of Canon Law Around 1100: Essays in Honour of Martin Brett*, ed. Bruce Clark Brasington and Kathleen Grace Cushing (CFC; Aldershot and Farnham 2008) 7–28, here at 7 (quote). In addition to the studies quoted above (n. 75) see idem 'The South Italian *Collection in Five Books* and Its Derivates: Maastricht Excerpta' MS 58 (1996) 273–284 for a fragment not listed in Kéry 157–161.

81. Fournier, 'Recueils canoniques italiens' 190–201; Reynolds, 'Five Books [1990]'.

82. See Jean Leclercq, 'Y at-il une culture monastique?', *Il monachesimo nell'alto Medioevo e la formazione della civiltà occidentale, 8–14 aprile 1956* (Settimane 4; Spoleto 1957) 339–356 and the discussion as documented ibid. 510–521. For a sceptic view, see Fuhrmann, *Einfluß und Verbreitung* 3.759 n. 3.

83. *Collectio canonum in V libris (lib. I–III)*, ed. Mario Fornasari (CCCM 6; Turnhout 1970). The most important criticism was raised by Fransen, 'Principes'.

84. In addition to the articles quoted in the last notes, see the studies in Roger E. Reynolds, *Studies on Medieval Liturgical and Legal Manuscripts from Spain and Italy* (CSS 927; Aldershot 2009).

85. See Kölzer, 'Prolegomena' 96–100.

3.3.1 Content and Structure

The collection, referred to simply as *Liber canonum* in medieval manuscripts, takes its modern name from its division into five large books.[86] Notwithstanding minor additions and omissions, and a certain amount of overlap between the individual books,[87] *5L* is a very large collection; covering some 300 folios, it contains a total of more than 2,000 proof texts. In addition, two of the three manuscripts are heavily glossed, and as the glosses were sometimes incorporated in *5L* derivative collections, they seem to have been regarded as an integral part of the collection.

The mass of material is divided according to subject matter into books. The first book presents the ecclesiastical hierarchy; it mainly deals with the ordinations of priests and bishops but also contains materials (not highlighted in the title) on kings and secular justice. The second book contains canons on the secular clergy, the celebration of synods (for which an appropriate *ordo* is inserted), on communities of monks and nuns, and the celibate life. Book three deals with the sacrament of baptism, feasts, and ecclesiastical property. The long fourth book is devoted to penance, the utility of which is highlighted not only in the book title but also in the preface to the whole collection. The last book is devoted to marriage and sexuality.

Further structuring elements make the mass of material accessible to the reader. Every book has a *capitulatio* which gives an overview of the numbered canons contained in the respective book. Importantly, the collection contains numerous prefaces and an epilogue: four prefaces at the very beginning, four at the beginning of the second book, one each to the other three books. Several prologues are lifted from other collections, but every book has a prologue that was written for or at least adopted to the book it introduces. All books are further subdivided into titles by 'structuring rubrics' (Reynolds), well above 400 in the case of book four, some 150 to 250 for most other books; the exact number varies with every copy. The canons themselves also are arranged in a way that facilitates the use, and indeed the understanding of the materials *5L* presents. In several cases, the compiler placed texts on the origin of an institution or the etymology of important terms at the beginning of a book, while more specialised materials are inserted later.[88] Finally, the empty pages 'inviting'

---

86. There also is another collection divided into five books, extant only in Vat. lat. 1348, which has nothing to do with *5L*. On the collection in Vat. lat. 1348 see Giuseppe Motta, 'Introduzione', *Liber canonum diuersorum sanctorum patrum sive Collectio in CLXXXIII titulos digesta*, ed. idem (MIC Corpus collectionum 7; Vatican City 1988) xvii–lxviii, here at xli–xliv.

87. As pointed out by Koal, *Studien* 78.

88. E.g. the very first canons in books one and four, taken from Isidore's *Etymologies*, or the first canon in the sub-section on royal office and secular judges (*5L* 1.139.1).

additions (Reynolds) may also be viewed as elements that facilitate a specific use of the collection.

Unusually for a canon law collection, the Vatican copy of *5L* is decorated with several miniatures showing individual church fathers or synods, with the emperors convening these synods depicted prominently.[89] Authors of penitential handbooks are likewise depicted.[90] These illustrations are all found in an unnumbered quire, which may suggest that they were added to the text only later; but they were made for a canon law collection, either for *5L* or a similar collection.[91]

3.3.2 Date and Place of Origin

The *terminus ante quem non* for *5L* in its extant form is 1014, the date of the most recent material the collection contains, five canons of an imperial synod held by Henry II at the very beginning of this year. The traditional view that it took place at Ravenna has been challenged in favour of Rome.[92] Reynolds pointed out that these canons are placed somewhat oddly in the manuscripts, possibly suggesting that they were *extravagantes* transmitted with the collection but only later integrated into the collection proper. If so, he held, *5L* may have been compiled earlier, perhaps even as early as the late tenth century.[93] As for a *terminus ante quem*, the extant manuscripts (none of which is the autograph) and early derivative collections like the *Toletana* suggest that *5L* already enjoyed considerable circulation in the mid-eleventh century.[94] While the collection therefore could have been compiled at any date between 1014 and *ca.* 1050, most scholars have preferred an early date within this range.[95] Mordek, Kölzer, and Reynolds tentatively suggested that the collection could be identical to the *Liber canonum* Theobald of Montecassino reports to have copied when he was prior at San Liberatore a Maiella.[96] If this identification

89. Roger E. Reynolds, 'Rites and Signs of Conciliar Decisions in the Early Middle Ages', *Segni e riti nella chiesa altomedievale occidentale, 11–17 aprile 1985* (2 vols. Settimane 33; Spoleto 1987) 1.207–247 (with several illustrations); Richard F. Gyug, 'The List of Authorities in the Illustrations of the *Collection in 5 Books* (MS Vat. lat. 1339)', *Ritual, Text and Law: Studies in Medieval Canon Law and Liturgy Presented to Roger E. Reynolds*, ed. Richard F. Gyug and Kathleen Grace Cushing (CFC; Aldershot 2004) 241–254.

90. Meens, *Penance* 177–179 (with illustration).

91. Reynolds, 'Rites' 215–221.

92. Wojtowytsch, 'Kanones'.

93. Reynolds, 'Further Evidence' 124.

94. The extant manuscript of the *Toletana* is from the mid-eleventh century: Douglas Adamson and Roger E. Reynolds, 'Introduction', *Collectio Toletana: A Canon Law Derivative of the South-Italian Collection in Five Books: An Implicit Edition with Introductory Study*, ed. iidem (PIMS Studies and Texts 159; Toronto 2008) 1–13, here at 11.

95. Fournier, 'Recueils canoniques italiens' 96; Koal, *Studien* 73 ('Datierung vor 1022 wahrscheinlich'); Fowler-Magerl, *Clavis* 82 ('shortly after 1014'); see next note.

96. Mordek, *Kirchenrecht und Reform* 100; Kölzer, 'Prolegomena' 50; Reynolds, 'Further Evidence'

holds, the collection in 1019 (when Theobald listed the *Liber canonum* in his *Commemoratorium*) was known in this priory of Montecassino in Abbruzzo.

The place of origin is equally difficult to determine with precision. It is generally agreed that the collection was compiled in Italy south of Rome.[97] All extant manuscripts come from southern Italy, and both the formal sources of *5L* and the mass of collections drawing on it are from these areas as well. The fact that one copy of *5L* and many *5L*-derivative collections are written in the Beneventan script (an unusual feature for canon law collections[98]) points to the old Duchy of Benevent and the neighbouring regions where this script was used.[99] On this basis, a number of south-Italian monasteries have been suggested as possible places of origin. Fornasari speculated that *5L* could come from Farfa, where he thought the Vatican copy of *5L* was written.[100] Koal suggested a south-Italian imperial monastery as a possible place of origin.[101] If *5L* was identical to the collection copied by Theobald of Montecassino before 1019 (as has been suggested, see above), this could imply a compilation at San Liberatore a Maiella.[102] At Montecassino itself, home of one of the three extant *5L* manuscripts, the same Theobald slightly later had a codex originally coming from Reims copied which is similar to a source used by the *5L* compilers.[103] Reynolds further pointed out that *5L* contained texts related to Henry II and to incidents at Montecassino at his time.[104]

3.3.3 Sources

The compilers of *5L* (it is hard to imagine that a single person achieved this work) drew on a wide range of sources, including the Bible, patristic authors, penitential books, monastic literature (Benedict of Nursia and

---

123 n. 14. The reference to Theobald and the *Liber canonicus* both in the chronicle of Leo Marsicanus (ed. Hoffmann, MGH SS 34.266) and the *Commematorium* of Theobald was first quoted by Mordek, *Kirchenrecht und Reform* 100.

97. Fournier, 'Recueils canoniques italiens' 188 (somewhere between Montecassino, Benevento, and Naples); Fornasari, 'Introduzione' xiii (Farfa); Reynolds, 'Five Books [1990]' 281–286 ('south of Rome to Chieti to Monte Cassino'); Koal, *Studien* 84 (south-Italian *Reichskloster*).

98. Reynolds, 'Canonistica Beneventiana' esp. 25. See now Virginia Brown, *Beneventan Discoveries: Collected Manuscript Catalogues, 1978–2008*, ed. Roger E. Reynolds (Toronto 2012).

99. Reynolds, 'Five Books [1990]' 291–292.

100. Mario Fornasari, 'Un manoscritto e una collezione canonica del secolo XI proveniente da Farfa' *Benedictina* 10 (1956) 199–210. On the use of *5L* at Farfa (outside the *Farfensis*), see Oliver Münsch, 'Die Orthodoxa defensio imperialis. Ein Beitrag zur Publizistik des Investiturstreits', *Quellen, Kritik, Interpretation. Festgabe zum 60. Geburtstag von Hubert Mordek*, ed. Thomas Martin Buck and Julia Herrmann (Frankfurt 1999) 135–154.

101. Koal, *Studien* 84.

102. Reynolds, 'Further Evidence' 123.

103. Zechiel-Eckes, *Concordia* 1.276.

104. Reynolds, *Collectio Casinensis* 4–5.

Smaragdus of Saint-Mihiel), hagiography, decretals, synodal canons, Roman law, plus Langobard, Frankish, and Ottonian royal legislation. Compared to non-monastic canon law collections, the use of biblical material, penitential books, and of course the Rule of Benedict appear as distinctively 'monastic'. The impact of secular legislation is relatively small compared to the mass of materials, but it is remarkable for an Italian collection that the compiler chose to integrated not only Roman law (nineteen canons) and some Langobard legislation (nine canons) but also 67 canons from Frankish capitularies.[105] With the sole exception of the five Henry II canons mentioned above, much of the *5L* material is ancient. Many materials found in *5L* are rare, but some of them became very widely distributed apparently because of the dissemination of *5L*. This is true, for example, for a handful of canons on baptism (including the question whether one might use wine instead of water) taken from the *Herovalliana* via *9L*.[106]

Among the less conventional materials found in *5L* there are a number of eastern Fathers. The interest in these Fathers certainly has to do with *5L* coming from an area in closer contact with Greek Christians, but interestingly, the Greek Fathers were mainly quoted from Latin collections that from north-western Europe like the *Hibernensis*.[107] Indeed, the latter collection contains much material (patristic or not) that ended up in *5L*: Some five hundred canons, dispersed over all books, ultimately come from the B (or 'beta') version of the *Hibernensis*.[108]

This brings us to the formal sources used by the *5L* compilers. Clearly a wide range of sources was used, but equally clearly, the most important one was the *Collection in Nine Books* as found in Vat. lat. 1349 (= the Vatican *9L*), though not this very manuscript.[109] The Vatican *9L* is a massive work (containing some 2,600 canons) and provided the *5L* compilers with most of their material, and may have informed the division into books too. In addition, the *5L* compilers also used a canon law collection similar to that extant in Vallicelliana, Tomus XVIII, best known as one of only two complete copies of the B version of the *Hibernensis*.[110] Actually, this 'collection'

105. Koal, *Studien* 84.

106. See Mordek, *Kirchenrecht und Reform* 138–139 on these canons and their odd transmission (including the *Caesaraugustana*). The material source is JE 2315 (calendared separately as JK †267 in the second edition of Jaffé's *Regesta pontificum*; it is not clear to me why this was retained in the third edition: J³ †630).

107. Reynolds, 'Influence'.

108. Reynolds, 'Transmission' 28 and 34.

109. Reynolds, 'Five Books [1990]' 280–281; idem, 'Transmission' 28; Koal, *Studien* 81; Adriaan H. Gaastra, 'Penance and the Law: The Penitential Canons of the *Collection in Nine Books*' *Early Medieval Europe* 14 (2006) 85–102, here at 89; idem, *Liturgy* 206–207. For the palaeography, see esp. Reynolds, 'Five Books [1990]' 280 (following Loew for an eleventh-century date).

110. Fowler-Magerl, *Clavis* 46–50; Reynolds, 'Penitentials' 68; Flechner, *Hibernensis* 1.141*–143*.

is not a uniform work; the Vallicelliana manuscript preserves a number of collections together with less reworked materials. Specifically, it contains the *Concordia* of Cresconius, a *Collection in 72 Chapters* (known only from this manuscript), the B version of the *Hibernensis*, a small collection known as *De episcoporum transmigratione*, and a large 'farraginous' collection of 448 items. As Zechiel-Eckes demonstrated for the Cresconius material in *5L*, both the arrangement of the canons and variant readings exclude a direct use of either the extant *9L* or Vallicelliana Tomus XVIII by the *5L* compilers; instead he pointed to similarities to a ninth-century copy of Cresconius' *Concordia*.[111]

In addition to these major sources, a number of other works provided *5L* with smaller number of canons. The Roman law in *5L* mainly comes from the *Epitome*; for other materials, the exact transmission remains obscure, and it is well possible that some of the materials found in *5L* but no other known canon law collection were taken directly from the material sources (e.g. canons taken from the writings of Augustine, Jerome, Isidore of Seville, and Caesarius of Arles).[112]

3.3.4 Monks on Marriage: The *Collection in Five Books* on Marriage, Sexuality, and Incest

The *Collection in Five Books* clearly is a 'monastic collection' and more specifically one that is 'highly penitential in nature', as Reynolds put it.[113] This is not only evident from the large share of penitential canons and the devotion of a whole book to these issues.[114] The compilers' concern with penance is also visible from the two prefaces at the very beginning of the collection that were specifically written for *5L*; they both highlight the importance and the necessity of penance.

The monastic background of the collection and its penitential character may also explain the general concern with sexual conduct that marks *5L*. Especially when compared to its main model (the Vatican *9L*), the devotion of a separate book on marriage and sexuality is striking.[115] Yet

---

111. Zechiel-Eckes, *Concordia* 1.269–277. The ninth-century manuscript is Vat. lat. 1347 from Reims which by the early eleventh century was at Montecassino, where it served as a model for the extant Montecassino, Archivio della Badia, MS 541 (Zechiel-Eckes, *Concordia* 1.276, following Franz Kerff, *Der Quadripartitus. Ein Handbuch der karolingischen Kirchenreform. Überlieferung, Quellen und Rezeption* [Quellen und Forschungen zum Recht im Mittelalter 1; Sigmaringen 1982] 18).

112. See Fowler-Magerl, *Clavis* 84–85.

113. Reynolds, 'Five Books [1990]' 294.

114. On book four of *5L*, see Davide Cito, *Collectio canonum in quinque libris libro IV* (Rome 1989). The edition Cito mentions (ibid. 34) seems not to have been published. The incipit/explicit list for book four (ibid. 59–116) is of limited use.

115. Fowler-Magerl, *Clavis* 84 saw this as indicating 'increasingly positive attitude toward marriage'; but scholars following Payer would perhaps see it as evidence for a repressive morality:

book five is not the only part of the collection that pays special attention to sexuality; book two on the clergy likewise devotes considerable space to the question of continence, as already reflected in the title:[116]

> On the prelates of the Church and the time of the synods, on the life and chastity of the clergy, above all the prohibition the life with women, and on women caught in fornication with clerics.

There is indeed an unusual stress in *5L* on clerical celibacy and its enforcement, which sometimes has been linked to the reforms of the later eleventh century.[117] However, it is also clear that clerical marriage in southern Italy continued well into the later Middle Ages. Of course it is possible that the *5L* compiler gathered his canons 'on the chastity of the clergy' because he was opposed to clerical marriage; but the unusual concern for sexuality and chastity in *5L* can much more elegantly be explained by the monastic background of the collection.[118]

While *5L* devotes special attention to the sexual activities of priests and monks, it also deals with marriage and sexuality of laypeople, including a short but interesting section on marriage prohibitons found at the very end of the collection. This part of the collection deals with marriage prohibitions on ground of serfdom, consanguinity, and spiritual kinship. The second of these three subsections deserves special attention, as it presents the marriage prohibitions between blood-relatives as extending very far. The same has been observed for Burchard's *Liber decretorum*, compiled at about the same time in Worms, and for this reason *5L* will be analysed here in comparison with this collection.[119]

The marriage prohibitions on ground of consanguinity are found in a short section containing only 32 canons (*5L* 5.209–240), preceded by two kinship diagrams adopted from Isidore's *Etymologies*.[120] Short as it may be,

---

Pierre J. Payer, *Sex and the Penitentials: The Development of a Sexual Code, 550–1150* (Toronto, Buffalo, and London 1984).

116. 'De primatibus ecclesie et de concilii temporibus, de vita et castitate clericorum, precipue de prohibitione consortii cum mulieribus et de feminis que in fornicatione cum clericis reprehense sunt.'

117. Johannes Laudage, *Priesterbild und Reformpapsttum im 11. Jahrhundert* (Beihefte zum Archiv für Kulturgeschichte 22; Cologne and Vienna 1984), here at 78–83; see already *Histoire* 1.429 (*5L* compiler as 'partisan de la Réforme'). Both have also stressed that Henry II jointly with the pope held synods concerned with clerical celibacy, most famously that of Pavia in 1022; for the latter, see Fournier, 'Recueils canoniques italiens' 186 and Laudage, *Priesterbild* 85–86.

118. See the classical study Jean Leclercq, *Monks on Marriage: A Twelfth-Century-View* (New York 1982). As for the 'strong monastic flavour' of the rules on sexual conduct as found in the penitentials (and hence *5L*), see Meens, *Penance* 46. See Gaastra, *Liturgy* 139 on the importance of sex and marriage in the penitentials from southern and central Italy in this period.

119. See the last chapter, and Ubl, *Inzestverbot*.

120. Vat. lat. 1339, fols. 303r–309v. For a facsimile of the second diagram (Vat. lat. 1339, fol. 303v), see Schadt, *Darstellungen* no. 34.

the section was evidently composed with great care; many texts are not found elsewhere, some are manipulated, and the whole arrangement of the texts is different from the known formal sources of *5L*. Concerning the content, however, there are important parallels to the *Liber decretorum*. Like Burchard, *5L* from the beginning presents canons on the seventh degree of kinship (*5L* 5.209, 211.1, 215). Isidore's account of kinship is manipulated as to extend to the seventh degree of kinship.[121] An important manipulation in favour of the seventh degree is a text taken from Gregory the Great (*5L* 5.215). Famously, Gregory in his *Libellus* had advised not to marry relatives in the third or fourth degree, even if such marriages were licit.[122] Yet according to *5L*, Gregory in fact had forbidden all marriages in the seventh degree of kinship.[123] *5L* is not the only collection to present a stricter version than the original, but goes further than any other known collection.[124]

Like Burchard of Worms, the *5L* compiler took definitions of kinship that originally applied to the law of inheritance and presented them as if these authorities dealt with the prohibition of kin marriage. The *Edictus Rothari* (from 643) in the passage quoted in *5L* indeed defined kinship as extending to the seventh degree (called *geniculum* here), but in the original context it is clear that this should apply to inheritance, not marriage prohibitions.[125] The same is true for the definition of kinship terms taken from Isidore's *Etymologies* and the relevant diagrams.[126] All in all, *5L* takes considerable effort to stress that the prohibitions to marry relatives extend to the seventh degree of kinship.

What is less clear is the way these degrees were to be counted according to *5L*. This, however, is crucial to understand *5L*, as there were two different computations.[127] The so-called Roman computation, adopted from

121. Schadt, *Darstellungen* 101; Gaastra, *Liturgy* 177.

122. Gregory I, JE 1843 (ed. Ewald and Hartmann, MGH Epp. 2.335): 'Unde necesse est, ut iam tertia vel quarta generatio fidelium licenter sibi iungi debeat; nam secunda quam praediximus a se omni modo debet abstinere.' On the *Libellus*, see Ubl, *Inzestverbot* 221–233 and Elliot, 'Boniface'; for further references, see Chapter 2.5.5.

123. Vat. lat. 1339, fols. 306v–307r as quoted by Gaastra, *Liturgy* 177 n. 6: 'Unde necesse est, ut iam tertia, quarta, quinta, sexta, septima generatio fidelium licenter sibi iungi nequaquam debeat. Graue est enim facinus, qui hec fecerit. Preterea cum cognata quoque, vel propinqua uxoris sue, vel propinquo viri sui misceri prohibitum est funditus, quia per coniunctionem priorum caro fratris fuerant facti.'

124. On the reception of JE 1843 in various collections, see Chapter 2.5.5.

125. *5L* 5.209 = *Edictus Rothari* c. 153 (ed. Bluhme, MGH LL 4.35), clearly dealing with inheritance, not marriage. The incest provisions found here in the *Edictus* do not apply to the seventh degree, see c. 185 (ed. Bluhme, MGH LL 4.44) as discussed by Ubl, *Inzestverbot* 209–211.

126. Isidore, *Etym.* 9.6.29 and the diagrams found there deal with the (Roman) law of inheritance; *5L* presents these authorities as relevant for marriage both implicitly (by inserting these diagrams in an incest section) and explicitly (in *5L* 5.211).

127. See Ubl, *Inzestverbot* ch. 1, also on the so-called 'Germanic' computation which according

ancient Roman law, counted the number of generations from ego to the common ancestor and down again to the relative in question; hence, for example, uncle and niece were related in the third degree and first cousins in the fourth. The so-called canonical computation counted only the number of generations to the common ancestor. Hence, uncle and niece were related in the second degree (as one of her grandparents was the common ancestor), and so were first cousins (having one grandparent in common). Yet to make things more complicated, there was some disagreement where to start with counting the degrees.

Which computation was used in *5L*? Both Gelting and Gaastra asserted that *5L* used the canonical computation,[128] but the evidence is not conclusive. Three passages of *5L* deserve special attention in this context. First, the kinship diagrams at the beginning of the incest section of *5L* taken from Isidore's *Etymologies*.[129] Second, the long canon (adopted from the Vatican *9L*) which explains these kinship diagrams and pretends to paraphrase Isidore's *Etymologies*.[130] Finally, Gelting brought to attention a canon containing the penance for killing one's blood-relatives.[131]

Both the diagrams and the canon that seeks to explain it (*5L* 5.211) present materials taken from Isidore's *Etymologies* in a partly manipulated version; the crucial change, however, is about context, as both Isidore's diagrams and his discussion of kinship terms was part of his discussion of Roman inheritance law and not marriage prohibitions.[132] In several cases, *5L* clearly goes beyond what Isidore had stated. Among other things, *5L* claims that one could conclude from Isidore's account that marriage was prohibited in the seventh degree of kinship, which is clearly not what Isidore had written.[133] Another oddity is that the list of direct descendants extends to the eighth generation, that is, ego's great-great-great-great-great-great-

---

to his findings should not be seen as a third computation but only a misguided theoretical construct of nineteenth-century scholarship.

128. Michael H. Gelting, 'Marriage, Peace and the Canonical Incest Prohibitions: Making Sense of an Absurdity?', *Nordic Perspectives on Medieval Canon Law*, ed. Mia Korpiola (Publications of Matthias Calonius Society 2; Saarijärvi 1999) 93–124, here at 103–106; Gaastra, *Liturgy* 177. Ubl, *Inzestverbot* does not consider *5L*.

129. Vat. lat. 1339, fol. 303r and 303v; for a facsimile of the latter, see Schadt, *Darstellungen* no. 34.

130. *5L* 5.211. My thanks are to Dr Adriaan Gaastra for pointing out the parallel to *9L* 7.21.2 (Vat. lat. 1349, fol. 144r–v) and generously making his transcriptions available to me.

131. Gelting, 'Marriage' 102–103. See below for discussion.

132. See Isidore, *Etym.* 9.5 and 6 (ed. Lindsay).

133. *5L* 5.211: 'Idcirco per hec dicta huius sanctissimi viri aperte datur intellegi, ut usque ad septimum gradum generationis nullatenus quilibet matrimonio iungi debet.' The Isidore passage in question is *Etym.* 9.6.29 (ed. Lindsay): 'Haec consanguinitas dum se paulatim propaginum ordinibus dirimens usque ad ultimum gradum subtraxerit, et propinquitas esse desierit, eam rursus lex matrimonii vinculo repetit, et quodam modo revocat fugientem.'

grandchildren.[134] In Isidore's *Etymologies*, which *5L* asserts to follow, the list had concluded with one's great-great-great-grandchildren.[135]

Yet neither the diagrams nor the 'explanatory' canon provide unambiguous evidence for the way the degrees of kinship were to be counted. For example, uncles and aunts are counted as the second degree, and great-uncles and great-aunts as the third; this would correspond to canonical rather than Roman computation. Yet first cousins once removed (*patrui nepotes*) are counted as related to ego in the fifth degree, and first cousins twice removed ('consubrini <vel> consubrine nepotes') as the sixth degree; this corresponds to Roman computation rather than the canonical. Second cousins (*sobrini* and *sobrinae*) are counted as related to ego in the fourth degree; this corresponds neither to Roman computation (sixth degree) nor the canonical (third degree). The list also contains some manifest errors; for example, it seems to assert that paternal great-great-uncles and great-great-aunts, paternal uncles, and maternal great-aunts (*propatruus, proamita magna, avunculus* and *materta magna* in the text) are all related to ego in the same degree, which does not make sense whatever computation is applied here.

Given that this canon is adopted from the Vatican *9L* and contains many inconsistencies, one has to be very cautious to take it as evidence which computation the *5L* compiler actually followed. By and large, *5L* in this canon seems to adopt (as Isidore had done) the Roman computation, but for closer kin sometimes seems to follow a computation closer to the canonical one; thereby, the marriage prohibitions in *5L* extend further than in collections that consistently use the Roman computation.

In the light of this, another *5L* canon on penances for killing one's blood-relatives may be taken into account here.[136] The canon has no known model and may thus reveal the way the *5L* compiler thought about kinship. It provides a long list of penitential tariffs for the killing of blood-

---

134. *5L* 5.211: 'trinepotis nepos, trinepotis neptis: septimus'. Apparently, 'trinepos' was dropped by accident, as the list jumps from 'adnepos' (as fifth degree) to 'trinepois fili, trineptis filie' (as sixth degree); thus, the 'trinepotis nepos' is counted as the seventh generation rather than the eighth.

135. Isidore, *Etym.* 9.6.23 (*trinepos/trineptis*). Isidore does not count the degrees of kinship in this passage.

136. *5L* 4.115–116 (FU04.115.04 in the *Clavis canonum* database) as discussed by Gelting, 'Marriage' 102–103. The canon was mentioned by Fournier, 'Recueils canoniques italiens' 297 and printed by Augustin Theiner, *Disquisitiones criticae in praecipuas canonum et decretalium collectiones: seu syllogus Gallandianae dissertationum de vetustis canonum collectionibus continuatio* (Rome 1836), here at 299 (from Vat. lat. 1339). Cito, *Collectio canonum* 76 counts this canon as 4.139.1; he prints incipit and explicit but gives no further information on the text or its sources. Schmitz, *Bussbücher* 2.816–817 edited the same provisions from the later *Poenitentiale Mediolanense* and indicated parallels to Anselm 11.47. While I was not able verify the latter, Anselm A' seem to have a version of the canon (AC07.175 in *Clavis*).

relatives, from parents to relatives in the seventh degree. According to the first part of this canon, the penance for killing one's parents is seven years of exile and lifelong penance; for someone who kills any of his or her children or siblings, five years of exile and 15 years of penance; twelve years of penance are given for killing 'one's grandfather, grandmother, male or female grandchild, paternal or maternal uncle, paternal or maternal aunt, the son or daughter or one's brother or sister, or one's male or female first cousin'.[137] It is highly significant that the latter group of relatives is treated together here, as they are all relatives in the second degree of kinship in canonical computation. The impression that the canonical computation was used is further confirmed by second part of the canon, listing provisions on killing more distant relatives. They are called 'relatives in the third to the seventh degree', and decreasing penitential tariffs are given for each degree.[138] So although no mention of 'degrees' is made in the first part of the canon, it is clear that the close relatives (up to and including first cousins) mentioned here are understood as being relatives in the first and second degrees of kinship. Indeed the relatives mentioned in the first part of the canon are exactly those counted as related in the first and second degree of kinship in canonical computation. If one assumed that Roman computation was used, the whole list would make no sense. For example, grandfather and granddaughter according to the Roman computation are related in the second degree, aunt and nephew in the third degree, and first cousins in the fourth degree; in *5L*, they all seem to be counted as related to each other in the second degree, and they certainly

137. *5L* 4.115 (as quoted and emended by Gelting, 'Marriage' 104 n. 50): 'Qui voluntarie genitorem suum aut genitricem occiderit, extra patriam septem annos exul fiat. Tunc demum usque ad mortem cum fletu et luctu peniteat. Si autem nolens hoc <accidit>, decem annos judicio sacerdotis peniteat. Qui voluntarie filium suum aut filiam, vel germanum aut germanam suam occiderit, quinque annos extra metas exul fiat ipsius terrae. Deinceps XV. annos inermis cum fletu et luctu peniteat. Si vera nolens, septem annos peniteat. Qui voluntarie avum suum aut avam suam, seu nepotem aut neptem suam, vel patruum aut avunculum, seu amittam sive materteram suam, vel filium aut filiam germani sui aut germanae, seu consobrinum suum sive consobrinam suam occiderit, duodecim annos inermis cum luctu et fletu peniteat. Si enim nolens, sex annos peniteat.' Note that first cousins are mentioned twice; however, this may well be explained with Latin kinship terminology as explained by Isidore, *Etym.* 9.6.13–14 (ed. Lindsay): 'Fratres patrueles dicti, eo quod patres eorum germani fratres inter se fuerunt. Consobrini vero vocati, qui aut ex sorore et fratre, aut ex duabus sororibus sunt nati, quasi consororini.' Adriaan Gaastra (private communication, 8 October 2020) suggested that these canons were coined by the *5L* compiler, working with *9L* material ultimately coming from the *Poenitentiale Ps.-Gregorii*, ed. Franz Kerff, 'Das Paenitentiale Pseudo-Gregorii III. Eine kritische Edition', *Aus Archiven und Bibliotheken. Festschrift für Raymund Kottje zum 65. Geburtstag*, ed. Hubert Mordek (Freiburger Beiträge zur mittelalterlichen Geschichte. Studien und Texte 3; Frankfurt 1992) 161–188.

138. *5L* 4.115 (ed. Gelting, 'Marriage' 104 n. 50): 'Qui voluntarie de propria cognatione sua occiderit, id est a tertia usque septimam. Si tertia fuerit duodecim annos inermis peniteat. Si quarta XI. Si quinta decem. Si sexta IX. Si septima VIII.'

are all treated the same in the sense that the same penance is given for killing one's grandfather, aunt or cousin. The assumption that the canonical computation was used does not lead to similar inconsistencies. Therefore, I have no doubt that *5L* in book four is indeed referring to the seventh degree of kinship in canonical computation.

It is in my opinion legitimate to conclude that *5L*, while retaining older materials and not achieving perfect consistency, all in all is clear about the seventh degree as the limit of kinship, and at least in the more original parts of the collection adopts the canonical computation. So unless the collection is considerably later than commonly thought, *5L* is an important witness that the canonical computation was known in Italy well before the time of Peter Damian.[139] It is also clear that *5L*, while expressing a doctrine very similar to Burchard, was independent of this German collection. In this context, it is significant that *5L* may contain marriage prohibitions very similar to those favoured by Burchard of Worms, but argues its case very differently. Not only is there no sign that Burchard was used; *5L* also draws prominently on secular legislation and penitential canons to support its position on incest prohibitions while Burchard, as far as he did use such materials, notoriously passed such authorities as synodal canons. In *5L*, the opposite is true. Not only does *5L* contain large shares of secular legislation (Justinian, Lombard law, and Frankish capitularies) and very many penitential canons; *5L* also often attributes these materials correctly, uses them as key authorities, and in several cases places them very prominently. For example, the very first canon of the incest section (*5L* 5.209) is from the *Edictus Rothari*. This suggests that *5L*, like Burchard, supported an extreme extension of marriage prohibitions, but did so independently of Burchard and indeed by using different arguments and sources. The question remains whether Burchard and *5L* may be linked in another way, that is, as canonical collections in the service of Henry II. Karl Ubl has forcefully argued that Burchard was the 'handbook of Emperor Henry II's anti-incest campaign', and the inclusion of the 1014 canons in *5L* and the very specific use of royal titles in the collection has led Valeska Koal to the conclusion that the *5L* compiler was an active supporter of Henry's Italian

---

139. Ubl, *Inzestverbot* 27 asserts that the canonical computation became common in Italy only with the reform papacy: 'Erst im frühen 11. Jahrhundert lassen sich wieder sichere Aussagen treffen. In dieser Zeit zählten alle Quellen innerhalb Deutschlands kanonisch oder in der von Burchard geprägten Abwandlung der kanonischen Zählung. In Italien und Frankreich setzte sich dagegen die kanonische Zählung erst durch die Anstrengungen des Reformpapsttums durch.' See also ibid. 470: 'Die Zählung in Generationen war in Italien eine erst durch Burchard und Petrus Damiani eingeführte Neuerung und traf deshalb auf lang anhaltenden Widerstand.'

politics.[140] The argument is ultimately speculative, but it is an interesting hypotheses that the unusual character of *5L*—one of the most influential canonical collections in Italy—may be explained by its role in Henry II's anti-incest politics.

3.3.5 The Reception of *5L*

5L Derivatives

As indicated above, *5L* was used by many later compilers to produce new collections in the eleventh and twelfth centuries. Some of them are best described as *5L* derivative collections, containing a selection of *5L* canons and little other material; others draw so extensively on other sources, and rearrange the material so thoroughly that the use of *5L* can only be established by careful analysis. The former collections are more common, and as many of these derivative collection are relatively short and had only a very limited circulation, they have attracted little scholarly interest. Only recently, some of these collections have been edited, namely the *Casinensis* (by Reynolds) and the *Toletana* (by Adamson and Reynolds). Reynolds also published an implicit edition of the short version found in Vallicelliana, Tomus XXI,[141] and edited the *capitulationes* of the *Collectio Angelica*, a collection mainly based on *5L*.[142]

One of the most common sources of these *5L* derivative collections is *74T*, another monastic collection.[143] Vice versa, copies of *74T* often come with excerpts from *5L*.[144] A rather famous manuscript of *74T*, the Montecassino copy Gilchrist used as his *Leithandschrift*, contains an appendix drawing on *5L*.[145] The other source commonly used to enhance *5L* derivatives was Burchard, and more specifically the penitential book found in this major collection.[146] These three collections—Burchard, *5L*, and *74T*—are among the very few canon law collections copied in the Beneventan script.[147]

---

140. See Ubl, *Inzestverbot* esp. 435 and Koal, *Studien* esp. 136, respectively.

141. Reynolds, 'Five Books [1992]'.

142. Reynolds, 'Angelica'.

143. Reynolds, 'Five Books [1992]' 77; idem, 'Angelica' 8; idem, *Collectio Casinensis* 9. The *Toletana*, in contrast, draws on Burchard, mainly for penitential texts: Adamson and Reynolds, 'Introduction' 4.

144. Reynolds, *Collectio Casinensis* 6–7.

145. Reynolds, 'Five Books [2001]', with an 'implicit edition' of this appendix.

146. Reynolds, *Collectio Casinensis* 9; Adamson and Reynolds, 'Introduction' 4.

147. Reynolds, 'Canonistica Beneventiana' 25, pointing out that only 25 of some 1,600 manuscripts in Beneventan script contain canon law, and none of them contained 'classical' canon law, even if the script as such was used well into the sixteenth century. See also Reynolds, *Collectio Casinensis* 19–29 and idem, 'Penitentials' esp. 83–84 for Beneventan manuscripts containing canon law and/or penitential canons.

The combination of *5L* with the pro-monastic *74T* and/or Burchard's penitential book suggests that these *5L* derivatives come from a monastic milieu, and the Beneventan script is known as 'chiefly monastic', too.[148] This impression is confirmed by other evidence. First of all, the manuscripts of *5L* derivative collections were produced and kept above all in monastic libraries. In several cases, the canon law material ultimately going back to *5L* is combined with privileges and other materials on monastic liberty. For example, the Montecassino copy of *74T* contains an appendix drawing on *5L* and a second one on the *libertas* of Montecassino.[149] Thus, *5L*, *74T*, and materials on the privileges of individual houses were transmitted together, and apparently seen as having something in common. The *Collectio Casinensis* in Montecassino MS 216 (to be discussed below in the context of *74T*) is a similar case; it was produced for Montecassino or one of its daughter houses drawing on Burchard, *5L*, and *74T*; among other things it contains a pro-monastic forgery concerned with monastic property.[150]

All these collections draw on similar sets of sources, often focussing on penance and monastic property, whether the latter issue was dealt with by canons taken from *74T*, by pro-monastic forgeries circulating outside major collections,[151] or materials pertaining to individual houses. This strongly suggests that *5L* and its derivatives were not only produced and kept but indeed used in a monastic context. While *5L* like any canon collection could also be read in different ways, monastic communities found this collection more attractive than other works of canon law, and copied it together with materials that supported the rights of their own house or indeed the monastic order as such.

This argument is strengthened by the sheer number of *5L*-derivative collections. However, these collections are not only evidence for the wide reception of *5L* and the way this collection was read in the eleventh and twelfth centuries; they are also collections in their own right. Even if it is impossible to study them at a detailed level here, a few remarks are necessary to understand this sub-group of monastic canon law collections. They are, on the whole, minor collections both in the sense of being relatively

---

148. Reynolds, 'Canonistica Beneventiana' 25.

149. Reynolds, 'Five Books [2001]' 355–356 (with incipit/explicit list of the appendix; it is also found in the Florence copy of *74T*).

150. On the collection, see below. The collection may well be described as a *5L* derivative, but to understand the collection it is necessary to compare it to *74T*; for this reason, I will present the collection found in Montecassino 216 only after the discussion of *74T*.

151. John T. Gilchrist, 'The Influence of the Monastic Forgeries Attributed to Pope Gregory I (JE †1951) and Boniface IV (JE †1996)', *Fälschungen im Mittelalter* (6 vols. MGH Schriften 33; Hanover 1988) 2.263–287.

small and having only a limited reception. Yet with monastic canon law collections as with so many other canonical collections one must be careful not to study only the major works which are found in very many manuscripts and/or stand out as innovative collections that shaped legal history by introducing new texts or new ideas into canon law. Most collections were much smaller, they are normally extant in one manuscript only, and they did not directly add to the corpus of legal material used by Gratian. While these collections are modest compared to works like *5L* and *74T*, it is also true that in many places canon law was known from such minor collections, and the growing canon law activity that in the end led to the emergence of law schools and universities began with the compilation of such minor works. Some of these 'minor collections' from monastic milieux will be studied below as 'derivative' collections of *5L*, Burchard, and *74T*; yet one will be studied here as it has especially close relations to *5L* without being a 'derivative' of it.

The Dossier in Montecassino MS 372: The Case Against
'Holy Simplicity'

The dossier in question is found in the miscellaneous manuscript Montecassino, Archivio della Badia, MS 372.[152] Like many other monastic collections, it has long been overlooked by canon law historians; significantly, the manuscript long was labelled 'penitential' rather than 'legal' in content.[153] The codex indeed contains various liturgical and penitential material, but also conciliar canons, papal letters, excerpts from the writing of Saint Jerome, and an almost complete *Vetus Gallica*.[154] In the context of the present chapter, however, mainly the canonical dossier found on pages 149 to 160 is relevant. It is uniquely known from this manuscript, and it may well have been compiled when the latter was written early in the eleventh century.[155] The manuscript comes from San Nicola della Cicogna, a priory of Montecassino, and may have been written there or in nearby Montecassino. The dossier draws on the *Hibernensis* (version B) and the Vatican

---

152. The following paragraph is based on Reynolds, 'Further Evidence' both for his analysis and the edition (ibid. 128–135) and Gaastra, *Liturgy* ch. 1; see also Luigi Tosti, *Storia della Badia di Montecassino divisa in libri nove, ed illustrata di note e documenti* (3 vols. Naples 1842–43), here at 1.295–303 (description) and Mordek, *Kirchenrecht und Reform* esp. 100 (analysis).

153. Reynolds, 'Further Evidence' 120.

154. Mordek, *Kirchenrecht und Reform* 100; Reynolds, 'Further Evidence' 126; Gaastra, *Liturgy* 19. Oddly, the section *De monachis* is missing from the *Vetus Gallica* in Montecassino, Archivio della Badia, MS 372; Reynolds suggested that the dossier on pages 149 to 160 compensated this lacuna. The manuscript seems to contain an otherwise unknown forgery (Leo [I?], JK –; J³ –), perhaps even as an autograph (Gaastra, *Liturgy* 22 n. 6); the odd text was printed by Tosti, *Storia* 1.296–297.

155. For the date, see Reynolds, 'Further Evidence' 122 and Gaastra, *Liturgy* 19–20.

Collection in Nine Books. Both the sources used and the selection criteria are similar to, but not identical with that of the *5L* compiler; the rubrics to the Pseudo-Clementine excerpts resemble those of *5L*, too. According to Reynolds, the Montecassino 372 collection and *5L* drew on a common source.[156] In addition, the compiler used a version of the False Decretals very similar to an extant Montecassino manuscript.[157]

The dossier contains 26 chapters, each consisting of one or, rarely, several proof texts. The first four chapters, drawn from the writings of Saint Jerome, Saint Augustine, and the Bible, deal with the question of 'holy simplicity'. Another four chapters provide a definition of the monastic order and the functions of an abbot. The remaining canons all deal with liturgical questions, mainly drawing on the second Pseudo-Clementine letter; this part of the collection begins with the Eucharist, contains a subsection on baptism (cc. 21–26), and at the end treats sacraments in general.

In our context, the most interesting part of the dossier is the opening section (cc. 1–4) containing a total of seven authorities on 'holy simplicity', a well-known topos going back to Jerome.[158] Conventionally, Jerome is quoted on 'holy simplicity' or indeed 'rusticity' to make the point that for a Christian, and certainly for a monk, learning was not the most important thing in life. Famously, Jerome had juxtaposed 'just simplicity' to 'learned malice' and 'holy rusticity' to 'sinful eloquence'.[159] In the Middle Ages, this often provided the basis for attacks on 'over-scholarly' monks, and specifically 'lawyer-monks', not least by other monks.[160] However, just like monastic theology, monastic canon law was based on the assumption that under certain conditions, 'holy simplicity is good, but holy knowledge is better'.[161] Indeed, the compiler of the Montecassino collection (who must have known Jerome's writing very well) was able to quote Jerome in this sense. The excerpts he chose to place at the very beginning of his work all agree that 'simplicity', even if 'holy', could be positively

156. Reynolds, 'Further Evidence' 125–127.

157. Reynolds, 'Further Evidence' 127.

158. Montecassino, Archivio della Badia, MS 372, p. 149 (ed. Reynolds, 'Further Evidence' 128–129). As already Reynold's apparatus makes clear, the section draws on *Hibernensis* 37.7–9 (ed. Flechner 1.281–282).

159. See Jerome's letters on the translation of the Bible and its 'simple' style for context, e.g. letters 53, 57, and 62 (all edited by Hilberg in CSEL 54).

160. For a monastic attack on 'lawyer-monks', see James A. Brundage, *The Medieval Origins of the Legal Profession: Canonists, Civilians, and Courts* (Chicago 2008), esp. 180. For monks (not) studying Roman law, see Robert Somerville, 'Pope Innocent II and the Study of Roman Law' *Revue des études islamiques* 44 (1976) 105–114.

161. See Jean Leclercq, *The Love of Learning of the Desire of God: A Study of Monastic Culture* (New York 1982), here at 205 on monastic theology; the quote is Leclercq's translation of Rupert of Deutz commenting on Ecclesiastes (PL 168.1218): 'Nam quamvis sanctis rusticitas bona sit, melior est tamen sancta scientia.'

dangerous. The rubricated title given to these excerpts is quite explicit in this respect: 'On learned justice being better than holy simplicity'.[162]

Only after having addressed this issue, and solved it quite cleverly by quoting Jerome in favour of 'learned justice', the compiler continued with more conventional material: what makes a monk, the sins monks could commit, the six different kinds of monks, and so on.[163] While this material may be proper to a monastic canon law collection, the opening section is perhaps even more important for its monastic character. In my interpretation, this should be read as a response to widely-spread opposition to the monastic study of canon law, and thus indicative of the Montecassino 372 collection not only being from a monastic perspective but, crucially, for a monastic audience. After all, who else but a monastic reader would need to be told that even Jerome, somehow, agreed with monks compiling and using canon law collections?

3.4 The *Collection in 74 Titles*: The 'Manual of Monastic Reform'

The *Diversorum patrum sententiae*, as the medieval title was, more commonly known as the *Collection in 74 Titles* (= *74T*), is an unusual collection in many respects. The number of extant manuscripts (some 25), the various revisions visible in these manuscripts, and the frequent quotations from *74T* in canon law and other works—mainly polemic literature—already show that the collection enjoyed considerable success in the late eleventh and early twelfth centuries. Found in relatively many manuscripts and available in print from early on, *74T* has also attracted more scholarly attention than most pre-Gratian collections. It is one of very few pre-Gratian collections to have been critically edited, and for decades was the only pre-Gratian collection to have been translated into any modern language.[164] Ever since Paul Fournier in 1894 in a seminal article called it the 'first manual' of (papal) reform, *74T* has been at the centre of the scholarly debates on 'law and reform'.[165] No other pre-Gratian collection has so frequently been studied with respect to its partisan character, and

---

162. Montecassino, Archivio della Badia, MS 372, p. 149 (ed. Reynolds, 'Further Evidence' 128): 'De eo quod melior est docta iustitia quam sancta rusticitas.' See *Hibernensis* 37.11 (ed. Flechner 1.283) which has the same rubric.

163. This section is similar to, and draws on, *Hibernensis* 38.

164. *Diuersorum patrum sententie siue Collectio in LXXIV titulos digesta*, ed. John T. Gilchrist (MIC Corpus collectionum 1; Vatican City 1973); *The Collection in Seventy-Four Titles: A Canon Law Manual of the Gregorian Reform*, tr. idem (Mediaeval Sources in Translation 22; Toronto 1980).

165. Paul Fournier, 'Le premier manuel canonique de la réforme du XIe siècle' *Mélanges d'archéologie et d'histoire de l'École française de Rome* 14 (1894) 147–223 and 285–290.

for no collection so utterly different interpretations have been offered.[166] It
was thought to have been issued by Gregory VII by some, and described
as anti-Gregorian by others, and claimed as 'pro-episcopal' as well as
anti-episcopal. Authorship, date, and place of origin were likewise subject
to very divergent interpretations.

The complicated historiography on *74T* need not to be studied here,
but it certainly is a warning against any attempt to characterize *74T* by a
simple label. Even if there is a growing consensus that *74T* is a monastic
collection,[167] many aspects of the collection were and often still are under
dispute; therefore, I will argue in greater detail than for other collections
what I think to be the most plausible model as to the origin, content, and
reception of this important collection.

3.4.1 Structure, Content, and Sources

Compared to other collections, *74T* is a short to mid-size collection, covering some fifty folios in many of the extant manuscripts; it contains 315
canons and takes its modern name from the seventy-four titles (*tituli*) of
very different length it is divided into. These titles, each with an individual

166. Most accounts of *74T* in the older literature follow Fournier's interpretation which was
canonised in *Histoire* 2.14–20. John Gilchrist, who edited and translated the collection, articulated
a much more nuanced view, and changed his mind several times concerning the main character
of *74T*; see his 'Canon Law Aspects of the Eleventh-Century Gregorian Reform Programme' JEH
13 (1962) 21–38, esp. 22–30; idem, 'Prolegomena', *Diuersorum patrum sententie siue Collectio in LXX-
IV titulos digesta*, ed. idem (MIC Corpus collectionum 1; Vatican City 1973) xvii–cxxv, esp. at xxi;
idem, 'Introduction', *Canon Law in the Age of Reform, 11th–12th Centuries* (CSS 406; Aldershot 1993)
xi–xix, here at xiv. For the abundant literature, see Kéry 204–210 and Fowler-Magerl, *Clavis* 110–119.

167. Already Lemarignier, 'Exemption monastique' argued that *74T* showed the Gregorians' concern for monastic reform, a claim he repeated e.g. in 'Les institutions ecclésiastiques en
France de la fin du Xe au milieu du XIIe siècle', *Histoire des institutions françaises au Moyen Âge*,
ed. Jean-François Lemarignier et al. (3 vols. Histoire du droit et des institutions de l'Eglise en
Occident 3; Paris 1962) 1–139, here at 115. Ovidio Capitani, *Immunità vescovili ed ecclesiologia in età
"pregregoriana" e "gregoriana": l'avvio alla "restaurazione"* (Biblioteca degli studi medievali 3; Spoleto 1966) doubted the 'Gregorian' character of *74T*, and instead stressed that it defended the
independence of 'monasteries and dioceses' alike. Horst Fuhrmann, 'Über den Reformgeist
der 74-Titel-Sammlung (Diversorum patrum sententiae)', *Festschrift für Hermann Heimpel zum
70. Geburtstag am 19. September 1971* (3 vols. Veröffentlichungen des MPI für Geschichte 36; Göttingen 1972) 2.1101–1120 too stressed the difference between *74T* and the *Dictatus papae*. Brigitte
Szabó-Bechstein, *Libertas ecclesiae. Ein Schlüsselbegriff des Investiturstreits und seine Vorgeschichte.
4.–11. Jahrhundert* (Studi Gregoriani 12; Rome 1985), here at 123 was the first to state unambiguously that *74T* was above all concerned with monastic *libertas* and that it had an anti-episcopal
tendency. Linda Fowler-Magerl, *Kanones. Ausgewählte Kanonessammlungen ausserhalb Italiens
zwischen 1100 und 1140: Eine Aufarbeitung mittels EDV* (Piesenkofen 1998) 56 added important arguments for a non-Italian origin of *74T*. For further references, see Christof Rolker, 'The *Collection
in Seventy-Four Titles*: A Monastic Canon Law Collection from Eleventh-Century France', *Readers,
Texts and Compilers in the Earlier Middle Ages: Studies in Medieval Canon Law in Honour of Linda
Fowler-Magerl*, ed. Kathleen Grace Cushing and Martin Brett (CFC; Aldershot and Farnham 2009)
59–72, esp. 60–62 and most recently Lotte Kéry, 'Kanonessammlungen aus dem lotharingischen
Raum', *Lotharingien und das Papsttum im Früh- und Hochmittelalter. Wechselwirkungen im Grenzraum
zwischen Germania und Gallia*, ed. Klaus Herbers and Harald Müller (Abh. Akad. Göttingen N.F.
45; Berlin and Boston 2017) 189–212 (pointing out a possible Lotharingian origin).

heading, group together canons according to subject matter. The heading both of the titles and the individual canons are repeated in a detailed table of content (*capitulatio*) at the beginning of the collection, making *74T* very easy to use.

As will be discussed in greater detail below, the compiler spent more attention on some sections; the first title devoted to the primacy of the Roman church, the title on monastic liberty (title 4), and that on the morality of the clergy (title 15) stand out as having been composed with particular care. While the Roman church and monastic liberty are at the focus at the beginning of *74T*, the moral standards for the clergy and procedural law are dealt with at some length in the middle part of the collection. In the last third of *74T*, the administration of sacraments and (much more briefly) a number of diverse topics are dealt with. Generally, the second half of the collection gives the impression of being less polished, and towards the end of the collection more and more titles often contain only single canons apiece.

Where was the material taken from? The overwhelming part of the canons are taken from Pseudo-Isidore. More specifically, the *74T* compiler exploited above all the False Decretals, as he systematically preferred papal documents to conciliar legislation.[168] In addition to Pseudo-Isidore, the *74T* compiler used genuine and forged the letters of Gregory I for another 41 canons. Other material sources include the *Constitutum Silvestri*, patristic fragments, and some rare materials including Hincmar of Reims (*74T* cc. 33–38). The latter source is unusual; while Hincmar was a prominent figure, it was not his canon law that was widely read.[169] This might suggest that the *74T* compiler spent some effort to gather his material, including relatively rare materials, when compiling his work. He certainly made unusual choices what *not* to use; specifically, the *74T* compiler seems to

---

168. No less than 252 of the 315 canons of *74T* are from Pseudo-Isidore (including 148 from the False Decretals). See Gilchrist, 'Prolegomena' xci and the additions by Roger E. Reynolds, 'Review of Schaafer William, *Codices Pseudo-Isidoriani*' *Speculum* 47 (1972) 821 (on *74T* c. 202) and Karl Georg Schon, 'Exzerpte aus den Akten von Chalkedon bei Pseudoisidor und in der 74-Titel-Sammlung' DA 32 (1976) 546–557 (on *74T* c. 306). On the latter canon, see also Klaus Zechiel-Eckes, 'Verecundus oder Pseudoisidor? Zur Genese der Excerptiones de gestis Chalcedonensis concilii' DA 56 (2000) 413–446. Unless otherwise noted, the following is based on Gilchrist, 'Prolegomena' ch. 3, esp. at xci–xcix. Note that *4L* reversed the decision of the *74T* by adding a separate book of conciliar canons to the *74T* material it retained largely unchanged in its first three books: Uta-Renate Blumenthal, 'Conciliar Canons and Manuscripts: The Implications of Their Transmission in the Eleventh Century', *Proceedings Munich 1992* MIC. Subsidia 10.357–379, here at 375.

169. On the rather limited reception of Hincmar's canon law writings, see Martina Stratmann, 'Zur Wirkungsgeschichte Hinkmars von Reims' *Francia* 22.1 (1995) 1–43, here at 16 and 18. As Stratmann rightly pointed out, Hincmar's reception in canon law calls for further studies. The *Clavis* database (key '3HI') suggests that such entreprise would be fruitful, and also revals the curious case of the collection in Paris, BnF, lat. 3858C where an excerpt of Hincmar's *Ep.* 135 (ed. Perels, MGH Epp. 8.1:88–90) is attributed to a 'Pope Hincmar' (<u>MY01.428</u> in *Clavis*).

have avoided conciliar legislation found in his formal sources, ending up with only a single canon taken from conciliar legislation in the whole collection. Finally, even a superficial comparison of *74T* to its formal sources shows that the *74T* was arranging his materials quite differently from any of these earlier works. Drawing on diverse, and sometimes rare materials, the compiler of *74T* therefore planned, and successfully composed a collection that arranged the traditional material in a genuinely new way.

3.4.2 Place and Date of Origin

Given that *74T* is an anonymous collection the early manuscript tradition of which remains difficult to understand, the best evidence for its area of origin are the sources used by the compiler, in particular the less common ones.[170] Here the excerpts from Gregory the Great provide important evidence, as the canons in *74T* can be traced back to a specific version, the so-called 'C+P' transmission.[171] The use of this formal source strongly tells against the traditional idea that *74T* was compiled in Italy, where these materials were apparently unknown. Rather, the extant manuscripts of and other works quoting from 'C+P' all come from the regions north of the Loire and west of (or along) the Rhine. In a similar way, the employment of the writings of Hincmar and Abbo points to Francia and her neighbouring regions as the most likely place of origin for *74T*. The exact place remains under debate, but scholars agree that the analysis of the formal sources points to north-western continental Europe.[172]

Other evidence (apart from the availability of formal sources) is less conclusive. The content of the collection, for example, gives hardly any clue towards the place of origin.[173] Evidence from the manuscript tradition is inconclusive. No single manuscript stands out as clearly having been pro-

---

170. Fowler-Magerl, 'Use of Gregory' 238 and eadem, *Clavis* 110–117 (against the method followed by Gilchrist).

171. See Paul Ewald, 'Studien zur Ausgabe des Registers Gregors I.' NA 3 (1878) 433–625, here at 485–486, and more recently Judic, 'Production' 79.

172. Fowler-Magerl, 'Fine Distinctions' 155 (Lotharingia, '[…] not far from Cologne. It might have been at Prüm, St-Hubert, Lüttich or Verdun, to name only a few possibilities'); eadem, *Clavis* 110 ('not far from Hirsau') and 117 ('vicinity of Cologne'); Rolker, 'Collection' 64 (northern France, perhaps the diocese of Reims); Kéry, 'Kanonessammlungen' 208–211 (Lotharingia); Sabine Strupp, *Die kanonistischen Quellen des 'Liber de unitate ecclesia conservanda'. Zu den Vorlagen und der Arbeitsweise eines hochmittelalterlichen Traktatverfassers* (Magisterarbeit; Johann Wolfgang Goethe-Universität, Frankfurt 2014), here at 46–50 (Lower Lotharingia).

173. One of the few references to a specific place (*74T* c. 235 'De auctoritate Arelatensis episcopi', an excerpt taken from Gregory I, JE 1843), seems not useful to localise the collection to Arles. Indeed, a reference to Arles was deleted in a different case. As Fowler-Magerl, 'Fine Distinctions' 158–159 has pointed out, *74T* c. 30 is from a letter of Gregory I that in the original mentioned a monastery in Arles. Interestingly, this passage, while absent from *74T* itself is found in two monastic collections drawing on *74T*, namely the *Sandionysiana* and the *Farfensis*. Could the reference still be found in the *74T* version used at Saint-Denis and Farfa?

duced soon after the collection was compiled; by the time the extant manuscripts were produced, the collection already existed in different versions in several places. More precisely, while relatively many manuscripts can be dated to the late eleventh century, none of them can be dated before *ca.* 1080; already the manuscripts themselves show that by this time the collection was known in many areas from northern France to southern Italy. In the late eleventh century, it was also known in Aquitaine and Catalonia.[174] John Gilchrist has pointed out that important early manuscripts containing a very good text were produced at Montecassino, but as Fowler-Magerl demonstrated, equally good manuscripts seem to have been available in France at about the same time.[175] This can be inferred from a number of French collections from the second half of the eleventh century which seem to have used early versions of *74T*.[176] Other examples of early uses of *74T* in northern France will be presented below, but in the end the argument for a French origin of *74T* rests on the availability of rare sources and not its manuscript tradition or its early reception.

Indeed, any attempt to infer the place of origin from the early reception of *74T* with greater certainty would require a more precise chronology of the genesis of *74T* than is available. Internal evidence does not help to establish a meaningful *terminus post quem*, as the compiler was (like many other compilers of the time) not specifically interested in recent materials. This has left room for speculations of a very early date of *74T*, most famously by Paul Fournier.[177] While he argued for a date around 1050, recent scholarship often asserts a date around or shortly before 1075. As for the *terminus ante quem*, the works of Bernold of Konstanz (d. 1100) are the most important witnesses, not because they are demonstrably

---

174. *74T*-dependend collections completed before *ca.* 1100 include the *Sandionysiana*, the collection in Paris, BnF, lat. 13658, the *4L*, the collection in Celle, Oberlandesgericht, C.8, the *Collectio canonum* of Anselm of Lucca, the *Tarraconensis*, the *Burdegalensis*, and the *Farfensis*. Establishing the date *74T* reached the Iberian Peninsula depends on the dating of the *Tarraconensis* (extant in manuscripts from the early twelfth century) and the collections in Tarragona, BP, 35, which may have been produced before 1100. For the latter two collections, see Fowler-Magerl, *Clavis* 133 and 137, respectively. Antonio García y García, 'Del derecho canonico visigotico al derecho comun medieval', *Iglesia, sociedad y derecho* (2 vols. Bibliotheca Salmanticensis: Estudios 74; Salamanca 1985) 1.29–43, here at 33 claimed that the 'liber ex diversis sententiis' mentioned in the *Historia Compostelana* was in fact a reference to *74T*, but the argument seems stretched to me.

175. Gilchrist, 'Prolegomena'; Fowler-Magerl, 'Fine Distinctions' 158–159; eadem, 'Use of Gregory' 238; eadem, *Clavis* 110–117.

176. These collections are the *Sandionysiana*, the collection in Paris, BnF, lat. 13658, and *4L*. On all three collections, see Fowler-Magerl, *Clavis* 110–117; for the *Sandionysiana*, also see below.

177. Fournier, 'Manuel' esp. 222 had argued for a date around 1050, partly because he (erroneously) thought that one could date the Engelberg copy to this time, but mainly because he saw *74T* as representing the needs of the early reforming papacy, in particular Leo IX. See also Paul Fournier, 'Les collections canoniques romaines de l'époque de Grégoire VII' *Mémoires de l'Institut National de France, Académie des Inscriptions et Belles-Lettres* 41 (1918) 271–395, here at 282. On Engelberg, Stiftsbibliothek, 52, see Gilchrist, 'Prolegomena' §41.

the earliest uses of *74T*, but because they can be precisely dated. Bernold used two different versions of *74T* in his writings, augmented the collection himself, and can be identified as the scribe of extant manuscripts of *74T*.[178] He is said to have used the collection in 1073/74.[179] In 1076, he clearly quoted from *74T*.[180] After 1077,[181] maybe after his return from the 1079 Lenten synod, Bernold augmented *74T* with the so-called Swabian Appendix, partly drawing on the register of Gregory VII.[182] This Appendix famously contains a note saying that papal legates had brought *74T* with them to Gaul ('in Gallias').[183] In the high Middle Ages, 'Gallia' could refer to the kingdom of France,[184] plus sometimes the kingdom of Burgundy;[185] scholars would also be aware of the rather wider area of Roman provinces called 'Gaul' on both sides of the Alps; finally, 'Gallia' increasingly was used to refer to Germany.[186] Partly because of this ambiguity, a rather long list of papal legates have been suggested to have brought *74T* with them,[187] yet none of them demonstrably knew *74T*. Vice versa, the only

178. Autenrieth, 'Bernold von Konstanz'; Gilchrist, 'Prolegomena'; Doris Stöckly and Detlev Jasper, 'Einleitung', *De excommunicatis vitandis, de reconciliatione lapsorum et de fontibus iuris ecclesiastici (libellus X)*, ed. iidem (MGH Fontes iuris 15; Hanover 2000) 1–69, here at 58–59. All four parts of Bernold's *Libellus X* draw on *74T* but will not be considered here as they are clearly later (see ibid. 44–47).

179. Fowler-Magerl, *Clavis* 110 asserted that Bernold copied *74T* c. 307 in 1073/74; I was not able to verify this claim. For c. 307, see Jasper in MGH Fontes iuris 15.171, nn. 393 and 396.

180. Autenrieth, 'Bernold von Konstanz' 390; Gilchrist, 'Prolegomena' xxviii; Fowler-Magerl, *Clavis* 110.

181. The most recent material quoted in the Appendix is a letter Gregory VII from 31 May 1077 (JL 5034), according to Gilchrist collated with a letter written the same day (JL 5035). The more recent texts found on p. 203 of the manuscript in its present form cannot be used to date the Appendix, as they are not part of the original manuscript, as Jasper has pointed out in the edition of Bernold's *De excommunicatis vitandis* (MGH Fontes iuris 15.60) and his 'The Deposition and Excommunication of Emperors and Kings: A Collection of Historical Examples from the Investiture Conflict', *Canon Law, Religion and Politics: Liber amicorum Robert Somerville*, ed. Uta-Renate Blumenthal et al. (Washington, D.C. 2012) 199–214, here at 209 n. 27.

182. Autenrieth, 'Bernold von Konstanz'; Stöckly and Jasper, 'Einleitung' 58.

183. *74T, capitulatio* (ed. Gilchrist 19): 'Incipiunt ecclesiastice regule ex sententiis sanctorum patrum deflorate a legatis ipsius sedis apostolice in Gallias pro ecclesiasticarum dispositione causarum deportate.'

184. See Manasses I of Reims, *Apologia* (= *Gallia Pontificia* 3.3:114), ed. Mabillon in *Museum Italicum seu collectio veterum scriptorum ex bibliothecis Italicis*, ed. Jean Mabillon and Michel Germain (2 in 3 vols. Paris 1687/89) at 1.2:119–127. Writing to Hugh of Die, Manasses argued that while he indeed had promised to attend a council in Gaul, he was not willing to leave the kingdom of France to do so: 'Quod dictum est "in partibus Galliarum", nullus aestimare debet de omni parte citra montes Alpium esse dictum.' He concluded (ed. Mabillon 124–125) 'quod de illis "Galliarum partibus" sine dubio dictum est, ubi regnum Franciae situm est.' For background, see Ott, 'Reims and Rome'.

185. Gregory VII (JL –, 4849, and –; *Gallia Pontificia* 3.3:2, 3, and 5) in 1075 made Hugh of Die legate for 'Gallia' (and to judge from Hugh's activities in his first years, this effectively meant the kingdoms of France and Burgundy. In 1078, Gregory VII made Hugh again legate, this time for 'France and Burgundy' (JL 5067; *Gallia Pontificia* 3.3:54).

186. See Margret Lugge, *"Gallia" und "Francia" im Mittelalter. Untersuchungen über den Zusammenhang zwischen geographisch-historischer Terminologie und politischem Denken vom 6.–15. Jahrhundert* (Bonner historische Forschungen 15; Bonn 1960), esp. 132–145 (Germany).

187. Older German scholarship long favoured the theory that Gregory VII equipped legates he sent to Germany in 1076/77 (cardinal Bernard and Bernard of Saint-Victor or Altmann of Pas-

papal legates to 'Gaul' who are known to have used *74T* have rarely been suggested in this context. The first is Anselm of Lucca, who drew on *74T* for his own canonical collection and was papal legate for Lombardy (thus in *Gallia cisalpina*).[188] The other candidate is Odo of Ostia, papal legate in Germany in 1084/85, who quoted from *74T* in a letter concerning the meeting at Gerstungen.[189] The idea that Odo was one of the legates the Swabian Appendix referred to is made even more attractive as he travelled to Konstanz where he ordained Bernold as priest.[190]

In any case, Bernold's note confirms that by *ca.* 1080 the collection was known relatively widely. At the very least, the note suggests that *74T* was known at the papal curia, by papal legates, and somewhere in 'Gaul'; this also means that *74T* by this time had crossed the Alps at least twice. In addition, in the 1080s, different versions of *74T* were used in northern France (*4L*), Lombardy (Anselm of Lucca), Aquitaine and/or Catalonia (*17L*, *Tarraconensis*). This all suggests that *74T* not long after 1080 already attracted considerable attention, and makes it likely that the collection was finished some time before its earliest datable use by Bernold. Indeed, there is a collection using *74T* that may plausibly (though not demonstrably) be dated earlier than 1076, namely the *Sandionysiana*. As Levillain argued long ago, this version of *74T* may have been produced by the monks of Saint-Denis in the context of a Roman synod in 1065.[191] While this hypotheses is attractive, it is too speculative to establish a precise date for *74T*.

----

sau and Sigehard of Aquileia) with a copy of *74T*, see Gilchrist, 'Prolegomena' xxvii–xxviii and Fuhrmann 'Reformgeist' 1104; this view was taken up again by Patrick Healy, *The Chronicle of Hugh of Flavigny: Reform and the Investiture Contest in the Late Eleventh Century* (CFC; Aldershot and Burlington 2006), here at 185–194. Fournier (*Histoire* 2.16) even proposed that Hildebrand himself brought *74T* to France. More recently, Fowler-Magerl, 'Fine Distinctions' 178 suggested that Hugh of Die was the legate in question. Healy, *Chronicle* 85–86 (translating 'Gallia' with 'Germany') in addition speculated on Gerald of Ostia and Hubert of Palestrina.

188. Some of the evidence on Anselm's legatine activity is doubtful, but I tend to trust Arnulf, *Liber gestorum recentium* (ed. Zey, MGH SS rer. Germ. 67.230); see below on Anselm's biography and a short discussion of his legation(s).

189. Odo in his letters quotes twice from *74T* (ed. Erdmann, MGH Briefe dt. Kaiserzeit 5.375–380, here at 377 lines 12–15 and 379 lines 34–40). Odo's knowledge of *74T* is little known, perhaps because it was overlooked by Horst Fuhrmann, 'Pseudoisidor, Otto von Ostia (Urban II.) und der Zitatenkampf von Gerstungen (1085)' ZRG Kan. Abt. 68 (1982) 52–69; yet it did not escape John T. Gilchrist, 'Introduction', *The Collection in Seventy-Four Titles: A Canon Law Manual of the Gregorian Reform*, tr. idem (Mediaeval Sources in Translation 22; Toronto 1980) 1–48, here at 47. On Odo's legation, see Alfons Becker, *Papst Urban II. (1088–1099)* (3 vols. MGH Schriften 19; Stuttgart 1964–2012), here at 1.62–77.

190. See Bernold's chronicle (ed. Robinson, MGH SS rer. Germ. N.S. 14.446). Bernold in his chronicle uses 'Gallia' to refer to France, not Germany.

191. See Léon Levillain, 'Études sur l'abbaye de Saint-Denis à l'époque mérovingienne. III: privilegium et immunitates ou Saint-Denis dans l'église et dan l'état' BEC 87 (1926) 20–97 and 245–346, here at 299–324 on the manuscript, and below on the collection.

3.4.3 The Character of *74T*: A Monastic Canon Law Collection

Yet before looking in detail how the collection was in fact used, let us first consider the internal evidence for the purpose of its compilation. For this, the collection will be studied from beginning to end, partly for sheer convention, but partly because it often is significant which topics were given prominence by being placed first in a collection. In the case of *74T*, a reader opening the collection or simply looking at the *capitulatio* would first encounter a title devoted emphatically to the primacy of the Roman church, followed by one on the passion of Saint Peter and Paul, a third one on the authority of privileges, and one on monastic liberties. As already mentioned above, the opening titles are more carefully reworked than other parts of *74T*, and more specifically they form a specific argument. The number of canons devoted to papal primacy may be small, but *74T* contains important new material on the issue and places it prominently towards the beginning of the collection.[192] The compiler also manipulated one of his proof text in order to stress the legislative power of the pope.[193] Thus, the emphasis on the Roman church has rightly been seen as an important feature of *74T*. In the late eleventh century, a considerable number of newly compiled collections began with books on Roman or papal primacy, but at the time *74T* was compiled, this clearly was an innovative move. Placing two titles on the Roman church and the authority of Saint Peter and Paul first also seems to fit well the tendency of *74T* to quote papal documents rather than synodal canons.

And yet, *74T* for a long time now has ceased to be seen as a 'papally- oriented collection' for good reasons.[194] For example, the opening titles stress Roman, not papal, primacy, and later on the collection contains traditional canons against the use of universal titles. The latter canons are directly at odds with claims found, for example, in the famous *Dictatus papae*.[195] Indeed, as I want to argue, the first titles do serve a specific argument that

192. Namely Gelasius, JK 664 as found in *74T* c. 10 (ed. Gilchrist 24).

193. *74T* cc. 291 and 307 (ed. Gilchrist 19), both times manipulating canons taken from the *Capitula Angilramni*. In addition, the latter canon also is given an anti-episcopal twist, turning Pseudo-Isidore's on his head, as Schon put it (Schon, *Capitula Angilramni* 60).

194. Already Gilchrist, 'Prolegomena' xxi in 1973 stated that 'the tendency to treat the *74T* as a papally oriented collection, that is, a special product of the Gregorian camp, is today in process of being dispelled'. See also idem, 'Review of Berschin, *Bonizo von Sutri*' ZRG Kan. Abt. 59 (1973) 427–432, here at 428: 'Gone are the days when Fournier could refer to this collection as "le premier manuel canonique de la reforme du XIe siècle", as though the collection stood in a direct line of development of a movement led and inspired by a devoted group of papal supporters, who had one aim, one ideology, one mission in mind.'

195. On contradictions between *74T* and the *Dictatus papae*, see Zelina Zafarana, 'Ricerche sul *Liber de unitate ecclesiae conservanda*' Studi medievali, serie terza 7 (1966) 617–700, here at 657–664, and Ian Stuart Robinson, '*Periculosus homo*: Pope Gregory VII and Episcopal Authority' Viator 9 (1978) 103–131, esp. 117.

becomes visible if one takes into account titles three and four. The first two titles had stressed the nature of Roman authority, title three turns to the authority of privileges (papal or not).[196] A closer look reveals that privileges in favour of religious communities are given special attention in this third title.[197] Partly, this focus on monastic privileges is the result of careful selection of relevant material, but significantly, two of the proof texts are manipulated to this end. The first text in title three is taken from a famous decretal of Pseudo-Anaclete (JK †2). Instead of protecting the privileges of 'churches and priests', as the version found in the False Decretals reads, the manipulated version in *74T* grants special protection to 'churches and monasteries'.[198] In like fashion, the next canon on the 'privileges of churches' in *74T* is changed into an authority protecting the privileges of 'churches and monasteries'.[199] Thus, two canons placed prominently at the beginning of the title, and taken from highly authoritative sources, are clearly manipulated in favour of monks, quite contrary to the original intention.

The selection criteria and manipulation of materials in title three link this section to title four 'On the liberty of monks', as this title consists of papal privileges in favour of monastic houses or the monastic order as such. This title is the most innovative title in the whole collection. For all others titles, the compiler could find his material in relatively common sources, and whether he knew them or not, other compilers of earlier canon law collections had arranged their material into sections that were more or less similar to the titles the *74T* compiler came up with. Not so in the case of title four; there is no earlier canon law collection that would have devoted a separate book or sub-section to monastic liberty. In fact, most pre-Gratian canon law collections do not even contain much material that could be gathered under such a heading; both the Pseudo-Isidorian forgeries and Burchard (to quote the collections that were most widely spread by the time *74T* was compiled) have little to say about monasteries, and as far as they do, they mainly affirm that monasteries should be under the firm control of the local bishop. The *74T* compiler, who mainly worked from Pseudo-Isidorian material, must have been very familiar with these texts, but evidently he was looking for other materials, and consequently he turned elsewhere for title four.

<hr>

196. Significantly, *74T* discusses the authority of papal documents in general only later on: *74T* tit. 23 has six canons 'De observatione decretorum pontificum Romanum'.

197. *74T* in title 3 contains 15 canons (*74T* cc. 24–38); many proof texts stress the inviolability of privileges for monastic houses in particular (*74T* cc. 24, 25, 27, 31, 34, 35).

198. Anaclete, JK †2 (ed. Hinschius 73): 'privilegia ecclesiarum et sacerdotum'; *74T* c. 24 (ed. Gilchrist 33): 'privilegia ecclesiarum et monasteriorum'.

199. Leo I, JK 481 (ed. Hinschius 610): 'privilegia enim ecclesiarum'; *74T* c. 25 (ed. Gilchrist 33): 'privilegia ecclesiarum et monasteriorum'.

As a result, title four also stands out compared to the rest of *74T* in containing material that is not found in any earlier canon law collection. So what did the title look which evidently was given special attention by the compiler? It gathers canons that all affirm the inviolability of monastic privileges and specifically monastic property, and in addition it contains one proof text in particular that makes even more general claims about monastic liberty. This is the famous forgery attributed to Gregory the Great with the incipit *Quam sit necessarium* (= *QSN*), which has been dubbed the 'Magna Carta of monasticism'.[200]

It is a pro-monastic forgery protecting specifically monastic property of all kinds from either secular or episcopal interference; according to this canon, Gregory forbade 'that any bishop or secular ruler henceforth presume to diminish the revenues, goods, or properties of monasteries [...] in any way or on any occasion'.[201] In this context, it is worth mentioning that *74T* manipulated another canon (c. 307) by adding bishops among the potential violators of papal privileges threatened by the anathema. For a monastery in conflict with its local bishop (but equipped with papal privileges), canons like this manipulated Pseudo-Isidorian text—and even more so *QSN*—were very valuable, and it is safe to assume that the compiler of *74T* was very well aware of this.

Indeed, the opening sections of his collection can be read as preparing the reader for the far-reaching claims found in *QSN* by first affirming the authority of the Roman church, then dealing with the nature of (monastic) privileges, and finally in title four, focussing specifically on papal privileges in favour of monastic communities. The compiler might have thought such a careful composition necessary as the contents of title four must have been very unfamiliar to his readers and maybe even suspicious to those of them familiar with traditional canon law. Indeed, compared to earlier collections, especially to those based on Pseudo-Isidore, *74T* gave monastic rights an unusual prominence, and protected monastic property in terms that went far beyond anything found in any major collection.

Compared to this opening section, the following parts of *74T* are somewhat more conventional. This is mainly true for the following ten titles on procedural law (titles 5 to 14). In this long section—no other area of

---

200. Pseudo-Gregory I, JE †1366. See Theo Kölzer, 'Codex Libertatis: Überlegungen zur Funktion des "Regestum Farfense" und anderer Klosterchartulare', *Il ducato di Spoleto: atti del IX congresso internazionale di studi sull'alto medioevo* (2 vols. Settimane 24; Spoleto 1983) 2. 609–653, here at 649 ('Magna Carta'); Gilchrist, 'Monastic Forgeries' 273, 274, 277, and esp. 286; Fowler-Magerl, 'Fine Distinctions' esp. 160–161; Giorgio G. Picasso, '"Quam sit necessarium monasteriorum quieti prospicere" (Reg. Epist. 8.17): sulla fortuna di un canone gregoriano', *Cristianità ed Europa: miscellanea di studi in onore di Luigi Prosdocimi*, ed. Cesare Alzati (2 in 3 vols. Rome 1994–2000) 2.95–105.

201. *74T* c. 39 (tr. Gilchrist 92).

the law is dealt with at greater length—*74T* is largely faithful to its main source, the False Decretals. Famously, Pseudo-Isidore had introduced an extremely large number of procedural norms into canon law, and often fabricated a large number of similar proof texts for those principles that were most dear to the forgers. For the law of process, then, the compiler of *74T* could draw on particularly rich materials, and freely did so. Following Pseudo-Isidore, the focus is on trials against bishops. However, a closer look shows that *74T* may have been interested in the same topics as Pseudo-Isidore, but gave its material a new twist in several cases. Famously, Pseudo-Isidore had protected bishops ('the eyes of the Lord') from unlawful litigation by making criminal accusation extremely difficult; if followed verbatim, the procedural law as found in Pseudo-Isidore made the accusation of, let alone a verdict against a bishop nearly impossible. In *74T*, the Pseudo-Isidorian material in several cases is changed so as to extend the protection specifically for bishops to all clergy (*74T* cc. 6, 78, 80, 86). Here, *74T* may be compared to the *Anselmo dedicata*, as it does, on the one hand, introduce important Pseudo-Isidorian materials into canon law while, on the other hand, manipulating at least some of these materials in a way that clearly went against the intentions of the forgers.

After these long sections on procedural law, *74T* continues with titles that are innovative in a different way. While the material is traditional, and not manipulated in any way, it is presented in such a way that it may well be read as addressing reform issues of the eleventh century. This is particularly true for the first of these titles on the morality of the clergy (title 15). Already the wording of the title makes clear that the high standards found in the ancient canons were all too often not met: 'About ignorant, unworthy, simoniacal, and neophyte prelates' ('De prelatis imperitis, indignis, symoniacis, neophytis'). The emphasis on simony and nicolaitism has been rightly seen as matching the 'reform issues' that became important in the late eleventh century, and *74T* is often seen as having contributed to this new awareness. The fact that *74T* in title 15 gathers more proof texts than any other single title of the collection adds to the impression that these issues were indeed of particular importance to the compiler.

While title 15 is clearly a programmatic one, the collection becomes gradually less structured afterwards. Titles 15 to 21 may be described as dealing with the reform of the clergy, so this subsection has at least a certain internal coherence to it. Then *74T* returns to the authority of the papal decretals (title 23), and gathers a handful of canons stating that the pope should not call himself 'universal' (title 24). This section has rightly been quoted as directly contradicting Gregorian claims as expressed in the *Dictatus papae*.[202] The following titles deal in this order with bishops, *chorepiscopi*, and priests (titles 25–28). After this, sacramental and liturgical issues are dealt with, but in an increasingly less structured way. One title, almost hidden away, combines a canon reserving the right to preach to priests with another canon which seems to assert the opposite.[203] Title 31 (on the consecration of churches) is the first of many titles to contain one canon only, and from here onwards *74T* gives the impression of a rather unsophisticated collection. Some titles do group material on specific topics together, and sometimes one discerns principles that seem to govern the arrangement of the titles. For example, title 36 gathers seven canons on baptism and confirmation, while the preceding title contains a canon on the preparation of chrism and title 37 one stating the prohibition of repeated baptisms. This is far from a complete account of baptism, but at least the nine excerpts are arranged in a meaningful way. However, such clusters of texts are rare and become even rarer towards the end of the collection; here, most titles contain only single canons, and two of the longer titles (titles 65 and 66) are evidently structured by the formal source the material is taken from, not the content.[204] No topic is dealt with at length, and there is nothing to suggest that the compiler spent considerable care to find unusual material for this part of *74T*.

3.4.4 The Reception of *74T*: A Monastic Collection with a Diverse Readership

If *74T* no longer is seen as the 'first manual of (papal) reform', as Fournier famously called it, should it be more correctly classified as the 'first manual of monastic reform' of the eleventh century? While this label would fit the programmatic character of *74T* as well as its influence in the monastic world, both internal evidence and its reception warn against seeing *74T* as a single-purpose collection. Clearly, the compiler had a special interest in the rights of monastic communities, and both his selection criteria and the way he manipulated a number of canons are strong evidence for his pro-monastic tendencies. The use of otherwise rare monastic authors like Abbo of Fleury likewise supports the idea that the compiler was working in a monastic library.

---

202. *Dictatus papae* c. 2 (ed. Caspar, MGH Epp. sel. 2.1:202) 'Quod solus Romanus pontifex iure dicatur universalis.' For the secondary literature, see above (note 195).

203. *74T* title 50 'On the authority of preaching'. In *74T* c. 242 one reads that 'God does not ask who preaches or how well, but whom he preaches', while c. 243 asserts that only priests should preach.

204. *74T* titles 65 and 66, containing cc. 276–307, are identical to the canons of Rome 721 (JE ante 2159) and the *Capitula Angilramni* as found in Pseudo-Isidore.

Nonetheless, *74T* contains not only monastic materials, and it was read and used well beyond the monastic world. Different readers may well have been interested in different sections of *74T*. For example, Fowler-Magerl imagined how monks brought *74T* to Gregory VII, and how the latter must have been pleased to read a collection beginning emphatically with Roman primacy.[205] While there are major differences between *74T* and 'Gregorian' thought,[206] the opening sections of *74T* may indeed have been similar to the collection Hildebrand had in mind when famously asking Peter Damian to compile a canon law collection on the prerogatives of the Roman church.[207] To take a non-fictitious example, Odo (the future Urban II) quoted from *74T* in an important letter concerning the meeting at Gerstungen.[208] Anselm of Lucca took the opening section of *74T* as a model for his own collection; a closer analysis shows that he employed *74T* material in a very independent way,[209] but no doubt his collection was shaped by *74T* and its approach to ecclesiastical hierarchy. Another group of *74T* readers may be identified as reformers concerned with clerical marriage and simoniacal entry into the clergy. Such a use of *74T* is made plausible by the *74T* quotations in the polemics of the late eleventh century which often revolved around these themes. Bernold of Konstanz is a good example how *74T* could be culled for authorities in this context.[210] Indeed, many polemicists of the late eleventh century drew on *74T*, and above all its sections on 'reform issues'; however, it is also clear that not only Gregorians used *74T*, and that Gregorians used many other sources too.[211]

205. Fowler-Magerl, *Kanones* 56: 'I suggest that the collection was brought to him [Gregory VII] by persons who were supporting their own interests, and that these persons were monks supporting the interests of their monasteries. Gregory must have been attracted by the beginning of the collection.'

206. On marked differences between *74T* and Gregory VII (and specifically the claims found in the *Dictatus papae*), see the literature quoted above (notes 194 and 195).

207. Peter Damian, *Ep.* 65 (ed. Reindel, MGH Briefe dt. Kaiserzeit 4.2:229), writing to Gregory VII: 'Frequenter a me [...] postulasti, ut Romanorum pontificum decreta vel gesta percurrens quicquid apostolicae sedis auctoritati specialiter competere videretur, hinc inde curiosus excerperem, atque in parvi voluminis unionem nova compilationis arte conflarem.'

208. Odo in his letters quoted twice from *74T* (ed. Erdmann and Ficker, MGH Briefe dt. Kaiserzeit 5.375–380, here at 377 lines 12–15 and 379 lines 34–40). This was overlooked by Fuhrmann, 'Gerstungen'; yet it did not escape Gilchrist, 'Introduction' 47. On Odo's legation, see Becker, *Urban II.* 1.62–77.

209. Cushing, *Papacy and Law* 78–85, concluding that '[s]ome, if not most' of the numerous changes Anselm made to his *74T* texts 'must be understood as deliberate correctives on the part of Anselm to what he perceived as the inadequacies of the *74T*'s transmission of texts and, more important, as the insufficiency of that collection in general as a guide to papally-inspired reform.'

210. Odo in his letter on Gerstungen (ed. Erdmann and Ficker, MGH Briefe dt. Kaiserzeit 5.375–380), see Gilchrist, 'Introduction' 47. For Gerstungen, see Fuhrmann, 'Gerstungen' (unaware of Odo's use of *74T*).

211. Zafarana, 'Ricerche'; Gilchrist, 'Introduction' esp. 44–45 and 47. More recently, Healy, *Chronicle* ch. 5 tried to argue that Hugh of Flavigny used *74T*. See the important corrections by Matthias Lawo, *Studien zu Hugo von Flavigny* (MGH Schriften 61; Hanover 2010) ch. III.

Likewise, the collection was used in the compilation of new collections, which in several cases preserved all (or almost all) of *74T*. For example, the *Collection in Four Books* and the *Sandionysiana* are essentially revised versions of *74T*; the much larger *Tarraconensis* and the Turin *Collection in Seven Books* (= Turin *7L*) incorporate almost every single canon of *74T*. These compilers often devoted, just as *74T* had done, separate sections on issues such as simony and nicolaitism. Indeed, *74T* visibly shaped the structure of many derivative collections, preserving the emphasis *74T* had placed on certain issues. For example, the Turin *7L* heavily used a Swabian version of *74T*, but treated different parts of it differently.[212] The first book of the Turin *7L* corresponds to *74T*, titles 1–4 (papal primacy, papal privileges, monastic liberty); the second book consists of titles 5–14 (all dealing with procedural law), left in the original sequence but added to with a handful of canons from Burchard; book three, finally, at the beginning corresponds to *74T*, titles 15–19 on clerical discipline, but continues with much more material taken from other sources. As for the remaing *74T* titles, these canons too are found in *7L*, but they are scattered over books 3–7 of the Turin collection without shaping the structure of this collection.

Finally, papal legates have often been mentioned as a group for which *74T* was of particular relevance. This idea—mainly going back to the Swabian *74T* as quoted above but supported by other evidence[213]—often went hand in hand with the idea of canon law collections as part of a centralized, papal reform. It is therefore worth mentioning that while there are papal legates like Odo who are known to have used *74T*, the collection was not particularly fit for the manifold obligations of a legate. For example, a key factor in legatine politics was the celebration of synods; yet *74T* was lacking material law on many of the diverse issues legates were confronted with and did not contain a synodal *ordo* (nor was such an order added to any *74T* copy). In contrast, a collection like Burchard's *Liber decretoum* contained more diverse material law, was transmitted with synodal orders, and praised by contemporaries as useful for the conduct of such gatherings. Hugh of Lyon probably was not the only papal legate to acquire a copy of Burchard's collection.[214]

So there is good evidence that *74T* was valued by church reformers, polemicists of different background, compilers of canon law collections,

<hr>

212. On this point, see Kriston R. Rennie, 'The Turin Collection Revisited' ZRG Kan. Abt. 98 (2012) 46–63.

213. See above on Bernold reporting that papal legates sent 'in Gallias' carried *74T* with them, and Odo of Ostia who used *74T* as a papal legate.

214. Rolker, *Canon Law* 62–63 and 64 n. 86.

and papal legates. All these groups showed interest in *74T*, and at least partly we see that they were attracted by different aspects of *74T*. Yet for a complete picture, we have to return to monastic circles. Not only does the majority of extant *74T* manuscript for which the transmission can be established come from monastic libraries (an unusual feature for any medieval canon law collection). It is also striking to see how many other collections compiled by monastic authors were inspired by *74T*, and some of these collections will be presented in the next section. As these and other monastic collections clearly show, monastic compilers working with *74T* strongly tended to concentrate on the first four titles including above all the *Quam sit necessarium* forgery. They also combined *74T* material (and again, above all *QSN*) with other monastic texts, pro-monastic forgeries and/or accounts of own their history and their possessions. The monks at San Sofia, for example, copied excerpts mainly from the first titles of *74T* (including *QSN*) and other pro-monastic forgeries into a manuscript that also contains the *Annales Beneventani* and the prologue to their own chartulary.[215] At Prüm, the *Liber aureus* (originally composed in 920) around 1100 was 'updated' with new privileges and a forgery based on *QSN*, apparently taken from *74T*.[216] The monks at Rheinau in 1125/26 compiled a chartulary that opened with *QSN* followed by other *74T* excerpts and a forgery on free abbatial elections, a disputed issue at the time the manuscript was produced.[217] At Fleury and at several other places, *QSN* was combined with two other major pro-monastic forgeries.[218] At Saint-Ouen in Normandy, the same three forgeries were combined with the letters of Gregory the Great.[219] At SS Mary and Benedict at Alberese in Tuscany, the

215. For an edition, see Ottorino Bertolini, 'La collezione canonica Beneventana del Vat. Lat. 4939', *Collectanea Vaticana in honorem Anselmi M. Cardinalis Albareda: a Bibliotheca Apostolica edita* (2 vols. Studi e testi 219/220; Vatican City 1962) 1.119–137. For further references on this monastic collection (known as *Beneventana*), see Kéry, *Collections* 288–289.

216. On the chartulary (Trier, Stadtbibliothek, HS 1709) see Hubertus Seibert, *Abtserhebungen zwischen Rechtsnorm und Rechtswirklichkeit. Formen der Nachfolgeregelung in lothringischen und schwäbischen Klöstern der Salierzeit (1024–1125)* (Quellen und Abhandlungen zur mittelrheinischen Kirchengeschichte 78; Mainz 1995), here at 419–423. The document in question is Pseudo-Nicholas JE 2733.

217. Hubertus Seibert, 'Eine unbekannte Überlieferung der 74-Titel-Sammlung aus Rheinau', *Deus qui mutat tempora. Menschen und Institutionen im Wandel des Mittelalters. Festschrift für Alfons Becker zu seinem fünfundsechzigsten Geburtstag*, ed. Ernst-Dieter Hehl et al. (Sigmaringen 1987) 87–100. See also Gilchrist, 'Monastic Forgeries' 278 for three Rheinau manuscripts containing JE †1951 and/or †1996.

218. Paris, BnF, lat. 2788; see Gilchrist, 'Monastic Forgeries' 273, 274, 275, 277, and 283. The Riccardiana florilegium is a similar case, see Giorgio G. Picasso, 'Ancora un florilegio patristico sulle prerogative dei monaci (Firenze, Riccardiana 3006, ff. 203r–205v)', *Noblità e chiese nel Medioevo e altri saggi: scritti in onore di Gerd G. Tellenbach*, ed. Cinzio Violante (Pubblicazioni del dipartimento di medievistica dell'Università di Pisa 3; Rome 1993) 223–232.

219. Rouen, BM, A.146 (517) according to Gilchrist, 'Monastic Forgeries' 275.

monks copied *74T* together with privileges of their own house as well as a pro-monastic Gregory I florilegium.[220]

These are only some examples of the monastic reception of *74T*; in addition, the reception of *74T* and *QSN* at Saint-Denis, Westminster, Chézal-Benoît, La Sauve Majeure, and Montecassino will be discussed in the context of various *74T*-derivative collections. Yet already now it should be clear that the monastic reception of *74T* was massive. *74T* may have had many readers, but above all monks copied, used, and reworked this collection, and it is abundantly clear that they were mainly attracted by the sections on (monastic) privileges. Even if *74T* had not been compiled with the intention to provide monasteries all over Latin Europe with a handbook of monastic canon law, the readers quickly treated it as such a manual of monastic reform.

3.5 Monastic 'Derivative Collections'

It is the exception rather than the rule for pre-Gratian canon law collections that they were composed from scratch; much more commonly, new collections emerged as older works were copied, added to, improved, abridged. In the following, three monastic canon law collections commonly seen as 'derivative' collections will be analysed. Compared to 'original' works like Abbo's collection, *5L* or *74T*, these collections are indeed 'derivative' in the sense that most characteristics of the collection—their contents and structure—were derived from the respective model collections. Yet it would not do justice to these works if they were only seen as evidence for the reception of this or that 'original' collection. Especially where we can see that compilers employed considerable time and skills, it is highly significant not only what they chose to change but also what they chose to retain when working with certain materials.

It is also worth remembering in this context why 'derivative' collections were much more common than 'original' works, and how these collections were actually made. More often than not, the process must have been slow and gradual. At some point, perhaps when a new copy of an old collection was planned, a careful reader would go through the collection marking canons that were less relevant for him as to reduce the labour of the next copyist; when this copy was made, these materials would be skipped, while at the same time this was an occasion to integrate glosses scribbled in the margins and additions crammed into originally empty pages, and perhaps

220. Firenze, BNC, Conv. Soppr. 91. For a similar florilegium, see Giovanni Miccoli, 'Un florilegio sulla dignità e i diritti del monachesimo: Cod. Pis. S. Cat. 59, ff. 1–16', *Volume in onore del Prof. Ottorino Bertolini* (Livorno 1967) 117–129.

additional materials on loose sheets kept alongside the old collection. Depending on the quantity and quality of the resulting changes, a modern scholar would classify the result essentially as a copy of the old collection, as a new collection or, frequently, as something in between.

Perhaps the process would be repeated as the copyists, maybe when compiling a *capitulatio*, began to have ideas how the many texts they had copied could be arranged differently; or another work came to their attention that provided new materials, and perhaps an alternative model of arranging the material. So again, canons would be added on empty pages, in the margins or on separate sheets, partly perhaps still in the sequence of the formal source, but partly according to the scheme the compilers may have in mind. If that scheme differed from that found in the collection(s) they were working with, they faced an important decision: Should they take one of the collections they were working with as their model, perhaps adding a new book or two but otherwise retaining the structure found there? Or should they embark on the difficult and laborious task of arranging all their material according to different principles? Even if they were working only with two mid-sized collections, this would imply the rearrangement of several hundred excerpts, and if they chose collections like Burchard as their basis, their desks would quickly fill with copies of thousands of proof texts. It was of course normally not necessary to assign a new place to every single text they chose to retain; the work would be greatly reduced if one left series of canons taken from one source in the sequence found there. Still, especially if one worked with larger collections, great care had to be taken if one had the ambition to avoid overlap, as many texts would be found in more or less identical versions perhaps in more than one of the formal sources the compilers were working with. With this in mind, let us look at three 'derivative' collections that emerged in the monastic milieu of the eleventh and twelfth centuries.

3.5.1 The *Sandionysiana*: Monastic Canon Law in Action

Sources, Content, and Structure

The *Collection of Saint-Denis* or *Sandionysiana* (as I will call it following Levillain) is a *74T*-derivative collection extant in one single manuscript from the second half of the eleventh century which also contains a chartulary of Saint-Denis, the abbey church most famous as the burial site of many kings of France.[221] Scholars have sometimes described it as a collection in its own

---

221. Paris, BnF, nouv. acq. lat. 326, fols. 26r–76v. Levillain, 'Études' 299–324; Rolf Große, *Saint-Denis zwischen Adel und König. Die Zeit vor Suger (1053–1122)* (Francia. Beihefte 57; Stuttgart 2002), here at 70–78; Kéry 206 and 278; Fowler-Magerl, *Clavis* 114–116.

right, sometimes as a version of *74T*.[222] It contains almost all canons of *74T* and very little other material; however, the arrangement of the canons is very different from *74T* and justifies the qualification as a separate work, comparable to the *Collection in Four Books*.

The *Sandionysiana* is clearly depended on a collection very similar to the extant form of *74T*. One text found only found in the *Sandionysiana* but not *74T* is the privilege of Philip I of France for Saint-Denis from 1068. The other material not found in *74T* are excerpts from papal letters, typically inserted in such a way that it complements *74T* canons attributed to the same pope. In the case of Miltiades and Gelasius, the Saint-Denis compiler added material from the very same decretal, suggesting that he deliberately was supplementing *74T* from the same sources the *74T* compiler had used.[223] This impression is further confirmed by the fact that with only one exception all canons found in Saint-Denis but not *74T* are also found in the *Collection in Four Books*, another French collection from about the same time that also can be described as a *74T*-derivative collection drawing on the same sources as *74T* itself.[224] In several cases, the *Sandionysiana*, the *Collection in Four Books* and other early *74T*-derivative collections preserve better texts than the extant manuscripts of *74T*.[225] This suggests that all these collections go back to a *74T* version, and also that the extant *74T* manuscripts all depend on an exemplar that had some defects. At least one of these errors looks like an eye-slip resulting in the omission of one line of a canon.[226]

How did the compiler treat his material, apart from these additions? Sometimes, the *74T* canons are rearranged as to present excerpts in chrono-

222. Levillain, 'Études' 301 ('collection de Saint-Denis'); *Histoire* 2.14 n. 2 and Fuhrmann, *Einfluß und Verbreitung* 2.490 (*74T* manuscript); Gilchrist, 'Prolegomena' xxviii ('re-arranged version of *74T*'); idem, 'Changing the Structure of a Canonical Collection: The Collection in Seventy-Four Titles, Four Books, and the Pseudo-Isidorian Decretals', *In iure veritas: Studies in Canon Law in Memory of Schafer Williams*, ed. Steven B. Bowman and Blanche E. Cody (Cincinnati 1991) 93–117, here at 96 (separate collection from *ca.* 1085); Große, *Saint-Denis* 70 (reworked *74T*); Fowler-Magerl, *Clavis* 114 ('rearrangement' of *74T*); Thomas G. Waldman, 'Charters and Influences from Saint-Denis, c. 1000–1070', *Bury St Edmunds and the Norman Conquest*, ed. Tom Licence (Woodbridge 2014) 22–30, here at 25 ('early version' of *74T*). Kéry 206 and 278, respectively, mentioned Paris, BnF, nouv. acq. lat. 326 both among the *74T* manuscripts and as a separate collection.

223. *Sandionysiana* cc. 245–246 (= Miltiades, JK †171) and 263–266 (= Gelasius, JK 632), with cc. 246 and 264 added from the source also used by the *74T* compiler, namely the False Decretals.

224. Fowler-Magerl, 'Fine Distinctions' 154–155 and 163. In *4L*, the canons found in *Sandionysiana* but not *74T* are part of longer canons.

225. Fowler-Magerl, 'Fine Distinctions' 163–165.

226. *74T* c. 207 (ed. Gilchrist 132), as pointed out by Fowler-Magerl, 'Fine Distinctions' 165. The passage should read (as in the material source and several *74T* derivative collections) 'Nam si vinum tantum quis offeret, sanguis Christi incipit esse sine nobis; si vero aqua sit sola, plebs incipit esse sine Christo', but in the 'standard' *74T* as edited by Gilchrist, the words 'nobis; si vero aqua sit sola, plebs incipit esse' are missing. The length of this omission fits well the typical layout of *74T* manuscripts (two columns).

logical sequence; sometimes, the titles of *74T* are left more or less intact; and sometimes, excerpts from the letters attributed to individual popes are grouped together; finally, some subsections of the *Sandionysiana* are best described as 'left over' sections, as the *74T* material not presented in any of the methods just mentioned was shuffled together regardless of content, date or authorship.

The first canons in the *Sandionysiana*, for example, are taken from the beginning of *74T*. Indeed, the opening section of the *Sandionysiana* (cc. 1–18) closely resembles the first title of *74T* with a few additions from the second title and the beginning of the third, but also a few omissions and some rearrangement of materials. The main result is that the *Sandionysiana* (unlike *74T*) presents its opening canons in chronological order. Some of the material from the first three titles of *74T* left out in the composition of this opening section is found immediately after it in no apparent order (*Sandionysiana* cc. 19–24). This 'left over' section ends with an excerpt attributed to Pope Julius, to which another canon (c. 25) from the same pope is added.[227] The next canons (cc. 26–36) are identical to titles 8 and 9 of *74T*, and already there present the material in the chronological order as found in the False Decretals. Only one canon is omitted (*74T* c. 76), and because of this omission, the next canon is misattributed.[228] After seven canons on diverse matters, apparently arranged chronologically, the *Sandionysiana* has a section that resembles *74T*, title 5 with only few omissions. The excerpts from Pope Stephen at the end are supplemented with canons of the same pope found in titles six and seven of *74T*. However, while the section contains almost all canons attributed to Pope Stephen in *74T*, two more excerpts from his letters are found towards the end of the *Sandionysiana* (cc. 229 and 299)

Not long after, the compiler of the *Sandionysiana* assembled nine canons from no less than eight different *74T* titles, all attributed to Pope Silvester. This short section contains all Silvester material of the *Sandionysiana*; *74T* has one more canon attributed to this pope only (*74T* c. 181). The sequence of the Silvester canons in the *Sandionysiana* follows the canon numbers given in the rubrics of *74T*, regardless of the different material sources these canons are taken from (the *Constitutum Silvestri* on the one hand, and the Pseudo-Isidorian *Synodalia gesta* of Nicaea on the other hand).

---

227. *Sandionysiana* c. 25, from *74T* title 12.

228. Paris, BnF, nouv. acq. lat. 326, fol. 32r, presenting c. 32 as if it were from the same source as c. 31 (Ps.-Anaclete) while in fact it is from Ps.-Alexander. In *74T*, the canon missing in the *Sandionysiana* contained the reference to Alexander (*74T* c. 76, ed. Gilchrist 59).

The longest section of this kind is the one gathering excerpts from Gregory the Great. Some Gregorian canons were already found as a group in the opening section, and some were left scattered over the whole collection; these scattered canons are typically found in the context of the same materials they are found with in *74T*. Most Gregory material of *74T*, however, is gathered in a separate section in the *Sandionysiana*, a total of 51 canons (cc. 169–219). The first of these canons is the forgery *Quam sit necessarium*, which is also marked with an unusually large initial, the only decorated initial in the whole collection. Within this section, the division of *74T* into titles is still visible.[229]

The compiler of the *Sandionysiana*, therefore, seems to have access to a very early and very good copy of *74T*. He spent some effort to change the structure of his model, mainly to create chronologically ordered subsections of the collection; the division of materials into titles, while still visible from the *Sandionysiana*, was greatly disturbed by this reworking. Similar examples of reworking collections so as to bring the materials into chronological order are known from the *Sinemuriensis* and the collection of Saint-Hilaire-le-Grand (also known as *17L*).[230] From internal evidence it is clear that the *Sandionysiana* does not preserve a chronologically arranged 'draft' of *74T* but must be dependent on a collection which was very similar to the extant *74T* in content and structure (only with better texts in some cases). The fact that the materials used to produce *74T* were available at Saint-Denis and also apparently in other places supports the idea that *74T* together with related materials circulated in northern France in the 1070s and may already have done so in the 1060s. While details of its origins remain obscure, the *Sandionysiana* adds to the impression that it may have been a monastic network that disseminated *74T* and *74T*-related materials.

Place and Date of Origin

Place and date of the *Sandionysiana* deserve special attention as the monks of Saint-Denis may have been among the first readers of *74T*.[231] The *terminus post quem* of the extant form of the collection is the 1068 privilege it contains; the *terminus ante quem* has to be inferred from the extant manuscript which also contains the chartulary compiled in preparation

---

229. E.g. *Sandionysiana* cc. 169–173 (identical to *74T* tit. 4) and cc. 181–189 (identical to all Gregory canons found in *74T* tit. 15, in the same sequence as there).

230. Fowler-Magerl, *Clavis* 129. On *17L*, see below section 3.7.3.

231. Levillain, 'Études' 299–324 (before 1065); for *74T*, Levillain followed the early date proposed by Fournier, 'Manuel' 192. Fowler-Magerl, *Clavis* 114 follows Levillain for the 1065 date of the *Sandionysiana* (not only the chartulary). Fuhrmann, *Einfluß und Verbreitung* 2.489–491 and Große, *Saint-Denis* 71 thought Levillain's arguments not cogent.

of the Lateran synod which according to Gresser took place in May 1066 (not 1065).[232] Levillain claimed that the collection too was produced in this context and copied in or very shortly after 1068.[233] While Levillain's palaeographical and codicological arguments are not cogent, it remains plausible that the *Sandionysiana* and the chartulary were both produced in the context the conflict between Saint-Denis and the bishop of Paris in the 1060s. That said, there is no compelling reason to exclude a later date, and hence the manuscript does not help to provide a secure *terminus ante quem* for *74T*.

The claim that the *Sandionysiana* was compiled in preparation of the Lateran synod remains speculative, but two of Levillain's arguments are still attractive. First, the collection would have been useful at the Lateran synod where the chartulary was presented.[234] Secondly, there are several parallels between *74T*, the *Sandionysiana*, and the chartulary, suggesting that the latter was compiled when *74T* was already available at Saint-Denis. The texts in question are *QSN* and two forgeries which draw on *74T* material also found in the *Sandionysiana*.[235] Große pointed out that all three *74T* parallels may be explained differently—the first two may have been taken from Pseudo-Isidore directly, and *QSN* may have reached Saint-Denis from an unidentified source rather than *74T*.[236] While this is true, the use of *74T* would provide an elegant explanation for the sources of several forgeries found in the chartulary. The chronology may be too speculative to establish the Lateran Council as the *terminus ante quem* for the compilation of *74T*, but in any case the monks of Saint-Denis belong to the earliest users of this important monastic collection.

To place the *Sandionysiana* into context, let us briefly consider the situation of the community that produced it in the eleventh century. Saint-Denis is well known, and rightly so, as one of the greatest among the major abbeys of northern Europe. However, its history was not without ups and downs, and in the time before the pontificate of Abbot Suger (from 1121 to 1151), Saint-Denis was under serious threat in several

---

232. Gresser, *Synoden und Konzilien* 77–82. The key document is Alexander II, JL 4565, ed. Rolf Große, *Papsturkunden in Frankreich N.F. Bd. 9: Diözese Paris II: Abtei Saint-Denis* (Abh. Akad. Göttingen. 3.225; Göttingen 1998) no. 18.

233. Levillain, 'Études' 299–324.

234. Große, *Papsturkunden* 117.

235. JE †1366 is contained in *74T* c. 39; it is found in Paris, BnF, nouv. acq. lat. 326, fols. 19r–20v (as part of the chartulary) and fols. 53r–54r (as part of the collection). Fowler-Magerl, 'Fine Distinctions' 163 pointed out differences between the two occurences of *QSN* in the Saint-Denis manuscript. The other forgeries are Zachary, JE †2294 and Ps.-Stephen II, JE – (J³ –); they are edited in Große, *Papsturkunden* 61–64 and 75–77, respectively. Waldman, 'Charters' 24 seems to treat them as genuine.

236. Große, *Saint-Denis* 71 and 77–78.

respects.[237] For the monks of Sankt Emmeran in Regensburg claimed that they possessed the relics of which Saint-Denis was so proud of.[238] At the same time, Saint-Denis was still weakened as a result of the fate of lords of Vexin, on whom they long had relied for protection; more generally, Saint-Denis did not fare well in the shifting balance of power between the dukes of Normandy and the kings of Francia in the eleventh century.[239] Some of the uncertainty is reflected in the genuine and forged privileges Saint-Denis collected in this period. As for genuine privileges, between the year 1000 and 1065 Saint-Denis had obtained two privileges from Robert II in 1000 and 1008 respectively, one from Leo IX in 1049, and two from Edward the Confessor in the 1050s. In the middle of the eleventh century, they forged one charter attributed to Offa, king of Mercia, one attributed to Edgar, king of England, and most importantly one attributed to Bishop Landry of Paris.[240] In the early 1060s, they forged papal privileges they attributed to Zachary and Stephen II, and obtained *QSN*.[241] So the monks of Saint-Denis seem to have looked to Normandy and England for protection but for a relatively long time failed to have their privileges confirmed by the Capetian kings.

In the 1060s the local bishop—the powerful Geoffrey of Boulonge—took advantage from the relatively weak position of Saint-Denis. Conflicts between Saint-Denis and bishop of Paris were nothing new; the disastrous synod of Saint-Denis in 995 is indicative of some of these tensions.[242] Geoffrey seems to have celebrated mass in the monastery and may also have tried to enforce *Gastung*.[243] After the king was unwilling or unable to help Saint-Denis, the monks turned to the pope and finally managed to have their case heard at the Lateran synod in 1066. In preparation of the trial, they produced the new chartulary, and copied all their charters including the genuine and forged documents mentioned above. The synod, not least because of the documents presented here, decided in favour of

237. Große, *Saint-Denis* passim; idem, 'Frühe Papsturkunden und Exemtion des Klosters Saint-Denis (7.–12. Jh.)', *Hundert Jahre Papsturkundenforschung. Bilanz – Methoden – Perspektiven, Akten eines Kolloquiums zum hundertjährigen Bestehen der Regesta Pontificum Romanorum vom 9.–11. Oktober 1996 in Göttingen*, ed. Rudolf Hiestand (Abh. Akad. Göttingen. 3. Folge 261; Göttingen 2003) 167–188.

238. Große, *Saint-Denis* 61–70.

239. See Große, 'Papsturkunden' 183 for the lords of Vexin and Lindy Grant, 'Suger and the Anglo-Norman World' *Anglo-Norman Studies* 19 (1996) 51–68 on the possessions of Saint-Denis in Normandy.

240. For the latter, see Levillain, 'Études' 35–53. For the (lost) genuine version, see Große, *Saint-Denis* 61–62.

241. See above.

242. See above; the main conflict was more generally about monastic tithes, but it is possible that privileges in favour of Saint-Denis were at issue (Große, *Saint-Denis* 64).

243. Große, *Saint-Denis* 64–65.

Saint-Denis. This, however, was not the end of the conflict; while the pope repeatedly urged King Philip to protect Saint-Denis against the bishop of Paris, it was only in 1068 that the king issued the important privilege already mentioned.

In the light of all this, Levillain's hypotheses are indeed attractive. There were many genuine and forged privileges Saint-Denis relied upon, including royal immunities dating back to Merovingian times and an exceptional number of papal privileges. Nonetheless, the *QSN* forgery must have been particularly attractive for the monks of Saint-Denis. This is not only suggested by the fact that copied it both in the chartulary and in the *Sandionysiana*. It is also evident that this document very neatly fit the situation Saint-Denis was in. In addition to the clauses on monastic property and free election of the abbot, *QSN* contains the prohibition for the bishop to have inventories made at the abbot's death, to celebrate mass in monasteries, to place his cathedra there, or to attempt to interfere with internal issues of the monastery by giving directives 'however trivial' ('ordinationem quamvis levissimam'). It is precisely this passage which is highlighted in the Paris manuscript,[244] which is all the more significant as it otherwise has very few nota signs. Whether or not the *Sandionysiana* was compiled in preparation of the Lateran synod, it certainly was shaped by the conflicts of the 1060s. *74T* may have been attractive to many monks, but at Saint-Denis in the 1060s it must have been recognised as a collection that was almost tailor-made for the situation the monks were facing.

Canon Law, Forgery, and Monastic Networks

However, the *Sandionysiana* not only is evidence of the monastic uses of *74T* or the way the monks of Saint-Denis used new law in the crises of the 1060s. Like Fleury's conflict with the bishop of Orléans, the Saint-Denis case was watched as a conflict that was important for the French Church at large. In several cases, other monasteries seem to have employed the very materials the monks of Saint-Denis produced in the context of this conflict. To quote only one example, Corbie found itself in a similar situation in the 1060s and was in close contact with Saint-Denis.[245]

---

244. Paris, BnF, nouv. acq. lat. 326, fol. 19v.

245. Ludwig Falkenstein, 'Alexander III. und die Abtei Corbie. Ein Beitrag zum Gewohnheitsrecht exemter Kirchen im 12. Jahrhundert' *Archivum Historiae Pontificae* 27 (1989) 85–195, here at 109–113; Laurent Morelle, 'Moines de Corbie sous influence sandionysienne? Les préparatifs corbéiens du synode romain de 1065', *L'Église de France et la papauté (X^e–XIIIe siècle) / Die französische Kirche und das Papsttum (10.–13. Jahrhundert): actes du XXVIe Colloque franco-allemand organisé en coopération avec l'École nationale des chartes par l'Institut historique allemand de Paris (Paris, 17–19 octobre 1990)*, ed. Rolf Große (Studien und Dokumente zur Gallia Pontificia 1; Bonn 1993) 197–218, here at 207–211; Falkenstein, *Papauté* 96–106; Große, 'Papsturkunden' 185.

The parallels are indeed striking: both monasteries had obtained a privilege from Leo IX in 1050; both were engaged in similar conflicts with their local bishops by 1060; both conflicts were heard at the Lateran synod of 1066; and both houses composed new chartularies in this context. A privilege forged at Saint-Denis before 1065 is suspiciously similar to the (genuine) 1050 privilege for Corbie; later, an extract of the Saint-Denis forgery was copied into a Corbie chartulary, with its text being adopted to local circumstances.[246]

These textual links are valuable evidence for the way texts and ideas travelled, and they are anything but unique.[247] Not much later (apparently after 1076, but before 1082), forgers at Westminster took the privileges for Saint-Denis as their model to articulate their rather lofty view of monastic liberty in general and that of Westminster in particular. For this, they used the (genuine) 1068 privilege of Philip I, forged charters as found in the Saint-Denis chartulary, and either the *Sandionysiana* itself or another *74T*-related collection; like other monastic users of these collections they particularly valued *QSN*.[248] Finally, a collection very similar to the *Sandionysiana* is extant in Paris, BnF, lat. 13658, a twelfth-century manuscript from the monastery of Chézal-Benoît in the diocese of Bourges.[249] It is possible that the collection was compiled at this house, which was founded in 1093. The collection is a *74T*-derivative work very similar to the *Sandionysiana* in size, content, and structure. Like the latter, the *74T* material is largely preserved but rearranged chronologically, and supplemented with a small number of canons from other sources including distinct Gregory I material it shares with the *Sandionysiana*.[250] In the collection in BnF lat. 13658, the *74T* canons are often 'shortened and copied badly'; twelve additional canons are taken from Regino of Prüm.[251] To some extent, the

---

246. Leo IX, JL 4212 for Corbie may have influenced the monumental forgery JL 4182 (= Böhmer-Frech †631) in favour of Saint-Denis; on the JL 4182 excerpt at Corbie, see Morelle, 'Moines de Corbie' 207–211. JL 4182 must have been forged before 1065 for the latest, the year Alexander II (JL 4565) confirmed a shorter version.

247. For instructive parallels, see also Robert F. Berkhofer, *Day of Reckoning: Power and Accountability in Medieval France* (The Middle Ages; Philadelphia 2004).

248. See Bernhard W. Scholz, 'Two Forged Charters from the Abbey of Westminster and Their Relationship with St. Denis' *English Historical Review* 76 (1961) 466–478 for edition and analysis of the forgeries. The passages Scholz identified as 'probably derived from some canonical collection' (ibid. 471) are in fact lifted from *74T*, see Rolker, 'Collection' 69–70. They are also found in the *Sandionysiana*. For relations between Saint-Denis and Westminster, see also Grant, 'Suger' 51–52 and Große, 'Papsturkunden' 185.

249. Fournier, 'Manuel' 218–219; Gérard Fransen, 'Autour de la collection en 74 titres' *Revue de Droit canonique* 25 (1975) 61–73, here at 65–66; Fowler-Magerl, 'Fine Distinctions' 157–159; eadem, *Clavis* 116; Kéry 293–294. My analysis is based on that of Fowler-Magerl and her *Clavis canonum* database.

250. Fowler-Magerl, 'Fine Distinctions' 158.

251. Fowler-Magerl, *Clavis* 116.

compiler continued the trends already visible in the *Sandionysiana*. To take the canons attributed to Gregory I as an example: In the *Sandionysiana*, this material is mainly found in two series of Gregory I canons, but partly scattered across the collection.[252] In the collection of BnF lat. 13658, all Gregory I material also found in the *Sandionysiana* is gathered in two separate sections.[253] While the genesis of the collection of BnF lat. 13658 and its relation to the *Sandionysiana* partly remains obscure, the two collections are clearly interrelated, supporting the idea that texts, ideas, and whole collections of canons travelled much more widely within monastic networks than it has so far been noticed by legal historians. Given that a use of the *Sandionysiana* can normally not be discerned from a use of *74T*, the examples quoted here are unlikely to be the only ones.[254]

To sum up, the *Sandionysiana* was a monastic canon law collection that emerged during a prolonged conflict with the local bishop, and was shaped directly by the issues under dispute in the 1060s. Saint-Denis was not the only monastery to face such a conflict, and monks at Corbie, Westminster, and Chézal-Benoît can be shown to have employed Saint-Denis materials to bolster their position vis-à-vis the local bishop. Genuine and forged privileges, pro-monastic forgeries like *QSN*, and canonical collections were exchanged between these houses. Yet it was not only the monks who read, copied, and used these texts; in the end, the monks had to convince synods, bishops, kings, and other magnates that their claims were justified. If individual houses successfully employed collections like *74T* this also contributed to the authority of both the collection and the materials found there. Gradually, therefore, even partisan forgeries like *QSN* were accepted as part of general Church law.

3.5.2 The *Burdegalensis*: A Monastic Burchard Version from Aquitaine

The *Collectio Burdegalensis* is a canonical collection compiled in the late eleventh century or not much later in Aquitaine.[255] It is extant in two

---

252. *Sandionysiana* cc. 11–18, 43, 75, 100, 169–219, and 307–308.

253. Canons 10–39 and 238–257 according to the *Clavis canonum* database, which follows the numbering found in Paris, BnF, lat. 13658. The only exception is a canon on fol. 64va; it is part of an appendix taken from Regino's *Libri duo*, manifestly an addition to the collection: the numbering of the canons does not extend to this appendix and the *capitulatio* does not refer to these texts (Fowler-Magerl, *Clavis* 116).

254. Grant, 'Suger' 51–52, Große, 'Papsturkunden' 185, and Waldman, 'Charters' have pointed out parallels and links to Bury St Edmunds which would be worth studying in greater detail.

255. Adolphe Tardif, 'Une collection canonique poitevine' NRHDFE 21 (1897) 149–216; Schneider, 'Einleitung' 41–42; Kéry 215–216; Fowler-Magerl, *Clavis* 129–132; Herbert Schneider, 'New Wine in Old Skins? Remarks on the *Collectio Burdegalensis*', *Canon Law, Religion and Politics: Liber amicorum Robert Somerville*, ed. Uta-Renate Blumenthal et al. (Washington, D.C. 2012) 41–55; for

near-contemporary manuscripts, the incomplete Bordeaux copy and the complete Würzburg copy.[256] Neither manuscript has been established as the 'original' or as the direct model of the other, but the version preserved in the Würzburg copy on the whole is closer to the formal sources.[257] Both manuscripts in addition to the *Burdegalensis* also contain materials most interesting for a monastic audience.[258]

The *Burdegalensis* is a substantial collection (covering almost 100 folios in the complete form) divided into sixteen books according to subject matter. Its main source is an Italian (though not a Milan) version of Burchard.[259] However, the collection is much more than an abbreviated Burchard; it is the result of a substantial and careful reworking of Burchard, selecting, rearranging, and reinterpreting the Burchardian material in an independent way, and adding to it from other sources. One of these sources is *74T* in a version similar or identical to that used for the *Tarraconensis I*.[260] Excerpts from the *Tarraconensis I* are found as additions to the collection proper in both manuscripts of the *Burdegalensis*.[261]

The compiler left out some books of Burchard completely (the last one, for example), gathered into one book what Burchard had divided into several books (most notably, marriage legislation), and introduced a new book on monastic liberty which has no model in Burchard but instead draws heavily on the *74T*. So while Burchard as a model is still visible, it is an independent and well-planned revision drawing on substantial materials (not only *74T*).

Date and Place of Origin

Where and when the collection was compiled and the extant copies were made, cannot be established with certainty. The most recent material

---

an analysis and an 'implicit' edition, see Kriston R. Rennie, *The Collectio Burdegalensis: A Study and Register of an Eleventh-Century Canon Law Collection* (Medieval Law and Theology 6; Toronto 2013); for some corrections to Rennie's analysis, see Schneider, 'New Wine' esp. 51.

256. Bordeaux, BM, 11, fols. 147r–171v (ending with *Burdegalensis* 7.16); Würzburg, UB, Mp.j.q.2, fols. 2v–95r.

257. Schneider, 'New Wine' 45.

258. The Bordeaux copy contains JE †1951 and (twice) JE †1996, see Detlev Jasper, 'Inveni in canonibus apostolorum. Zu einer mittelalterlichen Fälschung auf Papst Clemens I.', *Papsttum, Kirche und Recht im Mittelalter. Festschrift für Horst Fuhrmann zum 65. Geburtstag*, ed. Hubert Mordek (Tübingen 1991) 201–213, here at 205–206 and 209. (Gilchrist, 'Monastic Forgeries' 267 only mentioned the occurrence of JE †1996.) The Würzburg copy at the very end contains a short historical note on the origins of monasticism; it is edited in Hans Thurn, *Bestand bis zur Säkularisierung. Erwerbungen und Zugänge bis 1803* (Die Handschriften der Universitätsbibliothek Würzburg 5; Wiesbaden 1994), here at 114.

259. Schneider, 'New Wine' 49–50.

260. Fowler-Magerl, 'Fine Distinctions' 156, 163–165, and 166 n. 92.

261. Fowler-Magerl, *Clavis* 135.

the collection contains are canons from a Roman synod held in November 1078, the oath taken by Berengar of Tours in 1079, and canons from the famous Council of Poitiers of 1078.[262] The latter canons have attracted some attention in the context of the so-called Investiture Contest, but the *Burdegalensis* compiler seems not to have had a special interest in these texts.[263] The collection is commonly thought to have been compiled not long after this date, and the extant manuscripts may have been produced before 1100, although a later date cannot be excluded.[264] Thus, the collection in its extant form was compiled after 1079, but a precise *terminus ante quem* cannot be established.

As for the place of origin, scholarship for a long time tended to locate it in or around Poitiers. The argument was mainly based on the presence of 'Poitevin' material found in a number of collections, some of which can be traced to the Poitou region; but as more and more collections were discovered to contain some or indeed all 'Poitevin' features without showing other links to this region, the idea of a 'Poitevin school of law' was given up.[265]

Fowler-Magerl contemplated the idea that the collection may have been compiled in preparation of the council(s) of Bordeaux held in 1079/80.[266] Given that the *Burdegalensis* contains canons from the Roman synod held in November 1078 this would imply a very hasty compilation in early 1079 by someone familiar with very recent legatine and Roman legislation—a model which in turn would suggest that Hugh of Die was involved in the making of the collection.[267] Recently, Kriston Rennie has suggested that the *Burdegalensis* was compiled for La Sauve Majeure, a monastery some twenty kilometres east of Bordeaux. He assumed that the monastery was founded in 1079, and further suggested that the 1080 council may have

262. For an excellent study and edition, see Beate Schilling, 'Die Kanones des Konzils von Poitiers (1078) (mit Textedition). Ein Versuch' ZRG Kan. Abt. 103 (2017) 70–130, here at 75–77.

263. Rudolf Schieffer, *Die Entstehung des päpstlichen Investiturverbots für den deutschen König* (MGH Schriften 28; Stuttgart 1981), here at 166–167; Schneider, 'New Wine' 54–55.

264. Schneider (MGH Ordines 277) dates both manuscripts to the twelfth century.

265. Rolker, *Canon Law* 73–81 against the model proposed by Tardif, 'Collection' and Gabriel Le Bras, 'L'activité canonique à Poitiers pendant la réforme grégorienne (1049–1099)', *Mélanges offerts à René Crozet à l'occasion de son soixante-dixième anniversaire*, ed. Pierre Gallais (2 vols. Poitiers 1966) 1.237–239. See also Kriston R. Rennie, 'Poitevine Collections: Looking Behind the Manuscript Evidence' ZRG Kan. Abt. 97 (2011) 59–75.

266. Fowler-Magerl, *Clavis* 130. It is normally assumed that there were two separate councils, see Theodor Schieffer, *Die päpstlichen Legaten in Frankreich vom Vertrage von Meersen (870) bis zum Schisma von 1130* (Historische Studien 263; Berlin 1935), here at 126–127, followed by Herbert Edward John Cowdrey, *Pope Gregory VII, 1073–1085* (Oxford 1998), here at 367–368. The key evidence for the 1080 council is an entry in the late-medieval *Petit Cartulaire* of La Sauve Majeure; it is a forgery according to Ludwig Falkenstein, 'Das Grand Cartulaire der Abtei La Sauve Majeure und seine Papsturkunden' *Francia* 26 (1999) 155–183, here at 171–173. See also the following notes.

267. Fowler-Magerl, *Clavis* 130.

taken place at La Sauve Majeure rather than in Bordeaux.[268] The latter claim cannot be maintained,[269] whether or not his date for the foundation of La Sauve Majeure is accurate.[270]

Yet it is not impossible that the *Burdegalensis* was indeed compiled for or at La Sauve Majeure. The main reason to think so is the fact that the manuscript today kept in Bordeaux in the late fifteenth century was owned by the abbey, where it may have been already for a long time.[271] Unfortunately, its earlier history is rather obscure.[272] The manuscript itself commonly dated to the late eleventh or early twelfth century; on palaeographical grounds, it has been located to Aquitaine, but no more precise claims have been made.

For the Würzburg copy, the evidence is even less conclusive. Rennie suggested that the Würzburg copy may have been written as early as 1080 at La Sauve Majeure and brought to Saintes very quickly,[273] but evidence for all three claims is scarce. Even if the collection was compiled at La Sauve Majeure in or very soon after 1080, the place of origin and the later history of the Würzburg manuscript are still unclear.[274] The most important clue to its medieval history is a reference on folio 163r from the twelfth century pointing to a certain Peter of Saintes:

'Petrus Petrus [*sic*] presul Xantonensis salutat. Petrus.'

---

268. Rennie, *Burdegalensis* 19.

269. There is no evidence that the council was celebrated at the site of the monastery. Rennie's argument is based on the supposed confirmation of the foundation charter as edited in *Grand cartulaire de La Sauve Majeure*, ed. Charles Higounet et al. (2 vols. Études et documents d'Aquitaine 8; Bordeaux 1996), here at 1.34–35; yet the text is a forgery (see Falkenstein, 'Grand cartulaire' 171–173 and Constance H. Berman, '[Review of:] Charles Higounet and Arlette Higounet-Nadal, Eds., with Nicole De Peña, *Grand Cartulaire de la Sauve Majeure*' *Speculum* 72 (1997) 1183–1186, here at 1185). Even if the charter were genuine, it would not support the idea that the newly-founded monastery could entertain many guests; all there was in 1079 was a tiny church, an 'ecclesiola' (*Grand cartulaire*, ed. Higounet et al. 1.33). Second, and decisively, the charter in question clearly states it was issued at the council held in Bordeaux; the phrase 'Burdegalensi civitate' (*Grand cartulaire*, ed. Higounet et al. 1.35) cannot be read, as Rennie tried to do, as evidence for the council held at La Sauve Majeure.

270. The two key documents are edited in *Grand cartulaire*, ed. Higounet et al. 1.33–35. The first one is a forgery (see the last note); for second one, it is doubtful whether its original referred to La Sauve Majeure at all, see Berman, 'Sauve Majeure' esp. at 1185; she concludes that La Sauve Majeure was 'probably not founded in 1079' (ibid. 1186). The issue has not yet been critically studied.

271. Fowler-Magerl, *Clavis* 130 erroneously stated this for the Würzburg copy.

272. Jasper, 'Fälschung' 205 pointed out that the material found immediately before the *Burdegalensis* in the Bordeaux copy was once separate and only later combined with the collection.

273. Rennie, *Burdegalensis* 20.

274. The most recent catalogue cautiously gives 'eleventh- or twelfth-century Western France' as its time and place of origin: Thurn, *Bestand* 112. See also Brommer, 'Kurzformen' 28–29 and Schneider (MGH Ordines 277) (both 'saec. XII'), and Kéry 215 ('saec. XI^ex–XII^in').

As Schneider rightly pointed out, this does not look like an exlibris.[275] And even if one took it as an exlibris, the question remains who was the owner. Fowler-Magerl suggested Bishop Peter of Saintes, who took office around 1107.[276] However, not only in the Würzburg manuscript but also in the lists of bishops of Saintes there are several Peters, including another bishop of this name only a few years later.[277] So the Würzburg copy of the *Burdegalensis* may have been at Saintes (some 125 kilometres north of Bordeaux) in early the twelfth century, but this does not help in locating the collection itself.

This leaves the question where the *Burdegalensis* was compiled, open to speculation; given that both extant copies seem to have been produced in Aquitaine, this may also be taken as the home of the collection. It is also plausible that the collection was made for or indeed produced by a monastic community, but the available evidence does not allow to establish a specific house as the home of the *Burdegalensis*. Given that La Sauve Majeure owned the Bordeaux manuscript, and produced a forgery on monastic liberty,[278] it remains an attractive hypothesis that this house also is the home of the collection.

Analysis: Making Burchard More Monastic

However, wherever the *Burdegalensis* was compiled, internal evidence reveals something about the preoccupations of its compiler. As the main model of the collection was Burchard, I will first look at three examples how Burchard's materials were treated by the compiler of the *Burdegalensis*—book 15, the books on marriage, and Burchard's penitential—before looking specifically at the pro-monastic tendencies visible in the whole collection.

Burchard's book fifteen is a good starting point to highlight the independent character of the *Burdegalensis*. The book has no equivalent in the *Burdegalensis*, and it is plausible to assume that this has to do with its content. Burchard's book 15, containing canons on the cooperation of bishop and emperor, belongs to the books that most clearly are shaped by the compiler's existence as a bishop in the Ottonian-Salian Church. From the perspective of a compiler working in late-eleventh century Aquitaine, who was one of the first compilers to integrate a ban on lay investiture in his collections, these parts of Burchard must indeed have looked

---

275. Schneider, 'New Wine' 43 n. 48.
276. Fowler-Magerl, *Clavis* 130.
277. See Robert Favreau, 'Évêques d'Angoulême et Saintes avant 1200' *Revue historique de Centre-Ouest* 9 (2010) 7–142.
278. Falkenstein, 'Grand cartulaire' 171–173 did not suggest a date for the forgery.

strange.[279] For Burchard and many of his early readers in the Empire, good relations with the emperor were all-important, and the cooperation between the two powers was an accepted ideal. At the mouth of the Garonne, the emperor was far away and, in the late eleventh century, often identified as the adversary of the pope. It is a striking detail that the *Burdegalensis* compiler in one case replaced 'emperor' with 'king' in a canon he took from Burchard's book fifteen.[280] Therefore, I assume that the absence of an equivalent book to Burchard's book fifteen in the *Burdegalensis* is the result of a deliberate decision.

A different approach can be observed in the case of marriage legislation. Burchard's decision to treat marriage and sexuality in no less than three different books (four, if one counts the *Corrector*) largely reflects his preoccupation with incest legislation. Yet for most readers of Burchard around 1100, this division of the materials must have looked rather unmotivated. Why not treat separation of marriage on grounds of incest in the same book as separation on the ground of adultery? Why were sexual sins of married people dealt with in three books on marriage, and again in the penitential towards the end of the collection? Why was incest with in-laws treated in a book separate from incest with relatives by blood? And why did 27 (of some 1,800) canons merit a separate book, anyhow? These questions may have occurred to many readers and copyists; whatever his thoughts may have been, the compiler of the *Burdegalensis* took action and combined Burchard's books that treated marriage and sexuality, effectively reducing three books into one.

The *Burdegalensis* compiler also reworked book nineteen of Burchard (also known as the *Corrector*), and doing so displayed that he knew very well what he was doing. In Burchard's collection, there are penitential canons in almost every single book—and in addition to this, a separate penitential book (the *Corrector*) that contained nothing but penitential canons. Sometimes, the book was left out when Burchard was copied, sometimes the *Corrector* was copied separately, indicating that in the mind of many users of Burchard it was somewhat independent from the rest of the collection. The *Burdegalensis* compiler took yet another route; while dropping most of the *Corrector*, he retained some of the canons found there and carefully inserted them into books that dealt with the respective subject matter.

Last but not least, let us look at the most important change the com-

---

279. The Italian *Collection in 20 Books* in Vat. lat. 1350 also omits Burchard's book 15 (and book 20), see Brommer, 'Kurzformen' 27 and the discussion below.

280. *Burdegalensis* 13.4 = Burchard 15.8, as observed by Schneider, 'New Wine' 54 n. 52.

piler of the *Burdegalensis* made when turning Burchard into a new collection. As has been mentioned several times already, Burchard had little to say about monks and monasteries apart from stressing episcopal rights of control over religious communities in his diocese. The compiler of the *Burdegalensis*, who was familiar with rather different law from the *74T*, in this respect made important choices. After having made only minor changes to five Burchardian books, with book six the *Burdegalensis* compiler 'departs from the order provided by Burchard and conspicuously turns to monastic law under a separate title', as Schneider put it.[281] For this, he turned to *74T* for materials which were gathered in a separate book on monastic liberty; even the title of the book seems to have been inspired by *74T*.[282] Among the materials taken from *74T*, the forgery *QSN* is given special attention, as the *Burdegalensis* compiler (otherwise faithful to his formal sources) placed it first in this book. Interestingly, the canon was given a new rubric, calling it 'a general privilege in favour of monks'.[283] Technically, this might be a paradox, as a privilege by definition is a special right. And yet, the phrase is apt to describe *QSN* which may have begun as the forgery of a single monk but by 1100 was in the course of becoming universal law of the Church, bestowing a privileged position not to this or that monastic community but to the monastic order as such. Book six of the *Burdegalensis* was indeed a book asserting 'monastic liberty', and *QSN* was an appropriate opening canon.

Book seven, while modelled on a book of Burchard, continues the monastic theme. It is a short book, but interestingly, the compiler selected all of Burchard's material on nuns in this book. As it seems, the *Burdegalensis* compiler, after having composed a new book on monastic liberty which mainly was concerned with monks, deliberately supplemented it with a short book on nuns (and, in passing, canonesses). Such a book specifically on female religious communities is unique in the pre-Gratian collections, and indicative of the readiness to adapt the collections to the changing realities of the eleventh and twelfth centuries.[284]

A Mini-Collection Within the Collection: The *Burdegalensis* Appendix

Both *Burdegalensis* manuscripts after the collection also contain itself a number of texts which Rennie has rightly called a 'mini-collection' in its

---

281. Schneider, 'New Wine' 53–54.

282. *Burdegalensis* 6: 'De monasteriorum monachorumque libertate et eorum sancto proposito'; see *74T* title 4.

283. *Burdegalensis* 6.1, rubric: 'Privilegium generale monachis inductum a beato Gregorio papa'.

284. See also Rolker, 'Monastic Canon Law'.

own right.[285] Strictly speaking, the canons are not part of the collection, but as they are found in both manuscripts in similar form, and have no known transmission outside the *Burdegalensis*, it is reasonable to consider this evidence too.

The appendices have the following material in common: The miracle of Saint Hilary, a sermon attributed to Leo I, and canon law material taken from earlier collections. More specifically, one finds canons from Burchard (six canons in the Bordeaux copy, only three of which are also in the Würzburg copy), from the *Tarraconensis I* (nine and seven canons, respectively), from the *Tarraconensis II* (two and one), and above all from *74T* (some seventy and some sixty). This represents a large share of *74T* canons not already found in the main collection; the contents of the appendices are as diverse as the content of *74T*. What is remarkable, though, is that both appendices draw on a similar body of formal sources and make very similar choices. While there are differences (essentially the Bordeaux copy being more complete than the Würzburg one), the excerpts cannot be thought to have been made independently of each other; the appendix was transmitted with the *Burdegalensis*, and like the 'main collection' transmitted with some variants.

The parallels between this mini-collection and the two *Tarraconenses* collections is in all likelihood not to be understood as a use of two distinct collections; it is more probable that the *Burdegalensis* appendix draws on an unknown version of the *Tarraconensis I* that contains some of the material characteristic of the version known as *Tarraconensis II*. While the number of canons borrowed from this collection is too small (and the genesis of the *Tarraconenses* is too complex) to draw far-reaching conclusions, it links the *Burdegalensis* to collections compiled further south.

Crucially, the appendix draws for most texts on the very two canonical collections that already had provided the bulk of material for the *Burdegalensis*—namely Burchard and *74T*. This too can hardly be a coincidence. What is more, while the content of these canons is quite diverse, the compiler of the appendix carefully avoided overlap to the main collection—he almost only chose canons not already found in the *Burdegalensis* itself. So the compiler of the appendix not only worked with the same sources as the *Burdegalensis* compiler, he also knew that he did so, and he took the effort to check with the collection he added to. Given the size of the *Burdegalensis*, this required good memory. Unless one sees the appendix as the work of the original compiler who changed his mind about some omis-

---

285. Rennie, *Burdegalensis* 26–30; see already Fowler-Magerl, 'Fine Distinctions' 179.

sions (but too late to integrate these afterthoughts into his main work) one is tempted to see this as evidence of how compilers were learning from each other, simply by working with the same materials in different ways, and driven by the ambition to avoid overlap.

3.5.3 The *Collectio Casinensis* in Montecassino MS 216

The *Collectio canonum Casinensis duodecimi seculi*, as the modern editor called it,[286] is a collection that can be described as a derivative of *5L* drawing also on *74T*. It was compiled at Montecassino early in the twelfth century and is extant in a single copy from the end of the century. It contains 378 canons that are only partly organised according to subject matter; the canons are not numbered, nor divided into books; there is no *capitulatio*. The *fontes formales* include *5L*, *74T*, Burchard's *Liber decretorum*, and Ivo's *Decretum* or a collection similar to it; only a handful of canons are not taken from these collections.[287] This includes excerpts from the synods of Urban II and Paschal II found towards the end of the collection.[288]

The first part of the collection seems to have been ordered according to subject matter; the collection begins with canons on the necessity and utility of penance, and some rather general principles of penance. Penitential canons on murder, manslaughter, and abortion are grouped together, followed by a canons on various sexual sins committed by lay-people, monks, and secular clergy; another section seems to deal mainly with perjury. However, the same topics are also dealt with elsewhere, and it is not always clear whether the apparent order by subject matter was the result of deliberate arrangement. Especially in the middle of the collection, no principle of organisation can be discerned; the canons are neither in the sequence of the formal sources, nor arranged according to any discernible principle. Towards the end of the collection, however, a sub-section heavily drawing on *74T* is an exception to this rule.

This section (canons 301 to 321 in Reynold's numbering) can be described as a short version of the first six titles of *74T* augmented with further pro-monastic materials and privileges of Montecassino Abbey. The basic structure and argument of *74T* is still visible, as the short version preserves key texts of *74T* mostly in the original sequence; thus, it begins with

---

286. Reynolds, *Collectio Casinensis*. The following analysis is based on Reynold's study and edition.

287. Reynolds, *Collectio Casinensis* 4–9.

288. *Casinensis* cc. 326 and 327 (ed. Reynolds, *Collectio Casinensis* 99), taken from Piacenza 1095 and the Lateran Council of 1110, respectively. On the councils, see Uta-Renate 5986 *of Pope Paschalis II 1100–1110* (PIMS Studies and Texts 43; Toronto 1978) and Robert Somerville, *Pope Urban II's Council of Piacenza* (Oxford 2011), respectively.

the primacy of the Roman church,[289] the authority of (papal) privileges,[290] monastic liberty (JE †1366), and procedural law.[291] The selection criteria of the Montecassino compiler leave no doubt that he was specifically interested in monastic liberty. If *74T* in title three had gathered authorities on the immutability of papal privileges in favour of churches and monasteries, the Montecassino compiler selected all canons of this title that explicitly mention monasteries, and those canons only. Also, the additions from other sources point in the same direction. After the *Quam sit necessarium* forgery taken from *74T*, the Montecassino compiler inserted a canon attributed to Pope Leo,[292] the pro-monastic forgery attributed to Boniface (JE †1996), and four texts 'On the liberty of Montecassino'.[293] This strongly suggests that the compiler was well aware that the pro-monastic forgeries he found in *74T* and elsewhere could have immediate relevance for his own community.

The Montecassino collection is a modest, mid-size collection of the twelfth century. When it was compiled, Burchard was already available at Montecassino, and by the time the extant copy was made, the *Decretum Gratiani* already circulated widely. Compared to these works, the Montecassino collection may not be very sophisticated, but even in a place well-equipped with legal manuscripts like Montecassino, this kind of collection was useful enough to be compiled, to be copied (at least once), to be preserved and (to judge from the state of the manuscript) also to be

289. *Casinensis* cc. 301–304 (ed. Reynolds, *Collectio Casinensis* 93–94), taken from *74T* cc. 2, 8, 9, and 11.

290. *Casinensis* cc. 305–307 (ed. Reynolds, *Collectio Casinensis* 94–95) = *74T* cc. 24, 27, 25, and 31.

291. *Casinensis* c. 308 (ed. Reynolds, *Collectio Casinensis* 95) = *74T* c. 39 (JE †1366); *Casinensis* cc. 315–321 (ed. Reynolds, *Collectio Casinensis* 96–98)= *74T* cc. 44, 45, 46, 51, 48, 61, and 62.

292. *Casinensis* c. 309 (ed. Reynolds, *Collectio Casinensis* 98). This text, not identified by Reynolds, is Pseudo-Leo, JL 4327a (Böhmer-Frech †426). For an edition, see Horst Fuhrmann, 'Ein Papst Ideo (zu Collectio Lipsensis [*sic*] tit. 27, 5)', *Études d'histoire du droit canonique dédiées à Gabriel Le Bras* (2 vols. Paris 1965) 1.89–98 at 97–98. In addition to the *Lipsiensis* and the pre-Gratian collections listed by Fuhrmann (ibid., 97 n. 24), JL 4327a is also found in various versions in the *Francofurtana*, at least one *74T* manuscript, the Riccardiana florilegium, and Spanish manuscript on monastic discipline and property. See *Die Collectio Francofurtana: eine französische Dekretalensammlung. Analyse beruhend auf den Vorarbeiten von Walther Holtzmann* (†), ed. Peter Landau and Gisela Drossbach (MIC Corpus collectionum 9; Vatican City 2007), here at 192 (*Francofurtana* 26.4), Gilchrist, 'Prolegomena' xlv (transmission with *74T*), Picasso, 'Florilegio' 210–211 (Riccardiana florilegium), and Paul Ewald, 'Reise nach Spanien im Winter von 1878 auf 1879' NA 6 (1881) 217–398, here at 243. In the *Lipsiensis* it is attributed to 'Pope Ideo', but otherwise to a Pope Leo. As Fuhrmann argued convincingly, the attibution to Leo IX is unlikely (Fuhrmann, 'Papst Ideo' 94–95).

293. *Casinensis* cc. 310 and 311–314 (ed. Reynolds, *Collectio Casinensis* 95 and 96), respectively. See Gilchrist, 'Monastic Forgeries' 272 on c. 310 (JE †1996); for an edition, see Giles Constable, 'The Treatise "Hortatur nos" and Accompanying Canonical Texts on the Performance of Pastoral Work by Monks', *Speculum historiale. Geschichte im Spiegel von Geschichtsschreibung und Geschichtsdeutung. Johannes Spörl aus Anlass seines 60. Geburtstages dargebracht von Weggenossen, Freunden und Schülern*, ed. Clemens Bauer et al. (Freiburg and Munich 1965) 567–577.

used.[294] Also, even the modest degree of order the compiler was able to impose on his materials was the result of considerable labour; 5L, Burchard, and Ivo's *Decretum* are all massive compilations each containing thousands of canons; even if these three collections are well-structured, it is easy to get lost as they contain many canons in similar, but not identical versions. This all should warn against the idea to neglect 'minor' collections like that in Montecassino 216. Rather, we may take it as a useful source for the history of monastic canon law, and to take it seriously as evidence for the interest in legal materials. Like other compilers of monastic canon law collections, the monks of Montecassino displayed a special interest in penitential canons regulating marriage and sexuality, and also in papal letters protecting the liberty of Montecassino and the monastic order at large. Collections like that in Montecassino 216 show how monks were able to combine what modern scholarship has often studied separately—privileges for individual houses, pro-monastic forgeries, and canonical collections.

3.6 The Farfa Collection (*Farfensis*)

3.6.1 Gregory of Catino and the Register of Farfa Abbey

The *Collectio canonum regesto Farfensi inserta* ('Canon law collection inserted into the chartulary of Farfa'), or *Farfensis* for short, is a monastic canon law collection compiled around 1100 at Farfa,[295] an imperial abbey in the Sabine Hills some fifty kilometres north-east of Rome. As the modern title suggests, it is found in a monumental collection known as the *Regestum Farfense* (extant in Vat. lat. 8487) which documents the extended possessions of this monastery.[296] Containing more than 1,300 charters, the register is the most important source for the early medieval history of Farfa, which at times was the largest landowner among the great Italian abbeys.[297] In addition to charters documenting Farfa's possessions and the

---

294. See Reynolds, *Collectio Casinensis* 4 on signs of wear.

295. See Kölzer, 'Prolegomena' and his edition. For the manuscript, see Ignazio Giorgi, 'Prefazione', *Il regesto di Farfa*, ed. idem and Ugo Balzani (5 vols. Rome 1879–1914) 1.XXXIX–XLVII and Paul Fournier, 'La collezione canonica del regesto di Farfa' *Archivio della Società Romana di Storia Patria* 17 (1894) 285–301, here at 286–288. For bibliography, see Kéry 264–265 and Fowler-Magerl, *Clavis* 122–124. The most recent study is Lotte Kéry, 'Recht im Dienst der Reform. Kanonistische Sammlungen der Reformzeit und ihre "Adressaten"', *Brief und Kommunikation im Wandel. Medien, Autoren und Kontexte in den Debatten des Investiturstreits*, ed. Florian Hartmann (Papsttum im mittelalterlichen Europa 5; Cologne, Weimar, and Vienna 2016) 335–380 at 338–347.

296. Gregory gave it the slightly posh title 'Liber gemniagraphus sive cleronominalis ecclesiae pharphensis', explaining later that *gemniagraphus* meant 'topographic memory' and *cleronominalis* referred to Farfa's possessions (as opposed to leases which he later collected in a separate work): *Il regesto di Farfa*, ed. Ignazio Giorgi and Ugo Balzani (5 vols. Rome 1879–1914), here at 2.9.

297. There is no comprehensive study in English about this abbey; important studies include Toubert, *Latium médiéval*; Charles B. McClendon, *The Imperial Abbey of Farfa: Architectural Currents*

Farfensis itself, the *Regestum* contains a verse prologue, a preface, two catalogues of abbots and popes, and very brief historical notes (known as the *Annales Farfensis*).[298] It was compiled and written mainly by Gregory of Catino (d. after 1130) around the year 1100. The extant manuscript is Gregory's autograph, but the quires are not always in the original sequence. As Theo Kölzer established, originally the *Farfensis* was placed after the two prefaces, and the historical notes before the chartulary.[299]

With 280 proof texts, the *Farfensis* is a mid-sized collection—much larger than dossiers like the Riccardiana florilegium (containing some twenty canons), but much smaller than Burchard's *Liber decretorum* (containing almost 2,000 canons), to cite two collections Gregory was working with. The material is divided into four books, with the last being very short but the others roughly the same length. Books one and two were labelled as such by Gregory himself; books three and four have separate book titles but are not numbered, and it may be argued that they are in fact two halves of one book rather than two books.[300] While the *Farfensis* does cover a considerable range of topics, the focus is very clearly on monastic property. The first book is the only one with a somewhat broader scope; drawing mainly on the False Decretals, it deals with the sacraments, monastic clergy, procedural law, and church property. The remaining three books have in common that they concentrate on property, though drawing on different sources. Starting with the ancient provisions of the African councils, book two provides a rather traditional view on this issue, stressing the responsibility of the bishop for all ecclesiastical property in his diocese. The third book, while also concerned with ecclesiastical property, has a different approach as it mainly gathered canons attributed to Gregory the Great on monastic liberty, including some important pro-monastic forgeries. The last book, by far the shortest of all books, is likewise concerned with church property but draws on yet another set of sources, namely secular legislation.

---

of the Early Middle Ages (Yale Publications in the History of Art 36; New Haven and London 1987); Susan Boynton, *Shaping a Monastic Identity: Liturgy and History at the Imperial Abbey of Farfa, 1000–1125* (Conjunctions of Religion and Power in the Medieval Past; Ithaca, N.Y. 2006); Marios Costambeys, *Power and Patronage in Early Medieval Italy: Local Society, Italian Politics and the Abbey of Farfa, c. 700–900* (Life and Thought: Fourth Series 70; Cambridge 2007). For the possessions of Farfa, see Toubert, *Latium médiéval* esp. 2.1103–1126, Costambeys, *Power* ch. 2, and most recently Chiara Carloni, 'Celle e dipendenze del monastero di Farfa in area laziale', *Teoria e pratica del lavoro nel monachesimo altomedievale: atti del Convengno internazionale di studio, Roma - Subiaco, 7–9 giugno 2013*, ed. Letizia Ermini Pani (Spoleto 2015) 163–190.

298. See *Regesto* (ed. Giorgi and Balzani 2.3–19). The *Annales* contain numerous additions, see Kölzer, 'Prolegomena' 11.

299. Kölzer, 'Prolegomena' 9–16.

300. Fowler-Magerl, *Clavis* 123. Given the clear break marked by a title, I nonetheless retain the traditional classification of the four sections as books.

Both the codicological evidence and a first overview of the contents thus show that the *Farfensis* was an integral part of Gregory's attempts to document the possessions of his abbey. This is further confirmed by the reception of the collection; while it has no known circulation outside Farfa, Gregory reused some of the material he had gathered in the *Farfensis* in his later works (the *Liber Beraldi,* the *Chronicon Farfense,* and the *Liber Floriger*), a topic I will come back to.

3.6.2 Date

First, however, let us consider the date of the collection. As the *Farfensis* is an integral part of the *Regestum,* it is legitimate to infer the date the collection was compiled from this work. Codicological and palaeographical evidence suggest that the *Regestum* was written in several stages, but mainly by one hand (Gregory of Catino) and in a relatively short period of time. According to Kölzer's findings, the *Farfensis* grew out of a smaller work which now is extant as the second book of the whole collection and which was meant to supplement the chartulary proper.[301]

The most recent entry in the chartulary reports the election of Abbot Berardus III on May 23, 1099, so this date may be taken as the *terminus post quem.*[302] The list of popes contained in the *Regestum* strongly suggests that Gregory finished his work in 1100. The catalogue mentions the death of Wibert of Ravenna who died September 8 in Civita Castellana (not far from Farfa), but fails to mention his successors as anti-popes elected in late 1100 and early 1102, respectively. The monks of Farfa, loyal to the emperor and (with some reservations) to Wibert/Clement III, had a vital interest in these events; they must have heard about the election, imprisonment, and death of Theoderic of Albano in 1101/02 and likewise about the election and imprisonment of Albert of Silva Candida in 1102. It is therefore plausible to assume that Gregory would have mentioned these events if he had already known about them when working on the *Regestum.* Kölzer concluded that the oldest part of the *Farfensis* was finished by mid-September 1100, and the other books not long after.[303]

3.6.3 Structure and Content

As already mentioned, the *Farfensis* is divided into four books of unequal length; every book has a separate title indicating its content. Within the books, the canons are numbered (only exceptionally, small groups of

---

301. Kölzer, 'Prolegomena' 18.
302. Kölzer, 'Prolegomena' 26.
303. Kölzer, 'Prolegomena' 29.

canons are given one number).[304] The rubrics are largely Gregory's work, only some of the shorter ones are taken from the formal sources of the *Farfensis*. The rubrics are found not with the individual canons but only in the *capitulationes*. Those for book one and two are complete, providing a one-line rubric for every canon; that for book three is much more elaborate but incomplete, and that for book four is missing.[305] The *capitulatio* for book three is unusual in several respects. First, it has rather long rubrics (normally, some three to five lines instead of only one, and in one case no less than 18 lines), and second, instead of listing the rubrics of all canons in the sequence they are found in the collection itself, it first lists the rubrics for all canons attributed to Gregory the Great; the rest of book three and also book four, in contrast, are not covered by the *capitulationes*.

This imbalance and the special interest in Gregory the Great are also found in the collection itself. The title of book three announces a collection of 'decretals on the excellent liberty and security of monks by the blessed Roman Pontiff Gregory I' (while in fact it contains also other materials).[306] Compared to the other books, the beginning of this 'Gregory book' stands out; the script is almost twice the size as normal.[307] In addition, the first canon of book three is the only one in the *Farfensis* to be decorated with a portrait (of Gregory the Great).[308] The canon placed first in book three is also the canon which was given the unusually long entry in the *capitulatio*; it is no other text than *QSN*.

Material and Formal Sources

The *Farfensis* contains 273 numbered canons with a total of 280 proof texts. By far the largest share are canons attributed to councils (170 canons, or 61 percent); 60 are attributed to popes, 24 to secular rulers (mainly Justinian), 21 to other sources (e.g. Augustine, the *Canones Apostolorum*, Jerome); for seven texts no material source is indicated. The most recent material that can be securely dated is from 922, a fact that irritated Fournier but is not unusual for pre-Gratian collections.[309]

As for the formal sources, Gregory took his materials from a short form of Pseudo-Isidore, Burchard's *Liber decretorum*, the *Collection in Five Books* (= *5L*), and a dossier ultimately dependent on *74T* known as the

---

304. Kölzer, 'Prolegomena' 23.

305. Kölzer, 'Prolegomena' 23.

306. 'In nomine Domini incipiunt decreta beatissimi Gregorii pape urbis Rome de monachorum optima libertate sive securitate' (ed. Kölzer 216).

307. Kölzer, 'Prolegomena' 11.

308. Kölzer, 'Prolegomena' 11.

309. See Kölzer, 'Prolegomena' 82.

Riccardiana florilegium.[310] Concerning Pseudo-Isidore, Kölzer established that Gregory took many of his synodal and papal canons from a short version very similar to the Ottobonianus.[311] This could indicate a link to northern France.[312] In the case of *5L*, Gregory used a version very similar to (but not identical with) the extant Vat. lat. 1339.[313] Gregory took a total of 71 canons from *5L*, including all canons he needed to compile his book four. In six cases he retained not only the canon but also the glosses found in his source. The *Liber decretorum* of Burchard of Worms is the source of 32 canons in the *Farfensis*, 23 of which are found in one long series in book three;[314] three times, Burchard is mentioned by name.[315] As Kölzer demonstrated, Gregory used an Italian version of Burchard; more specifically, he may have used a copy similar to the extant Vat. lat. 1355. This is suggested by the fact that two of only three interpolated Burchard canons found in the *Farfensis* have a parallel in this copy; for the third, no parallel has been found.[316] The Burchard version used by Ivo of Chartres shares some peculiarities with the version used by Gregory of Catino but cannot possibly have been identical.[317] Finally, the beginning of book three on the *libertas* of the church and monastic privileges of the *Farfensis* has a number of parallels to *74T*.[318] The *Farfensis* here depends on the Riccardiana florilegium which in turn draws on an early version of *74T* also used by a number of French *74T*-derivatives including the *Collection in Four Books* and the *Sandionysiana*.[319] Other texts in the *Farfensis* cannot be traced to specific canon law collections. For example, the *Farfensis* includes a pro-monastic forgery (Boniface IV, JE †1996) which had an independent circulation but

310. Firenze, Biblioteca Riccardiana, 3006, fols. 203r–205v. For an edition, see Picasso, 'Florilegio' 207–211. For the manuscript, see Motta, 'Introduzione' xxiii–xxiv.

311. Ottobon. lat. 93; Kölzer, 'Prolegomena' 34–45.

312. Bischoff thought Ottobon. lat. 93 to have been at Chartres in the time of Fulbert (Kölzer, 'Prolegomena' 45 n. 87). Given that Fulbert quoted none of the canons which appear in a distinctive form in the Ottobonianus, this hypothesis is difficult to check.

313. Kölzer, 'Prolegomena' 50–51.

314. Kölzer, 'Prolegomena' 55. The series is *Farfensis* 3.54–76.

315. *Farfensis* 1.73.4: 'Bruchardi lib. XI t. [*sic*] LXVII' (ed. Kölzer 164), Farfa 2.88: 'Bruchardi lib. XI t. [*sic*] XXIII' (ed. Kölzer 208) and Farfa 3.73: 'Bruchardi lib. III t. [*sic*] CCXL' (ed. Kölzer 342). The canons are found in Burchard 11.67, 11.23, and 3.241, respectively.

316. Kölzer, 'Prolegomena' 60–62. *Farfensis* 3.74 is an otherwise unknown version of Burchard 8.67.

317. Rolker, *Canon Law* 110–112.

318. The title of book three reads: 'In nomine domini incipiunt capitula [...] de magna ecclesie libertate vel monachorum seu clericorum optima honestaque securitate, inprimis decreta beati Gregorii papae' (ed. Kölzer 211).

319. Fowler-Magerl, *Clavis* 122–124 (Farfa and Riccardiana florilegium); eadem, 'Fine Distinctions' 158–161 (*4L* and the *Sandionysiana*). Fowler-Magerl also pointed out that in a number of cases, these collections shared readings with the *Tarraconensis I* against *74T*. The use of the Riccardiana florilegium may explain some or perhaps even all *4L* and *Tarraconensis* parallels Kölzer noted in his edition; this question cannot be resolved here.

also was transmitted together in a number of florilegia dependent on *74T* and/or *5L*.[320] It is not impossible that the minor collections Gregory used already contained the Boniface forgery.

With the possible exception of the Riccardiana florilegium, none of Gregory's formal sources were very recent, and this comes as little surprise given that Gregory preferred ancient canons over new law even where he had such materials at hand. It is also true that Gregory's formal sources were fairly conventional. The use of Pseudo-Isidore, the 'Italian' Burchard version, and the *5L* confirm that Gregory mainly was working with relatively conventional materials; one would expect a well-equipped library like that of Farfa to have copies of these works by the time Gregory was working on the *Regestum*.

Character

The *Farfensis* no doubt is a monastic canon law collection. Its content is limited to material that was immediately relevant to the community at Farfa, and very directly supplements the chartulary of which it was indeed an integral part. Topics like episcopal elections, the celebration of synods or the celibacy of (secular) clergy are completely absent. In this sense, it is indeed 'local'.[321] The focus on Farfa's property also seems to be the reason why Gregory did not include any canons on penance or liturgy; even the sacraments are treated rather briefly in his collection. The main focus is monastic property, and books two to four treat the related issues on the basis of traditional canon law (mainly conciliar canons), genuine and forged letters of Gregory the Great, and secular legislation, respectively.[322] Gregory the Great is given special attention, as already indicated by a portrait of this monk-pope (the only such illustration in the whole collection); indeed, a complete book is presented as if it contained only Gregory material. The important pro-monastic forgery *QSN* (JE †1366) is placed very prominently at the beginning of book three, a presentation similar to (but not simply imitative of) that in *74T*, and Gregory of Catino also highlights this key document of monastic liberty in the *capitulatio*.

---

320. Kölzer, 'Prolegomena' 54–55 assumed JE †1996 was copied into *Farfensis* together with the surrounding material from an unknown collection. See Gilchrist, 'Monastic Forgeries' on the Boniface forgery, and Reynolds, 'Five Books [1990]' 294 on the (sometimes joint) transmission of JE †1366, JE †1951, and JE †1996. See also Hieronymus Frank, 'Zwei Fälschungen auf den Namen Gregors des Großen und Bonifatius IV. Ein Beitrag zur Ehrenrettung Erzbischof Lanfranks von Canterbury' *Studien und Mitteilungen zur Geschichte des Benediktiner-Ordens und seiner Zweige* 55 (1937) 19–47.

321. Kölzer, 'Prolegomena' 107. See Fournier, 'Collezione' 301.

322. This tripartite structure has a certain parallel in the *Anselmo dedicata*, as Kölzer, 'Prolegomena' 86 was the first to point out.

The pro-monastic forgeries (JE †1366 and †1996) link the *Farfensis* to other monastic collections, and like the *Sandionysiana*, it is found in the same manuscript as the chartulary.

The *Farfensis* contains but a few interpolations; whether or not they can be attributed to Gregory,[323] their pro-monastic character is significant. One of them deserves special attention because it cannot be explained by any of Gregory's possible sources and fits the specific situation of Farfa very well. In the original, the canon in question asserted that abbots are placed under episcopal control 'on account of humility', and this form is also found in Gregory's formal source, the *Liber decretorum* of Burchard of Worms. However, according to the version found in the *Farfensis*, an important exception is made here for 'those [abbots] who had papal and royal or imperial rights'.[324] In other words, the provisions on episcopal control simply did not apply to Farfa, which indeed boasted an impressive number of papal, royal, and imperial privileges. It is plausible to assume that this version emerged in an imperial abbey, and Farfa itself appears as a very likely candidate.

Yet the pro-monastic tendency of the *Farfensis* is not, or only exceptionally, visible in textual manipulations. All in all, Gregory's collection is selective but not overly partisan in character. Contrary to *74T* or *5L*, the *Farfensis* is much more concerned with the privileges of a specific community rather than the monastic order. Compared to these collections or even the *Sandionysiana*, it is indeed a 'local' collection, even if Gregory intended it for a wider use.[325] It is also more conservative in the sense that it generally preserved traditional canon law very faithfully, even where this implied far-reaching episcopal control over monastic property. However, it should also be noted that the local bishop for Farfa posed no threat; episcopal control over monastic houses was generally less tight in middle and southern Italy, and even ambitious bishops would have thought twice before attempting to 'control' great houses like Farfa. It is true that the *Farfensis* was less useful than, for example, *74T* in conflicts with the local bishop; but one should not forget that the *Farfensis* was supplemented by a chartulary of more than 1,000 entries all documenting Farfa's rights and

---

323. See Kölzer, 'Prolegomena' 81 who argued that Gregory should not be credited as the forger in the latter case, as he did not manipulate his material otherwise.

324. *Farfensis* 3.74 (with additions underlined): 'Abbates pro humilitate religionis his exceptis quos aut apostolica auctoritas vel regia sive imperatoria iura ad suam conservaverunt audientiam, reliqui in episcoporum potestate consistant [...].' Gregory's formal source was Burchard 8.67. Kölzer in his edition held that no (known) Burchard manuscript contained the addition, but later seemed to assert that the manipulation was already found in Gregory's Burchard; see Kölzer, 'Prolegomena' 60 against idem, 'Mönchtum' 139 as observed by Kéry, 'Recht' 344 n. 40.

325. Kéry, 'Recht' 347.

properties—including privileges that went beyond any canons found in
74*T*. Perhaps an abbey that had already been granted by Charlemagne free
abbatial elections, immunity, freedom from episcopal control, and other
privileges saw less need than other monasteries to rely on forged decretals
in such matters.[326]

Using Canon Law at Farfa

This brings us to the immediate context of the collection's compilation. Farfa was a great house with an ancient tradition, rich holdings, and a
large number of (genuine and forged, ancient and recent) privileges from
kings, emperors, and popes. In this, it is comparable to the great houses of
north-western Europe already mentioned earlier in this chapter (Fleury,
Saint-Denis, Westminster). A major difference to these houses concerned
the role of the bishop; both Fleury in Abbo's time and Saint-Denis in the
1060s were under serious pressure when conflicts with the local bishops
escalated. Farfa, in contrast, according to Gregory of Catino suffered from
abbots neglecting their duties, undue influence from the imperial court,
interference from Rome when it was held by Gregory VII, even from a
conspiracy supported by Clement III, and of course greedy local nobles;
yet the one institution that hardly figures in these narratives of property
dispute is the local bishop. This was indeed typical for the situation in Italy, especially south of Rome; it has been argued that the rarity of episcopal interference also accounts for the rather late date Italian houses sought
for 'full' exemption.[327] Another difference between Farfa and monasteries
north of the Alps was its rather peculiar position as being close to the
emperor and—spatially at least—to Rome. Compared to the French and
English communities just mentioned, the monks at Farfa were involved
much more directly into the great conflicts between pope and emperor
and the schisms of the eleventh and the twelfth centuries. Farfa remained
loyal to Henry IV throughout his prolonged conflicts with Gregory VII;
it accepted Wibert of Ravenna as Pope Clement III in 1084; perhaps as a
response, its liberty was called into question by Deusdedit in his *Collectio*;[328] as late as 1112, an unknown monk of Farfa wrote the *Orthodoxa defensio imperialis* to defend the imperial cause;[329] Paschal II was imprisoned

---

326. On Farfa's early medieval privileges see Costambeys, *Power* ch. 8.

327. See Ramseyer, *Transformation* (monasteries and bishops in general) and John Howe,
'Monasteria semper libera: Cluniac-Type Monastic Liberties in Some Eleventh-Century Central
Italian Monasteries' CHR 78 (1992) 19–34 (exemptions).

328. On Deusdedit 3.190 (149) (ed. Wolf von Glanvell 352–353), see below (Chapter Four, n. 143).

329. On the authorship see still Karl Heinzelmann, *Die Farfenser Streitschriften. Ein Beitrag zur
Geschichte des Investiturstreites* (diss. phil. Kaiser-Wilhelm-Universität, Strasbourg 1904), here at
119–120.

by Henry V at Tarano, one of Farfa's castles; and in 1159, (anti-)Pope Victor IV was consecrated in the abbey church.

This sometimes has given rise to the idea that Gregory of Catino, compiling his collection in the midst of these conflicts, produced an anti-Gregorian (or 'anti-reform', as Fournier held) collection.[330] This suspicion, however, is not confirmed by internal evidence. The pro-monastic character of the *Farfensis* could also make one think that it shared the anti-episcopal tendencies of collections like *74T*, but as already mentioned, this was not the case. So what did Gregory of Catino have in mind when he compiled his collection?

Fortunately, one does not have to speculate concerning the circumstances in which the *Farfensis* was compiled and used. First of all, the *Regestum* (including the *Farfensis*) can be linked to a bitter conflict with the counts of Palombara and Monticelli over some castles and other property in the very first years of the twelfth century.[331] As with all such conflicts, one should not overestimate the stability of the factions. The counts and their predecessors had long supported Farfa, and several family members had entered the monastery. Like so many conflicts over monastic property, it was only possible because of preceding cooperation; what was under dispute were the terms under which certain assets were given to the monastery. Apparently, the counts in 1103 gave certain castles and lands to the monastery, and received almost all of it back in long-term lease. According to Gregory of Catino—our only source for many aspects of the conflict—the counts had returned these assets which had been given to them in a similar long-term lease three generations before, and this claim seems to have enraged the counts. Indeed, there are good reasons to doubt the veracity of this account; contrary to what Gregory claims, not even the chartulary he compiled himself contains the relevant charters. Interestingly, Gregory himself condemned long-term leases, even if in this case he rested his case on the existence of such a contract; the counts in contrast would have agreed to a long-term lease in 1103 but apparently insisted that they had entered into such an arrangement by freely disposing over their property rather than 'returning' it to Farfa.

In any case, a prolonged conflict involving various local and not-so-local parties broke out. From a legal point of view, two claims of the counts of Palombara and Monticelli deserve special attention. First, they argued

---

330. Fournier, 'Collezione' 300–301, still followed e.g. by Boynton, *Shaping* 23.

331. For the following, see Heinzelmann, *Streitschriften* 65–98; Kölzer, 'Prolegomena' 108–112 (fundamental); Boynton, *Shaping* 1–41. For an excellent overview, see also Richard R. Ring, 'Review of Stroll, The Medieval Abbey of Farfa' *The Medieval Review* (1999) https://scholarworks.iu.edu/journals/index.php/tmr/article/view/14704.

that Farfa's privileges were valid only in the lifetime of the issuer; in addition, and spectacularly, they quoted the Donation of Constantine according to which, they held, Italy was papal property—and hence Farfa could not claim property over the disputed assets.[332] This highly unusual quotation of the Donation of Constantine also suggests that the counts (who otherwise supported Clement III) here either cooperated with Gregory VII or at least profited from his politics of claiming all of Latium as 'lands of Saint Peter'.[333] Without this backing, relying on the Donation of Constantine in a conflict over a handful of castles would have been a desperate lawyer's move at best.

Gregory of Catino was able to draw on his own works to respond directly to the claims of Farfa's opponents.[334] Six canons he lifted directly from the *Farfensis*, another 14 from one of its main sources, the False Decretals, and the selection was guided by the *Farfensis*. Later, Gregory turned again to the collection he had compiled as a young man; both the *Liber Beraldi* and his chronicle are informed by the legal arguments found in the *Farfensis*, especially when it comes to the inviolability of privileges. Given that the main conflict only broke out just after Gregory had finished his register-cum-collection, it cannot have been shaped by the course of these conflicts. However, one might legitimately speculate, whether Gregory—working through hundreds of charters—did not foresee some of the conflicts that were likely to occur, and indeed one could imagine that the very fact that the monks thanks to Gregory had a better overview over their possessions triggered some of the lingering conflicts.

However, one does not have to rely on such speculative arguments. If we are looking for lines of conflicts that already seem to have motivated Gregory when he compiled the *Farfensis*, we have to turn to the monastic community itself. Farfa around 1100 was a large community, and many of the conflicts outside the monastery were also fought within its wall. Reports about contested elections, exiled monks, conspiracies, and poisoned abbots leave little doubt that these conflicts in late eleventh century Farfa were indeed very violent.[335] Gregory himself was anything but an impartial observer; his contempt for most of the abbots of Farfa he served is manifest from his historiographical works. Abbot Berald II of Farfa is depicted as particularly corrupt by Gregory. The conflicts in which Berald II, Gregory of Catino, and many of their fellow brethren were involved were

---

332. Kölzer, 'Prolegomena' 108–115.
333. Toubert, *Latium médiéval* 2.1051–1080.
334. The following is based on Kölzer, 'Prolegomena' 108–112.
335. See Boynton, *Shaping* 25.

manifold.[336] At least to some degree, they can be linked to the content of the *Farfensis*. One of the reasons to think so is that some of the most violent attacks on Berald is found in Gregory's register, not his chronicle.[337] This part of the register is devoted to Gregory's criticism of abbots giving out Farfa's lands in a long-term lease, precisely the practice which in 1103 gave rise to the dispute just mentioned.[338] Secondly, several of the more specific charges Gregory brought against the abbot were related to Farfa's property. Gregory repeatedly reports that Berald violated the oath he had given at his (contested) election in 1090 not to give away any of Farfa's possessions.[339] Also, he singled out the giving away of castles and 'illicit' contracts with local counts—probably an allusion to what Gregory saw as the reason for the disputes with the counts of Palombara and Monticelli.[340] In this sense, monastic property and fairly specific questions of its management did shape the *Farfensis*. Yet the addressee of these canon law authorities Gregory had in mind was apparently not only the local nobility; it was also part of conflicts within the community of Farfa.

3.7 Regular Canons, Monks, and Canon Law

3.7.1 Regular Canons

The focus of this chapter is on monastic canon law and its contribution to the changing legal culture of high medieval Europe. The engagement with the normative traditions by monks and abbots was part and parcel of the reforms of religious life of the eleventh century. Yet it would be strange if this applied only to monastic communities; therefore, in what follows the contribution of regular canons will be studied. Two remarks are necessary in advance. First, the movement that transformed communities of clerks and canons into regular canons (or Augustinian canons) evidently began much later than the great monastic reforms; it was only in the late eleventh century that the Rule of Saint Augustine for canons played a role comparable to that of the Rule of Benedict for monastic communities, and that communities of canons supplemented it with customs (*consuetudines*) put down in writing in a similar way the monastic communities did. Among other things, this also implies that when canons

---

336. Kölzer, 'Prolegomena' 89–91; Boynton, *Shaping* 25–29.

337. Namely the gruesome vision Gregory reports of Berald devouring a child: *Regesto* (ed. Giorgi and Balzani 5.155–156).

338. Kölzer, 'Prolegomena' 113.

339. *Regesto* (ed. Giorgi and Balzani 5.155); *Il Chronicon Farfense di Gregorio di Catino*, ed. Ugo Balzani (2 vols. Fonti per la storia d'Italia 33/34; Rome 1903), here at 2.209–210 and 214–215.

340. *Regesto* (ed. Giorgi and Balzani 5.155): 'Castella [...] amisit et retinere neglexit, faciens cum R. comite pactum in futurum legaliter damnabile.'

began to engage with 'law' as found in the canonical collections, many of the monastic collections discussed earlier in this chapter were already widely used. They were all the more important for canons looking for materials as non-monastic collections were notoriously silent on the common life of the secular clergy; the only major exception was the collection of Anselm of Lucca.[341]

The second important point in the context of the present chapter is that the rise of regular canons was accompanied by conflicts between chapters and bishops,[342] but above all between canons and monks.[343] Replacement of canons by monks or vice versa in the eleventh and twelfth centuries frequently gave rise to fierce conflicts, and both the right to administer sacraments and claims to revenues related to pastoral care were contested issues between both groups. To make things more complicated, there was considerable disagreement within the monastic world on these issues too. Many authors articulated their views in learned tracts, polemic literature, and other forms; authorities quoted in these works—whether well-known, newly discovered, or newly forged—occasionally came to play a role in canonical collections.[344]

A number of pro-monastic forgeries have already been mentioned earlier in this chapter. Among other things, they asserted the right of monks to perform the cure of souls. Anti-monastic forgeries, in all likelihood produced by regular canons or their supporters, sought to counter precisely

341. Charles Dereine, 'Le problème de la vie commune chez les canonistes d'Anselme de Lucques à Gratien' *Studi Gregoriani* 3 (1948) 287–298, esp. 295; Gabriel Le Bras, 'Note sur la vie commune des clercs dans les collections canoniques', *La vita comune del clero nei secoli XI e XII: atti Mendola 1959* (2 vols. Miscellanea 3; Milan 1962) 1.16–18, here at 17; Picasso, 'Monachesimo' 135–142; Kathleen Grace Cushing, 'Polemic or Handbook? Recension Bb of Anselm of Lucca's *Collectio canonum*', *Bishops, Texts and the Use of Canon Law around 1100: Essays in Honour of Martin Brett*, ed. Bruce Clark Brasington and Kathleen Grace Cushing (CFC; Aldershot and Farnham 2008) 69–77.

342. Rudolf Schieffer, 'Spirituales latrones. Zu den Hintergründen der Simonieprozesse in Deutschland zwischen 1069 und 1075' *Historisches Jahrbuch* 92 (1972) 19–60.

343. Schreiber, *Kurie und Kloster*; Charles Dereine, 'Le problème de la *cura animarum* chez Gratien' SG 2 (1954) 305–318; Constable, *Monastic Tithes* esp. 145–186; Schieffer, 'Hintergründe'; Giles Constable, *The Reformation of the Twelfth Century* (Cambridge 1996) ch. 6; Julian Führer, *König Ludwig VI. von Frankreich und die Kanonikerreform* (Frankfurt 2008), here at 31–42. For the female canons, see Hedwig Röckelein, 'Die Auswirkung der Kanonikerreform des 12. Jahrhunderts auf Kanonissen, Augustinerchorfrauen und Benediktinerinnen', *Institution und Charisma. Festschrift für Gert Melville zum 65. Geburtstag*, ed. Franz J. Felten et al. (Cologne and Vienna 2009) 55–72.

344. See Dereine, 'Cura animarum' and Peter Landau, 'Seelsorge in den Kanonessammlungen von der Zeit der gregorianischen Reformen bis zu Gratian', *La pastorale della Chiesa in Occidente dall'età ottoniana al Concilio lateranense IV: atti Mendola 2001* (Ricerche: Storia 26; Milan 2004) 93–123, here at 118–121 who pointed out that Gratian in his account of monastic pastoral care relied above all not on ancient canons but relatively recent forgeries. For the career of a genuine quotation of Jerome, see Thierry Kouamé, '*Monachus non doctoris, sed plangentis habet officium*: l'autorité de Jérôme dans le débat sur l'enseignement des moines aux XIe et XIIe siècles' *Cahiers de recherches médiévales et humanistes* 18 (2009) 9–38.

these claims. For example, a forged canon attributed to the Council of Nicaea sought to exclude monks from the administration of penance and to forbid burials in monasteries.[345] Another forgery, attributed to a council of Pope Eugene (II) in the collections, in even more general terms prohibited monks from administering penance, baptising, from acting as godfathers, visiting the sick, offering burials, entering a collegiate church, or 'engaging in any business' ('neque qualibuscumque negotiis sese implicare').[346] According to Peter Landau, both forgeries emerged in Italy (perhaps Tuscany) in the 1060s, in direct response to the pro-monastic forgeries mentioned earlier in this chapter.[347] Another important authority quoted in these conflicts is a canon attributed to Leo IX (JL 4269) according to which laypeople taking the monastic habit had to bequeath at least half of their goods to their local parish. The text, which does not fit well Leo's politics towards the monastic order, is perhaps a forgery.[348] It was used (for example, at synods) in cases against monasteries, and in some canonical collections it is found with the rubric 'On the greed of monks'.[349] This points to the conflict over revenues that were at issue in these conflicts over baptism, burial, and the care of souls in general. In the context of the present chapter, these forgeries mainly matter as the way they were dealt with may be used to understand the preoccupations of the compilers of individual collections. As in the case of monastic collections, special attention will be given to the actual use of these works, but internal evidence nonetheless is important to establish the milieu in which a collection may have emerged.

345. Gratian, C.16 q.1 c.1 (ed. Winroth 508; ed. Friedberg 761). See Landau, 'Seelsorge' 112.

346. Gratian, C.16 q.1 c.8 (ed. Winroth 510; ed. Friedberg 763). See Landau, 'Seelsorge' 112. Both canons are also found together in Anselm C 5.65 (Ps.-Eugene) and 66 (Ps.-Nicaea); for other occurences, see the *Clavis* database. On Ps.-Eugene (JE –; J³ –) see also Frank, 'Zwei Fälschungen' 45–46, Kuttner, 'Roman Manuscripts' 11, and Reynolds, 'Five Books [1996]' 276–277. The textual history of this forgery calls for further studies.

347. Landau, 'Seelsorge' 116 (*pace* Kuttner, 'Roman Manuscripts' 11 who argued for a later date). For the relevant pro-monastic forgeries (above all JE †1366, JE †1951, and JE †1996), see above, esp. notes 200, 235, and 320.

348. See Ludwig Schmugge, 'Die Dekretale Papst Leos IX. "Relatum est auribus nostris" (JL 4269) in der kanonistischen Tradition (1052–1234)' ZRG Kan. Abt. 73 (1987) 41–69, here at 68–69 for doubts on the authenticity. However, idem, 'Leo IX, JL 4269: An Attempt at an Edition', *The Two Laws: Studies in Medieval Legal History Dedicated to Stephen Kuttner*, ed. Laurent Mayali and Stephanie A. J. Tibbetts (SMCL 1; Washington, D.C. 1990) 31–39 and even more so Böhmer-Frech 954 argued that the letter may be genuine. It is found in numerous pre-Gratian collections (including the *Sinemuriensis*, Deusdedit, Anselm, *Britannica*, *183T*, *Polycarpus*, and *Caesaraugustana*) but also many post-Gratian collections like the *Francofurtana* 26.6 (ed. Landau and Drossbach 193). Gratian is exceptional for *not* containing JL 4269, although he must have known it (Schmugge, 'Dekretale Leos' 50–51).

349. On the use of JL 4269, see Schmugge, 'Dekretale Leos' 67. The first collection containing the rubric 'De rapacitate monachorum' seems to be Ivo's *Decretum* 7.150, from where it passed to *Tripartita* B, *Panormia*, *10P*, the *Pragensis I*, and the *Ambrosiana II*.

3.7.2 The *Collection in Twenty Books* (Vat. lat. 1350)

The *Collection in Twenty Books* extant in Vat. lat. 1350 (= *20L*) is a canon law collection based on an Italian version of Burchard.[350] It contains 689 canons, more than 500 of which are taken from Burchard (often truncated). The extant manuscript was made after 1139; the collection itself seems to have been compiled around or perhaps even before the year 1100, maybe in Tuscany.[351] As *20L* draws on the collection of Anselm of Lucca, it cannot have been compiled before *ca.* 1086. Bellini argued that the apparent non-use of the Ivonian collections implied 1096 as the *terminus ante quem*, but this cannot be maintained.[352] It is rich in penitential materials and has been characterized as a practical handbook for the use of regular canons.[353]

Books one to fourteen can be described as abbreviated versions of the respective books of Burchard with more or less additions. The canons are often in the sequence also found in Burchard. In the case of Burchard's books six (a short book on homicide) and fourteen (an extremely short book on debauchery), only a very small number of canons were retained by the *20L* compiler. Books fifteen to twenty of the *20L* all draw on Burchard's *Corrector* (his book 19), and contain single canons from Burchard's books 16, 17, and 18. Burchard's book fifteen 'On emperors, lords and other laymen' in contrast has no equivalent in *20L*, and none of its canons were retained in *20L*. The book may have been left out as it was of little practical use for the compiler, or perhaps because it was perceived as anachronistic.[354]

Like many monastic collections discussed earlier in this chapter, *20L* is rich in penitential material. Two features suggest that the community that produced and/or used *20L* was a chapter rather than a monastic house. First, book two contains excerpts from a rule for canons (sometimes erroneously attributed to Gregory VII).[355] Secondly, the beginning of the last book of *20L* contains several texts against monastic cure of souls, including JL 4269.[356]

---

350. Paul Fournier, 'De quelques collections canoniques issues du *Décret* de Burchard', *Mélanges Paul Fabre: études d' histoire du moyen âge* (Paris 1902) 189–214, here at 198; Brommer, 'Kurzformen' 27; Roberto Bellini, 'Un abrégé del Decreto di Burcardo di Worms: la collezione canonica in 20 libri (Ms. Vat. Lat. 1350)' *Apollinaris* 69 (1996) 119–195; idem, 'Tra riforma e tradizione: un abrégé del Decreto di Burcardo di Worms' *Aevum* 72 (1998) 303–334; Fowler-Magerl, *Clavis* 179–180. *20L* is not mentioned in Kéry.

351. Bellini, 'Abrégé' 126.

352. Bellini, 'Abrégé' 125–126.

353. Fowler-Magerl, *Clavis* 180.

354. See above on the *Burdegalensis*.

355. Bellini, 'Abrégé' 124; see Charles Dereine, 'La prétendue Règle de Gregoire VII pour chanoines réguliers' *Revue bénédictine* 71 (1961) 108–118 on this rule.

356. *20L* 20.4; see Bellini, 'Abrégé' 122 (not reported by Schmugge, 'Dekretale Leos').

Another part of *20L* that deserves attention is an appendix which contains a marriage tract taken from the *Sententiae magistri A.* and a tract on penance (*Augustinus in libro vite*) from the same source.[357] The marriage tract is also found in the collection known as *Ambrosiana II*, a small collection containing some 400 proof texts apparently compiled in late eleventh-century Milan.[358] Like *20L*, it draws on an Italian Burchard version and seems to have been compiled for a house of canons.[359] Linda Fowler-Magerl pointed out that a number of shared texts links *20L*, the *Ambrosiana II*, the *Collection in Seventeen Books* (from Saint-Hilaire), and the *Collectio canonum* extant in Clm 16068; all these collections and their manuscripts seem to come from communities of canons.[360]

All in all, *20L* is not a partisan collection, but may legitimately be seen as a collection compiled for a community of canons. It shares materials with other collections used in this milieu, and this may indicate an exchange of texts and ideas between such communities, comparable to the monastic networks studied earlier in this chapter.

3.7.3 The *Collection in Seventeen Books* from Saint-Hilaire

The *Collection in Seventeen Books* (*17L*) or *Collection of Saint-Hilaire* is a collection from the second half of the eleventh century largely modelled on Burchard's *Liber decretorum*. Containing some 1,200 canons and filling some 80 to 100 folios in the manuscripts it is relatively large, but in many respects also a 'raw' work. Contrary to its conventional title, *17L* is divided into fifteen (not seventeen) books, and only imperfectly so, as will be discussed below.[361] There are three complete copies and two short forms;[362] excerpts are transmitted with copies of *4L*.[363] *17L* is linked to the house of canons of Saint-Hilaire in Poitiers for two reasons. First, the canons owned the Berlin copy of *17L* (Berlin, SBPK, Phillips 1778). Second, *17L* contains three canons which in the Berlin and Reims copies of *17L* are

357. On the marriage canons, see Bellini, 'Abrégé' 124. For an edition of the tract *Augustinus in libro vite*, see John Wei, *Gratian the Theologian* (SMCL 13; Washington, D.C. 2016) 303–309. On the *Sententiae magistri A.* in general see Pauline Henriëtte Joanna Theresia Maas, *The Liber sententiarum Magistri A.: Its Place Amidst the Sentences Collections of the First Half of the 12th Century* (Middeleeuwse studies 11; Nijmegen 1995).

358. Fowler-Magerl, *Clavis* 124–126.

359. Fowler-Magerl, *Clavis* 224.

360. Fowler-Magerl, *Clavis* 124, 126, 179, and 180, respectively. The collection Fowler-Magerl refers to as the '*Collectio canonum* of the canonry Saint-Hilare-le-Grand' is *17L*, on which see the next pages.

361. The traditional title goes back to Fournier (see *Histoire* 2.230). Roger E. Reynolds, 'The *Turin Collection in Seven Books*: A Poitevin Canonical Collection' *Traditio* 25 (1969) 508–514 was the first to point out that Fournier's division into books is questionable at least.

362. Kéry 213.

363. Fowler-Magerl, *Clavis* 128.

interpolated so they refer to Saint-Hilaire. The 'canons' in questions are *formulae* taken from the *Liber decretorum*; in Burchard's version, the template of the datum clause refers to the cathedral of Worms, dedicated to Saint Peter ('Actum in illa civitate in domo sancti Petri, Kalendis illis, anno [...]'). In the *17L* manuscripts now at Reims and Berlin, the text is altered to Saint-Hilaire ('in domo sancti Hilarii').[364] This strongly suggests that *17L* was reworked at Saint-Hilaire, but not that the original form of *17L* was compiled there.[365] Behind the change may also be the conflict of the canons of Saint-Hilaire with the chapter of the local cathedral—also dedicated to Saint Peter.[366]

The collection essentially is a reworked form of Burchard's *Liber decretorum*, of which a Milanese version was used. Many of Burchard's canons were abbreviated, simplified, or omitted; a smaller number of texts were added from other sources. The Burchard version used for *17L* must have come from Italy, as the synodal *ordo* clearly shows.[367] *17L* is also linked in a slightly complicated way to the Milan version of Burchard, a subgroup of the so-called *deteriores* manuscripts. While *17L* does not have all gaps typical of the *deteriores*,[368] it contains materials which are typically found with the Milan version of Burchard. They may have been part of the Burchard model, or only combined with the Burchard material in the making of *17L*. Fowler-Magerl, pointing out at the use of the Milanese *Ambrosiana II* and the independent circulation of the materials used to augment the Italian Burchard versions, assumed that *17L* took the canons in question from a version of the *Ambrosiana II*.[369] Yet it is possible that *17L* used a Burchard

364. Burchard 2.26, 27, and 30 = *17L* 2.16, 17, and 20. See Linda Fowler-Magerl, 'Vier französische und spanische vorgratianische Kanonessammlungen', *Aspekte europäischer Rechtsgeschichte. Festgabe für H. Coing zum 70. Geburtstag*, ed. Christoph Bergfeld (Ius commune. Sonderhefte 17; Frankfurt 1982) 123–146, here at 143. The change (in the Berlin manuscript) was first observed by Tardif, 'Collection' 159 who on these grounds argued that *17L* was from the Poitou and, by extension, also the *Burdegalensis* (even though, as he acknowledged, the latter did not contain this variant). Tardif knew *17L* only from the Berlin manuscript.

365. The third complete copy (Hereford, Cathedral Library, o.2.VII) and the short form in Bern, Burgerbibliothek, 314 contain the canons without any reference to Saint-Hilaire; see Fowler-Magerl, *Clavis* 126.

366. For the conflict of Saint-Hilaire with chapter of Saint-Pierre and the bishop of Poitiers, see Ovidio Capitani, 'Episcopato ed ecclesiologia nell'età gregoriana', *Le istituzioni ecclesiastiche della «Societas Christiana» dei secoli XI–XII: papato, cardinalato ed episcopato: atti Mendola 1971* (Miscellanea 7; Milan 1974) 316–373, here at 323–331 and Fowler-Magerl, *Clavis* 126.

367. Schneider (MGH Ordines 44).

368. The '*deteriores*' lack Burchard 12.10–20, but *17L* 9.1–14 contains (in this order) Burchard 12.3–6, 8–9, 11–12, 15, 18, 20, and 25.

369. Fowler-Magerl, 'Fine Distinctions' 148–150, pointing at the 'Milanese form of CES' in *17L* 1.21 and *Erga simoniacos* as found in *17L* 1.32 (here attributed to Pope Leo). She assumed that *17L* took these texts from the *Ambrosiana II*, but also related that *17L* has the same version of the canon as the Burchard copy Milano, Ambrosiana, E.144.sup. (ibid. 149). She assumed that *17L* 1.32 was likewise taken from *Ambrosiana II*, although *17L* has a version closer to the Italian Burchard

exemplar already augmented in this way. There are manuscripts ultimately depending on so-called *deteriores* models and containing the additions typical for this version of Burchard, but with some or all missing canons inserted from more complete exemplars.[370] While it is true that *17L* used the *Ambrosiana II*, it is also true that the extant version of this collection does not contain the very form found in *17L*, and *17L* inserted the canons in a way very similar to the Milan Burchard.

Other sources are the *Abbreviatio Ansegisi et Benedicti Levitae*, the *Dacheriana*, and the *Collection in 342 Chapters*, all of which are contained in a manuscript now preserved at Montpellier which may even be the compiler's exemplar.[371] In addition, another Italian source similar to the core of the *Ambrosiana II* was seemingly used for several canons on simony.[372] This collection also provided the most recent material contained in *17L*, an excerpt of Pope Alexander II (1063–1071).[373] Two *17L* manuscripts in addition contain conciliar canons taken from the *Hispana*, but not as part of the collection.

Burchard's *Liber decretorum* provided not only most material but also the basic structure of the collection. Like its model, *17L* is divided into books, but less clearly so than its traditional title suggests.[374] The first three books largely correspond to the first three books of Burchard; they have a discernible title indicating the book number ('Liber primus' etc.) and its content, a *capitulatio* at the beginning of each book, and the canons they contain are numbered. Compared to the rest of the collection, these three books are long (making up more than half of *17L*) and more carefully composed. Indeed, the second part of the collection (the forth to thirteenth book) is less structured. To begin with, the book numbers are missing (or only given as 'liber imus'), and sometimes the beginning of a

which Fransen called 'Burchard grégorien'. In addition, *17L* is closer this Burchard version in the placing of the canon: In the 'Burchard grégorien', *Erga simoniacos* is added after Burchard 1.112; in *17L*, *Erga simoniacos* is found just before this canon (Burchard 1.112 = *17L* 1.23). Finally, *17L* inserts one sentence (*Porro ecclesiae – prece*) slightly earlier in the canon than usual; this would support Fowler-Magerl's own idea that this sentence original was a (marginal) comment in a Burchard manuscript which later was inserted in the canon itself.

370. Fransen, 'Tradition manuscrite' 9–11; Rolker, *Canon Law* 62 and 111.

371. Montpellier, Bibliothèque interuniversitaire, Section de Médecine, H.137. See Fowler-Magerl, *Clavis* 126 for further references.

372. Fowler-Magerl, 'Fine Distinctions' 175–176; eadem, *Clavis* 126. An incipit/explicit edition of the *Ambrosiana II* is found in Giorgio G. Picasso, *Collezioni canoniche milanesi del secolo XII* (Pubblicazioni dell'Università cattolica del S. Cuore. Saggi e ricerche. Scienze storiche 2; Milan 1969), here at 81–143.

373. JE †1948 as found in *17L* 1.26 (perhaps from *Ambrosiana II* c. 236). The canon, often attributed to Alexander II in the collections, lacks an inscription in *17L*. Only in Gratian C.1 q.4 c.11 (ed. Friedberg 420; ed. Winroth 261) the first part of the canon is attributed to Gregory.

374. See Fowler-Magerl, *Clavis* 126–127, who for this reason preferred to refer to *17L* as '*Collectio canonum* of the canonry of Saint-Hilaire-le-Grand'.

new book is not marked at all.[375] Many of the books in this part of the collection are very short—the fifth and thirteenth 'book' hardly exceed one page. While there are signs of thoughtful rearrangement in many cases the canons are distributed without any discernible rationale. The end of *17L* consists of one book containing all non-Burchardian material and, as the last book, a version of Burchard's *Corrector*. Compared to the middle part of the collection, these last two books are more carefully composed and fuller.

The varying degree of order in the different parts of the collection seem to reflect the compiler's interest in the respective topics. This is most evident where *17L* 'updates' Burchard in the sense of inserting canons from different sources. In particular, the first book on bishops, ecclesiastical hierarchy, and ordinations, contains canons dealing with simony not found in the *Liber decretorum*. The title of this book, while evidently modelled on the title of Burchard's first book, is also changed by inserting a reference to simony. This apparent interest of the *17L* compiler in simony seems to have motivated him to rework Burchard's first books with greater care. Conversely, the middle part of *17L* not only lacks clear division into books and similar elements, but the compiler was much more selective in his use of the corresponding books of Burchard. He left out most of Burchard's canons concerning the administration of sacraments of baptism and the Eucharist, and retained only very few canons on marriage (mainly incest prohibitions). Burchard's book on speculative theology has no equivalent in *17L*, and none of its canons are found here. Burchard's penitential book, in contrast, was largely retained in *17L*, and indeed augmented by inserting penitential canons dispersed in other books of Burchard, in particular those not having an equivalent in *17L*.

In the context of the present chapter, special attention should be given to Burchard's book eight on monastic affairs. First of all, unlike other books found before and after in Burchard, it is largely retained in *17L*, where it is the sixth book. Given that Burchard in this book mainly gathered material stressing episcopal control over monastic property, the *17L* compiler's decision to retain it should not be understood as reflecting a pro-monastic tendency; if anything, the opposite is true. Already Fournier pointed out what he interpreted as an anti-monastic manipulation of a Burchard canon in *17L*.[376] Indeed *17L* contains a canon, ultimately modelled on one of Burchard's rubrics, which prohibits monks to administer

---

375. Reims, BM, 675, fol. 60r ('Incipit liber de periurio [...]', no number) and fol. 61v ('Liber imus'). See Fowler-Magerl, *Clavis* 127.

376. *Histoire* 2.233–234.

penance for lay people; yet the manipulated version of the canon is presumably not the work of the 17L compiler. The very same canon is found in at least three other collections.[377]

While the canon against pastoral care by monks was not produced by the 17L compiler, the decision to retain this canon may still be indicative of the compiler's interests. After all, the canon touched upon a delicate issue which was frequently debated and in the case of many other collections gave rise to canonical proof texts being forged, manipulated, and omitted. In this context, it may also be significant that all manuscripts of 17L (including the Hereford and Bern copies) have shorter *formulae* than Burchard because they omit the variant clauses he provided for charters issued by monastic communities.[378] In the light of the link between 17L and the canons of Saint-Hilaire, one can tentatively take this as evidence supporting the idea that 17L emerged and circulated among regular canons (rather than in monastic circles).

As for the origin and character of 17L, one should be even more careful than in the case of other anonymous collections. Whoever compiled 17L, for whatever reasons, did not rework his materials very thoroughly, and some traits of 17L may well be the result of neglience rather than careful planning. As for the individual canons, many are abbreviated and simplified; likewise, many inscriptions in 17L are missing or simply wrong. In the middle part of the collection in particular, it is often difficult to understand which canon a specific inscription belongs to. Generally speaking, 17L gives the impression of an unfinished collection; the uneven treatment of different books may at least in part go back to the lack of time or resources.

3.7.4 The *Collection in Thirteen Books* (Vat. lat. 1361) and Related Collections

The *Collection in Thirteen Books* (=13L) extant in Vat. lat. 1361 is a sizeable Italian collection from the middle of the twelfth century.[379] The manuscript

---

377. Burchard 19.142 (*editio princeps*, fol. 217rb): 'Liberi sunt monachi ad dandam penitentiam secularibus'. The rubric is 'Quod monachi secularibus penitentiam dare non debeant'. 17L 15.53 (Reims, BM, 675, fol. 84r), Berlin 13L 1.108, Vienna 7L 5.52, and Turin 7L 4.229 all have a canon reading 'Quod monachi secularibus penitentiam dare non possunt'. Fournier claimed that the 'non' was only found in 17L; in fact, the interpolation was the change from 'non debeant' to 'non possunt'. On the Turin 7L weakening the pro-monastic tendency of 74T (its main model), see also Rennie, 'Turin Collection' 60.

378. The clause 'vel in monasterio illo, indictione illa' found in Burchard 2.27 is absent from all three complete 17L manuscripts and the Bern short version according to Fowler-Magerl, 'Vier Kanonessammlungen' 143.

379. Stephan Kuttner, 'Some Roman Manuscripts of Canonical Collections' BMCL 1 (1971) 7–29, here at 9–13, esp. 10; Johanna Petersmann, 'Die kanonistische Überlieferung des Constitutum Constantini bis zum Dekret Gratians. Untersuchung und Edition' DA 30 (1974) 356–449, here

seems to come from Bergamo, where the collection in all likelihood was compiled.[380] The collection will be studied here in conjunction with two smaller works related to it by shared texts—namely a short version of Anselm of Lucca's *Collectio canonum* and a small work which will be referred to as 'the Pisa florilegium' in the following.[381] As will become clear, *13L* is a pro-monastic collection but also an important document for the reception of anti-monastic forgeries produced by regular canons in the twelfth century, and for this reason is here treated in the context of regular canons and their collections.

In addition to Ivo's Prologue, *13L* contains some 1,600 canons which are divided into thirteen books and made accessible by a *capitulatio*. The main sources of the collection are two relatively recent collections, that of Anselm of Lucca, and the French *Panormia*. Both collections were relatively widely spread in Lombardy.[382] The division of the material is strongly influenced by the collection of Anselm of Lucca, which seems to have been an attractive collection for canons.[383] The division into thirteen books is that of Anselm's collection; the book titles are largely retained, and many books in *13L* begin with material taken from this source and left in the original sequence. The *Panormia* was mainly used for additions, including

at 388–389; Uta-Renate Blumenthal, 'Decrees and Decretals of Pope Paschal II in Twelfth-Century Canonical Collections' BMCL 10 (1980) 15–30; Detlev Jasper, *Das Papstwahldekret von 1059. Überlieferung und Textgestalt* (Beiträge zur Geschichte und Quellenkunde des Mittelalters 12; Sigmaringen 1986), here at 52–54; Kéry 291–292; Fowler-Magerl, *Clavis* 225–226. The Vatican *13L* in Vat. lat. 1361 ('AH' in the *Clavis* database) should not be confused with the Berlin *13L* extant in Berlin, SBPK, Savigny 3 ('SA' in the *Clavis* database). Both collections are similar as they are both strongly influenced by the collection of Anselm of Lucca; however, the Berlin *13L* does not display the pro-monastic tendency of the Vatican *13L*.

380. See Jasper, *Papstwahldekret* 52–54 and Fowler-Magerl, *Clavis* 225–226, pointing out that not only the extant manuscript comes from Bergamo but also the Papal Election Decree is found in the form otherwise known from a Bergamo manuscript, and that the Vatican *13L* contains a letter of Paschal II (JL –; *Italia Pontificia* –) relating to Bergamo (*13L* 13.45, ed. Kuttner, 'Roman Manuscripts' 28–29).

381. The Pisa florilegium is found in Pisa, Biblioteca del Seminario S. Catarina, 59, fols. 1–16 [not seen]; an 'almost identical' florilegium is found in the *74T* manuscript Firenze, BNC, Conventi Soppressi 91, fols. 1–18 according to Fowler-Magerl, *Clavis* 224. The Pisa manuscript also contains the short version of Anselm's collection (by a different hand and on a separate quaternio). See Miccoli, 'Florilegio' for the Pisa manuscript and Fowler-Magerl, *Clavis* 224 for that from Florence.

382. Peter Landau, 'Erweiterte Fassungen der Kanonessammlung des Anselm von Lucca aus dem 12. Jahrhundert', *Sant'Anselmo, Mantova e la lotta per le investiture: atti di convegno internazionale di studi (Mantova 23–24–25 maggio 1986)*, ed. Paolo Golinelli (Bologna 1987) 323–337, here at 328 (A Aucta version of Anselm used); idem, 'Kanonessammlungen in der Lombardei im frühen und hohen Mittelalter', *Atti dell'undecimo congresso internazionale di studi sull'alto medioevo. Milano, 26–30 ottobre 1987* (2 vols. Spoleto 1989) 1.425–457, here at 448 (*Panormia* in Lombardy).

383. Anselm of Lucca was virtually the first compiler to include more than a few scattered authorities on the regular life of the secular clergy, as already Dereine, 'Vie commune' 295 made clear. See Cushing, 'Polemic or Handbook' on Anselm Bb, apparently produced for a house of canons. The C version contains Ps.-Eugene and Ps.-Nicaea (Anselm C 5.65–66).

rare materials like the list of general councils known as *Sancta octo*.[384] The *capitulatio* sometimes does not reflect well the addition of non-Anselmian materials. For example, the first book of *13L* begins with a series of canons on the basic articles of faith lifted from the very beginning of the *Panormia*.[385] Yet the *capitulatio* only mentions the canons that follow on Roman primacy (lifted from Anselm's collection), and the book title ('de primatu et potestate apostolice sedis et eius dignitate') likewise is modelled on that of Anselm's collection, thus ignoring the opening canons of *13L*.

The *13L* compiler was aware of the overlap that resulted from parallels between Anselm's collection and the *Panormia*. For example, he copied the Donation of Constantine from the *Panormia* into the first book of his collection (*13L* 1.13); in book four, he copied the rather different version of the Donation from Anselm's collection, but at this occasion left out those passages which he already had copied into his first book.[386] On the whole, the compiler succeeded to avoid overlap resulting from the fact that many of his proof texts were found more than once in his formal sources.[387]

Scholars early on noticed that *13L* displayed a 'strong monastic bias',[388] and there are indeed a number of reasons to see the collection as a partisan collection strongly in favour of the monastic order. Some pro-monastic material was taken into *13L* from *74T* via Anselm's collection.[389] Additional pro-monastic materials were taken from other sources which cannot be identified with any major collection. This applies to two canons on monastic tithes (*13L* 13.41 and 43), and two important forgeries in favour of monks exercising the cure of souls, JE †1951 and †1996; only the latter is also found in the Pisa florilegium. The presence of JE †1951 is remarkable, as it makes *13L* one of only two pre-Gratian collections to include this forgery (widely

---

384. *13L* 6.125 (Vat. lat. 1361, fol. 145ra–rb). Given the unstable textual transmission of this text, it may be worth noting that *13L* reads 'Constantinopolitanim' where almost all *Panormia* manuscripts have 'constanter'. See *Panormia* 2.103 (ed. Brett) and, for discussion, Chapter 5.5.5.

385. *13L* 1.1–6 (Vat. lat. 1361, fols. 33ra–34rb) based on *Panormia* 1.1–7. The Ambrosian material that follows (*13L* 1.7–11) is not taken from the *Panormia*.

386. Petersmann, 'Überlieferung' 388–389.

387. Sometimes, however, a canon was copied twice into *13L*. For example, *13L* 5.91 is taken from *Panormia* 3.183, but *13L* 13.35 contains the same text from a different source; *13L* 10.34k is taken from Anselm (part of a series of Gregory I canons), but in *13L* 13.91 the same canon (attributed to Gregory II, and with slightly different text) is repeated, this time from *Panormia* 8.61. Sometimes, such doublets were already present in *13L*'s formal sources; for example, *13L* 10.39 and *13L* 13.23 overlap, but this is already found in Anselm.

388. Kuttner, 'Roman Manuscripts' here at 10 (quote); Gilchrist, 'Monastic Forgeries' 279–288.

389. E.g. *13L* 4.1, rubric (Vat. lat. 1361, fol. 93va): 'Ut privilegia ecclesiarum et monasteriorum inviolata permaneant'. The canon, ultimately from Pseudo-Isidore (JK †2), is taken from Anselm 4.1 (ed. Thaner 193), which retains the pro-monastic changes introduced by the *74T* compiler: *74T* c. 24 (ed. Gilchrist 33).

transmitted separately from collections).[390] The *13L* compiler also incorporated the tract *Apologeticus monachorum* attributed to Peter Damian (d. 1072). The *Apologeticus* is otherwise only known from the Pisa florilegium and the Anselm abbreviation found in the same manuscript.[391]

These texts contribute to the partisan character of *13L*, and closely link it to the Pisa manuscript. Yet one of the most interesting aspects are not the pro-monastic materials *13L* contains, but the way anti-monastic polemic texts are treated. Specifically, *13L* 5.37 contains a canon attributed to Leo IX (JL 4269) already mentioned above; it is found in many collections, sometimes with the title 'On the greed of monks'.[392] In *13L*, no such polemic rubric is found,[393] but the presence of this canon nonetheless is surprising at first. Yet one should never assume that canonical collections contained only texts the compiler agreed with. In the case of JL 4269, the opposite may be true for the *13L* compiler. This at least is suggested by two other canons found in *13L* (5.58 and 68). Both canons go back to anti-monastic forgeries similar to JL 4269, but in *13L*, these forgeries are themselves manipulated; rather than restricting the care of souls by monks, in *13L* the texts are changed as to endorse such monastic activities.[394] This is a striking example how such forgeries were not only read and used in their milieu of origin but read and re-used in the very group targeted by these texts.

390. Gilchrist, 'Monastic Forgeries' 283. JE †1951 was copied in manuscripts of various collections but only in *4L* and *13L* it is part of the collections proper.

391. The authenticity of this tract (also known as *Opusculum 28*) is relevant for the dating of JE †1951 and JE †1996; if the *Apologeticus* were written by Peter Damian (d. 1072), this would the earliest securely datable use of the two forgeries. It was long accepted as genuine, for example by John Joseph Ryan, *Saint Peter Damiani and His Canonical Sources: A Preliminary Study in the Antecedents of the Gregorian Reform* (PIMS Studies and Texts 2; Toronto 1956), here at 54 and Stephan Kuttner and Robert Somerville, 'The So-Called Canons of Nîmes (1096)' *Tijdschrift voor rechtsgeschiedenis* 38 (1970) 175–189, here at 177–178, but see Reindel's edition (MGH Briefe dt. Kaiserzeit 4.1:61 and 296 n. 18) and most recently Christian Lohmer, 'Pseudoepigraphica of Peter Damian: Truly and Falsely Attributed Works of a Church Reformer', *Proceedings Washington 2004* MIC Subsidia 13.108–126, here at 124–125. For an edition, see PL 145.511–518 (a flawed reprint of the 1606 *editio princeps* by Caetani).

392. On this rubric ('de rapacitate monachorum'), see above, note 349.

393. According to the *Clavis* database, the rubric to *13L* 5.37 ('ut quicumque converti voluerit medietatem rerum suarum ecclesie cui subiectus est dimittat sicque ad monasterium vadat') is also found in the A version of Anselm's *Collectio* (not the A Aucta version!) and the Berlin *13L* 5.47. See database entries AH05.037, AA05.047, and SA04.047.

394. Kuttner, 'Roman Manuscripts' 12, observing that 'the prohibition for monks to exercise any pastoral or clerical ministry, from baptism to burial, has been turned into an unrestricted permission, to be respected by all; and the monastic life is held up as a model to all canons regular, even to the point that "nullus quippe dici potest canonicus qui monachus rennuit fore" (5.68).'

3.7.5 The *Collection in Ten Parts*: A Canonical Collection for Canons

The *Collection in Ten Parts* (= *10P*) belongs to the rare specimen of pre-Gratian collections visibly shaped by the compiler's concern for regular canons.[395] It was compiled in northern France after 1124 and contains some 2,200 canons, divided into ten books (referred to as *partes* in the preface). All complete manuscripts of *10P* contain two prefaces, a first one lifted from the *Panormia*, the second one apparently written for *10P*. As the first preface mentions Ivo of Chartres as the author, *10P*—like the *Panormia* and other collections containing Ivo's *Prologue*—was often thought to have been compiled by Ivo. While this hypothesis has long been given up, no other author has been identified.[396] All in all, six complete manuscripts and one fragment of *10P* are known.[397] The latter may represent an earlier draft, but no cogent evidence is available to date this version with any precision.[398] The number of extant manuscripts, and also the use of *10P* by other compilers,[399] suggest that *10P* enjoyed some pop-

395. Robert Somerville, 'The Councils of Pope Calixtus II and the *Collection in Ten Parts*' BMCL 11 (1981) 80–86; Kéry 263–264; Fowler-Magerl, *Clavis* 209–214; Joaquin Sedano Rueda, *La colección canónica en 10 partes* (diss. iur. can.; Pontificia universitas Sanctae Crucis, Rome 2008); idem, 'The Manuscript Tradition of the *Collection in Ten Parts*', *Proceedings Esztergom 2008* MIC Subsidia 14.261–272; Melodie Harris Eichbauer, 'A Desire for the Latest and the Greatest: Papal Decretals and Roman Law in the *Collectio decem partium*' BMCL 36 (2019) 195–208.

396. Theiner, *Disquitiones criticae* 165 suggested Hildebert of Lavardin as the compiler, but see already Fournier, 'Collections attribuées à Yves' BEC 58.441 for arguments against this idea (and ibid. 441–442 against Hugh of Châlons as the author). Joseph Marie de Smet, *De heilige Jan van Waasten en de Gregoriaansche hervorming in het bisdom Terwaan* (Mémoire de licence; Université catholique de Louvain, Leuven 1943) 125–143 suggested that the *Atrebatensis* and the Wolfenbüttel *9L* were essentially preparatory collections for *10P*, and that all three collections emerged in Thérouanne when John of Warneton (d. 1130) was bishop there; specifically, he argued *10P* was compiled by Walter of Thérouanne. This model, strongly inspired by Fournier's model of the three Ivonian collections, has rightly been criticized by Laurent Waelkens and Dirk van den Auweele, 'La collection de Thérouanne en IX livres à l'abbaye de Saint-Pierre-au-Mont-Blandin: le Codex Gandavensis 235' *Sacris erudiri* 24 (1980) 115–153 and Sedano Rueda, *Colección* 100–108. However, Eichbauer, 'Desire' 199 stressed that some of the recent material in *10P* may well fit the idea that *10P* was compiled in Thérouanne or indeed by Walter.

397. See Kéry 263 (omitting Berkeley, Robbins collection, 103) and Sedano Rueda, *Colección* 81–94.

398. Paris, BnF, lat. 14145, fols. 1–14, containing the *capitulatio* and *10P* 1.1.1–1.5.1 (but not the prefaces normally found with *10P*). The fragment breaks off in mid-line at the end of a verso, strongly suggesting that it is physically incomplete. The *capitulatio* implies that this version did not yet contain canons from the councils of Poitiers (1100) and Toulouse (1119), nor book ten. From this, however, it is not possible to conclude that the version extant in Paris, BnF, lat. 14145 was compiled before 1110 as had been argued by Fowler-Magerl, *Clavis* 209–210. See Rolker, *Canon Law* 277.

399. *10P* was used by the compilers of the two *Catalaunenses* collections and by Haimo of Bazoches (d. 1153), see *Histoire* 2.306–313 and Sedano Rueda, 'Manuscript Tradition' 44–45. For chronological reasons, I do not think that Hugh of Châlons (d. 1113) was involved in the making of the *Catalaunensis* (pace Fowler-Magerl, *Clavis* 238).

ularity in the twelfth century, mainly in northern France but also beyond these regions.[400]

Structure and Content

Evidently, the *10P* compiler began his work by enlarging a copy of the *Panormia*, a collection compiled in northern France around the year 1115.[401] Eight of the ten books of the *10P* are *Panormia* books with only minor changes and moderate additions; only the other two *10P* books were newly composed and contain substantial materials from other sources. The compiler seems to have begun his work by inserting single canons from other sources in the appropriate *Panormia* book; in a second step, he gathered materials on topics not dealt with in this collection into new books, thus gradually moving from enlarging the *Panormia* to composing a new collection. In the end, *10P* almost doubled the length of the *Panormia* by adding new materials namely from the Wolfenbüttel *Collection in Nine Books*[402] and the *74T*-derivative *Collection in Four Books*.

In many respects, then, *10P* can be seen as an augmented *Panormia* adopted to the needs of a cathedral chapter. Compared to the *Panormia*, the most obvious change *10P* made was the addition of two books, one on regular canons and episcopal administration (inserted as book four) and one on penance (at the very end). The latter addition directly reverted one of the changes the *Panormia* compiler had imposed on his materials. While the *Panormia* compiler very carefully eliminated the numerous penitential canons found in the collections he worked with,[403] and even shortened canons containing penitential tariffs, the *10P* compiler specifically searched for penitential canons to supplement his main model, the *Panormia*. The result was a separate book on penance, similar to that found in collections like Burchard or *5L*. It is possible that this last book of *10P* was only added at a late stage of compilation.[404]

The second major change is the addition of book four which deals with various aspects of the episcopal office and church property, but most prominently with regular canons. The substantial book contains 299 canons, none of which is taken from the *Panormia*; the most important formal

---

400. Cambridge, CCC, 94 comes from Christ Church Canterbury; Firenze, BNC, Conv. Soppr. D. 2. 1476 was annotated in Italy, probably at Rome, according to Sedano Rueda, *Colección* 82.

401. On the *Panormia*, see Chapter 5.7.

402. On the Wolfenbüttel *9L*, see Waelkens and van den Auweele, 'Collection de Thérouanne' and Fowler-Magerl, *Clavis* 207–209.

403. See Rolker, *Canon Law* esp. 253 and 268.

404. The *capitulatio* in Paris, BnF, lat. 14145 does not refer to book ten, and unlike other elements missing in this *10P* fragment, this cannot be explained by the manuscript being physically incomplete.

(with more than 100 canons) is *9L*.[405] The book begins with excerpts from the Rule of Saint Augustine. The book title also highlights that this book dealt with the 'Rule of Saint Augustine and its observation'. This is highly unusual; no earlier collection is known to contain a separate book or a sub-section on regular canons. The other material in this book deals mainly with episcopal property, episcopal elections, possessions of the (secular) clergy and so on, it is plausible to see this as a kind of manual for a cathedral chapter, especially useful in times of a vacancy. In fact, a series of canons specifically deals with the situation after the bishop's death.[406] Book four of *10P* is a very independent work, not drawing on any known models. However, one could speculate whether the *Collection in Four Books* may have provided some inspiration; while *4L* did not deal with regular canons at all, it was a collection that could serve as an example of how to compile a canonical collection specifically dealing with the needs of single groups within the Church. Whatever his source of inspiration was, the *10P* compiler by compiling his book four provided what regular canons working with various canon law collections may indeed have felt missing.

There are other elements in *10P* which indicate the collection was compiled, and may have been used, by regular canons. As mentioned above, conflicts between regular canons and monks in the eleventh and twelfth centuries gave rise to a number of polemic writings and forgeries, including an anti-monastic canon attributed to Leo IX (JL 4269) which is also found in *10P*. The canon is very widely spread and in itself, its presence in *10P* would not necessarily show that the *10P* compiler shared the anti-monastic sentiments expressed in JL 4269. However, if one understands the rubrics as a form of comment, it seems plausible to assume that the *10P* compiler indeed approved of the anti-monastic tendency of the Leo canon: *10P* belongs to the relatively small group of collections preserving a rubric first found in Ivo's *Decretum*, namely 'On the greed of monks'.[407]

Finally, the addition of a penitential as a last book may be seen as a sign that *10P* was compiled as a practical handbook for the secular clergy. Of course, penitential canons could be and were used to many ends—in pas-

---

405. Sedano Rueda, *Colección* 105–106.

406. *10P* 4.28 gathers nine canons under the heading 'Quomodo defunctus episcopus humetur et res eius fideliter conscribantur nec a clericis vel laicis rapiantur'.

407. *10P* 2.34.1 ('De rapacitate monachorum'); see Ivo 7.150. The same rubric is also found in *Tripartita* B 11.10, *Panormia* 2.28, the *Pragensis I*, and the *Ambrosiana II*. The latter according to Picasso was compiled in Milan in the first half of the twelfth century, 'probably by canons' (Fowler-Magerl, *Clavis* 124). It is closely linked to the Vatican *13L*, also seen as having been produced for regular canons. On the latter collection, see below.

toral care, by monastic communities, in the education of confessors, as a law book in ecclesiastical courts, and so on. Yet in the case of *10P*, there is evidence that the penitential was indeed compiled for 'internal' use of in a community of canons. Already the title to book ten highlights the penance of the clergy ('De penitentia et [...] quomodo clerici peniteant [...]'), and this fits the contents very well. While several sections specifically deal with priests and secular clergy doing penance (e.g. *10P* 10.7–9), only very few canons specifically deal with lay penitents (*10P* 10.6.1–2), and no mention is made of monks or nuns. Contrary to the penitential books found in many monastic collections, sexuality and marriage are not particularly prominent in the penitential of *10P*. In the light of the addition of book four, it therefore seems plausible to interpret the penitential found in *10P* as a book intended for the use by a community of canons.

10P and the 'New Law'

As Beryl Smalley once put it, 'new' in the course of the twelfth century 'ceased to be a dirty word'.[408] In canon law history, scholars long assumed that there was a marked difference between pre-Gratian collections (gathering 'old law') and the so-called decretals collections (focussing more or less exclusively on 'new law'). More recent research suggests that the change was less of a break, as 'decretal collections' in fact contain large shares of old, sometimes ancient, materials while manuscripts of pre-Gratian collections contain additions of recent conciliar materials in particular.[409]

In this context, the place of 'new' law in *10P*, or its 'desire for the latest and the greatest' (as Eichbauer put it) deserves attention. To begin with, both the formal and the material sources of *10P* are relatively recent. The *Panormia*, the most important formal source of *10P*, was compiled around the year 1115, and the compared to most pre-Gratian collections, *10P* contains a relatively high share of recent conciliar legislation (Toulouse 1119, Reims 1119). Book three contains prohibitions of investiture and other 're-form legislation' by Urban II and his predecessors, including the relevant decrees from Clermont 1095; these canons were not 'new' but *10P* is the first major collection to include them.[410] What is even more unusual, *10P*

---

408. Beryl Smalley, 'Ecclesiastical Attitudes to Novelty *c.* 1100–*c.* 1250', *Church, Society and Politics*, ed. Derek Baker (Studies in Church History 12; Oxford 1975) 113–131, here at 115, commenting that by *ca.* 1200, '*new* has ceased to be a dirty word [...]. God has changed sides; he is no longer safely conservative'.

409. See Brett, 'Margin' and Summerlin, 'Old Law'.

410. See Eichbauer, 'Desire' 196–199 ('reform legislation' in *10P*) and the discussion of 'Papal Elections and Investiture' in Chapter 5.7.4 (for the delayed reception of investiture prohibitions).

also contains excerpts from a letter of Ivo of Chartres (d. 1115).[411] Unlike contemporary theological works,[412] pre-Gratian canon law collections did hardly ever insert the opinions of *magistri moderni*. The letter itself is an expertise on the possible reconsecration of an altar; it is part of a discussion initiated by Abbot William of Fécamp but later involving a surprising number of participants.[413] In *10P*, Ivo's letter seems to be treated as an authority in its own right. One is reminded of the collections of theological *sententiae* like the *Liber pancrisis*, where the 'modern masters' William of Champeaux, Ivo of Chartres, Anselm of Laon, and his brother Raoul famously are listed alongside the fathers like Augustine, Ambrose, and Gregory the Great.[414] It may also be significant that *10P* left space for the addition of materials, and that this was used to supplement the collection with yet more recent materials: the Florence manuscript contains an excerpt from a tract of Bernard of Clairvaux (dated to 1124), and one Paris copy integrates canons from the Council of Reims held in 1131.[415]

This said, *10P* also contains a high share of patristic materials, above all, from the writings of Saint Augustine; almost 300 canons in the collection are attributed to him. Partly, this may be explained by the interest of the compiler in Saint Augustine and his rule, but evidently patristic authorities were valued in many contexts, in particular concerning the administration of the sacraments. In this, *10P* continued a trend visible in many collections of the late eleventh century, above all the *Decretum* of Ivo of Chartres. Compared to the latter, however, the number of misattributions

411. *10P* 2.11.3.2, being the middle part of Ivo's *Ep.* 80 (on which see below note 413). The preceding canon (*10P*, 2.11.3.1) is a proof text Ivo quoted in the section of letter 80 not taken into *10P*; interestingly, *10P* has the correct inscription as found in the Ivonian collections and not the erroneous one found in Ivo's letter. For another collection (in Cambridge, CCC, 442) containing excerpts from Ivo's *Ep.* 16, see Brett, 'Collectio Lanfranci' 169–170.

412. Writing early in the 1120s, Abelard in his *Sic et non* quoted Ivo twice by name, and inserted his opinions among excerpts culled from decretal letters and patristic writings: *Sic et non*, qq. 125 and 131 (ed. Boyer and McKeon, 430 and 453–454). Abelard also used the canon law Ivo quoted in *Ep.* 16. For general background, see the excellent study by Cédric Giraud, *"Per verba magistri": Anselme de Laon et son école au XIIᵉ siècle* (Bibliothèque d'histoire culturelle du Moyen Âge 8; Turnhout 2010).

413. See Rolker, *Canon Law* 152 on Anselm of Canterbury, Urban II, and his cardinals involved in the discussion which Ivo dealt with in his *Epp.* 72 and 80 (the former being quoted in *10P*).

414. London, BL, Harley MS 3098, fol. 1r, here quoted from the edition in Giraud, *Anselme de Laon* 503: 'Incipit liber Pancrisis id est totus aureus, quia hic auree continentur sententie vel questiones sanctorum patrum Augustini, Jheronimi, Ambrosii, Gregorii, Ysidori, Bede et modernorum magistrorum Guillelmi Catalaunensis episcopi, Ivonis Carnotensis episcopi, Anselmi et fratris eius Radulfi'. See also Cédric Giraud and Constant J. Mews, 'Le *Liber pancrisis*, un florilège des Pères et des maitres modernes du XIIᵉ siècle' *Bulletin du Cange* 64 (2006) 145–191 who rightly points out that the attribution of texts to Ivo in the *Liber pancrisis* is untenable in most cases.

415. An excerpt from Bernard's *De gradibus humilitatis* is found as an addition to book five in the manuscript Firenze, BNC, Conventi soppressi D.2.1476; Paris, BnF, lat. 10743 contains the Reims canons. See Fowler-Magerl, *Clavis* 213.

in *10P* is significant. For example, *10P* follows the *Panormia* in attributing a number of canons of Lanfranc of Bec and Saint Ambrose to Saint Augustine.[416] A famous marriage canon commonly attributed to Leo the Great in *10P* is attributed to Saint Augustine too; the error may be due to an eye-slip.[417]

In the case of *10P*, therefore, the openness towards recent authorities—including 'modern masters' like Ivo and Bernard—went hand in hand with the continued interest in patristic authorities. In this, *10P* is representative of the collections of the twelfth century compiled both before and after Gratian's *Decretum*.

3.8 Conclusions

Law was not the most important aspect of monastic culture, and monastic collections not the most important ones in pre-Gratian legal history. Nonetheless, both our understanding of monastic culture and of canon law history in the eleventh and twelfth centuries profits from taking into account monastic canon law collections. First of all, it should have become clear that collections specifically compiled for the use by religious communities are a significant group, and that they are linked to each other both at the textual level and by the milieu in which they emerged. At the textual level, the collections are linked by common sources (including many letters of Gregory the Great), by joint transmission (e.g. in the case of *5L* and *74T*) or by direct dependence on each other, as in the case of the *Sandionysiana* and *74T*.

As for the link to the monastic milieu, the evidence is often more indirect, but all in all there are enough hints that the collections discussed in the present chapter were produced by monks and for monks. Internal evidence (selection criteria, textual manipulations, arrangement, rubrics) as well as the manuscript tradition and in several cases the use of these collections by monks provide sufficient evidence to establish the background of these (mostly anonymous) collections. In several cases, they were clearly shaped by the situation of the communities producing them; this was most visible in cases that involved open conflict—as in the case of Abbo of Fleury and Arnulf of Orléans, between the monks of Saint-Denis and the bishop of Paris, or between monks and canons over pastoral care.

416. On these misattributions, see Christof Rolker, 'The Earliest Work of Ivo of Chartres: The Case of Ivo's Eucharist Florilegium and the Canon Law Collections Attributed to Him' ZRG Kan. Abt. 93 (2007) 109–127 and idem, *Canon Law* 271–272.

417. Jean Gaudemet, 'Recherche sur les origines historiques de la faculté de rompre le mariage non consommé', *Proceedings Salamanca 1980* MIC Subsidia 6.309–331, here at 326–327 (on JK 544).

These conflicts have been given considerable attention in this chapter not because they were representative of the relations of monks and their environment, but because they help to situate collections compiled at these houses in context.

More importantly, though, the collections can be shown to have been used sometimes well beyond their place of origin and both by monastic and non-monastic readers. Partly, this was already visible from the manuscript tradition of individual works. Some monastic collections may have been very local (e.g. the *Farfensis*) but some decisively not so, circulating in monastic networks (e.g. *5L* or the *Sandionysiana*) or in social groups well beyond the monastic world (*74T* and *4L*). Indeed, *5L* and *74T* are among the most influential collections of the eleventh century. Even relatively 'minor' collections like *10P* still can be seen to have been used by later compilers of canonical collections, to have been copied well beyond their region of origin, and to have been 'updated' for a long time, indicating that they were indeed used and not simply preserved. Vice versa, well after the emergence of the *Decretum Gratiani* religious communities continued to value pre-Gratian collections, and sometimes reworked them according to their specific needs. The *Appendix Seguntina*, which awaits detailed analysis, may be such a case of post-Gratian reworking of pre-Gratian materials by regular canons.[418]

These finding alone would justify the assumption that monastic canon law collections contributed to the development of 'mainstream' canon law. The most striking example here are probably the monastic forgeries integrated into canon law by collections such as *74T* and *13L*, but the same holds also for quite different areas of the law. For example, monastic collections like *5L* helped to establish a stricter version of the marriage prohibitions on ground of consanguinity in Italy even before Burchard was known there. Likewise, monastic collections played an important role to introduce (*9L*, *5L*) or indeed to re-introduce (*10P*) penitential canons into canon law tradition. Finally, almost all monastic collections show a predilection for the letters of Gregory the Great which surely helped to make these materials more widely available not only in monastic circles.

In many cases, such reception of new materials into the monastic collections was motivated by the specific needs of the compilers, and in the case of monastic property in particular, the partisan character of both the

---

418. See Gérard Fransen, 'Appendix Seguntina, Liber Tarraconensis et Décret de Gratien' *Revista española de derecho canónico* 45 (1988) 31–34, here at 31–32 (regular canons) and Arturo Bernal Palacios, 'La redacción breve del c. "In die surrectionis" en las colecciones canónicas pregracianas', *Proceedings Munich 1992* MIC Subsidia 10.923–952, here at 936 (date).

relevant texts (like *Quam sit necessarium* or *QSN* for short) and the collections containing them (especially *74T*) was manifest. As has been discussed at some length in the case of *QSN*, there is ample evidence that (monastic) users not only read and copied these canons, but used them very specifically in lawsuits (e.g. at the Lateran Council), in the making of chartularies (e.g. at Prüm, Rheinau, and Farfa) or to produce further forgeries (e.g. at Westminster). Perhaps even more important was the reception of these texts outside monastic circles. *QSN* was a controversial text, and Deusdedit may not have been the only one to have doubts about its authenticity; but while others may have silently dropped the canon, Deusdedit chose to articulate his views very clearly in his own canonical collection.[419] Yet *QSN* gradually was accepted as genuine not only by monks who for obvious reasons argued that *QSN* was a 'general privilege' for the monastic estate.[420]

Pro-monastic forgeries like *QSN*, composed by monks and introduced into canon law tradition by monastic collections, are an example of very direct influence of monastic canon law collections. Other forms of influence can only be inferred indirectly. For example, it should not be forgotten that monasteries as served as schools. Many popes, cardinals, and bishops, including many compilers of collections not treated in this chapter, had lived in religious communities before. Likewise, monastic libraries and scriptoria were valued widely; the revival of keeping of registers in the papal chancery has plausibly been linked to the contribution of monks from Montecassino.[421] Abbots of major houses were also judges and advisors, and some of their letters are in themselves canonical dossiers (e.g. Abbo's *Letter 14*). Learned abbots were asked for legal advice, and sometimes would give their advice even if not asked. Siegfried of Gorze, for example, opposed the marriage of Henry III and Agnes of Poitou in 1043 as uncanonical, and intervened accordingly.[422] Given that monasteries preserved the genealogical knowledge of many noble families, it is plausible to assume that abbots often played an important role in cases of kin mar-

---

419. Deusdedit, 3.105–106 (90) (ed. Wolf von Glanvell 314–315, here at 315): 'Hoc privilegium cuidam monasterio Ravennatis tantummodo concessum fuisse legitur in registro et quedam sunt ei iuncta, que contraria sunt canonibus et registro eiusdem.' See Uta-Renate Blumenthal, 'Päpstliche Urkunden, Briefe und die europäische Öffentlichkeit', *Erinnerung – Niederschrift – Nutzung. Das Papsttum und die Schriftlichkeit im mittelalterlichen Westeuropa*, ed. Klaus Herbers and Ingo Fleisch (Abh. Akad. Göttingen N.F. 11; Berlin and New York 2011) 11–30, here at 22.

420. See the rubric to *QSN* in *Burdegalensis* 6.1: 'Privilegium generale monachis inductum a beato Gregorio papa'.

421. Dietrich Lohrmann, *Das Register Papst Johannes' VIII. (872–882). Neue Studien zur Abschrift Reg. Vat. I, zum verlorenen Originalregister und zum Diktat der Briefe* (Bibliothek des Deutschen Historischen Instituts in Rom 30; Tübingen 1968); Blumenthal, 'Register'.

422. Max Büdinger, *Zu den Quellen der Geschichte Kaiser Heinrichs III.* (Vienna 1852), here at 7–16.

riages—whether they helped to avoid them in the first place, to denounce them afterwards, or indeed to deal with them in other ways.

Monastic law, therefore, was not confined to the cloister. This is also an important point for the question of 'law and privileges'. For good reasons, privileges (as opposed to general laws) are seen as typical for the Middle Ages, and monastic privileges are a prime example of this. Papal or royal politics towards monks, for example, is not normally studied from general decrees, but the numerous privileges conferred to individual houses. The compilers of monastic canon law collections clearly valued privileges very highly, and their works would often be transmitted jointly with chartularies. Yet importantly, they went beyond accumulating (and occasionally forging) privileges for their own houses. As they gathered the relevant documents protecting the 'liberty' of their houses—privileges, but also hagiography, historiography, and other materials[423]—they also thought about monastic 'liberty' more generally. What was the common foundation of the 'liberties' of an individual house or indeed the monastic order? These were fundamental questions, and compiling a canon law collection provided some monks with an opportunity to address them. Abbo, for one, while evidently engaged in securing royal and papal privileges for Fleury, in his canonical collection also argued very generally about royal office, legal change, and the relations between monasteries and secular rulers. The 74T compiler likewise linked specifically monastic concerns about 'monastic liberty' with more general ecclesiological arguments in his collection. Even the modest dossier in Montecassino MS 372 made a general point in collecting material on the study of law by monks. As monks and nuns copied and exchanged such works, they help each other to define more clearly the place of the cloistered clergy in the Church at large. As the law came to the monks, monastic affairs became part and parcel of canon law.

---

423. In addition to the examples quoted above, see Cushing, 'Polemic' (Anselm), eadem, 'Law, Penance, and the "Gregorian" Reform: The Case of Padua, Biblioteca del Seminario Vescovile MS 529', *Canon Law, Religion and Politics: Liber amicorum Robert Somerville*, ed. Uta-Renate Blumenthal et al. (Washington, D.C. 2012) 28–40 (Burchard), and Berkhofer, *Day of Reckoning* (chartularies).

4

The 'Gregorian' Collections

4.1 'Gregorian Collections': A Working Definition

In his massive *Histoire du droit canonique*, Jean Doujat (d. 1688) between two chapters on Burchard of Worms and Ivo of Chartres inserted a note of two pages on 'less famous collections', referring to the collections of Anselm of Lucca and Deusdedit.[1] In the second half of the nineteenth century, this perception had dramatically changed. Wilhelm von Giesebrecht may have been the first to argue that Anselm, Deusdedit, and others compiled their collections in order to support the politics of Gregory VII.[2] Yet above all, it was Paul Fournier who developed this idea into a fully-fledged historiographical model enshrined in his magisterial *Histoire*.[3]

1. Jean Doujat, *Histoire du droit canonique: avec l'explication des lieux qui ont donné le nom aux Conciles, ou le surnom aux Autres Ecclesiastiques et une chonologique canonique* (Paris 1680), here at 74–75: 'De quelques Collections moins connues'.

2. Wilhelm von Giesebrecht, 'Die Gesetzgebung der römischen Kirche zur Zeit Gregors VII.' *Historisches Jahrbuch* (1866) 91–194, esp. 151–154 (Atto, Anselm, Bonizo, Deusdedit, and Bernold as 'Gregory's canonists'). Among the German-language literature of the late nineteenth century, see also Janus [= Johann Joseph Ignaz von Döllinger], *Der Papst und das Concil* (Leipzig 1869), here at 108–116 (Anselm, Deusdedit, Bonizo, and Gregory, but not Ivo); Ernst Sackur, 'Der *Dictatus papae* und die Canonsammlung des Deusdedit' NA 18 (1893) 137–153, here at 141 (Anselm and Deusdedit as Gregorian canonists). Paul Scheffer-Boichorst, *Die Neuordnung der Papstwahl durch Nikolaus II. Texte und Forschungen zur Geschichte des Papstthums im 11. Jahrhundert* (Strasbourg 1879) and Theodor Sickel, *Das Privilegium Otto I. für die römische Kirche vom Jahre 962* (Innsbruck 1883) highlighted close textual relations, especially between Anselm and Deusdedit.

3. *Histoire* esp. 2.1–14 (74T, Atto, Anselm, and Deusdedit as Gregorian collections), 106–114 (Ivo as 'moderate' Gregorian), and 177–179 (*Polycarpus* as 'reform collection'). For discussion, see Christof Rolker, 'Fournier's Model and Its Merits', *New Discourses in Medieval Canon Law Research:*

Rather than being 'collections moins connues', the collections compiled in the environment of the reform papacy between the mid-eleventh century and *ca.* 1120 became very prominent in scholarship. For Fournier their emergence was nothing less than the 'turning point' in medieval canon law history,[4] and even more importantly, the Gregorian collections were accepted by many scholars (not only legal historians) as important sources for the so-called Gregorian reform.

Since the 1970s, however, this model has increasingly been called into question.[5] The seminal studies of Fuhrmann and Gilchrist have convinced scholars that there was a considerable gap between Gregory VII and canon law.[6] Specialized studies on individual collections have equally cast doubt on Fournier's model. The most dramatic case was *74T*, once dubbed 'the first manual of papal reform' but since around 1970 less and less seen as a 'papally oriented' or 'Gregorian' collection.[7] Increasingly, scholars realized that Fournier had exaggerated the number, the unity, and the importance of the Gregorian collections. For all these reasons, scholars have made qualifications concerning the role of the papacy,[8] the

---

Challenging the Master Narrative, ed. idem (Medieval Law and Its Practice 28; Leiden and Boston 2019) 4–32.

4. Paul Fournier, 'Un tournant de l'histoire du droit 1060–1140' NRHDFE 41 (1917) 129–180. The most famous reply is Stephan Kuttner, 'Urban II and the Doctrine of Interpretation: A Turning Point?' SG 15 (1972) 55–86.

5. John T. Gilchrist, 'Was There a Gregorian Reform Movement in the Eleventh Century?' *Study Sessions of the Canadian Catholic Historical Association* 37 (1970) 1–10; Horst Fuhrmann, 'Das Reformpapsttum und die Rechtswissenschaft', *Investiturstreit und Reichsverfassung*, ed. Josef Fleckenstein (Vorträge und Forschungen 17; Sigmaringen 1973) 175–203; idem, 'Reformgeist'; Hubert Mordek, 'Kanonistik und Gregorianische Reform. Marginalien zu einem nicht-marginalen Thema', *Reich und Kirche vor dem Investiturstreit. Vorträge beim wissenschaftlichen Kolloquium aus Anlaß des 80. Geburtstags von Gerd Tellenbach*, ed. Karl Schmid (Sigmaringen 1985) 65–82; Gerd Tellenbach, '"Gregorianische Reform". Kritische Besinnungen', ibid. 99–113; Horst Fuhrmann, 'Papst Gregor VII. und das Kirchenrecht. Zum Problem des Dictatus Papae' *Studi Gregoriani* 13 (1989) 123–149; Uta-Renate Blumenthal, 'The Papacy and Canon Law in the Eleventh-Century Reform' CHR 84 (1998) 201–218. For a very good recent overview, see Lotte Kéry, 'Recht im Dienst der Reform. Kanonistische Sammlungen der Reformzeit und ihre "Adressaten"', *Brief und Kommunikation im Wandel. Medien, Autoren und Kontexte in den Debatten des Investiturstreits*, ed. Florian Hartmann (Papsttum im mittelalterlichen Europa 5; Cologne, Weimar, and Vienna 2016) 335–380, here at 347–380.

6. Fuhrmann, 'Reformpapsttum' and John T. Gilchrist, 'The Reception of Pope Gregory VII into the Canon Law (1073–1141)' ZRG Kan. Abt. 59 (1973) 35–82. See also Mordek, 'Kanonistik'.

7. Gilchrist, 'Prolegomena', *Diuersorum patrum sententie siue Collectio in LXXIV titulos digesta*, ed. idem (MIC Corpus collectionum 1; Vatican City 1973) xvii–cxxv, here at xxi: 'the tendency to treat the 74T as a papally oriented collection, that is, a special product of the Gregorian camp, is today in process of being dispelled'. For full discussion, see Chapter Three.

8. Fuhrmann, 'Reformpapsttum' 200; Gerd Tellenbach, *The Church in Western Europe from the Tenth to the Early Twelfth Century* (Cambridge Medieval Textbooks; Cambridge 1993), here at 315: 74T, Anselm, Atto, Bonizo, and Deusdedit 'affected by contemporary trends' but none of them 'commissioned by the curia'; Mordek, 'Kanonistik' 68; Ian Stuart Robinson, *The Papacy 1073–1198: Continuity and Innovation* (Cambridge Medieval Textbooks; Cambridge 1990), here at 208: *74T*,

Gregorian character of indivdual collections,[9] and the impact these collections had.[10] At the same time, no alternative paradigm has won acceptance; as a result, the term 'Gregorian collections' is still used, and well into the 1990s was applied to very many collections, though increasingly often with some reservation.[11]

Special care is therefore needed if the concept of 'Gregorian collections' is used. Yet the basic idea that some of the collections of the eleventh and twelfth centuries can be seen as the product of a specific milieu close to Gregory VII should not be dismissed. After all, an impressive number of these collections were compiled by prelates close to Gregory and his successors. In addition, one should take seriously contemporary sources describing some of these compilers as a group, and specifically mentioning the use (or abuse) of canon law in this context. Cardinal Beno of San Silvestro and a number of other cardinals in their polemic writings from the late 1090s singled out Gregory VII, Urban II ('Turbanus'), Anselm of Lucca, and Deusdedit for perverting canon law 'in their fraudulent compilations'.[12] While clearly polemic in nature, this label is evidence that contemporaries saw 'Gregorian' prelates as attempting to shape canon law by compiling collections. Therefore, the idea of 'Gregorian canon law collections' should not be dismissed.[13]

So which collections should be counted as 'Gregorian'? Traditionally, four different criteria have been used to qualify a collection as Gregorian:

Anselm, Atto, Bonizo, Deusdedit, Bonizo, and *Polycarpus* 'inspired by the reform programme of Gregory VII' but 'not commissioned by the pope'.

9. E.g. Ian Stuart Robinson, *Authority and Resistance in the Investiture Contest: The Polemical Literature of the Late Eleventh Century* (Manchester 1978), here at 39–49: Anselm and Atto but not Deusdedit compiled 'Gregorian' collections; Walter Berschin, 'Nachwort', *Bonizo von Sutri, Liber de vita christiana, hg. von Ernst Perels. Mit einem Nachwort zur Neuauflage*, ed. idem (Hildesheim 1998) 405–410, here at 407: Bonizo's *Liber* not Gregorian.

10. Mordek, 'Kanonistik' 69–70; Kathleen Grace Cushing, *Reform and the Papacy in the Eleventh Century: Spirituality and Social Change* (Manchester Medieval Studies; Manchester and New York 2005) 85 (74T, Anselm, Deusdedit, and *Polycarpus* 'more works of propaganda than practical manuals').

11. E.g. both Jean Gaudemet, *Les sources du droit canonique, VIIIᵉ–XXᵉ siècle: repères canoniques, sources occidentales* (Paris 1993) 84 and Kéry 203 (Part III) avoid the term 'Gregorian collections'. Gaudemet divides the pre-Gratian collections of the eleventh and twelfth centuries in five categories: 'regional' collections (six, including Burchard), 'Collections dites de la "Réforme grégorienne"' (27 items), the three Ivonian collections, 'non-Gregorian collections' (in fact only one, the *Farfensis*), and 'collections of the twelfth century' (18 collections). Kéry lists 67 'Collections of the Gregorian Reform period', 37 of which are labelled as 'collections of local importance'. Most collections Gaudemet called 'regional' (Burchard, *12P*, and *5L*) are listed among the 'Carolingian and post-Carolingian collections' in Kéry's volume.

12. Beno, *Gesta* (ed. Francke, MGH Ldl 2.399 and 414): 'in compilationibus suis fraudulentis'; on this passage, see Sackur, 'Dictatus papae' 141, Uta-Renate Blumenthal, 'Fälschungen bei Kanonisten der Kirchenreform des 11. Jahrhunderts', *Fälschungen im Mittelalter* (6 vols. MGH Schriften 33; Hanover 1988) 2.241–262, here at 242, and Cushing, *Papacy and Law* 103.

13. See Blumenthal, 'Fälschungen' and Kéry, 'Recht'.

that the collection was compiled at the request of Gregory VII (or at least inspired by him); that the compiler was close to the reform papacy and supported its policies; that the collection, its content, and its structure, reflected these policies; and that the collection disseminated these texts and ideas. All four criteria deserve attention, and should be considered seperately, as the different aspects are not necessarily congruent.

Inspiration by the pope (an idea dear to Fournier) is generally thought to be unlikely for any canonical collection,[14] and in any case would be difficult to prove, even if one takes into account that some collections can indeed be traced to the papal curia—Atto of San Marco, Deusdedit, and later Gregory of San Grisogono all compiled canonical collections during their time as cardinals. The idea of 'papal inspiration' is mainly based on Peter Damian's report that Hildebrand asked him to compile a small collection of excerpts on the prerogatives of the apostolic see.[15] Yet even Peter Damian, a radical reformer well familiar with canon law, either did not want, or felt unable to fulfil Hildebrand's repeated requests. The episode can thus be quoted as evidence for Gregory's will to have new collections compiled, but also for the apparent difficulties in compiling such a work. A similar ambiguity sourrounds the other source often quoted in this context, the *Dictatus papae*.[16] Dictated by Gregory VII himself, and transmitted in the register of his letters, the *Dictatus* consists of twenty-seven short sentences, mainly claims concerning papal prerogatives. Both in content and in style it resembles the *capitulatio* of a (very short) canonical collection, and for this reason has often been compared to such collections. These comparisons, however, in the end have clearly shown that many of these propositions had no firm support by canonical tradition, and some directly contradicted it.[17] No doubt those of Gregory's supporters who were familiar with canon law were aware of this problem. Thus, while Damian's letter and the *Dictatus papae* do support the idea that Gregory was interested in canon law, both sources also point to the fact that the collection Gregory wished for was never compiled, and at least in part could not have been compiled.

Closeness to Gregory himself and political support for the Gregorian cause is easier to establish, at least for those collections which can be

14. See above notes 3–4 (Fournier) and 8 (modern research).

15. Peter Damian, *Ep.* 65 (ed. Reindel, MGH Briefe dt. Kaiserzeit 4.2:228–247, here at 229), writing to Gregory VII: 'Frequenter a me [. . .] postulasti, ut Romanorum pontificum decreta vel gesta percurrens quicquid apostolicae sedis auctoritati specialiter competere videretur, hinc inde curiosus excerperem, atque in parvi voluminis unionem nova compilationis arte conflarem.'

16. Gregory VII, *Dictatus papae* (ed. Caspar, MGH Epp. sel. 2.1:202–208).

17. There is an abundant literature on the *Dictatus*; on its relation to canonical collections, see Fuhrmann, 'Papst Gregor VII.', Blumenthal, 'Papacy' esp. 214, and Fowler-Magerl, *Clavis* 158–159.

attributed to known compilers. Atto of San Marco, Anselm of Lucca, Deusdedit, and Bonizo of Sutri all can be shown to have supported Gregory in various ways just as Hildebrand/Gregory supported Atto, Anselm, and Bonizo in their (ultimately failed) attempts to take or retain their episcopal sees, and in all likelihood he made both Atto and Deusdedit cardinals. No doubt this suggests that these prelates were close to Gregory in some sense. However, there also are a number of important caveats. First, closeness and even loyalty to Gregory VII was not the same as loyalty to the reform papacy. Bonizo, for example, had supported Gregory VII for a long time but was a vocal critic of Urban II. Secondly, political factions were likely to change, sometimes dramatically so. Atto may have been an 'ardent Gregorian' for a long time, but in 1084 he broke with Gregory and was excommunicated by him. Finally, and most importantly, political allegiance can take us only so far. Both opponents and supporters of Gregory VII disagreed among themselves on important issues, including fundamental problems of canon law. For example, Deusdedit fiercely opposed the Papal Election Decree of 1059 which is often seen as a key text of papal reform. More importantly, reformers like Peter Damian, Bernold of Konstanz, Anselm, Deusdedit, and Bonizo of Sutri all disagreed over the validity of sacraments administered by schismatics. Generally, as Mirbt noted long ago, political allegiance played no role in this important debate on the sacraments.[18] Therefore, even the most loyal Gregorians may have compiled very different collections.

Even greater attention has, therefore, be paid to the **content and structure** of the collections themselves. As for the content, the idea that a high share of Pseudo-Isidorian material was a distinct feature of Gregorian (or 'reform') collections has long been given up. Another criterion is the inclusion of recent papal legislation, in particular material going back to Gregory VII himself. His letters, on the whole, had little impact on canon law; yet precisely for this reason, parallels to the *Dictatus papae* and the relatively high share of canons taken from Gregory's register in Deusdedit and a number of anonymous collections deserves attention.[19] Also, the

18. Carl Mirbt, *Die Publizistik im Zeitalter Gregors VII.* (Leipzig 1894), here at 430: 'Der Parteigegensatz der Gregorianer und Antigregorianer erweist sich als völlig neutral gegenüber den Gegensätzen, welche in der Behandlung der einzelnen Unterfragen [zur Wiederholbarkeit der von Häretikern gespendeten Sakramente, CR] zu Tage treten.' See also John T. Gilchrist, '*Simoniaca haeresis* and the Problem of Orders from Leo IX to Gratian', *Proceedings Boston 1963* MIC Subsidia 1.209–235 and Robinson, *Authority and Resistance* 47–48.

19. See Gilchrist, 'Reception'. Out of 82 pre-Gratian collections, nine contain ten or more canons from Gregory's letters, namely Deusdedit (39 canons according to Gilchrist), *3L* and Turin *7L* (24 canons each), San Pietro *9L* (17 canons), Berlin *13L* (16 canons), *Tarraconensis II* (11 canons), and *Tarraconensis I* (10 canons).

Tarraconensis has rightly been identified as a 'unique direct transmitter of the policies of pope Gregory VII',[20] and together with a handful of closely related collections (including Turin 7L and Berlin 13L) contributed to the dissemination of the relevant materials. To a lesser degree this is also true for the *Taurinensis*.[21] If we turn from content to structure, the attention paid to papal prerogatives and the importance of the Roman church is the most important structural element of Gregorian collections, especially where a relevant book is placed prominently at the beginning of a collection. In this respect, the collection of Anselm of Lucca stands out. Also, as will become clear, cardinals like Deusdedit or Gregory of San Grisogono clearly distinguished between 'papal' and 'Roman' prerogatives; the mere fact that they devoted special attention to the Roman church cannot be taken as evidence for 'papalist' views, as it has sometimes been done in the literature.

Finally, even if both the person of the compiler and the collection itself merit the label 'Gregorian', one should ask whether the collection in question had any **impact** on canon law history. The collection of Atto of San Marco, for example, has sometimes been given great attention, but any discussion of this work has to take into account that it had no discernable influence on later collections. The collections of Anselm and Deusdedit, while extant in relatively few manuscripts, did have such an influence, mainly in Italy; the *Polycarpus* by Gregory of San Grisogono seems to have been more influential. None of these three collections, however, contains key texts of Gregory VII as the *Tarraconensis* and a number of anonymous related collections did.

As can be seen from this short survey, the collections compiled by Atto, Anselm, Deusdedit, Bonizo, and Gregory of San Grisogono, and the *Tarraconensis*, all meet one or more of the criteria for Gregorian canon law collections, but none meets all of them. This does not mean that they are not Gregorian; rather, it underlines the diversity in content, structure, and dissemination of the works, and the diffuse content of the term 'Gregorian' in much of the modern literature.

4.2 Atto of San Marco

Atto of San Marco was a prelate whose ecclesiastical career is closely tied to Hildebrand/Gregory VII. In 1072, he had been elected archbishop

---

20. Fowler-Magerl, *Clavis* 133.

21. On the collection, which would deserve a separate study, see Giuseppe Motta, 'Una silloge canonistica del sec. XII tra Deusdedit ed Anselmo di Lucca (Torino, Biblioteca Nazionale E.V.44)', *De iure canonico medii aevi. Festschrift für Rudolf Weigand*, ed. Peter Landau (SG 27; Rome 1996) 413–442 and Fowler-Magerl, *Clavis* 172–173.

of Milan with the support of the Patarenes upon Hildebrand's advice, but met resistance both locally and from the imperial court. Unable to take office, Atto fled to Rome where Gregory made him cardinal, perhaps to compensate him for this loss. Atto no doubt was loyal to Gregory; but in 1082, he was among the cardinals who protested against Gregory's use of ecclesiastical property, and in 1084, Atto (together with a number of other cardinals) defected from him to Wibert/Clement III.[22] He was excommunicated by Gregory VII and died in 1085 or 1086 with the excommunication still in force.[23]

Apart from his involvement in the Milan affair, Atto is mainly known for having compiled a small canonical collection called *Breviary* (or sometimes *Capitulare*).[24] It is commonly thought to have been compiled after *ca.* 1075 but before 1084. It contains some 500 canons on a wide range of subjects, most notably Roman primacy. The materials are largely left in the sequence of Atto's formal sources.[25] These were the False Decretals (by far his most important source), the register of Gregory the Great, the *Dionysio-Hadriana* for (relatively few) conciliar canons, a dossier of letters of Gelasius I, and a single letter of Nicholas I.[26] For his Pseudo-Isidore, Atto apparently relied on a intermediate source also used by Deusdedit,[27]

22. On the 1082 protest, see Zelina Zafarana, 'Sul *conventus* del clero romano nel maggio 1082' *Studi medievali, serie terza* 7 (1966) 399–403. Michael E. Stoller, *Schism in the Reform Papacy: The Documents and Councils of the Antipopes, 1061–1121* (PhD thesis; Columbia University, New York 1985), here at 228 in addition argued that Atto belonged to the cardinals who 'almost certainly' participated in Wibert's Roman synod of 1084 for three reasons: because they protested against Gregory in 1082, because they were mentioned by Beno (ed. Francke, MGH Ldl 2.369), and because they subscribed a privilege of Wibert/Clement III. However, contrary to what Stoller suggests, the latter is not true of Atto.

23. This is reported by Hugh of Lyon in a letter preserved in the chronicle of Hugh of Flavigny (ed. Pertz, MGH SS 8.367), see Lawo, *Studien* 245.

24. Kéry 233–234; Fowler-Magerl, *Clavis* 138–139; in addition, see Rebekka Gotter, *Das Breviar Attos von San Marco* (MA thesis; Rheinische Friedrich-Wilhelms-Universität, Bonn 2018).

25. Fournier, 'Collections romaines' 288–292, 335–336, and 388–390; John Joseph Ryan, 'Observations on the Pre-Gratian Canonical Collections: Some Recent Work and Present Problems', *Congrès de droit canonique médiéval: Louvain et Bruxelles 22–26 Juillet 1958*, ed. Stephan Kuttner et al. (Bibliothèque de la revue d'histoire ecclésiastique 33; Leuven 1959) 88–103, here at 99; Fuhrmann, *Einfluß und Verbreitung* 2.532.

26. As Robert Somerville, 'Pope Nicholas I and John Scottus Eriugena: JE 2833' ZRG Kan. Abt. 83 (1997) 67–85, here at 73–76, demonstrated, Atto in the preface (but not the collection) quoted from Nicholas I, JE 2833. The quotation from this rather rare letter can not be traced to any of the formal sources of the *Breviary*.

27. Fuhrmann, *Einfluß und Verbreitung* 2.532. To the canons quoted by Fuhrmann one could add Atto 30.6 (ed. Mai 73) = Deusdedit 4.333 (156) (ed. Wolf von Glanvell 568–567). Not only is the canon very rare, but (as Gotter, *Breviar* 29 n. 197 observed) Atto and Deusdedit also share the misattribution to Pope Siricus; in fact, the source is Ps.-Damasus, JK †245 (ed. Hinschius 519–520). The same misattribution also occurs in the collection in Roma, Vallicelliana, B.89 (not seen; key VL150 in the *Clavis* database) which seems to have an even shorter excerpt than Atto and Deusdedit. Fuhrmann, *Einfluß und Verbreitung* 3.905 n. 770 pointed to Ps.-Calixtus.

while the Gelasius dossier was also used by both Deusdedit and Anselm.[28] This rather modest set of sources and the strong predilection for papal—not conciliar—legislation fits Atto's radical views on papal authority expressed in the preface. According to Atto, any canon 'not confirmed by the Roman pontiff is not an authoritative writing', and councils in particular needed papal approval.[29]

The *Breviary* is extant in only one medieval manuscript (Vat. lat. 586), which may even be Atto's exemplar;[30] the collection had no discernible influence.[31] Given the manifest difficulty to use the collection, this comes at no surprise. Nonetheless, the *Breviary* is relatively prominent in modern scholarship mainly for three reasons. First, it was available in print from very early on.[32] Second, it is one of the relatively few collections to come with a preface and to be attributed to a named author—two features that greatly facilitate the analysis. Finally, for Fournier in particular the *Breviary* was important because Atto in his preface seemed to criticize the *Liber decretorum* of Burchard of Worms—something which Fournier thought to be typical of the reformers but for which there is in fact very little evidence. In any case, the passage is worth quoting:[33]

> It is, therefore, evident that the Roman Penitential is not valid [...]. But the transalpine councils one reads in Burchard do obtain validity in the places where they were enacted, provided that they are contrary neither to reason nor to the regulations of the Roman church. But otherwise, if they are not confirmed by this church they are not valid except with the agreement of both parties. Nevertheless, many things there [*ibi*], though true, are attributed to an

28. Fournier, 'Collections romaines' 389 on Atto 39.21–35 (ed. Mai 81–82); Fuhrmann, *Einfluß und Verbreitung* 2.532 n. 291. Four of Atto's Gelasian fragments have no parallel either in Anselm or in Deusdedit (Atto 39.27, 30, and 31); three are not in *Britannica*, fols. 9v–38r (Atto 39.26, 32, and 35).

29. Atto, *Praefatio* (ed. Mai 61): 'Sicut enim secundum Iob est locus ubi conflatur aurum, ita apud nos locus est ad faciendam hanc monetam, ut non sit scriptum authenticum quod a Romano pontifice non fuerit confirmatum. [...] Si enim secundum Iulium papam, nullum ratum est concilium aut erit, quod huius sedis non est fultum auctoritate, nec sine huius sedis auctoritate rata sunt scripta, quibus fieri solent concilia.' The translation is taken from Somerville and Brasington, *Prefaces* 118.

30. Gotter, *Breviar* 38.

31. Fowler-Magerl, *Clavis* 138–139 and 142 followed the *Histoire* on Anselm and Deusdedit using Atto's *Breviary*, but Fournier did not provide sufficient evidence for this claim. The question of a shared source for some of their Gelasian material, in contrast, merits a new study.

32. Mai published his edition in 1836 without quoting the base manuscript. His edition essentially is a transcript of Vat. lat. 586, but Mai occasionally altered the Latin.

33. Atto, preface (ed. Mai 61): 'Unde patet quod paenitentiale Romanum non est ratum [...]. Transalpina vero concilia, quae in Burcardo leguntur, si non sunt contra rationem aut contra instituta Romanae ecclesiae, in locis suis ubi facta sunt, obtinent firmitatem. Alias autem si non sint hac confirmata, non valent, nisi ex partis utriusque consensu. Multa tamen ibi, licet vera, falso nomine auctoris titulantur, alia re ipsa falsa leguntur, alia vero turpissima scribuntur, quae sanctis viris solet esse pudor dicere et pudor audire.' My translation is largely adopted from Somerville and Brasington, *Prefaces* 120 but also taking into account Fournier's translation (see below, note 35) and comments by Martin Brett (private communication).

author falsely; others are plainly false; others concern so foul a matter as to be for holy men a disgrace to utter and a disgrace to hear.

This is a striking, and unusual, diatribe. Atto's disdain for the (or a?) Roman Penitential,[34] and his low esteem for transalpine councils are evident. The last sentence is less clear, as the 'ibi' could refer to the Roman Penitential, the transalpine councils, or Burchard. Most scholars have followed Fournier, who removed any ambiguity by inserting 'in Burchard's *Liber decretorum*' in his translation of the passage.[35] There are good reasons to think that Atto's critique extends to Burchard.[36] The latter does indeed contain many canons from Frankish councils, and book nineteen contains excerpts from penitentials including the Roman Penitential, which may also be the passages perceived by Atto as too detailed and therefore 'a disgrace to hear'.[37] In addition, many of Burchard's inscriptions (especially in his penitential book) are manipulated,[38] and this may well have been noted by Atto. At least indirectly, therefore, Atto's diatribe is aiming at Burchard, and the 'ibi' may indeed refer to Burchard's collection.[39] Atto's contempt of the *Liber decretorum* in turn may explain why he did not use the latter as a source for his own collection. Both the criticism of Burchard and the decision not to use it are extremely unusual. Most collections compiled in Italy in the second half of the eleventh century used it, sometimes heav-

34. For context, see Meens, 'Bußbücher'. On the penitential Atto was referring to, see below (note 36).

35. Fournier, 'Décret' 691–692: 'Burchard, qui représente l'Église soumise au pouvoir impérial, est évidemment très suspect aux réformateurs. Un membre important du parti de la réforme, le cardinal Atton, en fait l'aveu sans détours, dans un passage trop intéressant pour que je m'abstienne de le citer. "Nous admettons, écrit-il, qu'on observe dans les provinces pour lesquelles ils ont été rédigés les canons des conciles transalpins recueillis par Burchard, s'ils ne sont contraires ni à la raison ni aux institutions de l'Église romaine. Au-delà de cette limite, ils ne valent qu'autant qu'ils ont été confirmés par le Saint-Siège ou ont été acceptés par le libre consentement des intéressés. On trouve d'ailleurs dans le *Décret* de Burchard une foule de textes qui, quoique reproduisant exactement les règles du droit, portent des attributions fausses à tel ou tel auteur; d'autres qui contiennent des règles erronées; d'autres enfin traitant de matières si honteuses que la pudeur défend aux hommes religieux de s'entretenir".'

36. Jasper, 'Burchards Dekret' 180–184.

37. Burchard's penitential, like all penitentials, contains more or less straightforward references to various sins; there is a tradition of warning against the use of too explicit language in hearing confession which Atto may belong to. For a thirteenth-century example, see *Robert of Flamborough, Liber poenitentialis*, ed. J. J. Francis Firth (PIMS Studies and Texts 18; Toronto 1971) 196–197. Dr Adriaan Gaastra (private communication, 15 October 2020) kindly pointed out to me the parallel in Theodulf of Orléans, *Capitula altera*, c. 14 (ed. Brommer, MGH Capit. episc. 1.176). He also raised the point that Atto by 'Roman penitential' may well have referred to a minor penitential like the *Poenitentiale Vallicellianum I* or the *Poenitentiale Vaticanum* which are known to have circulated in Rome.

38. Schmitz, *Bussbücher* 1.764.

39. In my PhD thesis, I was inclined to read the 'ibi' as a reference to the transalpine councils: Rolker, *Canon Law* 64 n. 83. My thanks are to Dr Cushing, who in discussion made me rethink the issue. See also her 'Law and Reform' 41.

ily so.[40] Peter Damian, who is closest to Atto in his disdain of penitential canons,[41] never blamed Burchard for including such materials in his *Liber decretorum*.[42]

Atto's radical views may partly explain why his collection had little if any impact. Even readers sharing Atto's views would still have found it difficult to use the *Breviary*; the collection is not organised by any discernable principle, lacks a *capitulatio*, and does not even provide rubrics. Looking up the relevant canon law on any given issue is, therefore, unnecessarily difficult. Even if one finds the text one was looking for, Atto normally quotes so heavily abbreviated a version that many readers (assuming for the moment they existed) would have found it of little help. The *Breviary* is therefore mainly valuable as a source for Atto's own opinions, perhaps also for Gregorian ecclesiology more generally, but not as an important document of legal history. In this context, it may be worth noting that the manuscript of the *Breviary* also preserves the protocol of the 1082 gathering of cardinals who protested against Gregory's use of ecclesiastical property.[43] Atto was one of these cardinals, and if he already had his *Breviary* at hand, he could have quoted a canon supporting the cardinals' position from it.[44] It is plausible that Atto was responsible for the 1082 protocol finding its way into the sole copy of his collection.

However, while Atto's influence on later canon law history was minimal, his collection still is an important source for the integration of 'new' canon law in the late eleventh century. In particular, his use of the letters of Gelasius I deserves special attention. Thanks to the overlap between Atto, Anselm, and Deusdedit, it is possible to reconstruct a source behind all three collections with some certainty. Specifically, a series of fifteen Gelasius fragments in Atto's *Breviary* contains material mostly not found in earlier collections; yet all but four are also in Anselm or Deusdedit (or both), and the *Britannica* has all but three of Atto's fifteen canons.[45] The

40. Jasper, 'Burchards Dekret' passim; Rolker, *Canon Law* 62–68.

41. Peter Damian, *Ep.* 31 (ed. Riedel, MGH Briefe dt. Kaiserzeit 4.1:284–330, esp. 300–301) famously rallied against too lax penances for sexual misconduct, and violently criticized penitentials on this account; in ridiculing these book, he also raised the point of dubious origin of many of these canons. For background, see Gaastra, 'Penitentials'.

42. On Damian's use of Burchard, see John Joseph Ryan, *Saint Peter Damiani and His Canonical Sources: A Preliminary Study in the Antecedents of the Gregorian Reform* (PIMS Studies and Texts 2; Toronto 1956) esp. 160–161 and Ubl, *Inzestverbot* 451–460.

43. Vat. lat. 586, fol. 125v.

44. Atto 41.2 (ed. Mai 82–83; Vat. lat. 586, fol. 109r). In the *Clavis* database, this canon is presented as being attributed to Gelasius, but this is an error.

45. Atto 39.21–35 (ed. Mai 81–82). Only canons 27, 30, and 31 have no parallel in Anselm and/or Deusdedit; canons 26, 32, and 35 are not in the *Britannica* (London, BL, Add. MS 8873, fols. 9v–38r).

series, first noted by Fournier,[46] is unusual for a number of reasons. First of all, while Gelasius I was a prolific writer, his letters were rarely quoted in pre-Gratian collections. Only the so-called *Generale decretum* (JK 636) and a handful of letters transmitted with the Pseudo-Isidorian forgeries were relatively widely accessible; the *Avellana* contained more materials, but was rarely used before the late eleventh century.[47] Yet Atto's series does not even overlap with these traditions, and in fact cannot be taken from *any* known collection. The only parallels are the *Britannica* (extant only in a later version from the twelfth century), and the collections of Anselm and Desdedit compiled before 1086/87. As far as the letters are datable, they all seem to stem from the later years of Gelasius' pontificate (late 494 to 496), and intriguingly, they seem to be in chronological sequence.[48] Atto thus seems to preserve—although much more imperfectly than the *Britannica*—the order of the lost register from which these excerpts were taken. A relatively direct use of Gelasius' register is also suggested by Deusdedit, who in two cases claimed to have taken canons from this series 'ex registro'; these are the only references to Gelasius' register in his *Collectio*.[49] The parallels between Atto, Anselm, and Deusdedit are best explained by the use of a common source, as direct influence of one collection on the other can largely be excluded. In particular, Atto's collection (presumably the earliest of the three) cannot have been the source for either Anselm or Deusdedit; this is evident already from the way Atto abbreviates most canons. At the same time, Atto could not have arranged

46. Fournier, 'Collections romaines' 389–390 was the first to point out that Atto's series was unusual and suggested access to otherwise unknown sources also available to Anselm and Deusdedit. Indeed, the overlap of Atto's series with Anselm, Deusdedit, and the *Britannica* is much greater than Fournier assumed.

47. Maassen, *Quellen* 281–282 (JK 636); Jasper, 'Beginning' 59–60 (JK 636), 60–62 (*Avellana*), 64 (Pseudo-Isidore), and 64–65 (eleventh-century collections). Jasper does not discuss Atto in this context, or any of the letters from which the excerpts in Atto 39.21–35 are taken.

48. The ultimate sources of Atto 39.21–35 are the following letters: JK 643 = J³ 1292 (dated between 494 and 495), JK 692 = J³ 1333, JK 648 = J³ 1295 (494/495), JK 735 = J³ 1392 (496), JK 651 = J³ 1297 (494/495), JK 677 = J³ 1340, JK 658 = J³ 1302 (494/495), JK 668 = J³ 1307 (494/495), JK 706 = J³ 1364 (495/496), JK 711 = J³ 1367 (496), JK 712 = J³ 1368 (496), JK 694 = J³ 1335, JK 725 = J³ 1381 (496), JK 728 = J³ 1384 (496), and JK 680 = J³ 1357 (495/496). The dates given in brackets are that of the third edition of Jaffé; Ewald and Kaltenbrunner proposed a more narrow timeframe for many letters, especially for JK 641–663 (late 494 to August 495), but their arguments are not convincing. See Paul Ewald, 'Die Papstbriefe der Brittischen Sammlung' NA 5 (1880) 275–414 and 505–596, here at 526–529 and Kaltenbrunner in *Regesta pontificum* JK 641–663. Note that the odd 'extended' form of JK 694 in Atto 39.34 (ed. Mai 82; Vat. lat. 586, fol. 108v) can be explained by the combination here with an excerpt from JK 728 (Martin Brett, private correspondence). See also Peter Landau, 'Die Rezension C der Sammlung des Anselm von Lucca' BMCL 16 (1986) 17–54, here at 30 who must have spotted this but did not comment. (J³ 1335 relies on pre-1880 scholarship and editions here.)

49. Atto 39.28, 32, and 34 = Deusdedit 2.54 (40) and 4.339 (156) (ed. Wolf von Glanvell 211 and 570), taken from JK 668 and JK 694, respectively. On the second half of Deusdedit 4.339 (156) (ed. Wolf von Glanvell 570) and Atto 39.34, see the last note.

the Gelasian material in chronological sequence (not even imperfectly) if he had lifted his canons from a collection which presented these materials even remotely similar to Anselm and Deusdedit. As for Anselm and Deusdedit, the latter collection cannot have been the source of the former as it lacks some Gelasius fragments completely and also tends to have shorter versions than Anselm.[50] Indeed, of three compilers, Anselm normally preserves the best and/or longest versions of these excerpts; but occasionally, Deusdedit has a better text than Anselm.[51] More decisively, there are parallels between Atto's Gelasius series and Deusdedit not matched by Anselm's collection.[52] It would be possible in principle that a lost, fuller version of Anselm was used by Deusdedit, but this question cannot be solved here.

All in all, the evidence from Atto, Deusdedit, and the various versions of Anselm strongly points towards a dossier of excerpts ultimately taken from the lost register of Gelasius which contained, in chronological sequence, fuller versions of the canons of Atto 39.21–35, and perhaps more Gelasius fragments. Given that Atto for *other* papal registers seems not to have had access to the shared sources of Anselm and Deusdedit, the series of Gelasian material also suggests that these intermediate sources were extant as small dossiers rather than in the form of one large collection containing excerpts from many papal registers.[53] Although the Gelasius material in the end was combined with many other excerpts from papal registers in the *Britannica*, the shared intermediate source behind Atto, Anselm, and Deusdedit must have been much more modest. Otherwise— if one assumed that *all* dossiers of papal letters and other shared materials were available in one rather large collection to all three compilers—one would have to assume that all three chose to use only very small parts of what they must have recognised as a first rate source, and instead decided to spend much more time excerpting canons from the same popes from

50. See Atto 39.26 (ed. Mai 82; Vat. lat. 586, fol. 108r), Anselm 7.79 (ed. Thaner 397–398), and Deusdedit 1.172 (141) (ed. Wolf von Glanvell 109). Anselm has much more than Atto, and more than Deusdedit; but Atto cannot depend on Deusdedit. The ultimate source is JK 677; for an edition see *Epistolae Romanorum pontificum genuinae et quae ad eos scriptae sunt*, ed. Andreas Thiel (Braunsberg 1868) 485.

51. Anselm 6.110 (ed. Thaner 322) is longer than Deusdedit 1.170 (139) (ed. Wolf von Glanvell 108), and much fuller than Atto 39.24; yet only Deusdedit preserves the 'et post pauca' marking a significant omission in the letter (JK 677 = *Fragmentum 5*, ed. Thiel 485).

52. Atto 39.32 and 34 (ed. Mai 82; Vat. lat. 586, fol. 108v) = Deusdedit 4.339 (156) (ed. Wolf von Glanvell 570), but not in Anselm.

53. The same is true for other intermediate collections, see Busch, *Liber de honore* 102–114 (the 'error series', a mini-collection small in size but widely used) and Christof Rolker, 'Bonizo von Sutri, die "Sammlung in zwei Büchern/acht Teilen" und das Gespenst der gregorianischen Zwischensammlung' BMCL 37 (2020) 55–105, here at 101–102 ('mehrere[] unabhängig entstandene[] Kleinstsammlungen' behind the collections of Anselm, Bonizo, and Deusdedit).

various other collections. The Gelasius fragments in Atto, Anselm, and Deusdedit therefore are evidence how relatively small dossiers were, occasionally at least, available to several compilers of systematic canon law collections, but also suggest that these dossiers travelled independently from each other.

4.3 Deusdedit

4.3.1. Biography

Little is known about Deusdedit's biography.[54] According to Berengar of Tours, he was monk in Tulle in the Limousin before he came to Rome and was already a cardinal when participating in the Roman synod of November 1078.[55] His titular church was San Pietro in Vincoli; significantly, Deusdedit himself preferred the ancient name 'SS. Apostolorum in Eudoxia' for his church, stressing its dedication to both Saint Peter and Paul. At some point before 1087 he was in Lower Saxony,[56] perhaps when travelling with the papal legate Odo in 1084/85.[57] Apart from his *Collectio canonum*, his extant works include a *Libellus theopoeseos* (a collection of poems) and the *Libellus contra invasores*, a polemic against Wibert/Clement III written *ca.* 1097.[58] Unlike other lower-ranking cardinals, who as a group initially supported Gregory VII but over the years deserted him in relatively large numbers, Deusdedit remained loyal to Gregory. Above all, however, Deusdedit was loyal to the Roman church, as will also become evident from the analysis of his collection. He died on 3 March 1098 or 1099.[59]

54. Walther Holtzmann, 'Kardinal Deusdedit als Dichter' *Historisches Jahrbuch* 57 (1937) 217–232, here at 230–232 (early biography); Rudolf Hüls, *Kardinäle, Klerus und Kirchen Roms 1049–1130* (Bibliothek des Deutschen Historischen Instituts in Rom 48; Tübingen 1977), here at 114 (overview); Becker, *Urban II.* 2.49–62 (later life).

55. Berengar's letter, ed. R. B. C. Huygens, 'Bérenger de Tours, Lanfranc et Bernold de Constance' *Sacris erudiri* 16 (1965) 355–403, here at 390–391; repr. in CCCM 171.239–255.

56. Deusdedit 4.420 (161) (ed. Wolf von Glanvell 596): 'Hoc sacramentum invenit scriptor huius libri in Saxonia in monasterio, quod dicitur Luineburg.'

57. Fuhrmann, *Einfluß und Verbreitung* 2.523–524; Fuhrmann, 'Gerstungen' 60–61. Odo convened a synod at Quedlinburg on Easter 1085; he may have travelled further, perhaps to Arras, before returning to Italy according to Becker, *Urban II.* 1.76–79. There is no evidence that Deusdedit himself was papal legate either to Germany or to Spain. The latter claim (found e.g. in *Histoire* 2.38) goes back to a confusion with a cardinal of the same name who in the twelfth century was legate to Spain.

58. *Die Carmina des Kardinals Deusdedit († 1098/99)*, ed. Peter Christian Jacobsen (Editiones Heidelbergenses 31; Heidelberg 2002); *Libellus* (ed. Sackur, MGH Ldl 2.300–365); for Roman and canon law in the *Libellus*, see Hermann Heinrich Fitting, 'Über die Stellen des römischen Rechtes in einer Streitschrift des Cardinals Deusdedit' ZRG Rom. Abt. 9 (1888) 376–381 and Ernst Sackur, 'Zu den Streitschriften des Deusdedit und Hugo von Fleury' NA 16 (1891) 347–386.

59. Hartmut Hoffmann, 'Der Kalender des Leo Marsicanus' DA 21 (1965) 82–149, here at 94 and 134.

4.3.2 Deusdedit's *Collectio canonum* (Overview)

Deusdedit's *Collectio canonum* has an important place in the history of canon law.[60] The complete collection is extant in only one medieval manuscript (Vat. lat. 3833) from the early twelfth century; the quality of the text is modest.[61] The most recent datable material it contains is a letter of Gregory VII from 1081, and the collection may have been more or less finished by that time.[62] Blumenthal suggested that a draft version of Deusdedit's collection could have been available as early as 1078.[63] As the dedication to 'Pope Victor and all Roman clergy' shows, the *Collectio* was completed during the short pontificate of Victor III, who after long delay was consecrated only in May 1087 and died in September the same year.

Deusdedit's collection consists of a preface,[64] a sophisticated *capitulatio*, and four books containing a total of 703 numbered canons. Wolf von Glanvell in his edition split many canons and renumbered the fragments.[65]

60. See in general Kéry 228–233 and Fowler-Magerl, *Clavis* 160–163. Among the more recent literature, see in particular Jasper, 'Beginning' esp. 60, 64, 66, 78, 129, and 131; Robert Somerville, 'Cardinal Deusdedit's *Collectio canonum* at Benevento', *Ritual, Text and Law: Studies in Medieval Canon Law and Liturgy Presented to Roger E. Reynolds*, ed. Richard F. Gyug and Kathleen Grace Cushing (CFC; Aldershot 2004) 281–292 (fragments not listed by Kéry); Uta-Renate Blumenthal, 'Reflections on the Influence of the *Collectio canonum* of Cardinal Deusdedit', *Mélanges en l'honneur d'Anne Lefebvre-Teillard*, ed. Bernard d'Alteroche et al. (Paris 2009) 135–148; Ulrich Schludi, *Die Entstehung des Kardinalkollegiums. Funktion, Selbstverständnis, Entwicklungsstufen* (Mittelalter-Forschungen 24; Ostfildern 2014); Nowak, 'Papsttum'; idem, 'Recent Work on the *Dagome Iudex* in the *Collectio canonum* of Cardinal Deusdedit', *Sacri canones editandi: Studies on Medieval Canon Law in Memory of Jiří Kejř*, ed. Pavel Otmar Krafl (2nd edition Nitra 2020) 25–39.

61. For fragments and later works preserving better readings, see Victor Wolf von Glanvell, 'Einleitung', *Die Kanonessammlung des Kardinals Deusdedit, I. Die Kanonessammlung selbst*, ed. idem (Paderborn 1905) IX–LIV, here at XXVIII (Paris, BnF, lat. 1458) and Wilhelm Maria Peitz, *Das Originalregister Gregors VII. im vatikanischen Archiv (Reg. Vat. 2) nebst Beiträgen zur Kenntnis der Originalregister Innozenz' III. und Honorius' III. (Reg. Vat. 4–11)* (Sb. Akad. Wien 165.5; Vienna 1911), here at 247–252 (*Liber censuum*). On Vat. lat. 1984—a miscellaneous manuscript that is also an important source for the lost registers of Paschal II—see Uta-Renate Blumenthal, 'Bemerkungen zum Register Paschalis II.' QF 66 (1986) 1–18 at 9–15.

62. The reference in Deusdedit 4.420 (161) (ed. Wolf von Glanvell 596) to a stay in Lüneburg cannot be dated (see above, notes 56 and 57). The reference to a certain Gebizo as 'former' ('tunc') abbot in the rubric to Deusdedit 3.278 (150) (ed. Wolf von Glanvell 383) and also the reference found in some manuscripts to him as bishop of Cesana in principle could be used to date the rubric, but research on Gebizo's career so far has not been conclusive. See Carlo Dolcini, 'La storia religiosa fino al secolo XI', *Storia di Cesena II,1: Il Medioevo (secoli VI–XIV)*, ed. Augusto Vasina (Storia di Cesena 2.1; Rimini 1983) 25–73, here at 69–73.

63. Uta-Renate Blumenthal, '*De praua consuetudine*: A Fragment of the Council of 1078?', *Grundlagen des Rechts. Festschrift für Peter Landau zum 65. Geburtstag*, ed. Richard H. Helmholz et al. (Rechts- und Staatswissenschaftliche Veröffentlichungen der Görres-Gesellschaft N.F. 91; Paderborn, Munich, Vienna, and Zurich 2000) 141–154, here at 151–152. The parallel is indeed striking, but as Blumenthal herself concedes, it was in principle possible that the quotations was cobbled together from other sources.

64. Somerville and Brasington, *Prefaces* 122–129.

65. Wolf von Glanvell, 'Einleitung' XII and LIII was convinced that the numbers as found in the manuscripts were not the original ones. Yet the numbers are not only found manuscripts

While this gives a better impression of the diversity of the materials—sometimes, Deusdedit assigned only one number to dozens of excerpts taken from very diverse sources[66]—the original numbers are important in using and analysing the collection. Indeed, they are the only link between the rubrics as found in the *capitulatio* and the actual canons; Deusdedit also used them for cross-references within the collection. In the scholarly literature, Deusdedit is quoted sometimes by the numbers found in the manuscripts (and Martinucci's edition), sometimes by those introduced by Wolf von Glanvell; this can be confusing, especially if no indication is given which of the two is used, or if both are used interchangeably.[67] To facilate comparisons with both the collection itself and the secondary literature, I will always provide both numbers.[68]

Deusdedit divided his material into four books which at least roughly correspond to different topics as outlined in the preface. Within these books, the material is (again, roughly) organized by material sources: Conciliar canons and biblical texts precede long series of excerpts from papal letters (often in chronological sequence), followed by patristic texts and/or Roman law towards the end. Often, series of canons seem to be left in the sequence of Deusdedit's formal sources. The individual 'canons' in fact often are groups of texts, sometimes from diverse sources, but normally concerning the same legal matter. Yet otherwise, there is no attempt to arrange the material according to subject matter. Unusually for a 'systematic' canon law collection, the canons have no rubrics to guide the reader, either. Instead, at the beginning of the collection there is a *capitulatio*; for every single book, Deusdedit provides a long list of

---

of Deusdedit's *Collectio*, but also in works drawing on it, namely the *Ambrosiana I* and Albinus of Albano. See Fowler-Magerl, *Clavis* 177 (*Ambrosiana*), Sickel, *Privilegium* 79 (Albinus), and Peitz, *Originalregister* 257–258 (general).

66. For the extreme case of Deusdedit 3.184–267 (149) (ed. Wolf von Glanvell 348–377), see the excellent analysis in Przemysław Nowak, '*Dagome iudex* w *Zbiorze kanonów* kardynała Deusdedita' *Studia Źródłoznawcze - Commentationes* 51 (2013) 75–94 [with English summary], esp. 78–81 (table of sources).

67. For example, the third edition of Jaffé's *Regesta* uses both numbers interchangeably; e.g. J³ 4008 refers to 'Deusdedit Coll. can. III c. 258', and J³ 4236 to 'Coll. can. II c. 131', but in the first case the numbers are those introduced by Wolf von Glanvell, while in the latter those found in the manuscript (and Martinucci's edition) are used.

68. For this reason, all references to Deusdedit in the present study give first book and canon number of the edition, then (in brackets) the number found in Vat. lat. 3833, and finally (also in brackets) the reference to the edition. The printing errors in Wolf von Glanvell's chapter numbers, another source of confusion, have been silently corrected; for example, Deusdedit 1.240 (193), 241 (194) and 144 (196) (ed. Wolf von Glanvell 140–141) are misnumbered '113', '114', and '116' in the edition. The missing (second) chapter number for example in Deusdedit 4.376 ([157]) (ed. Wolf von Glanvell 582) has been supplied from the manuscript. Without the numbers found in the manuscript, it would be difficult to make sense of Deusdedit's cross-references in the *capitulatio*.

rubric-like captions referring to one or more canons. The rubrics here are not in sequence of the canons in the collection,[69] but grouped more or less thematically. Many rubrics refer to several canons (up to sixteen),[70] some canons (especially in book one) are mentioned more than once,[71] while others (especially towards the end of the collection) are not mentioned at all in the *capitulatio*.[72] Some rubrics refer to canons found in several or even all four books,[73] which also means that rubrics to canons in one book sometimes are only found by looking up the *capitulatio* to another book.[74] So, the *capitulatio* helps the reader to find canons on a specific topic, but for some materials more so than for others. As far as the *capitulatio* does impose some order on the material, it works if and only if the numbers in both the *capitulatio* and the collection itself are faithfully copied.[75] Deusdedit was aware that the risk of confusion was very real.[76]

The first book is devoted to 'The privilege of the Roman church' (251 canons in the manuscript, 327 canons in the edition), book two deals with the Roman clergy (131 or 163 canons), book three with property of the Roman church (159 or 289 canons), and the last book on the 'liberty' of the Church and again church property (162 or 437 canons). These topics are also dealt with in the preface, where Deusdedit leaves little doubt that his main concern was to exalt the Roman church by gathering authorities on her venerable tradition, her legal primacy, her clergy, and her property.

Deusdedit's emphasis on the primacy of the Roman church is matched by several contemporary collections; yet the focus on church property

69. For example, the very first rubric ('Quod Romana ecclesia a Christo primatum optinuit', ed. Wolf von Glanvell 6) refers to four different canons.

70. Deusdedit, *capitulatio* (ed. Wolf von Glanvell 41): 'De reverentia antiquorum imperatorum erga eandem', referring to sixteen canons of books one and four.

71. Deusdedit 1.27 (22) (ed. Wolf von Glanvell 41) from the Council of Serdica, for example, is alluded to in the preface (ed. Wolf von Glanvell 2), figures three times in the *capitulatio* (ed. Wolf von Glanvell 7, 9, and 16), and is mentioned once again in a cross-reference in canon 1.51 (41) (ed. Wolf von Glanvell 59). See the following notes for more examples.

72. Deusdedit, *capitulatio* (ed. Wolf von Glanvell 6, 15, 19, and 24).

73. Deusdedit, *capitulatio* (ed. Wolf von Glanvell 13): 'Ut laicalis potestas se non interserat electioni vel promotioni pontificis', referring to *Collectio* 1.244, 2.131, 3.152–154, 4.11, 4.16–18, and 4.20. See next note.

74. The rubric quoted in the last note is found twice; once in the *capitulatio* of the first book (as quoted above) and once in that of the third book (ed. Wolf von Glanvell 25), but this time referring to fewer canons, and partly to different ones (Deusdedit 3.152–153, 4.16, 4.136, and 4.146 only).

75. The same holds for the small number of cross-references found in Deusdedit 1.51 (45), 4.246 (131), 4.326 (156), 4.330 (156) and 4.348 (156) (ed. Wolf von Glanvell 59, 533, 566, 567, and 573, respectively). In one case, there indeed is a scribal error in Vat. lat. 3833; the cross-reference reads: 'Quere supra in eodem libro, cap. XX' (ed. Wolf von Glanvell 566), but the canon in question is in fact Deusdedit 4.39 (33) (ed. Wolf von Glanvell 417).

76. Deusdedit, *Praefatio* (ed. Wolf von Glanvell 3 lines 7–11) urged future copyists to pay special attention to the canon numbers; but to little avail (see last note).

is unusual. In this aspect, the *Collectio* is comparable only to the collections of great monastic houses that also combine canon law and charters: the *Farfensis*, the *Sandionysiana*, and various copies of *74T*.[77] Just as *74T* is concerned with 'monastic liberty', Deusdedit gathers canons on the preeminence, the privileges, and the property of the Roman church, including the apostolic tradition of this church, her primacy, liturgy, relics, feudal titles, property, and revenues under the title 'On the liberty of the church'.[78] By the time he completed the *Collectio*, the city of Rome (after recently having been pillaged by the Normans) was held by Wibert/Clement III; the dedicatee of Deusdedit's work, in contrast, was hardly able to set foot in the eternal city during his pontificate. So while Deusdedit's *Collectio* conveys an impressive view of the rights and property of the Roman church, this property was partly lost and partly held by the opponents of the pope to whom Deusdedit dedicated his work. The conflicts of the 1080s may well have been an additional incentive for Deusdedit to list this property so extensively—a phenomenon also known from more modest chartularies, often compiled when property was lost or challenged.[79]

4.3.3 Legal Learning

The *Collectio* has been described as clumsy and difficult to use,[80] and not without reason; nonetheless, it reveals the dedication and learning of its compiler. Deusdedit had a profound understanding of the canonical texts he gathered, their authenticity (or lack of it), and the complexities of their transmission. For example, he inserted comments and cross-references that clearly show his knowledge of canon law extended far beyond the materials selected for his collection.[81] In the preface, he makes an elaborate case in favour of the authenticity of the Pseudo-Clementine letters to Saint James, perhaps as a direct response to Bernold of Konstanz.[82] He evidently compared his materials very carefully, and occasionally could not resist comment. For example, in the very first canon of his collection Deusdedit quotes two different translations of the acts of Nicaea I,[83] making clear from the beginning that he knew his material very well. His excerpts

---

77. Kölzer, 'Prolegomena' 18–29 (Farfa); Große, *Saint-Denis* 65–78 (Saint-Denis); Rolker, 'Collection' (*74T*).

78. Deusdedit 4, title (ed. Wolf von Glanvell 397): 'De libertate ecclesie et rerum eius et cleri'.

79. For instructive examples, see Kölzer, 'Codex'.

80. Fuhrmann, *Einfluß und Verbreitung* 2.524; Mordek, 'Kanonistik' 60 ('etwas plump').

81. Fuhrmann, *Einfluß und Verbreitung* 2.526.

82. Deusdedit, *Praefatio* (ed. Wolf von Glanvell 4) on JK †10–11. See Fuhrmann, 'Gerstungen' 63.

83. Deusdedit 1.1 (ed. Wolf von Glanvell 30 line 21): 'Alia translatio sic habet: [. . .]'. Deusdedit also adds a pro-Roman interpretation to the *Versio Prisca*, see the comment in Blumenthal, 'Fälschungen' 245 n. 18.

from the Donation of Constantine are introduced by a brief note which contains a quotation from the *Vita Sancti Silvestri*, and a cross-reference to the *Decretum Gelasianum*, where this *Vita* is mentioned.[84] When copying one letter of Gregory VII (JL 5201), he evidently checked the quotations contained in this letter, found some of them inaccurate,[85] and inserted two additional cross-references, one of them apparently quoting from the lost register of Nicholas I.[86] In the case of the pro-monastic forgery *Quam sit necesssarium* Deusdedit likewise must have double-checked the text he inserted in his collection; as a result, he duly warned his readers that it differed from the version found in Gregory's register, and also remarked that the interpolations were against canon law.[87]

Deusdedit was keenly aware of the complexities of transmission and the danger of manipulation. His access to papal archives explains the exceptional quality and rarity of some of his material; for the very same reason it is also difficult to check whether texts first found in Deusdedit go back to lost sources or are Deusdedit's invention. The *Liber diurnus* excerpts found only in his collection (but none of the *Liber diurnus* manuscripts) are an example of this kind of problem. Deusdedit is normally normally seen as a faithful reporter of his sources.[88] Nonetheless, for a

84. Deusdedit 4.1 (ed. Wolf von Glanvell 397 lines 1–6). Lines 2–3 are a quotation from the *Decretum Gelasianum* (ed. von Dobschütz 43); lines 3–6 are a quotation from the *Vita Silvestri* as found in *Sanctuarium seu vitae sanctorum*, ed. Boninus Mombritius (2 vols. Paris 1910), here at 2.513 lines 517–519. Anselm 4.33 (ed. Thaner 206) not only has the same excerpts from the Donation of Constantine but also the same introduction.

85. Gregory VII, JL 5201 (ed. Caspar, MGH Epp. sel. 2.2:546–562, here at 550–551) stated that already Gregory I had excommunicated kings for their disobedience. Deusdedit did not tamper with this passage (ed. Wolf von Glanvell 489 lines 19–21), but in the *capitulatio* (ed. Wolf von Glanvell 27 line 18), he correctly stated that Gregory I had *threatened* kings with excommunication only. However, Gregory VII was not the only one to interpret Gregory the Great in this way. An extract from the very letter quoted by Gregory VII in JL 5201 (Gregory I, JE 1875) according to Fowler-Magerl, *Clavis* 154 in *2L/8P* 1.14 has the rubric 'Quod papa possit reges deponere et excommunicare etiam per scriptum.' See also ibid. on the transmission of this canon in *3L*, the San Pietro *9L*, and the *Taurinensis*.

86. Deusdedit 4.184 (106) (ed. Wolf von Glanvell 490 lines 3–8 and 17–18). The first cross-reference is to Ps.-Anaclete, JK †4; the second reads: 'Innocentius papa Archadium imperatorem [...] excommunicavit, sicut ait primus Nicholaus papa in suo registro I in epistola ad imperatorem Hludoichum'; the reference to a lost letter of Nicholas (JE –; Böhmer-Herbers 482) was first pointed out by Ernst Perels, 'Die Briefe Papst Nikolaus' I. Die kanonistische Überlieferung' NA 39 (1914) 43–153, here at 77 n. 8.

87. Deusdedit 3.105–106 (90) (ed. Wolf von Glanvell 314–316, here at 315) on JE †1366: '[...] quedam sunt ei iniuncta que contrario sunt canonibus et registro eiusdem'. Wolf von Glanvell divided the canon into two, taking Deusdedit's comment (found in the margin of the manuscript) as his guide. The comment is found precisely where the interpolations begin. See Blumenthal, 'Register' 22 (on Deusdedit) and Rolker, 'Collection' 66–68 (on *QSN* as found in *74T*).

88. Dvornik, *Photian Schism* 321 (asserting that Deusdedit 'dared not touch the profession of faith which he copied from his *Liber Diurnus*'); Hans Foerster, 'Die Liber Diurnus-Fragmente in der Kanones-Sammlung des Kardinals Deusdedit', *Lebendiges Mittelalter. Festgabe für Wolfgang Stammler* (Fribourg 1958) 44–55, here at 53–55.

relatively large number of canons it is almost certain that the differences between Deusdedit's text and that found elsewhere in the transmission is best explained by Deusdedit's interference with his material, as these changes conform to consistent patterns.[89] As will be discussed below, Deusdedit was particularly ready to manipulate his proof texts when it came to the role of cardinal priests and deacons.

4.3.4 Formal Sources

The formal sources of Deusdedit's *Collectio* still are only partially understood.[90] Deusdedit evidently had access to a wide selection of canon law (including Pseudo-Isidore,[91] Burchard,[92] but probably not *74T*[93]), Roman law (derived ultimately from the Institutes, the Code, and the Novels via the *Epitome Juliani* and the *Authenticum*),[94] royal and imperial charters, church fathers, and various texts for the use of the Roman church (*Ordines Romani, Liber pontificalis, Liber diurnus*). Even more importantly, he had direct access to the papal archives (both the Lateran *Patriarchium* and the *Cartularium iuxta Palladium*), from which he took much material.[95]

For about one in seven of his canons, Deusdedit claims to have taken them from papal registers.[96] In some cases, this assertion can be checked

89. This was first advanced by Blumenthal, 'Fälschungen'. See below for details.

90. Wolf von Glanvell died shortly after the publication of his edition and thus could not, as he had announced, publish a second volume of commentary. Fournier only relatively late in his life devoted more attention to Deusdedit: Fournier, 'Collections romaines' esp. 327–380. For the following, see Wolf von Glanvell, 'Einleitung' XII–XV; Fuhrmann, *Einfluß und Verbreitung* 2.527–533 and 540 n. 312 (*Barberiniana*); Jasper, 'Beginning' s.v. Deusdedit; Blumenthal, 'Fälschungen'; eadem, 'Rom in der Kanonistik', *Rom im hohen Mittelalter. Studien zu den Romvorstellungen und zur Rompolitik vom 10. bis zum 12. Jahrhundert. Reinhard Elze zur Vollendung seines siebzigsten Lebensjahres gewidmet*, ed. Bernhard Schimmelpfennig and Ludwig Schmugge (Sigmaringen 1992) 29–39; eadem, 'Reflections'; Nowak, 'Dagome iudex'; idem, 'Work'.

91. Fuhrmann, *Einfluß und Verbreitung* 2.527 asserted that Deusdedit used more than one version, but Dr Przemysław Nowak (private communication) found that in fact he only used the A1 version of the False Decretals.

92. Fournier in the *Histoire* failed to mention Deusdedit's use of Burchard, even though Deusdedit twice mentioned him by name ('Ex libro Burchardi'), see Deusdedit 2.153 (123) and 4.229 (126) (ed. Wolf von Glanvell 265 and 521, respectively).

93. *Histoire* 2.46; Fuhrmann, *Einfluß und Verbreitung* 2.528. In addition to Fuhrmann's examples, see Deusdedit 3.36 (35), 105–106 (90), 165 (134) (ed. Wolf von Glanvell 284, 314–316, 340) = *74T* cc. 25, 39, and 38 (ed. Gilchrist 33, 39, and 38). Nonetheless, these parallels do not demand a direct knowledge of *74T*.

94. Jean Gaudemet, 'Le droit romain dans la *Collectio Canonum* du Cardinal Deusdedit', *Etudes d'histoire du droit medieval en souvenir de Josette Metman* (Mémoires de la Société pour l'Histoire du Droit et des Institutions des anciens pays bourguignons, comtois et romands 45; Dijon 1988) 155–165.

95. On the building, see Wilhelm Kurze, 'Notizen zu den Päpsten Johannes VII., Gregor III. und Benedikt III. in der Kanonessammlung des Kardinals Deusdedit' QF (1990) 23–45, here at 38–40. For the *tomi*, see below (note 103). On Deusdedit's use of the registers of Urban II (JL 5396 as quoted in *Libellus contra invasores*, ed. Sackur, MGH Ldl 2.338), see Becker, *Urban II*. 2.51 n. 88.

96. Rudolf Schieffer, 'Tomus Gregorii papae. Bemerkungen zur Diskussion um das Register Gregors VII.' *Archiv für Diplomatik* 17 (1971) 169–184, here at 172–173.

against extant registers or parts thereof. For the register of Gregory I, Deusdedit used the form know as 'R'. In the case of Gregory VII, he often used the extant register (Reg. Vat. 2) directly,[97] but in some cases also original charters.[98] This also seems to be the case for the letters of Alexander II.[99] The register of John VIII is an interesting case, not least because Victor III (the dedicatee of the *Collectio*) had it copied when he was still abbot of Montecassino. Yet like other compilers of canonical collections, Deusdedit did not use this incomplete register or its Montecassino copy (Reg. Vat. 1).[100] On the other hand, the letters of John VIII he quotes 'ex registro' are not found in the Montecassino manuscript.[101] For the so-called Photian schism Deusdedit quoted John VIII from the acts of Constantinople IV, and hence in a version which was very different from that of the papal registers.[102] Other genuine papal letters from the mid-tenth to the mid-eleventh centuries are taken from original papyrus *chartae* which Deusdedit found in the Lateran library (*ex tomis Lateranensis bybliothece*) and occasionally the papal archives near the Palatin Hill (*cartularium iuxta Palladium*).[103] Finally, it is possible that Deusdedit by 'ex registro' referred to

97. For Gregory I, see Wilhelm Maria Peitz, *Das Register Gregors I.: Beiträge zur Kenntnis des päpstlichen Kanzlei- und Registerwesens bis auf Gregor VII.* (Stimmen der Zeit 2; Freiburg 1917); idem, *Originalregister* 133–147; Jasper, 'Beginning' 78. For Gregory VII, see Erich Caspar, 'Studien zum Register Gregors VII.' NA 38 (1913) 143–226, here at 168–169; Schieffer, 'Tomus' 172–174; Othmar Hageneder, 'Papstregister und Dekretalenrecht', *Recht und Schrift im Mittelalter*, ed. Peter Classen (Vorträge und Forschungen 23; Sigmaringen 1977) 319–347, here at 323–326; for a recent overview, see Rudolf Schieffer, 'Die päpstlichen Register vor 1198', *Das Papsttum und das vielgestaltige Italien. Hundert Jahre Italia Pontificia*, ed. Klaus Herbers and Jochen Johrendt (Abh. Akad. Göttingen N.F. 5; Berlin and Boston 2009) 259–274.

98. Peitz, *Originalregister* 136–140; Caspar, 'Register Gregors' 196 n. 2. See also Caspar's apparatus, normally referring to *Archivüberlieferung* to explain the differences, e.g. the more complete version of JL 5206 in Deusdedit 4.422 (161) (ed. Wolf von Glanvell 597–598) as opposed to *Reg.* 9.3 (ed. Caspar, MGH Epp. sel. 2.2:573).

99. Tilmann Schmidt, *Alexander II. (1061–1073) und die römische Reformgruppe seiner Zeit* (Päpste und Papsttum 11; Stuttgart 1977), here at 220–224, esp. on Deusdedit 3.288 (159) (ed. Wolf von Glanvell 395–396). Schmidt also claims (wrongly, in my opinion) these letters were found in the *Privilegiensammlung*.

100. Lohrmann, *Register* 113–114; Blumenthal, 'Register' 19.

101. For example, a letter John VIII (JE 2995; Böhmer-Unger 125), only preserved in Deusdedit 2.90 (74) (ed. Wolf von Glanvell 225), is quoted 'ex registro'. Also see the next note.

102. Lohrmann, *Register* 112–114. The excerpts from John's letter (JE 3271; Böhmer-Unger 551) in Deusdedit 4.434 (162) (ed. Wolf von Glanvell 612–614) are clearly distinct from that found in the register (ed. Caspar, MGH Epp. 7.1:166–176); they are a retranslation from the Greek acts of the 879 Council of Constantinople. Note in particular the difference concerning the 869 synod of Constantinople (ed. Caspar 169–170); according to Deusdedit, the pope bluntly stated that 'synodus etiam synodum soluit [...]' (ed. Wolf von Glanvell 613 line 13)—as in the Greek text (ed. Caspar 170 line 6)!

103. Nowak, 'Papsttum' 336–338. The main evidence are the documents (including *Dagome iudex*) in Deusdedit 3.191–204 (149) (ed. Wolf von Glanvell 353–362), which Deusdedit refers to as taken 'ex tomis Lateranensis bybliothece' or found 'in cartico thomo inventa iuxta Palladium'. The meaning of 'tomus' in Deusdedit has been subject to considerable debate (see Schieffer, 'Tomus' esp. 172–181), but Nowak has argued convincingly that it refers to orginal documents, not copies, written on papyrus. See Nowak, 'Papsttum' 337 n. 18 (peculiarities of *chartae*), idem,

dossiers of excerpts also available to other compilers. This seems to be the case for some of his Gelasius letters, apparently taken from a small dossier also available to Anselm of Lucca and Atto of San Marco;[104] some of them appear in Deudedit as 'ex registro'.

For other canons, it is often less clear where Deusdedit found his material. Some hints are provided by Deusdedit's tendency to leave canons in the sequence of his formal sources. For example, the first book contains a long series of canons taken from Pseudo-Isidore left in chronological order, most of which have a parallel in Anselm, Bonizo, and/or 2L/8P.[105] The series in Deusdedit continues largely in historical order, but with material taken from diverse sources and few if any parallels to other collections.[106] However, they include rare materials sometimes found in the same sequence in Anselm, Bonizo and/or 2L/8P, suggesting common sources.[107] The Pseudo-Isidore excerpts shared with Bonizo and Anselm may have inspired the chronological arrangement of the material.

Only relatively few texts are taken from Roman law (some thirty canons); yet a relatively large porportion of those text are not found in earlier collections.[108] Some have a parallel in Anselm, including in one case a significant omission.[109] As Deusdedit presents his Roman law in three series apparently in the order of his formal source, while they are scattered in Anselm's collection, it seems unlikely that Deusdedit relied on Anselm for the canons they have in common.[110]

Deusdedit at least partly relied on sources also available to other compilers, above all Anselm of Lucca. The parallels between both collections for their canon law, Roman law, and also liturgical material clearly demands

---

'Dagome iudex' 82–83 (with fuller references), and idem, 'Work' 26. See also the summary in Nowak, 'Dagome iudex' 94: '*Dagome iudex* was drawn from the original of a Roman document on papyrus (*tomus*), present in the library of the Lateran Palace during the papacy of Gregory VII (1073–1085). The document had been written down by a scribe in Rome in the time of Pope John XV (985–996), before 25th May 992, the day Mieszko I died. *Dagome* is most probably an error resulting from Deusdedit having misread the first words of the intitulation (*Ego Misica iudex*).'

104. On Atto 39.21–35 (ed. Mai 81–82), see above (notes 45–48).

105. Deusdedit 1.57 (48)–96 (78) (ed. Wolf von Glanvell 60–78).

106. Deusdedit 1.97 (79)–164 (133) (ed. Wolf von Glanvell 78–106).

107. Deusdedit 1.114 (94), 126 (103), 132–133 (108), and 161–164 (130–133) (ed. Wolf von Glanvell 85, 88, 91, and 104). See Rolker, 'Bonizo' 89–96. Schon, *Capitula Angilramni* 66 suggested that the *Capitula Angilramni* canon and the JE 2785 fragments as found in Deusdedit 1.147 and 161–164 were transmitted together with Sickel's *Privilegiensammlung*, but I do not find the argument convincing.

108. Gaudemet, 'Deusdedit'.

109. Deusdedit 4.278 (144) (ed. Wolf von Glanvell 548) = Anselm 3.106 (*sic*) (ed. Thaner 184), omitting the important clause 'quantum ad causas tamen ecclesiasticas pertinet' from *Constitutio Sirmondiana* III (ed. Mommsen and Meyer 1.2:909). The canon was later widely disseminated via Gratian, C.9 q.1 c.5 (ed. Friedberg 627). For an interesting parallel in Hincmar of Reims, see Fuhrmann, *Einfluß und Verbreitung* 1.121 n. 177.

110. *Pace* Gaudemet, 'Deusdedit'.

some explanation.[111] How much overlap between the two collections can be explained by the common use intermediate collections, and whether Anselm perhaps used Deusdedit, remains to be studied. However, it is also clear that both prelates used sources not available to the other; most notably, Deusdedit (but not Anselm) had access to the Lateran archives, but seems not to have used *74T* directly (an important source for Anselm). To take another example, Deusdedit apparently did not know a set of letters of Pelagius similar to that extant in *2L/8P* used by Anselm.[112]

4.3.5 Themes and Tendencies

Roman and Papal Primacy

Deusdedit's main concern was the primacy of the Roman church, both in the sense of the Latin Church at large and that in the city of Rome.[113] This is evident from the preface, the *capitulatio*, and the collection itself. The opening canons of book one and four are key texts on Roman primacy, and the *capitulatio* likewise begins with this topic.[114] The first book in particular contains an unusually large number of proof texts that Rome was the head (*caput*), 'mother and teacher', and the 'foundation' of all churches, that all major cases should referred to her judgement, and so on. While it was not rare to begin canon law collections with these topics, Deusdedit gathered unusually many, including very radical and/or rare texts on Roman primacy. At the very beginning of his collection, Deusdedit inserted decrees from the Council of Nicaea, but interspersed with (forged) material stressing that even the decrees of this venerable council had to be confirmed by Pope Silvester I and his successors.[115] According to one of his rubrics, the eight universal councils had been celebrated 'by papal authority'.[116] In another rubric, Deusdedit claimed that separating oneself from and acting against the Roman church was tantamount to heresy, and provided an appropriate proof text not found in major collections before his time.[117] Similar language is best known from the *Dictatus*

---

111. For the legal material, see above; for liturgical text found in both collections see Michel Andrieu, *Les Ordines Romani du haut Moyen Âge* (5 vols. Spicilegium sacrum Lovaniense. Études et documents 11, 23, 24, 28, and 29; Leuven 1931–61) here at 1.519–522.

112. Rolker, 'Bonizo' 89.

113. For an excellent discussion, see Kéry, 'Recht' 360–365.

114. The very first rubric alone is referring to four canons (Deusdedit 1.18, 50, 76, and 4.92), see Deusdedit, *capitulatio* (ed. Wolf von Glanvell 6). The sixth canon from the Council of Nicaea on Roman primacy and the Donation of Constantine are placed at the beginning of books one and four, respectively.

115. Deusdedit 1.1–30 (1–34) (ed. Wolf von Glanvell 30–42), esp. 1.7 (5–6) (ed. Wolf von Glanvell 32–33). On these sixth-century forgeries, see still Maassen, *Quellen* 412.

116. Deusdedit, *capitulatio* (ed. Wolf von Glanvell 7): 'Quod eius auctoritate iam VIII universales sinodi celebrate sunt.'

117. Deusdedit, *capitulatio* (ed. Wolf von Glanvell 8): 'Quod heretici sint, qui Romane ecclesie

papae, the letters of Gregory VII, and Peter Damian's writings.[118] Indeed, one of Deusdedit's proof texts was a manipulated excerpt lifted from Damian but attributed to Nicholas II in his collection.[119] As to the foundations of Roman primacy, Deusdedit strongly emphasized that both Peter and Paul as 'princes of the Apostles' stood at the beginning of the Roman church;[120] he carefully selected canons which mentioned both apostles, and occasionally manipulated his material by adding 'Saint Paul' where his proof texts only mention Saint Peter,[121] or omitting references to Peter alone.[122] Famously, Deusdedit also introduced into canon law a fragment from an obscure source—*De sancta Romana ecclesia*, sometimes erroneously attributed to Humbert of Silva Candida[123]—which praised Rome in the highest terms; here too the stress is on Peter and Paul rather than Peter alone. This stress on both apostles is remarkably, especially in contrast to contemporary attempts to justify papal prerogatives by stressing their succession to Saint Peter as the sole 'prince of the apostles'.[124]

non concordent et qui eius privilegia nituntur auferre.' For parallels, see *TC* c. 129c (Paris, BnF, lat. 13368, fol. 14rb) and numerous collections drawing on this collection (Rolker, 'Genesis' 87 and the table in the appendix). Anselm does not have this canon but a similar rubric, see Cushing, *Papacy and Law* 188.

118. For Gregory VII, see JL 5167 (ed. Caspar, MGH Epp. sel. 2.2:504–505) and *Dictatus papae* c. 26 (ibid. 2.1:207). For Peter Damian, see e.g. Robinson, *Authority and Resistance* 27–28 and Othmar Hageneder, 'Die Häresie des Ungehorsams und das Entstehen des hierokratischen Papsttums' *Römische historische Mitteilungen* 20 (1978) 29–47, here at 36–37.

119. Ps.-Nicholas II, JL 4424 as found in Deusdedit 1.167 (136) (ed. Wolf von Glanvell 106–107) repeats Peter Damian's claim (ed. Reindel, MGH Briefe dt. Kaiserzeit 4.2:234 lines 1–4): 'Qui autem Romanae ecclesiae privilegium [...] auferre conatur, hic proculdubio in heresin labitur.' The third edition of Jaffé (in J³ 10340) seems to claim that the letter was genuine.

120. See also Deusdedit, *Preface* (ed. Wolf von Glanvell 2 lines 15–23 esp. 22) on the merits of both 'princes of the Apostles'.

121. Blumenthal, 'Fälschungen' 243–250. In addition to her examples, it may be noteworthy that the version of Donation of Constantine Deusdedit selected likewise mentions both apostles where other versions only referred to Saint Paul: *Constitutum Constantini* (ed. Fuhrmann, MGH Fontes iuris 10.16).

122. For example, Deusdedit 4.1 (1) (ed. Wolf von Glanvell 398 line 23), taken from the 'Leo-Humbert-Gruppe' of the Donation of Constantine (see last note) omits the reference to future popes as 'successors of Saint Peter' (ed. Fuhrmann, MGH Fontes iuris 10.57 lines 2–3). JK †2 as found in Deusdedit 1.61 (50) (ed. Wolf von Glanvell 63 lines 25–26) omits another reference to Peter. Note that Anselm 1.66 and 4.33 (ed. Thaner 34 and 207) has the same gaps as Deusdedit.

123. The claim that Deusdedit 1.306 (231) and 327 (251) were taken from a lost work *De sancta Romana ecclesia* by Humbert of Silva Candida was first made by Anton Michel, *Humbert und Kerullarios: Studien* (2 vols. Paderborn 1924/30), here at 1.vi and repeated in Percy Ernst Schramm, *Kaiser, Rom und Renovatio. Studien zur Geschichte des römischen Erneuersgedankens vom Ende des karolingischen Reiches bis zum Investiturstreit* (2 vols. Studien der Bibliothek Warburg 17; Leipzig 1929), here at 2.134–136. Although the argument was extremely weak, Schramm himself followed Michel's assertion (ibid. 1.239 and 2.124) and thus lent credibility to this claim. On Michel's methods, see Fuhrmann, *Einfluß und Verbreitung* 2.503 n. 215 ('Anhäufung von Mißverständnissen'; 'belanglose, falsche oder geradezu grotesk irreführende Parallelstellen', 'sinnentleerte[] Buchstabenstecherei').

124. See, for example, Tellenbach, *Church* 305–307. Gregory VII sometimes referred to both Peter and Paul, but much more frequently to Peter alone in the context of his primacy claims. See also Leo Meulenberg, *Der Primat der römischen Kirche im Denken und Handeln Gregors VII.* (Mededelingen van het Nederlands Historisch Instituut te Rome 33.2; The Hague 1965) esp. 26–29.

Roman Clergy

Indeed, Deusdedit did not identify the Roman church with the pope. Instead, he focused on the Roman church as a 'corporate entity'.[125] This may also explain the dedication of the collection both to Pope Victor and 'all the clergy of the holy Roman church'. In practice, Deusdedit was mainly concerned with the rights of cardinal priests and deacons,[126] who according to him 'govern' and 'move the people of God to the love of God' by means of their teaching.[127] To give another example, he changed a well-known Pseudo-Isidorian rubric to the effect that deacons (not bishops) were 'the eyes of the pope'.[128] Deusdedit's collection is further evidence that in the late eleventh century, the three orders of cardinals—deacons, priests, and bishops—acted as groups, but the 'college of cardinals' was not yet a corporate body as it would be in the twelfth century.[129]

Specifically, Deusdedit defended the rights of the lower-ranking cardinals against what he saw as an unjust exaltation of the cardinal-bishops. Most textual manipulations in the *Collectio* are changes in favour of cardinal priests.[130] These twists, in particular those in favour of Deusdedit's

---

125. See esp. Blumenthal, 'Rom' 33–39 and more recently eadem, 'Reflections'. See also Cowdrey, *Gregory VII* 324: 'Deusdedit gave little place to the pope's personal authority, but made him the spokesman of a sancta Romana ecclesia in which, as a corporate entity, the prerogatives of the apostolic see were embodied; it was the Roman church, rather than the pope himself, that its primacy was vested.' In contrast, Giuseppe Alberigo, *Cardinalato e collegialità: studi sull'ecclesiologia tra l'XI e il XIV secolo* (Testi e ricerche di scienze religiose 5; Florence 1969) quotes Deusdedit as an example how the cardinals gained importance as a collegiate body at the expense of the episcopate.

126. Scheffer-Boichorst, *Neuordnung* 79; Stephan Kuttner, 'Cardinalis: The History of a Canonical Concept' *Traditio* 3 (1945) 129–214, here at 189 and 194; Blumenthal, 'Rom' esp. 34; Schludi, *Entstehung* 152–169.

127. Deusdedit 2.160 (130) (ed. Wolf von Glanvell 267–268). Only the first sentence is from Isidore, the rest is Deusdedit's own comment: 'Sicut a basibus, que sunt future columnarum a fundamento surgentes, basilei idest reges dicuntur, quia populum regunt: ita et cardinales derivative dicuntur a cardinibus ianue, qui tam regunt et movent, quod plebem Dei, ut superius diximus, doctrinis sanctis ad amorem Dei moveant.'

128. Deusdedit, *capitulatio* (ed. Wolf von Glanvell 16): 'Quod diacones sunt oculi pontificis'. Pseudo-Isidore had called deacons 'eyes of their bishops' in JK †10 (ed. Hinschius 34; see Fuhrmann, *Einfluß und Verbreitung* 1.146), and several collections used this phrase as a rubric to the relevant part of JK †10 (e.g. Anselm 7.58).

129. According to Klewitz (and many scholars following him), the cardinals already in the mid-eleventh century began to form a collegiate body: Hans-Walter Klewitz, 'Die Entstehung des Kardinalkollegiums' ZRG Kan. Abt. 25 (1936) 115–221, here 117. More recently, Becker, *Urban II.* 3.98–217 esp. 102, 119, and 136 and Claudia Zey, 'Entstehung und erste Konsolidierung. Das Kardinalskollegium zwischen 1049 und 1143', *Geschichte des Kardinalats im Mittelalter*, ed. Jürgen Dendorfer and Ralf Lützelschwab (Päpste und Papsttum 39; Stuttgart 2011) 63–94, here at 80, stressed that by 1100 there was a marked tendency that all cardinals (not only bishops) were involved in papal affairs. Schludi, *Entstehung* 105–118 and 361–375 has argued convincingly that the 'college of cardinals' was only to emerge in the twelfth century (perhaps in the 1120s).

130. See Blumenthal, 'Fälschungen' esp. 246, 252–253, 260–261 with the respective footnotes. The

own titular church, may be explained as *pro domo* manipulations. Yet Deusdedit did much more than find (and occasionally manipulate) canonical authoritiy in favour of his own church and the status of cardinal priests. The distinction he made between the Roman church and the papacy, and the attention he paid to the Roman clergy, are integral to his ecclesiology.

Deusdedit's views on the Roman clergy and its importance are most evident from the second book of his collection devoted entirely to this group, containing above all canons on the role and the privileges of cardinal priests and, to a lesser degree, cardinal deacons.[131] The sheer mass of these canons, and the fact that Deusdedit (unlike any other compiler before him) devoted a separate book to this issue, is in itself significant. The rubrics in the respective *capitulatio* in addition show how Deusdedit himself understood these canons, and how he wished the users of his collection to understand them. The Roman clergy, Deusdedit noted in one such rubric, had to honour the pope—and vice versa.[132] According to Deusdedit, the pope addressed the cardinal priests as his 'brothers' and 'co-presbyters'.[133] Their participation was necessary in consecrations.[134] Cardinal priests and deacons had to sign papal decisions.[135] Together, cardinal priests and deacons formed the 'senate' of the Roman church.[136] During a vacancy it was up to the Roman clergy to exercise papal rights, and in particular to decide cases of appeal.[137]

---

most important manipulations are the rubric to Deusdedit, *Collectio* 2.41 (28 and 205, line 16) (ed. Wolf von Glanvell 15) and the text of the following canons: *Collectio* 1.261 (210) (ed. 153 line 26); *Collectio* 2.1 (1) (ed. 193 line 6), 43 (30) (ed. 206 lines 7–8 and 11–12), 75 (59) (ed. 220 line 3), 88 (72) (ed. 224 lines 4–5), 104 (87) (ed. 229 lines 14–15), 109 (92) (ed. 234 line 6 and 235 lines 1–9), 2.110 (93) (ed. 235 line 14), 110 (93) (ed. 236 lines 5 and 21–24), 160 (130) (ed. 267–268). In contrast, only a handful of manipulations cannot be explained that way. Three times, Deusdedit added Saint Paul where the original mentioned only Saint Peter: twice in *Collectio* 2.111 (94) (ed. 237–238), and once in 3.58 (55) (ed. 293); two cases are manipulations in favour of Deusdedit's own titular church: *Collectio* 2.103 (86) and 108 (91) (ed. 229 lines 5–6 and 230 lines 23–24); two cases, mentioned above (but not discussed by Blumenthal), are in favour of the Roman church and the pope: *Collectio* 1.167 (136) and 2.112 (95) (ed. 106–107 and 239–240). See also Schludi, *Entstehung* 152–169.

131. For the following, see Ernst Hirsch, 'Die rechtliche Stellung der römischen Kirche und des Papstes nach Kardinal Deusdedit' AKKR 88 (1908) 595–624, here at 597; Blumenthal, 'Fälschungen' esp. 187, 250–252, and 260–262; Kéry, 'Recht' 362–364; Dusil, *Wissensordnungen* 100.

132. Deusdedit, *capitulatio* (ed. Wolf von Glanvell 17): 'Ut clerci honorent suum episcopum et ipse eos.'

133. Deusdedit, *capitulatio* (ed. Wolf von Glanvell 16): 'Quod Romani pontifices presbiteros suos fratres et compresbiteros appellant.'

134. Deusdedit, *capitulatio* (ed. Wolf von Glanvell 17): 'Ut episcopus absque consilio presbiterorum suorum clericos non ordinet.'

135. Deusdedit, *capitulatio* (ed. Wolf von Glanvell 17): 'Ut sententia episcopi presbiterorum et diaconorum subscriptione firmetur.'

136. Deusdedit, *capitulatio* (ed. Wolf von Glanvell 17): 'Inde Romani clerici locum antiquorum habent patriciorum.' The preceding rubrics all refer to (cardinal) priests and deacons; Deusdedit is silent on 'cardinal bishops'. See also Deusdedit 1.322 (246) (ed. Wolf von Glanvell 188), where Deusdedit adds a reference to the Roman senate in his version of the *Constitutio Romana* (ed. Boretius, MGH Capit. 1.323, no. 161 c. 5).

137. Deusdedit, *capitulatio* (ed. Wolf von Glanvell 9 and 17): 'Quod appellationis causas ipsa

Indeed, already in the preface Deusdedit had stressed that during the vacancy after death of Pope Fabianus (between January 250 and March 251) the priests and deacons of Rome governed the Church, convened a synod, and won acceptance even from African churches.[138] For Deusdedit, this was an important argument both for the primacy of the Roman church (which was even accepted when Christians were still persecuted) and the importance of the priests and deacons at Rome (evidently able to govern this church, if need be, and to defend her primacy). Of course, one has to bear in mind that Deusdedit finished his collection during a prolonged vacancy following the death of Gregory VII. He may have hoped to strengthen the rights of all cardinals during such circumstances, but he must have been aware that in practice cardinal bishops were much more likely to exercise papal rights during a vacancy.[139]

Ecclesiastical Property

Deusdedit likewise insisted that 'the Church is unable to exist without the clergy, nor the clergy without possession',[140] and gathered indeed rich materials on church poperty and its administration. For this reason, and uniquely for a canonical collection, Deusdedit's work is an important source for administrative and economic history.[141] The 'canons' in books three and four include (among many other documents) donations made to the Roman church including the Donation of Constantine; many of them are extremely valuable for preserving information not found elsewhere. This is true for the famous *Dagome iudex regestum*,[142] but also (for example) an alleged donation of the imperial monastery Farfa to the Roman church,[143] or the unique granting of the use of the mitre to a

---

finire possit etiam absente pontifice' and 'Quod absente Romano pontifice clerus eius quorumlibet causas diiudicat'.

138. Kéry, 'Recht' 362–364, quoting Deusdedit, *Praefatio* (ed. Wolf von Glanvell 2).

139. An interesting case is the pallium grant for Renaud II of Reims during the vacancy of 1087/88 (later confirmed by Urban, JL 5415); see Becker, *Urban II.* 3.110–111.

140. Deusdedit, *Praefatio* (ed. Wolf von Glanvell 2): 'Et quoniam ecclesia sine clero suo esse non potest, nec clerus absque rebus, quibus temporaliter subsistat: huic subiunxi secundum et tertium de clero et rebus eiusdem ecclesie.' The translation is taken from Somerville and Brasington, *Prefaces* 124.

141. Karl Jordan, 'Zur päpstlichen Finanzgeschichte im 11. und 12. Jahrhundert' QF 25 (1933/34) 61–104; Jürgen Sydow, 'Untersuchungen zur kurialen Verwaltungsgeschichte im Zeitalter des Reformpapsttums' DA 11 (1954/55) 18–73; Thomas Wetzstein, 'Noverca omnium ecclesiarum. Der römische Universalepiskopat des Hochmittelalters im Spiegel der päpstlichen Finanzgeschichte', *Rom und die Regionen. Studien zur Homogenisierung der lateinischen Kirche im Hochmittelalter*, ed. Jochen Johrendt and Harald Müller (Abh. Akad. Göttingen N.F. 19; Berlin 2012) 13–62.

142. Deusdedit 3.199 (149) (ed. Wolf von Glanvell 359). See now Nowak, 'Dagome iudex' and idem, 'Work'.

143. Deusdedit 3.190 (149) (ed. Wolf von Glanvell 352–353). The authenticity of this document is doubtful. See Claudia Märtl, 'Einleitung', *Die falschen Investiturprivilegien*, ed. eadem (MGH

duke.[144] Deusdedit was also keen to document feudal oaths,[145] and many details of administration.[146] At the time Deusdedit compiled his collection, these issues were of special urgency; Gregory VII and his successor were in desperate need of income and military support.[147] The financial breakdown of the Roman church was an issue between the pope and the cardinals already in 1082,[148] and the conflicts over the city of Rome in the late 1080s put ecclesiastical property at risk. If the Roman church ever were to regain control, not only money, but also written documents for her property were useful, indeed necessary.

Yet the documents on church property Deusdedit collected had more than practical value. This is particularly true of the canon which Deusdedit clearly regarded as one of the most important documents in his collection, the Donation of Constantine. He was among the first compilers to include this famous forgery in a canonical collection, and placed it prominently at the beginning of his book four.[149] A total of no less than fourteen rubrics, scattered over all four of his *capitulationes*, refer the reader to this document.[150] What was so interesting about the Donation of Constantine? First, and most generally, it was a welcome proof that the Roman church had extensive property, and the Christian rulers at least in ancient times generously bestowed land and titles on the pope. Second, the specific version Deusdedit cites (Fuhrmann's 'Leo-Humbert-Gruppe') has two peculiarities: It enhanced the glory of Rome at the expense of Constantinople, and it refers to Saint Peter and Paul where other versions mention only Saint Paul.[151] Given that this matches Deusdedit's general tendency, we can assume that he made a conscious choice here, too. Finally, the rubrics indicate very precisely what Deusdedit thought the Donation proved. Among other things, his rubrics to this canon claim that the

---

Fontes iuris 13; Hanover 1986) 7–124, here at 91, pointing out that Deusdedit's collection was known at Farfa (ibid. n. 298). The excerpts in Rome, Biblioteca Casanatense, 2010, fols. 93v–102r omit the canon. On Farfa, see also Chapter Two.

144. Deusdedit 3.279 (150) (ed. Wolf von Glanvell 385), see Nowak, 'Papsttum' 347.

145. E.g. Deusdedit 3.284 (156) (ed. Wolf von Glanvell 393), containing Robert Guiscard's oath, is the only source to mention Norman obligation to pay subsidies. See Graham A. Loud, *The Age of Robert Guiscard: Southern Italy and the Northern Conquest* (London and New York 2014) ch. 5 and Robinson, *Papacy* 369–371.

146. Sydow, 'Untersuchungen' 22, 24–30, and 33; Wetzstein, 'Universalepiskopat' 24 n. 33, 41, 56, and 58.

147. Loud, *Robert Guiscard* ch. 5.

148. Robinson, *Papacy* 244.

149. Deusdedit 4.1 (1) (ed. Wolf von Glanvell 397–401). On the transmission in canonical collections, see Horst Fuhrmann, 'Einleitung', *Das Constitutum Constantini (Konstantinische Schenkung). Text*, ed. idem (MGH Fontes iuris 10; Hanover 1968) 7–54 and Petersmann, 'Überlieferung' passim.

150. Deusdedit, *capitulatio* (ed. Wolf von Glanvell 8 lines 2 and 11; 17 lines 24 and 27–28; 23 lines 1–2; 24 lines 6–10, 12–14, and 21)

151. *Constitutum* c. 12 (ed. Fuhrmann, MGH Fontes iuris 10.82–83 lines 171–174 and 184–185). On this 'Leo-Humbert-Gruppe' see also Fuhrmann's comment ibid. 15–17.

pope was 'pontifex of all pontifices' and that he was called 'universal' from ancient times, but also that the Roman clergy had taken the place of the senate.[152] The first two rubrics remind one of Gregory's *Dictatus papae*,[153] the other is an example of Deusdedit's attempts to strengthen the position of the Roman clergy, specifically the lower-ranking cardinals.[154]

Papal Elections

Papal elections were a topic Deusdedit had a natural interest in as a long-serving cardinal, especially so as his titular church was San Pietro in Vincoli, where Stephen IX, Alexander II, and later Gregory VII were elected.[155] It comes therefore as no surprise that Deusdedit was drawn into the conflicts around the Papal Election Decree of 1059 which (in its genuine version) effectively made the cardinal bishops the most important electors.[156] Deusdedit both in his *Libellus* and his *Collectio canonum* passionately argued that the whole decree was invalid because it violated ancient canon law.[157] In the preface to his collection, he specifically mentioned this issue,[158] and to substantiate his claims, he gathered ancient texts on papal election from a wide range of sources, namely the Roman synod of 499,[159] the *Ordo IX*, the *Liber pontificalis*, the *Liber diurnus*, an interpolated version of the *Constitutio Romana*,[160] and the Lateran synod of 769.[161] The latter

152. 'Quod sicut Petrus est princeps omnium apostolorum ita Romanus pontifex omnium pontificum' (ed. Wolf von Glanvell 8) and 'Item quod ante eam [scil. Nicaeam synodum, CR] vocatus sit papa universalis' (ibid.); 'Inde Romani clerici locum antiquorum habent patriciorum' (ibid. 17).

153. *Dictatus papae* c.2 (ed. Caspar, MGH Epp. sel. 2.1:202); see above.

154. All three claims can indeed be substantiated from the Donation of Constantine cc. 2 and 15 (ed. Fuhrmann, MGH Fontes iuris 10.58 and 88–89) = Deusdedit 4.1 (1) (ed. Wolf von Glanvell 397 and 399, respectively).

155. Schmidt, *Alexander II.* 89–91.

156. Ed. Jasper, MGH Conc. 8.383–393; see in general Jasper, *Papstwahldekret*.

157. Mirbt, *Publizistik* 555; Scheffer-Boichorst, *Neuordnung* 103; Francisco Wasner, 'De consecratione inthronizatione coronatione summi pontificis' *Apollinaris* 8 (1935) 86–125, 249–299, and 428–439, here at 100; Klewitz, 'Entstehung' 164–166; Kuttner, 'Cardinalis' esp. 149–151; Blumenthal, 'Fälschungen' esp. 257–258; Schludi, *Entstehung* 153–160. For background, see Schieffer, *Entstehung* 64–84 (JL 4405/4406) and Schludi, *Entstehung* (cardinals).

158. Deusdedit, *Praefatio* (ed. Wolf von Glanvell 4–5): 'Preterea antiquum ordinem electionis seu consecrationis Romani pontificis et cleri eius huic operi inserere libuit. Nam quidam olim in dei et sanctorum patrum sanctionibus contemtum [...] scripserunt sibi novam ordinationem eiusdem Romani pontificis [...].'; tr. Somerville and Brasington, *Prefaces* 128: 'Moreover I was happy to insert in this work the ancient order of election and consecration of the Roman pontiff and his clergy. For once upon a time certain men, in contempt of the sanctions of God and the holy Fathers [...] wrote for themselves a new ordination [procedure] for the same Roman pontiff.'

159. Symmachus, JK ante 752; this decree clearly describes the designation by the reigning pontiff as the standard procedure.

160. Deusdedit 1.318–326 (242–250) (ed. Wolf von Glanvell 187–189) are select and partly interpolated excerpts of the *Constitutio Romana* of 824 (ed. Boretius, MGH Capit. 1.322–324, no. 161). The references to imperial supervision of Roman affairs (c. 4) are suppressed, and the papal oath is omitted completely.

161. Deusdedit 1.255 (206), 2.109 (93), 2.113 (96), and 2.161–163 (131) (ed. Wolf von Glanvell 146, 233–235, 239–240, and 268–270).

provided him with important proof texts that only cardinal priests and deacons of the Roman church could be elected pope; these canons are extremely rare.[162] Other texts, while not containing binding law, contained valuable evidence for the practicalities of an election; in the oaths taken by Welf of Bavaria and Robert Guiscard (uniquely preserved here) one finds a reference to the 'better cardinals' electing the pope.[163]

In Deusdedit's collection, the relevant texts are far apart from each other, but the *capitulatio* provides the necessary cross-references.[164] Taken together, these canons indeed contain rules for papal elections against which Nicholas' decree must seem unnecessary at best. The first key passage was the requirement that any candidate had to be 'made cardinal deacon or priest' before he could become pontiff; the other is the rule that the candidate had be 'one of the cardinal priests or deacons'.[165] The 1059 decree, in contrast, allowed non-Romans to be elected pope and very considerably strengthened the position of cardinal bishops.[166] For Deusdedit, it was clear that not even the pope could legislate against ancient canon law, and he regarded the 1059 decree as invalid for this reason alone.[167] Yet Deusdedit did not stop here. While he did not include the Papal Election Decree itself in his collection, he did insert excerpts from the synodal letter of Nicholas II which summarized its content; Deusdedit's version of

162. See the edition of the synodal acts (ed. Werminghoff, MGH Conc. 2.1:74–92) based on the *Liber pontificalis*, Deusdedit, Anselm, Rather of Verona, and the collection in Wolfenbüttel, HAB, Cod. Guelf. 454 Helmst. [not seen]. The collection was misnamed 'Collection of Rotger of Trier' by Wasserschleben, *Beiträge* 162–163. On the Wolfenbüttel manuscript, see Rudolf Pokorny and Hans Jakob Schuffels, 'Kirchenrechtliche Materialsammlung (233-Kapitel-Sammlung)', *Bernward von Hildesheim und das Zeitalter der Ottonen. Katalog der Ausstellung Hildesheim 1993*, ed. Michael Brandt and Arne Eggebrecht (2 vols. Hildesheim and Mainz 1993) 2.486–489. The provisions on cardinals (ed. Werminghoff, MGH Conc. 2.1:77 lines 1–3 and 86 lines 21–23) are only known from the *Liber pontificalis* and Deusdedit (assuming that Anselm depends on the latter here).

163. Deusdedit 3.285 (142) and 4.422 (161) (ed. Wolf von Glanvell 394 and 598–599). For background on Robert's oath, see Loud, *Robert Guiscard* 185; on JL 5206, containing a different version of Welf's oath, see below (n. 181).

164. While he placed the canon in book two ('De Romano clero'), and specifically among the canons concerning the cardinals, in his *capitulatio* to the first book, in the context of papal elections twice refers to canon 2.161 (131): Deusdedit, *capitulatio* (ed. Wolf von Glanvell 18 lines 30 and 33).

165. Deusdedit 1.255 (206) (ed. Wolf von Glanvell 146), prohibiting to elect anyone 'nisi per distinctos gradus ascendens diaconus aut presbiter factus fuerit cardinalis'. The excerpt is taken from the *Liber pontificalis* (ed. Duchesne 1.468–476); Deusdedit greatly abbreviates the narrative of the *Liber pontificalis* but quotes the synodal decree on papal election it contains in full (ed. Duchesne 1.476 lines 1–3). The second key text taken from the synodal acts is Deusdedit 2.161 (131b) (ed. Wolf von Glanvell 268): 'Oportebat, ut […] unus de cardinalibus presbiteris aut diaconibus consecraretur.'

166. This is above all true for the genuine version; yet even the so-called imperial version gave cardinal bishops a stronger position than Deusdedit was willing to accept as valid. On the versions of the 1059 decree see Jasper, *Papstwahldekret* esp. 4–8 and Thier, *Hierarchie und Autonomie* 294–308.

167. Blumenthal, 'Fälschungen' esp. 255–258.

this letter was clearly manipulated in favour of the lower-ranking cardinals.[168] Even if he did not falsify the text himself, Deusdedit must have been aware of the manipulation. At the textual level, the change was minute: Simply by dropping the word 'bishops' twice, the excerpts as found in Deusdedit's *Collectio* speak of 'election by the cardinals' instead of 'election by the cardinal bishops'.[169] This manipulated version, which sought to strengthen the position of lower-ranking cardinals, gained considerable circulation mainly in Italian collections up to and including Gratian.[170]

As the case of the Papal Election Decree makes clear, Deusdedit's loyalty to the Roman church and ancient canon law in some cases clashed with his loyalty to the pope. In his opposition to the 1059 decree, he not only criticized Pope Nicholas II but also his successors, in particular Pope Victor III to whom he dedicated his collection.[171] At the same time, in some respects he argued much as cardinals supporting Wibert/Clement III did. The most prominent examples are Beno of San Martino e Silvestro, who like Deusdedit had long served as a cardinal under Gregory VII but in 1084 deserted him, and Hugh Candidus, created cardinal by Urban II but in 1098 defecting to Wibert/Clement III. Both strongly emphasized the equality of the cardinals and that the privileges of the Roman church were not vested in the pope alone.[172] Yet while these parallels are important, it is equally important that Deusdedit, unlike Beno and Hugh, remained loyal to Gregor VII and his successors.

168. Nicholas II, JL 4405 and 4431a (ed. Jasper, MGH Conc. 8.402–404 and 382–383) as found in Deusdedit 1.168–169 (137–138) (ed. Wolf von Glanvell 107). The manipulations (see next note) correspond to the omission of 'episcopi' in the forged version of the Papal Election Decree itself (ed. Jasper, MGH Conc. 8.385). The importance of JL 4405 was first pointed out by Klewitz, 'Entstehung' 165.

169. Deusdedit 1.169 (138) (ed. Wolf von Glanvell 107 lines 15 and 17). In the preceding canon, Deusdedit replaced 'electione cardinalium, religiosorum et laicorum' by 'electione cardinalium eiusdem' (ibid. lines 8–9). See Scheffer-Boichorst, *Neuordnung* esp. 57–61 and 79–80; Kuttner, 'Cardinalis' 174 n. 99; Blumenthal, 'Fälschungen' 258–259; eadem, 'History and Tradition in Eleventh-Century Rome' CHR 79 (1993) 185–196, esp. 194–195. Fournier, in his detailed account of how Deusdedit and Anselm reworked their materials, significantly did not mention this canon: Fournier, 'Collections romaines' 327–371, esp. 354–364 and 370–371. Jasper, *Papstwahldekret* 73–78 argued that Deusdedit and others were loyal to Gregory VII and his successors, and for this reason thought their opposition to the 1059 Decree 'völlig unwahrscheinlich' (ibid. 77); in his opinion, the similarities to the imperial version of the decree in their collection was only a coincidence (ibid. 78): 'Offenbar ging es Anselm, Deusdedit und Bonizo nicht um Rangfragen innerhalb des Kardinalkollegiums [...]. Wir können hier lediglich die zufällige [*sic*] Verwendung desselben Wortes *cardinales* in der Verfälschung und in den Reformsammlungen konstantieren.'

170. Among the major collections, see Anselm 6.12–13 (ed. Thaner 272–273), Bonizo 4.87 (ed. Perels 156), *Caes. I* 3.9, *Polycarpus* 1.4.4, and Gratian, D.79 cc. 1 and 9 (ed. Winroth 176 and 177, ed. Friedberg 276 and 278–279).

171. Desiderius of Montecassino, the future pope, was one of the few lower-ranking cardinals to have signed the 1059 decree (ed. Jasper, MGH Conc. 8.388); see Blumenthal, 'Fälschungen' 258 and eadem, 'History' esp. 194–195.

172. Becker, *Urban II.* 3.98–106; Zey, 'Entstehung' esp. 87–89.

Gregory VII in Deusdedit's Collection

Deusdedit's collection has often been quoted as a prime example of a 'Gregorian' collection. There is ample evidence to test this. To begin with, the collection stands out for containing an unusually high number of canons taken from Gregory VII.[173] Many of them are quoted as coming from the register ('ex registro').[174] The way Deusdedit quoted from the registers leaves little doubt that he used the very volume still extant today (Reg. Vat. 2).[175] To understand what this use of the register means, let us first look at the 'Gregorian' material as a whole. Ironically perhaps, these canons often do not contribute to the 'Gregorian' character of Deusdedit's *Collectio*. The reason for this is simple: Most of them concern church property or oaths (mainly oaths of fidelity).[176] So while it is technically true that Deusdedit introduced more Gregory VII canons into canon law than any other compiler,[177] the explanation for this is not his preference for 'Gregorian' materials but rather his unique interest in the property of the Roman church; if Gregory VII figures prominently here, this is simply due to the availability of his registers and related documents to Deusdedit.

This is not to say that Deusdedit was not interested in those affairs which modern scholarship has identified as 'Gregorian'. In particular, Deusdedit quoted from Gregory's letter on the excommunication of Henry IV (JL 5201), and the letter to Gebhard of Salzburg containing the oath of obedience by Welf IV of Bavaria (JL 5206).[178] There are a number of ('Gregorian') collections containing these canons, and it is plausible at least that Anselm of Lucca and Deusdedit both rely on a shared source here. At first sight, therefore, both canons are a perfect case of the use of a 'Gregorian intermediate collection' in action: the texts come from a papal register, are certainly 'Gregorian' in nature, were disseminated via Gregorian collections, some of them relying on shared intermediary sources.

---

173. Gilchrist, 'Reception' 38–43.

174. For an overview, see Peitz, *Originalregister* 136–141 (who assumed Deusdedit quoted from original letters in all cases where his *Collectio* differed from the extant register); Schieffer, 'Tomus' 172–183; Hageneder, 'Papstregister' 324–327. On Deusdedit's 'tomus carticus', see now Nowak, 'Papsttum' 336–339 (esp. 337 n. 18), identifying it with original charters (specifically, *chartae* written on papyrus).

175. Deusdedit frequently quoted the letters by book and number, and in doing so replicates the numeration in Reg. Vat. 2 including all errors found in the first two books. See Peitz, *Originalregister* 141 for details.

176. The canons in questions are Deusdedit 3.259–267 (149), 3.270 (150), 3.272–278 (150) (ed. Wolf von Glanvell 376–377, 378, and 379–385) and Deusdedit 3.284–288 (156–157), 4.421–422 (161), 4.424–426 (162) (ed. Wolf von Glanvell 393–396, 597–598, 600–601), respectively. See Hageneder, 'Papstregister' 324–325.

177. Gilchrist, 'Reception' 38–43.

178. Deusdedit 4.184 (106) and 422 (161) (ed. Wolf von Glanvell 489–491 and 598–599), respectively.

Yet if we take a closer look at the canons in question, the story changes considerably. The first canon is taken from Gregory's famous letter of 1081 in which the popes justifies the excommunication and deposition of Henry IV. Famously, Gregory VII in this letter (as found in the register) asked the rhetorical question who would criticize him 'for having deposed and excommunicated Henry'.[179] In Deusdedit's collection, the canon is quoted as 'ex registro', but in fact the text has a significant variant. Deusdedit's version, and indeed the version found in all 'Gregorian' canonical collections, lacks the crucial phrase referring to the king's deposition ('deposuisse et').[180] In other words, the canon as found in Deusdedit (and other Gregorian collections) does not support Gregory's claims to have the right to depose kings.

A similar case can be made for Gregory's letter containing the oath of obedience by Welf IV of Bavaria. It is found in Deusdedit's *Collectio*,[181] but no other canon law collection. According to the register version, Welf pledged obedience to Gregory VII, and specifically to observe faithfully whatever he, the pope, may command.[182] In Deusdedit's version, Welf swears to be faithful to Gregory and to his successors who 'take office by the election by the better cardinals'.[183] Thus, both the adressee and the content of the oath are different in Deusdedit's version of the letter.

Both canons, therefore, have small but highly significant variants in Deusdedit's collection (and other collections containing them) which diminish the specifically personal authority of the pope, as found in the register text, against the rights of the Roman church more generally. It is not immediately clear who is responsible for these substantial changes.[184] De-

179. Gregory VII, JL 5201 as found in *Reg.* 8.21 (ed. Caspar, MGH Epp. sel. 2.2:544–563, here at 551 line 7): 'quis nos H. [...] deposuisse et excommunicasse reprehendat'.

180. Gregory VII, JL 5201 as found in Deusdedit 4.184 (106) (ed. Wolf von Glanvell 489–491, here at 490) = Anselm 1.80 (ed. Thaner 53–55). Caspar, while commenting on other variants in Deusdedit, is silent on this significant omission; Blumenthal, 'Fälschungen' does not discuss it either. See, however, Kéry, 'Recht' 293.

181. See Gregory VII, JL 5206 as found in *Reg.* 9.3 (ed. Caspar, MGH Epp. sel. 2.2:573–577, here at 576), Deusdedit 4.422 (161) (ed. Wolf von Glanvell 598–599, here at 598), and *Le Liber censuum de l'église romaine*, ed. Paul Fabre and Louis Duchesne (2 vols. Bibliothèque des Écoles françaises d'Athènes et de Rome 6; Paris 1889–1910) here at 1.419, respectively. Caspar asserted that an intermediate collection kept in the papal archives would explain the distinct variants found in Deusdedit and the *Liber censuum* (ed. Caspar, MGH Epp. sel. 2.2:573 n. 1).

182. Gregory VII, JL 5206 as found in *Reg.* 9.3 (ed. Caspar, MGH Epp. sel. 2.2:573–577, here at 576) 'Et quodcumque mihi ipse papa preceperit sub his videlicet verbis per veram obedientiam, fideliter sicut oportet christianum, observabo.'

183. Gregory VII, JL 5206 as found in Deusdedit 4.422 (161) (ed. Wolf von Glanvell 598–599, here at 598): 'et successoribus eius meliorum cardinalium electione intrantibus'.

184. Peitz, *Originalregister* 139–140 assumed that Deusdedit relied on lost original letters wherever his texts differed from the register, but did not specifically discuss JL 5201 and 5206. Hageneder, 'Papstregister' 324–325 claimed that Deusdedit quoted JL 5201 from an intermediate collection he 'maybe' had compiled himself. Lotte Kéry, 'Kanonessammlungen als Fundorte für päpstliche

usdedit's *Collectio* is among the earliest documented appereances of both canons, but does not clearly predate other collections. Yet Deusdedit certainly was prepared to adapt his Gregorian material elsewhere, sometimes by textual manipulation. For example, Deusdedit in his collection seems to contain two oaths by Wibert of Ravenna as archbishop. The first is an oath of obedience Wibert had professed to Alexander II.[185] The second is presented as a model oath for deposed bishops from Gregory's register; in fact, it is an altered version of the oath of bishop Robert of Chartres, apparently altered by Deusdedit to discredit Wibert.[186] To take another example, a decree of the Lenten synod of 1078 in Deusdedit's collection has a reference to 'the Apostles Saint Peter and Paul' instead of 'Saint Peter, the prince of the Apostles' in the version found in Gregory's register.[187] This kind of textual manipulation is typical of Deusdedit, and there can be little doubt that he changed the text of this synodal decree as well.

So was Deusdedit also responsible for the altered versions of Gregory's letters found in his collection? In the case of Gregory's letter on the excommunication and deposition of Henry IV (JL 5201), this can be ruled out. The omission of the crucial 'deposuisse' is shared by all canonical collections containing this canon;[188] but Deusdedit's version of the canon contains additions (cross-references to other letters) only found here.[189] Thus, Deusdedit's *Collectio* cannot be the source of the other canonical collections for the 'watered down' version of JL 5201; they all, including

---

Schreiben', *Das Papsttum und das vielgestaltige Italien. Hundert Jahre Italia Pontificia*, ed. Klaus Herbers and Jochen Johrendt (Abh. Akad. Göttingen N.F. 5; Berlin and Boston 2009) 275–298, here at 293 assumed an intermediate collection used by Deusdedit and Anselm. Caspar in his edition (MGH Epp. sel. 2.2:573 n. 1) claimed that Deusdedit quoted JL 5206 from an 'Archivversion' but did not discuss Deusdedit's version of JL 5201. Blumenthal, 'Fälschungen' did not discuss these variants.

185. Deusdedit 4.423 (162) (ed. Wolf von Glanvell 599). The same formula was used when Diego Gelmírez received the pallium in 1105, see Ludwig Vones, *Die "Historia Compostellana" und die Kirchenpolitik des nordwestspanischen Raumes 1070–1130. Ein Beitrag zur Geschichte der Beziehungen zwischen Spanien und dem Papsttum zu Beginn des 12. Jahrhunderts* (Kölner historische Abhandlungen 29; Cologne 1980) 162.

186. Deusdedit 4.424 (162) (ed. Wolf von Glanvell 600) vs. Gregory VII, *Reg.* 3.17a (ed. Caspar, MGH Epp. sel. 2.1:282–283). Caspar, once more, asserted that Deusdedit reproduced the version of the oath as found in the Lateran archives ('Archivüberlieferung'); but I find it more likely that Deusdedit changed the text, as already suggested by Löwenfeld, 'Canonsammlung' 321.

187. Deusdedit replaces 'beati Petri apostolorum principis' by 'beatorum apostolorum Petri et Pauli', and 'principis beati Petri' by 'beatis apostolis' [*sic*]. See Rome 1078 c. 11 (ed. Caspar, MGH Epp. sel. 2.2:405 lines 17 and 22) and Deusdedit 3.58 (55) (ed. Wolf von Glanvell 293 lines 14 and 19), respectively. Anselm 4.37 (ed. Thaner 217) has the version found in Gregory's register. See Blumenthal, 'Fälschungen' 246.

188. In addition to Deusdedit, see Anselm 1.80 (ed. Thaner 54), 13L (Berlin) 1.79 (AH01.079c), 3L 1.1.66 (DS01.01.066c), 7L (Vienna) 6.2.1 (SV06.002.01c), Polycarpus (PX01.20.11c), Sinemuriensis appendix (SO651a), and *Tarraconensis II* (TA01.214a).

189. Deusdedit 4.185 (106) (ed. Wolf von Glanvell 491–492).

Deusdedit, ultimately seem to rely on a source which already lacked the reference to Gregory having deposed Henry IV.

Things are different with the second example quoted above, the oath of obedience sworn by Welf of Bavaria as quoted in another letter of Gregory VII (JL 5206).[190] The reference to future popes 'elected by the *melior pars* of the cardinals' replaces the far-reaching profession of obedience to 'whatever the pope may command', strongly suggesting that the same person was responsible for omission of the latter phrase and the insertion of the former. Deusdedit's *Collectio* is the only canonical collection to contain this version; the only other transmission in the *Liber censuum* depends on Deusdedit.[191] More importantly, both the selection of the canon and the kind of manipulation fit what can be observed elsewhere in Deusdedit's collection. He was generally interested in oaths which popes, bishops, kings, and magnates took on various occasions, and in particular gathered oaths sworn by lay magnates to Gregory VII. Frequently, he changed the wording of these oaths.[192] Finally, and probably most significantly, the insertion of a reference to the cardinals as papal electors in JL 5206 fits Deusdedit's well-attested tendency to select and occasionally manipulate proof texts in order to bolster the collective authority of the cardinals. Indeed, this was the most frequent reason for Deusdedit manipulated his proof texts.[193] This all strongly suggests that there is no need to assume an intermediate collection here; Deusdedit himself changed the text of JL 5206.

So while Deusdedit took up a comparatively large number of texts from the letters and councils of Gregory VII, he was mainly interested in documents concerning ecclesiastical property, including the oaths of lay magnates and papal privileges for individual churches; as far as he also turned to 'programmatic' letters, he presented modified versions which were less radical than the versions found in Gregory's register. Given that Deusdedit worked with this register, his decision to retain the 'watered down' version of JL 5201 is almost as interesting as his manipulation of the text of JL 5206. In both cases, if on the one hand he contributed to the reception of Gregory VII into canon law, on the other hand he did so using distinctly less Gregorian versions of the relevant letters.

190. Gregory VII, JL 5206 as found in *Reg.* 9.3 (ed. Caspar, MGH Epp. sel. 2.2:573–577, here at 576).

191. Peitz, *Originalregister* 247–252 (though not on this canon in particular).

192. See Philipp Hofmeister, *Die christlichen Eidesformen. Eine liturgie- und rechtsgeschichtliche Untersuchung* (Munich 1957), here at 45–46.

193. Blumenthal, 'Fälschungen' 246, 252–253, and 260; for details, see above, note 130.

The 'Universal' Pope and Papal Immunity

Let us now return to place of the pope in Deusdedit's collection. As the treatment of Roman primacy, papal elections, and Gregory VII suggests, Deusdedit's view of the papacy was nuanced. It is important to bear in mind that Deusdedit distinguished between Roman and papal primacy; but of course the two issues are related. Obviously, many of Deusdedit's canons on the privileges of the Roman church were also relevant to specifically papal rights. Indeed, Deusdedit's interpretation of papal prerogatives as found in his preface even goes beyond what these canons assert.[194] Sometimes, he interfered with the canons directly; for example, he manipulated the text of an oath bishops should take so that they specifically pledged loyalty to the 'Roman church and the pope'.[195] The version of *De privilegio Romanae ecclesiae* Deusdedit inserted in his collection (JL 4424) is likewise manipulated in favour of Rome and the papacy.[196] In his rubrics, Deusdedit used language similar to the *Dictatus papae* to assert the primacy of the Roman church and of the pope, whom he called 'the pontiff of all pontiffs'.[197] As quoted above, he called those separating themselves from the Roman church 'heretics', and quoted from rare sources to substantiate this claim.[198] Deusdedit also affirmed that no 'writing' (*scriptura*) should be called 'authentic' unless confirmed by the pope.[199] Even more telling are two rubrics asserting that the pope is to be called 'universal', referring the reader to the Donation of Constantine and a letter of Greg-

194. Deusdedit, *Praefatio* (ed. Wolf von Glanvell 1); Dusil, *Wissensordnungen* 104–105.

195. Deusdedit 2.112 (95) (ed. Wolf von Glanvell 239–240), taken from the *Liber diurnus* V75 (ed. Foerster 246). Instead of promising not to consent to any acts 'contra rem publicam vel piissimum principem' (ibid. lines 26–27) the passage in Deusdedit refers to acts 'contra Romanam ecclesiam vel contra honorem domini papae' (ed. Wolf von Glanvell 240 lines 6–7)!

196. Deusdedit 1.167 (136) (ed. Wolf von Glanvell 106–107), also found in a handful of collections including Anselm 1.63 (ed. Thaner 31–32) and Bonizo 4.82 (ed. Perels 146–147). It is attributed to Nicholas II in the collections but in fact lifted from Peter Damian, *Ep.* 65 (ed. Reindel, MGH Briefe dt. Kaiserzeit 4.2:228–247, here at 232 line 14 to 325 line 17). In addition to Reindel's apparatus and the literature quoted there, see also Cushing, *Papacy and Law* 25–26 and 37 (though with no discussion of the collections) and Stephan Freund, *Studien zur literarischen Wirksamkeit des Petrus Damiani* (MGH Studien und Texte 13; Hanover 1995), esp. 90–95. Contrary to what Freund (ibid. 91 and 102) suggests, both Anselm and Deusdedit have the same form of the letter and both attribute it to Nicholas II. The third edition of Jaffé's *Regesta* (J³ 10340) seems to return (*pace* Perels, Reindel, Berschin) to Ewald's position that the letter was genuine (JL 4424); no reason is given for this contentious assertion.

197. Deusdedit, *capitulatio* (ed. Wolf von Glanvell 8): 'Quod sicut Petrus est princeps omnium apostolorum, ita Romanus pontifex omnium pontificum.'

198. Ibid.: 'Quod heretici sint, qui Romane ecclesie non concordent et qui eius privilegia nituntur auferre.'

199. Deusdedit, *capitulatio* (ed. Wolf von Glanvell 10): 'Quod nulla scriptura sit autentica, nisi illius iudicio sit roborata.' On *Dictatus papae* c. 17 (ed. Caspar, MGH Epp. sel. 2.1:205), see Kuttner, 'Liber Canonicus'.

ory the Great.[200] The point here is that Gregory the Great in fact objected to the use of 'universal' titles.[201] Indeed, the very letter from which Deusdedit's canon is taken was commonly quoted as a proof that *no one* should be called 'universal'.[202] Yet Deusdedit in his collection presents an abbreviated version apparently saying the opposite.[203] Even if Deusdedit was not responsible himself for the abbreviation, he must have know the original form one way or the other and chose the shorter form, knowing that it misrepresented the main point of Gregory's letter. So Deusdedit used language similar to the *Dictatus papae* in his rubrics, spent considerable effort to find corresponding canons, and did not refrain from using manipulative abbreviations of certain materials.

The emphasis on papal power, and in particular the parallels between Deusdedit's *Collectio* and the *Dictatus papae* have long been observed;[204] they have frequently been quoted to show that Deusdedit's collection was above all 'Gregorian'.[205] Yet at the same time, Deusdedit introduced into canon law texts which one would rather expect to have been quoted by the opponents of Gregory VII. To begin with, Deusdedit was quite clear that the pope was bound by canon law. The authority of universal synods

200. Deusdedit, *capitulatio* (ed. Wolf von Glanvell 8): 'Item quod ante eam [scil. Nicaeam synodum, CR] vocatus sit papa universalis', referring to Deusdedit 4.1 (1) (ed. Wolf von Glanvell 397–401), and 'Quod a Calcedonensi sinodo DC XXX patrum universalis sit appellatus', referring to Deusdedit 1.185 (149) (ed. Wolf von Glanvell 114). For Gregory VII, see *Dictatus papae* c. 2 (ed. Caspar, MGH Epp. sel. 2.1:202).

201. Gregory I, JE 1360 (ed. Ewald and Hartmann, MGH Epp. 1.322–323): 'Certe pro beati Petri apostolorum principis honore per venerandam Chalcedonensem synodum Romano pontifici oblatum est. Sed nullus corum umquam hoc singularitas nomine uti consensit, ne, dum privatum aliquid daretur uni, honore debito sacerdotes privarentur universi.'

202. The JE 1360 excerpt in the collection in Vat. lat. 3829 (*Clavis*, PG63.046) has the rubric 'Ut nemo universalis vocetur', and gathers a number of canons on the same issue. Indeed, canons with similar rubrics and content are commonplace in collections including Burchard of Worms and *74T*, to quote only two of the collections circulating most widely around the time Deusdedit completed his work.

203. Deusdedit 1.185 (149) (ed. Wolf von Glanvell 114): 'Certe pro beati Petri apostoli honore per venerandam Chalcedonensem sinodum universalis nomen Romano pontifici oblatum est.' See Stephan Kuttner, 'Universal Pope or Servant of God's Servants: The Canonists, Papal Titles, and Innocent III' *Revue de Droit canonique* 32 (1981) 109–149, here at 113–114. Fournier, in his detailed account of how Deusdedit reworked his materials, significantly did not mention this canon: Fournier, 'Collections romaines' 327–371, esp. 354–364 and 370–371.

204. Parallels between Deusdedit and *Dictatus papae* were highlighted already by Sackur, 'Dictatus papae', by Wolf von Glanvell in his edition of Deusdedit, by Caspar in his edition of the *Dictatus* (MGH Epp. sel. 2.1:202–208), and others. Yet as Horst Fuhrmann, '"Quod catholicus non habeatur, qui non concordat Romanae ecclesiae". Randnotizen zum Dictatus Papae', *Festschrift für Helmut Beumann zum 65. Geburtstag*, ed. Kurt-Ulrich Jäschke and Reinhard Wenskus (Sigmaringen 1977) 263–287 pointed out, many articles of the *Dictatus* were not, and could not have been, supported by canonical authorities.

205. Sackur, 'Dictatus papae' esp. 140–141; Fournier, 'Collections romaines' 360, repeated verbatim in *Histoire* 2.51: 'Que Deusdedit ait composé son œuvre avec le dessein d'élever un monument au pouvoir suprême du Pontife romain, fondement nécessaire et indispensable instrument de là Réforme ecclésiastique, c'est là un fait trop évident pour qu'il soit besoin d'y insister.'

'celebrated by four or five patriarchs' was paramount; not even the pope could abrogate their decrees.[206] Even more importantly, the pope was *subject* to canon law and could be brought to trial. Indeed, Deusdedit's *Collectio* is the first collection in church history to contain a canon stating that the pope could be judged 'if he deviated from the faith'.[207] While the Roman church 'never erred from the true faith' according to one of Deusdedit's rubrics,[208] he evidently thought this possible for the pope in person. The canon Deusdedit introduced into canon law had a remarkable impact on medieval political thought.[209] Taken up by Gratian 1, the canon in the later Middle Ages became a founding text of conciliarism.[210] Whether or not he forged the fragment himself,[211] Deusdedit ultimately provided the medieval Church with the sole canon containing what for centuries was accepted as the only exception to papal immunity, and sometimes was even perceived as an anti-papal statement.[212] The deposition of popes in

206. Deusdedit, *Praefatio* (ed. Wolf von Glanvell 3 lines 16–20), clearly referring to the ancient pentarchy; at the same time, he spoke of universal synods as being 'celebrated by papal authority' in his *capitulatio* (ibid. 7 lines 28–29).

207. Deusdedit 1.306 (231) (ed. Wolf von Glanvell 177–178, here at 177): 'Cuius [papae, CR] culpas istic redarguere presumit mortalium nullus, quia cunctos ipse iudicaturus a nemine est iudicandus, nisi forte deprehendatur a fide devius.' The idea may go back to Pseudo-Isidore, where bishops are protected against accusations from their subjects—safe for cases of 'deviation from the faith', in which they exceptionally are allowed. See for example Ps.-Fabian, JK †93 (ed. Hinschius 166) as found in *74T* c. 78 (ed. Gilchrist 60): 'Si [episcopus, CR] a fide deviaverit, erit corrigendus prius secrete a subditis. Quod si incorrigibilis, quod absit, apparuerit, tunc erit accusandus ad primates suos aut ad sedem apostolicam.' *Panormia* 4.40 contains this text (via *4L*) as part of a short series of canons on this matter (*Panormia* 4.38–41). For a parallel, see also Henry IV, *Ep.* 12 (ed. Erdmann, MGH Deutsches Mittelalter 1.16), who likewise claimed immunity except in cases of 'deviation from the faith' (ibid., line 23: 'nisi a fide, quod absit, exorbitaverim').

208. Deusdedit, *capitulatio* (ed. Wolf von Glanvell 10): 'Quod Romana ecclesia numquam a vera fide erraverit.'

209. The canon is also found in *Tarraconensis II* 1.93, *Britannica* (London, BL, Add. MS 8873, fol. 191r), and Ivo, *Decretum* 5.23; they presumably all depend directly or indirectly on Deusdedit. From Ivo it passed to Gratian D.40 c.6 via *Tripartita* B3.8.3.

210. See Brian Tierney, *Foundations of the Conciliar Theory: The Contribution of the Medieval Canonists from Gratian to the Great Schism* (Studies in the History of Christian Thought 92; Cambridge 1955) and most recently Dusil, *Wissensordnungen* 431–438 on Gratian D.40 c.6 and later canon law. The pre-Gratian history of the canon has received rather less critical attention. See James M. Moynihan, *Papal Immunity and Liability in the Writings of the Medieval Canonists* (Analecta Gregoriana 120; Rome 1961), here at 30–33 for a short but useful analysis. Salvatore Vacca, *Prima sedes a nemine iudicatur. Genesi e sviluppo storico dell'assioma fino al Decreto di Graziano* (Miscellanea historiae pontificiae 61; Rome 1993) quotes a number of relevant sources, including Deusdedit. Tierney, Moynihan, and Vacca all follow Michel's mistaken idea that Humbert of Silva Candida forged the canon. On the authorship of the canon (also known as 'fragment A of *De sancta Romana ecclesia*'), see above note 123.

211. Blumenthal, 'Reflections' 140 rightly pointed out that Deusdedit was at least a better candidate than Humbert of Silva Candida.

212. See, for example, Johannes Nauclerus, *Chronica succinctim compraehendentia res memorabiles seculorum omnium ac gentium* [...] (Cologne 1544), here at 1.610: 'Huius [Bonifacii, CR] etiam celebre ac vulgatum contra Romanos pontifices dictum, ab ecclesia est receptum, quo scripsit, papam a fide devium, iudicari posse [...].'

practice may have had little to do with canon law as found in the collections,[213] but nonetheless it is remarkable that Deusdedit chose to insert this text in his collection. After all, in the 1080s and 1090s the question how to deal with a pope who overstepped his competences, 'deviated from the faith', or even lapsed into heresy was anything but academic. To take just one example from Deusdedit's immediate environment, Cardinal Beno of San Martino e Silvestro in 1098 argued precisely that Gregory had 'manifestly deviated from the faith' and could have been accused and deposed by the cardinals.[214] Unlike Beno, Deusdedit had remained loyal to Gregory VII, but he must have been aware that the canon he chose to introduce in his collection would be welcome above all to Gregory's opponents. So while Deusdedit more than any other compiler of a major canon law collection gathered canons in accordance with the *Dictatus papae*, his canonical activity as a whole displays a distinct and more nuanced tendency.

4.3.6 Influence

Scholars often take the number of extant manuscripts as a crude measure of how influential a given collection was. In the case of Deusdedit's *Collectio*, of which only one complete manuscript written in the Middle Ages is extant, this method would give a much distorted impression. This is suggested by the number of manuscripts containing fragments and excerpts—twenty such manuscripts are known, suggesting the collection was read and used relatively widely.[215] Deusdedit's interest in church property and its administration was not lost to the emerging bureaucracy at the papal curia. Indeed, Deusdedit's account of papal revenues was highly valued here, and in the later twelfth century it became the kernel of the *Liber censuum*.[216] Pope Paschal II, a former cardinal priest himself, quoted

213. See Harald Zimmermann, *Papstabsetzungen des Mittelalters* (Graz, Vienna, and Cologne 1968).

214. Beno, *Gesta* (ed. Francke, MGH Ldl 2.370): 'manifeste a fide catholica erravit'; on Beno's arguments and the similarities to Deusdedit, see Robinson, *Authority and Resistance* 47–49. Deusdedit was silent on the question who could judge the pope, but later canonists like Huguccio agreed with Beno that if anyone could judge the pope it would be the cardinals.

215. For manuscripts, see Kéry 229–230, Martin Brett, 'Editions, Manuscripts and Readers in Some Pre-Gratian Collections', *Ritual, Text and Law: Studies in Medieval Canon Law and Liturgy Presented to Roger E. Reynolds*, ed. Richard F. Gyug and Kathleen Grace Cushing (CFC; Aldershot 2004) 205–224, here at 209 n. 13, Blumenthal, 'Reflections' 137–138, eadem, 'Handbook' 20–21 (Roma, Vallicelliana, F.54, part III), Somerville, 'Deusdedit', and Kéry, 'Recht' 367–370. References to a Montecassino manuscript with excerpts from all four books are erroneous, see Blumenthal, 'Reflections' 137 n. 11. At least indirectly, fragments of Deusdedit were known even north of the Alps, see Märtl, 'Einleitung' 103–104. These fragments (in Dresden, Sächsische Landesbibliothek, F 168) may depend on Vat. lat. 1984.

216. See Sickel, *Privilegium* 79. Peitz, *Originalregister* 247–252. and more recently Blumenthal, 'Reflections' 140–145, who makes a very strong case that both Albinus of Albano and Cencius Savelli used Deusdedit directly.

from Deusdedit.[217] It was probably this milieu of cardinals and the curia in general where Deusdedit's collection had most impact in the long run. Yet various compilers of canonical collections valued Deusdedit as well. A number of anonymous collections took material from Deusdedit; the most famous one among them is the *Britannica*, while others (for example the *Taurinensis* and *Ambrosiana I*) remain to be studied.[218] Other collections (for example the *Caesaraugustana*) were improved either from Deusdedit's collection itself or various intermediate collections drawing on it.[219] In addition to providing evidence for the reception of Deusdedit's collection, collections like the Turin 7L can therefore be used to reconstruct lost earlier versions of Deusdedit's collection. However, even the Deusdedit canons in Turin 7L display some features which one would otherwise blame on the scribe of Vat. lat. 3833. A series of excerpts from Saint Augustine, for example, not only contains Deusdedit's comment, presumably found already in the earliest version of his collection, but also a misguided inscription to Pope Victor which must have been added at a later stage.[220] Given that Turin 7L cannot depend on the extant Vat. lat. 3833, this indicates a lost version of Deusdedit's collection which had some, but not all of the peculiar features of Vat. lat. 3833.

In addition, the *Britannica* deserves special mention both because it contains substantial excerpts from Deusdedit and because it passed considerable materials via the Ivonian collection into 'mainstream' canon law. To judge from the *Britannica*, Deusdedit's collection was valued as a trustworthy source of rare materials, above all ancient papal letters. Finally, Deusdedit was influential by virtue of his cooperation with Anselm of Lucca, with whom he evidently exchanged texts and ideas. Scholars have often referred to 'Gregorian intermediate collections' to explain the parallels between both collections, but this should not obscure the fact that some canons found in both collections bear the mark of Deusdedit's learning,

---

217. Blumenthal, *Early Councils* 82–83 (on four Deusdedit canons in JL 6145, issued at Troyes 1107).

218. On the *Britannica*, see Chapter Five; note that Ewald, 'Brittische Sammlung' 582 contemplated the idea that it used a more complete version of Deusdedit. For a comparison of Deusdedit with the first part of the *Taurinensis*, see Motta, 'Silloge' 423–434 (noting fuller versions of several canons in the *Taurinensis*). The dependence of *Ambrosiana I* on Deusdedit was demonstrated by Picasso, *Collezioni* 171–173; note that one could add Deusdedit 4.13 and 15 to his table on account of *Ambrosiana I* cc. 69–70. In addition, see Fowler-Magerl, *Clavis* 162–163 and 177 on the Turin 7L, *Ambrosiana I*, *Taurinensis*, and the collections in Roma, Vallicelliana, B.89 and Vat. lat. 3829.

219. Linda Fowler-Magerl, 'The Version of the *Collectio Caesaraugustana* in Barcelona, Archivo de la Corona de Aragón, MS San Cugat 63', *Ritual, Text and Law: Studies in Medieval Canon Law and Liturgy Presented to Roger E. Reynolds*, ed. Richard F. Gyug and Kathleen Grace Cushing (CFC; Aldershot 2004) 269–280, here at 179–180 and Blumenthal, 'Reflections' 136–145 (*Caesaraugustana*); Fowler-Magerl, *Clavis* 162–163 (*Sinemuriensis* in Orléans, BM, 306).

220. Turin 7L 6.56–57 = Deusdedit 4.222–225 (126–128) (ed. Wolf von Glanvell 522–525).

for example elaborate cross-references,[221] or are shaped by Deusdedit's concern for lower-ranking cardinals.[222] Missing references to Saint Peter are also more likely Deusdedit's than Anselm's work.[223] The exact relationship deserves (and demands) further study; in any case, it is clear that Deusdedit and Anselm together were sucessful in introducing many proof texts into canon law, including many key texts mentioned in the preceding pages, e.g. the 'Leo-Humbert' version of the Donation of Constantine, or the striking canon stating that the pope could be judged if 'deviating from the faith'.[224] In particular, Deusdedit would have been pleased to see how far the canons he manipulated in favour of the lower-ranking cardinals spread; they are found in Anselm's *Collectio*, the *Caesaraugustana*, the *Collection in Three Books*, and a number of collections including ultimately Gratian 2.[225] In contrast, the Papal Election Decree of 1059, against which Deusdedit railed, was not taken into any major canon law collection before the twelfth century, at least not in Italy. In fact, the first Italian collection to quote it was the *Decretum Gratiani*—compiled some 80 years after the election of Nicholas II, and well after the disputed election of 1130. Both directly and indirectly, therefore, Deusdedit's collection (and his canon law activity more generally) had considerable influence both in Rome and beyond.

4.3.7 Summary

While Deusdedit was a loyal supporter of Gregory VII, his *Collectio canonum* as a whole cannot be called 'Gregorian'. The point is not that this would do injustice to the complex nature of this work; this would be true for any major collection. Rather, it turned out that even the elements

---

221. E.g. the introductory notes in Deusdedit 4.1 (1) (ed. Wolf von Glanvell 397 lines 1–6) = Anselm 4.33 (ed. Thaner 206); on other cross-references, see above (notes 68, 71, 75, 81, 84, and 86). For another example, see already Ernst von Dobschütz, 'Untersuchung', *Das Decretum Gelasianum de libris recipiendis et non recipiendis*, ed. idem (Texte und Untersuchungen zur Geschichte der altchristlichen Literatur 38.4; Leipzig 1912) 135–357, here at 191.

222. E.g. Deusdedit 1.255 (206) (ed. Wolf von Glanvell 146).

223. E.g. Deusdedit 1.61 (50) (ed. Wolf von Glanvell 63 lines 16 and 25–26) = Anselm 1.66 (ed. Thaner 34).

224. On the canon itself, see above (note 207). It has sometimes been assumed that Gratian took this canon from Deusdedit directly, but evidence is not cogent. See Blumenthal, 'Reflections' 136.

225. The second part of Deusdedit 1.255 (206) as quoted above (note 165) is found in Anselm 7.27, *Polycarpus* 1.4.6, and Vienna 7L 1.6.6; slightly different versions are found in Anselm A Aucta 6.195a, Anselm B 6.25, *Caes. I* 3.6, 3L 1.4.6, San Pietro 9L 1.1.73, and Gratian D.79 c.4 (ed. Friedberg 277). Deusdedit 2.161 (131b) (ed. Wolf von Glanvell 268) has an even wider distribution: Anselm A Aucta 6.195b, Anselm B 6.25a, 13L (Vat. lat. 1361) 1.47b, 3L 1.4.7, San Pietro 9 1.1.74, the collections in Firenze, Biblioteca Medicea Laurenziana, Ashburnham 1554 (= LM044 in *Clavis*), Paris, BnF, lat. 3858C (= MY01.028) and Vat. lat. 3829 (= PG37.001), *Polycarpus* 1.4.5, 13L (Berlin) 5.143a, 7L (Vienna) 1.6.5; Gratian D.79 c.3 (ed. Friedberg 277). On the transmission, see Kuttner, 'Cardinalis' 149 n. 22; Hans-Georg Krause, *Das Papstwahldekret von 1059 und seine Rolle im Investiturstreit* (Studi Gregoriani 7; Rome 1960), here at 246–247; Jasper, *Papstwahldekret* 76–78.

that at first sight seemed to make Deusdedit's collection 'Gregorian' effecticely do not. In particular, while Deusdedit did focus on Roman primacy, he more than any other compiler of a canon law collection stressed the difference between the Roman church on the one hand and the pope on the other. He devoted considerable effort to finding, and occasionally manipulating proof texts on the role of the cardinals and all Roman clergy; they, as a corporate group, profited from the privileges and property of the Roman church he so carefully documented. Partly, these efforts can be explained by Deusdedit's taking sides in conflicts within the cardinalate, or the fact that his collection was finished during a vacancy; but there can be no doubt that strenghtening the cardinals as the 'senate' of the Roman church was one of Deusdedit's main goals.[226] As for the Gregory VII material found in Deusdedit's collection, it turned out that it overwhelmingly documents Deusdedit's interest in the property of the Roman church. In addition, where Deusdedit did quote from letters referring to Gregory's more contentious politics, he quoted adapted versions, and in one case at least was directly responsible for the alteration. So the *Collectio* was shaped by Deusdedit's support for Gregory VII, but also by the conflicts between Gregory and his cardinals, by conflict and solidarity within the cardinalate, by Deusdedit's critique of Gregory's successor Victor III, by the troubled situation of the Roman clergy after 1081, and by special circumstances of the vacany of 1086/87. Occasionally, this is visible in contentious and even polemic elements Deusdedit introduced in his collection; but on the whole he concentrated on ancient canon law, procedure, and well-documented property. The lasting success of his collection, particularly at the curia, suggests that these texts were useful beyond the partisan interest that may have played a role in the composition of the collection.

4.4 Anselm of Lucca

4.4.1 Biography

Anselm was born to a noble family, probably in Milan, perhaps in the 1030s.[227] He presumably was a relative of Pope Alexander II,[228] whom he

---

226. See one of the rubrics Deusdedit wrote (for the Donation of Constantine): 'Inde Romani clerici locum antiquorum habent patriciorum' (ed. Wolf von Glanvell 17).

227. For the following, see Schmidt, *Alexander II.* 28; Hagen Keller, 'Le origini sociali et famigliari del vescovo Anselmo', *Sant'Anselmo vescovo di Lucca (1073–1086) nel quadro delle trasformazioni sociali e della riforma ecclesiastica: atti del convegno internazionale di studio, Lucca 25–28 settembre 1986*, ed. Cinzio Violante (Istituto storico Italiano per il medio evo. Nuovi studi storici 13; Rome 1992) 27–50 (and other contributions in the same volume); Cushing, *Papacy and Law* ch. 1; eadem, 'Events That Led to Sainthood: Sanctity and the Reformers in the Eleventh Century', *Belief and Culture in the Middle Ages: Studies Presented to Henry Mayr-Harting*, ed. Richard Gameson and Henrietta Leyser (Oxford 2001) 187–196.

228. For discussion, see Schmidt, *Alexander II.* 28.

succeeded as bishop of Lucca. From early on, he was in close contact with Gregory VII and many of his supporters including Peter Damian, Hugh of Die, Matilda of Tuscany, Bonizo of Sutri, and Deusdedit. In 1073, Anselm was elected bishop of Lucca; however, his investiture and consecration were delayed at the request of Gregory VII. The pope was concerned that Henry IV at the time was in contact with the advisers the pope had excommunicated over the Milan affair. Only after this conflict (temporarily at least) was resolved, Anselm received royal investiture and papal consecration in late 1074 or early 1075. According to his biographers, he entered a monastery around that time; if so, this did not stop him from travelling widely during the 1070s. In 1077, he was active as papal legate in Lombardy, and was briefly imprisoned in this context.[229] His pontificate is relatively obscure; as so often, conflicts are more visible than peaceful relations. Apparently, struggles between the new bishop and local elites escalated quickly. Anselm could rely on his family and on external support—including Matilda of Tuscany and Gregory VII—but the cathedral clergy took advantage of the Wibertine schism, joined with imperial forces, and effectively exiled Anselm in 1080.

By that time, Anselm already was one of the most prominent supporters of Gregory VII who famously named him as a possible successor. The claim that Anselm acted (again) as papal legate in 1082 is at least plausible.[230] It was at this time of conflict he both compiled a canonical collection and wrote a polemic tract against Wibert/Clement, his *Liber contra Wibertum* of 1085/86. Anselm died on 18 March 1086, during the vacancy following the death of Gregory VII, in Mantua; at the intervention of Bonizo, he was buried in the cathedral church of Mantua rather than the monastery of Polirone, as he apparently had wished. Soon, Anselm was venerated as a saint, at least among Gregorians, many of whom remembered him in their writings.

4.4.2 Anselm's *Collectio canonum* (Overview)

Anselm's collection has attracted considerable attention in the context of 'law and reform', not least because it is the only 'Gregorian' collection

---

229. Arnulf, *Liber gestorum recentium* (ed. Zey, MGH SS rer. Germ. 67.230); *Vita Anselmi* c. 17 (ed. Wilmans, MGH SS 12.18); Bernold of Konstanz, *Chronicon* (ed. Robinson, MGH SS rer. Germ. N.S. 14.410 and 413). Cushing, *Papacy and Law* ch. 1 seems not to take these sources as sufficient evidence for Anselm's legation; see also next note.

230. The only source for this legation is the *De thesauro Canusinae ecclesiae* transmitted with the *Vita Mathildis* in Vat. lat. 4922, fol. 1v (ed. Bethmann, MGH SS 12.385 n. 14). For this (second) legation I agree with Cushing, *Papacy and Law* 136–138, esp. 136 n. 54 that the evidence is not beyond doubt.

extant in more than a few manuscripts.[231] It is a massive collection of more than 1,100 canons filling some 250 folios in the extant copies. The collection consists of a short preface, and thirteen books of canons, each preceded by a *capitulatio* mostly composed of numbered rubrics. The first book is emphatically devoted to the primacy of the Roman church.[232] Books two to six are devoted to the ecclesiastical hierarchy—the relation between papacy and local churches, ordinations, and procedure. Considerable parts, mainly based on Pseudo-Isidore, deal with procedural law; a complete book is devoted to the validity of (papal) privileges. Book seven and eight deal with the clergy, more specifically with communal living and celibacy (book seven) and how to deal with those who fall short of the high standards of clerical discipline (book eight 'de lapsis'). Both books are short, but highly unusual in their design. Book nine rather briefly treats the Eucharist and baptism, with a comparatively large number of canons concerning the validity of sacraments administered by heretical or schismatic clergy. The next book, equally short, deals with marriage; book eleven is a penitential book not unlike Burchard's *Corrector sive medicus*. The last two books are devoted to excommunication (book twelve) and use of force by ecclesiastical and secular authorities (book thirteen); both are manifestly shaped by the bitter conflicts around 1080.[233]

Anselm's authorship has occasionally been doubted,[234] as only one manuscript containing a short version ('Bb') of the collection names him as the author, and even this note was added by a later hand.[235] However, the claim is plausible from what is known about Anselm's career and learning, and there are several near-contemporary sources referring to a collection compiled by Anselm.[236] In addition, there are also parallels

<hr>

231. Kéry 218–226; Fowler-Magerl, *Clavis* 139–148, 157–158, 169–171, 218–224, and 227.

232. Fowler-Magerl, *Clavis* 140 emphasized that Anselm devoted his first book neither to 'papal primacy', nor the 'authority and primacy of the apostolic see', but to the 'primacy of the Roman church'. In the secondary literature, the title of the first book is often quoted in the form of the A' and Bb versions of Anselm which, as Fowler-Magerl stressed, Anselm 'had nothing to do with' (ibid.).

233. Edith Pásztor, 'Lotta per le investiture e "ius belli": la posizione di Anselmo di Lucca', *Sant'Anselmo, Mantova e la lotta per le investiture: atti di convegno internazionale di studi (Mantova 23–24–25 maggio 1986)*, ed. Paolo Golinelli (Bologna 1987) 375–421; Cushing, *Papacy and Law*.

234. Gérard Fransen, 'Anselme de Lucques canoniste?', *Sant'Anselmo vescovo di Lucca (1073–1086) nel quadro delle trasformazioni sociali e della riforma ecclesiastica: atti del convegno internazionale di studio, Lucca 25–28 settembre 1986*, ed. Cinzio Violante (Istituto storico Italiano per il medio evo. Nuovi studi storici 13; Rome 1992) 143–155.

235. Barb. lat. 535, fol. 14v; see Fowler-Magerl, *Clavis* 139–140. On Anselm Bb in general, see Cushing, 'Polemic or Handbook' and eadem, 'Looking Behind Recension Bb of the *Collectio canonum* of Anselm of Lucca' ZRG Kan. Abt. 95 (2009) 29–47.

236. Beno mentioned 'compilationes' of Anselm and Deusdedit (ed. Francke, MGH Ldl 2.399); Bardo, *Vita Anselmi* (ed. Wilmans, MGH SS 12.14) claimed that Anselm compiled a canonical collection called *Apologeticus*: 'Apologeticum unum diversis ex sanctorum patrum voluminibus

between Anselm's *Liber contra Wibertum* and his *Collectio*,[237] and also between the *Liber* and the sources used for the *Collectio*, namely the *Barberiniana*.[238] All in all, it is plausible to assume Anselm indeed compiled the
collection traditionally attributed to him. Like several other compilers of
canon law collections, Anselm seems to have (still) worked on his collection late in life. The *terminus post quem* for the completion is the same as
for Deusdedit's *Collectio*; the most recent material in both cases is a letter
of Gregory VII of 1081. The *terminus ante quem* is Anselm's death in 1086
and thus slightly earlier than that of Deusdedit's *Collectio*.

In the decades after Anselm completed his work, it was frequently copied and, almost equally frequently, reworked. There are 18 complete manuscripts, mostly from the twelfth century, and a number of fragments.[239]
Several versions can be distinguished, commonly referred to as A, A' (or A1),
A Aucta (or A Ven), B, Bb, and C; in addition, scholars have suggested further subdivisions of these versions and argued about lost versions behind
(or between) those found in the extant manuscripts.[240] The complex, and

compilavit, quibus domni papae sententiam et universa eius facta atque praecepta canonicis de-
fenderet rationibus et approbaret orthodoxis auctoritatibus.' Sigebert of Gembloux, *Chronicon*
(ed. Bethmann, MGH SS 6.365) is more ambivalent; the *liber* he mentioned could well be Anselm's *Liber contra Wibertum*.

237. See Cushing, *Papacy and Law* 223–224 for parallels between Anselm's *Liber contra Wibertum*
and books 12–13 of his *Collectio*. Parallels extend to other books, too. For example, the citations
from Cyprian (ed. Bernheim, MGH Ldl 1.521 lines 19–22 and lines 32–41) correspond exactly to
Anselm 5.1 and 6.56, respectively. For the manuscript tradition of the *Liber*, see the important
study of Claudia Märtl, 'Zur Überlieferung des *Liber contra Wibertum* Anselms von Lucca' DA 41
(1985) 192–202 (also against Robert Somerville, 'Anselm of Lucca and Wibert of Ravenna' BMCL
10 [1980] 1–13).

238. A series of quotations in the *Liber contra Wibertum* (ed. Bernheim, MGH Ldl 1.526 line 16
to 527 line 9) for which neither Bernheim nor Cushing found the source are in fact a version of
the so-called 'error series'; they have a parallel in Deusdedit 4.56–65 (48) (ed. Wolf von Glanvell
427–429) but also in the *Barberiniana* 2.1–9 which contains many materials used by Anselm.

239. Landau, 'Erweiterte Fassungen' 325–333; Kéry 218–221; Fowler-Magerl, *Clavis* 139–148 (A
and C versions), 157–158 (Barb. version, elsewhere known as 'Bb'), 169–171 (B), 218–221 (A'), 221–224
(Pisa abbreviation of A'), 227 (A' subgroup). Note than Thaner also saw Vat. lat. 1361 as a copy
of Anselm; the collection, while based on Anselm's, is today counted as a separate work (the
'Vatican 13L').

240. See Landau, 'Erweiterte Fassungen' on Anselm A Aucta (his 'A Ven.'); John T. Gilchrist,
'The *Collectio canonum* of Bishop Anselm II of Lucca (d. 1086): Recension B of Berlin Staatsbib-
liothek Preussischer Kulturbesitz Cod. 597', *Cristianità ed Europa: miscellanea di studi in onore di
Luigi Prosdocimi*, ed. Cesare Alzati (2 in 3 vols. Rome 1994–2000) 1.2:377–403 on B; Fowler-Magerl,
Clavis 157 on Barb. lat. 535 as a separate version of the A version (not Bb), and ibid. 218–221 and
227 on subgroups within the A' version; Cushing, 'Polemic or Handbook' on Bb. On Fournier's 'Anselm C' as a product of the sixteenth century, see Landau, 'Rezension C' esp. 19.; Klaus
Zechiel-Eckes, 'Eine Mailänder Redaktion des Kirchenrechtssammlung Bischof Anselms II. von
Lucca (1073–1086)' ZRG Kan. Abt. 81 (1995) 130–147 on 'Y'. On the Vatican copies, see Stephan Kuttner and Reinhard Elze. *A Catalogue of Canon and Roman Law Manuscripts in the Vatican Library, vol.
1: Codices Vaticani Latini 541–2299* (Studi e testi 322; Vatican City 1986) and Gero Rudolf Dolezalek
and Martin Bertram, *Catalogue of Canon and Roman Law Manuscripts in the Vatican Library, Vol. III
Resuscitated [Vat. lat. 3137–11527]* (2009), https://home.uni-leipzig.de/jurarom/manuscr/Vatican-
Catalogue/historyvaticancatalogue.html.

sometimes changing, nomenclature reflects the vivid debate on the genesis of Anselm's collection, and occasionally has led to confusion.[241] The debate continues, but most scholars follow Thaner and Fournier that the A version reflects Anselm's legal thought best.[242] Three manuscripts of the A version are known,[243] eight more manuscripts contain reworked and enlarged forms of this version (= A' and A Aucta).[244] Thaner used the A version version for the text of the canons in his (incomplete) edition, but for the rubrics drew on various forms of the collection including A'.[245] As the rubrics are an important element of the collection, it is crucial that Anselm had nothing to do with the A' rubrics or the *capitulatio* found in this version.[246]

4.4.3 Formal Sources

Anselm's collection is based on a broad selection of formal sources.[247] They include *74T*, one or more versions of Pseudo-Isidore, Burchard's *Liber decretorum*, the register of Gregory the Great, the so-called *Capitula iudicorum* penitential, and various intermediary collections today only preserved in the so-called *2L/8P*. Many of these sources were also used by the anonymous compiler responsible for the so-called Bb version of Anselm's collection.[248] The additions in the A manuscripts themselves also seems to draw on sources used for the A version, suggesting that reworking began early

241. The complexities of the manuscript tradition have evidently confused Mitrofanov, who variously claimed 'A, Bb, and C', 'A, B, and C', or 'A, A Aucta, B, and C' to be closest to the original; see Andrey Mitrofanov, *L'ecclésiologie d'Anselme de Lucques (1036–1086) au service de Grégoire VII: genèse, contenu et impact de sa «Collection canonique»* (Instrumenta patristica et mediaevalia 69; Turnhout 2015), here at 80, 81, and 86, respectively. These asssertions reflect the sometimes contradictory statements found in the secondary literature. Likewise, Szuromi's study is seriously marred by the confusion of different versions of Anselm's collection: Szabolcs Anzelm Szuromi, *Anselm of Lucca as a Canonist* (Adnotationes in ius canonicum 34; Frankfurt 2006). Both works should be used with caution and always checked against the sources.

242. *Histoire* 2.26–27; Landau, 'Erweiterte Fassungen' 326; Cushing, *Papacy and Law* 5–7.

243. The manuscripts are Vat. lat. 1363, Paris, BnF, lat. 12519, and Cambridge, CCC, 269, all from the twelfth century. According to Landau, 'Erweiterte Fassungen' 326 they contain 'Form A [...] in der ursprünglichen Fassung ohne Zusätze'. However, as will be discussed below, even these three manuscripts contain a few additions, i.e. canons not mentioned in the *capitulatio* and/ or not found in other manuscripts of the A version.

244. Landau, 'Erweiterte Fassungen' 326.

245. *Anselmi episcopi Lucensis collectio canonum una cum collectione minore*, ed. Friedrich Thaner (Innsbruck 1906–15). Thaner's edition extends only to the first part of the penultimate book. For an 'implicit edition' of the missing parts, see Cushing, *Papacy and Law* Appendix II and the *Clavis* database; for a partial edition of book 13, see Pásztor, 'Lotta'. Unless otherwise stated, I have used Thaner's base manuscript Vat. lat. 1363 to supplement the edition.

246. This was stressed by Fowler-Magerl, *Clavis* 139–140.

247. Fournier, 'Collections romaines' 301–327 (summarized in *Histoire* 2.29–32); Fuhrmann, *Einfluß und Verbreitung* 2.511–519; Cushing, *Papacy and Law* 70–75 and 95–102; Jasper, 'Beginning' s.v. Anselm; Cushing, 'Anselm and Burchard'; Fowler-Magerl, *Clavis* esp. 140–141 and 150–155. See also the intriguing suggestions by Schon, 'Redaktion' 506 suggesting that Anselm may have used, and also reworked, the Cluny version of Pseudo-Isidore.

248. Cushing, 'Recension Bb'.

on in the very workshop that had produced the first version of the collection. The *Barberiniana*, while not a source of Anselm, is linked to many of the collections with which Anselm's *Collectio* shares material.[249]

Perhaps the single most important of these collections was *74T*. This relatively recent collection provided Anselm with both material and structure; no less than 250 of *74T*'s 314 canons, above all from Pseudo-Isidore and Gregory the Great, are also found in Anselm's collection.[250] Clearly, *74T* was a model for Anselm. Both the title and the content of his first book on Roman primacy ('De primatu Romanae ecclesiae') have a parallel in *74T*;[251] indeed no less than four of Anselm's books begin with canons taken from *74T* and found there as the first canons of the respective *tituli*.[252] Evidently, Anselm's book four on privileges is modelled on the third title of *74T* and contains it in its entirety.[253] Yet it is also true that Anselm used *74T* (like other formal sources) independently. While he did model some of his books on *74T*, others have no such model, and while he took most canons of *74T* into his collection, he rearranged them almost completely, and generously supplemented them with other materials. After all, *74T* was a small collection, and virtually silent on several issues Anselm was interested in, in particular marriage and penance.[254]

For these topics in particular, Anselm used Burchard's *Liber decretorum*.[255] While none of Anselm's books is directly modelled on Burchard's collection, he clearly engaged with this work. Significantely, Anselm chose the canon found at the beginning of Burchard as the opening canon of his own collection.[256] While using the same text, Anselm put the canon in a very different context. The excerpt is taken from Pseudo-Anaclete on the beginning of priesthood in Saint Peter, but while Burchard stressed

249. Kathleen Grace Cushing, '"Intermediate" and Minor Collections: The Case of the *Collectio canonum Barberiniana*', *Readers, Texts and Compilers in the Earlier Middle Ages: Studies in Medieval Canon Law in Honour of Linda Fowler-Magerl*, ed. eadem and Martin Brett (CFC; Aldershot and Farnham 2009) 73–85, here at 81. See also Giuseppe Fornasari, 'Collectio canonum Barberiniana' *Apollinaris* 36 (1963) 127–141 (description) and 214–297 (edition).

250. Fuhrmann, *Einfluß und Verbreitung* 2.516; Fowler-Magerl, *Clavis* 141.

251. Compare Anselm 1.1–2 (ed. Thaner 6) to title, c. 21, and c. 2 of *74T* (ed. Gilchrist 19, 30, and 20). The material source is JK †4 for both canons (*pace* Thaner), but Anselm 1.1 seems to be taken from Burchard 1.1 while Anselm 1.2 is taken from *74T* c. 2. Note that Thaner's edition is not faithful to the A version when it comes to rubrics; the title of the Anselm A version is 'Liber de primatu sancte Romane ecclesiae' (Vat. lat. 1363, fol. 3v).

252. Anselm 2.1, 4.1, 6.1, and 9.1 = *74T* cc. 1, 24, 174, and 205 (= the opening canons of *tituli* 1, 3, 22, and 30), respectively.

253. Anselm 4.1–9 and 13–18 = *74T* cc. 24–38 (= *74T* tit. 3).

254. *74T* cc. 251–254 (penance) and 271–275 all figure in Anselm's collection, too, but evidently contribute very little to his book 10 (on marriage), and nothing to book 13 (the penitential).

255. Fuhrmann, *Einfluß und Verbreitung* 2.516 (five of Anselm's Pseudo-Isidorian canons from Burchard); Fowler-Magerl, *Clavis* 141 (Burchard mainly used for penance).

256. Anselm 1.1 from Burchard 1.1; the ultimate source is Ps.-Anaclete, JK †3.

the equality within this order, Anselm very clearly took this text as one proof text among many others for the primacy of the Roman church and papal supremacy. Anselm's first book mixes canons on the primacy of the Roman church, the Apostolic See, Saint Peter, and the pope in a way that strongly suggests that it was above all the pope in whom all these privileges rested. This also marks a contrast between Anselm and Deusdedit; unlike the latter, Anselm very clearly put the focus on Saint Peter.[257]

It has long been observed that Anselm must have shared materials with other compilers, above all Deusdedit. The shape, content, and influence of these lost 'intermediate collections' ('collections intermédiaires' or 'Zwischensammlungen') has been subject to scholarly debate since the late nineteenth century.[258] Fournier in particular made far-reaching claims about a very large intermediate collection available to many Gregorian compilers.[259] Subsequent research has often explored this issue but only relatively rarely confirmed the use of identifiable *Zwischensammlungen*. Sickel famously introduced the hypothetical *Privilegiensammlung* to explain some of the overlap between Anselm and Deusdedit, and Fuhrmann asserted that Anselm used various intermediate collections for his Pseudo-Isidore.[260] For other materials, less speculation is needed. Anselm clearly shared manipulated versions of letters of Nicholas II and Gregory VII with Deusdedit.[261] As for excerpts from papal registers, Perels was able to demonstrate with great clarity that Anselm and Deusdedit must have used an intermediate source for the letters of Nicholas I; this source may also have been available to Bonizo, but if so, he used in only sporadically.[262] Almost equally interestingly, the evidence is less decisive for other papal letters. In the case of Stephen V, Anselm may have used an intermediary source also available to Deusdedit.[263] Anselm also used a source similar to *2L/8P*, or several sources which ended up in this collection. The exact relation between *2L/8P* and Anselm remain to be studied, but for

---

257. Saint Paul is only mentioned in Anselm 1.66–69.

258. The literature is vast. See *Histoire* 2.9–13; Ryan, *Peter Damiani* 10–11; Fuhrmann, *Einfluß und Verbreitung* 2.518–519, 526–527, 531–532, and 538–539; Hageneder, 'Papstregister' 322–326; Horst, *Polycarpus* 46–54; Jasper, 'Beginning' esp. 78–79 and 121–122; Fowler-Magerl, *Clavis* esp. 14, 140–141, 150–155, and 162–163; Kéry, 'Kanonessammlungen' 291–293; Rolker, 'Bonizo' 59–78.

259. Fournier, 'Collections romaines' esp. 391–392 (various intermediary sources nothing but 'diverses parties d'une vaste collection' available to many Gregorian compilers of canon law collections).

260. Sickel, *Privilegium* 76–81 (*Privilegiensammlung*); Fuhrmann, 'Constitutum' 16–18 (Donation of Constantine); idem, *Einfluß und Verbreitung* 2.519 (Pseudo-Isidore).

261. Nicholas II, JL 4405 and 4431a as found in Deusdedit 1.168–169 (137–138) (ed. Wolf von Glanvell 107) = Anselm 6.12–13 (ed. Thaner 272–273); Gregory VII, JL 5201 as found in Deusdedit 4.184 (106) (ed. Wolf von Glanvell 489–491, here at 490) = Anselm 1.80 (ed. Thaner 53–55). On the manipulations, see above (notes 168–170).

262. Perels, 'Briefe' 78–86 and 92–94.

263. Jasper, 'Beginning' 133.

a number of excerpts from Saint Augustine and the letters of Pelagius it seems clear that Anselm and Bonizo (but not Deusdedit) used a source similar to *2L/8P*.[264] This collection also contains a large number of canons taken from the *Capitula Angilramni*; the only other collection from which this selection is known is Anselm's collection.[265] Finally, *2L/8P* preserves pseudo-Isidorian material which has parallels in Anselm, Deusdedit, and Bonizo.[266] It may be that *2L/8P* compiler, working around 1100, had access to a set of smaller collections used by Anselm (with some also known to other compilers) and united them into one collection.

Another collection also provided Anselm with very rare letters of Gelasius ultimately coming from the ancient *Avellana*.[267] In addition, Anselm also seems to have used another intermediary collection for (other) letters of Gelasius. This can be inferred from a comparison of the collections of Anselm and Deusdedit with a series of fifteen Gelasius fragments in Atto's *Breviary*, contains material mostly not found in earlier collections; yet all but four are also in Anselm or Deusdedit (or both), and the *Britannica* has all but three of Atto's fifteen canons.[268]

In any case, Anselm and Deusdedit clearly drew on common sources. While it is not possible to prove who compiled these intermediate collections, at least in some cases Deusdedit seems a plausible candidate. Some of the material that scholarship has assumed to show evidence Deusdedit and Anselm relied on shared sources is highly relevant to those issues which were of special significance to Deusdedit and on which he was ready to tamper with his proof texts. This is particularly true for the supposed *Privilegiensammlung*, the unusual version of the Donation of Constantine, and materials on papal elections which Deusdedit gathered mainly to refute the Papal Election Decree of 1059. If one assumes the *Privilegiensammlung* was available to Deusdedit and Anselm (and not compiled by Deusdedit himself), Deusdedit clearly made much fuller use of it than Anselm. Likewise, Deusdedit was more keenly interested in papal elections, the important role of Saint Paul, and the position of the lower-ranking cardinals. If Deusdedit was not responsible for the manipu-

---

264. See Rolker, 'Bonizo' 83–84 (Augustine) and 84–89 (Pelagius). In fact, *2L/8P* is the lost intermediary sources Berschin postulated (though his assumptions about Deusdedit are partly misguided); see Berschin, *Bonizo von Sutri* 73–74.

265. Rolker, 'Bonizo' 89. The series is found in Assisi, Biblioteca del Sacro Convento, 227, fols. 110vb–112rb (but not Vat. lat. 3832); it was unknown to Schon, *Capitula Angilramni*.

266. See Bonizo 4.48–75 (ed. Perels 133–144) and the corresponding canons found in Deusdedit 1.57 (47) to 1.132–133 (108) (ed. Wolf von Glanvell 60–91); many of these canons are found in Anselm's collection, too. For details, see Rolker, 'Bonizo' 89–96.

267. Otto Günther, *Avellana-Studien* (Vienna 1896), here at 102–110; Jasper, 'Beginning' 85 (cautiously noting that *2L/8P* 'may have used the *Avellana* for some Gelasian excerpts').

268. On Atto 39.21–35 (ed. Mai 81–82), see above note 48.

lations found in these texts, it is still true that the selection of these (very rare) materials suited his interests very well. For Deusdedit, this can be shown from his canonical collection as well as his polemic writings, while the same is not true for Anselm. For the dossiers of excerpts quoting papal letters 'ex registro' Deusdedit also seems to be the more likely candidate of the two to have compiled them.[269] After all, Deusdedit (but not Anselm) had access to the Lateran archives, and some of the shared materials can be seen as preparatory works for Deusdedit's collection much more than for Anselm's. On the whole, Anselm seems to take more texts from Deusdedit's working materials than vice versa.

Nonetheless, whatever the direction of borrowing, Anselm clearly had his own mind on many issues. This is perhaps most evident from the first books of the two collections, which at a first glance are so similar (both opening with Roman primacy) but in the end make very different points. While for Deusdedit it was fundamentally important to stress the difference between the pope and the Roman church, Anselm rather merged the two, effectively presenting Roman primacy as vested much more in the pope alone than Deusdedit had done.

While a complete study of Anselm's formal sources would be far beyond the scope of the present study, a short view on the *Liber contra Wibertum* may be helpful, as it can shed light on the way Anselm worked with his canon law material. Specifically, the *Liber* contains a series of eight very short canons from various fathers which evidently are taken from the so-called 'error series', a mini-collection which had some independent circulation.[270] Interestingly, Anselm did not use it for his *Collectio*, but it was taken up by both Deusdedit and the *Barberiniana*.[271] The versions of the 'error series' in Anselm's *Liber*, Deusdedit's *Collectio*, and the *Barberiniana* are related but not identical; none of the three works can directly depend on either of the others for these texts. The canons Anselm quotes in the *Liber* are also found in Deusdedit's *Collectio* and in the *Barberiniana*, which both contain more of the series. The sequence of the (shared) canons is the same in Deusdedit and *Barberiniana*; Anselm has a different one. In one case, the *Barberiniana* shares a common misattribution with Anselm

---

269. Peitz, *Originalregister* 133–146 und 246–265.

270. *Liber contra Wibertum* (ed. Bernheim, MGH Ldl 1.526 line 16 to 527 line 9). On the 'error series', see Fowler-Magerl, 'Vier Kanonessammlungen' 132–135; eadem, *Clavis* 96 (calling it a 'mini-collection'); Busch, *Liber de honore* 61–62 and 102–114; Cushing, 'Intermediate Collections' 76 and 83. The 'error series' was used in polemic writings, e.g. Wido of Ferrara (ed. Dümmler MGH Ldl 1.544), *De unitate ecclesiae conservanda* (ibid. 2.223), Deusdedit's *Contra invasores* (ed. Sackur ibid. 2.335–336), and Placidus of Nonantola (ed. Heinemann and Sackur ibid. 2.627). It takes its name from the incipit of the first canon: 'Error cui non resistitur, approbatur', which later became widely know via Gratian D.83 c.3 (ed. Friedberg 293).

271. Deusdedit 4.56–65 (48) (ed. Wolf von Glanvell 427–429); *Barberiniana* 2.1–9.

not found in Deusdedit's *Collectio* but, interestingly, in Deusdedit's *Libellus contra invasores*.[272] In another case, however, Anselm's *Liber* shares a rare variant with Deusdedit's collection against the *Barberiniana*.[273] It is possible that Anselm used a collection similar to the *Barberiniana* for his *Collectio*,[274] but the 'error series' offers no cogent proof for this.

4.4.4 Anselm on Papal Elections

As mentioned above, Anselm compiled his collection almost at the same time as Deusdedit, worked often with the same materials, and like Deusdedit was a loyal supporter of Gregory VII. These similarities have rightly been noted by grouping Anselm and Deusdedit among 'Gregorian' canonists; at the same time, these very similarities make it also possible to study how differently 'Gregorian' canonists treated important issues. The most evident case is perhaps the canon law on papal elections. As mentioned above, Deusdedit opposed the Papal Election Decree of 1059 and sought to strengthen the position of the Roman clergy (above all that of the cardinal priests) in papal elections. To this end, he chose not to insert the Papal Election Decree of 1059 in his collection, but instead drew on the synodal decrees of 769 and manipulated letters of Nicholas II.

While few compilers of canonical collections were so preoccupied with papal elections as Deusdedit was, many made similar choices concerning their proof texts. Indeed, most compilers of canon law collections traditionally labelled 'Gregorian'—namely Anselm of Lucca, Bonizo of Sutri, and Gregory of San Grisogono—all ignored the 1059 decree, quoted from the 769 Lateran synod, and have Nicholas' letters in the form found in Deusdedit. (Atto of San Marco did not deal with papal elections in his collection.) Yet only in the case of Gregory—a cardinal priest like Deusdedit—can this readily be explained by a desire to strengthen the position of cardinal priests. For Anselm and Bonizo, two (exiled) bishops, their choices are less readily

272. *Liber contra Wibertum* (ed. Bernheim, MGH Ldl 1.526 lines 36–37 and 37–39); Deusdedit 4.56–57 (48) (ed. Wolf von Glanvell 427–428); *Barberiniana* 2.1–2. The sources are Pope Felix III (II), JK 595 (ed. Thiel 236) and Pseudo-Eleutherus JK †68 (ed. Hinschius 127). The *Liber* and the *Barberiniana* attribute both canons to Innocent. Deusdedit in his *Collectio* attributes the canon to Eleutherus, but in his *Libellus contra invasores* apparently ('Item idem') to Innocent (ed. Sackur, MGH Ldl 2.335)! Busch, *Liber de honore* 107–108 assumed that Deusdedit relied on a version which attributed the canon to Innocent, but later corrected it from Pseudo-Isidore. However, Deusdedit's collection predates his *Libellus*.

273. *Liber contra Wibertum* (ed. Bernheim, MGH Ldl 1.529 line 9) and Deusdedit 4.56–65 (48) (ed. Wolf von Glanvell 428 line 14) have 'non occurrit' while the *Barberiniana* has the more common 'concurrit'. Busch, *Liber de honore* 106 n. 140 pointed out that Alger of Liège and Gratian have this version, too. According to the *Clavis* database, the only other collection to have the 'non occurrit' version is the Turin 7L (TU06.068.04 in *Clavis*).

274. Cushing, 'Recension Bb' 81 took up Fowler-Magerl's suggestions that the question of a 'direct use by Anselm in any version or Deusdedit, though largely discredited, may [...] merit reinvestigation'.

explained. In fact, given that the 1059 decree is often seen as a key text of the 'Gregorian reform', scholars have seen a contradiction between the Gregorian attitude of Anselm and Bonizo, on the one hand, and the contents of their collections. In the case of Bonizo, it is clear that he knew the 1059 decree; while he did not include it in his canonical collection, he quoted from it in his polemic *Liber ad amicum*. Indeed, the *Liber ad amicum* shows him to be an outspoken critic of the Papal Election Decree. In the light of Bonizo's loyalty to the reform papacy, some scholars tried to explain the perceived contradiction by claiming that Bonizo did in fact not know the *genuine* version of the 1059 decree; his criticism, Krause and Berschin asssumed, rather was directed against anti-Gregorian interpretations of Nicholas's decree, or against the (forged) imperial version of the decree.[275]

The case is different again with Anselm of Lucca. Unlike Deusdedit or Bonizo, he is not known to have criticized the Papal Election Decree; unlike Atto, Deusdedit, and Gregory of San Grisogono he was not a cardinal himself, so less involved in conflicts within this group. It may also be relevant that Anselm was close to Alexander II, who directly succeeded Nicholas II in 1061; he was elected by the very cardinal bishops whose position the 1059 decree had strengthened. One could also argue that Gregory VII, in naming Anselm as potential successor, evidently was not concerned by the synod of 769 provisions that only Romans were *papabiles*. However, this all does not tell us much about Anselm's own position. For this, we have to turn again to his canonical collection.

Fortunately for such an analysis, Anselm's collection contains rich materials on almost every aspect of papal office. Book six in particular is relevant as it deals with episcopal elections in general and, especially in its first part, the election of the Roman pontiff. On these topics, Anselm largely used the same kind of sources as Deusdedit. Specifically, he gathered excerpts from the Roman synod of 499, the *Epitome Juliani*, Justinian's Code, the *Constitutio Romana*, a manipulated version of letters of Pope Nicholas II, the account of the *Liber pontificalis* on the Lateran synod of 769, the acts of the same synod, and many other authorities. Concerning Anselm's view of the 1059 decree, the manipulated letters of Nicholas are perhaps the most straightforward case: Anselm inserts them at the beginning of his book six,[276] and his rubric highlights what also is clear from the canons

---

275. Krause, *Papstwahldekret* 192–193; Berschin, *Bonizo von Sutri* 50.

276. Nicholas II, JL 4405 and JL 4431a as found in Anselm 6.12–13 (ed. Thaner 272–273). While the first canon is absent from some manuscripts (see Thaner's edition), both canons are in all version A manuscripts including the Cambridge manuscript unknown to Thaner: Cambridge, CCC, 269, fol. 107r.

themselves: The pope is elected by the cardinals.[277] Crucially, no mention is made of any special rights of the cardinal bishops (a key point of the 1059 decree). From these canons alone, one could suspect Anselm followed Deusdedit in his opposition to Nicholas's Papal Election Decree.

Yet if we turn to the Lateran synod of 769 in Anselm's collection, a different picture emerges. The synod provided Deusdedit with what he valued as key texts on the the role of cardinal deacons and priests in papal elections, specifically the requirement that any candidate had to be 'made deacon or cardinal priest' before he could become pontiff (Deusdedit 1.206) and that the candidate had be 'one of the cardinal priests or deacons' (Deusdedit 2.131b).[278] So what did Anselm make of these fairly straightforward canons? As for the second key text (Deusdedit 2.131b), it apparently was absent from the orginal version of Anselm's collection. Only two manuscripts of the 'A' version of Anselm's *Collectio* contain it as part of an addition to book one ('canon 91'). This canon belongs to a set of three texts which are found in one, two, or all three of the manuscripts of the A version at the very end of the first book.[279] However, even in the manuscripts which contain canon 91, the *capitulatio* does not mention it. This all strongly suggests that book one originally ended with canon 89, although the addition of canons 90–92 seems to have happened early.

Before we can speculate on the textual history of 'canon 91', let us first turn to Deusdedit's second key text on the role of cardinal deacons and cardinal priests (Deusdedit 1.206). This canon does appear in different Anselm versions and derivative collections like the Vatican 13L.[280] The text of the canon is the same in all collections: no one can be promoted to the 'pontificate' (*honor pontificatus*) unless he was first cardinal deacon or priest.[281] Yet there is some room for interpretation, as the canon itself does not tell whether 'pontificate' referred to the episcopal office in general or the papal office in particular. This information can only be deduced from the context or the rubrics. Deusdedit in his rubric made it quite clear that

277. Anselm 6.12 (ed. Thaner 272; Cambridge, CCC, 269, fol. 107r).

278. Deusdedit 1.255 (206) (ed. Wolf von Glanvell 146) as quoted above; Deusdedit 2.161 (131b) (ed. Wolf von Glanvell 268): 'Oportebat, ut [...] unus de cardinalibus presbiteris aut diaconibus consecraretur' (ibid, 268).

279. Cambridge, CCC, 269, fol. 27v (Anselm 1.90, also in the *capitulatio*); Paris, BnF, lat. 12519, fol. 60ra–rb (Anselm 1.90–91, neither of which is mentioned in the *capitulatio*); Vat. lat. 1363, fols. 26v–27v (canons 90–92, none of them mentioned in the *capitulatio*). Canons 90 and 91 are numbered in the manuscripts containing them, but the third text is not.

280. Anselm 7.27 (ed. Thaner 375; Cambridge, CCC, 269, fol. 146r–146v); Anselm A Aucta 6.195; Anselm B 6.25; 13L (Vatican) 4.48; 7L (Vienna) 1.6.6; *Polycarpus* 1.4.6.

281. Deusdedit 1.255 (206) (ed. Wolf von Glanvell 146) = Anselm 7.27 (ed. Thaner 375): '[...] ut nullus unquam laicorum neque ex alio ordine presumat, nisi per distinctos gradus ascendens diaconus aut presbiter factus fuerit cardinalis, ad sacrum pontificatus honorem promoveri'.

the 'pontificate' in question was the papal office;[282] Gregory of San Grisogono likewise left no doubt.[283] Anselm, in contrast, has a rubric presenting
the canon as being directed against rash promotion of laymen.[284] Perhaps
even more important is his decision to place the canon not at the beginning
of book six (where papal elections are dealt with) but rather in book *seven*,
and more specifically in the midst of a long series of canons on ordinations
of priests and bishops.[285] If read in this context, there is nothing to suggest
that the *honor pontificatus* in question had anything to do with papal office;
vice versa, any reader of Anselm's collection looking up the canons on papal elections in the relevant book six would not come across this canon.

In other words, Anselm apparently dropped one of Deusdedit's key
texts completely (Deusdedit 2.131b), and presented the other in a way
that effectively neutralized the provision that only priests and deacons of
the Roman church could become pope (Deusdedit 1.206). Thus, no one
looking up the relevant book six of Anselm's collection on papal elections
would find either of Deusdedit's key texts. Here, only the (relatively uncontroversial) provision that the cardinals had the right to elect the pope
was found.

Yet the story does not end here. The original form of Anselm's collection may have dropped or hidden the excerpts from the 769 synod Deusdedit had collected, but these texts reappear in later versions. As already
mentioned, some of the 769 provisions (including Deusdedit 2.131b) are
found appended at the end of book one in two manuscripts of the A version of Anselm's collection.[286] The same material is also found in the A
Aucta, B, and C versions of Anselm's collection, and also in the *Collection in Three Books*.[287] In the Venice manuscript of the A Aucta version,
the canon is found not at the end of book one, but rather at the end of
book six; it is slightly more complete than the version in the manuscripts

282. Deusdedit, *capitulatio* (ed. Wolf von Glanvell 18 line 29): 'Ut de presbiteris vel diaconis
eiusdem [scil. Romane] ecclesie eligatur episcopus'. Deusdedit refers the reader to no less than
six canons on this topic.

283. *Polycarpus* 1.4.7 (ed. Erdmann and Horst 30) belongs to the canons 'De electione et ordinatione Romani pontificis' (ed. Erdmann and Horst 24).

284. Anselm 7.27 (ed. Thaner 375): 'ut nullus laicus nisi per distinctos gradus ad presbiteratum
ascendat'. Anselm 7.1–106 are canons on the lower clergy (priests, regular canons, minor orders)
in general, and specifically the requirements for ordinations; none of them refers to episcopal, let
alone papal, ordinations.

285. On papal elections, see in particular Anselm 6.1–2, 6, and 12–14 (ed. Thaner 265–266, 270,
272–273).

286. Anselm 1.91 as found in Paris, BnF, lat. 12519, fol. 60ra and Vat. lat. 1363, fol. 27r–v.

287. Anselm A Aucta 6.195a. See Giuseppe Motta, 'La redazione A *"aucta"* della *Collectio An-
selmi episcopi Lucensis*', *Studia in honorem eminentissimi Cardinalis Alphonsi M. Stickler*, ed. Rosalio
J. Castillo Lara (Studia e textus historiae iuris canonici 7; Rome 1992) 375–449, here at 404–405
(Anselm A Aucta, B, and C); Fowler-Magerl, *Clavis* 146 (Anselm A Aucta, *3L*).

Table 2: Deusdedit and Anselm on Papal Elections: Key Proof Texts found in their Canonical Collections

Material source	Deusdedit	ed. Wolf von Glanvell	Anselm A[1]	ed. Thaner
Nicholas II, JL 4405 (ed. Jasper, MGH Conc. 8.402 lines 19–24)	1.168 (137)	107 lines 8–12	6.12	272
Nicholas II, JL 4431a (ed. Jasper, MGH Conc. 8.383 lines 2–13)	1.169 (138)	107 lines 14–24	6.13	272–273
Liber pontificalis (Stephen III) / Lateran 769 (ed. Duchesne 1.468 line 1 to 476 line 3)	1.255 (206)	146 lines 2–11	7.27 (!)	375
Lateran 769, *actio* III (ed. Werminghoff, MGH Conc. 2.1:86–87)	2.161 (131a)[2]	268 lines 9–10	*deest*	
dito	2.161 (131b)	268 lines 11–14	*deest*	
dito	2.162 (131c)	268 lines 17–30	*deest*	
Lateran 769, *actio* IV (ed. Werminghoff, MGH Conc. 2.1:87–88)	2.163 (131d)	269 lines 3–7	*deest*	
dito	2.163 (131e)	269 lines 7–9	*deest*	
dito	2.163 (131f)	269 lines 10–15	*deest*	
dito	2.163 (131g)	269 lines 15–16	*deest*	
dito	2.163 (131h)	269 lines 16–18	*deest*	
dito	2.163 (131i)	269 lines 18–20	*deest*	
dito	2.163 (131j)	269 lines 21–26	*deest*	
dito	2.163 (131k)	269 lines 26–28	*deest*	
dito	2.163 (131l)	269 line 28–270 line 2	*deest*	
dito	2.163 (131m)	270 lines 2–5	*deest*	

1. In the context of the present study, I assume that Anselm A as edited by Thaner is the 'original version', and specifically that the canons found at the end of book one in some manuscripts were only added later (see below for discussion).

2. Both in the edition and in the *Clavis* database, the texts numbered 'CXXXI' in the manuscript are divided into three canons; Wolf von Glanvell's '161', '162', and '163' correspond to 'DU02.131a', '131b', and '132' in Clavis. In the manuscript, however, all of them are numbered 'CXXXI'; this section is divided into thirteen sub-sections by 'item' and, in one case, 'Actio IIII'. For this reason, I count Wolf von Glanvell's '161–162' as '131a–b' and have subdivided his '163' into canons '131c' to '131m'.

of the A version.[288] In the only other manuscript of the A Aucta version (the Mantua copy), most of this canon was added in the margin at the beginning of book six.[289] The canons are still very visibly additions, but the insertion of this material in book six is significant, as this was where Anselm's collection (in all versions) dealt with episcopal and papal elections. We may assume that this was a conscious choice as the A Aucta version in book six also contains another canon from Lateran 769 which in the A version was (mis-)placed in book seven and presented (by the rubric) as a canon against rash promotions.[290] In the A Aucta version, however, it is placed into book six and given a new rubric unmistakably referring to papal elections.[291] Much of these observations on the A Aucta versions also hold for the B version which closely linked to the A Aucta version by virtue of shared additions and rubrics.[292] The canons on papal election found as additions to book six in the A Aucta version in the B version are part and parcel of this book, and placed towards at the beginning of book six among other canons on episcopal and papal elections.[293] Finally, the Vatican *Collection in Thirteen Books*, a collection from the mid-twelfth century which heavily draws on Anselm's collection (and the *Panormia*), also contains the additional canons on papal elections of the A Aucta version, but this time in book one, where they are found in one block following canons on papal primacy.[294] Unlike the A Aucta and B versions of Anselm's collection, the Vatican 13L retains the rubrics of the A version for the first excerpt from the Roman synod at least in the *capitulatio*.[295]

288. Motta, 'Redazione' 404–405. The first sub-canon (Motta's 6.195a) is less complete in Vat. lat. 1363 and Paris, BnF, lat. 12519.

289. According to the *Clavis* database, Anselm A Aucta 6.195 is found in the margins of the Mantua manuscript (AD06.195a–e). Yet the canon found in Mantova, BC, 318, fol. 189v is considerably shorter than in Venezia, Biblioteca Marciana, lat. IV.55. The error in *Clavis* is apparently due to a misunderstanding of Motta's apparatus that first seems to suggest that all of canon 6.195 were found in the Mantua manuscript but in fact later on reports the omissions (Motta, 'Redazione' 405). For details, see Table 3 below.

290. Anselm 7.27, rubric (ed. Thaner 375): 'Ut nullus laicus nisi per distinctos gradus ad presbiteratum ascendat' as discussed above.

291. Anselm A Aucta 6.195a, rubric: 'Ut nullus laicorum presumat venire in electione Romani pontificis'. See Anselm B 6.25, rubric: 'Ut nullus eligatur pontifex Romanus nisi unus ex cardinalibus, presbiteris aut diaconibus'. The information is taken from the *Clavis* database (AD06.195a and AE06.025, respectively).

292. Fowler-Magerl, *Clavis* 146.

293. Anselm B 6.12 (JL 4405), 13 (JL 4431a), and 25–25d (Lateran 769) according to the *Clavis* database (AE06.012).

294. Vatican 13L 1.46 (JL 4405), 47a (JL 4431a), 47b–48 (Lateran 769) (Vat. lat. 1361, fol. 42ra–va). Note that one excerpt of the Roman synod (= Deusdedit 2.131b) was merged with the manipulated version of JL 4431a; this may indicate that the material was inserted, perhaps first as a marginal addition which was imperfectly integrated in the main text by a later scribe.

295. Vatican 13L 1.48, *capitulatio* (Vat. lat. 1361, fol. 10va–vb): 'Ut nullus presumat ad ordines nisi per distinctos gradus accedere.' The rubric is not repeated in the collection itself (Vat. lat. 1361, fol. 42ra). See the rubrics to Anselm 7.27 (ed. Thaner 375), Anselm A Aucta 6.195a, and Anselm B 6.25 as quoted above (notes 292 and 293).

Table 3: The Canon Law on Papal Election in Different Anselm Versions

Material Source	Deusdedit	ed. Wolf von Glanvell (page and line)	Anselm A (original form)	Anselm A (Vatican and Paris mss)	Anselm A Aucta (Venice ms)	Anselm A Aucta (Mantova ms)	Anselm B	13L (Vatican)
JL 4405	1.168 (137)	107.8–12	6.12	6.12	6.12	6.12	6.12	1.46
JL 4431a	1.169 (138)	107.14–24	6.13	6.13	6.13	6.13	6.13	1.47a
Liber pontificalis	1.255 (206)	146.2–11	7.27	7.27	6.195a[1]	ad 6.3–4 (marg.)[2]	6.25	1.48
Lateran 769, *actio* III	2.161 (131a)	268.9–10	*deest*	*deest*	*deest*	*deest*	*deest*	*deest*
dito	2.161 (131b)	268.11–14	*deest*	1.91a[3]	6.195b	ad 6.3–4 (marg.)	6.25a	1.47b
dito	2.162 (131c)	268.17–30	*deest*	1.91b[4]	6.195c[5]	*deest*	*deest*	*deest*
Lateran 769, *actio* IV	2.163 (131d-i)	269.3–20	*deest*	*deest*	*deest*	*deest*	*deest*	*deest*
dito	2.163 (131j)	269.21–26	*deest*	1.91b	6.195d	ad 6.3–4 (marg.)	6.25b	*deest*
dito	2.163 (131k)	269.26–28	*deest*	*deest*	*deest*	*deest*	*deest*	*deest*
dito	2.163 (131l)	269.28-270.2	*deest*	1.91c	6.195d	*deest*	*deest*	*deest*
dito	2.163 (131m)	270.2–5	*deest*	1.91c	6.195e	ad 6.3–4 (marg.)	6.25c	*deest*
Pontificale Romanum	1.250 (201)	144.15–23	*deest*	*deest*	6.196 (to 'electio fiat' only)	*deest*	6.11 (to 'electio fiat' only)	*deest*
Rome 862	1.149 (123)	98.19–22	*deest*	*deest*	6.197	ad 6.3–4 (marg.)	6.25d	*deest*

1. From 'Nullus' on only.

2. In Mantova, BC, 318, the canons under discussion here are not found in the collection itself but were added in the margin of fol. 189v, next to Anselm A Aucta 6.3–4 (dealing with papal elections); the sequence of the texts is the same as in the other manuscript of the A Aucta version (Venezia, Biblioteca Marciana, lat. IV.55).

3. Anselm 1.90–92 are absent from Thaner's edition; canon 91 is found in Vat. lat. 1363, fol. 27r–v and Paris, BnF, lat. 12519, fol. 60ra–rb, but not Cambridge, CCC, 269. Canon 91a only begins with 'Quod'.

4. Vat. lat. 1363, fols. 26v–27v and Paris, BnF, lat. 12519, fol. 60rb share a gap here. Some three lines (assuming his exemplar was written in long lines) were lost because of a homeoteleuton. 'Deductus' is the last word of the line; the next would have been 'tunc', but the scribe instead jumped to 'cuncti', thus omitting 'tunc optimates – in eo'. In addition, the canon ends with 'observandum'.

5. According to *Clavis*, the canon in Venezia, Biblioteca Marciana, lat. IV.55 too ends with 'observandum'; I was not able to check whether it also shares the 'tunc optimates – in eo' gap with Vat. lat. 1363, fols. 26v–27v and Paris, BnF, lat. 12519, fol. 60rb (see last note).

So Deusdedit in his *Collectio* presented unusually rich materials on papal elections, including two canons clearly stating that only cardinal priests and deacons could be elected pope. These materials in all likelihood were all known to Anselm of Lucca, who however in his collection dropped one of Deusdedit's two key texts and altered the meaning of the other, which he placed in book seven of his collection. Yet the texts Anselm dropped were quickly (re-)introduced. Already the version behind the Paris and the Vatican manuscript of the A version has more canons on papal elections from the 769 Lateran synod, though not in book six. In the A Aucta version all canons on papal elections discussed above are united in one book (rather than scattered over three books), although still very much as additions. Only in the B version are these canons integrated into the collection again, and find their place at the beginning of book six among other canons on episcopal and papal elections.

Step by step, and presumably independently from each other, these compilers undid most of Anselm's editorial choices concerning the papal election law coming from the 769 synod as found in Deusdedit's collection. It is possible that these canons absent from the original version of Anselm's collection but found in manuscripts of the A, A Aucta, and B versions were transmitted in a mini-collection similar to (or perhaps even related to) the one extant in the Mantua copy of the A Aucta version of Anselm's collection.[296] In any case the different versions show that Anselm's collection was indeed a 'living text', with canons being dropped, added to (at the end of a book, in the margins, or in separate florilegia), moved from one book to the other, and given changing rubrics. All these changes, even if they concerned only a handful of texts, required very careful reading and can often be understood as expressing changing attitudes towards delicate legal issues such as papal elections. In particular, Anselm of Lucca himself—while closely cooperating with Deusdedit— did not adopt those canons which could be understood as challenging the Papal Election Decree, but later compilers reworking Anselm's collection undid most of his editorial decisions in this respect, re-entering canons he had omitted and bringing (again) together what he separated in different books. This suggests that these anonymous compilers took part in the ongoing debate on the status of the Papal Election Decree, which for decades was not taken into any major canon law collection.

---

296. On the florilegium in Mantova, BC, 318, fols. 2r–3v, see Fowler-Magerl, *Clavis* 147. The florilegium contains some canons which are also in the A Aucta version (but not the A version), but not the canons on papal elections under discussion here.

4.4.5 Reception: 'From Polemic to Handbook'

As the example of the canons on papal elections has made clear, the various versions of Anselm's collection differ—sometimes only in detail, but sometimes very considerably. This is true of many canonical collections, but Anselm's collection stands out as being reworked extremely quickly in very different ways.[297] They have attracted very different degrees of scholarly attention, mainly not because of their merit as important collections in their own right. The A version has attracted most attention for the simply reason that Theiner's edition largely presents this version of Anselm's collection, though he sometimes followed other traditions and omitted the last part of the collection. The A' version, as Peter Landau dubbed it, has attracted special attention as the version used by Gratian.[298] More research is also needed into the way Anselm's collection became relatively widely diffused (as least compared to other Gregorian collections), but the extant manuscripts suggest that the collection was mainly known in twelfth-century northern Italy. Evidence for reception outside Italy is relatively scarce, except for two Italian manuscripts making their way across the Alps.[299]

Much more scholarship is needed into the various versions, their genesis, and their reception. In the context of the present book, a few examples must suffice to indicate the fate of Anselm's collection as a 'living text'. For this, let us turn to the rubrics, an important element of the collection. These 'headlines' to individual canons could be used merely to summarize the content of a canon, but also could influence its interpretation. Anselm was well aware of the latter possibility, and in many cases composed pointed rubrics for the canons in his collections. For good reasons, scholars have regarded them as an important source for his ecclesiology.[300] It is therefore very interesting to see that Anselm's readers not only read these comments, but also felt motivated to change them relatively often.

297. Fowler-Magerl, *Clavis* esp. 139–148; Cushing, 'Polemic or Handbook' (Anselm Bb).

298. Landau, 'Erweiterte Fassungen' 327 followed by Winroth, *Making* 15–16. See also Peter Landau, 'Gratian and the *Decretum Gratiani*', *The History of Medieval Canon Law in the Classical Period, 1140–1234: From Gratian to the Decretals of Pope Gregory IX*, ed. Wilfried Hartmann and Kenneth Pennington (HMCL; Washington, D.C. 2008) 22–54, here at 32 for a number of canons which Gratian could have taken from Anselm Bb.

299. Cambridge, CCC, 269 was at Pipewell in the fifteenth century according to the note found fol. 258v and may have reached the house before *ca.* 1200; Graz, UB, 351 was given to Seckau by Gottschalk of Diernstein who is attested in charters dating before 1184, see Anton Kern, *Die Handschriften der Universitätsbibliothek Graz: Band 1* (Leipzig 1942) 208; see also the Seckau necrology (ed. Herzberg-Fränkel, MGH Necr. 2.387).

300. Kathleen Grace Cushing, 'Anselm of Lucca and the Doctrine of Coercion: The Legal Impact of the Schism of 1080?' CHR 81 (1995) 353–371 and eadem, *Papacy and Law* esp. 68, 76, and 84–85. Mitrofanov, *Ecclésiologie* tried to take a similar approach.

Take, for example, Anselm's first book containing 89 canons, all with a rubric. Of these 89 rubrics, no less than 43 (including six of the first ten) are changed in the A Aucta, A', and/or B versions. Many changes seem minute: whether the Roman church was made head of all churches and received her primacy 'from the Lord and no one else', or only was made head of all churches by the Lord;[301] whether Saint Peter was 'first' or 'head' among the apostles;[302] whether his see surpassed that of other bishops or 'all' other bishops.[303] Indeed, not only the rubrics in book one but also the title of this opening section of the collection oscillated: Was it about the 'primacy of the Roman church', her 'primacy and excellence' or her 'dignity'? Or rather the 'power and primacy of the apostolic see', or perhaps the 'primacy of the Roman see and the pope'?[304] These changes seem minute, but apparently the readers and users of Anselm's collection had their reasons to interfere. The frequency with which they took the effort to make relatively subtle changes indicates that the issue of the primacy of the Roman church was as important to Anselm's readers as it had been to the compiler, and shows that both compilers and readers paid great attention to the precise wording of these claims.

If we turn to individual versions and manuscripts of Anselm's collection, we get a glimpse at the motives behind such changes. Take, for example, the Mantua copy of the A Aucta version.[305] The A Aucta version is one of the earliest versions of Anselm's collection, extant in only two manuscripts kept today in Mantua and Venice, respectively. The version may be the product of San Benedetto in Polirone, a monastery with close ties to Anselm, an excellent library, and apparently a community which was thoroughlyfamiliar with canon law. Many rubrics are different from those of the A version—sometimes closer to the B version—and canons

301. Anselm A 1.2, rubric (Vat. lat. 1363, fol. 3v): 'Quod Romana ecclesia caput est omnium ecclesiarum et ab ipso Domino non ab alio primatum obtinuit'; in the A Aucta and B versions (according to *Clavis*, here checked against Vat. lat. 1364, fol. 6v) the rubric is: 'Quod sacrosancta Romana ecclesia caput omnium ecclesiarum a Domino est constituta.'

302. Anselm 1.7, rubric (Vat. lat. 1363, fol. 3v): 'Quod Christus sancto Petro concessit [...] ut primus esset' as opposed to 'Quod beato Petro a Domino concessum est ceteris preesse' in the A Aucta and B versions (Vat. lat. 1364, fol. 7r).

303. Anselm 1.8, rubric (Vat. lat. 1363, fol. 3v): 'Quod [...] omnibus beati Petri sedes preminet', with 'omnibus' lacking in A Aucta and B versions (Vat. lat. 1364, fol. 7r).

304. 'De primatu sancte Romane ecclesie' (Vat. lat. 1363, fol. 3v; this is also the rubric to *74T* c. 1); 'De primatu et excellentia Romane ecclesie' (Vat. lat. 1364, fol. 6v; Mantova, BC, 318, fol. 102r); 'De ordine et primatu Romane sedis et de eiusdem pontifice' (Cambridge, CCC, 269, fol. 1r); 'De dignitate Romane ecclesie' (Venice manuscript of A Aucta according to Fowler-Magerl, *Clavis* 146); 'De potestate et primatu apostolice sedis' (A' and Bb/Barb. according to *Clavis* database; this is also the beginning of the title of the first book of Burchard's *Liber decretorum*; Anselm 1.1 = Burchard 1.1).

305. The following is based on Landau, 'Erweiterte Fassungen' 328–330; Motta, 'Redazione'; Fowler-Magerl, *Clavis* esp. 145–148.

found in A Aucta and B strongly suggest that both go back to a lost, more complete version than the extant A version. Also, the title of book seven is changed from 'De communi vita clericorum' to the more general 'De vita et ordinatione clericorum' in A Aucta.

Whether or not the A Aucta version originated at Polirone, the Mantua copy definitely comes from this monastery. It contains a large number of additions; in almost every book of Anselm's collection it has at least some canons which are not found in other manuscripts, not even the Venice manuscript. These additions come from different sources and cover very diverse subjects, but a considerable number are genuine and forged letters of Gregory the Great, and many of them deal with monastic property and other canon law aspects of monastic life. Anselm's book four 'On privileges' contains 55 canons; the book title corresponds to the third titulus of *74T*, which Anselm incorporated completely in this book. In the Mantua manuscript, no less than sixteen canons are added, mainly on monastic issues, including Pseudo-Boniface (JE †1996) and Pseudo-Gregory's *Quam sit necessarium* (= *QSN*; JE †1366).[306] The two pro-monastic forgeries were often transmitted together, and often added to monastic copies of canonical collections.[307] A possible source for *QSN* is *74T*; it is therefore significant that the Mantua manuscript contains, outside Anselm's collection, the very first canon of *74T*.[308] In addition, there is a shorter excerpt from *QSN* attributed to Gregory III here; the same version (with the same misattribution and same rubric) is found in Bonizo.[309] Given that A Aucta also preserved *QSN* as found in book five of the A version of Anselm's *Collectio*,[310] *QSN* is quoted in three canons—all written in different hands according to Fowler-Magerl.[311] The impression is that this reflects intense, but not very coordinated reworking by monastic readers who found the same text in different source and wanted to make sure it was in 'their' canon law collection.

A rather different Anselm in found in the Bb version, which extends only to the first seven books of the collection and is extant in a single manuscript of the early twelfth century.[312] The manuscript has some notority

---

306. Anselm A Aucta 4.61A and 4.70A (ed. Motta, 'Redazione' 394 and 395), respectively.

307. See Gilchrist, 'Monastic Forgeries' (though not on this manuscript).

308. Mantova, BC, 318, fol. 101v according to Motta, 'Redazione' 383 n. 15.

309. Anselm A Aucta 4.59a (ed. Motta, 'Redazione' 394) = Bonizo 6.6. (ed. Perels 212). Polirone had at least one Bonizo copy in the Middle Ages, see Walter Berschin, 'Zwei neue Bonizo-Handschriften' *Scriptorium* 41 (1987) 87–90, here at 58.

310. Anselm 5.54 (ed. Thaner 252–254; taken from *74T*).

311. Fowler-Magerl, *Clavis* 147.

312. The following is based on Landau, 'Erweiterte Fassungen' 331–332, Fowler-Magerl, *Clavis* esp. 145–148, Cushing, 'Polemic', and eadem, 'Recension Bb'.

as it is the only medieval manuscript of the collection that actually mentions Anselm as the compiler.[313] Large parts of the Bb version are structurally early—arranging material closer to the sequence of the sources than other versions of Anselm[314]—and some of the material peculiar to Bb may go back to a lost version of Anselm. Other materials seem to be additions, specifically those materials referring to canons regular, and particularly to those at San Frediano at Lucca.[315] Compared to the A aucta version, the additions—in the main text, but also the margins and appendices to individual books—are massive, especially in books six and seven, and are taken from a variety of formal sources including Burchard and the *Anselmo dedicata*.[316] The new material includes disciplinary canon law (penance!), canons on ecclesiastical property, and other 'practical' issues, but significantly not marriage (another area on which Anselm A had rather little to say). The careful reworking resulted, as Cushing put it, in an Anselm version that was 'more of a practical canonical handbook and less of a polemical *libellus de lite*'.[317]

Anselm's collection was polemic in nature, and strikingly incomplete in some key areas of canon law,[318] but from the beginning it also was a very well-structured, copious collection of canon law; many of the topics Anselm paid special attention to (including Roman primacy) evidently struck a cord with contemporary readers and users. As the various Anselm versions—only two of which have been taken into account here—demonstrate, Anselm's early readers recognised and valued the high quality of his collection, and adopted them for their own use; this reduced some of the polemic quality, added to its character as a manual, and doing so produced a remarkable variety of versions.

4.5 Bonizo of Sutri

4.5.1 Biography

Bonizo was born *ca.* 1045 in Lombardy, and after studies in Cremona joined the Milanese *pataria* in the 1060s and early 1070s.[319] During the pon-

---

313. This gave rise to the theory that the Anselm perhaps only compiled a short version of his collection, see Fransen, 'Anselme' 144 (with further references).

314. My special thanks are to Martin Brett, who alerted me to the problem and generously shared with me his notes on Anselm Bb.

315. Cushing, 'Polemic' 73.

316. Cushing, 'Polemic' 73–77.

317. Cushing, 'Polemic' 72; see also ibid. 77.

318. Fransen, 'Anselme' esp. 146.

319. The following is mainly based on the excellent overview in Berschin, *Bonizo von Sutri* ch. 1. See also more recently Ian Stuart Robinson, 'Introduction', *The Papal Reform of the Eleventh Century: Lives of Pope Leo IX and Pope Gregory VII*, ed. idem (Manchester Medieval Sources; Manchester 2004) 1–95, here at 36–64.

tificate of Alexander II and Gregory VII, he attended several papal synods. Before 1078, he was elected bishop of Sutri, but soon exiled, perhaps without having taken office—Sutri was a stronghold of Wibert/Clemens III. Like Anselm of Lucca (whom he held in the highest regard), Bonizo was supported by Matilda of Tuscany and Gregory VII, who appointed him as papal legate. Bonizo also shared Anselm's experience of exile and, in 1082, imprisonment. His earliest work was the *Paradisus*, a collection of excerpts from Saint Augustine. Shortly after the death of Gregory VII, he wrote the *Liber ad amicum*, and around that time also composed a tract on investiture and a lost polemic *Liber in Ugonem*. In 1088/89 he was elected bishop of Piacenza with the luke-warm support of Urban II, but was mutilated and blinded by his opponents. Only after this cruel attack, again in exile, Bonizo compiled his canonical collection and some smaller works on marriage prohibitions, sacraments, and penance. In this period, he clearly was disappointed by Pope Urban II (with whom he also disagreed on the delicate issue of reordinations), and turned against his former guardian Matilda of Tuscany. He died in Cremona, perhaps in 1094.

4.5.2 The *Liber de vita christiana* (Overview)

Bonizo's *Liber de vita christiana* is a large and unusual canonical collection extant in five medieval manuscripts, plus one incomplete copy and another one containing excerpts.[320] It is available in Perels' 'semi-critical' edition that has stood the test of time very well.[321] *De vita christiana* is composed of a preamble, ten books on individual topics, and a short epilogue; the preface is lost. Unusually for a pre-Gratian canonical collection, it not only contains series of canons taken from other collections but also long comments by Bonizo himself; books two, four, and seven are at least in part tracts more than collections of canons. Frequently, the passages authored by him are introduced as 'Bonizo episcopus', and the original form of the collection may have consistently done so. Comparing these comments to those of Gratian, scholars sometimes refer to them as Bonizo's 'dicta'.[322]

---

320. Kéry 234–237; Fowler-Magerl, *Clavis* 174–176. The incomplete copy (olim Toronto, Bergendal Collection, 79) is now New Haven, Yale University, Beinecke MS 1154; the excerpts (not listed by Kéry) are found in Troyes, Trésor de la cathédrale, 4 according to Berschin, 'Nachwort' 408*.

321. See Perels, 'Einleitung' LXXIII–LXXVIII on the editorial principles. Berschin, *Bonizo von Sutri* 58–59 was able to supplement the edition from a manuscript unknown to Perels (Matova, BC, 439), and in doing so confirmed Perels' hypothesis concerning the textual losses in Bonizo 5.7 (ed. Perels 178).

322. Above all, Ursula Lewald, *An der Schwelle der Scholastik. Bonizo von Sutri und das Kirchenrecht seiner Tage* (Weimar 1938), 18–34; but see Berschin, *Bonizo von Sutri* 99 and 102. See also William L. North, 'Bonizo of Sutri, the *Dicta Bonizonis* and the Development of the Jurisprudence of Canon Law Before Gratian', *The Use of Canon Law in Ecclesiastical Administration, 1000–1234,*

There is good evidence that *De vita christiana* originally began with what is now book two, and ended in book nine.[323] Most books are devoted to the canon law on specific groups (*ordines*) within the Church—bishops (book two), metropolitans and primates (books three), popes (book four), priests and deacons (book five), monks and nuns (book six), and 'kings, judges, and other lay magnates' (book seven). Book eight mainly deals with the law of marriage, but Bonizo himself introduces it as a book on 'ordinary lay people'.[324] This division of the material reflects a model Christian society, divided in clergy and laypeople, with both groups sub-divided according to dignity and power. Only the beginning and the end of the collection do not fit this pattern, as the first book is devoted to baptism and the last two to penance. While Bonizo clearly paid attention to the administration of the sacraments, and was familiar for example with the teaching of Berengar of Tours,[325] no separate section of *De vita christiana* is devoted to the Eucharist. The books on bishops and ecclesiastical hierarchy, but also the book on lay magnates, seem to have worked upon most intensively, with books two and seven also containing the highest share of Bonizo's own comments. Books one, five, six, and eight through ten, in contrast, are less refined.[326]

The canons are not numbered, and there is no detailed *capitulatio*. However, the whole collection is straightforward to use. The epilogue contains an overview over the collection, and with the exception of books one and three, all books begin with more or less elaborate introductions by Bonizo, often containing comments on the place of the respective book in *De vita christiana* as a whole. In addition to the rubrics, Bonizo's comments guide the reader, sometimes very firmly so.[327] Even if the beginning and the end of the collection are additions which do not exactly fit the original plan, and there is some overlap between the books,[328] *De vita christiana* is a well-structured work.

As for the content, Bonizo employed canon law in a very broad sense; compared to other Italian collections of his time, he used an unusually

ed. Danica Summerlin and Melodie Harris Eichbauer (Medieval Law and Its Practice 26; Leiden 2018) 159–182; this study could have profited from more profound engagement with Lewald's and Berschin's monographs.

323. Berschin, *Bonizo von Sutri* 62. See in particular the cross-reference in Bonizo 5.1 (ed. Perels 175) and the note 'Explicit liber' after Bonizo 9.74 (ed. Perels 302).

324. Bonizo 8.1 (ed. Perels 252): 'Quia vero superiori libro de prelatis in laicali ordine positis, prout potuimus, breviter enarravimus, superest nunc in ulteriori libro, qualiter subditi vitam debeant instituere, breviter indagare.'

325. Berengar of Tours mentioned him among the participants of the Roman synod of 1078, see Huygens, 'Bérenger' 390.

326. Berschin, *Bonizo von Sutri* 67.

327. E.g. Bonizo 5.48 and 6.47 (ed. Perels 193 and 224).

328. Berschin, *Bonizo von Sutri* 61–62.

high share of theological texts drawn from Saint Augustine and other Church Fathers.[329] An even more unusual feature for a canonical collection is that Bonizo in *De vita christiana* remarkably often argues from history (as he also does in his other works).[330] The first half of book four is an account of the popes from Saint Peter until his own time, books six and seven begin with short accounts on the origin of monasticism and secular power, respectively. Several times, Bonizo comments on the changing laws and institutions, e.g. concerning the consecration of churches, clerical marriage, and female asceticism.[331] In a similar way, Bonizo in his tract on marriage prohibitions sketched the history of incest prohibitions and the calculation of the relevant degrees from the earliest time to Alexander II.[332] This attention to historical development may also explain why Bonizo paid great attention to custom.[333] At the same time, many of his comments refer to his own lifetime; he twice mentions Anselm of Lucca, praising him as a saintly bishop.[334] His comments on bishops in exile can be assumed to reflect his own experience.[335] The passages on female rulers are a thinly-veiled criticism of Matilda of Tuscany.[336] Finally, to a passage explaining that only lighter fasting should be imposed on the sick and frail, and no fasting was prescribed for the frailest ones, Bonizo adds that he himself belonged to this category.[337] Yet while the narrative passages and comments frequently refer to Bonizo's own times, recent legislation is completely absent from his *De vita christiana*.[338]

4.5.3 Christian Society According to Bonizo

Bonizo's *Liber de vita christiana* is often called 'more theological than legal' in nature, and indeed it is best described as a book on an ideal Christian society. This is also reflected by the organisation of the material. The

329. See von Giesebrecht, 'Gesetzgebung' 154 ('Mittelding zwischen einer Kanonensammlung und einem theologischen Tractat'); a similar case is the *Liber de misericordia et iustitia* of Alger of Liège, on which see Chapter Five.

330. Thomas Förster, *Bonizo von Sutri als gregorianischer Geschichtsschreiber* (MGH Studien und Texte 53; Hanover 2011)

331. Bonizo 4.98, 5.77, and 6.30 (ed. Perels 164–165, 203, and 218–219).

332. Berschin, *Bonizo von Sutri* 85–91. For a second manuscript of the tract, see Schadt, *Darstellungen* 124.

333. E.g. Bonizo 4.47, 129–130.

334. Bonizo 2.30 and 5.77 (ed. Perels 48 and 204).

335. Bonizo 2.37 (ed. Perels 50).

336. Bonizo 7.29 (ed. Perels 250); see Walter Berschin, 'Herrscher, "Richter", Ritter, Frauen … Die Laienstände nach Bonizo', *Love and Marriage in the Twelfth Century*, ed. Willy van Hoecke and Andries Welkenhuysen (Mediaevalia Lovaniensia. Studia 8; Leuven 1981) 116–129, esp. 123–124.

337. Bonizo 5.80 (ed. Perels 206): '[…] infirmis et debilibus, de quorum numero ego sum, non est lex.'

338. The most recent material is JL 4405 as found in Bonizo 4.87 (ed. Perels 156). In his *Liber ad amicum* and *De parentela*, Bonizo also quotes letters of Alexander II (namely JL 4500 and 4637). See also Alexander II, JL 4506.

first book is devoted to the sacrament of baptism, while later books are devoted to the different orders within the Church, that is, the different ranks of both clergy and laypeople.[339] Bonizo, following traditional canon law, identifies 'prelates' mainly with bishops, and at first sight seems to downplay hierarchical differences within this order, for on account of their ordination 'the bishop of Nepi is equal to the bishop of Rome'.[340] (The bishop of Nepi, the neighbouring diocese of Sutri, may have found this comparison very flattering; his diocese was so small that it was merged with Sutri in the late Middle Ages.) In line with this, Bonizo's second book, mixing commentary and proof texts, is devoted to bishops. Only in books three and four, the differences are dealt with. Book three is devoted to metropolitan bishops, devoting more attention to this order of bishops than other collections. The first nineteen canons of book three all deal with the rights and duties of metropolitans, including two canons stressing that obtaining the pallium was not so much an honour as a duty. Drawing on the concept of *plenitudo potestatis*, Bonizo asserted that metropolitans received their 'share of the responsibility' only from the pope. This echoes his arguments in the *Liber ad amicum* where he employs the same argument—including a misquotation of Leo's JK 411—against German metropolitans opposed to Gregory VII. In book four, Bonizo gathers rich material on the primacy of the Roman church. The key proof texts are those also found in Anselm, taken from Pseudo-Isidore (JK †10 and †4), Gelasius (JK 664), (Pseudo-?)Gregory (JE †2579), Pseudo-Nicholas II (JE 4424), and other genuine and forged papal letters.[341]

If we turn from the clergy to laypeople, it is striking to see that Bonizo devoted almost equal attention to what he described as different *ordines* of laypeople, earning the *Liber de vita christiana* the label 'sociological'.[342] While this mainly refers to Bonizo's own comments, the actual canons are clearly ecclesiastical law for the laity, not secular laws. Bonizo seems to have held Roman law in high regard, but does not seem to have been very familiar with it (or preferred canon law for other reasons). Like Peter Damian a generation earlier, Bonizo sought to disseminate the excessive

---

339. Bonizo 2.3 (ed. Perels 35): 'Christianorum alii sunt clerici, alii laici, et in his conditionibus alii subditi, alii prelate.' On Bonizo's role in medieval debates on the sacrament of baptism, see Marcia L. Colish, *Faith, Fiction and Force in Medieval Baptismal Debates* (Washington, D.C. 2014) 27–29.

340. Bonizo 2.4 (ed. Perels 35): 'Episcopatus licet unus sit toto orbe diffuses et licet secundum episcopalem benedictionem talis sit Nepesinus ut Romanus talisque Laudensis ut Mediolanensis.'

341. See in particular Bonizo 4.48–86 (ed. Perels 133–148). The 'canons' before are in fact Bonizo's introduction, including a lengthy catalogue of popes from Saint Peter to Urban II (ed. Perels 111–133).

342. Berschin, 'Herrscher' 102; Claire Cabaillot, 'De la theorie des trois ordres à la revue des états: Rathier de Vérone et Bonizon de Sutri' *Revue des études italiennes* 39 (1993) 35–51; Berschin, 'Nachwort' 408*–409*.

incest prohibitions as found in Burchard and endorsed by Alexander II.[343] Bonizo's account of marriage prohibitions indeed is very complete,[344] and in his own comment he further stresses that these prohibitions outlawed marriages between free and unfree, abducted women and their abductors (*raptores*), Jews and Christians, and so on.[345] He here mentions even more prohibitions than Burchard, includings some relatively obscure ones, for example between the children of two persons who served as godparents of the same child.[346] While this comment strongly stresses how many impediments to marriage there were, elsewhere in *De vita* Bonizo makes clear that the application of canon law always was subject to 'mercy and justice',[347] and in a separate tract on the degrees on consanguinity specifically stressed the power of the bishop to grant dispensation from the rather excessive prohibitions.[348]

Bonizo's *Liber de vita christiana*, containing an unusual share of historical argument and patristic theology, only had a limited impact on canon law. No doubt Bonizo's work had some circulation, at least in Italy; but only very few canonical collections seem to have been influenced by it. Instead, it was Bonizo's account of papal history in *De vita* which seems to have attracted the most attention; it was copied separately, and quoted in several medieval chronicles and other works. In particular, Cardinal Boso (d. 1178) was interested in the papal history in both the *Liber ad amicum* and the *De vita*; the relevant excerpts Boso inserted in his reworking of the *Liber pontificalis* are probably the most influential branch of the transmission of Bonizo's works.[349] Even canon law collections concentrated on this part of *De vita christiana*, for example in the case of additions to the Vienna *Collection in Seven Books*.[350]

343. For background, see Ubl, *Inzestverbot* esp. 451–459 (on Peter Damian) and 469–470 (on Alexander II and the uncertain date of JL 4500). Bonizo quotes JL 4500 in his marriage tract (ed. Berschin, *Bonizo von Sutri* 84). Like Burchard's collection, Bonizo's *De vita christiana* and his *De arbore* are illustrated with diagrams on which see Schadt, *Darstellungen* esp. 124–127.

344. See Ursula Lewald, 'Das Eherecht in Bonizos von Sutri *Liber de Vita Christiana*' ZRG Kan. Abt. 27 (1938) 560–598 and Berschin, *Bonizo von Sutri* 85–93 (mainly on *De parentela*) and 102.

345. Bonizo 8.11 (ed. Perels 256–257, here at 256): 'Legitimum vero coniugium non potest esse inter inequales, hoc est, inter servum et liberam vel inter liberum et ancillam, nec inter raptam et raptorem, nec inter Iudeam et Christianum nec inter paganum et Christianum, nec inter catholicum et hereticam, nec inter compatres et commatres, nec inter filios et filias compatrum et commatrum, qui fratres spirituales nominantur.' The materials Bonizo quotes in his collection do not substantiate all of these impediments, and even where they do, often make clear that there were important exceptions.

346. Bonizo 8.11 (ed. Perels 256–257) as quoted in the last note.

347. See his comments in Bonizo 9.1, 9.74, 10.1, and 10.17 (ed. Perels 277, 302, 305, and 313).

348. Bonizo, *De arbore*, ed. Giovanni Miccoli, 'Un nuovo manoscritto del *Liber de vita christiana* di Bonizone di Sutri' *Studi medievali*, serie terza 7 (1966) 371–398, here at 390–398, here at 397 and 399. See Berschin, *Bonizo von Sutri* 82–84 for important corrections.

349. Berschin, *Bonizo von Sutri* 97–101.

350. Peter Landau, 'Die Quellen der mittelitalienischen Kanonessammlung in sieben Büchern

4.5.4 Formal Sources

The *Liber de vita christiana* adopts a structure unlike any previous collection, and rarely did Bonizo leave materials he took from other collections in the sequence found there. This thorough reworking also makes it more difficult to establish the formal sources of the *Liber* in greater detail.[351] An additional difficulty is related to Bonizo's mutilation in 1089; as he compiled *De vita christiana* only after he was blinded, he may have frequently quoted from memory, and certainly had to delegate more tasks than other compilers. Finally, as Bonizo's comments are sometimes only distinguished from 'normal' canons by the inscription, and these notes were easily overlooked (especially in their abbreviated form: 'B. dix.'), it is not always possible to distinguish between materials from unknown sources, forgery, and Bonizo's comment.[352]

For all these reasons, Bonizo's formal sources are only known imperfectly. As so often, the use of Burchard is relatively easy to discern, even more so as it is Bonizo most important formal source. His exemplar does not seem to have had the gaps typical for Italian Burchard copies.[353] A direct use of the Pseudo-Isidorian forgeries is plausible, but only for a few dozens canons. Bonizo also seems to have known *5L*.[354] Many of Bonizo's patristic quotations seem to have been taken directly from these works rather than canonical collections. In the case of Saint Augustine at least, some of his quotations are taken from the florilegium of Eugippius (d. 535).[355] In addition, Bonizo drew on his own writings (specifically *Paradisus* and *Liber ad amicum*), and perhaps preparatory materials, though far less

---

(MS Vat. Lat. 1346)', *Ritual, Text and Law: Studies in Medieval Canon Law and Liturgy Presented to Roger E. Reynolds*, ed. Richard F. Gyug and Kathleen Grace Cushing (CFC; Aldershot 2004) 255–268, here at 261–262.

351. For the following, see in general Perels, 'Briefe' esp. 90–95; Fournier, 'Bonizo' esp. 124–127; Ernst Perels, 'Einleitung', *Bonizo von Sutri, Liber de vita christiana*, ed. idem (Texte zur Geschichte des römischen und kanonischen Rechts im Mittelalter 1; Berlin 1930) ix–lxxix, esp. xxx–xxxi; *Histoire* 2.143–144; Fuhrmann, *Einfluß und Verbreitung* 2.537–540; Berschin, *Bonizo von Sutri* ch. 2; Fowler-Magerl, *Clavis* 174–176; Rolker, 'Bonizo' 78–103.

352. See the 'Ambrosius' text in Bonizo 2.48 (ed. Perels 57–58) and Pseudo-Innocent, JK – (J³ –) in Bonizo 4.47 (ed. Perels 133). For discussion, see Perels, 'Einleitung' XXIII and LXXVI (general) and Berschin, *Bonizo von Sutri* 65 (Bonizo 4.47 'apokryph, vielleicht eine Prägung Bonizos selbst') and 69 (Bonizo 2.48 a summary of Augustine).

353. Bonizo 6.43–44 and 52–58 (ed. Perels 222–223 and 225–228) are taken from Burchard 8.38–49, absent in the so-called *deteriores* tradition as described by Fransen, 'Essai de classement'.

354. Gaastra, *Liturgy* 183 and 215; Dr Gaastra (private communication, 16 October 2020) pointed me *5L* 2.79 and 75 as plausible sources of Bonizo 10.46 and 48 (ed. Perels 321 and 322). The material source of the former canon is JK †382; the latter, beginning *Si qua femina*, has no inscription in Bonizo but is commonly misattributed to Hormisdas in other collections. It was printed by Theiner, *Disquisitiones criticae* 293–294 but seems not to have been calendared by Jaffé (JK –; J³ –).

355. Berschin, *Bonizo von Sutri* 68–70.

than one could have expected.[356] Finally, *De vita christiana* contains rich historical material, including an expanded catalogue of popes based on the *Liber pontificalis*.

It had long been assumed that Bonizo used intermediary collections also available to other compilers, namely Anselm and Deusdeudit. This assumption was shared by Berschin, who assumed that all three used shared sources (*Zwischensammlungen*) but in the end conceded that their shape remained vague. Following an observation of Erdmann, Berschin postulated another source for the Augustinian and Pelagian materials shared by Anselm and Bonizo only, and accepted Perels' claim for yet another *Zwischensammlung* of Pseudo-Isidorian material. With only minor qualifications, Berschin's assumptions proved right. Some of Bonizo's Pseudo-Isidorian material indeed comes from a source also available to Anselm and Deusdedit (Bonizo 4.48–82), some from a source he shared with Anselm but not Deusdedit (Bonizo 7.17–27). Strikingly, by far the most of these materials (Bonizo 4.48–75 and 7.17–27) are also found *2L/8P*, and a comparison of all collections involved and their material sources makes clear that the source used by Bonizo and Anselm was most similar to the extant version of *2L/8P* (as found in two manuscripts of the twelfth century).[357]

Given that Anselm and Bonizo knew each other, and *De vita christiana* specifically mentions Anselm twice, one may assume that these textual relations reflect a certain cooperation between the two prelates. The fact that Deusdedit seems to have had access to some, but not all of this *2L/8P* material (while sharing other materials with Anselm not found there) indicates that the diverse materials were not yet transmitted together, but rather circulated in the form of small dossiers.

4.5.5 Bonizo as a Moderate Ex-Gregorian

Bonizo in many respects was a 'radical Gregorian' around 1080, when he must already have collected much material he later used for the *Liber de vita christiana*. Evidently, he was deeply involved in the conflicts between supporters of Gregory VII and Henry IV during the 1080s, and had to suffer exile and mutilation as a result of his support for the papal cause. However, even at this time, Bonizo's concept of secular and ecclesiastical hierarchy was much more traditional than that of Gregory VII.[358] Both in

---

356. Berschin, *Bonizo von Sutri* 68 (*Paradisus*) and 70–71 (*Liber ad amicum*).

357. Rolker, 'Bonizo' 79–83 (on Berschin), 83–100 (general discussion), and 104–106 (concordance table).

358. Berschin, *Bonizo von Sutri* esp. 110–111.

his *Liber ad amicum* and in his tract on investiture, Bonizo argued that the papal right to change canon law was limited. He raised this point in the discussion on the Papal Election Decree, and specifically to defend Gregory VII against attacks based on the imperial version of this decree.[359] The decrees he was condemning were not the False Investiture Privileges,[360] but the imperial version of the Papal Election Decree and a canon of 'Pope Stephen' transmitted with it.[361] Bonizo not only suspected that these canons were forgeries; crucially, he independently of this claim made a general point that such canons 'even if proclaimed validly' would not change the law.[362] Like Deusdedit (and to a lesser degree Anselm), Bonizo quoted *ancient* canon law on papal elections in his *De vita christiana*,[363] and he was very clear that he regarded these provisions as immutable.[364] This also means that he regarded the genuine version of the 1059 Papal Election Decree invalid.[365] So while Bonizo defended Gregory VII with his canonical learning, his insistence on the limits of papal legislation was clearly not 'Gregorian'.

By the time Bonizo compiled his *Liber de vita christiana*, his relation with the reform papacy was even more distant; yet more importantly, he in many respects had become more moderate in the sense that he came to accept the kind of compromises that were found after the death of

---

359. Förster, *Bonizo* 145–163.

360. Märtl, 'Einleitung' 61–63 (*pace* Berschin, *Bonizo von Sutri* 76 and others).

361. For his severe criticism of the imperial version of the Papal Election Decree, see Bonizo's *Liber ad amicum* (ed. Dümmler, MGH Ldl 1.615 lines 15–24) and his tract on investiture (ed. Berschin, *Bonizo von Sutri* 76): 'Quamvis falsissimus esse nulli dubium sit sciolo, sunt tamen qui dicunt decretis Romanorum pontificum Sergii et Stephani et Nicolai iunioris hoc regibus esse concessum.' The reference to Stephen and Nicholas II fits the combination of JE †ante 2543 and the 1059 decree as found in *Panormia* 3.1 and in Köln, Historisches Archiv, 101* [not seen] as discussed by Claudia Märtl, 'Die kanonistische Überlieferung der falschen Investiturprivilegien (Ivo, Panormia 8.135 und 136; D. 63 c. 22 und 23)' BMCL 17 (1987) 33–44, here at 38–42. Bonizo's reference is vague; perhaps he was only reacting to rumours ('sunt qui dicunt'); it cannot be used to date the tract (Märtl, 'Einleitung' 61–63).

362. Bonizo, *Liber ad amicum* (ed. Dümmler, MGH Ldl 1.615 line 18), evidently referring to the so-called *Königsparagraph*: 'etsi verum esset, tamen nullius momenti esset'.

363. Bonizo 2.18–19 (Symmachus, JK ante 752). Bonizo, *Liber ad amicum* (ed. Dümmler, MGH Ldl 1.586 lines 8–19, esp. 8–13) quotes the Lateran 769 decrees as found in Deusdedit 2.161–162 (131a–c) (ed. Wolf von Glanvell 268).

364. In his tract on investiture, Bonizo specifically quoted papal elections as an example of canons which popes could not change under whatever circumstances (ed. Berschin, *Bonizo von Sutri* 76 lines 15–16): 'Necessarii enim nullo modo possunt inflecti, nullave ratione immutari vel leviari, ut ille de pontificali electione.' More generally, he held (ibid.) that the making of 'new law' was restricted to adopting old law to new circumstances; in support he quoted Pseudo-Leo I. (JK –; J³ –): 'Novos canones possunt [Romanorum pontifices, CR] quidem cudere, sed tales, qui veteribus non obvient, et veteres non destruere, sed pro consideratione temporum immutare: hoc est in melius et non in peius mutare.' On this canon (perhaps even forged by Bonizo?), see already Perels, 'Einleitung' XXXIII n. 4.

365. Berschin, *Bonizo von Sutri* 49–50 assumed that Bonizo did not know the genuine version, but only the manipulated summary (JL 4405) as found in Anselm and Deusdedit.

Gregory VII. For example, Bonizo still thought that schismatics (i.e. supporters of Wibert/Clement III) could not confer valid ordinations, and was severely critical of Urban II in this respect; nonetheless, in his canonical collection he (however grudgingly) accepted that such reordinations, even if against canon law, fell within papal powers.[366] More generally, Bonizo's *De vita christiana* is not a polemical work. Bonizo, like Deusdedit, firmly believed that ancient papal election law was still valid; but unlike Deusdedit, he in his collection did not elaborate on this issue. For example, he probably still held that the election of Clement II (a non-Roman) was against the canons, and that Henry III abused his position as *patricius*, but did not repeat the polemic as found in his *Liber ad amicum* in this context.[367] Or, to take another example, Bonizo was clear that lay magnates had no right to interfere with episcopal elections;[368] yet like most compilers of canon law law collections he avoids mention of the radical Gregorian decrees against lay investiture. However, it is also true that Bonizo inserted 'historical' examples of papal excommunications of (Greek) emperors in *De vita christiana*, examples which he had originally collected as precedent for the excommunication of Henry IV by Gregory VII.[369] Several of Bonizo's canons and rubrics concerning Roman primacy also are 'Gregorian' in their far-reaching claims; for example, Bonizo shares a manipulated proof text claiming that 'all churches were founded by Rome'.[370] The passages on the use of force in *De vita christiana* (the canonical proof texts and historical examples he selected as well as his comments) may likewise be linked to the bitter struggles of the times around 1080, and in particular to Bonizo's support of Countess Matilda at that time. So *De vita christiana* still contains materials which Bonizo once excerpted in the context of the conflict between Gregory VII and Wibert/Clement III; it also contains several passages which show his disappointment with former allies, above all Matilda of Tuscany. His attacks on female rulers are clearly directed against his former patroness.[371] All in all, the *Liber de vita christiana* was neither Gregorian nor anti-Gregorian; essentially it was Bonizo's vision of a hierarchically structured Christian society, containing his own arguments and proof texts taken from the canonical tradition of the Church.

366. Bonizo 5.6 (ed. Perels 177); see, more generally, Berschin, *Bonizo von Sutri* 14–18.

367. Bonizo, *Liber ad amicum* (ed. Dümmler, MGH Ldl 1.586 lines 8–19); Bonizo 4.45 (ed. Perels 132) cross-references to this passage but does not repeat the polemic attack on Henry, who instead is praised for his intervention at Sutri 1046.

368. Bonizo 2.23 (ed. Perels 43), containing Bonizo's own comment on canons like Bonizo 2.18–18 (ed. Perels 42–43).

369. Berschin, *Bonizo von Sutri* 107 n. 490.

370. Bonizo 4.82 (ed. Perels 146–147). The canon is attributed to Nicholas II (JE 4424) in the collections but in fact lifted from Peter Damian; see above (note 196).

371. Berschin, *Bonizo von Sutri* 16–17.

4.6 Canon Law in Aquitaine: The *Tarraconensis* and Related Collections

While there are a number of Italian collections which can be traced to the immediate environment of Gregory VII, one has to look beyond Italy to trace the reception of Gregorian texts and ideas into canon law. Indeed, the 'unique direct transmitter of the policies of pope Gregory VII' into canon law was found not among the many Italian collections of the late eleventh century, but in a collection that circulated in southern France and Catalonia.[372] This collection (known as the *Tarraconensis*) is part of a group of canonical collections which all emerged somewhere between Catalonia, Aquitaine, and southern Burgundy between *ca.* 1080 and the middle of the twelfth century; none can be tied to known compilers, and both place and date of origin remain to some degree uncertain. What is more certain is that these collections are closely related to each other by a number of shared characteristics, not least the inclusion of otherwise rare 'Gregorian' materials. These collections are the *Burdegalensis*, both versions of the *Tarraconensis*, a collection in thirteen books ('Berlin 13L'), another one in seven books ('Turin 7L'), and finally the second and third versions of the *Caesaraugustana*.[373]

This group largely overlaps with the collections often referred to as 'Poitevin' in the literature.[374] This label, however, is a misnomer; there is very little evidence to link any of the so-called Poitevin collections to Poitiers.[375] Given that the concept played a central role in the research relevant to the following pages, a short note on historiography may be helpful here. Both the term and the concept of 'Poitevin collections' go

372. Fowler-Magerl, *Clavis* 133 (quote), 133–136 (collection).

373. My usage of '*Caes. II/III*' corresponds to the 'second and third versions' as defined by Fowler-Magerl, *Clavis* 242–244. For details, see Chapter Five.

374. Gilchrist, 'Changing the Structure'; Le Bras, 'Activité'; Rennie, 'Poitevine Collections'; idem, *Burdegalensis* 42–51; Reynolds, 'Turin 7L'; Tardif, 'Collection'; Fowler-Magerl, 'Fine Distinctions' 174–182; Joseph Goering, 'Bishops, Law, and Reform in Aragon, 1076–1126, and the Liber Tarraconensis' ZRG Kan. Abt. 95 (2009) 1–28; Uta-Renate Blumenthal, 'Codex 173, Biblioteca Alessandrina, Rome: The Pontifical of the Gregorian Reform?', *Procession, Performance, Liturgy, and Ritual: Essays in Honor of Bryan R. Gillingham*, ed. Nancy van Deusen (Wissenschaftliche Abhandlungen 62.8; Ottawa 2007) 65–81; eadem, 'Poitevin Manuscripts, the Abbey of Saint-Ruf and Ecclesiastical Reform in the Eleventh Century', *Readers, Texts and Compilers in the Earlier Middle Ages: Studies in Medieval Canon Law in Honour of Linda Fowler-Magerl*, ed. Kathleen Grace Cushing and Martin Brett (CFC; Farnham and Aldershot 2009) 87–100; Uta-Renate Blumenthal and Detlev Jasper, 'Licet nova consuetudo. Gregor VII. und die Liturgie', *Bishops, Texts and the Use of Canon Law Around 1100: Essays in Honour of Martin Brett*, ed. Bruce Clark Brasington and Kathleen Grace Cushing (CFC; Aldershot and Farnham 2008) 45–68; Schilling, 'Kanones' 89; Rolker, *Canon Law* 73–75; Fowler-Magerl, 'Vier Kanonessammlungen'. See also eadem, *Clavis* on the individual collections.

375. Rennie, 'Poitevine Collections' 61.

back to an article of Adolphe Tardif, published in 1897.[376] His original argument was that 17L, *Burdegalensis*, and *Tarraconensis II*[377] were all from one 'school' because they used the same formal sources (namely Burchard and 74T), and included otherwise rare materials—a miracle story of Saint Hilary of Poitiers, a liturgical text of Gregory VII (*Licet nova consuetudo*), and the canons of the 1078 Council of Poitiers. Crucially, Tardif argued that this 'school' was to be sought at Poitiers because all three collections contained texts linked to Poitiers, namely interpolated Burchard canons (in the case of 17L) or the Saint Hilary miracle and the Poitiers 1078 canons (in *Burdegalensis* and *Tarraconensis II*). Later scholarship added more and more collections to the 'Poitevin' group, which can be divided into two classes: collections related to *Tarraconensis II* by virtue of shared rare materials, and collections related to these *Tarraconensis*-related collections in one way or the other. Only for the first group, scholars made a strong case that they were 'Poitevin';[378] for the collections of the second group, such assertions were more tentative in nature, sometimes even casual, and need not to be discussed here. Interestingly, none of these collections added to Tardif's list contained either the interpolated Burchard canons or the miracle of Saint Hilary. As a result, the debate on 'Poitevin' collections in practice became a discussion on *Tarraconensis*-related collections.

As it turned out, the *Tarraconensis* group, while much larger than the original set of three collections, nonetheless was much more coherent in the sense that the collections shared many rare texts and distinct features. Reynolds, Fowler-Magerl, Blumenthal, and Goering in particular identified texts characteristic of the 'Poitevin' collections and works directly influenced by them.[379] In addition to the interpolated Burchard canons,[380] the miracle of Saint Hilary,[381] Gregory's *Licet nova consuetudo*,[382] and the de-

---

376. Tardif, 'Collection'.

377. Before 1959, no complete manuscript of the first version was known, and only in 1982 the chronology was established. See Fransen's remark in the discussion to Ryan, 'Observations' 102 and Fowler-Magerl, 'Vier Kanonessammlungen' 142, respectively.

378. Le Bras, 'Activité' (Berlin 13L); Reynolds, 'Turin 7L' (Turin 7L); Fowler-Magerl, *Clavis* 120 (*Tarraconensis I*); Blumenthal, 'Poitevin Manuscripts' 90 (Tarragona, BP, 35); Rennie, 'Poitevine Collections' 62 (*Caes. II/III*).

379. Reynolds, 'Turin 7L' 509–513; Fowler-Magerl, 'Fine Distinctions' 174–181; Goering, 'Bishops' 2–3; Blumenthal, 'Poitevin Manuscripts' 87–90. The account of Blumenthal (ibid. 88) could suggest that already Paul Fournier, 'Le *Liber Tarraconensis*: étude sur une collection canonique du XIᵉ siècle', *Mélanges Julien Havet: recueil de travaux d'érudition dédiés à la mémoire de Julien Havet (1853–1893)* (Paris 1895) 259–281 expanded the list of 'Poitevin characteristic', but in fact in this article he was only concerned with the *Tarraconensis* which he did not (yet) link to Poitiers.

380. For the interpolations in two 17L manuscripts, see above (Chapter Three, notes 377–378).

381. On the transmission (outside canonical collections) see Horst Fuhrmann, 'Die Fabel von Papst Leo und Bischof Hilarius. Vom Ursprung und der Erscheinungsform einer historischen Legende' *Archiv für Kulturgeschichte* 43 (1961) 125–162; for the version found in the *Burdegalensis*, see Rennie, *Burdegalensis* 204.

382. On *Licet nova consuetudo* (= JL 5290), see Blumenthal and Jasper, 'Licet' (with edition).

crees of Poitiers (i.e. the texts identified by Tardif), the list came to include also another letter of Gregory VII (*In die resurrectionis*),[383] a formula for the consecration of bishops (*Ordo Romanus XXXVB*),[384] another liturgical text (*De septem gradibus*),[385] Berengar's oath of 1079,[386] the *Dictatus papae*,[387] and a unique version of the Donation of Constantine.[388] All these texts are rare, and some are very rare indeed, so the joint appearance of several of them in any given collection is indicative of close textual relations.[389]

If one adopts these criteria, and systematically tests all collections ever referred to as 'Poitevin' (nineteen in total) by these standard, the vast majority quickly turn out to contain none, or only one, of these texts. Table 4 gives an overview over the most important shared materials,[390] as found in both the collections Tardif originally labelled 'Poitevin', and those which contain at least two of the defining criteria listed above.

As this table makes clear, the interpolated Burchard canons (the only clear textual link to Poitiers itself in any 'Poitevin' collection!) cannot be used to define *any* group. They do not even link Tardif's original set of three collections, nor have they been found in any other collection studied in relation to these collections. In contrast, other canons Tardif pointed

---

Cowdrey for some time doubted the authenticity: *Epistolae vagantes of Pope Gregory VII*, ed. and tr. Herbert Edward John Cowdrey (Oxford Medieval Texts; Oxford 1972), here at 159; but see also his 'Pope Gregory VII (1073–85) and the Liturgy' *Journal of Theological Studies* 55 (2004) 55–83, esp. 66–68.

383. On the two versions of *In die resurrectionis* (JL –), see Bernal Palacios, 'Redacción breve', Blumenthal and Jasper, 'Licet' 49–50, Cowdrey, 'Liturgy' 60 and 69–71, and Fowler-Magerl, 'Version' 276–277 (pointing out an expanded form of the long version).

384. Blumenthal, 'Codex 173'.

385. See Reynolds, 'Turin 7L' 512 (with edition). In addition to 5L 1.2, the text only seems to be found among the 5L excerpts in Vat. lat. 4977 according to the *Clavis* database.

386. See Robert Somerville, 'The Case Against Berengar of Tours: A New Text' *Studi Gregoriani* 9 (1972) 55–75 and Herbert Edward John Cowdrey, 'The Papacy and the Berengian Controversy', *Auctoritas und ratio. Studien zu Berengar von Tours*, ed. Peter Felix Ganz et al. (Wolfenbütteler Mittelalter-Studien 2; Wiesbaden 1990) 109–138.

387. Blumenthal, 'Poitevin Manuscripts' 90 was the first to add it to the 'Poitevin characteristics'.

388. Goering, 'Bishops' 2, whose list of 'noteworthy documents' is not meant to define 'Poitevin' origin (of which Goering is sceptical) but largely overlaps with the criteria established by Reynolds, 'Turin 7L' 509–513, Fowler-Magerl, 'Fine Distinctions' 174–181, and Blumenthal, 'Poitevin Manuscripts' 87–90. On the *Donation* in canon law, see Petersmann, 'Überlieferung'.

389. Reynolds, 'Turin 7L' 510–512 also pointed at a sermon attributed to Pope Leo I, and a version of the so-called *Epistola ad Leudefredum*, lifted from Burchard. Both canons are relatively common and will not be taken into account in the following. Fowler-Magerl, *Clavis* 96 seemed to regard a specific transmission of the Roman synod of November 1078 as linking several 'Poitevin' collections, but did not discuss this in detail.

390. Corrected from Rennie, *Burdegalensis* 48–50. *Licet nova consuetudo* and the Poitiers canons are found in more collections than he lists (ibid. 48); his list of occurrences of Berengar's 1079 oath also includes references to the 1059 oath (ibid. 48); contrary to what Rennie suggests, the Berlin 13L and the Vatican 13L are two different collections (ibid. 49), and neither of them is 'also known as the 17L' (ibid. 50).

Table 4: Shared Rare Materials in the 'Poitevin' Collections

	Interpolated Burchard canons	Miracle of Saint Hilary	Poitiers 1078	Licet nova consuetudo	In die resurrectionis	Ordo Romanus XXXVB	De septem gradibus	Berengar's 1079 oath	Dictatus papae	Donation of Constantine
17L	(+)[1]									
Burdegalensis		(+)[2]	+	+				(+)[3]		(+)[4]
Tarraconensis I		+	+	+	(+)[5]	+		+[6]	+	+
Tarraconensis II		+	+	+	+	+		+	+	+
Berlin 13L			+	(+)[7]	+		+			
Turin 7L			+		+	+	+	+	(+)[8]	+[9]
Caes. II/III			(+)[10]	+	+[11]			+		
Tarragona, BP, 35 I			+	+						
Other collections	none	none	one[12]	few	few	none	none	few	none	none

1. Only in two manuscripts, see above (Chapter 3.73, notes 377–378).

2. Addition of a version different from that in the *Tarraconensis*, see Rennie, *Burdegalensis* 46.

3. Addition in one manuscript only, see Rennie, *Burdegalensis* 48.

4. Addition in one manuscript only, see Goering, 'Bishops' 2 n. 3.

5. Addition in one manuscript only, see Bernal Palacios, 'Redacción breve' 943.

6. All manuscripts contain the canon. Gilchrist, 'Reception' 55–56 overlooked Tarragona, BP, 26, fols. 111v–112r (in main hand, but not numbered)

7. Excerpts only, see Blumenthal and Jasper, 'Licet' 61.

8. Later addition, and excerpts only, see Fowler-Magerl, *Clavis* 158–159.

9. Rennie, 'Turin Collection' 54 claimed that 7L did not contain the Donation of Constantine, but see Fuhrmann, 'Constitutum' 18 n. 34, Petersmann, 'Überlieferung' 381–382 and 404, and the *Clavis* database on Turin 7L 6.25 (= Torino, BNU, D.IV.33, fols. 99v–100v [not seen]) containing it. A handwritten note in the MGH copy of Fuhrmann's edition relates that Turin 7L 6.25 was incomplete due to a loss of one folio. If so, this seems to have happened after Fuhrmann and Petersmann worked with the manuscript: Petersmann, 'Überlieferung' 416–445 collated the Turin manuscript for her edition, reporting no major gaps (beyond those also found in the *Tarraconensis* and the *Burdegalensis*).

10. *Caes. II/III* contains canons 9, 8, 3, 6–7, and 1b of the Council of Poitiers. Schilling, 'Kanones' 90–94 employed Tarragona, BP, 26 and Paris, BnF, lat. 3876 for her edition.

11. *Caes. II/III* and *Tarraconensis I/II* share an expanded version of the long form of *In die resurrectionis*, see Fowler-Magerl, 'Version' 276.

12. The only other occurrences are the *other* collection in Tarragona, BP, 35 (three canons) and Paris, BnF, lat. 2050 (two and a half canons found in a copy of Augustine); see Schilling, 'Kanones' 81–82 and 86.

out (the Poitiers decrees and Gregory's *Licet nova consuetudo*), while generally rare, have a joint transmission in the collections listed above but only very rarely, if at all, are found in collections outside the *Tarraconensis* group.

For this reason alone, these 'Gregorian' texts, not the (rather weak) links to Poitiers, should be seen as the defining characteristics of the *Tarraconensis* group. This effectively excludes 17L from the group, which by any criteria is different from the other collections listed above.[391] In the case of the *Burdegalensis*, it is more the texts transmitted with the collection than the collection itself that constitute the link to the other collection;[392] nonetheless, it should be counted as *Tarraconensis*-related. The two short collections in Tarragona, BP, 35 are also borderline cases; they both contain the canons of Poitiers, and the first additionally has Gregory's *Licet nova consuetudo*, but neither has any other of the texts listed above. In the following, therefore, only the first collection in Tarragona, BP, 35 will be counted as part of the *Tarraconensis* group. For the remaining collections, the evidence is more straightforward. The *Burdegalensis*, both versions of the *Tarraconensis*, the Berlin 13L, the Turin 7L, and the second and third versions of the *Caesaraugustana* share sufficient unusual material to justify treating them as a distinct group.

The main evidence comes from the rarity of the shared materials, which can hardly be exaggerated. For the *Dictatus papae*, the *Ordo Romanus XXXVB*, *De septem gradibus*, and the Donation of Constantine version, no other pre-Gratian canonical collection is known to contain them; the Poitiers canons are only found in the *Tarraconensis* group and its immediate context (namely in the second collection in Tarragona, BP, 35), and *Licet nova consuetudo* is still very rare.[393] *In die resurrectionis* is somewhat more common, but the extended form is only known from *Tarraconensis*-related collections.[394] All this strongly indicates that shared sources were employed in the compilation of these collections. In addition, there are other intertextual relations suggesting, sometimes intriguingly so, that the collections were compiled and reworked from shared materials, including perhaps even shared manuscripts. Namely, there are *Tarraconensis I* excerpts in both *Burdegalensis* manuscripts, and *Dictatus papae* excerpts appended to the Turin 7L.[395] The latter collection and the *Tarraconensis I* show signs

---

391. See already Fowler-Magerl, *Clavis* 130.

392. See Rennie, *Burdegalensis* 47, who rightly pointed out the distance between the *Burdegalensis* and other so-called Poitevin collections.

393. Blumenthal and Jasper, 'Licet'.

394. Fowler-Magerl, 'Version' 276.

395. Fowler-Magerl, *Clavis* 131 (*Burdegalensis*), 158–159 (Turin 7L).

of cross-contamination.[396] Equally intriguingly, the Donation of Constantine version found in *Tarraconensis I* and Turin *7L* is found in the Bordeaux manuscript of the *Burdegalensis* (outside the collection proper), while no other occurrence is known.[397] The appendix of one *Caesaraugustana II* manuscript contains excerpts from the ninth-century *Quadripartitus* otherwise only known from *Tarraconensis II* and one of its formal sources.[398]

Yet the argument becomes even stronger, if we look not only at the rarity of these texts, but also at their quality. Most of them date from the late 1070s, many concern liturgical questions, and almost all are linked to Gregory VII. In fact, it is no exaggeration to say that most of them are key texts for his concept of church reform. In the case of the Donation of Constantine and the *Dictatus papae*, there can be little doubt about their importance for Gregorian politics.[399] The legatine synod held at Poitiers in 1078, though perhaps not as famous as the *Dictatus*, marks a turning point in Gregory's relation with lay rulers, as it issued the earliest extant prohibition of lay investiture.[400] It also contains decrees against simony and unusually harsh canons on clerical celibacy. Berengar's 1079 oath was not only important for the medieval theology of the Eucharist (famously introducing the term 'substantialiter' into the debate), but also marked the end of Gregory's support for Berengar.[401] This was an extremely delicate issue; the 1080 Council of Brixen, for example, accused Gregory of continously supporting Berengar, and cited this as a reason to depose him.[402] The letters *In die resurrectionis* and *Licet nova consuetudo* (perhaps both from the Lenten synod of 1078) are two decrees on liturgical matters, mainly on the number of psalms to be chanted in the canonical hours and the date of the Ember Days. Both decrees show how central liturgical uniformity was for Gregory, and that liturgical and political aspects of reform cannot be separated. The long version of *In die resurrectionis* links the diversity of liturgy even at Rome to deterioration 'above all in the time the Germans were allowed to govern our church'.[403] *Ordo Romanus XXXVB* is likewise a

---

396. Fowler-Magerl, *Clavis* 134; Blumenthal, 'Poitevin Manuscripts' 90; Goering, 'Bishops' 6.

397. Goering, 'Bishops' 2 n. 3.

398. On the *Quadripartitus* excerpts as found in *TC* cc. 240–304, *Tarraconensis II*, and Paris, BnF, lat. 3876 (the latter two drawing on *TC*), see Rolker, 'Genesis' 92–95. On the ninth-century *Quadripartitus* in general see Kerff, *Quadripartitus*.

399. See above (note 84) on the use Deusdedit made of the Donation of Constantine, especially in the context of claims also found in the *Dictatus*.

400. Schieffer, *Entstehung* 153–176; Schilling, 'Kanones' 95–99.

401. See Somerville, 'Berengar' and (for background) Nikolaus M. Häring, 'Berengar's Definitions of *sacramentum* and Their Influence on Medieval Sacramentology' MS 10 (1948) 109–146.

402. Synodal decree (ed. Erdmann, MGH Deutsches Mittelalter 1.72). The synod did however not actually depose Gregory.

403. This passage is found only in the long version of *In die resurrectionis* (ed. and tr. Cowdrey,

document for the history of the liturgy as well as for the relation between the papacy and the Roman kings. As Blumenthal has argued convincingly, it is the result of a 'Gregorian' reworking of the Romano-German Pontifical 'adapted ruthlessly to Roman usages', and excluding the usual *ordo* for the coronation of the Roman king.[404] *Ordo* XXXVB itself was a newly created rite for the consecration of bishops from the Patrimony of Saint Peter; it contains several references to simony, and the protocol forsees that the pope examined the suitability of the bishop-elect.[405] To sum up, the canons used as textual markers for the *Tarraconensis* group are diverse in nature, but they all touch upon topics which for Gregory VII and his supporters were important aspects of reform—papal power, lay investiture, simony, clerical celibacy, the Berengar controversy, liturgical unity, and the relations between popes and kings.

Given that the links to Poitiers are weak, the question remains where this group of collections emerged. Some clues to the areas in which they likely emerged already are found in the formal sources employed. Like most pre-Gratian collections, the *Tarraconensis*-related collections both individually and collectively draw on very diverse materials (much of which cannot be dated or localised with certainty); one therefore has to be cautious to draw conclusions from the supposed origin of the sources employed in the making of one or more of these collections. The employment of different versions of relatively common collections (namely *74T*, *4L*, and/or Burchard) mainly shows that the *Tarraconensis*-related collections were probably compiled in different places, but do not help to locate any of them precisely. As far as rare formal sources offer any hint to their place of origin, it is mainly the south of modern France and Catalonia. Some of the formal sources ultimately come from Italy, but are known to have been quickly available in France and Spain.[406] The decrees of Poitiers 1078 are the most recent, or almost most recent, materials in several of the collections.[407] More decisively, the close relation between the *Exceptiones*

Epistolae vagantes 60): 'Romani autem diverso modo agere ceperunt maxime a tempore quo teutonicis concessum est regimen nostrae aecclesiae.' See Blumenthal and Jasper, 'Licet' 49–50 and Cowdrey 'Liturgy' 60 and 70–71 (both with further literature) on the question whether the passage is an interpolation. The *Tarraconensis* has the short version while *Caes. II/III* contain the long version.

404. Blumenthal, 'Codex 173' 65 (quote).

405. Blumenthal, 'Codex 173' 69.

406. Several *Tarraconensis*-related collections use an Italian version of Burchard, *Ambrosiana I/II*, the canonical collection and/or polemic writings of Deusdedit, and the *Polycarpus*. For the availability of these materials in France and Spain, see Fowler-Magerl, *Clavis* esp. 133–135 and 160–167.

407. Fowler-Magerl, *Clavis* 129 and 137 (Poitiers 1078 in *Burdegalensis* and Tarragona, BP, 35), 133–134 (Poitiers 1078 and Rome 1080 in *Tarraconensis I/II*), 155 (Poitiers 1078 and JL 5393 in *13L*).

Petri and all versions of the *Caesaraugustana* points to Burgundy (Valence or Die).[408] Materials on the boundaries of dioceses in a copy of the *Tarraconensis*, and forgeries concerning the primacy claims of Arles (JK †446) and Bourges (JE 2765) in all versions of the *Caesaraugustana* strongly point to compilers and users interested in the (re-)organisation of the ecclesiastical hierarchy on both sides of the Pyrenees around 1100.[409] It is clear that none of these materials is cogent proof for a specific place of origin; all these materials travelled with the collections under discussion here, and may have done so before. Yet the overall impression is that the places where these sources were most readily available at the time the collections were compiled are to be sought clearly south of the Loire, and perhaps not too far from the Mediterranean coast.

In addition to the formal sources, the provenance of the manuscripts provides some evidence where the respective collections circulated. To judge from the medieval home of the extant manuscripts, this area stretched from northern Italy to northern Spain.[410] Both copies of the *Burdegalensis* seem to come from Aquitaine, and one was owned by a monastery near Bordeaux in the late Middle Ages.[411] The manuscripts of the Turin 7L and the Berlin 13L may have been at Turin and Poitiers already in medieval times, though neither provenance is certain. The copy of the *Tarraconensis I* which preserves the most archaic form of the collection comes from Tulle in southern France; the second manuscript was produced for use in Roda/Barbastro (Aragon) and later held by the monastery of Santes Creus in Catalonia;[412] the third one comes from the library of Bobbio. There are two manuscripts of the second version which can be traced to southern France (Toulouse?) and Catalonia (Poblet). As for the *Caesaraugustana II/III*, most manuscripts come from southern France and Catalonia; an unidentified version of the *Caesaraugustana* seems to have been in Marseille in the Middle Ages.[413] The provenance of several manuscripts may also point to the canons of Saint-Ruf in Avignon, who

---

408. Fowler-Magerl, *Clavis* 242; Uta-Renate Blumenthal, 'The *Collectio canonum Caesaraugustana* and Roman Legal Sources', *Canon Law, Religion and Politics: Liber amicorum Robert Somerville*, ed. Uta-Renate Blumenthal et al. (Washington, D.C. 2012) 15–27, here at 17.

409. Goering, 'Bishops' (*Tarraconensis*); Fowler-Magerl, *Clavis* 239 (*Caesaraugustana*). For background, see Ludwig Vones, 'Kardinal Rainer von San Clemente als päpstlicher Legat in Katalonien und Südwestfrankreich. Politische und diplomatische Aspekte', *Aspects diplomatiques des voyages pontificaux*, ed. Bernard Barbiche and Rolf Große (Studien und Dokumente zur Gallia Pontificia 6; Bonn 2009) 203–218.

410. In addition to the literature quoted for specific collections, the following is based on the consensus of Kéry's and Fowler-Magerl's repertories.

411. On the *Burdegalensis*, see above in Chapter 3.

412. Goering, 'Bishops' esp. 5–6 on Tarragona, BP, 26.

413. Fowler-Magerl, *Clavis* 240–243. On the *Caesaraugustana*, see Chapter Five.

may have had some of these collections disseminated in the Pyrenee regions.[414]

So these collections in the Middle Ages were known in a relatively large area for which there is no easy denominator. It stretched from the very north of Italy and the Kingdom of Burgundy via southern France and Aquitane to the Iberian peninsula; if there is a discernible 'centre', it would be the Aquitaine and Catalonia. In the case of the *Tarraconensis* and the *Caesaraugustana*, it is very likely that the collections were compiled, reworked, and used on either side of the eastern Pyrenees; these areas also were the medieval home of relatively many manuscripts. Northern Italy (Bobbio, Milan?) and Burgundy (Valence/Die, Avignon, Marseille) seem to have played a role in providing formal sources, and also in the dissemination of copies, but cannot be established as the home of any *Tarraconensis*-related collection.

While a more precise localisation remains difficult, the evidence for the compilation and use of these collections in mainly Occitan language areas is solid enough to take it into account if we now turn to the content of these collections. As mentioned above, the 'Gregorian' materials in the *Tarraconensis*-related groups stand out both for their rarity in pre-Gratian collections, and for containing a considerable number of key texts for Gregory's pontificate around 1080. Some of them, namely the *Dictatus* and several of the Poitiers decrees, were also extremely contentious texts, even by the high standards of the late 1070s and early 1080s. The best evidence is available for the Poitiers decrees. The council itself was resented by King Philip, and one may assume that the outbreak of violence at the council was related to the content of these decrees, too.[415] More specific evidence is available from the letters of Manasses I of Reims and a number of prelates from Thérouanne, Cambrai, and Noyon who in their writings used elaborate argument, biblical examples, and a wide array of patristic and legal authorities to argue against specific decrees, in particular on clerical marriage.[416]

Why is this opposition to the decrees of Poitiers important in our analysis of the *Tarraconensis*-related collections? The point is that even with

414. Blumenthal, 'Poitevin Manuscripts'; see also Fowler-Magerl, *Clavis* 134–136 and Schilling, 'Kanones' 89.

415. See Hugh's letter in Hugh of Flavigny (ed. Dümmler, MGH SS 8, 418–419).

416. Erwin Frauenknecht, *Die Verteidigung der Priesterehe in der Reformzeit* (MGH Studien und Texte 16; Hanover 1997), here at 105–125; Brigitte Meijns, 'Opposition to Clerical Continence and the Gregorian Celibacy Legislation in the Diocese of Thérouanne: *Tractatus pro clericorum conubio* (c. 1077–1078)' *Sacris erudiri* 47 (2008) 223–290; John Stephens Ott, *Bishops, Authority and Community in Northwestern Europe, c. 1050–1150* (Life and Thought: Fourth Series 102; Cambridge 2015), here at 58–64.

less contentious materials, we often see that compilers of canon law collections made conscious choices what to retain and what to drop in the compilation of their collections. Indeed, the process of selection began much earlier; as Somerville put it, canons 'unappealing or uninteresting to certain parties' were less likely to became canon law.[417] Even prelates attenting the same council would bring home very different versions of the decrees, and often the silence from some areas is telling.[418] This certainly applies to Hugh's synods, less so, perhaps, for the decrees being 'uninteresting' but all the more for their being 'unappealing to certain parties'. One group which may be assumed to have taken a critical stance were those prelates who were suspended, deposed, or excommunicated at these synods. In 1078, the group of recently deposed or suspended prelates included the archbishops of Besançon, Bordeaux, Bourges, Lyon, Tours, Reims, Rouen, and Sens; the bishops of Amiens, Autun, Beauvais, Châlons-en-Champagne, Chartres, Laon, Noyon, Poitiers, Rennes, Senlis, Soissons, and Thérouanne, plus several abbots of great houses.[419] However, opposition to the decrees of Hugh's legatine synods was not restricted to those immediately affected by this 'decapitation of the French Church'.[420] For King Philip, the novel prohibition of lay investiture was a source of grave concern; the clergy at Cambrai and Noyon, and the authors of the *Tractatus pro clericorum cunubio* specifically took issue with Hugh's decrees concerning clerical marriage.[421] The tracts of the *Norman Anonymous* are later echoes of the protests against both what Hugh sought to implement and the measures he took.[422]

In the light of this wide-spread protest against the decrees of Autun and Poitiers, the presence of the latter in the *Tarraconensis*-related collections is indeed significant. None of the many canonical collections compiled in northern France in the same time included them, although the writings

417. Robert Somerville, *The Councils of Urban II, Vol. 1: Decreta Claromontensia* (AHC. Supplementum 1; Amsterdam 1972), here at 39: '[...] aspects of the decrees might have been unappealing or uninteresting to certain parties. Those portions could be omitted from any record the prelate carried home.'

418. A striking example is the prohibition for clerics to do homage at Clermont 1095; see Somerville, *Decreta Claromontensia* 38–39, 45–71, 83–98 (discussion), 145 (concordance table), and the summary by Jörg Peltzer, *Canon Law, Careers and Conquest: Episcopal Elections in Normandy and Greater Anjou, c. 1140–c. 1230* (Life and Thought: Fourth Series 71; Cambridge 2008), here at 24. See also Becker, *Urban II.* 3.323–330.

419. In total, Hugh and other papal legates between 1075 and 1082 suspended or deposed thirty-four French archbishops and bishops, and excommunicated eighteen of them. See Hiestand, 'Légats pontificaux' 57.

420. Hiestand, 'Légats pontificaux' 58 ('une véritable décapitation de l'Église de France') ; Tellenbach, *Church* 209–211 (French church); Ott, *Bishops* 59–64 (esp. Cambrai).

421. Frauenknecht, *Verteidigung* 105–125; Meijns, 'Opposition'; Ott, *Bishops* 59–63.

422. Frauenknecht, *Verteidigung* 125–149.

against these decrees themselves are good evidece that they were known. The presence of the Poitiers canons, and more generally the 'Gregorian' materials in the *Tarraconensis*-related collections need not reflect approval of every single text by every single compiler of the various collections. However, it is striking to see that all collections containing the decrees were compiled outside the sphere of royal influence. King Philip had clashed directly with Count William VIII of Poitiers over the assembly of the council, but in the end could not prevent Hugh from holding another of his 'so-called councils', as Philip preferred to call them.[423] When it came to the compilation of collections—and thus the 'enduring legacy' of any decree[424]—many more parties were involved. No king, count, or papal legate could control which prelates copied (or ignored), preserved (or lost), remembered (or forgot) which parts of the synodal acts.

Given that the corpus of Gregorian materials found in many *Tarraconensis*-related collections was hardly ever taken into any canonical collection compiled in northern France (specifically, in the provinces of Tours, Sens, Reims, and Rouen), it seems legitimate to come to the conclusion that these differences reflect wider-ranging differences concerning canon law in these large areas. Gregory's politics, and many of his letters were well known in all of modern France; but when it came to the integration of these canons into canon law collections, northern and southern France were clearly different areas.

This is not the place to fully discuss the regional differences in legal culture; a short notice on parallel evidence must suffice here. To take one example, the prohibition of investititure at Poitiers may be compared to the similar prohibitions of the Roman synods of 1078 and 1080. Most *Tarraconensis*-related collections (namely *Tarraconensis II*, *Caesaraugustana II/III*, Berlin 13L, Turin 7L, and that in Tarragona, PB, 35) contain at least one or the other of the Roman prohibitions, and the same is true for a considerable number of Italian collections, many of which draw on Anselm and/or Deusdedit. However, hardly any of the collections compiled in northern France contains these prohibitions; the only notable exception is the *Atrebatensis* (and the Wolfenbüttel 9L depending on it) for the 1078 prohibition, and the twelfth-century 10P for the 1080 decree.[425] Significant-

---

423. As reported by Hugh of Die (ed. Dümmler, MGH SS 8.418 line 26): 'conventicula et quasi concilia'.

424. See Somerville, *Piacenza* 81.

425. See Schieffer, *Entstehung* 198–201 and Stefan Beulertz, *Das Verbot der Laieninvestitur im Investiturstreit* (MGH Studien und Texte 2; Hanover 1991), esp. 47–49. Contrary to what Beulertz (ibid. 50) suggests, 4L does not contain the prohibitions of Rome 1078; only an appendix found in one 4L manuscript does so according to Gilchrist, 'Reception' 53–54.

ly, the Wolfenbüttel *9L* and *10P* also are the only pre-Gratian collections to contain the radical prohibitions of Clermont 1095 to do homage to any layperson.[426] In general, only very few pre-Gratian collections compiled north of the Alps contained the prohibitions of investiture, and the three collections just mentioned (*Atrebatensis*, *9L*, *10P*) are closely related to each other.[427] More importantly, these collections—even taken together—were not very influential, especially if compared to the *Panormia* which was compiled around the same time (clearly after *Atrebatensis* but not long before *10P*). The *Panormia* not only contains none of the investiture prohibitions issued between 1078 and 1107, but in its most common form instead contains the so-called False Investiture Privileges, which asserted that the Roman king had the right to invest bishops.[428] In Aquitaine and Catalonia, in contrast, the *Tarraconensis*-related collections made Gregory's prohibitions of investiture relatively widely known, but no manuscript containing the False Investiture Privileges is known from these regions, let alone a canon law collection compiled there. All this suggests that while canon law collections travelled widely, the reception and non-reception of specific materials sometimes followed regional patterns, which, at least in the case of sensitive issues like investiture, could coincide with the spheres of royal influence.

4.7 Gregory of San Grisogono and his *Polycarpus*

4.7.1 Biography

Little is known about Gregory's biography except that he was archdeacon at Lucca (until at least 1109), before he became cardinal priest of San Grisogono at some point before April 1111; he died 30 November 1113.[429] Most of the sources on his life date from his last years, mainly because he was involved in the chaotic events of 1111. This year, King Henry V had come to Italy and famously negotiated a radical settlement concerning

---

426. Somerville, *Decreta Claromontensia* 38–39, 45–71, 83–98 (discussion), 78 (edition of the prohibition), and 145 (concordance table). The only other transmission of the complete decrees (Somerville's 'LL') is the *Codex Lamberti* containing a large number of documents relating to the foundation of the diocese of Arras on which see Lotte Kéry, *Die Errichtung des Bistums Arras 1093/1094* (Francia. Beihefte 33; Sigmaringen 1994) (analysis) and *Le registre de Lambert, évêque d'Arras (1093–1115)*, ed. Claire Giordanengo (Sources d'histoire médiévale 34; Paris 2007) (edition).

427. Fowler-Magerl, *Clavis* 206–214; see also Oliver Münsch, 'Ein Streitschriftenfragment zur Simonie' DA (2006) 619–629. Like the *Codex Lamberti* (see last note), these collections are associated with Lambert of Arras and John of Thérouanne.

428. *Panormia* 8.135–136 (ed. Brett). See Märtl, 'Überlieferung' 35–36 and Chapter Five for discussion.

429. On Gregory's biography, see Klewitz, 'Entstehung' 212, Hüls, *Kardinäle* 169–170, and Horst, *Polycarpus* ch. 1.

royal investiture with Pope Paschal II: Henry was ready to renounce investiture at his coronation as emperor, but bishops would have had to return all regalia to the crown. This attempt to solve the 'Investiture Contest' is mainly famous because it failed so spectacularly; when the agreement was read out on 12 February 1111 in Saint Peter, it was immediately faced with opposition from both sides. Violence broke out, the planned coronation failed, and in the end the king imprisoned the pope and his cardinals. After two months, Paschal II gave in and promised to issue a privilege granting the king the right to invest bishops and abbots before their consecration, to crown Henry, and never to excommunicate him for violation of prohibitions of investiture. Gregory was among the cardinals to sign the 'privilege of Ponte Mammolo' in April 1111 which soon was known as 'pravilegium'.[430] In the long run, it may have helped to end the conflict over investiture,[431] but for Paschal II this course of events spelt disaster; for the remainder of his pontificate he faced severe criticism for having granted the 'pravilegium'. The Lateran council of March 1112 condemned it in no uncertain terms; Paschal II was made to renounce the *pravilegium*, profess his faith, and to pledge to follow the policies of his predecessors Gregory VII and Urban II. A few months later, Guido of Vienne convened a council that declared the *pravilegium* void, excommunicated Henry, and declared any form of lay investiture a heresy; the council openly threatened the pope with disobedience unless he confirmed these decrees.[432] Geoffrey of Vendôme, likewise, declared no obedience was owed to a pope 'deviating from the faith', and the danger of a French schism was real.[433]

This was the situation in which Gregory completed the influential canonical collection known as *Polycarpus*, available in a provisional edition.[434]

430. See the proceedings of Lateran 1112 (ed. Weiland, MGH Const. 1.572): 'Privilegium illud, quod non est privilegium sed vere debet dici pravilegium [...] a domno papa Paschali per violentiam Henrici regis extortum [...] iudicio sancti Spiritus dampnamus et irritum esse iudicamus atque omnino cassamus [...].' The second recension has almost the identical text, see *Liber pontificalis* (ed. Duchesne 2.370).

431. Tellenbach, *Church* 281–283, stressing that Henry V insisted on conferring regalia, not churches.

432. Beate Schilling, *Guido von Vienne – Papst Calixt II.* (MGH Schriften 45; Hanover 1998) 362–373.

433. Carlo Servatius, *Paschalis II. (1099–1118). Studien zu seiner Person und seiner Politik* (Päpste und Papsttum 14; Stuttgart 1979) 289–291.

434. Kéry 266–269; Fowler-Magerl, *Clavis* 229–232. The fundamental study is Horst, *Polycarpus*; see in addition Horst Fuhrmann, 'Kurzinformation', *Die Sammlung "Policarpus" des Kardinals Gregor von S. Grisogono. Angelegt und gestaltet von Carl Erdmann (†). Zum Druck vorbereitet von Uwe Horst, unter Mitarbeit von Michael Klein, herausgegeben von Horst Fuhrmann* ([ca. 2004]), https://www.mgh.de/index.php/mgh-digital/digitale-angebote-zu-mgh-abteilungen, Somerville, *Piacenza* 31–32, Kéry, 'Recht' 371–380, and most recently Uta-Renate Blumenthal, '1111 and Canon Law in Rome' BMCL 36 (2019) 157–173. All quotations are from the provisional edition prepared by Erdmann in the 1930s and Horst in the 1970s, available at www.mgh.de. This edition is based on a

In many respects, the *Polycarpus* is a decisively Roman collection. It was compiled by a cardinal of the Roman church, in the immediate context of a conflict between imperial and papal parties, and addresses many issues of special relevance for the papal curia. At the same time, the collection is evidence for the contacts between the curia and the Latin Church at large, as Gregory dedicated it to Diego Gelmírez, the bishop and (from 1120) archbishop of Santiago de Compostella. As the dedication is also important evidence for the date of the collection, it is worth quoting it in full:[435]

> Here begins the prologue by Gregory, cardinal priest of San Grisogono, [dedicated] to Diego, bishop of Santiago de Compostella. Gregory, the most humble of priests, to the beloved lord Diego of Santiago de Compostella, worthily decorated with the pontifical chasuble, greetings.

The first sentence (the 'incipit' clause) is absent from most manuscripts and may be a later addition. The most unusual part of the dedication is the reference to 'the pontifical chasuble' (*infula*). While the translation as 'chasuble' is the most straightforward possibility, it sometimes has been translated as 'mitre' or seen as an allusion to the pallium that Diego was granted in 1105. Horst with good reasons rejected the latter interpretations and argued that Gregory used the ambiguous 'chasuble' to avoid the term 'bishop' (so not to embarrass the dedicatee).[436] This is an attractive argument, provided that the first sentence of the prologue was indeed a later addition and that Diego had tried to become archbishop already in 1105.[437]

---

broad selection of *Polycarpus* manuscripts but lacks an *apparatus fontium*, so it should be used in conjunction with the concordance tables in Horst, *Polycarpus* 103–198. It seems that there were two different versions of the edition available for download in the past; I have used, and archived, the version available in early 2020. The update announced by Fuhrmann, 'Kurzinformation' 3 was never published. Note that the canon numbers in the *Clavis* database (which follows Madrid, BN, 7127) are different from those of Erdmann and Horst. References to a partial edition by Angelo Mai (Kéry 267; Fowler-Magerl, *Clavis* 231) are misguided.

435. *Prologus* (ed. Erdmann und Horst 1): 'Incipit prologus Gregorii cardinalis presbiteri tituli sancti Grisogoni ad Didacum sancti Iacobi ecclesie episcopoum. Dilecto domino D. sancti Iacobi ecclesie pontificali infula digne decorato Gregorius presbiterorum humillimus [*sic*] salutem.' The translation is adopted from Somerville and Brasington, *Prefaces* 129 (which seems to be based on the shorter Ballerini text, not Hüffer's; see Ballerini and Ballerini, 'De antiquis collectionibus' here at PL 56.346–352 vs. Hermann Hüffer, *Beiträge zur Geschichte der Quellen des Kirchenrechts und des Römischen Rechts im Mittelalter* (Münster 1862) 75.

436. Horst, *Polycarpus* 4 against Paul Fournier, 'Les deux recensions de la collection canonique romaine dite le *Polycarpus*' *Mélanges d'archéologie et d'histoire de l'École française de Rome* 37 (1918/19) 55–101, here at 62.

437. The first sentence, where Diego is called 'bishop', is found in four manuscripts including Madrid, BN, 7127 [not seen] and Köln, Erzbischöfliche Diözesan- und Dombibliothek, Cod. 126, fol. 3r, two codices valued highly by Erdmann and other scholars. On Diego's 1105 (not 1104, as the older scholarship thought) trip to Rome, see Vones, *Historia Compostellana* 161 n. 60a (date of JL 5986) and 289–292 (Diego's aims). Blumenthal, *Early Councils* 23–31 does not discuss JL 5986 (the pallium grant for Santiago), but see Gresser, *Synoden* 359.

4.7.2 The *Polycarpus* (Overview)

The *Polycarpus* is a large collection of eight books, divided into nine to forty-two titles each, containing a total of 1,540 canons; it has a short preface and contains a *capitulatio* listing the titles (not the canons) of all books. The canons have inscriptions, which in the first two books sometimes are more precise than those in earlier collections; they are not numbered and (with two exceptions) have no rubric. Rather, the titles are numbered both in the *capitulatio* and the main text; they have rubrics normally coined by Gregory himself. Most titles only contain a handful of canons, but some are very long indeed, namely those on episcopal elections (*Polycarpus* 2.1.1–41), ordinations (2.31.1–56), baptism (3.10.1–52), celebration of mass (3.16.1–40), lower clergy (4.32.1–83), abbatial elections (4.35.1–44), procedure (5.1.1–59), and marriage (6.4.1–74). The composition of these titles need not reflect special interests on Gregory's side; for example, the long series on episcopal and abbatial elections represent the relevant canon law very well, but seventy-four canons on marriage contain little more than the basic rules of ecclesiastical marital law. In fact, the first book, which in many respects gives the impression of being reworked thoroughly, has only short *tituli* (the longest of which contains sixteen canons).

According to the preface, the 'Greek' title of the collection refers to its composite nature,[438] and indeed the *Polycarpus* covers many areas of canon law. Let us briefly look at the individual books. The first one—to be discussed in greater detail below—deals with the Roman church, its internal organisation as well as its relationship with the Latin Church at large. Book two focusses on the clergy; it treats episcopal elections, outlines the respective rights and duties of priests, bishops, and metropolitans, covers ordinations (and reordinations), simony, and the prohibition of investiture. It contains a separate title on 'the use and the authority of the pallium' (*Polycarpus* 2.20) and canons on the respective roles of bishops and archbishops; but none of the canons can be linked to the case of Santiago de Compostella in particular, as one would perhaps have expected from the dedication of the *Polycarpus* to Diego Gelmírez. The long third book is devoted to churches, ecclesiastical property (including monastic property and exemption),[439] and liturgy; the sacraments of the Eucharist and baptism are treated here too. The next book contains disciplinary canons;

---

438. *Prologus* (ed. Erdmann und Horst 1).

439. See *Polycarpus* 3.15 in particular, with many parallels to *74T* tit. 3–4 on 'monastic liberty'. Kuttner, 'Roman Manuscripts' 11 suspected that the pro-monastic forgeries attributed to Eugene II (JE –; J³ –) made their 'first appearance in the *Polycarpus*', but in fact they are only found in the second version (PY01.35.01 in the *Clavis* database). Landau, 'Seelsorge' 112 suggested they emerged in the mid-eleventh century in Italy (Tuscany?).

it mainly deals with the clergy (bishops, priests, monks and nuns) including the *lapsi*, clergy 'fallen into heresy' but returning to the catholic faith. Book five deals with accusations and procedural law on the basis of the False Decretals and *Capitula Angilramni*. The next book, the longest of the *Polycarpus*, gives an overview of the rights and duties of laypeople, marital law, various sins and their penance, and penance in general. In the context of obedience due to the Church Gregory here also addresses the role of the emperor (*Polycarpus* 6.1 *De imperatoribus*) and the protection of church property. Book seven, clearly inspired by Anselm of Lucca, presents different ways to treat those outside the Church (heretics, schismatics, Jews), namely excommunication, the use of (military) force, but also dispensation. The very short last book, again more conventional in content, is devoted to death, burial, and the afterlife; it may be compared to the last book of Burchard's *Liber decretorum* from which Gregory took the bulk of the material. Three in four canons are taken from Burchard, more than in any other book of the *Polycarpus*.[440]

4.7.3 Date, Structure, and Content

Date

Like with other major collections, we may assume that the *Polycarpus* was compiled over an extended period of time, which in Gregory's case strongly suggests he began his work at Lucca. This is supported by the fact that he used the collection of Anselm of Lucca and apparently a Luccese copy of Burchard. The main question is when the *Polycarpus* was finished.[441] Most scholars agree that this was only after Gregory was made cardinal, but the exact date is still open to discussion. Horst's interpretation that Gregory avoided calling Diego 'bishop' would fit a date after 1105 (when Diego had failed to become archbishop) better than an earlier date. Gregory's assertion that Diego had urged him to compile a collection 'for a long time' may refer back to Diego's stay at Rome, but also could be topical. Fortunately, stronger arguments in favour of a late date are at hand. The fact that Gregory in the dedication refers to himself as 'most humble priest' suggests that he was already cardinal priest, and thus a date after September 1109, the last time he was referred to as archdeacon in the sources. Internal evidence from the collection also supports the idea it was compiled by Gregory after he had become cardinal priest, as the

---

440. Horst, *Polycarpus* 25–26.

441. Fournier, 'Polycarpus' 61 proposed an early date (shortly after 1104), but see Horst, *Polycarpus* 1–6; Blumenthal 'IIII' 172–173.

Polycarpus gives special attention to the lower-ranking cardinals.[442] Above all, Horst and Blumenthal have argued convincingly that the *Polycarpus* was finished only after April 1111 as it contains materials which seem to be tailor-made to defend Pope Paschal II and his cardinals against the criticism they faced after the events of Ponte Mammolo.[443] For example, right at the beginning of the collection there is a text on Saint Peter's denial (*Polycarpus* 1.1.2) that echoes the argument made by Paschal's supporters that the pope like Saint Peter may have been guilty but also could correct his error. Also, the rubric to *Polycarpus* 1.22 asserts papal immunity, even if the pope had acted 'reprehensibly'—a point that would seem unusual in a collection compiled at the papal curia, but in the years after 1111 was an important argument to defend Paschal II. Another canon on 'forced oaths' is highlighted by a separate rubric; this is significant, as normally only titles (not canons) have rubrics in the *Polycarpus*. The canon, not found in any earlier collection, declared void promises and oaths made under threat.[444] Finally, a rare excerpt from the Digest (*Polycarpus* 3.12.36) holds that anyone leaving behind his property and is prevented upon his return from entering, is regarded as 'driven out by violence', which echoes Paschal's demands that Henry returned ecclesiastical patrimony. None of these canons alone would allow to link the *Polycarpus* to any specific situation, but taken together they fit the line of defence taken by Paschal II and his cardinals so well that they can best be explained if we assume that the *Polycarpus* was only finished after April 1111.[445]

The First Book of the *Polycarpus*: A Cardinal's View of the Roman Church *ca.* 1112

Let us take a closer look the first book, which deals with the primacy of the Roman church, papal elections, and the papacy in general. By the early twelfth century, choosing these topics for the opening book of a canonical collection was fairly conventional, at least in the environment of the papal curia. For his material, Gregory therefore could draw on the opening sections of *74T*, Deusdedit, Anselm, and anonymous Italian collections.[446] In most respects, the first book of the *Polycarpus* is similar to the respective

---

442. Horst, *Polycarpus* 5.

443. Horst, *Polycarpus* 5–6; Blumenthal '1111' 172–173.

444. *Polycarpus* 6.10.31 (ed. Erdmann und Horst 425), with the rubric 'De iuramento iniuste extorto' to JL 4447. See the *Liber pontificalis* (ed. Duchesne 2.370) as quoted below note 449.

445. Horst, *Polycarpus* 1–6, especially 6 (followed by Blumenthal, '1111' 170–171): none of the arguments was conclusive in itself, 'doch sie sind so auffällig und ungewöhnlich, daß ihre Erklärung am besten gelingt, wenn man für den Abschluß der Kanonessammlung die Zeit nach 1111 ansetzt.'

446. Horst, *Polycarpus* 56 (calculating that 83 per cent of the material in book one was from 'reform collections', a much higher share than in any other part of the *Polycarpus*).

sections of these collections, but with some exceptions. Namely, there are unusually rich materials on the right of the pope to consecrate, translate, or depose bishops and to create, relocate, or merge episcopal sees (titles 5, 6, and 9–14); this may well reflect that the interference with episcopal elections and even the diocesan structure had become routine business for the papal curia by the early twelfth century.[447] Also, the *Polycarpus* in book one contains several titles on papal and imperial power that echo anti-imperial polemics of Gregory's time (titles 20, 21, 23, and 29). While Gregory thus in some respects emphasizes papal prerogatives very strongly, other titles are rather apologetic, reflecting the uncomfortable situation of the papal curia after Ponte Mammolo. For example, while Gregory stressed the right of the pope 'and other prelates' to excommunicate the emperor—Paschal II had taken an oath not to do this himself—, no mention is made of the 'Gregorian' claim that the pope may *depose* kings and emperors.[448] Even more significantly, the *Polycarpus* has a separate title stressing that the pope may not be judged 'even if he had acted reprehensibly' (*Polycarpus* 1.22; JE 2796). Gregory had to take into account that Paschal was severely attacked by many reformers. Also, as mentioned above, the opening section of the *Polycarpus* contains a canon on Saint Peter's denial that in the context of the first book may well be understood as an apologetic argument on papal fallibility. After all, Paschal II himself had professed at the Lateran synod of 1112 to have done wrong and that he hoped for correction.[449] This probably saved him from being put to trial for heresy, as heresy commonly was defined as 'obstinate' deviation from the faith. The principle of papal immunity, in contrast, would probably not have saved him, as accusations of heresy posed an exception to this rule; it may be significant that Gregory avoided this topic introduced into canon law by Deusdedit a generation earlier. Instead, he carefully distinguished 'schism' and 'heresy'.[450] In this context, it may also be noteworthy that Gregory chose to compose a title (*Polycarpus* 1.3) on the 'purity of the faith of the Roman church'—not 'of the pope'. Paschal II used a similar argument to defend himself against accusations of heresy.[451]

---

447. See Becker, *Urban II.* 3.352–368 (politics of Urban II in general) and Kéry, *Errichtung* esp. 307–333 (Arras). The foundation of Arras was still discussed during Paschal's pontificate (ibid. 129–134).

448. *Polycarpus* 1.23 (ed. Erdmann und Horst 62): 'Quod pape aliisque presulibus sit potestas excommunicandi imperatores.' While Paschal II felt bound by the oath he had given, the council of Vienne 1112 did not, and excommunicated Henry V (see Schilling, *Guido von Vienne* 362–373).

449. See Paschal's profession to have done wrong at the 1112 Lateran council reported by the *Liber pontificalis* (ed. Duchesne 2.370).

450. *Polycarpus* 7.5.5 (ed. Erdmann and Horst 482).

451. See Blumenthal, 'Opposition' 98 on Paschal's arguments at the 1116 Lateran council.

While all these canons are best understood as reflecting the difficulties Paschal II and his cardinals experienced after Ponte Mammolo, the first book of the *Polycarpus* also contains other elements that deserve attention. For example, it has a very short title on papal legates (*Polycarpus* 1.15), an issue of great relevance for papal government around 1100.[452] The legations of Hugh of Die and Lyon (interrupted by his own excommunication in 1087) followed a 'trial and error' approach to canon law.[453] Popes, legates, and those they interacted with remained uncertain about legatine powers; for example, could papal legates depose bishops, or only suspend them from office?[454] In the decades that followed, legations became a much more routine business, but were not adequately covered by canonical collections before Gratian. The *Polycarpus* did not fundamentally change this, but as the first collection to devote a separate sub-section to this issue at least made clear that legates had an important place in canon law.

The short title on papal elections (*Polycarpus* 1.4) deserves attention because it is manifestly shaped by the desire to enhance the position of the lower-ranking cardinals. Like other Italian compilers of canonical collections, Gregory in this context ignored the 1059 Election Decree but instead followed Deusdedit's lead in presenting the ancient canon law of papal elections, specifically the 769 election decree, and manipulated letters of Nicholas II (JL 4405 and 4431a).[455] Therefore, no mention is made of any leading role of the cardinal bishops in papal elections; in fact, the way Gregory presented the law strongly calls into question whether they could be elected pope at all.[456] In practice, of course, cardinal bishops were a dominant group at the papal curia. Gregory had first-hand experience

452. The literature is vast. See Schieffer, *Legaten in Frankreich*; Robinson, *Papacy* ch. 4; Zey, 'Augen'; Becker, *Urban II.* 3.157–179; Ludwig Vones, 'Legation und Konzilien. Der päpstliche Legat Richard von Marseille und die konziliare Tätigkeit auf der Iberischen Halbinsel', *Das begrenzte Papsttum. Spielräume päpstlichen Handelns. Legaten – "delegierte Richter" – Grenzen*, ed. Klaus Herbers et al. (Abh. Akad. Göttingen N.F. 25; Berlin 2013) 213–236 (all with further literature).

453. On Hugh's legation see now the relevant entries in *Gallia Pontificia* 3 (with further literature); Schilling's introduction (ibid. 130–139) provides an excellent overview.

454. On this question, see Robert Somerville and Hartmut Zapp, 'An "Eighth Book" of the Collection in Seven Books', *Grundlagen des Rechts. Festschrift für Peter Landau zum 65. Geburtstag*, ed. Richard H. Helmholz et al. (Rechts- und Staatswissenschaftliche Veröffentlichungen der Görres-Gesellschaft N.F. 91; Paderborn, Munich, Vienna, and Zurich 2000) 163–177 quoting Urban II (JL –; *Italia Pontificia* –) to the effect that legates could only suspend bishops from office. Becker, *Urban II.* 3.165 assumed this was a general rule, but if so, this left no trace in canon law collections, and evidence from other sources is scarce.

455. See Klewitz, 'Entstehung' 165–166 and Horst, *Polycarpus* 92 ('starkes Eigeninteresse'); for fuller discussion, see above (in the discussion of 'Papal Elections' in Deusdedit's collection) on these documents being introduced into canon law by Deusdedit.

456. *Polycarpus* 1.4.6–7 (ed. Erdmann and Horst 17) assert that only 'unus de cardinalibus presbiteris aut diaconibus' may be elected pope; the same canons (excerpts taken from the 769 election decree and the *Liber pontificalis*) are also found in Deusdedit 2.161 (131) and 1.255 (206) (ed. Wolf von Glanvell 268 and 146, respectively).

how important they were for papal government, and also how powerful they were as adversaries;[457] and of course he was well aware that Paschal's predecessor Urban II had been cardinal bishop before his election. As in the case of Deusdedit, Gregory's account of papal elections should not be taken as 'the law' but as a statement, based firmly on ancient canon law, by the cardinal deacons and priests eager to guard their position vis-à-vis the cardinal bishops.

Gregory on Canonical Authority, Dispensation, and Legal Theory

Neither the preface nor the collection contain much legal theory, but dispersed over the *Polycarpus* one finds several titles which contain canons relevant for any scholar interested in legal hermeneutics; in several cases, there are parallels to the writings of Bernold of Konstanz, Ivo of Chartres, and Alger of Liège. Specifically, at or towards the end of books one, three, and seven, the *Polycarpus* contains a number of titles dealing with the sources of the law and the correct understanding of canonical texts. Specifically, the canons in *Polycarpus* 1.26–27 deal with the sources of the law and the concept of 'authority and reason'. The distinction between different kinds of canonical norms (precept, admonition, council) in *Polycarpus* 1.26 echoes similar distinctions by Ivo of Chartres and Bernold of Konstanz, while the next title on 'authority and reason' was later taken up by the *Caesaraugustana* compiler in his book on the sources of the law. *Polycarpus* 3.20, 21, and 23 all contain canons on the sources of the law. This includes numerous lists of biblical books, excerpts from the *Decretum Gelasianum*, Gregory's *Synodica* (JE 1092), and the catalogue of sources of canon law which Leo IV declared as admissible in ecclesiastical courts (JE 2599).[458] At the end of book seven (in titles 14 and 15), Gregory gathers canons on dispensation, legal change, and the principle that what was done 'out of necessity' was no longer binding once this 'necessity' had ceased.[459]

In addition to these titles, there are other materials in the *Polycarpus* which would have been of interest to any medieval scholar trying to understand the nature of canon law. In the case of penance, it is obvious that Gregory in his collections was more interested in discussing what 'true'

457. See Schludi, *Entstehung* 107–108 commenting on the strong position of the cardinal bishops during Paschal's pontificate in general, and Uta-Renate Blumenthal, 'Opposition to Pope Paschal II: Some Comments on the Lateran Council of 1112' AHC 10 (1978) 82–98, here at 84–85, 90, and 92 on the role of cardinal bishops in orchestrating the opposition against the pope.

458. *Polycarpus* 3.20.5 (ed. Erdmann and Horst 218). The only earlier collection to contain this part of JE 2599 is Ivo 4.72 (on which see below, Chapter Five).

459. For the principle of 'cessante necessitate' see the discussion below in the context of Alger of Liège.

penance was rather then simply providing a list of penitential tariffs for individual sins.[460] Another case may be the law on episcopal translations, a topic Gregory deals with at no less than four occasions (*Polycarpus* 1.9–10, 2.14, and 3.30). He may well have had in mind the tumultuous events in many disputed sees around 1100, or valued these canons as evidence for papal prerogatives in this area of the law. At the same time, the question of episcopal translations is also a classical topic in the discussion of exceptions—out of 'necessity' or for the greater good—to general prohibitions, and scholars from Hincmar of Reims to Bernold of Konstanz took this as a starting point to discuss the very nature of canon law.[461] Finally, the *Polycarpus* is the earliest known collection to contain *Duae sunt*.[462] In this famous text, Pope Urban II distinguished 'public law' as found in the writings of the fathers from 'private law' (*lex privata*) of individual conscience. Strikingly, the pope argued that 'private law is more worthy than public law' and therefore conscience can override positive canon law, at least in the case under discussion in *Duae sunt* (entry into monastic life). In the course of the twelfth century, different forms of *Duae sunt* circulated widely, and the instability of the text may at least partly be due to the tantalizing assertion that conscience can prevail over written law.[463] As with all canonical collections devoid of explicit comment, any interpretation why the compiler chose to bring together the canons he inserted in his collection remains to some degree speculative; but one may well conclude that Gregory of San Grisogono was willing and able to include a considerable number of texts that provided food for thoughts on fundamental legal questions. To judge from the later career of the titles he composed (for example, the afterlife of *Polycarpus* 1.27 in the *Caesaraugustana*) and the canons he introduced into canon law (for example *Duae sunt*), the choices Gregory made struck a chord with legal scholars of the twelfth century.

Compadrazgo in the Early Twelfth Century

The *Polycarpus* may be strongly influenced by Gregory's role as a cardinal close to Paschal II in tumultuous times, but one should not forget that

---

460. See Horst, *Polycarpus* 29 on *Polycarpus* 6.19 as a tract on penance rather than a penitential ('eher schon wie eine theoretische Abhandlung zum Thema Buße').

461. See Scholz, *Transmigration* (general); for Hincmar, Abbo, Bernold, and others, see Chapter Three (see Chapter 3, note 68).

462. *Polycarpus* 4.32.79 (ed. Erdmann and Horst 292–293). On *Duae sunt* (JL 5760) see in general Robert Somerville, 'Canon Law, Inspired Law, and Papal Authority', *Netti'ot le-David: Jubilee Volume for David Weiss Halivni* (Jerusalem 2004) 119–134 (with further literature). Its authenticity was doubted by Peter Landau, 'Die "duae leges" im kanonischen Recht des 12. Jahrhunderts', *Officium und Libertas christiana* (Sb. Akad. München 1991.3; Munich 1991) 55–96, here at 72–73.

463. On the many versions of JL 5760, see Titus Lenherr, 'Zur Überlieferung des Kapitels *Duae sunt*' AKKR 168 (1999) 369–374.

it was a well-structured collection covering very many everyday questions of canon law. Therefore, the final example to illustrate Gregory's approach to canon law is taken from marital law. Book six of the *Polycarpus* contains a fairly complete account of the law of marriage, including many canons on the various impediments to marriage. Like most collections compiled after *ca.* 1050, the *Polycarpus* contains the excessive prohibitions of kin marriage as found first in Burchard's *Liber decretorum*, and in addition other prohibitions. An interesting case are the prohibitions on account of spiritual kinship, relations resulting from sponsorship at baptism (or confirmation). Title six contains three canons on this impediment to marriage, specifically those resulting from the bond between the parents of the baptised on the one hand and the godparents on the other.[464] The relationship to the godparents of one's own children in medieval societies was an important social institution; by acting as godparent, one became the parent's 'co-parent' (*compater* and *commater*, *compère* and *commère*, *Gevatter* and *Gevatterin*); in English-language scholarship, the Spanish *compadre* and *commadre* are often used, and the relationship is known as 'compadre relationship' or *compadrazgo*.[465] At the same time, the spiritual relationship between the baptised and godparents was an absolute impediment to marriage,[466] and the main question the *Polycarpus* addressed in this section was whether and how this also affected marriages among the parents and godparents of the baptisee. The first canon asserts that if someone acted as godfather or godmother, the bond of spiritual kinship also extended to his or her spouse; both partners therefore are co-parents of the parents of the baptised, suggesting that no marriage was possible between any of them even as widowers and widows. The second canon, in contrast, allowed the marriage between a man and the widow of the godfather of his child (his *compadre*), if the widow had not acted as godmother herself. In the third canon, finally, Pope Paschal II (JL 6436) confirmed this and additionally discussed the case of a man who wants to marry the daughter of his *compadre*. According to Paschal, such a marriage was allowed if and only if this daughter was born before the bond of spiritual kinship had been established; but one was not allowed to marry any children born to the godparents of one's own children. Later medieval canon law ad-

---

464. *Polycarpus* 6.6 (ed. Erdmann and Horst 403).

465. See Jussen, *Patenschaft* and Lynch, *Christianizing Kinship*.

466. See still Joseph Freisen, *Geschichte des canonischen Eherechts bis zum Verfall der Glossenlitteratur* (Paderborn 1893), here at 507–532. Modern studies on the legal aspects are rare, especially for pre-Gratian times; for an account of the classical canon law, see de Enrique León, *La «cognatio spiritualis» según Graciano* (Pontificio Ateneo delle Santa Croce. Monografie giuridiche 11; Milan 1996).

opted this solution first found in the *Polycarpus*.[467] Small as it is, the title on *compadrazgo* shows that Gregory at this occasion at least was keen to insert the newest canon law into his collection, and the arrangement of the canons strongly suggests that Gregory saw the most recent canons as binding, even where they seemed to contradict the ancient canon law he quoted at the beginning of the title.

Formal Sources and Method

The collections Gregory used most frequently were, in this sequence, Burchard, Anselm, *74T*, and *2L/8P*; taken together, they provided nearly two thirds of his canons.[468] His working library must have been considerable, and presumably included the False Decretals, the *Dionysio-Hadriana*, the register of Gregory the Great, and perhaps other papal registers. The relatively large share of unidentified sources is probably due to Gregory working with numerous smaller collections and his tendency to rework his sources independently, sometimes abbreviating material, sometimes combining different sources, and rarely taking long series of canons from only one formal source.

Horst made a strong case that Gregory's Burchard manuscript was very similar to an extant copy today kept at Lucca.[469] The Anselm version he used may also point to Lucca.[470] It may further be that Gregory, who had been archdeacon in Lucca until 1109, had access to some of Anselm's working materials. In any case his use of *2L/8P* extends to a series of excerpts taken from Augustine's *Contra Donatistas* and the letters of Pelagius I which was also used by Anselm and Bonizo (but not Deusdedit) and is best preserved in *2L/8P*.[471] Gregory seems also have had access to a small

467. See Gratian 1 C.30 q.4, mainly containing the same canons; c. 5 is an addition by Gratian 2.

468. Horst, *Polycarpus* ch. 2 and 3, esp. 25 and 55 (tables). I follow Horst in including doubtful cases and the parallels to unidentified intermediate collections; disregarding them would affect the numbers less than one might think, as many canons Horst counts as coming from intermediate collections could well have come from Anselm or *2L/8P* instead. My own assumption is that *2L/8P* or a collection very similar to it played an important role in the making of the *Polycarpus*; see, for example, the series in *Polycarpus* 7.5.8–31. According to Fowler-Magerl, *Clavis* 101 and 174, Gregory also used *183T* and Bonizo, but she did not provide further arguments.

469. Lucca, Biblioteca Capitolare Feliniana, 124. See Blumenthal and Jasper, 'Licet' 52 on JE †1989 as found in the Lucca manuscript and *Polycarpus* 3.25.4.

470. Horst, *Polycarpus* 45–46 highlighted similarities to Anselm Barb. but stopped short of calling it Gregory's source. According to Fowler-Magerl, *Clavis* 231, Ludwig Schmugge linked Gregory's Anselm version to Anseln A' and specifically the manuscript Firenze, BML, Ashburnham 53; I was not able to verify this claim from the article quoted by Fowler-Magerl (Schmugge, 'Dekretale Leos').

471. The two series *Polycarpus* 7.5.11–21 and 7.10.6–19 correspond in this sequence to Bonizo 7.20–27 and 7.17–19, respectively; the material found in the *Polycarpus* but not Bonizo seems to be taken from a source similar to *2L/8P*. See Horst, *Polycarpus* 50–51 (discussion), 191–192, and 194 (concordance tables), Berschin, *Bonizo von Sutri* 54, and now Rolker, 'Bonizo' 81–89.

intermediate collection that provided Deusdedit, Anselm, and Bonizo with a series of Pseudo-Isidorian excerpts.[472] Compared to the other three compilers, Gregory only took a few canons from this source, and only chose canons also found in Anselm; the text is often closer to Anselm than to the other collections. Gregory's use of this source, therefore, seems to have been not entirely independent from Anselm, but on the other hand he cannot simply have taken these canons from Anselm's collection (at least not any known version of this work). Not only are Gregory's inscriptions fuller and more often correct than Anselm's, the *Polycarpus* also (like Bonizo, Deusdedit, and *2L/8P*, but unlike Anselm) preserved the sequence of the material source.

In the case of Gregory I, he seems to have double-checked material he found in his formal sources by looking it up in the register.[473] This does not mean that Gregory corrected his sources, however. To take a famous forgery as an example, the *Polycarpus* contains, like many collections compiled in the decades around 1100, the forgery *Quam sit necessarium* (JE †1366). It was first introduced into canon law by *74T*, and in the *Polycarpus* is found as part of a series of *74T* canons.[474] Gregory's inscriptions, while not wholly correct, are more precise than in *74T* and other collections. Did Gregory double-check with the register in his hand? If so, he must have noticed the difference between the forgery as found in *74T* (JE †1366) and the register version of the letter (JE 1504), as others had done: Deusdedit alarmed his readers in a comment that the canon he quoted was different from the register, and the Anselm B version substituted JE †1366 with JE 1504 altogether.[475] Gregory adopted another approach; while he remained faithful to the *74T* tradition for his text, he largely abbreviated the canon, quoting only the beginning, which has a parallel in the genuine version, and left out the more contentious forged passages on monastic liberties. As a result, his version of the forgery did not go much beyond the genuine letter the forgers had taken as their starting point (JE 1504).

4.7.4 Influence

The *Polycarpus* is a fascinating source for the dramatic events of Ponte Mammolo and its aftermath, but of course it also was an important col-

---

472. Horst, *Polycarpus* 49 n. 171 on *Polycarpus* 1.6.3–11. On the series, which was first brought to attention by Perels, 'Einleitung' XXX, see now Rolker, 'Bonizo' 89–97.

473. Fowler-Magerl, *Clavis* 231.

474. *Polycarpus* 3.15.9–11 (ed. Erdmann and Horst 196–197) = *74T* cc. 38–40 (ed. Gilchrist 39–42). The material sources are JE †1366, 1504, and 1307.

475. Anselm B 5.53 (Vat. lat. 1364, fols. 108v–109v). This was first reported by Thaner in his edition: Anselm 5.54 (ed. Thaner 252, here note b). The version of *Quam sit necessarium* in the Pisa florilegium (not seen; *Clavis* database, CT23) may be a parallel, or even related, case.

lection of canon law in its own right. Both the extant manuscripts and the numerous collections influenced by the *Polycarpus* suggest that it was valued by many readers throughout the twelfth century. There are no less than twelve medieval manuscripts of the *Polycarpus*, including one (Paris, BnF, lat. 3882) containing a revised version. The second version contains pro-monastic forgeries and seems to have been valued in monastic circles.[476] Twelve medieval manuscripts may not sound like a large number, but compared to the other collections discussed in the present chapter—mostly extant in only one or two manuscripts—it indeed is.

Where was the *Polycarpus* read and used? The provenance of the manuscripts points to Italy and southern France as the main areas of influence. Interestingly, although Gregory had dedicated his collection to Diego Gelmírez, evidence on the reception of the *Polycarpus* in Galicia is scarce. In fact, apart from the *Historia Compostellana*, which perhaps draws on the *Polycarpus*,[477] there is no direct evidence that a dedication copy of the collection made it to Santiago. We may assume that Gregory's collection was available elsewhere on the Iberian Peninsula, but again the evidence is mostly indirect. The three manuscripts known from Spanish libraries were not produced in Spain,[478] so the employment of the *Polycarpus* in the making of the *Caesaraugustana I* is in fact the only solid evidence for a medieval use of the *Polycarpus* on the Iberian Peninsula. For the Italian reception, the evidence is much fuller, as a large number of twelfth-century collections from Italy used the *Polycarpus*. The list includes the Vatican *13L*, the *Pragensis I, 3L*, the San Pietro *9L*, the Vienna *7L*, very famously the *Decretum Gratiani*, plus perhaps the *Gaddiana* and the collection in Vallicelliana F.54.[479] One could also quote a twelfth-century *ordo iudicarius* which

476. See Fournier, 'Polycarpus' 57 on Paris, BnF, lat. 3882 as a second recension and Fowler-Magerl, *Clavis* 236 on the use of this version for the pro-monastic dossier in Leipzig, UB, 276 [not seen].

477. Richard A. Fletcher, 'Magister Geraldus, Geraldus Episcopus Salamanticensis, Geraldus Scriptor: A Suggestion', *Life, Law and Letters: Historical Studies in Honour of Antonio García y García*, ed. Peter Linehan (2 vols. SG 28/29; Rome 1998) 1.249–264, here at 251, claimed the use of the *Polycarpus*. He quoted *Historia Compostellana* 1.79 (ed. Falque Rey, CCCM 70.145), perhaps taken from *Polycarpus* 6.10.23 (ed. Erdmann and Horst 423), to support this claim; I was not able to verify his only other example, *Historia Compostellana* 1.96 (ed. Falque Rey, CCCM 70.157).

478. García y García, 'Derecho' 34–36 does not discuss the *Polycarpus* (although he mentions the Madrid manuscript in the context of Lateran II). The statement of Florencio Marcos Rodríguez, 'Tres manuscritos del siglo XII con colecciones canónicas' *Analecta sacra Tarraconensia* 32 (1959) 35–54, here at 44, is probably still true: '[Este] presumible que en las bibliotecas de nuestra patria se conservase, aunque ignorado, algún ejemplar más.'

479. See Fowler-Magerl, *Clavis* 215 (*Gaddiana*), 225 (Vatican *13L*), and 231 (*Pragensis I, 3L*, San Pietro *9L*), and Blumenthal, 'Handbook' 16 (Roma, Vallicelliana, F.54, part III). For *7L* see Erdmann as quoted by Horst, *Polycarpus* 9 n. 32 (against Fournier, 'Polycarpus' 65) and Landau, 'Quellen' esp. 259. For Gratian's use of the *Polycarpus*, see Titus Lenherr, *Die Exkommunikations- und Depositionsgewalt der Häretiker bei Gratian und den Dekretisten bis zur "Glossa Ordinaria" des Johannes*

refers to a passage from *Polycarpus* 5.1 as being found 'in Policarpo libro quintus [*sic*] primo'.[480] In the case of Gratian, Lenherr has shown that Gratian used the *Panormia* and the *Polycarpus* for the 'kernel' of his Causa 24, which was later added to from other sources (namely *Tripartita* and *3L*), suggesting that the *Polycarpus* had a special importance for the compiler today known as 'Gratian 1'.[481]

Like other collections, the *Polycarpus* was added to and reworked. The pro-monastic 'second recension' has already been mentioned. Three manuscripts of the 'French group' of *Polycarpus* manuscripts contain a long series of decrees from the councils of Urban II and Calixtus II, from Melfi 1089 to Lateran I (1123). Some of the Urban II material seems to come from his register, and several of Urban's successors from Paschal II to Eugene III quoted from the same source; a lost copy of the *Liber censuum* also contained some of the material found in the *Polycarpus* appendix.[482] This evidence adds to the impression that the collection not only emerged in the immediate environment of the papacy but indeed continued to be used and 'updated' in this milieu; however, as the extant *Polycarpus* manuscripts and the numerous collections drawing on the collection testify, its reception was clearly not limited to the papal curia.

4.8 The Gregorian Collections Between Polemic and Canon Law

4.8.1 Unity and Diversity of the Gregorian Collections

The idea that collections compiled by known supporters of Gregory VII for this very reason shared an ideological bias strong enough to treat them as a group ultimately goes back to the times when these collections were compiled in the first place.[483] Yet it was only in the late nine-

---

Teutonicus (Münchener theologische Studien, Kanonistische Abteilung 42; Sankt Ottilien 1987) esp. 87–93 and Winroth, *Making* esp. 16 and 48–50.

480. As quoted by Bruce C. Brasington, '*Crimina que episcopis inpingere dicis*: The Contribution of the *Collectio Polycarpus* to an Early *Ordo iudiciorum*', *Readers, Texts and Compilers in the Earlier Middle Ages: Studies in Medieval Canon Law in Honour of Linda Fowler-Magerl*, ed. Kathleen Grace Cushing and Martin Brett (CFC; Farnham and Aldershot 2009) 123–135, here at 132. The canon in question is *Polycarpus* 5.1.23 (ed. Erdmann and Horst 333), overlapping with Gratian C.2 q.7 cc.23 and 52 (ed. Friedberg 488 and 500–501).

481. Lenherr *Exkommunikations- und Depositionsgewalt* 89–90 (summary); Winroth, *Making* ch. 2 and esp. 125 (Lenherr's 'kernel' and 'Gratian 1').

482. For the '*Polycarpus*-Cencius' transmission, see Somerville, *Decreta Claromontensia* 119–121. See also Blumenthal, 'Conciliar Canons' 371, Somerville, 'Deusdedit' 290–291, and Becker, *Urban II.* 3.709–710. Both the appendix and the link to Eugene III (JL 9660) were first reported by Hüffer, *Beiträge* 79 and 143–144.

483. Beno, *Gesta* (ed. Francke, MGH Ldl 2.399 and 414), as quoted above.

teenth century, in the midst of the *Kulturkampf,* the concept of 'Gregorian reform collections' rapidly gained traction, and has dominated much of twentieth-century scholarship. The question is whether modern research should still use this category, and if so, in which sense.

As for the content and structure, the collections studied in this chapter are certainly very diverse. For example, among those that they divide their material into books, some start emphatically with the privileges of the Roman church, but Bonizo for one placed the sacraments first. As for the material sources, only some of these collections (all belonging the *Tarraconensis* group) preserve significant 'Gregorian' materials, while the other collections show a stronger interest in ancient canon law or, in the case of Deusdedit, a very peculiar mix of ancient canon law and more recent documents (oaths, leases, charters, *formulae*). More importantly for Fournier's argument, there is very little evidence for 'papal inspiration', not even in the case of the most ardent Gregorians. Also, contrary to what Fournier had claimed, an analysis of the formal sources does not support the idea of the papacy providing canonists with pre-selected materials in the form of 'Gregorian intermediate collections'. Only relatively rarely, two or even three Gregorian collections depend on shared lost collections, and these collections were typically very small; there is nothing to suggest that these collections were comissioned or disseminated by the papacy. Fournier's concept of one giant intermediate collection available to all Gregorian compilers should be given up once and for all.[484]

This, however, is not to deny that the collections studied here were shaped by the desire to support the papacy and individual popes. Deusdedit, Anselm, and Bonizo all reused texts and arguments from their polemical writings when they compiled their collections, some of which directly supported Gregory's legitimation; Gregory of San Grisogono in his collection defended Paschal II as well as he could. Indeed, in the case of the *Tarraconensis*-related collections, Fournier for once even underestimated their Gregorian content. Yet even in their support for Gregory VII, compilers took very different routes, and it would be completely misguided to interpret their work as an enterprise guided, or even inspired, by the reform papacy. They all had their own interests, and worked under specific circumstances. Deusdedit's claims on the superiority of the general council, his opposition to the 1059 Papal Election Decree, and his bold decision to include in his collection a canon challenging the immunity of the pope can not be explained by his support for Gregory VII, but have to

---

484. See also Rolker, 'Bonizo' esp. 75–77 on this point.

be seen as expressions of his own views, some of which may have had the support of other prelates, some less so. As in other contexts, one should distinguish between 'Gregorian' ideology, loyalty to Gregory VII in particular, and support for ecclesiastical reforms in general—positions that sometimes went hand in hand but often did not.

4.8.2 The Prohibitions of Investiture

On average, the Gregorian collections were not very influential. The number of extant copies is relatively low, and while Deusdedit in particular was more influential than the existence of only one medieval manuscript would suggest, it is also true that his collection did not influence any later collection the way that Burchard or *74T* shaped a number of derivative collections. Anselm's collection—the only Gregorian collection that actually did have a stronger impact on 'mainstream' canon law—was itself changed substantially in the course of its dissemination; to adopt Cushing's categories, it was transformed 'from polemic to handbook'.[485] This already indicates that the meagre reception of the Gregorian canon law collections and their ideological content were linked. This assumption demands further thought as it can help to understand better both the unity of the Gregorian collections and the complicated process by which individual canons did, or did not, became universal law in the decades around 1100.

Here, the prohibitions of lay investiture promulgated by Gregory VII, Urban II, and Paschal II provide valuable evidence. It has long been noted that most Gregorian collections do contain them, while many other collections do not. Gilchrist, Schieffer, and Beulertz have carefully established which pre-Gratian collections contained any of the numerous investiture prohibitions issued since 1077, and found a dozen collections or roughly half of their sample to contain at least one of these prohibitions.[486] This is valuable evidence, but a fuller picture emerges if we take into account the manuscript tradition of the collections in question. First, it is evident that most collections containing the prohibitions are extant in exactly one manuscript.[487] This is more than for canons of many other

---

485. Cushing, 'Polemic or Handbook'.

486. Gilchrist, 'Reception'; Schieffer, *Entstehung* 198–203; Beulertz, *Verbot*. Schieffer, *Entstehung* 198 noted the absence of the prohibitions from the Ivonian collections, but in the end stressed the number of collections that contained them: 'Immerhin ist aber doch festzuhalten, daß gut die Hälfte der kirchlichen Rechtsbücher, die im Zeitalter der gregorianischen Reform entstanden sind, die päpstlichen Dekrete gegen die Investitur rezipiert haben.'

487. Beulertz, *Verbot* listed fourteen collections containing at least one canon against lay investiture, to which one could add the Vatican *13L* 6.44 (containing Rome 1080), while *4L* has to be eliminated. Contrary to what Beulertz suggests, only one manuscript of *4L* contains the 1078

papal councils,[488] but not much in comparison to the number of surviving copies for collections like Burchard, the *Tripartita*, or the *Panormia*. Perhaps even more interesting, the collections that do contain canons against lay investiture have in common that almost all were compiled in southern Europe, and were largely unknown north of the Loire. The only exceptions before *ca.* 1125 are the *Atrebatensis* and the closely related Wolfenbüttel *Collection in Nine Books* (both compiled around 1100 in or around Arras),[489] and the *Britannica* (compiled in the early 1090s). Significantly, while the latter was used intensively by several major collections in northern France, none of them retained the prohibition of lay investiture found there.[490] Therefore, the reception of the prohibitions of lay investiture follows a clear geographical pattern. In Italy, Catalonia, and Aquitaine a relatively high number of collections very quickly included the prohibitions of investiture, and taken together had a significant dissemination;[491] in France, Normandy, England, and Germany, the reception of these prohibitions was delayed by decades and limited to collections of modest influence. This can be partly explained by the reluctance of Ivo of Chartres in particular, who as late as 1096 (shortly after having participated in the Council of Clermont!) claimed not to be aware of any prohibitions that would make royal investiture a real problem.[492]

Yet Ivo as a person should not be overrated; he may have been influ-

---

prohibition, and only in an appendix; see Gilchrist, 'Reception' 53 (Canterbury, Cathedral Library, B VII). Of Beulertz' remaining thirteen collections, eight are extant in only one medieval manuscript, two more in two copies each: Berlin *13L*, Deusdedit, San Pietro *9L*, *Caesaraugustana I*, *Britannica*, and the collections in Clm 16085, Vat. lat. 3829, and Barb. lat. 538 are all extant in one medieval manuscript only; *2L/8P* is extant in two manuscripts (one unknown to Beulertz), and the *Collectio Catalaunensis* is likewise extant in two manuscripts (one manuscript each of both versions).

488. See Robert Somerville (in collaboration with Stephan Kuttner), *Pope Urban II, the Collectio Britannica, and the Council of Melfi (1089)* (Oxford 1996), here at 213 on councils of Urban II, some of which 'are little more than a few lines in narrative sources'.

489. Schieffer, *Entstehung* 199 n. 128 and Beulertz, *Verbot* 15 and 53. The *Atrebatensis* is extant in one manuscript, the Wolfenbüttel *9L* in two. On the collections, see Waelkens and van den Auweele, 'Collection de Thérouanne' and Rolker, *Canon Law* 72–73. Significantly perhaps, both also contain excerpts from a polemical tract of Peter Damian, see Münsch, 'Streitschriftenfragment'. See also Robert Somerville, 'Prolegomena', *Decreta Claromontensia* 3–41, here at 58 on the possible involvement of Lambert of Arras.

490. Melfi 1089 c. 8 (ed. Somerville, *Urban II* 254) is found in the *Britannica* (London, BL, Add. MS 8873, fol. 152r), but none of the Ivonian collections.

491. Schieffer, *Entstehung* 195 (reception mainly 'im Bannkreis Gregors VII.'); Schilling, 'Kanones' 89: reception of Poitiers 1078 in rather limited areas, specifically where the canons Saint-Ruf were active. On this point, see also Blumenthal, 'Poitevin Manuscripts'.

492. Ivo, *Ep.* 60 (ed. Leclercq 246; ed. Giordadegno, http://telma-chartes.irht.cnrs.fr/yvesde-chartres/notice/20997). See Schieffer, *Entstehung* 198 (commenting on Ivo's 'Zurückhaltung [...], die keinesfalls auf bloßer Unkenntnis beruhen kann'). For Ivo's presence in Clermont, see Robert Somerville, 'The Council of Clermont (1095), and Latin Christian Society' *Archivum Historiae Pontificiae* 12 (1974) 55–90, here at 67.

ential, and able to make specific provisions widely known, but he hardly could hinder other compilers working between the 1070s and 1115 to include material in their collections as they saw fit. However, when it came to the much-debated investiture prohibitions, these compilers almost unanimously decided not to insert them into their collections. The Loire valley effectively was a *cordon sanitaire* preventing the most disruptive papal politics from being disseminated.[493] Only after the Concordate of Worms (1122), the first major collections containing canons against lay investiture were compiled north of the Loire, too. The first collection to do so was *Collection in Ten Parts*, compiled some time after the Lateran Council of 1123; to judge by the six extant manuscripts, it had a relatively wide circulation, at least compared to other collections containing prohibitions of lay investiture. The collection has been discussed above as a collection which to an unusual extent was ready to integrate recent conciliar legislation and, in some manuscripts, even the statement of *magistri moderni* like Ivo of Chartres and Bernhard of Clairvaux.[494] At least in northern Europe, therefore, the investiture prohibitions only entered 'mainstream' canon law after the political conflict around investiture had cooled down. Indeed, among the collections including prohibitions against investiture, the chronologically next major collection with a notable circulation outside Italy was the *Decretum Gratiani*, compiled two generations after the synod of Autun in 1077.

For decades, then, the investiture prohibitions in large parts of Europe were known, but never integrated into major canon law collections. Those compilers who did include these prohibitions, sometimes clearly perceived them as general laws;[495] but their works were either not known, or consciously ignored by the majority of compilers of canonical collections north of the Loire. This fits the geographical pattern of the places where the prohibitions were promulgated in the first place, including the failed attempts to convene legatine councils in the kingdom of France; it fits also the pattern for how differently participants remembered the decisions of such councils after their return home.[496] This also means that the decision of the Gregorian compilers to include the controversial in-

---

493. Jean-Hervé Foulon, *Église et réforme au Moyen Âge: papauté, milieux réformateurs et ecclésiologie dans les Pays de la Loire au tournant des XIe–XIIe siècles* (Bibliothèque du Moyen Âge 27; Brussels 2008), passim. An excellent study on the underlying episcopal networks is found in Ott, *Bishops*.

494. See above, Chapter Three on 'Regular Canons'.

495. Schilling, 'Kanones' 88 (quoting Paris, BnF, lat. 2050 [not seen] and the *Burdegalensis*).

496. Somerville, 'Prolegomena' 46–98, including the example of King Philip's excommunication being only reported in sources from 'outside the sphere of royal influence' (ibid. 87).

vestiture prohibitions can rightly be seen as a distinctive feature of these works which already contemporaries may have perceived as unusual. In this sense, the idea that the Gregorian collections indeed formed a meaningful group is confirmed; yet the same evidence also makes clear that the texts found in these collections were not necessarily part of general canon law.

5

The Schools of Northern France and Beyond

5.1 The Schools: Masters, Methods, Milieux

From the eleventh century on, Italy and northern France in particular saw a considerable rise of schools and the emergence of what later would be dubbed 'scholastic method'. There were cathedral schools at Reims, Liège, Chartres, Beauvais, Laon, Paris, Orléans, and many other places; religious houses like Bec, Saint-Quentin, and Saint-Victor were likewise places of learning and scholarship. Even more importantly perhaps, teachers and students travelled between these centres, gradually forming social groups with their own habits, norms, and (much later) institutions. It was in this milieu that contemporary debates about the Eucharist, episcopal elections, new heresies, and ecclesiastical reforms were transformed into learned debates, rich in quotations of ancient authorities as well as recent masters—teachers, friends, colleagues, and enemies (sometimes in changing roles) included. It was also this milieu where copies of the Bible, patristic writings, canon law collections, and other texts were in high demand, and where these often ancient texts were annotated, introduced by new prefaces, reorganised in new collections, and supplied with glosses. By its very nature, this emerging scholastic culture was not limited to any specific region, and the eventual rise of a smaller group of centres of exceptional and international importance was a slow process. Even so it is clear that in the second half of the eleventh century, French and Norman schools surpassed those in Germany.

This development involved all areas of learning, and turned some of them into 'disciplines' by the end of the twelfth century—complete with their own textbooks, degrees, careers, and institutions. Change was well underway already in the eleventh century, and the canonical collections studied in the present chapter were influenced by changing attitudes to 'reason and authority'.[1] The sheer number of canonical collections compiled in or around northern France in the century before Gratian is in itself impressive (*74T*, *4L*, *Tripartita*, Ivo's *Decretum*, *Panormia*, *10P*, and Alger's *De misericordia*). These collections gained wide circulation, suggesting that they were attractive to a wider audience including most famously the Bolognese milieu in which the Gratians were working around 1140.

Most of what has been said about canonical collections here also applies to 'sentence collections', which are traditionally seen as belonging to the pre-history of academic theology rather than canon law. These collections of excerpts from the Fathers as well as 'modern masters' commenting on the apparent discrepancies of tradition and various dogmatic questions are indeed different from 'canon law'; they contain much more discursive elements, discuss questions like the creation of the world or eschatology rarely treated in canon law, and contain little procedural law and no disciplinary canons (notably no penitential canons, although some of them discuss the *nature* of penance in great detail). This said, they often address the same issues as canonical collections, using the same proof texts and similar techniques of reconciling contradictory canons as do the compilers of canon law collections. Marriage and penance, but also baptism, ordination, and the Eucharist are areas where there was considerable overlap and mutual influence; Gratian used 'theological' sentence collections just as Abelard used 'legal' materials, to take two famous examples.[2] The influence of Abelard on Gratian has often been exaggerat-

---

1. Toivo J. Holopainen, *Dialectic and Theology in the Eleventh Century* (Studien und Texte zur Geistesgeschichte des Mittelalters 54; Leiden 1996).

2. See still Joseph de Ghellinck, *Le mouvement théologique du XIIᵉ siècle: sa préparation lointaine avant et autour de Pierre Lombard, ses rapports avec les initiatives des canonistes: études, recherches et documents* (Museum Lessianum. Section historique 10; 2nd edition Bruges 1948). Recent studies include Cédric Giraud, *"Per verba magistri": Anselme de Laon et son école au XIIe siècle* (Bibliothèque d'histoire culturelle du Moyen Âge 8; Turnhout 2010); Thomas M. Izbicki, *The Eucharist in Medieval Canon Law* (Cambridge 2015); Atria Ann Larson, *Master of Penance: Gratian and the Development of Penitential Thought and Law in the Twelfth Century* (SMCL 11; Washington, D.C. 2014); Philip L. Reynolds, *How Marriage Became One of the Sacraments: The Sacramental Theology of Marriage from Its Medieval Origins to the Council of Trent* (Cambridge Studies in Law and Christianity; Cambridge 2016); John Wei, *Gratian the Theologian* (Studies in Medieval and Early Modern Canon Law 13; Washington, D.C. 2016). On the older historiography, see in particular idem, 'Of Scholasticism and Canon Law: Narratives Old and New', *New Discourses in Medieval Canon Law Research: Challenging the Master Narrative*, ed. Christof Rolker (Medieval Law and Its Practice 28; Leiden and Boston 2019) 105–126.

ed, but the influence of exegetical literature (tracts, sentence collections, the Gloss to the Bible) on canon law collections including the *Decretum Gratiani* was indeed profound.[3]

The common background, and also the close textual relations, of canonical collections and *sententiae* are important to understand the development of canon law in the decades around 1100. In many respects, canon law collections did not change; the canons they assembled were still normally supplied with short inscriptions and rubrics, usually divided into books, sometimes provided with *capitulationes,* or introduced by a preface to guide the reader; only rarely did the compilers intervene to insert their own dicta or similar forms of comment (as Abbo of Fleury had done around 1000). Nonetheless, the comparison with the *sententiae* helps to emphasise two changes in the collections, even where they contain traditional material and follow established forms of layout. Around 1100 a very substantial number of 'new' canons were culled from the Church Fathers, above all Saint Augustine, and inserted into canonical collections. The motives for this notable widening of the net of authorities, and the effect they had on the collections, changed the ways in which the whole body of canons was read and studied. The treatment of baptism and marriage in the *Panormia* will be discussed below as an example of this development.

5.2 Lanfranc and the *Collectio Lanfranci*

5.2.1 The Collection Itself

The canonical collection traditionally attributed to Lanfranc of Bec (d. 1089) and for this reason known as the *Collectio Lanfranci* is a very large canonical collection of the second half of the eleventh century.[4] Covering some 200 folios in the extant manuscripts, it contains almost 1,900 canons. Almost all of them are taken from a long version of Pseudo-Isidore; many texts are shortened and others left out completely, but the chronological

3. See in general Wei, *Gratian,* and specifically idem, 'Gratian and the School of Laon' *Traditio* 64 (2009) 279–322 demonstrating that Gratian passages often quoted as evidence for Abelard's influence can be explained much more elegantly by Gratian's use of the sentence collection *Deus itaque summae.* Wei also was able to show that the parallels between the Florence copy of the *Sententiae magistri A.* and Gratian may well be the result of the former drawing on Gratian I (not the other way round). For Gratian and the glossed Bible, see Titus Lenherr, 'Die "Glossa ordinaria" zur Bibel als Quelle von Gratians Dekret' BMCL 24 (2000) 97–129 and Tatsuchi Genka, 'Hierarchie der Texte, Hierarchie der Autoritäten. Zur Hierarchie der Rechtsquellen bei Gratian' ZRG Kan. Abt. 95 (2009) 101–127. For the influence of Gratian on sentence collections in the later twelfth century, see Larson, *Master.*

4. Kéry 239–243; Fowler-Magerl, *Clavis* 181–182; Álvarez de las Asturias, *Collectio Lanfranci.* The collection was labelled 'Lanfranc's Collection' and given prominence by Zachary Nugent Brooke, *The English Church and the Papacy: From the Conquest to the Reign of John* (Cambridge 1931), ch. 5.

arrangement is left intact. The whole collection is divided into two parts based on different models. The first part contains excerpts from papal letters from Clement to Gregory II, all taken from the False Decretals, and at the very end decrees of the 1059 Easter synod including Berengar's oath taken there.[5] The second part consists of conciliar canons from Nicaea to Seville II, with a peculiar mix of the *Hispana* and the *Dionysio-Hadriana* versions. For the Greek councils (except Ephesus), the *Collectio Lanfranci* follows the *Dionysio-Hadriana*, for all other councils it follows Pseudo-Isidore and hence the *Hispana*.[6] The bipartite structure links the *Collectio Lanfranci* to a specific version of Pseudo-Isidore,[7] and in particular a manuscript today at Eton.[8]

All in all, the *Collectio Lanfranci* preserves the spirit of the model, too; it is strong on episcopal rights and procedure and contains many canons on the papacy, but is relatively short on issues such as marriage. The compiler tended to omit Pseudo-Isidorian forgeries on dogmatic issues.[9] By virtue of the material related to Nicholas' 1059 Easter synod, however, the *Collectio Lanfranci* also contains at least some materials directly related to eleventh-century reforms: a version of the Papal Election Decree, canons against simony, prohibitions against cousin marriage, and Berengar's oath concerning the Eucharist.

The main links between Lanfranc and the collection attributed to him are the following. First, the Trinity manuscript contains several references to Lanfranc, and is normally thought to have been his personal working copy.[10] The most important evidence is a note that Lanfranc had the manuscript bought from Bec and given to Christ Church, Canterbury.[11]

5. The decrees are taken from Nicholas' letters: JL 4405 (ed. Jasper, MGH Conc. 8.402–404); JL 4431a (ibid. 382–383); Berengar's oath (ibid. 398–399).

6. Brooke, *English Church* 61. The *Dionysio-Hadriana* does not contain canons from Ephesus.

7. For manuscripts of Pseudo-Isidore which divide the material into papal and conciliar canons (instead of the usual tripartite structure), see Paul Hinschius, 'De collectione decretalium et canonum Isidori Mercatoris', *Decretales Pseudo-Isidorianae et Capitula Angilramni*, ed. idem (Leipzig 1863) xi–ccxxxviii, here at lxxiii–lxxvi.

8. Eton, College Library, B.1.1.6 [not seen]. It also shares the 1059 material with the *Collectio Lanfranci*. See Brooke, *English Church* ch. 6, Joachim Richter, 'Stufen pseudo-isidorischer Verfälschung. Untersuchungen zum Konzilsteil der pseudoisidorischen Dekretalen' ZRG Kan. Abt. 64 (1978) 1–72, esp. 25–27 (Eton manuscript), Fuhrmann, 'Forgeries' 144–149 (on *Hispana Gallica Augustodunensis*), and Álvarez de las Asturias, *Collectio Lanfranci* 24–30. Álvarez de las Asturias in his *Appendice I* also provides an 'implicit edition' (rubrics, inscriptions, implicit, and explicit) of the canons taken from the False Decretals in the Eton manuscript (his **Eb**).

9. Fuhrmann, *Einfluß und Verbreitung* 2.421, contrasting the *Collectio Lanfranci* with the *Anselmo dedicata* in this respect.

10. Cambridge, Trinity College, B.16.44 (405) [not seen].

11. Brooke, *English Church* esp. 60 and 70–71; see also T.A.M. Bishop in Christopher Nugent Lawrence Brooke, 'Archbishop Lanfranc, the English Bishops and the Council of London of 1075' SG 12 (1967) 39–59, here at 57. The manuscript also contains a letter of Nicholas to Lanfranc (JL 4469), but in a later hand.

This entry (of *ca.* 1070) provides a strong link between Lanfranc and the collection. It is all the more important as the Canterbury copy is early not only palaeographically, but also structurally: the two parts of the *Collectio Lanfranci* (papal letters and councils) were written by different scribes, perhaps for the first time uniting what previously existed only in separate codices.[12] Second, some of the canons in the Trinity manuscipt are marked by nota signs ('A' and 'a' for 'attende') in the margin; some of these canons are quoted by Lanfranc in his letters. Brooke took this as evidence that the Trinity manuscript was used and annotated by Lanfranc himself.[13] However, while there is overlap, not all canons marked by an 'a' appear in his letters, nor do all the canons Lanfranc cites bear such a mark.[14] Third, Lanfranc in his Eucharist tract quotes Berengar's 1059 oath and other authorities in the distinctive forms of the *Collectio*, suggesting that the collection in its extant form (i.e. with both parts already combined) was already available to him at Bec.[15] So even if he did not compile the collection, he clearly was familiar with it from early on, used it at Bec and probably at Canterbury too, and had an important role in its dissemination.

5.2.2 Multiple Uses of the *Collectio Lanfranci*

The *Collectio Lanfranci* certainly circulated early and widely, especially in England. There are twenty extant copies, and strikingly all complete versions are found in English libraries.[16] It is likely that Lanfranc had a very direct role in disseminating the collection, and the copy he gave to Canterbury probably was the first to combine the excerpts of papal letters with the conciliar canons in one codex.[17] The relatively rapid dissemination of the *Collectio Lanfranci* is especially remarkable as the influence of continental collections in England was very limited before Lanfranc's time.[18] The False Decretals were virtually unknown in pre-conquest England,[19]

---

12. Schafer Williams, *Codices Pseudo-Isidoriani: A Paleographico-Historical Study* (MIC Subsidia 3; Vatican City 1971); Brett, 'Collectio Lanfranci' 159–160.

13. Brooke, *English Church* esp. 67–70, stating that they were Lanfranc's autograph.

14. Gullick, 'Lanfranc' esp. 82.

15. Brooke, *English Church* 65 (oath) and Álvarez de las Asturias, *Collectio Lanfranci* 65–71 (canon law). Brooke, *English Church* 65 also argued that the 1059 materials were added by Lanfranc, assuming that Lanfranc had attended the council; the latter claim, while based on the *Vita Anselmi*, seems unlikely.

16. On the lost Chartres copy (Chartres, BM, 409; saec. XIV) see Williams, *Codices* 91 and Álvarez de las Asturias, *Collectio Lanfranci* 79–80; according to https://www.manuscrits-de-chartres.fr, only fragments have survived.

17. Brett, 'Collectio Lanfranci' 159–160.

18. Brooke, *English Church*; Brett, 'Collectio Lanfranci' 169; Richard H. Helmholz, *The Canon Law and Ecclesiastical Jurisdiction from 597 to the 1640s* (The Oxford History of the Laws of England 1; Oxford 2004), here at 27; Elliot, *Canon Law*.

19. Fuhrmann, *Einfluß und Verbreitung* 1.231 n. 126 (summarized in idem, 'Forgeries' 183), quoting

and even Burchard's *Liber decretorum*, which by *ca.* 1050 was very widely spread on the continent had no demonstrable impact in England before the end of the century. In fact, a considerable part of the evidence for the reception of continental collections in eleventh-century England is linked to Lanfranc and the *Collectio Lanfranci*. First, the Trinity manuscript of the *Collectio Lanfranci* itself contains a Burchard fragment.[20] Second, Ernulf of Rochester, who had studied with Lanfranc and in a different context used the *Collectio Lanfranci*, in his *De incestis coniugiis* quoted from Burchard.[21] Finally, there may have been a copy of Burchard at Bec already in Lanfranc's time as prior, although this remains speculative.[22] In any case, the modest reception of the Pseudo-Isidorian forgeries and Burchard in England before Lanfranc's time is evident; this clearly contrasts with what happened in the early twelfth century (let alone the later twelfth century). Most strikingly, compilers in England drew on the works of Ivo of Chartres and the collections attributed to him relatively quickly after they emerged in northern France. The earliest dateable and complete copy of Ivo's *Decretum* (Cambridge, CCC, 19) was written at Canterbury around 1125. By that time, Rochester possessed copies of Ivo's *Decretum* (or another collection with Ivo's preface attached to it) and his letter collection; the latter manuscript is still extant.[23] Extracts from Ivo's *Decretum* are found in one manuscript of the Canterbury abbreviation of *Collectio Lanfranci*.[24] Copies of the *Tripartita* were held by several Anglo-Norman libraries, and it was used in the composition of new collections. The collection in Bodley 561 depends on the *Collectio Lanfranci* and the *Tripartita*, including Ivo's *Prologue*.[25] The collection in Cambridge, CCC, 442 is linked to the *Tripartita* and takes at least one canon from a letter of Ivo of Chartres.[26] The *Leges Henrici primi* use the pseudo-Ivonian *Panormia*; indeed, they are the earliest datable collection to do so.[27] Gilbert Crispin used the *Collectio*

Ælfric of Eynsham and the *Wigorniensis*. However, the evidence for Ælfric's knowledge of the forgeries is very slight, and Elliot has called into question the date for the quotations from the *Capitula Angilramni*: Elliot, *Canon Law* 449.

20. Gullick, 'Lanfranc' 84.

21. Cramer, 'Ernulf of Rochester'; Brett, 'Finding' 68; idem, 'The *De corpore et sanguine Domini* of Ernulf of Canterbury', *Canon Law, Religion and Politics: Liber amicorum Robert Somerville*, ed. Uta-Renate Blumenthal et al. (Washington, D.C. 2012) 163–182.

22. Délivré, 'Ombre' 89.

23. Rolker, *Canon Law* 128 (London, BL, Royal MS 6 B VI from Rochester) and 265 n. 80 (*Decretum* at Rochester).

24. Brett, 'Collectio Lanfranci' 161 n. 14 (London, Lambeth Palace, MS 351).

25. Brett, 'Collectio Lanfranci' 159.

26. Brett, 'Collectio Lanfranci' 170.

27. Rolker, *Canon Law* 278–279. The date for the *Quadripartitus* (on which I had followed Liebermann), one of the sources of the *Leges*, has since been called into question by Richard Sharpe, 'The Dating of the Quadripartitus Again', *English Law Before Magna Carta: Felix Liebermann and Die Gesetze der Angelsachsen*, ed. Stefan Jurasinski et al. (Medieval Law and Its Practice 8;

Lanfranci, and the *Collection in 74 Titles*; his treatment of the Eucharist has close textual parallels in Ivo's work.[28] So while continental collections had little impact in England before Lanfranc's time, from soon after 1100 other collections, particularly the Ivonian collections, gained considerable influence, apparently replacing the *Collectio Lanfranci* in many contexts. This also explains why the evidence for the practical use of the *Collectio Lanfranci* is limited despite its wide diffusion.[29]

So not everyone in England who may have had the *Collectio Lanfranci* at his disposal chose to use it, and the largely chronological arrangement of the material may partly explain this reluctance. Yet this is not to say that the *Collectio Lanfranci* was not used. Indeed, it is striking to see how different readers found it useful in very different contexts. This of course already applies to Lanfranc himself, who quoted from the collection at Bec when writing on the Eucharist, but later, as archbishop, must have been much more interested in the Pseudo-Isidorian material on procedural law, episcopal office, and the respective rights of metropolitan and primates. Importantly, however, the collection was hardly tailor-made for the use by the archbishop of Canterbury. Yet the canons on primates may indeed have been attractive for readers in Canterbury. Both the False Decretals and the (genuine) Toledo canons which the *Collectio Lanfranci* took from Pseudo-Isidore may indeed have been 'important source of inspiration for Lanfranc' in the primacy dispute between Canterbury and York.[30] In one of his letters, Lanfranc in the context of primatial rights seems to refer to the *Collectio Lanfranci*,[31] and at the Council of London 1075, the collection was used in the conciliar decrees concerning the archbishop of York.[32] At the same time, like any collection containing substantial parts of the False Decretals, the *Collectio Lanfranci* in great detail spelled out the rights of all bishops, and in this sense did not directly help an archbishop trying to establish his primacy.

In particular, the *Collectio Lanfranci* contained ample materials useful specifically for bishops accused by secular lords and/or other prelates.

Leiden and Boston 2010) 81–93. Liebermann's original argument is found in his *Quadripartitus. Ein englisches Rechtsbuch von 1114* (Halle 1892) esp. 41 and *Über das englische Rechtsbuch Leges Henrici* (Halle 1901) 19 and 28–29.

28. Brett, 'Collectio Lanfranci' 168.

29. Brett, 'English Abbeys' 301–302.

30. Fabrice Delivré, 'The Foundations of Primatial Claims in the Western Church (Eleventh–Thirteenth Centuries)' JEH 59 (2008) 383–406, here at 386.

31. *The Letters of Lanfranc, Archbishop of Canterbury*, ed. and tr. by Helen Clover and Margaret T. Gibson (Oxford Medieval Texts; Oxford 1979), here at no. 47 as quoted by Delivré, 'Foundations' 386.

32. Martin Brett, 'Gundulf and the Cathedral Communities of Canterbury and Rochester', *Canterbury and the Norman Conquest: Churches, Saints and Scholars 1066–1109*, ed. Richard G. Eales and Richard Sharpe (London and Rio Grande 1995) 15–25, here at 23.

This was indeed the situation William of Saint Calais (d. 1096), bishop of Durham, found himself in when he was accused to have participated in the 1088 rebellion against the king. Before he was brought to trial, the king had seized his lands. The famous treatise *De iniusta vexatione Willelmi* details William's elaborate defence.[33] Here, William argued that he could only be tried after this rights had been restored to him (*exceptio spolii*); in a next step, he appealed to Rome. Lanfranc countered these arguments—famously claiming that William was accused as vassal, not as bishop[34]—but must have been aware that William's claims had ample support in canon law as found, inter alia, in the *Collectio Lanfranci*. Indeed, Philpott has shown that this very collection was used in the composition of the *De iniusta vexatione*, and hence probably in the trial itself.[35] Like the Trinity copy, William's exemplar of the *Collectio Lanfranci* also contains nota marks, but this time they correspond very neatly to the canon law quotation of *De iniusta vexatione*.[36] The *Collectio Lanfranci* contains all canons quoted in this tract, and in William's copy, almost all of them are marked. Even if William was unsuccessful in the end, his *De iniusta vexatione* clearly shows that the *Collectio Lanfranci* was at least as useful to one of Lanfranc's political opponents as it may have been for himself.

5.3 The *Collectio Britannica*

The *Collectio Britannica* is one of the most famous pre-Gratian canon law collections, and rightly so.[37] It contains a large number of excerpts from papal letters and Roman law which for centuries had been virtually

33. 'De iniusta vexacione Willelmi episcope primi per Willelmum regem filium Wellelmi magni Regis,' ed. H.S. Offler, revised for publication by A.J. Piper and A.I. Doyle, *Chronology, Conquest and Conflict in Medieval England* (Camden Miscellany 34 / Camden Fifth Series 10; Cambridge 1997) 49–104. The edition documents the Pseudo-Isidorian quotations and parallels; for the use of the *Collectio Lanfranci*, see Mark Philpott, 'The *De iniusta vexacione Willelmi episcopi primi* and Canon Law in Anglo-Norman Durham', *Anglo-Norman Durham, 1093–1193*, ed. David W. Rollason et al. (Woodbridge 1994) 125–137.

34. See, for example, Herbert Edward John Cowdrey, *Lanfranc: Scholar, Monk, and Archbishop* (Oxford 2003), here 219–222.

35. Philpott, 'De iniusta vexacione'.

36. Philpott, 'De iniusta vexacione' 131 (on Cambridge, Peterhouse, 74). Note that Offler's edition of *De iniusta vexacione* was posthumously printed and not yet available to Philpott at the time. I agree with Philpott, 'De iniusta vexacione' 127 that the report is indeed contemporary to the events (*pace* Offler).

37. For bibliography, see Kéry 237–238 and Fowler-Magerl, *Clavis* 184–187. Ewald, 'Brittische Sammlung' remains fundamental. For recent overviews, see Somerville, *Urban II* 3–21, Jasper, 'Beginning' 122–124, Kéry, 'Kanonessammlungen' 286–292, Martin Brett, 'Some New Letters of Popes Urban II and Paschal II' JEH 58 (2007) 75–96 at 77–79, and my own article 'The *Collectio Britannica* and its Sources: Reviewing the Trustworthiness of a Key Witness of Medieval Papal Letters' ZRG Kan. Abt. 108 (2022) 111–169. Dr Steven Schoenig (Saint Louis) is preparing a new study and edition of the *Britannica*.

unknown in the West. While the *Britannica* itself was not widely spread, the materials it made available became part and parcel of medieval canon law via the Ivonian collections. The rarity of the ancient texts it contains and the wide diffusion they ultimately had makes the question of the authenticity of the material particularly urgent. Is the *Britannica* especially valuable because it uniquely preserved papal letters otherwise completely lost—or should one suspect these letters as forgeries precisely because there is no parallel transmission? Was the *Britannica* a crucial element of the 'revival' of legal studies by reintroducing large shares of genuine ancient legal texts, or is it representative of an early medieval culture where 'forgery' was an important mode of legal change?[38] These question repeatedly have attracted debate, and occasionally heated argument, ever since Ewald boldly proposed that the *Britannica* was compiled directly from lost papal registers.[39]

5.3.1 The *Britannica* as Found in the London Manuscript

To understand the *Britannica*, it is crucial to distinguish between the extant form of the collection and earlier versions of it. The extant version is found in the sole surviving copy of the *Britannica* (London, BL, Add. MS 8873). While this codex was produced in the early twelfth century, with the most recent material dating after August 1108,[40] the existence of earlier *Britannica* version(s) can be inferred from *Tripartita* A, the first *Arsenal Collection*, Ivo's *Decretum*, and some of Ivo's letters which all in the 1090s drew on a collection very similar, but not identical to that found in the manuscript today kept in the British Library.

Let us begin with the collection as found in the London copy.[41] The manuscript consists of an incomplete index and the collection itself, which is divided into nine sections on the basis of the material they contain (see Table 5).[42]

38. See Fournier (*Histoire* 2.155–163) for the former idea and Peter Landau, 'Gefälschtes Recht in den Rechtssammlungen bis Gratian', *Fälschungen im Mittelalter* (6 vols. MGH Schriften 33; Hanover 1988) 2.11–49, here at 40–42, for the latter.

39. For fuller discussion, see Rolker, 'Collectio Britannica'.

40. See Christof Rolker and Marcel Schawe, 'Das Gutachten Ivos von Chartres zur Krönung Ludwigs VI. Quellenstudium und Edition von ep. 189' *Francia* 34 (2007) 147–157 and Christof Rolker, 'History and Canon Law in the *Collectio Britannica*: A New Date for London, BL Add. 8873', *Bishops, Texts and the Use of Canon Law Around 1100: Essays in Honour of Martin Brett*, ed. Bruce Clark Brasington and Kathleen Grace Cushing (CFC; Aldershot and Farnham 2008) 141–152.

41. The best analysis is Somerville, *Urban II* 3–21; see also the important observations by Martin Brett, 'Urban II and the Collections Attributed to Ivo of Chartres', *Proceedings San Diego 1988* MIC Subsidia 9.27–46, idem, 'The Sources and Influence of Paris, Bibliothèque de l'Arsenal MS 713', *Proceedings Munich 1992* MIC Subsidia 10.149–167, and idem, 'New Letters' 77–79.

42. Ewald, 'Brittische Sammlung' 279 and passim. The statistics are based on the *Clavis canonum* database, not Ewald, who occasionally was misled by Bishop's transcript. In the Varia 2 sec-

Table 5: The Contents of London, BL, Add. MS 8873

BL Add. 8873	Content
fols. 1r–8v	Incomplete index for 135+88+47+74+122 items (on which see below)
fols. 9r–38v	136 numbered excerpts taken from the letters of Gelasius I and Pelagius I
fols. 38v–52r	87 numbered excerpts taken from the letters of Alexander II; the heading fol. 38v is 'Ex registro Alexandri pape II'
fols. 52r–120r	Varia 1; 47+77+117 numbered canons in three subsections (Varia 1A–C)
fols. 120r–126v and 127r–136v	53 excerpts taken from the letters of John VIII (on the break after fol. 126 and the numbering of the canons see below)
fols. 136v–142r	18 excerpts taken from the correspondence of Saint Boniface
fols. 142v–153r	53 excerpts taken from the letters of Urban II
fols. 153r–159v	33 excerpts taken from the letters Stephen V
fols. 160v–171r	45 excerpts taken from the letters of Leo IV
fols. 171r–210v	Varia 2 (incomplete); 165 canons

Within the individual sections, the material appears to be left largely in the sequence of the formal sources. All sections containing excerpts from the letters of individual popes with few exceptions are in chronological sequence; the excerpts from the correspondence of Saint Boniface retain the sequence of this collection.[43] The two Varia sections, finally, also seem to preserve the sequence of their formal sources, as far as these are known. The first begins with a subsection (= 'Varia 1A') containing twenty-three excerpts from the Digest and twenty-four more from Justinian's Institutes. This Roman law in Varia 1A seems to be taken from a separate intermediary source which preserved the sequence of the *fontes materiales*.[44] The second and third sub-sections (= 'Varia 1B–C') contain a total of almost 200 excerpts from papal letters and patristic literature, above all Saint Augustine. The excerpts from papal letters found here seem to be taken from

tion, *Clavis* reports only 163 items, omitting the last two texts on fol. 210v and the erased text (on which see below, note 49).

43. The most detailed discussions of the chronological order are Pius M. Gassó and Columba Batlle, 'Prolegomena', *Pelagii I papae epistulae quae supersunt (556–561)*, ed. iidem (Scripta et documenta 8; Montserrat 1956) XXI–CXIV, here at XXXII–XXXV and Somerville, *Urban II* 41–172 (summary at 23). On Boniface, see Michael Tangl, 'Studien zur Neuausgabe der Bonifatius-Briefe' NA 40 (1916) 639–790 and 41 (1919) 23–101, here at NA 41.91–98 (stressing similarity to Clm 8112) with additions and important corrections by Brett, 'Urban II' 37 n. 33 and Jasper, 'Beginning' 100.

44. Max Conrat (Cohn), *Der Pandekten- und Institutionenauszug der brittischen Dekretalensammlung, Quelle des Ivo* (Berlin 1887), summarized and added to by idem, *Geschichte* 345–347, 352–354, and 370–372; see also Carlo Guido Mor, 'Il Digesto nell'età preirneriana e la formazione della *Vulgata*', *Per il xiv centenario delle Pandette e del Codice di Giustiniano* (Pavia 1934) 559–697.

different earlier collections. Indirectly at least, Varia 1B depends on the ancient *Collectio Arelatensis*.[45] Varia 1C contains, inter alia, excerpts from three letters of Hadrian I which cannot be traced to any known transmission of Hadrian's letters.[46] The second Varia section (the longest of all nine sections of the *Britannica*) contains similarly mixed materials. The first sixteen canons are excerpts from papal letters, patristic literature, the Digest, and a dossier of historical notes based on the *Continuatio Haimonis*.[47] The Digest excerpts are taken from the same intermediary source already used for Varia 1A. Yet the main part of Varia 2 is taken from Deusdedit, and largely left in the sequence of this collection.[48] At the very end, more material from unknown sources was added, and to judge from the erasure on the last verso, the section was slightly longer than it is today.[49]

The extant manuscript, in many respects, is a careless copy, and was evidently left unfinished. The *capitulatio* (on a separate quire) contains numbered headings to individual canons; but it only extends to the first letters of John VIII and does not exactly match the content of the collection. The letters of Gelasius and Pelagius are here numbered continuously, and the last rubrics are numbered as if they were part of Varia 1C, not

45. *Britannica* Varia 1B.17–19 are otherwise only known from the *Arelatensis*. See also below (n. 55) on *Britannica* Varia 2.11.

46. *Britannica* Varia 1C.34, 35, and 55 (London, BL, Add. MS 8873, fols. 100r–104r), taken from JE 2448, 2483, and 2449; see Erich Lamberz, 'Studien zur Überlieferung der Akten des VII. ökumenischen Konzils: Der Brief Hadrians I. an Konstantin VI. und Irene (JE 2448)' DA 53 (1997) 1–43 and idem, 'Einleitung', *Concilium Universale Nicaenum Secundum 1*, ed. idem (ACO, Series II, vol. 3.1; Berlin and Boston 2008) VII–LXX, esp. LI, who demonstrated that the *Britannica* cannot depend on Anastasius Bibliothecarius for JE 2448 and 2449, and further claimed that the *Britannica* excerpts were taken from Hadrian's register. The latter idea is worth further investigation; so far, no conclusive evidence has been found. My thanks are to Professor Evangelos Chyros (Athens) for making me think about this problem; unfortunately, I can still not offer any precise model on the transmission of the letters. For references, see also J³ 4494, which curiously quotes the letter from Mansi, not the critical editions cited.

47. *Britannica* Varia 2.14 (London, BL, Add. MS 8873, fols. 177r–180r). For the dossier, its content, and the date, see Rolker and Schawe, 'Gutachten' and Rolker, 'History'. In the light of *Tripartita* A2.13, I should clarify that parts of Varia 2.14 may well have been composed before 1108; but the section on the coronation of Frankish kings outside Reims was compiled in 1108 when the coronation of the future Louis VI outside Reims became an issue, or at least a possibility.

48. Ewald, 'Brittische Sammlung' 582. Note that Ewald thought it possible that the canons at the very end of the *Britannica* may go back to a more complete version of Deusdedit's collection; see next note.

49. Somerville, *Urban II* 15. Dr Steven Schoenig (private communication, 2 October 2019) kindly informed me that the erased text is actually *Tantam saeculi* (CPL 483; ed. Munier, CCL 148.136), a letter of Leo of Bourges commonly attribtued to Pope Leo I well into modern times (JK –; J³ –) on which see now Charles West, 'Pope Leo of Bourges, Clerical Immunity and the Early Medieval Secular' *Early Medieval Europe* 29 (2021) 86–108. Steve Schoenig is preparing an article in which he will argue that *Tantam saeculi* links the end of the *Britannica* not with Deusdedit (who quoted *Tantam saeculi* in his *Libellus contra invasores*) but with Hincmar of Reims. See his 'An Erased Canon and Roman Law in the *Collectio Britannica*', *The Making and Influence of Canon Law in the Long Twelfth Century (c. 1073–1234)*, ed. Travis Baker [forthcoming].

the John VIII section. In the collection itself, there are no rubrics indicating the content. The canon numbers in the first sections (written in red ink) seem to have been copied from the index, not the other way round.[50] Some numbers are omitted, others found twice.[51] Inscriptions are normally written in a slightly darker red ink. Some canons have no inscription at all in the London manuscript, and some inscriptions are erroneous. The texts of many canons contains manifest errors, some of which were corrected; many corrections are in a very dark ink, while others are in the same brown ink as the main text, or exceptionally in the same red ink as the inscriptions.[52] The second part of the manuscript (from fol. 127) was possibly written by the same scribe but clearly in a darker ink. The break is mid-text but corresponds to the beginning of a new quire.[53] The canons in this second part of the manuscript mostly lack initial letters, are not numbered, and have no inscriptions (except for an occasional 'item' written in the main hand), though space is left for these elements. Only in the outer margins, in very small script, the main hand has written fuller inscriptions; no doubt, they were meant for the rubricator who never completed his work. Unfortunately, they were largely cut off when the manuscript was trimmed.

5.3.2 The *Britannica* Used for *Tripartita* A, *Arsenal I*, and Ivo's *Decretum*

Both *Tripartita* A and *Arsenal I* depend on a source that was very similar, but clearly not identical, to the extant *Britannica*,[54] and Ivo of Chartres seems to quote from an early *Britannica*, too. Specifically, it is evident that *Tripartita* A depends on a version very similar to that preserved in the London manuscript for the correspondence of Gelasius I, Pelagius I, John VIII, Saint Boniface, Stephen V, and Leo IV, and also for most of the materials found in the Varia 2 section. (For the letters of Alexander II and Urban II, see below.) As in other cases, the *Tripartita* A contains these canons in long series left in the sequence of its formal sources, thus also confirming

---

50. Ewald, 'Brittische Sammlung' 582.

51. For example, the 87 excerpts taken from the letters of Alexander II are numbered 'I' to 'LXXXVIII', with two numbers omitted ('VI' and 'LXXVII') while one is found twice ('XVIII'). (Corrected from Ewald, 'Brittische Sammlung' 282; see London, BL, Add. MS 8873, fols. 40r, 42r, 43r, and 50v.)

52. London, BL, Add. MS 8873, fol. 18v, correcting 'Christiani' to 'Christianis'.

53. Somerville, *Urban II* 11.

54. Ewald, 'Brittische Sammlung' 325–326 provided many arguments but stopped short of claiming that *Tripartita* A used the *Britannica*; this was established by Paul Fournier, 'Les collections attribuées à Yves de Chartres' BEC 57 (1896) 645–698 and BEC 58 (1897), 26–77, 293–326, 410–444, and 624–676, here at BEC 57.656–661. See also Perels, 'Briefe' 102 (*Britannica*) and Brett, 'Sources' (*Arsenal I*).

that the individual sections of the lost *Britannica* not only must have contained much of the material found in the extant version but also arranged the materials within the individual sections just like the extant version does; the *Britannica* material in *Arsenal I* confirms this, but as *Arsenal I* rearranges its material according to subject matter, only short series are left in the sequence of the *Britannica*. From both collections—*Tripartita* A and *Arsenal I*—it is clear that the *Britannica* version they used frequently had better inscriptions and occasionally a better text than the London copy preserves. For example, the letters of Gelasius I and Pelagius I in Add. 8873 often lack inscriptions; yet the compiler of *Tripartita* A evidently had no problem to attribute them correctly. To take another example, Varia 2.11 in the London manuscript is misattributed to Pope Hilary; nonetheless, both *Tripartita* A and *Arsenal I* correctly attribute it to Zosimus, and so does Ivo in his *Decretum* and two of his letters.[55] Likewise, an excerpt from Gelasius I is correctly inscribed 'Rustico' in *Tripartita*, while the extant *Britannica* has 'Rufino'.[56] On the other hand, the *Britannica* version used to produce *Tripartita* A already seems to have contained some errors which one would otherwise perhaps blame on the scribe of the London copy. For example, Varia 2.94–95 are taken from Deusdedit, where the canons are attributed correctly to Gelasius I and the 869 Council of Constantinople, respectively. In the London copy, Varia 2.94 still has a fragmentary inscription (ending 'Gelasii'), while the following inscription incorrectly reads 'item'. The *Tripartita* misattributes the second canon to Gelasius, and thus placed both fragments together in the same section.[57] This is best explained by *Tripartita* A relying on an earlier *Britannica* version which already had the 'item' introducing Varia 2.95.

Such a comparison between the London copy of the *Britannica* and the Ivonian collections strongly suggests that the latter all used a *Britannica* version very similar to the extant copy in content and arrangement, but with better inscriptions and sometimes a better text. The most important question that remains is whether *Tripartita* A, on the one hand, and Ivo of Chartres and his collaborators, on the other hand, really used the same

<hr>

55. *Britannica* Varia 2.11 (London, BL, Add. MS 8873, fol. 71r); *Tripartita* A1.39.2 (ed. Brett and Nowak); *Arsenal I* (Paris, Bibliothèque de l'Arsenal, 713, fol. 144v); Ivo 4.226 (ed. Brett); Ivo, *Epp.* 60 (ed. Leclercq 240) and 77 (PL 162.99). The material source is JK 334 (ed. Gundlach MGH Epp. 3.11), which has no known transmission outside the *Arelatensis* (but was not entirely 'ignored' as Jasper, *Beginning* 40 suggested). In the third edition of the *Regesta pontificum*, this JK 334 excerpt errorneously was registered as a separate letter of Pseudo-Hilary (J³ †1161); the entry should be deleted.

56. JK 729 as found in *Britannica* Gelasius I.52 (London, BL, Add. MS 8873, fols. 18v–19r) = *Tripartita* A1.46.43.

57. Deusdedit 2.54 (40) and 3.11 (9) (ed. Wolf von Glanvell 211 and 275–276); *Britannica* Varia 2.94–95 (London, BL, Add. MS 8873, fols. 194v–195r; Ewald's no. 86–87); *Tripartita* A1.46.22–23.

Britannica version or not. The answer to this question is relevant for the authorship of the Ivonian collections—could Ivo have compiled *Tripartita A*?—but also for the *Britannica*, as the existence of yet another lost version of the collection would indicate a more prolonged genesis.

The evidence for two different *Britannica* versions behind *Tripartita A*, on the one hand, and, on the other, the Ivonian œuvre—*Arsenal I*, Ivo's *Decretum*, his letters, and his *Prologue*—is found in three of the nine *Britannica* sections, namely the first Varia section, the Alexander II section, and the Urban II section. There are two reasons why one could think that these sections were later additions not found in the version used by the *Tripartita A* compiler. First, the three sections contain the most recent materials of the *Britannica*; second, the *Tripartita A* seems to take only very little material from these three sections. More precisely, there are only three canons in *Tripartita A* taken from the Varia 1 section (comprising 241 canons in the extant *Britannica*), two from the Alexander II section (eighty-seven canons), and two more from the Urban II section (fifty-three canons). Given that *Tripartita A* draws so extensively on other sections, this finding demands some explanation. Fournier argued that the *Britannica* version used to produce *Tripartita A* simply lacked the most recent materials found in the extant copy.[58] This, however, was to a large degree based on Fournier's strong belief that compilers of 'reform collections' were especially keen on inserting the most recent papal legislation, an assumption that has been disproven since.[59] Ivo's *Decretum* itself is a good counter-example for Fournier's idea; there can be no doubt that he knew much more recent material than he chose to include in his *Decretum*. Therefore, from *Tripartita A* alone one cannot deduce (as Fournier had done) that the sections containing excerpts from the letters of Alexander II and Urban II were lacking in the lost *Britannica* version of the 1090s.

Additional evidence on the development of the *Britannica* in general, and the question of the letters of Alexander II and Urban II in particular, is available from the first of the two canonical collections in Paris, Bibliothèque de l'Arsenal, 713 which I refer to as '*Arsenal I*' (and which will be discussed below as one of the formal sources of the *Decretum* of Ivo of Chartres). This collection dates from the late eleventh century; it draws on all parts of the *Britannica* and was used to produce Ivo's *Decretum* in *ca.* 1095. In general, the *Britannica* version behind *Arsenal I* must have looked very similar to that used for *Tripartita A*. Compared to the latter, *Arsenal I* contains more recent material, including excerpts taken from the *Britanni*-

---

58. Fournier, 'Collections attribuées à Yves' BEC 57.661, followed by Jasper, 'Beginning' 101.
59. Brett, 'Urban II' 30.

ca: it has thirty-two excerpts from letters of Alexander II, all of which are also found in the extant *Britannica*, and twenty-two excerpts from letters of Urban II, sixteen of which are also found in the *Britannica*.[60] Evidently, *Arsenal I* relied heavily on a version of the *Britannica* for these canons. It thus seems very plausible that the *Britannica* version available in the early 1090s contained the same excerpts of letters of Alexander II and Urban II as that are found in the extant London copy. As in the case of *Tripartita* A, the *Britannica* canons in *Arsenal I* also confirm that this *Britannica* version had often fuller inscriptions and occasionally a better text than the extant manuscript.[61]

What does this mean for the question whether or not *Tripartita* A and Ivo used the same version of the *Britannica*? The short period of time in which all these collections emerged, and also the intimate relation of both *Tripartita* A and *Arsenal I* to Ivo's *Decretum*, in my view make it even more likely that they used the same version of the *Britannica*. While it remains remarkable that *Tripartita* A ignored some sections of the *Britannica* almost entirely, the evidence from *Arsenal I* suggests that this was due to the selection criteria of the *Tripartita* A compiler, not because the relevant material was absent from his source. The *Britannica* version available early in the 1090s had more and better inscriptions, and occasionally a better text than the extant London manuscript, but otherwise must have been almost identical to it. Apart from some historical notes in Varia 2.14, none of the materials found in the London manuscript can be shown to have been absent from the earlier *Britannica*. Likewise, while the Varia 2 section is slightly incomplete in the extant copy, no solid evidence is available on substantial materials contained in an Ur-*Britannica* but dropped before the extant manuscript was produced.

5.3.3 Date and Place of Origin

If, therefore, there is only one *Britannica* version predating the extant version which we can reconstruct from other sources, when and where was this version compiled? The *Britannica* version used for *Tripartita* A and *Arsenal I* contained the canons of the 1089 Council of Melfi and excerpts from letters of Urban II, several of which date to *ca.* 1090.[62] It therefore cannot have been compiled before 1090, even if one assumes a very early date for all of Urban's letters in question. This *Britannica* version cannot

---

60. Somerville, *Urban II* 19 and idem, 'Papal Excerpts in Arsenal MS 713B: Alexander II and Urban II', *Proceedings Munich 1992* MIC Subsidia 10.169–184, here at 181–184.
61. Somerville, *Urban II* esp. 18; idem, 'Papal Excerpts' 174–180. See also above on JK 334.
62. Somerville, *Urban II* 23.

have been compiled much later, either, because in the mid-1090s both *Tri-partita* A and *Arsenal I* were available to Ivo of Chartres in the compilation of his *Decretum*.[63] This provides a narrow timespan in the early 1090s during which the *Britannica* as Ivo knew it could have been compiled.

As for the place of origin, the large number of otherwise unknown excerpts from genuine papal letters point to Rome and its archives; the Roman law in the *Britannica* likewise suggests Italy as the place of origin. The use of Deusdedit's collection supports an Italian and perhaps even a Roman origin of the *Britannica*, as it was only finished in 1087 (though Deusdedit had largely finished his work years before that date). At the same time, there are substantial parts of the *Britannica* that indicate a reworking with materials much more readily available outside Italy, and more specifically in France north of the Loire. In particular, while the letters in the John VIII section have no parallel in the extant copy of the register (made at Montecassino in the late eleventh century), the only places where John's letters are known to have been current in the Middle Ages are Reims, Dol, and Tours.[64] Dol is also the most likely place for the address of one of John's letters as preserved in the *Britannica* to have been manipulated (JE 3003, to be discussed below). It is also noteworthy that while most of John's letters deal with Italian affairs, this holds for less than a third of his letters in the *Britannica*.[65] All this suggests that the relevant *Britannica* section draws on a non-Italian dossier of the letters of John VIII and / or the *Britannica* compiler himself was less interested in Italian affairs. Similar observations can be made for other sections of the *Britannica*. In the case of the letters of Leo IV, the lack of a register copy makes it more difficult to establish any selection criteria, but at least some pieces may well have been selected because of their special relevance for Frankish affairs.[66] The section also contains highly suspicious materials which may go back to ninth- or tenth-century forgeries in favour of Hincmar of Reims. The Boniface section almost certainly goes back to a manuscript from north-western Europe. Ewald and Tangl asserted the use of

63. Brett, 'Urban II'; Rolker, *Canon Law* 96.

64. On Dol and Tours see below in the context of JE 3003; on Reims see Unger, 'Einleitung', Böhmer-Unger, VII–XVI, here at X.

65. Schieffer, 'Register' 270, commenting that this suggested 'daß sich die Redaktoren der Collectio Britannica überproportional für Betreffe nördlich der Alpen interessiert haben.'

66. See Brett, 'Urban II' 37 n. 33 on *Britannica* Leo IV.28 (London, BL, Add. MS 8873, fol. 167v), an excerpt praising the military prowess of the Franks. In addition, letters like JE 2608 (a pallium grant for Hincmar of Reims) were of course of special interest for the French church, but the *Britannica* also contains pallium grants for numerous non-French prelates too (see Schoenig, *Bonds* passim), so I hesitate to quote these letters as evidence for the Frankish contribution to the *Britannica*.

a source very similar to one from Mainz (Clm 8112, corrected by Otloh of Sankt Emmeran) with no known reception in Italy.[67] Contrary to Tangl's speculations,[68] the easiest explanation is that the *Britannica* indeed relies on a model very closely related to Clm 8112.[69] As for the Varia 2 section, it contains excerpts from the *Rotula prolixa* by Hincmar of Laon. This work is extant in only one manuscript, and there is no evidence that it was known in Italy.[70] The Varia 2 section also contains excerpts from Frankish historiography.[71] Finally, the Latin translation of Nicaea II in the Varia 2 likewise points to Frankish sources rather than Rome; the *Britannica* may here depend on a source related to that used by the synod of Paris in 825.[72]

All in all, the *Britannica* made extensive use of essentially 'Roman' materials—excerpts from the Digest, ancient registers of Gelasius I and Pelagius I, recent letters of Urban II, and Deusdedit's collection—but likewise draw on a broad variety of material circulating mainly north of the Loire: letters of John VIII on Frankish affairs, a forgery in favour of Dol, perhaps another one from Reims, the correspondence of Boniface, Hincmar's *Rotula*, Frankish historiography, and a peculiar (Carolingian?) translation of Nicaea II. There is no uniform selection criterion that seems to govern the *Britannica*, but the materials just mentioned clearly were more interesting—and much more readily available—to readers north of the Loire than south of the Alps. If the *Britannica* had a separate existence before it was added to from these Frankish materials, it must have been a substantially shorter collection; but no evidence is available for such a proto-*Britannica*. To sum up, the *Britannica* version used by *Tripartita A*, *Arsenal I*, and Ivo was not an 'Italian' collection but already a combination of both Roman

---

67. Ewald, 'Brittische Sammlung' 285 and 288; Tangl, 'Studien' NA 41.91 n. 1, 93, and 97. For corrections, see Jasper, 'Beginning' 99–100.

68. Tangl, 'Studien' NA 40.695. For criticism, see Reinhold Rau, 'Einleitung', *Briefe des Bonifatius. Willibalds Leben des Bonifatius*, ed. and tr. idem (FSGA 4B; Darmstadt 1968) 3–15, here at 12–13, Brett, 'Urban II' 37 n. 33, and Jasper, 'Beginning' 100. As for the case of JE 2160 as found in Deusdedit, Tangl himself conceded that it offers no cogent evidence as to which branch of the transmission was available in Italy. See Tangl, 'Studien' NA 40.695 and 41.90.

69. Vice versa, Tangl's claim ('Studien' NA 41.97) that Ivo drew on Otloh's manuscript for his Boniface letters has to be rejected in favour of the *Britannica*. For JE 2251, the *Britannica* (London, BL, Add. MS 8873, fol. 137r) has the same variant ('a patre vel episcopo') also found in *Tripartita* A1.57.2 = Ivo 6.117 which Tangl thought be found in Ivo's *Decretum* only and to have been derived from Otloh's correction 'aperte' in Clm 8112.

70. See Brett, 'Urban II' 37, quoting the passages as evidence for a non-Italian origin of the *Britannica*. On the sole manuscript of the *Rotula* (Paris, BnF, lat. 5095 [not seen]), see Schieffer (MGH Conc. 4 suppl. 2.364), who also points out that the *Britannica* must have used a different, slightly more complete copy.

71. Brett, 'Urban II' 37 ('Frankish sources with little obvious relation to papal interests'). While Varia 2 on the whole predates the Ivonian collections (ibid. 37 n. 33), parts of Varia 2.14 were only added later, see Rolker, 'History' 145–148.

72. Lamberz, 'Einleitung' L–LII.

and Frankish materials, and this decisive step in producing the *Britannica* took place north of the Loire in 1090 or very shortly after.

5.3.4 The Reliability of the *Britannica*: Short Remarks on a Long Debate

Thanks to the ongoing edition of the Ivonian collections, the genesis of the *Britannica* today can be studied in greater detail than ever before; it thus is possible to reconstruct the content, structure, date, and place of origin of the *Britannica* version available in the mid-1090s with some precision. However, the crucial question remains whether this collection can be trusted to faithfully preserve excerpts of original papal letters.

As already has been mentioned, Ewald in his pioneering study was confident that the relevant sections in the *Britannica* were composed from lost papal registers and therefore could be trusted to contain genuine papal letters in chronological sequence in the sections under discussion here.[73] This model initially was widely accepted, not least by a number of MGH scholars and also by Fournier.[74] Research on papal letters confirmed some of Ewald's hypothesis. For example, Carl Erdmann was able to find independent evidence for Ewald's claim based soley on the *Britannica* that three documents on the primacy claim of Toledo were found in the first book of Urban's registers.[75] However, from the late 1940s to the early 1980s in particular, a number of scholars also raised doubts on Ewald's model by claiming that individual letters in the *Britannica* were manipulated or forged, perhaps even by the *Britannica* compiler. More recent studies have dispelled most of these doubts,[76] but a cloud of suspicion still surrounds the *Britannica* even in some recent accounts.[77] What is more important, however, is the growing consensus on a 'multi-stage genesis' of the *Britannica*, meaning that the formal sources from which the *Britannica* took its

73. See Ewald, 'Brittische Sammlung' 279–280 (Rome), 289 (chronology), and passim.

74. In addition to the editions of von Hirsch-Gereuth, Perels, and Caspar (in MGH Epp. 5, 6, and 7) and the respective introductions, see Fournier in *Histoire* 2.155–163.

75. Carl Erdmann, *Papsturkunden in Portugal* (Abh. Akad. Göttingen 20.3; Göttingen 1928) esp. 107 and 381–382 on JL – (incipit 'Hoc tempore Toletanus'), 5370, and 5371, all dealing with the primacy of Toledo; see Uta-Renate Blumenthal 'Papal Registers in the Twelfth Century', *Proceedings Cambridge 1984* MIC Subsidia 8.137–151, here at 140–141, Michael Horn, 'Der Streit um die Primatswürde der Erzbischöfe von Toledo. Ein Beitrag zur Geschichte der älteren Papstregister' *Archivum Historiae Pontificiae* 29 (1991) 259–280, here at 266–267, and Somerville, *Urban II* 80–83.

76. For fuller discussion, see Rolker 'Collectio Britannica'.

77. For example, Jasper, 'Beginning' 110. See also the balanced view of Schieffer, 'Register vor 1198' 264: 'Da die Sammlung auch mit Stücken von anderer Herkunft (wie etwa aus dem Briefbuch des Bonifatius) und mit mutmaßlichen Fälschungen angereichert ist, wird sie kaum unmittelbar und vollständig auf die verlorenen Registerbände zurückzuführen sein, spiegelt aber eben doch die Fülle von deren Inhalten in der weiten zeitlichen Spreizung von den 490er bis zu den 1090er Jahren wider.'

papal letters from had been composed, copied, and occasionally reworked over an extended period of time and at different places.[78] Instead of a dichotomy of 'direct use of original registers' versus 'forgery', the question now is what these sources of the *Britannica* looked like, whether they were united before they were used to produce the *Britannica*, and how confident we are that they faithfully preserve the letters from which they seem to be taken. This also means that the answers may well be different for different sections of the *Britannica*.

In this context, the above-mentioned evidence for the *Britannica* being reworked from materials circulating in France, north of the Loire, is of crucial importance. First of all, the interpolations in some letters of John VIII and Leo IV, however small they are, clearly tells against Ewald's idea of a direct use of papal registers for all 'ex registro' sections of the *Britannica*. At the same time, the use of formal sources which emerged and circulated north of the Loire may also explain some of the textual oddities that older scholarship sometimes took as evidence for the *Britannica* compiler manipulating his material. This is true, for example, for a letter of Nicholas I in the second Varia section which Kuttner thought the *Britannica* compiler had 'conflated' with excerpts from Hincmar of Laon (JE 2785).[79] While it is true that the end of Nicholas's letter and the beginning of Hincmar's comment on this very letter are not marked, this need not be the result of the *Britannica* compiler combining these two texts. Rather, he may well have found both in one single formal source, specifically Hincmar's *Rotula prolixa*, which contains very long quotes from this letter combined with Hincmar's comment—and only someone very familiar with either Nicholas's letters or Hincmar's writing could tell where JE 2785 ended and where the comment began. Assuming that the *Britannica* compiler, once more, drew on Frankish sources for his papal letters elegantly explains the evidence; rather than 'interpolating' the papal letter, the scribe of the London manuscript simply overlooked or failed to copy the break (or inscription?) that marked the beginning of the Hincmar pas-

---

78. Brett, 'Urban II' 34–39; Herbers, *Leo IV.* 49–51 and 89; idem, 'Einleitung', *Böhmer-Herbers* VII–XIV, here at X–XI. See also Hageneder 'Papstregister' 325–326 and Blumenthal, 'Päpstliche Urkunden' 21.

79. The passage in question is the *Rotula prolixa* excerpt (ed. Schieffer, MGH Conc. 4 suppl. 2.394 line 24 to 406 line 27) as found in *Britannica* Varia 2.159a (from 'Porro sicut scripsisti') to 162 (London, BL, Add. MS 8873, fols. 209r–210r) on which see Kuttner, 'Turning Point' 74, Brett, 'Urban II' 37 n. 33, and Jasper, 'Beginning' 123. Perels first (in 1912) treated the Hincmar passages as another possible letter of Nicholas ('Ep. 160', MGH Epp. 6.683–684) but corrected himself later ('Briefe' 89–90; MGH Epp. 6.811); Schieffer came to the same conclusion (MGH Conc. 4 suppl. 2.365). The letter appears to be treated as genuine in the third edition of Jaffé's *Regesta* (J³ 6097) for reasons unclear to me.

sage. This seems to be a better explanation than the assumption of a wil-ful interpolation which would in addition raise the question of why the *Britannica* compiler would tamper with his text in this way.

As this example shows, the assumption of 'forgery' in the *Britannica* in the older literature has to be carefully reassessed in the light of more recent discoveries. Two more examples may suffice here. The first rep-resents those alleged manipulations that are simply the result of the poor state of the London manuscript. The letter in question is by Nicholas I (JE 2796), and according to Kuttner was 'interpolated' with a letter of Saint Cyprian by the *Britannica* compiler.[80] However, there is good evidence that the *Britannica* version of the 1090s neatly separated Nicholas's letter and the supposed 'interpolation'. To begin with, even the extant London manuscript contains a fragmentary inscription marking the Cyprian pas-sage as a separate text. The break must have been more clearly visible be-fore the London manuscript was trimmed, and crucially, the inscription can be assumed to have been found in the model of this copy. In addi-tion, *Tripartita A*, *Arsenal I*, and Ivo in one of his letters all drew on the *Britannica* passages in question, with none of them falling victim to the supposed interpolation. All available evidence suggests that the *Britannica* version available in the 1090s marked the Cyprian quotation as such by an appropriate inscription ('Ciprianus Iubiano') and did not pretend that this passage was part of Nicholas' letter, as Kuttner had thought.

The idea that the text of JE 2796 as found in the London manuscript was best explained by the *Britannica* compiler interpolating a papal letter can only be understood if one takes into account the influential studies of Walter Ullmann, who since the 1950s had argued that the *Britannica* con-tained many forged and manipulated letters. This brings us to our second example of supposed forgeries, namely JE 2646. For Ullmann, this frag-ment of a letter of Leo IV was a forgery, and he thought the evidence for this assumption so convincing that he suspected other papal letters as forgeries mainly because they were similar to or simply transmitted with JE 2646. His main reasons to suspect forgery was that JE 2646 called papal immunity into question and that it first emerged (as he thought) in the context of pro-imperial propaganda of the late 1070s or early 1080s, name-

---

80. Kuttner, 'Turning Point' 81–83 on *Britannica* Varia 2.127 (London, BL, Add. MS 8873, fol. 200v). The fragmentary inscription in the margin was overlooked by Kuttner, 'Turning Point' and Rolker, *Canon Law* 153. It can be reconstructed from Paris, Bibliothèque de l'Arsenal, 713, fol. 143v = Ivo 4.188 (ed. Brett) and Ivo, *Ep.* 60 (ed. Leclercq 252), edited most recently by Geneviève Giordadegno at http://telma-chartes.irht.cnrs.fr/yves-de-chartres/notice/20997. The material source of the 'interpolation' is Cyprian, *Ep.* 73.15, edited in *Saint Cyprien, Correspondence*, ed. and tr. Louis Bayard (2 vols.; Paris 1925) 2.278.

ly a tract *De investitura regali*.[81] As it turned out, JE 2646 is not unique in calling papal immunity into question, and the supposed pro-imperial tract Ullmann quoted is neither a tract, nor pro-imperial, nor from the time of Gregory VII. Crucially, the supposed title of the tract is an artefact of the edition Ullmann relied on (not found in the sole manuscript), and the JE 2646 text found here cannot be taken from the supposed formal source of the *Britannica* but instead can be shown to rely on the second version of the *Tripartita* A, thus a source clearly later than the *Britannica*.[82]

This last example has been quoted partly because the textual transmission allows to refute Ullmann's idea with great clarity, but also because the assumption that JE 2646 was very influential. Well into the 1980s, Ullmann's idea was so widely accepted that in several cases papal letters preserved uniquely in the *Britannica* were thought suspicious only because of their joint transmission with 'forgeries' like JE 2646. In a similar way, Kuttner's assertion that the *Britannica* compiler was ready to 'interpolate' letters as in the case of JE 2785 and JE 2796 made him and other scholar quick to assume that other letters in the *Britannica* were manipulated. Yet in all three cases (JE 2646, 2785, and 2796) the evidence clearly tells against the *Britannica* compiler manipulating, let alone forging, the excerpts in question.

This is not the place to discuss all papal letters in the *Britannica* which as some point were called 'suspicious' by some scholar. All too often, the sole reason to doubt their authenticity was their joint transmission with alleged 'forgeries' like JE 2646, and sometimes no reason was given at all (Ullmann famously ignored all Gelasian letters in the *Britannica* without much discussion in his monograph on Gelasius I).[83] Instead, let us turn to those few letters where there, in my opinion, is actual reason to suspect the *Britannica* did preserve manipulated versions. First, there is a letter of John VIII, which in the *Britannica* has a manipulated address (JE 3003); second, a number of related Leo IV fragments uniquely preserved in the *Britannica* (JE 2607 and 2608) are highly suspicious.

---

81. See Walter Ullmann, '"Nos si aliquid incompetenter …"': Some Observations on the Register Fragments of Leo IV in the Collectio Britannica' *Ephemerides iuris canonici* 9 (1953) 3–11 on *Britannica* Leo IV.10 (London, BL, Add. MS 8873, fol. 170r–170v) and *De investitura regali* (ed. Böhmer, MGH Ldl 3.610–614). The title of the latter is an artefact of the edition, see Bamberg, SB, Msc. Can.9, fol. 109r–109v. For important corrections to Ullmann's argument see Claudia Märtl, 'Ein angeblicher Text zum Bußgang von Canossa' DA 38 (1982) 555–563; see also Herbers, *Leo IV.* 65.

82. See *Tripartita* A1.60.23 (ed. Brett and Nowak). The same is true for the other parallels between the Bamberg manuscript and the *Britannica*, namely JE 2613 and JL 3446, see *Tripartita* A1.60.20 and A1.64.7 (ed. Brett and Nowak). For details, see my 'Britannica' article.

83. Walter Ullmann, *Gelasius I. (492–496). Das Papsttum an der Wende der Spätantike zum Mittelalter* (Päpste und Papsttum 18; Stuttgart 1981), esp. 218 n. 3, 225–226, and 227 n. 36. See Patrick Amory, *People and Identity in Ostrogothic Italy, 489–554* (Life and Thought: Fourth Series 33; Cambridge 1997), here at 198–200, esp. 200 n. 22 for a short but powerful critique.

First, JE 3003, a letter by John VIII written to Dol. Its address as found in the *Britannica* almost certainly is not genuine as it addresses the recipient as 'archbishop'.[84] Yet neither John VIII nor other popes ever accepted Dol's claims to this title. The clergy of Dol are known to have quoted the JE 3003 address to support their claims to independence from Tours—but this backfired, as the address is indeed at odds with the rest of the letter, as the archbishop of Tours was quick to point out.[85] There can be little doubt that some unknown scribe at Dol was responsible for changing 'episcopo' to 'archiepiscopo'; the clergy at Dol are known to have forged papal letters (for example, JE †2950) in their prolonged conflict with Tours which was only settled in 1198/99 by Innocent III.[86] Some dossiers produced in the context of this conflict were still extant in early modern times, including copies of JE 3003.[87] The *Britannica* therefore in the John VIII section seems to depend on a version of JE 3003 that ultimately was produced at an unknown time in Dol; the rest of the John VIII section shows no signs of Dolois influence, but as already mentioned the share of letters on Italian affairs is clearly lower compared to the extant copy of John's register. The manipulated address of JE 3003 in the *Britannica* does not suggest that the *Britannica* compiler interfered with the letters found in the John VIII section, not even that the text of the letter was forged (indeed, a forger could easily have produced a text more coherent with the address). Rather, the best explanation is that the John VIII depends, at least in part, on materials compiled apparently north of the Loire and ultimately under the influence of the forgers at Dol. It should therefore be seen as another example of the multi stage-genesis of the *Britannica*.[88]

Finally, there is the delicate question of the Leo IV letters in the *Bri-*

84. *Britannica* John VIII.41 (London, BL, Add. MS 8873, fol. 132r, ed. Caspar, MGH Epp. 7.299–300). See Ewald, 'Brittische Sammlung' 312; Caspar, 'Register Johanns VIII.' 106; Julia M. H. Smith, *Province and Empire: Brittany and the Carolingians* (Life and Thought: Fourth Series 18; Cambridge and New York 1992), here at 180; Herbers, *Leo IV.* esp. 79; Böhmer-Unger †35. For background (and pallium grants for Dol), see also Schoenig, *Bonds* 112–114 and 314–316.

85. See *Mémoires pour servir de preuves à l'histoire ecclésiastique et civile de Bretagne* [...], ed. Hyacinthe Morice (3 vols. Paris 1742–46), here at 1.753–759.

86. Innocent III, Potthast no. 726; for an edition, see *Die Register Innocenz' III., 2. Band: 2. Pontifikatsjahr. Texte*, ed. Othmar Hageneder et al. (Publikationen des Österreichischen Kulturinstituts in Rom 2.1:2; Rome and Vienna 1979), here at 153–154.

87. See *Veterum scriptorum et monumentorum moralium, historicorum, dogmaticorum, ad res ecclesiasticas, monasticas et politicas illustrandas, collectio nova*, ed. Edmond Martène (Rouen 1700), here at 51 and *Thesaurus novus anecdotorum*, ed. idem and Ursin Durand (5 vols. Paris 1717), here at 3.849–850 for slightly different versions of JE 3003. There also is a seventeenth-century dossier in Paris, BnF, français 22322 [not seen], first reported by Lohrmann, *Register* 155 n. 170 which according to Böhmer-Unger 410 contains JE 3003 and 3144.

88. See Herbers, *Leo IV.* 79 n. 83, commenting on JE 3003: '[...] erscheint es mir nicht ganz ausgeschlossen, daß bretonischer neben Reimser Einfluß bei der Zusammenstellung der Coll. Brit. oder eher noch im Vorfeld vermutet werden könnte'.

tannica, and above all the question whether Leo's 'second pallium grant' to Hincmar of Reims (JE †2610) was genuine, forged, or manipulated.[89] What makes the letter so contentious is the rather unusual provision that the pope seemed to allow Hincmar to wear the pallium 'every day' rather than restricting its use to special occasions. The privilege is only known from Flodoard of Reims, but a handful of fragments found in the Leo IV section of the *Britannica* (JE 2607 and 2608) seem to confirm its authenticity—unless of course they were themselves forged.[90] Herbers, and even more so Schoenig, thought an interpolation possible.[91] After all, Leo had granted Hincmar the pallium, and it is possible that JE 2608 goes back to a genuine letter with only the phrase 'daily' inserted by Hincmar or his circle.[92] In the context of the *Britannica*, it is crucial that whatever had happened to JE 2607 and 2608, it must have happened long before the *Britannica* was compiled and indeed before the time of Flodoard of Reims.[93] Thus, even if one assumes that JE 2607 and 2608 are forged, this does not at all suggest that the *Britannica* compiler forged or manipulated any of his materials.

As in the case of JE 3003, the presence of JE 2607 and 2608 (or any other forgery) in the Leo IV section of the *Britannica* is a strong argument against Ewald's idea of direct use of lost papal registers. In both cases, the manipulation took place in different places and presumably at different times long before the *Britannica* was compiled; the presence of these fragments in the Leo IV and John VIII sections are best explained by 'multi-stage genesis' of the *Britannica* as argued by Brett and Herbers. Both sections also seem to have been shaped by an interest in Frankish rather than Italian affairs, adding to the impression that they emerged north of the Loire, like other materials the *Britannica* ultimately came to incorporate. Nothing suggests that the *Britannica* compiler himself

89. From the vast literature, see Ewald, 'Brittische Sammlung' 381–382; Herbers, *Leo IV.* 347; Böhmer-Herbers †(?)240; Brett, 'New Letters' 81–82; Ludwig Falkenstein, 'Zu verlorenen päpstlichen Privilegien und Schreiben: Palliumverleihungen an die Erzbischöfe von Reims (8.–12. Jahrhundert)', *Eloquentia copiosus: Festschrift für Max Kerner zum 65. Geburtstag*, ed. Lotte Kéry (Aachen 2006) 181–224, here at 187–190 and 221; Schoenig, *Bonds* esp. 106–107 and 224.

90. See Flodoard, *Historia Remensis ecclesiae* 3.10 (ed. Stratmann, MGH SS 36.206) and *Britannica* Leo IV.12–13 (London, BL, Add. MS 8873, fol. 163r–v).

91. Böhmer-Herbers †(?)240; Herbers, *Leo IV.* 346–347: '[…] denkbar, daß eine Pallienverleihung Leos IV. weiter "bearbeitet" wurde'; Schoenig, *Bonds* 106: '[…] probably forged or interpolated by the archbishop's circle (or by his enemies).'

92. Herbers, *Leo IV.* 347. Schoenig, *Bonds* esp. 106–107 is slightly more sceptical than Herbers on JE 2608 but agrees that in the case of JE 2607 'the removal of two words, *cotidianum* and *cotidie*, renders it mostly unobjectionable.' See also Falkenstein, 'Palliumverleihungen' 188–190 (making a strong argument against the authenticity from JE 2823 and Hincmar's reply) and Brett, 'New Letters' 81–82 on both JE 2608 and Leo (IV?), JE – (J³ –), another grant of pallium.

93. Falkenstein, 'Palliumverleihungen' 187–188.

manipulated any material, and Ullmann's idea about 'manipulated papal registers' should be given up as an unsubstantiated hypothesis built on assumptions that have been largely debunked. Even more importantly, it is far from clear that the cloud of suspicious that surrounds the Leo IV and John VIII sections should extend to any other section of the *Britannica*. Compared to the other 'ex registro' sections, these two sections stand out for their 'French' character, both in content and with respect to their sources. None of the other sections is similarly shaped by any discernable selection criterion, and none of them contains any known forgeries.

5.3.5 Summary

Any judgement on the *Britannica* has to distinguish carefully between the collection as found in the London copy, the *Britannica* version used for *Tripartita* A (and other works around Ivo of Chartres), and the dossiers from which this latter version was compiled. It seems safe to assume that the formal sources of the *Britannica*, even if they contained excerpts from genuine papal letters in chronological sequence, were not composed by directly exploiting papal registers. Instead, the material seems to have reworked, apparently in several stages, before it reached the *Britannica*. In the case of the Leo IV section and also the John VIII section, such a multi-stage genesis is the best explanation for the small number of manipulated or suspicious letters they contain. In the case of the other 'ex registro' sections, no signs of interference have been discovered; for the sections containing excerpts from the letters of Gelasius I, Pelagius I, Alexander II, Urban II, and Stephen V one can still assume that they depend on sources very close to the lost registers. It is unclear at which stage the individual sections were united, but more and more evidence has been found that the *Britannica* originated outside Italy. Already the version used for *Tripartita* A shows signs of having been compiled by someone with a special interest in Frankish affairs having access to diverse materials circulating in north-western France but not in Italy.

The *Britannica*—both the extant copy and the version available in the 1090s—is clearly more distant from the papal registers than Ewald claimed. Some parts show signs of having been reworked several times, and at every stage may have been subject to alterations, losses, and additions. This said, the number of cases were the *Britannica* can be shown to differ from the papal registers is very small, even for those registers where the evidence is relatively good (John VIII, Urban II). A few letters of Pelagius I may no longer be in chronological sequence, the address of one letter of John VIII was manipulated, and the Leo IV fragments on Hincmar's pallium are suspicious. Yet neither the compiler of the *Britannica* nor the scribe of the London manuscript show any tendency to deliberate manipulation. Papal letters found only in the *Britannica* in general can be trusted to be genuine, and normally the series of fragments in the sections under discussion here can be assumed to preserve the chronological arrangement of their ultimate sources. If it comes to reliability of the text, one has to take into account that the London copy contains numerous scribal errors; here, parallels in *Tripartita* A, *Arsenal I*, and the works of Ivo of Chartres often provide crucial evidence for the original text. While the London manuscript alone can be confusing, the comparison with the Ivonian collections commonly allows us to reconstruct a very reliable text of the papal letters in question, and to attribute them correctly. The *Britannica* not only is an important canonical collection, it remains one of the most import single sources for papal letters from the fifth to the eleventh century.

5.4 The *Tripartita*

5.4.1 Content, Structure, Date

The *Collectio Tripartita* (sometimes *Collectio trium partium*) is a large canonical collection compiled around 1100. It is both a key witness to the genesis of Ivo's *Decretum* and an important work in its own right. An edition of the collection, long hampered by its complicated transmission, is under way.[94] Based on Brett's work and meticulous studies of the transmission, Nowak has recently identified two codices (Paris, BnF, lat. 13656 and Reg. lat. 973) as *Leithandschriften* for any future edition.[95]

The structure of the collection is unusual, and reflects an equally unusual genesis, as the *Tripartita* combines both a source of Ivo's *Decretum* and a digest of it. This intimate relation to Ivo's *opus magnum* also provides the date of the *Tripartita*; the first part must have been available by

94. The on-going edition by Brett and Nowak is found at https://ivo-of-chartres.github.io/ (revision stamp '20150923 / 898fb'). My thanks are to both editors for their unfailing generosity with texts, time, and expertise which has informed much what follows here; all remaining errors are, of course, my own. On the collection, see Kéry 244–250, Fowler-Magerl, *Clavis* 187–190, Brett, 'Urban II' 27–46, and most recently Przemysław Nowak, 'A Legation of Galo, Bishop-Elect of Beauvais, to Poland in 1104 and the Collectio Tripartita', *Proceedings Paris 2016* MIC Subsidia 16.347–355.

95. See Nowak, 'Legation' 355, asserting that 'the *Leithandschriften* for any further draft edition online should be Paris, BN, lat. 13656 (for the earliest state) and Vatican, Reg. lat. 973 (for the latest).' My thanks are to Dr Nowak for generously sharing with me his knowledge of the *Tripartita*. Following his advice, I have checked all quotations from the *Tripartita* against Paris, BnF, lat. 13656 (= Brett's J). Curiously, a previous attempt to edit the *Tripartita* had already been based on this very manuscript in the early eighteenth century, see Rolker, *Canon Law* 40 n. 177.

ca. 1095, while the latter cannot have been added before that date. The *Tripartita* is extant in twenty-three medieval manuscripts, making it one of the more widely used pre-Gratian collections. It was used for both recensions of the *Decretum Gratiani*, giving some of the materials it contains a very wide circulation.[96] The manuscripts divide about equally between two versions; the more recent one added *capitulationes* to the individual sub-sections, has fuller rubrics, and makes minor improvements to the collection itself. For example, just as in the *Decretum*, several canons were dropped to avoid repetition.[97] As the earliest dated manuscript of the second version was written early in the twelfth century (before 1118 according to Nowak),[98] the revision of the collection must have happened very soon after its completion.

The *Tripartita* takes its name from the three major sections into which it is divided. The first part ('*Tripartita* A1') consists in excerpts from papal letters and the correspondence of Saint Boniface.[99] This part is divided into sixty-seven subsections for individual popes from Clement I to Urban II, including one for a fictious pope Chrysogonus or Grisogonus (A1.27). The second part of the *Tripartita* (known as 'A2') in a similar way is divided into fifty subsections; forty-eight of them contain conciliar canons from Nicaea to the second Council of Seville (only partly in chronological sequence). Between the Greek and the Latin councils, there is a section of miscelleaneous *sententiae* of Greek Fathers (A2.14), and a similar one is found at the very end, drawing on Latin Fathers (A2.50). Many papal letters in *Tripartita* A1 and most conciliar canons in A2 are taken from Pseudo-Isidore (hence ultimately the *Hispana* in the case of the councils), but both parts of *Tripartita* A also draw on other *fontes materiales*.

While no physically complete manuscript contains only *Tripartita* A, for some time at least such a bipartite version of the collection must have

96. Winroth, *Making* esp. 76 and 125–126 on Gratian 1 knowing *Tripartita* but only Gratian 2 making heavy use of it.

97. For example, the short canons *Tripartita* A1.1.8A and 9A are found in only four manuscripts (Brett's **GHQZ**) and apparently were dropped because they overlapped with *Tripartita* A1.1.1–2.

98. See Nowak, 'Legation' on Kraków, Archiwum Krakowskiej Kapituły Katedralnej, Ms. 84 (Brett's **P**; not seen): 'The *terminus ante quem* for the three-part version of this law collection is given by the two inventories of the cathedral treasury (of 1101 and 1110) included in the Cracow manuscript of the *Tripartita* written under Bishop Maurus (1110–1118).' See also idem, 'The Manuscripts of the *Collectio Tripartita* in Poland', *Bishops, Texts and the Use of Canon Law Around 1100: Essays in Honour of Martin Brett*, ed. Bruce Clark Brasington and Kathleen Grace Cushing (CFC; Aldershot and Farnham 2008) 91–109; for the French origin of the Cracow manuscript, see idem, 'Papsttum' 356 n. 91.

99. *Tripartita* A1.57. Contrary to what Tangl thought ('Studien' NA 41.98), *Tripartita* A1.57 takes all its eight canons from the *Britannica*, preserving the order of its model, that is, the sequence of the letters in the Boniface section (for cc. 1–6) and the Varia 2 section (cc. 7–8), respectively.

had an independent existence, as Ivo of Chartres employed it for his *Decretum*.[100] The third part of the *Tripartita* ('*Tripartita* B'), in contrast, is an abridged version of Ivo's *Decretum*, divided into twenty-nine sub-sections of very unequal length. The canons are left in the sequence of the *Decretum* and only very rarely (for four canons) does *Tripartita* B draw on other sources; thus, it preserves the character of its model very faithfully.

5.4.2 The *Tripartita* A

As indicated above, *Tripartita* A must have had a separate existence, even if no extant manuscript documents this stage of the work; its content and structure have to be carefully reconstructed. While the division between parts A and B is relatively straightforward (only *Tripartita* B draws on the *Decretum*), great care is needed to distinguish between *Tripartita* A as found in the extant manuscripts, and the hypothetical *Tripartita* A version used in the compilation of Ivo's *Decretum*.

Partly, the earliest version of *Tripartita* A can be established from a careful analysis of the extant manuscripts, some of which retain archaic features that were later lost; in addition, the *Decretum* provides valuable evidence what *Tripartita* A looked like in the mid-1090s. In addition, Martin Brett was able to identify the *Collectio Brugensis* as a formal source and indeed a model of *Tripartita* A.[101] The overall structure of *Tripartita* A (decretals followed by councils), and largely also the subdivisions within both parts are modelled on the *Brugensis*. In addition, the *Tripartita* retains the *Brugensis* preface, without adopting it to the extended content of the collection.[102] *Tripartita* numbers the popes in the same way as the *Brugensis*, and the section reserved for 'Pope Chrysogonos' also goes back to this collection. The earliest form of the *Tripartita* may have looked very similar to the *Brugensis*, but gradually new material was added, often resulting in *Brugensis* material being dropped. One important source for this reworking was a long version of Pseudo-Isidore, another one the *Britannica*; the excerpts from the correspondence of Gelasius I, Pelagius I, Saint Boniface, Leo IV, John VIII, and Stephen V in the relevant *Britannica* sections reappear in the *Tripartita*, often preserving the order of the older collection, but added to from material found in the Varia sections.

---

100. The *Collection in Ten Parts* in Köln, Historisches Archiv, 199 (*olim* W 199) largely draws on *Tripartita* A, see Petersmann, 'Überlieferung' 448–449 and Fowler-Magerl, *Clavis* 191–192. However, Brett has found that the collection also contains *Tripartita* B material; see his introduction to the *Tripartita* edition at https://ivo-of-chartres.github.io/. Also, the use of Ivo's *Prologue* and the *capitulatio* to the *Decretum* in the Cologne *10P* very strongly suggests that the *Tripartita* version employed here postdated the *Decretum*.

101. Brett, 'Urban II' 39–41, esp. 39 n. 41.

102. Brett, 'Urban II' 41.

By the time Ivo compiled his *Decretum*, the *Tripartita* therefore still was structured very much like the *Brugensis* but that apart had become a completely different work. So what did this version look like? The preface plus the Pseudo-Isidorian material in *Tripartita* A1.1–54, A2.1–13, and A2.15–49 can safely be assumed to have been part of the *Tripartita* A from the beginning of its existence. The sections mainly drawing on the *Britannica* (*Tripartita* A1.56–64) also must have been part of the *Tripartita* used for Ivo's *Decretum*, already containing all or most material found in the extant versions. The long Gregory I section (*Tripartita* A1.55) is a special case. It seems to have been used for the *Decretum*, and thus been part of *Tripartita* A from early on, but it is also noteworthy that it draws on different formal sources than the rest of *Tripartita* A. Most of the canons at the beginning of the section are taken from the *Sinemuriensis*; the canons at the end are from a source so far unidentified. In between, some sixty canons seem to be taken from a minor collection known as 'TC',[103] a source otherwise only used for the *sententiae* sections of the *Tripartita* (for which see the next paragraphs). One explanation, though not the only one, would be that these sections—A1.55 and the *sententiae* sections—drawing on a different set of formal sources were composed at a later stage and/or by a different compiler.

Further evidence for the genesis of *Tripartita* A comes from a handful of excerpts from the letters of Alexander II and Urban II (= *Tripartita* A1.66–67) and the two *sententiae* sections (= *Tripartita* A2.14 and 50). In the case of A1.66–67, there is reason to suspect their absence in the *Tripartita* version used for the *Decretum* as the latter did not draw on either section, which is at odds with Ivo's heavy use of the rest of *Tripartita* A. These sections contain ten canons including the most recent material found in *Tripartita* A, specifically excerpts from a letter Urban II wrote in 1091 or 1093 (JL 5730). As these ten canons are found in the extant *Britannica*, the possible absence of these materials from an early *Tripartita* A also raises the question whether the *Britannica* version employed for the earliest form of the *Tripartita* may have lacked the corresponding sections.[104] If, however, *Tripartita* A1.66–67 were added by a different compiler, it is also possible that this simply represents the different selection criteria of the two compilers.

As for the *sententiae* sections in *Tripartita* A2, there is no clear evidence that they were used in the making of the *Decretum*. In addition, both draw

---

103. Rolker, 'Genesis' 83–86. *Tripartita* A seems to use the version I have called 'complete TC' which contained the materials found in Paris, BnF, lat. 13368, fols. 9v–18v (ibid. 76–77).

104. See Brett, 'Urban II' 39 on this 'key difficulty'.

on a set of formal sources not otherwise used in *Tripartita* A—book four of the *Quadripartitus* and the collection known as *TC*. In the case of the second *sententiae* section (*Tripartita* A2.50), it is almost certain that it is a later addition. The reason to think so is a note found just before these *sententiae* apparently marking the end of one part of the collection:[105]

> Thus far the collection of canons. What follows are either sentences of orthodox Fathers, or laws of the catholic kings, or acts of councils held in Gaul and Germany.

This note—found in all extant manuscripts—would fit *Tripartita* B, or the *sententiae* plus *Tripartita* B, but clearly not the *sententiae* alone. It is best understood as referring to *Tripartita* A2.50 and *Tripartita* B: The 'sentences' could well refer to the material in *Tripartita* A2.50 und B1–2 in particular, while the 'laws of catholic kings' here may designate the Roman law in *Tripartita* B29 and elsewhere.[106] Finally, the Burchardian material scattered all over *Tripartita* B contains a high share of canons from 'councils held in Gaul and Germany'; indeed the same phrase is found in Burchard's preface.[107] It therefore seems that the note was only inserted after *Tripartita* B was already added to *Tripartita* A—that is, at some point after *ca.* 1095. This in turn implies that the second *sententiae* section, and probably also the first, were only added at this time.

Two more points may also be significant in this context. First, those sections in *Tripartita* A which seem to have been additions (the middle part of A1.55; A1.66–67; A2.14; A2.50) do not draw on the *Brugensis* or the *Sinemuriensis*, but on the *Britannica*, *TC*, and the *Quadripartitus*. Second, three of these sections also stand out from the rest of *Tripartita* A for containing very recent material. This applies not only to *Tripartita* A1.66–67 (Alexander II and Urban II), but also the second *sententiae* section, which surprisingly contains an excerpt taken from a letter of Gregory VII of 1078, misattributed here to Gregory the Great.[108] Neither aspect can prove who was involved in the reworking of these sections, but the differences to the rest of *Tripartita* A suggest that these sections are the work of someone working partly with material not available to the compiler of the original *Tripartita* A and, as far as he was using the same formal sources (*Britannica*), followed different selection criteria.

---

105. *Tripartita* A, after A2.49.6 (ed. Brett and Nowak): 'Hactenus de corpore canonum. Ea que sequuntur aut sententie sunt orthodoxorum patrum aut leges catholicorum regum aut synodice sententie Gallicanorum aut Germanorum pontificum.'

106. See also the list of authorities in Ivo's *Prologue* (ed. Brasington 115).

107. Burchard, 'Praefacivncvla' (ed. Fransen and Kölzer 49).

108. *Tripartita* A2.50.21 (from JL 5081); see Brett, 'Sources' 39 n. 39.

For all these reasons, I assume that the last two sections in *Tripartita* A1 and the two *sententiae* sections in *Tripartita* A2 were added to the *Tripartita* version used for the *Decretum* at a later stage by a different compiler, perhaps at the same time as part B was composed. While there is nothing to suggest that Ivo was involved in the compilation of the earliest form of *Tripartita* A, the close relation between the mature form of *Tripartita* and his own *Decretum* raises the question whether he was involved in some or all steps that turned the original *Tripartita* A (the version he employed for his *Decretum*) into the mature form of this collection, that is, a *Tripartita* A version containing the Gregory I material taken from *TC*, the Alexander II and Urban II excerpts taken from the *Britannica*, and also the *sententiae* section. This idea is supported by the fact that Ivo clearly knew the formal sources used for the middle part of *Tripartita* A1.55, A1.66–67, A2.14, and A2.50 (*Britannica*, *TC*, and *Quadripartitus*) as he employed them in his *Decretum*, his *Prologue*, and also his correspondence.[109] In this case, the reworking of *Tripartita* may have occurred parallel to Ivo's canon law activities that ultimately produced the *Decretum*. Improving *Tripartita* A certainly continued after the *Decretum* was made.[110] However, it is also noteworthy that the reworking of *Tripartita* A was done apparently by someone not using Burchard, Ivo's most important model for his own *Decretum*. This, however, is not a very strong argument against Ivo's authorship as Burchard contained but very few canons relevant for the *sententiae* section, and evidently could not be used for recent materials as found in *Tripartita* A1.66–67. In the end, one can be relatively certain that Ivo was not responsible for the earliest form of *Tripartita* A, while his involvement in the reworking of *Tripartita* A remains speculative; the overlap in the formal sources (*Britannica*, *TC*, and *Quadripartitus*) is balanced by the absence of further evidence one would demand before asserting that Ivo was involved in reworking *Tripartita* A.

5.4.3 The *Tripartita* and the 'Eight General Councils'

The Importance of the *Tripartita* for the History of Councils

Collections which arrange their materials largely in chronological order rarely reveal the preoccupations of their compilers as directly as do some of the collections arranged by subject matter. Yet one area where compiling a chronological collection obliged compilers to make decisions shap-

---

109. Rolker, *Canon Law* s.v. canonical collections (with sub-entries for *Britannica*, *Quadripartitus*, and *TC*).

110. This is suggested by Ivo's use of canons like *Tripartita* A1.1.8A, 9A, and 12A–C (= Ivo 3.64–66) which were later eliminated in *Tripartita* to avoid overlap.

ing very visibly the structure of their collection was the question which popes and councils they recognised as sources of the law. The evolving nature of the 'canon'—and also the considerable uncertainties on historical circumstances—in practice forced every compiler of a chronological collection to make sense of contradicting accounts of which fathers had actually established canon law. Any reader of medieval canon law manuscripts with their abundance of scribal errors when it comes to names of popes and councils in particular will understand how difficult this task, if taken seriously, must have been for medieval compilers working from such works. Partly, there were practical problems; in other cases, however, there were theological, ecclesiological, and political reasons either in favour or against the reception of certain popes and councils, and in this respect too compilers had to make choices. In the following, this will be studied for one small part of *Tripartita* A, specifically the 'sixth, seventh, and eighth synods' and their canons as found in sections A2.10A to A2.13.

The reception of these synods into canon law is related to the larger question of which synods were recognised as 'universal' or 'general' in the course of time. For the first five synods today recognised as ecumenical, this can be answered relatively straightforwardly. Yet for those synods convened after Constantinople II (553), and in particular the addition of the seventh and eighths synods, the story is more complicated.[111] Given that the recognition of the councils held after Constantinople II differs among the churches, research is often influenced by denominational and ecclesiological debates, with historians and theologians often adopting different approaches in their research. The most evident examples are the discussions around the critical editions of the conciliar acts directed, for half a century, by Giuseppe Alberigo (COD and COGD).[112]

As far as (Western) pre-Gratian canon law is relevant for this debate, scholarship has studied both the textual history of Gratian's list of 'eight holy synods' often known by its incipit *Sancta octo*, and the reception of individual councils. The *Tripartita* plays a critical role for both aspects of

---

111. The literature is vast. See Joseph Hergenröther, *Photius, Patriarch von Constantinopel. Sein Leben, seine Schriften und das griechische Schisma* (3 vols. Regensburg 1867–69); Dvornik, *Photian Schism*; Daniel Stiernon, *Constantinople IV* (Histoire des conciles œcuméniques 5; Paris 1967); Hermann Josef Sieben, *Die Konzilsidee des lateinischen Mittelalters (847–1378)* (Konziliengeschichte. Untersuchungen 2; Paderborn 1984); idem, *Studien zum ökumenischen Konzil. Definitionen und Begriffe, Tagebücher und Augustinus-Rezeption* (Konziliengeschichte. Untersuchungen; Paderborn 2010) 153–190; Danica Summerlin, *The Canons of the Third Lateran Council of 1179: Their Origins and Reception* (Life and Thought: Fourth Series 116; Cambridge 2019) ch. 1. See also the introductions to the individual councils in the critical editions (ACO Series secunda, COD, and COGD).

112. For a very brief introduction to the debate, see Alberto Melloni, 'Essence, Concept, or History: What Is at Stake in a Dispute over the COGD' CHR 101 (2015) 578–587.

the history of the canon of 'general councils' for two principal reasons. First, the *Tripartita* (after the *Britannica*) was only the second collection to contain *Sancta octo*, and disseminated this text widely; crucially, the *Tripartita* also passed the canon on to Gratian.[113] By virtue of the pervasive influence of the latter, the *Sancta octo* list became a key document in Western debates about the definition of general councils, and in particular the ecumenicity of Constantinople IV.[114] Second, and perhaps even more importantly, the *Tripartita* was the first canonical collection which systematically strove to include the canons of all eight general councils. To this end, the compiler drew on rare, sometimes extremely rare documents, many of which were later taken up by Gratian. This strongly suggests that the compiler not only copied the above-mentioned list but made a serious effort to assemble the relevant enactments of these councils as well. This in turn also helps to clarify which councils were 'holy and general', as the *Sancta octo* list gives no details about the councils except for the place where they were held and their sequence.

Given that in eleventh-century Latin Europe several lists of general synods circulated, but none was widely known, and that very little was known about the canons of the fifth, sixth, seventh, and eighth universal synods, the importance of the *Tripartita* can hardly be exaggerated. Nonetheless, mainly because the *Tripartita* was not available in a printed edition, its role in the history of the canon of general councils has not been studied in detail yet.[115] Also, as the following paragraphs will demonstrate, despite the relative wealth of internal evidence, it is surprisingly difficult to establish which assemblies the *Tripartita* compiler actually referred to as the sixth, seventh, and eighth general councils.

---

113. *Tripartita* A2.10A.1 (on which see below) = Gratian D.16 c.8 (ed. Winroth 38; ed. Friedberg 45). For discussion, especially of the sigma group manuscripts, see Regula Gujer, *Concordia discordantium codicum manuscriptorum? Die Textentwicklung von 18 Handschriften anhand der D. 16 des Decretum Gratiani* (Forschungen zur kirchlichen Rechtsgeschichte und zum Kirchenrecht 23; Cologne, Weimar, and Vienna 2004) 69–78. On *Britannica Varia* 2.147 see Rolker, 'Britannica'.

114. The presence of Constantinople IV in *Tripartita* A2 was already noted by Theiner, *Disquitiones criticae* 157, Johann Friedrich Schulte, *Das katholische Kirchenrecht* (2 vols. Giessen 1856–60), here at 1.315, Hergenröther, *Photius* 2.131 n. 94; *Histoire* 2.62–63. Dvornik, *Photian Schism* rightly recognised the importance of *Britannica Varia* 2.147 but had no direct knowledge of *Tripartita* (see next note).

115. Dvornik, *Photian Schism* 323 relied on the brief notes in Fournier, 'Collections attribuées à Yves' BEC 57.687 n. 2 for his knowledge of the *Tripartita*. Hofmann, Stiernon, and Sieben did not take into account the *Tripartita* at all: Georg Hofmann, 'Ivo von Chartres über Photios' *Orientalia Christiana Periodica* 14 (1948) 105–137; Stiernon, *Constantinople IV*, Sieben, *Konzilsidee* and idem, *Studien* 153–190. This is all the more important as Sieben was positive that Ivo's *Decretum* was the first collection to have Gratian's list. However, this claim relies on printed editions in which *Sancta octo* was 'corrected' from Gratian.

Which Councils Were There? (*Tripartita* A2.10A)

To understand the choices the *Tripartita* compiler made, and his contribution to the canon of general councils, let us first consider the structure of the collection. The first part of *Tripartita* A2 (sections A2.1–13) contains excerpts from Greek councils, arranged roughly in chronological sequence. The first ten entries are devoted to councils from Nicaea to Chalcedon.[116] This part of the *Tripartita*, following the Pseudo-Isidorian model, includes the first four general councils (Nicaea I, Constantinople I, Ephesus I, Chalcedon) but not Constantinople II (533) which was commonly counted as the fifth.[117] Like other Pseudo-Isidorian collections, *Tripartita* A2.1–10 does not number the councils or separate general synods from other assemblies, except that Nicaea is consciously placed first. Where the manuscripts identify individual councils (in inscriptions, headlines to individual sections, and sometimes running titles), they do so simply by the respective place names.

This, however, changes with following section (*Tripartita* A2.10A), which interrupts the long series of synodal enactments by a small set not of conciliar canons, but canons about conciliar authority. While not clearly marked as a separate section in all manuscripts,[118] the change in content itself is notable. One finds here:

1. *Sancta octa*, the list of eight universal councils mentioned above; it lists Nicaea, Constantinople I, Ephesus I, Chalcedon, Constantinople II and III, Nicaea II, and Constantinople IV.[119]
2. Bede's account of Constantinople III, with an truncated version of Bede's list of the first five general synods: Nicaea, Constantinople I, Chalcedon, and Constantinople II.[120] Ephesus is omitted for no

116. The synods in question are Nicaea I (325), Ancyra (314), Neocaesarea (315), Gangra (355), Serdica (343), Antioch (324), Laodicea, Constantinople I (381), Ephesus I (431), and Chalcedon (451). Ephesus is only represented by the Creed of Union.

117. See, for example, the *Indiculus* in *Liber diurnus* A59 (ed. Foerster 335): 'Sancta quoque universalia concilia: Nicenum, Constantinopolitanum, Ephesinum primum, Chalcedonensem et secundum Constantinopolitanum.' For a more detailed list, see the *Fides papae* in *Liber diurnus* A60 (ed. Foerster 338–352). On the absence of Constantinople II from Latin collections before Ivo's *Decretum*, see Rudolf Schieffer, 'Das V. ökumenische Konzil in kanonistischer Überlieferung' ZRG Kan. Abt. 59 (1973) 1–34. None of the four canons Ivo quotes from this council (Ivo 14.49a, 49b, 62a, and 63) is found in the *Tripartita*.

118. See the edition for the lack of a title and sometimes also missing canon numbers. In addition to the edition by Brett and Nowak, I have used Paris, BnF, lat. 13656 (Brett's J). Here the break is relatively clear: *Tripartita* A2.10A begins on a new recto (J, fol. 137r), and has a separate title at the top of the page 'De octo synodis'; unlike in the previous section, the items in A2.10A are not numbered, and the elaborate rubrics in the margin stop, too.

119. See above on *Britannica* (the formal source of *Tripartita* A2.10A.1) and other collections.

120. Bede, *De temporum ratione* (ed. Jones, CCL 123B.528). The *Tripartita* lacuna was reported

obvious reason in the *Tripartita*, and no mention is made of Bede's vitriolic attack on the Quinisextum as 'erroneous'.[121]

3. Gregory's *Synodica* (JE 1092), comparing the first four councils (Nicaea, Constantinople, Ephesus, Chalcedon) to the four Gospels and professing to venerate the fifth, though he does not mention where it met.

4. A short text from the 'seventh synod' (Nicaea II) on the sixth synod having gathered twice.[122]

5. Another canon from Nicaea II against the 'so called seventh synod' (the Council of Hieria of 754).[123]

6. A letter of Pope Hadrian I (JE 2449 as transmitted with the acts of Nicaea II) on the authority of the sixth synod 'and all its canons'; the canon Hadrian quoted is from the Quinisextum.[124]

7. A 'letter of the sixth synod' (Constantinople III) to Pope Agatho, sending him the acts for approval.[125]

8. Another 'letter of the sixth synod' (the Quinisextum) to Emperor Justinian II, and excerpts from canon two of this council, confirming earlier canon law (the complete *Canones Apostolorum*, councils from Nicaea to Carthage, and Greek Fathers).[126] The list

---

by Friedberg as it is also found in Gratian 2: D.16 c.9 (ed. Friedberg 45). Interestingly, Ivo 4.125 (ed. Brett) has a *longer* excerpt from Bede with the same lacuna (with two manuscripts mending the gap, see Brett's apparatus), while Gratian 1 had an even shorter text (ed. Winroth 38). See also below note 390 on the *Caesaraugustana I*.

121. Bede, *De temporum ratione* (ed. Jones, CCL 123B.529): 'Hic [Justinian II, CR] beatae memoriae pontificem Romanae ecclesiae Sergium, quia aerraticae suae synodo, quam Constantinopoli fecerat, fauere et subscribere noluisset, misso Zacharia protospatario suo iussit Constantinopolim deportari.' If the *Tripartita* compiler knew this passage, he either failed to identify the council, or chose to ignore Bede's judgement. Ivo likewise chose to ignore this passage, although he seems to have read some Bede for book four of his *Decretum*.

122. On *Tripartita* A2.10A.4–6, see also Erich Lamberz, 'Die Überlieferung und Rezeption des VII. Ökumenischen Konzils (787) in Rom und im lateinischen Westen', *Roma fra Oriente e Occidente. 19–24 aprile 2001* (2 vols. Settimane 49; Spoleto 2002) 2.1053–1099, here at 1088–1091. The text established by Brett and Nowak, not yet available to Lamberz, confirms his findings (based on Friedberg's apparatus).

123. Nicaea II, *refutatio* (ed. Lamberz, ACO, Series II, vol. 2.3 p. 609 lines 10–14); on the unusual Latin translation, see below.

124. On JE 2449 and the Quinisextum, see below.

125. Peter Landau, 'Überlieferung und Bedeutung der Kanones des Trullanischen Konzils im westlichen kanonischen Recht', *The Council in Trullo Revisited*, ed. George Nedungatt and Michael Featherstone (Kanonika 6; Rome 1995) 215–227, here at 219; a different version of this letter is found in Mansi 11.683 and 686, as Landau pointed out.

126. *Tripartita* A2.10A.8a–c. These three texts seem to be based on the *Logos prosphonetikos* (8a) and canon 2 (8b–c) of the Quinisextum; in the first version manuscripts only, the correct canon number is retained (J, fol. 138v). For the material source, see the editions by Nedungatt and Agrestini (COGD 1.222 lines 137–146, p. 223 lines 195–198, p. 229 lines 410–419, and pp. 229–230 lines 436–487) and Ohme (ACO, Series II, vol. 3.4 p. 19 lines 13–18, p. 20 lines 11–12, p. 24 lines 2–6, and p. 24 line 14 to p. 25 line 6). In addition, I have used *Concilium Quinisextum / Das Konzil Quinisextum, griechisch-deutsch*, ed. and tr. by Heinz Ohme (Fontes Christiani 82; Turnhout 2006). Note that the *Tripartita* text not only is an abbreviation but generally differs from the Greek acts; for example,

lacks a reference to Constantinople found in its Greek original, and is partly confused.[127] The second part of this canon, or even all of it, may in fact already belong to the next section of *Tripartita* A (see below).

These eight (or perhaps seven) canons may be described as material concerning the definition of universal synods in general, and the status of the sixth to the eighth synods in particular. Despite some discrepancies, these texts taken together strongly suggest that there were not only five, but indeed eight general synods, and that the last three had taken place in Constantinople (with two separate meetings), Nicaea, and again Constantinople. For the sixth and the seventh synods, the texts also provide enough historical detail to date them with some precision. Only then follow three sections containing actual canons attributed to these three synods.

The Quinisextum as the Sixth Synod (*Tripartita* A2.11)

With no clear break in the early manuscripts, *Tripartita* A2.11 next presents canons of the 'sixth synod'.[128] They are all from the Quinisextum council of 691 (also known as *Concilium Trullanum*, 'Council in Trullos' or 'in Trullo').[129] The *Tripartita* quotes from a total of nineteen of the 102

---

the reference to the preceding councils as 'fifth' and 'sixth' is only found in the *Tripartita*. Perhaps this indicates knowledge of Quinisextum c. 1 (ed. Ohme, ACO, Series II, vol. 3.4 p. 23 lines 2–3) where Constantinople 680/681 is called the 'sixth holy synod'?

127. Quinisextum c. 2 (ed. Ohme, ACO, Series II, vol. 3.4 p. 24 lines 22–25) contains a reference to Constantinople 394 which is dropped in the *Tripartita*; the list of 'canons of bishops' which the Quinisextum confirmed is turned into a list of *opuscula* in the *Tripartita*, with many details confused.

128. Paris, BnF, lat. 13656 (= J in the edition) largely confirms what Brett and Nowak report for other first version manuscripts (namely their **ZOGHQA**, 'which run this section straight on from the last'). In J there seems to be a break, but not clearly marked; if there is one, it is after *Tripartita* A2.10.7: there is an inscription 'Canones sexte synodi' in the margin next to *Tripartita* A2.10A.8a (J, fol. 138r); canon 8 continues on fol. 138v, where the running title 'De sexta synodus' is found in the upper margin. The second version of *Tripartita*, in contrast, has a *capitulatio* after *Tripartita* A2.10A.8, clearly marking that the new section begins only with *Tripartita* A2.11.1.

129. On *Tripartita* A2.10A.8b–c, which contains excerpts from Quinisextum c.2, see above. On the council and its enactments, see Erich Caspar, *Geschichte des Papsttums von den Anfängen bis zur Höhe der Weltherrschaft* (2 vols. Tübingen 1930/33), here at 2.632–636, Heinz Ohme, *Das Concilium Quinisextum und seine Bischofsliste. Studien zum Konstantinopeler Konzil von 692* (Arbeiten zur Kirchengeschichte 56; Berlin and New York 1990), esp. 35–54, Janet L. Nelson, 'Law and Its Applications', *Early Medieval Christianities, c. 600–c. 1100*, ed. Thomas F. X. Noble and Julia M. H. Smith (The Cambridge History of Christianity 3; Cambridge 2008) 299–326, here at 299–308, and Heinz Ohme, 'Sources of the Greek Canon Law to the Quinisext Council (691/2): Councils and Church Fathers', *The History of Byzantine and Eastern Canon Law to 1500*, ed. Wilfried Hartmann and Kenneth Pennington (HMCL; Washington, D.C. 2012) 24–114, here at 77–84. On the transmission in the West, see Landau, 'Überlieferung' (*Tripartita* and Gratian), Nicolae Dură, 'The Ecumenicity of the Council in Trullo: Witnesses of the Canonical Tradition in East and West', *The Council in Trullo Revisited*, ed. George Nedungatt and Michael Featherstone (Kanonika 6; Rome 1995) 229–262, and Heinz Ohme, 'Einleitung', *Concilium Constantinopolitanum a. 691/2 in Trullo habitum (Concilium Quinisextum)*, ed. idem (ACO, Series II, vol. 3.4; Berlin and Boston 2013) VII–CIX.

canons of the council.[130] This is surprising, given that earlier Latin canon law collections had not contained any canons of this council, and indeed there had been considerable opposition to it in the West.[131] Of course, Nicaea II had recognised the Council in Trullos, but this canon too was unknown in the West.[132] Famously, Humbert of Silva Candida in 1054 even claimed that the apostolic see had refuted the Quinisextum canons.[133] Yet if the *Tripartita* compiler knew these polemics against the council or its 'anti-Roman canons' (as they are sometimes called),[134] he was unimpressed. In any case he inserted canon 36 asserting that in the order of the patriarchal seats, Constantinople was second only to Rome—even if the latter see is called 'inferior Rome' in his translation![135]

The *Tripartita* compiler was the first to introduce canons from the council in Trullos into Latin canon law and to accept the council as 'general'. His source remains unknown, and with only one exception,[136] no other canons of the Quinisextum were taken into Latin canon law collections of the next centuries. Ohme concluded that the *Tripartita* compiler must have had access to a complete translation, different from (and later than) that of 873.[137] The identification of this council as the sixth general council

130. Landau, 'Überlieferung' 220–221 (followed by Ohme, 'Einleitung' LXXXV) listed only 17 canons, to which one should add the excerpts from canon 2 in *Tripartita* A2.10.8 (authenticity of *Canones Apostolorum*, list of synods and Greek Fathers) and the quotation from canon 82 in *Tripartita* A2.10A.6 (prohibition to depict Christ as lamb). On the possible allusion to canon 1, see above.

131. The *Liber pontificalis* (ed. Duchesne 1.372–373) reports that Pope Sergius opposed the council, though his legates were tricked into subscribing; see Caspar, *Geschichte* 2.634–635 and Ohme, *Quinisextum* 55–75. On Bede's opposition to the Quinisextum, see above (note 121).

132. Nicaea II c. 1 (ed. Lamberz, ACO, Series II, vol. 3.3, pp. 899 line 14–19 = DOGC 1.318 lines 267–278).

133. Humbert (PG 120.1030) as quoted by Ohme, 'Einleitung' LXXXV n. 403: 'Capitula quae nobis sub ejus (scil. Sextae synodi) auctoritate opponitis omnino refutamus, quia prima et apostolica sedes nec aliquando ea accepit nec observat hactenus; et quia aut sunt nulla, aut ut nobis libuit, depravata sunt.'

134. See also Ohme, *Quinisextum* 3–4 and idem, 'Die sogenannten "antirömischen Kanones" des Concilium Quinisextum (692) – Vereinheitlichung als Gefahr für die Einheit der Kirche', *The Council in Trullo Revisited*, ed. George Nedungatt and Michael Featherstone (Kanonika 6; Rome 1995) 307–321, here at 309–310 on various (modern) lists of supposedly 'anti-Roman' canons, often including c. 36; more importantly, see his analysis (ibid. 310–317) and conclusion that the canons on the whole are not 'anti-Roman' (ibid. 317).

135. *Tripartita* A2.11.17 (ed. Brett and Nowak): '[…] petimus, ut Constantinopolitana sedes similia priuilegia que inferior Roma accipiat.' As already Landau, 'Überlieferung' 223 spotted, the council (quoting Chalcedon c. 28) had in fact called Rome 'the see of the older Rome' (πρεσβυτέρας Ῥώμης θρόνο[ς])! See Quinisextum c. 36 (ed. Ohme, ACO, Series II, vol. 3.4 p. 39 lines 13–14) and the comment. See also *Anselmo dedicata* 1.117–118 (ed. Besse 293) for a parallel.

136. *Panormia* 3.86, apparently from *Arsenal II* (Paris, Bibliothèque de l'Arsenal, 713, fol. 132r), is the only Quinisextum canon not found in *Tripartita* A2 later taken into Gratian D.31 c.13 (ed. Winroth 79; ed. Friedberg 144–115).

137. See Ohme, 'Einleitung' LXXXV: 'Mit einiger Wahrscheinlichkeit muss Ivo [i.e. the *Tripartita* compiler, CR] ein vollständiger lateinischer Text des Quinisextums vorgelegen haben, ohne dass sich bislang sagen liesse, woher Ivo diesen Text hatte. Es lässt sich nur feststellen, dass dieser lateinische Text wohl erst nach 873 entstanden sein wird.'

in the *Tripartita* goes back to Hadrian I (JE 2449). In this letter, as transmitted in the *Tripartita* A2.10A, the pope quoted c. 82 of the Quinisextum (a canon not found in *Tripartita* A2.11) and, importantly, recognised it as the sixth synod.[138] While today Constantinople III and the Quinisextum are often seen as two distinct synods (and only the former is accepted as ecumenical by the Roman Catholic Church in modern times), Gratian would follow the *Tripartita* in that he called the latter council a continuation of the former.[139] Indeed, Gratian strongly relied on the *Tripartita* both for his canons of the Quinisextum and for its identification with the sixth synod; eighteen of his nineteen canons are taken from *Tripartita*.[140]

Nicaea II as the Seventh Synod (*Tripartita* A2.12)

The next section, discernible as such in the early manuscripts,[141] begins with an unnumbered text on the date of the seventh synod, followed by fourteen canons of Nicaea II (787). The enactments of this council were famously opposed by Charlemagne and the *Libri Carolini* but for some time at least defended by Pope Hadrian I (JE 2483).[142] Some of the Carolingian opposition was based on imperfections of the first Latin translation issued by the pope, and the second translation by Anastasius Bibliothecarius was meant to mend these errors.[143] This translation, in turn, from the late eleventh century on provided several compilers of canon law collections with their Nicaea II material.[144] However, *Tripartita* A2.12

138. Hadrian I, JE 2449 (ed. Lamberz, ACO, Series II, vol. 3.1, pp. 174–182, here at 176 line 10–178 line 4) quoting from Quinisextum c. 82 (ed. Ohme, ACO, Series II, vol. 3.4, p. 54). Crucially, JE 2449 is quoted in *Tripartita* A2.10A.6 (ed. Brett and Nowak): 'Sanctam sextam synodum recipio cum omnibus canonibus suis, in quibus dicitur: "In quibus scripturis sanctarum imaginum agnus precursoris [. . .]".' (Here checked against J, fol. 138r; the interpunctation is my own.)

139. Gratian D.16 d.p.c. 6 (ed. Winroth 37; ed. Friedberg 44).

140. Landau, 'Überlieferung' 220–221 listed only 18 canons, but earlier (ibid. 216) had mentioned the quotation from Quinisextum c. 82 via the acts of Nicaea II in Gratian D.16 c.4 (ed. Winroth 36–37; ed. Friedberg 42). Friedberg and Landau overlooked that this canon too is taken from the *Tripartita* (see above, note 138).

141. To take Paris, BnF, lat. 13656 (J) as my guide again, the inscription to *Tripartita* A2.12.1 'Actio prima septime synodi' is longer than most of J's inscriptions for *Tripartita* A2; in addition, the page where this canon is found has 'De septima synodo' in the upper margin (J, fol. 140r). The beginning of a new section is clearly visible.

142. Nicaea II (ed. Lamberz, ACO, Series II, vol. 2.1–3); *Libri Carolini* (ed. Freeman, MGH Conc. 2, suppl. 1). See Ann Freeman, 'Carolingian Orthodoxy and the Fate of the *Libri Carolini*' Viator 16 (1985) 65–108 and Lamberz, 'Einleitung'.

143. For an edition of the Greek canons and Anastasius' translation, see Nicaea II, ed. Lamberz and Uphus (COGD 1.297–345).

144. Jean Gaudemet, 'Le deuxième concile de Nicée (787) dans les Collections canoniques occidentales' AHC 20 (1988) 278–288; Lamberz, 'Überlieferung'; idem, 'Einleitung' L–LII. Both Gaudemet and Lamberz used the *Tripartita* via Friedberg's apparatus and quoted Ivo from PL 161; but all important readings they quote are also found in the manuscripts according to Brett's edition.

does not fit this pattern; it was clearly not using Anastasius's translation.[145] Rather, it seems to use the first translation otherwise known only from quotations in Carolingian sources.[146] The same source may also have been used for the letters of Hadrian transmitted in the Greek acts of the council (JE 2448 and 2449 as found in *Tripartita* A2.10A).

Constantinople IV as the Eighth Synod (*Tripartita* A2.13)

Finally, the section on the eighth synod, again marked (if imperfectly) as a separate segment in the early manuscripts, is introduced by an unnumbered text on the synod.[147] According to this note, Pope Hadrian had sent legates (accompanied by Anastasius Bibliothecarius) to Emperor Basilius and his sons in Constantinople, where they celebrated the eighth synod; this synod, according to the *Tripartita* excerpt, 'calmed the schism' by anathemising Photios.[148] This passage is taken from the Varia 2 section of the *Britannica*, where it is part of a larger excerpt 'Ex gestis Francorum'.[149] The passage found in the *Tripartita* is taken from the *Annals of Saint-Bertin* and goes back to Hincmar. It describes the 869 synod as favourable towards Rome but also as self-contradictory concerning image worship; the latter part is ignored by the *Tripartita*.[150] As the *Tripartita* is

145. Lamberz, 'Überlieferung'. However, the *Tripartita* compiler did use Anastasius' translation in different parts of his collections; see *Tripartita* A2.14.3–4 for two letters of Saint Cyrill as transmitted with Nicaea II, but with no indication of this origin.

146. Lamberz, 'Einleitung' LI: '[...] scheint die Schlußfolgerung unausweichlich, daß seine [Ivos, CR] Zitate aus den Akten des Nicaenum II einer anderen Quelle als Anastasius entnommen sind. Diese Quelle kann, wenn nicht alles täuscht, nur die erste lateinische Fassung der Akten sein, die in Nordfrankreich, wo sie für die Pariser Synode von 825 benutzt worden war, noch zugänglich gewesen sein muß.'

147. In J, fol. 144r, the new section is marked (like the previous ones) by a relatively long inscription to the first canon ('Cap. ix. Ex octava synodo') and a corresponding title in the upper margin ('De octava synodo')

148. *Tripartita* A2.13 (ed. Brett and Nowak, checked against J, fol. 140r): 'Adrianus papa secundus [*sic*] quod Nicholaus decessor eius disposuerat missos suos, Donatum scilicet Ostiensem episcopum et Stephanum Nephesinum episcopum et Marinum dyaconum sancte Romane ecclesie ad Basylium imperatorem et ad filios eius, Constantinum et Leonem augustos Constantinopolim direxit. Cum quibus et Anasthasius bybliothecarius sedis Romane utriusque lingue, Grece scilicet et Latine peritus perrexit, et synodo congregata quam octauam uniuersalem synodum illuc conuenientes appellauerunt exortum scisma de Ignatii depositione et Fotii ordinatione sedauerunt, Fotium anathematizantes et Ignatium restituentes.' The error at the beginning may actually be informed by historical knowledge, as the pope in question was indeed Hadrian II; however, the sentence still demands 'secundum'. The material source are the *Annales Bertiniani*, a. 872 (ed. Grat et al. 187).

149. *Britannica* Varia 2.14 (London, BL, Add. MS 8873, fols. 177r–180r, here at fols. 177v–178r). For a transcription, see Rolker, 'History' 149–152, here at 150. *Britannica* Varia 2.14 also preserves a source compiled only after 1108 from which Ivo quoted in one of his letters (*Ep.* 189, ed. in Rolker and Schawe, 'Gutachten' 154–157). This indicates that Varia 2.14 is more composite than has been assumed; it clearly deserves further study. Friedberg's assumption (in his apparatus to Gratian D.63 c.2, ed. Friedberg 235) that the passage in *Tripartita* was taken 'ex actis Concilii' is unsound.

150. The *Britannica* (London, BL, Add. MS 8873, fol. 178r), in contrast, preserves the passage: 'In qua sinodo de imaginibus ordinandis [*sic*] aliter quam orthodoxi doctores antea diffinierant

one of the first canonical collections to include the eighth synod, this excerpt may have served as a proof text that the synod was indeed 'general', approved by the pope, and attended by papal legates. When it came to the enactments of the synod, however, the *Tripartita* is rather short; it only quotes two canons. The first is the canon which in the late eleventh century was most strongly associated with Constantinople 869/870 and which probably contributed to the increasingly favourable reception of the synod, namely canon 22 against lay intervention in episcopal elections.[151] The only other canon *Tripartita* attributes to this council is in fact taken from the synod that took place ten years later—the very synod which abrogated the 869/870 synod and restored Photios to his office.[152] A similar phenomenon can be found in the collection of Deusdedit which clearly had influenced *Tripartita*, though the exact textual relationship is obscure.[153] The canon itself, strongly abbreviated in *Tripartita*, states that a bishop who resigned and became monk should never be received as bishop again.

The account of the eighth synod in the *Tripartita*, therefore, is considerably confused. Apparently, the *Tripartita* compiler was unaware that the synods of 869/870 and 879/880 had made utterly different decisions in the Photian affair. Although the inscription to *Tripartita* A2.13.1 could have made him suspicious,[154] he treated these two synods as one. It is not clear what his immediate source for this section looked like. Clearly it was very similar to the extant *Britannica*, and must have depended ultimately

statuerunt et quedam pro fauore Romani pontificis, qui eorum uotis de imaginibus adorandis annuit et quedam contra antiquos canones et contra ipsam suam sinodum constituerant, sicut qui eandem sinodum legerit patenter inueniet.' See *Annales Bertiniani*, a. 872 (ed. Grat et al. 187), where one reads 'adorandis' instead of 'ordinandis'; but otherwise, the *Britannica* has only trivial variants.

151. *Tripartita* A2.13.1 (ed. Brett and Nowak, checked against J, fol. 144r–v) = Constantinople 869/870 c. 22 (ed. Gemeinhardt, COGD 2.1:44–45). The canon is also found in Deusdedit 4.18 (16) (ed. Wolf von Glanvell 409–410), Anselm 6.20 (ed. Theiner 276–277), and Bonizo 2.17 (ed. Perels 42). The *Tripartita* clearly has the text of Deusdedit (via *Britannica* Varia 2.107). On the reception of canon 22, see Dvornik, *Photian Schism* 319–326.

152. *Tripartita* A2.13.2 (ed. Brett and Nowak, checked against J, fol. 144v) = Deusdedit 4.437 (162) (ed. Wolf von Glanvell 617 lines 6–13). *Tripartita* and Deusdedit share many gaps and variants against the apparent source, Constantinople 879/880 c. 2 (ed. Gemeinhardt, COGD 2.1:70 lines 44–57). In J, *Tripartita* A2.12.12 is inserted here, but with a note referring back to the correct place: 'Hec sententia debet poni ubi superius uideris hoc signum: Φ.' Indeed one finds the Φ-like sign in the appropriate place (J, fol. 143v). Brett and Nowak report the same displaced canon with the same note for their manuscript A (Alençon, BM, 135 [not seen]).

153. Both canons (*Tripartita* A2.13.1–2) have a parallel in Deusdedit, but only the former is also in the *Britannica* (see last notes). Note also that Deusdedit 4.437 (162) is the very last canon in Vat. lat. 3833, and may well have been an addition; it is not mentioned in Deusdedit's sophisticated *capitulatio*.

154. This inscription mentions, correctly, that the synod was convened during the pontificate of John VIII, while the excerpt from the *Annales Bertiniani* quoted above related that Pope Hadrian II, as had already been planned by his predecessor Nicholas I, sent legates to Constantinople.

on Deusdedit. Given that the compiler was eager to include canons of all eight general synods, one may tentatively assume this source did not contain much more material linked to either the 869/870 or the 879/880 synod than the two canons in *Tripartita* A2.13.[155] If true, this would be strong case for a difference in learning, and also in attitude, between the *Tripartita* compiler and Ivo of Chartres. The latter, while certainly familiar with *Tripartita* A2.13, also displayed considerable knowledge of the whole Photian affair, and quoted his restoration to office (apparently unknown to the *Tripartita* compiler) as a prime example of dispensation in his *Prologue*.[156] Ivo in his *Decretum* also quoted material from sources outside the *Tripartita* on the revocation of the 869/870 synod.[157] While these texts need not express Ivo's own opinion, his favourable presentation of Photios suggests that he indeed was more likely to regard the 879/880 synod as 'general', rather than the 869/870 synod as the *Tripartita* A compiler seems to have done.

Summary: Chances and Choices

The four sections A2.10A–13 of the *Tripartita* contain highly unusual materials, often from obscure but apparently ancient sources. The compiler evidently took great pains to make sense of the incomplete and confusing transmission of his material. The short, but powerful introductory texts in *Tripartita* A2.10A addressed these problems. They asserted the authenticity of the 'sixth, seventh, and eighth synods', and may have helped readers who struggled, like the *Tripartita* compiler himself did, to distinguish the various councils referred to by these numbers. The fact that four relevant councils—Constantinople III, Quinisextum, and the two synods known as Constantinople IV—had taken place in the same city must have added to the confusion.

Some of the conflicts of, and about, these councils must likewise have been difficult to understand from the perspective of the compiler. Nonetheless, some of the theological and political issues were still, or again, well known in the eleventh century,[158] and the *Tripartita* shows signs that

---

155. The second version of the *Tripartita* would add a *capitulatio* that seems to announce no less than 32 canons of the eighth synod, but in fact only repeats the rubrics to both the two canons in *Tripartita* A2.13 and the 30 items in *Tripartita* A2.14; it also adds running numbers for both sections. This is surprising, as in both versions the boundary between these sections is clearly marked by a short note (in J, fol. 144r, even in red ink): 'Huc usque de conciliis Grecorum. Deinde sequuntur quedam sent--tie Grecorum doctorum.'

156. Ivo, *Prologue* (ed. Brasington 135–140; tr. Somerville and Brasington, *Prefaces* 152–156).

157. John VIII, JE 3273 and 3276 as found in Ivo 4.76–77 (ed. Brett). For both canons, Ivo's text is that of the acts of Constantinople 879/880; see John VIII, *Epp.* 209 and 211a (ed. Caspar, MGH Epp. 7.186 lines 3–8 and 189 lines 26–29, respectively).

158. Evidently, the *filioque* condemned by the 879/880 synod was still a contentious issue in

the compiler was aware of this fact. The material he introduced had been subject to sometimes vehement opposition, but the *Tripartita* compiler boldly introduced it as coming from 'universal' synods. In doing so, he shaped Western canon law profoundly. The acceptance of the Quinisextum, Nicaea II, and Constantinople IV as 'general' synods, plus the introduction of their canons was mainly due to the decisions the *Tripartita* compiler took, and it was a leap forward in the history of the sources of canon law. There had been occasional assertions that some or even all of these synods were 'holy and universal', and single canons were found in collections before the *Tripartita*. However, the *Tripartita* went far beyond what Anselm, Deusdedit, or even the *Britannica* had to offer in this respect. Only the *Tripartita* contained a clear list of the 'holy eight synods' matched by sections for every single one of them, clarified (to considerable extent at least) the identity of the synods in question, and provided at least a selection of their enactments. Given the lasting impact his choices had, for better and for worse, it is no exaggeration to call this short section of *Tripartita* A an important document for canon law history and indeed for ecclesiastical history in general.

5.4.4 The *Tripartita* B

Compared to *Tripartita* A, part B of the collection can be defined relatively easily, as it is a faithful abbreviation of Ivo's *Decretum*; all books except for the last one (on speculative theology, essentialy a copy of Burchard's book 20) are used for *Tripartita* B. The sequence of its 29 sub-sections, and also the arrangement of the canons within these sections, manifestly is that of the *Decretum*. Many of these sub-sections correspond to one book of the *Decretum*, but some books of the *Decretum* are turned into two or or more sub-sections in *Tripartita* B. For example, Ivo in book seven of his *Decretum* had gathered 158 canons on monastic life; in *Tripartita* B, no less than four sub-section draw on this book: *Tripartita* B11 has fourteen canons 'On monks', B12 eight canons 'On nuns', B13 another eight canons 'On monks and nuns', and B14 nine canons 'On virgins'. Nonetheless, as in similar cases, the sequence of canons is still that of the *Decretum*. There is some evidence that *Tripartita* B retains more fully those materials which Ivo himself tended to quote more frequently in his cor-

---

1054 when Humbert of Silva Candida and the other papal legates in the bull of excommunication against Patriarch Michael Keroullarios famously blamed Greek Christians to have 'dropped' this addition to the Creed. For an edition of the bull, see *Acta et scripta quae de controversiis ecclesiae Graecae et Latinae saeculo undecimo composita extant*, ed. Cornelius Will (Leipzig and Marburg 1861) 153a–154b, here at 153b: 'Sicut Pneumatomachi vel Theumachi absciderunt a symbolo Spiritus sancti processionem a Filio.'

respondence, for example on marriage.[159] On the whole, *Tripartita* B is a very faithful abbreviation of the *Decretum*, much shorter but still covering many issues, and considerably easier to use.

Given that neither part A nor part B of the *Tripartita* had a separate existence, at least none visible in the extant manuscripts, it seems plausible to assume that *Tripartita* B was produced and added to part A not long after the latter had been used to produce the *Decretum*. Indeed, the *Decretum* version used to produce *Tripartita* B manifestly was an earlier version than that extant in any manuscript. It contained several canons which can be assumed to have been contained in the earliest form of the *Decretum* but were later deleted in an effort to reduce overlap within the collection.[160] This places the composition of *Tripartita* B even closer in time and space to the composition of the *Decretum*; *Tripartita* B seems to have been compiled shortly after 1095, and it is difficult to imagine that this happened outside Chartres. While all this is circumstantial evidence in favour of Ivo's authorship, this hypothesis is surprisingly difficult to test. The reason for this is precisely that *Tripartita* B faithfully preserves the structure and content of the *Decretum*. For this reason, it is almost impossible to decide whether the parallels to *Tripartita* B found in Ivo's letters are really taken from this collection rather than the *Decretum* (which Ivo can be shown to have used). There are letters where the use of *Tripartita* B would explain all of Ivo's canonical quotations—a finding that has some weight given that *Tripartita* B is much shorter than the *Decretum*. In general, the parallels between the canon law in Ivo's letters and the materials found in *Tripartita* B suggest that Ivo's interests matched those of the *Tripartita* B compiler, but this in itself cannot be taken as proof that he compiled the collection.[161] The knowledge of the sources from which *Tripartita* B was compiled in principle would be a stronger argument, but this line of inquiry is hampered by the fact that all canons are taken from *Decretum* (which Ivo compiled himself) and only four texts are taken from different sources. While it is dangerous to argue on such a small basis, it is at least interesting that two of Ivo's latest letters (apparently going back to the

---

159. Rolker, *Canon Law* 245–248.

160. Ivo 16.9A (a doublet to Ivo 5.7) was omitted by the archetype of some *Decretum* manuscripts (Brett's **CMR**) but is present in others (Brett's **BPV**). Interestingly, the position of the canon in *Tripartita* B suggests that the latter was using a *Decretum* similar to manuscript **B**, the only extant manuscript where this canon is found after Ivo 9.16 (in **PV**, it is found after Ivo 16.11). Ivo 16.57, 74, 76–79, 127–129, 142, 144, 145a, 159–162, parts of 163–166, 228, 248, 324–325, 329, all found in *Tripartita* B29, were among the canons dropped by the archetype of *Decretum* manuscripts **PV**, mostly because they overlapped with other canons in books 8 or 16. For details, see Rolker, *Canon Law* 260–261.

161. See Rolker, *Canon Law* 145–147.

same draft) quote a canon found in *Tripartita* B but not the *Decretum*.[162] Perhaps Ivo knew these texts because he was involved in the making of *Tripartita* B, but it could equally be the case that the *Tripartita* B compiler had access not only to the *Decretum* but also other materials Ivo was working with. Given that the link is based on a sole canon, one should not speculate too much on it.

5.5 Ivo and his *Decretum*: Pastoral Canon Law at Chartres

5.5.1 Ivo and the Ivonian Collections

Ivo of Chartres (d. 1115) was born to a family of relatively low rank in or around Chartres.[163] He entered religious life, apparently early, and in 1067 became abbot of the newly founded community of Saint-Quentin near Beauvais. For more than two decades, he very successfully acted as abbot of this house, which was widely seen as a model of reform. His position at Saint-Quentin brought Ivo in contact with the royal court, bishops, secular lords, and reform communities across France. It was also a place of scholarly debate and teaching; Ivo taught *sacra scriptura* here, composed a tract on the Eucharist, and in nearby Beauvais met scholars like Roscelin. In 1090, Ivo became bishop of Chartres with the help of King Philip and Pope Urban. Having received royal investiture and papal consecration, he almost immediately was drawn into conflicts between secular and ecclesiastical factions, and quickly had to choose sides—but also to seek compromise in many conflicts. Despite considerable resistance from his own chapter (filled with canons from some of the most powerful French baronial families), his predecessor as bishop, and even the metropolitan bishop, Ivo established himself as bishop of this important see, an office he held until his death on 23 December 1115.

Ivo's canon law activities, above all the completion of his *Decretum* in the mid-1090s, have to be seen against this sometimes tumultuous background. No doubt, Ivo was familiar with various aspects of canon law well before 1090. The biographer of John of Thérouanne, one of Ivo's pupils, reports that Ivo was held in high esteem both by John and indeed 'universally' on account of his teaching in Saint-Quentin.[164] Urban II in

---

162. See Rolker, *Canon Law* 147–148 on *Tripartita* B29.284 as found in Ivo's *Epp.* 255 and 'Add. III'.

163. Rolf Sprandel, *Ivo von Chartres und seine Stellung in der Kirchengeschichte* (Pariser historische Studien 1; Stuttgart 1962) ch. 1.

164. *Vita Iohannis* (ed. Holder-Egger, MGH SS 15.2:1140 lines 18–20): '[…] alter vero, qui et maior ab universis habitus est, domnus Ivo, qui […] quantae religionis quantaque scientiae temporibus suis culmen tenuerit'.

1090 praised Ivo's learning including his acquaintance with the canons.[165] Very soon after his, Ivo displayed his familiarity with procedural norms when facing accusations from his metropolitan and a local synod; his first extant letter to Richer of Sens already quotes a wide range of canon law.[166] Other conflicts—over King Philip's marriage affair, the rights of papal legates, and so on—followed quickly and must have been a matter of discussion and rumour in many cathedral chapters, monasteries, and secular courts in northern France and well beyond. From the late 1090s for the latest, Ivo's ability to quote from and comment on the vast canonical tradition of the Western Church was widely known, and his correspondence shows how he was asked to produce legal opinions, act as arbitrator, or otherwise intervene in conflicts ranging from the marriages (and 'unmarriages') of local nobility to the relations between pope and king. Even more importantly perhaps, Ivo acquired the reputation of being able to extract from this tradition guidelines of how to apply canon law sometimes strictly, but sometimes with moderation, 'according to the needs of the time'. In an age ripe with controversies and deeply divided factions, the ability to balance seemingly contradictory norms, to moderate rules without giving up their authority, and generally the ability to find compromise, was in high demand.

This also helps to understand why Ivo's œuvre seemed to grow considerably after his death in 1115, as more and more works were attributed to him—including various theological *sententiae*, a chronicle, and other works. As far as canon law collections are concerned, this was mainly due to his *Prologue* being attached to many (anonymous) collections; given that the *Prologue* mentions Ivo by name and refers to a subsequent collection, it is easy to see how this created the illusion that Ivo compiled all the collections found with the preface he had written for his *Decretum*. The most famous *Decretum*-derivative, which—mainly for this reason—was attributed to Ivo, was the *Panormia*. In addition, the *Tripartita* was attributed to Ivo partly (in the Middle Ages) because of the *Prologue* found with some copies of it, but mainly (in modern times) because it is intimately related to Ivo's *Decretum*. Following scholarly convention, I will refer to all three collections, and also the first Arsenal collection (on which see below) as 'Ivonian collections' in this chapter, without denying their different nature and relation to Ivo.

---

165. Urban II, JL 5438 (PL 162.13): 'Scimus autem quod ab infantia sacris es litteris eruditus et canonum institutis edoctus.'

166. Ivo, *Ep.* 8; see Rolker, *Canon Law* 14–15 (background) and 73–74, 131–132, 157–158 (canon law).

5.5.2 The *Decretum* (Overview)

Ivo's *Decretum* is one of the largest canonical collections of the Middle Ages, containing 3,760 canons in seventeen books, covering more than 300 folios in most extant copies.[167] It comes with a preface (the celebrated *Prologue*) which also contains a very summary overview over the collection. The *Decretum* covers almost all aspects of church life a prelate may become involved in. Compared to its main model—the collection of Burchard of Worms—Ivo's *Decretum* contains much more, and more refined, sacramental theology, quotes important Roman law texts not found in earlier collections, and generally introduces many new materials into canon law tradition.

The *Decretum* emerged over a long period of time. Most of the work was done at Chartres in the early 1090s, but there is good evidence that Ivo turned to smaller works he prepared when still at Saint-Quentin (though not necessary with the *Decretum* in mind) and that the process of improving the *Decretum* went on for a long time and at more than one place. Around 1095, Ivo seems to have had a version of the *Decretum* similar to that extant today at his disposal. The formal sources of the *Decretum* (to be discussed in detail below) include Burchard of Worms, *Arsenal I*, *Tripartita A*, the *Britannica*, *TC*, Ivo's own Eucharist florilegium, and a large number of diverse sources (canon law, patristic writings, historiography, penitential books, capitularies, a letter of Fulbert of Chartres on the oath of fealty,[168] and so on).

As one can see from his correspondence, Ivo himself used his *Decretum* in various contexts, ranging from runaway monks to royal marriages.[169] Yet not only these letters, but also the *Decretum* itself must have been circulating outside Chartres very quickly. Contrary to what the relatively small number of complete copies may suggest, the success of the *Decretum* was wide and rapid. Only five complete (or almost complete) manuscripts of Ivo's *Decretum* have survived; but in addition, there are two large

---

167. The on-going edition by Brett and his collaborators is found at https://ivo-of-chartres.github.io/; see in particular Brett's 'Prefatory Note'. All quotations from this site have been checked again in late February 2020; the revision stamp of all files used for the present study is '2015-0923 / 898fb'.—For literature, see Kéry 250–253; Fowler-Magerl, *Clavis* 192–198; Rolker, *Canon Law* esp. 107–121.

168. Fulbert of Chartres, *Ep.* 51 (ed. Behrends 90–92) as found in Ivo 12.76; first spotted by Fournier, 'Collections attribuées à Yves' BEC 58.60 n. 7.

169. *Yves de Chartres, Correspondance: tome I (1090–1098)*, ed. and tr. by Jean Leclercq (Les classiques de l'histoire de France au Moyen Âge 22; Paris 1949) [all published]; for letters not edited by Leclercq, I refer to Migne (PL 162) for the sake of convenience. All quotations have been checked against manuscripts and the new edition by Geneviève Giordadegno at http://telma-chartres.irht.cnrs.fr/.

fragments (one containing most of the first six books, one most of the last nine), and the 1561 *editio princeps* was based on two manuscripts, both now lost. To these manuscripts one should add several short versions—most famously the *Tripartita* B and the *Panormia* (to be discussed below), but also the 'Harley abbreviation' extant in four manuscripts (plus a fifth containing an even shorter version), the 'Lincoln abbreviation', and two large collections of excerpts in Vallicelliana, B.7 and Paris, BnF, lat. 14809, respectively. Many of the 'short' versions are massive collections which still cover some 100 folios and must have provided many readers with the material law they needed. The sheer number of such abbreviations suggests that Ivo's *Decretum* was not only copied, but also used relatively widely. Smaller fragments have been found in collections in Columbia, Koblenz, Oxford, Straubing, Soest, and most recently Prague.[170] To judge from the provenance of the manuscripts, the *Decretum* was successful in northern France and England but also known well beyond this area from early on. Most copies and versions were produced in the twelfth century, but the Siguenza manuscript clearly belongs to the thirteenth century; in any case Ivo's *Decretum* remained of considerable interest well after Gratian was available.

5.5.3 The Formal Sources

Ivo's Eucharist Florilegium

Ivo's *Decretum* is a massive collection that emerged over an extended period of time—five or six years at the very least, but probably much longer. In the course of this work, many preparatory collections and draft versions must have been produced, and some will be discussed in the following. Let us begin with a small collection which Ivo compiled when still at Saint-Quentin, and later integrated into his *Decretum*, where it formed the opening part of the second book on the Eucharist. This makes it the oldest datable contribution Ivo made to the *Decretum*, and indeed the earliest known work of Ivo to survive.[171] In the modern division of the canons, the collection makes up only ten canons, but many canons combine several excerpts, and together they fill almost half of the second book of Ivo's *Decretum*. Indeed, these canons are a substantial, carefully composed florilegium of key texts on the Eucharist. We know that Ivo composed this florilegium before he became bishop of Chartres because he quoted from it in a letter written during his time at Saint-Quentin. A comparison of the

170. My thanks are to Prof Marek Jindřich (private communication, 5 February 2016) who first made me aware of the fragment Praha, Národní muzeum, 1 D a 2/16 (a single folio, saec. XIII).
171. For the following, see Rolker, 'Earliest Work'.

letter (ep. 287 in the modern editions) and *Decretum* 2.1–10 allows us to reconstruct this florilegium. Unsurprisingly perhaps, Ivo took the writings of Lanfranc of Bec and Berengar of Tours as his starting point, and culled many patristic quotations from them. Interestingly, he can be shown to have compared these quotations against the original sources; in the end, Ivo selected longer excerpts than Lanfranc had quoted for his own florilegium. When Ivo compiled his Eucharist florilegium, he probably did so in preparation of the extant letter, and perhaps was already involved in the debates on Berengar's teaching that continued well into Ivo's time at Saint-Quentin (1067–90). There is no evidence that Ivo already planned a major canonical collection, but he already was building a reputation as a teacher of *sacra scriptura*.

Burchard

Ivo's Eucharist florilegium may be the oldest work of Ivo that became part of the *Decretum*, and with hindsight one can call this work a preparatory collection for the *Decretum*. Yet it was only when Ivo began to engage with the collection of Burchard of Worms that a first version of what later became the *Decretum* began to take shape. It is not certain whether this had happened already at Saint-Quentin, where Ivo had the time to prepare the huge task of compiling a major collection, or only at Chartres, where he may have found more resources. In any case, his promotion to the new office (and the challenges to his election) must have been an important stimulus for Ivo to make himself familiar with canon law on episcopal elections, accusations against bishops, and the conduct of synods—topics for which Burchard's *Liber decretorum* was an excellent starting point. Reading through the twenty books of the *Liber decretorum*, contemplating what may be missing from this collection, noting where better versions of certain materials were available, rethinking the arrangement of materials, and occasionally perhaps marking canons which could be dropped in an improved version were important steps in the making of Ivo's *Decretum*. This process of reading and comparing Burchard may have started with one or two other canonical collections but in the end involved working through a considerable number of diverse books, including not only canonical collections but also patristic works (above all from Saint Augustine), a number of chronicles, and many other books. In many cases Ivo and his collaborators found two or more versions of the same canons, and saw many different ways to arrange materials; but it was Burchard that remained the most important source and at the same time the most important model of how to arrange materials. In the end, Ivo preserved almost all of Burchard's material, but added about the same amount of material from other sources, above all *Tripartita* A and the *Britannica*. Most of Ivo's seventeen books correspond to one or two books of Burchard, and in most cases the Burchardian material is found in long series largely in the original sequence;[172] canons Ivo took from other formal sources are normally added before and after (and sometimes between) such series.

Take, for example, Burchard's first book.[173] It contains 234 canons on ecclesiastical hierarchy which Burchard had carefully selected and arranged, often taking the opportunity to strengthen episcopal rights (see the discussion in Chapter 2 on 'The Ecclesiastical Hierarchy in the *Anselmo dedicata*, Burchard, and *12P*'). Burchard's first book served as the model of Ivo's book five, as content, structure, and even the book title makes evident. The vast majority of Burchard's 234 canons reappear here, most of them in long series lifted without change from Burchard; in addition, one canon is found in another book of Ivo's *Decretum*, and two more canons are quoted in Ivo's *Prologue*. All but thirteen canons (more than ninety-four percent) of Burchard's first book figure somewhere in Ivo's *Decretum* in at least some manuscripts. As a closer analysis further shows, the omission of single canons mainly was due to rather 'technical' reasons, namely the attempt to avoid overlap within Ivo's *Decretum*.

Let us look at the thirteen canons from Burchard's first book Ivo did *not* retain, namely Burchard 1.1, 63, 132, 143, 152, 155, 176, 192, and 227. The opening canon of Burchard's collection may not be found in Ivo's *Decretum*, but only because Ivo took a longer version of the same canon from a different source, namely *Tripartita*.[174] So while technically Ivo 'dropped' Burchard's first canon, he in fact affirmed Burchard's choice of placing an excerpt from the second letter of Pseudo-Anaclete (JK †3) at the beginning of his book on ecclesiastical hierarchy. In similar fashion, the omission of Burchard 1.63, 132, 143, 152, 176, and 192 can be explained by Ivo preferring *Tripartita* A as his source; here, many of Burchard's canons were found in fuller, sometimes better versions and with more precise references to their (putative) sources. Some of these parallels are rather hidden; for example, Burchard 1.63, if retained, would have overlapped with the middle part of Ivo 5.54 (from *Tripartita* A1.9.3–6)—a canon which begins differently,

---

172. The first book of Burchard's *Liber decretorum* is almost completely incorporated in Ivo's book 5, Burchard 2 in Ivo 6, Burchard 3 in Ivo 3, Burchard 4 in Ivo 1, Burchard 5 in Ivo 2, Burchard 6 in Ivo 10, Burchard 7 and 17 both in Ivo 9, Burchard 8 in Ivo 7, Burchard 9 in Ivo 8, Burchard 10 in Ivo 11, most of Burchard 11 in Ivo 14, Burchard 12 in Ivo 12, Burchard 13 in Ivo 4, Burchard 14 in Ivo 15, Burchard 15 in Ivo 16, Burchard 18 and 19 in Ivo 15, Burchard 20 in Ivo 17.

173. The following is based upon (and improved from) Rolker, *Canon Law* 110 and 194–195.

174. Ivo, *Decretum* 5.1 = *Tripartita* A1.1.14–15, not Burchard 1.1. The *fons materialis* is JK †3.

ends differently, and ended up in a different book of the *Decretum*. So eleven of thirteen Burchardian canons 'missing' from Ivo's fifth book were dropped because of a painstaking comparison of different collections and the strong desire to avoid overlap within the Ivonian *Decretum*. For one of the two remaining canons from the *Liber decretorum* (Burchard 1.155) the reason for their omission is obscure. In theory, Ivo's Burchard copy could have been defective, but the Chartres copy of Burchard, in fact, seems to have contained the canon.[175] Ivo certainly did not exclude the canon from his collection because he disapproved of its content; indeed, he quoted this very canon as part of his argument in one of his letters.[176] Maybe Burchard 1.155 was dropped by accident. In any case, this only leaves one canon from Burchard's first book (Burchard 1.227) where one could even suspect that Ivo omitted a text because he disagreed with Burchard's choice of material.[177]

The *structure* of Ivo's book five is also close to Burchard's book in the sense that Burchard's material was simply left in the sequence of the model. Ivo's book five has a 'sandwich structure'—it contains a large block of material taken almost without change from one of Burchard's books, with material from other sources mainly added before and after this block of Burchardian canons. There are relatively long series of non-Burchardian materials at the beginning (Ivo 5.1–56 and 77–134) and the end (Ivo 5.345–378) of the book, but in the middle there is a very large block (Ivo 5.135–344) which is almost completely taken from Burchard and already contains most of his first book.[178] In this respect, book five is typical of Ivo's *Decretum*; in fact, most books are even closer to Burchard in the sense that the corresponding books of Burchard's collection are retained with even longer series left in Burchard's sequence and with even fewer canons dropped or replaced from other sources.[179]

If one looks, then, for the changes Ivo made to his great model, it is

175. Chartres, BM, 161, image nos. 9–10: Several of the rubrics to Burchard 1.148 to 157 are still legible. Unfortunately, Burchard 1.155 seems to have been written on the lost upper-right part of the verso, above of what is left of the inscription, rubric, and incipit of Burchard 1.156 ('Ex epistola <Damasi papae ad Stephanum et ad concilia Affrice>. De v<ocatione accusati episcopi>. V<ocatio enim>'). The last word of the preceding canon seems to have begun with 'diffin', which would fit Burchard 1.155 (ending 'definirent').

176. Ivo, *Ep.* 236 (PL 161.238) quotes Ps.-Clement, JK †10 (ed. Hinschius 39) as found in Burchard 1.155, *Tripartita* A1.1.7, and many other canonical collections. See Rolker, *Canon Law* 194.

177. To judge from Chartres, BM, 161, image no. 24, Ivo's Burchard almost certainly contained Burchard 1.227. The canon allowed clergy to dispose relatively freely over certain goods they acquired from secular lords (rather than having to pass it to their own church). The material source is Hohenaltheim 916 c. 37 (ed. Fuhrmann, MGH Conc. 6.1:38–39).

178. More specifically, Ivo 5.57–77, 135–234, 250–280, and 289–344 are all taken from Burchard's first book.

179. See Rolker, *Canon Law* 173–176.

neither the suppression of Burchard's material nor the rearrangement of materials within individual books. Rather, the main change is found in the material Ivo added from other sources, the different arrangement of the books, and partly also in the structure of individual books. To take Burchard's first book as our example again, Ivo obviously deviated from his model by *not* placing his own book on the ecclesiastical hierarchy at the beginning, as so many other compilers had done. Instead, Ivo placed four books on the sacraments, on church property, and feasts and fasting first; significantly, these books belong to the books Ivo took special pains in composing. The second important change, equally obviously, was that Ivo drew on other sources (namely *Tripartita* A and *Britannica*) both to find longer and better versions of Burchard's canons, and to add new material not found there. In the case of his book on the ecclesiastical hierarchy, Ivo retained 221 of Burchard's 234 canons, but added another 157 (often longer) excerpts from non-Burchardian sources. Finding and excerpting these materials from chronologically arranged collections, like *Tripartita* A, or small, farraginous collections like *TC*, evidently took more time and effort than using collections that presented the canons according to subject matter. For this reason, it can also be assumed that Ivo thought these materials particularly important, and at least in some cases their insertion may reflect his own preferences. This idea is supported by the fact that the material found at the beginning of individual books of Ivo's *Decretum* is quoted more frequently in Ivo's letters than other parts of the collection.[180] Some of the canons Ivo placed very prominently at the beginning of individual books are so frequently quoted in his letters and are so central to some of his arguments that one can label them his favourite canon law quotations. For example, at the very end of the first section of Ivo's book five (the non-Burchardian material in Ivo 5.1–56), there is a canon attributed to Nicholas I which severely limits the rights of primates; according to Pseudo-Nicholas, primates could only claim such rights as were found in positive canon law. In practice this meant that the 'primacy' itself conferred few if any prerogatives, as Ivo on his letters against the primacy claims of Lyon in particular made abundantly clear.[181]

Ivo's rather conservative treatment of his main source also helps to reconstruct the version of Burchard he was working with. To begin with, Ivo worked with a complete Burchard copy with canons in the so-called Frankfurt order, the most common arrangement found in the extant man-

180. Rolker, *Canon Law* 146–148, 205, and 255.
181. Ivo quoted from a manipulated version of JE 2765 (ed. Perels, MGH Epp. 6.633–636) as found in his *Decretum* 5.56 in *Epp.* 60, 65, 83, and 236; see Rolker, *Canon Law* 195, 204, and the concordance table in the Appendix.

uscripts. A number of interpolated, displaced, or added canons (Burchard 1.21, 2.23, 3.15A, 3.178–179, and *Ordo 5*) in Ivo's *Decretum* all suggest that his copy of Burchard ultimately depended on an Italian model, and more specifically the so-called Milan branch of the transmission. At the same time, Ivo's *Decretum* contains none of the gaps which are typical for most Italian copies of Burchard (the so-called '*deteriores* group'). So, either Ivo was working both with an Italian Burchard and a more complete ('German') exemplar from which he managed to mend all the gaps, or he relied on a copy of Burchard where this had already been done. As many copies of the *deteriores* group show signs of having been corrected against more complete exemplars, the latter possibility is more likely. Also, Ivo's *Decretum* contains canons of Seligenstadt 1023 in a form that Jasper calls the French branch of the second recension.[182] Apart from the fragmentary Chartres manuscripts, none of the known French Burchard copies can be linked to Ivo.[183] The Burchard manuscript from which Ivo took these canons seems to have contained the Seligenstadt canons after book 19 (not 20); whether his exemplar also contained the peculiar version of Burchard 11.9 which Jasper lists as another defining feature is impossible to verify as Ivo did not retain this canon in his *Decretum*.

The Chartrain Burchard Manuscript (Chartres, BM, 161)

The obvious candidate for Ivo's working copy of Burchard is codex 161 of the Bibliothèque municipale of Chartres (= 'Chartres 161' in the following), the only manuscript of Burchard's *Liber decretorum* known to have been at Chartres in the Middle Ages. It belonged to the cathedral chapter and may even have been written in Ivo's time. Unfortunately, the library burnt down in 1944, and like so many Chartrain manuscripts, codex 161 only survives in fragments, with most of the codex completely lost and other parts damaged by fire (and water). For a long time, all that was known about the codex was found in the brief description of the nineteenth-century catalogues and scattered comments in the literature.[184] Thanks to the careful restoration and subsequent digitization of the fragments by the IRHT, it is now possible to study the surviving parts of the codex.[185] For a sizeable part of Chartres 161 (some thirty-five folios),

---

182. Jasper (MGH Conc. 8.29).

183. See Rolker, *Canon Law* 112 n. 143 esp. on Reims, BM, 673 and 674.

184. *Catalogue des manuscrits de la bibliothèque de la ville de Chartres* (Chartres 1840), at 139–140 (as no. 154); *Catalogue général* 11 (1890) 89. See now Michela Galli and Christof Rolker, 'Destroyed but not Lost: A Digital Reconstruction of the Chartrain Copy of Burchard's *Liber decretorum* (Chartres BM 161)' BMCL 39 (2021) 19–58.

185. In the following, individual fragments of Chartres, BM, 161 will be quoted by the number of the images as found online at https://bvmm.irht.cnrs.fr/.

the contents can be reconstructed with some certainty; these folios contain the second half of Burchard's book one, books two and three, and most of book four. In many cases, the rubrics are legible, and sometimes even parts of the canons themselves. The order of canons is largely the so-called 'Konstanzer Ordnung' of 'Order of Worms, type B' as found in almost all extant copies.[186] In particular, the sequence of canons at the end of books two and three corresponds to that found in the Frankfurt and Freiburg manuscripts, not the sequence of Pal. lat. 585/586.[187]

Pokorny assumed that Chartres 161 belonged to the 'German branch of the Order of Worms, type B' tradition,[188] but there is good evidence that it in fact belongs to the larger 'Italian' branch. While Chartres 161, as far as we can tell, did not have the gaps characteristic of the Italian *deteriores* manuscripts,[189] other elements in Chartres 161 clearly point to an Italian model. In particular, Chartres 161 contains an *Ordo synodalis* (almost certainly Schneider's *Ordo 5*) at the end of book three;[190] Burchard 2.23 was apparently found between canons 18 and 19;[191] at the beginning of book three, two canons are switched, and an excerpt from a letter of Gregory (JE 1317) is added;[192] finally, the interpolated versions of Burchard 3.179–180 are probably Italian, too.[193] All these features are absent from the early manuscripts produced at Worms and most German copies of Burchard; instead, they go back to the reworking of Burchard in Italian scriptoria between between the middle of the eleventh century and the 1080s. Some or all of these features are found in extant Burchard manuscripts written in medieval Italy (and Spain), and often also in French manuscripts. While

186. Out of almost one hundred extant manuscripts, only Pal. lat. 585/586 and two Würzburg manuscripts (plus the *editio princeps*) preserve 'Type A'. On 'Type A' and 'B', and the various sub-groups of type 'B', see Pokorny's list of manuscripts in Kéry 132–148.

187. Chartres, BM, 161, image nos. 51–55: Burchard 2.226, 234, 227–233, 236, 239; c. 235 is found after Burchard 2.197, while cc. 238 and 237 are found after Burchard 2.201. Chartres, BM, 161, image no. 87–93: Burchard 3.217–222, 227–228, 225–226, 230–238, 240, 239, 223–224, 241. Almost exactly the same sequence of canon is behind Ivo 6.269–271 (= Burchard 2.197, 201, 198), 6.301–310 (= Burchard 2.226, 234, 228–233, 236, 239), and 4.267–284 (= Burchard 3.227–228, 225–226, 230–238, 240, 239, 223–224, 241).

188. Pokorny in Kéry 136.

189. On the *deteriores*, see most recently Fransen, 'Décret de Burchard' 9–11. Chartres, BM, 161, image nos. 215–216 have Burchard 12.1–13, including the canons absent from the *deteriores* manuscripts, with no visible signs of corrections. See Ivo 12.58–70 (= Burchard 12.1–13),

190. Chartres, BM, 161, image nos. 93–95. On *Ordo 5* and its transmission with Burchard and Ivo, see *Konzilsordines*, ed. Schneider 230–241.

191. Chartres, BM, 161, image nos. 28–29. See Ivo 6.37–39 (= Burchard 2.18, 23, and 19).

192. Chartres, BM, 161, image no. 58 has Burchard 3.6–8, 10, 9, 11–15, 15A, and 16–18. Burchard 3.10 is found between canons 8 and 9 as in some, but not all Italian manuscripts (see e.g. Vat lat. 1355, fol. 79v). On canon '15A' (from JE 1317), see Fransen, 'Décret de Burchard' 39. See Ivo 3.8–21 (= Burchard 3.6–8, 10, 9, 11–15, 15A, and 16–18).

193. Kölzer, 'Prolegomena' 60–62. See Ivo 3.240–241 (= Burchard 3.179–180).

the handwriting of Chartes 161 seems to point to a French scriptorium, the Burchard version it contains ultimately must go back to an Italian exemplar.

Crucially, all 'Italian' features just mentioned also are found in Ivo's collection; Chartres 161 fits exactly the Burchard version that had been reconstructed from Ivo's *Decretum*.[194] This alone would be enough to suspect that Chartres 161 must be very closely related to, perhaps even a direct copy of, Ivo's 'Italian' Burchard. This assumption is further supported by the fact that Ivo shares very many variant readings with Chartres 161, although it is not clear how many of them were perhaps common among Italian Burchard manuscripts. Another important argument to assume that Ivo's working copy of Burchard was very similar to Chartres 161 is the presence of rare additional materials which are otherwise only known from Ivo's *Decretum*.[195] As far as the text of Chartres 161 is legible, it often agrees with Ivo's *Decretum*. For example, on Fragment 18 most of the rubrics and some of the other text of Burchard 1.189–191 are still legible. For the rubric and the inscription to Burchard 1.189, Chartres 161 seems to be closer to Ivo's exemplar than other Burchard manuscripts are.[196] Burchard 1.190 both in Chartres 161 and Ivo 5.306 begins 'et' instead of 'ut'.[197] The inscription to Burchard 1.191 in Chartres 161 and Ivo refers to 'Antherus' while the consensus of early Burchard manuscripts has 'Etherius'.[198] All these variants are minute, and may well be found in many Burchard manuscripts; nonetheless, it is noteworthy that Chartres 161 in all four cases is closer to Ivo's *Decretum* than to early Burchard manuscripts.

This is not to say that Ivo's copy of Burchard looked exactly like Chartres 161; indeed, one can find a large number of minor differences. Namely, Ivo's inscriptions are sometimes more reliable than those found in Chartres 161. For example, Chartres 161 confuses the register of Greg-

---

194. Rolker, *Canon Law* 110–112.

195. Chartres, BM, 161, image no. 42 after Burchard 2.118 contained additional material including two canons which seem to be the source for Ivo's addition in the respective part of his *Decretum* (Ivo 6.194A–194B, found only in Brett's manuscripts **P** and **V**).

196. The rubric to Burchard 1.189 in Chartres, BM, 161 ends 'loco altero subiugato', and the inscription to refers to 'cap. <cc>xxxviiii'; Ivo 5.305 has 'loco altero subrogato' and 'cap. 239'. Pal. lat. 585/586 (according to *Clavis*): 'loco alteri surrogato'; *editio princeps*, fol. 26rb 'loco altero subrogato'; Bamberg, fol. 44rb: 'loco altari subrogato'; Frankfurt, fol. 38rb: 'loco altero subrogato'; Freiburg, fol. 41ra: 'loco alteri subrogata' but corrected by a later hand to 'loco altero subrogato'. All these Burchard manuscripts refer to 'cap. 238'.

197. Pal. lat. 585/586 (according to *Clavis*), the *editio princeps*, fol. 26vb, Bamberg, fol. 44vb, Freiburg, fol. 41va, and Frankfurt, fol. 38vb all have 'ut'.

198. Chartres, BM, 161, image no. 18: 'Ex registro ad Antherum epiiscopum cap. CCXXX-<III>'. Ivo 5.307 'Ex registro Gregorii ad Anterum episcopum' (but no chapter number). Pal. lat. 585/586 (according to *Clavis*), the *editio princeps*, fol. 26vb, Bamberg, fol. 44vb, Frankfurt, fol. 38vb, and Freiburg, fol. 41va all have 'Ex registro ad Etherium episcopum cap. 233'.

ory I with his *Regula pastoralis*, renders a council of Orléans as 'Pope Au-relianus', and in another misguided inscription refers to a council that allegedly took place in Babylon; Ivo does not repeat these errors.[199] Some-times, however, Ivo seems to have faithfully copied erroneous inscriptions which go back to the tendency in Chartres 161 to confuse papal and concil-iar material.[200] This may suggest that Ivo's copy already contained some errors preserved in Chartres 161; it may also be that Ivo in some cases was able to correct them. In the cases just quoted, common sense and some familiarity with canon law would probably have been sufficient to guess the correct inscriptions, but other cases demand a different explanation. In particular, Chartres 161 relatively frequently lacks the chapter numbers when quoting from papal letters or conciliar acts.[201] If these gaps were already found in Ivo's exemplar, he found a way to supplement the in-formation from other sources—either a better copy of Burchard or other canonical collections containing the same canons. All in all, it seems that many of the erroneous inscriptions of Chartres 161 were already present in Ivo's Burchard copy, but that he was able to mend most of these errors when copying these canons into his own *Decretum*.

Finally, Ivo's Burchard canons contain errors that are also found in Chartres 161. Burchard 2.38 contains a long list of works not to be done on Sundays; in both the Chartres manuscript and Ivo's *Decretum*, the can-on lacks the prohibition to build houses and to work in the garden.[202] Burchard 2.59 is attributed to canon six of a Council of Rouen in Chartres 161 and *Decretum* 6.155, while the German Burchard manuscripts agree that it was the first canon of this council.[203]

---

199. In Chartres, BM, 161, image no. 52, the inscription to Burchard 2.201 (from JE 1845) has 'Ex regula' instead of 'Ex registro Gregorii'. The inscription to Burchard 3.6 in Chartres, BM, 161, image no. 58 is 'Ex concilio Aureliani papae' instead of 'Ex concilio Aurelianensi'. The inscrip-tion to Burchard 3.146 in Chartres, BM, 161, image no. 78 has 'Ex concilio Babillonensi' instead of 'Cabilonensi'. See Ivo 6.274, 3.8, and 3.211, respectively, for the inscriptions as also found in most Burchard manuscripts. The material source of Burchard 3.6 is obscure, see Hoffmann and Pokorny, *Dekret* 190; Burchard 3.146 is ultimately from Toledo III, but in the form of Benedic-tus Levita 3.468; see Emil Seckel, 'Studien zu Benedictus Levita VIII (Studie VIII, Schlußteil V), ergänzt und aus dem Nachlass herausgegeben von Josef Juncker' ZRG Kan. Abt. 24 (1935) 1–112.

200. The inscription to Burchard 3.43 (from JK †139) in Chartres, BM, 161, image no. 62 has 'Ex concilio Dionisii cap. iv' instead of 'Ex decretis Dionisii'; the same error is also found in Ivo 3.47.

201. E.g. in Chartres, BM, 161, image no. 72, the inscription to Burchard 3.100 lacks the chapter number; Ivo 3.135 has 'cap. xliii' as in Burchard. Pal. lat. 585, fol. 192ra; *editio princeps*, fol. 66rb; Frankfurt, fol. 89ra; Freiburg, fol. 92ra all have '42'. Likewise, the inscriptions to Burchard 3.186–187 in Chartres, BM, 161 lack chapter numbers but Ivo 3.246–247 has them (i.e. the numbers found in most Burchard manuscripts).

202. Pal. lat. 585, fol. 131ra; *editio princeps*, fol. 42va; Bamberg, fol. 64va; Frankfurt, fol. 58va; Freiburg, fol. 62va all have 'nec domos struere nec in horto laborare'. Chartres, BM, 161, image no. 38 and Ivo 4.65 lack this phrase.

203. Pal. lat. 585, fol. 125vb; *editio princeps*, fol. 40ra; Bamberg, fol. 62ra; Freiburg, fol. 60ra all

Chartres 161 was probably only written in the twelfth century and cannot itself be the copy of Burchard Ivo used for the *Decretum*, yet evidently it resembled that exemplar in a number of significant respects. In all likelihood, Chartres 161 was copied directly from Ivo's Burchard, which may well have been quite worn once Ivo completed his own collection; the scribes responsible for making this copy produced a beautiful new copy, although the rubricator evidently was not among Ivo's brightest students.

The First Arsenal Collection

If Burchard was the single most important formal source Ivo employed for his *Decretum*, the first of the two so-called Arsenal collections (= *Arsenal I*) is the best witness of the working materials Ivo and his team must have produced in the course of compiling the *Decretum*.[204] The Arsenal collections take their name from the only extant manuscript (Paris, Bibliothèque de l'Arsenal, 713) which consists of two originally separate codices. The first, or 'Arsenal 713A', is a twelfth-century copy of the *Panormia* covering the first 116 folios; the second, or '713B' (covering fols. 117r–192v), was long seen as a canonical collection somehow related to, and presumed to depend on Ivo's *Decretum*. Yet as Brett discovered, the long series of canons in Arsenal 713B which correspond very neatly to parts of Ivo's *Decretum* cannot conceivably have been excerpted from it. The main argument is that the parallels extend only to Ivo's non-Burchardian material—that is, canons taken mainly from the *Britannica* and *Tripartita A*.[205] At the same time, Arsenal 713B contains texts and variants which strongly suggest that it is related to an archaic version of Ivo's *Decretum* still containing some canons dropped very early in its history. Both Brett and Somerville found that the Arsenal manuscript sometimes has better inscriptions than any extant *Decretum* copy.[206]

As Brett was able to establish, Arsenal 713B contains a preparatory col-

---

have 'Ex concilio Rotomagensi, cap. i'. The inscription in Frankfurt, fol. 56ra is almost illegible in the digital version I have used. The attribution to Rouen goes back to Burchard; the material source is the *Admonitio generalis* c. 80 (ed. Mordek et. al., MGH Fontes iuris 16.234). Burchard took the canon from Regino 2.205 and may have been inspired by Regino 2.202 for his inscription.

204. The following is mainly based on Brett, 'Sources', the notes Dr Brett kindly made available to me, and my own research. See also Greta Austin, 'Were There Two Arsenal Collections? Arsenal 713B and the Ivonian *Panormia*', *Canon Law, Religion and Politics: Liber amicorum Robert Somerville*, ed. Uta-Renate Blumenthal et al. (Washington, D.C. 2012) 3–14; Blumenthal, 'Caesaraugustana'; Martin Brett, 'Creeping up on the *Panormia*', *Grundlagen des Rechts. Festschrift für Peter Landau zum 65. Geburtstag*, ed. Richard H. Helmholz et al. (Rechts- und Staatswissenschaftliche Veröffentlichungen der Görres-Gesellschaft N.F. 91; Paderborn, Munich, Vienna, and Zurich 2000) 205–270; Somerville, 'Papal Excerpts'; idem, *Urban II* 16–18.

205. Brett, 'Sources' 154.

206. For example, in the case of JL 5277, attributed to Gregory VII in Ivo's *Decretum* but to Urban II in *Arsenal I*, it seems that *Arsenal I* is correct. See Somerville, 'Papal Excerpts' 177–180.

lection containing almost all non-Burchardian material that was to be included in Ivo's *Decretum*. Such a collection can only have conceived with a mature vision of the future *Decretum* in mind, and all major collections used to produce the *Decretum* at hand.[207] Recent scholarship has refined this model and established that this preparatory collection (now dubbed *Arsenal I*) was later combined with other material not used by Ivo, including a collection which seems to have been used to produce the *Panormia* (= *Arsenal II*).[208] At some point in the twelfth century, substantial parts of both Arsenal collections (seemingly in the form of unbound material) were combined, mixed up, and copied together in a single hand to produce the extant Arsenal manuscript, the only textual witness to both collections.

While *Arsenal I* material is found throughout the codex, *Arsenal II* material only occurs between fols. 129 and 152.[209] Generally, though not invariably, canons from the two Arsenal collections are still found on separate pages and folios in the extant manuscript.[210] Some, but not all breaks between the two collections are marked by blank folios and/or the beginning of a new quire, adding to the impression that *Arsenal I* and *Arsenal II* both existed in the form of sheets and quires before they were copied into what today is Arsenal 713B.[211] It is almost certain that Arsenal 713 only preserves parts of *Arsenal I* and *Arsenal II*, while at the same time it contains (especially from quire six on) materials which were not used for the making of either Ivo's *Decretum* or the *Panormia*. In any case, already the series that have a parallel to Ivo's *Decretum* fill dozens of folios in the extant manuscript and cannot possibly have been extracted from Ivo's collection.

The first Arsenal collection was thus produced specifically to prepare Ivo's *Decretum*, and therefore should be counted among the 'Ivonian collections'. The last stage before Ivo's *Decretum* began to exist as a collection in its own right probably was a copy of Burchard, *Arsenal I*, and a number of smaller preparatory works. These materials would have contained notes and signs on which canons were to be copied into which book of

207. Brett, 'Sources' 155: 'it must preserve almost the last stage before a complete *Decretum* was copied out'.

208. This account is based on Brett, 'Sources' 157–160, Rolker, *Canon Law* 124–125, and Austin, 'Arsenal'. See also below on *Arsenal II* and the *Panormia*.

209. Paris, Bibliothèque de l'Arsenal, 713, fols. 117r–122r, 125r–128r, 129r–130r, 135v–137r, 139r–144v, 146r–149r, 152v–153, 154r–157v, 158v–171v, 172v–173v, and 175r–192v contain *Arsenal I* material; *Arsenal II* material is found on fols. 129r, 131r–135v, 136v–138v, 139v–140r, and 149r–152r.

210. For *Arsenal I/II* being mixed up, see Paris, Bibliothèque de l'Arsenal, 713, fols. 136v–137r containing, in this sequence, three canons also found in Ivo 4.81–83, two *Panormia* canons (*Panormia* 2.134–135), a canon found in neither collection, and four more *Decretum* canons (Ivo 4.84–87).

211. Brett, 'Sources' 154.

the new collection; the moment they all were copied into a single collection was the birth of Ivo's *Decretum*.

Ivo, Burchard, and *Arsenal I*: The Sandwich Structure of Ivo's *Decretum*

To understand which role *Arsenal I* played in the making of Ivo's great collection, the 'sandwich' structure of many books of the *Decretum* provides important evidence. While individual books of Burchard's *Liber decretorum* frequently form the kernel of individual books of the *Decretum*, the Arsenal material typically is found before and after this kernel. This suggests that normally Ivo started with Burchard, in a second step collected new material from other collections (above all, *Britannica* and *Tripartita* A), which was arranged in long series and placed before and after the Burchard material; the resulting 'sandwich' books—sometimes added to with material which for one reason or the other was not included in *Arsenal I*—already resembled the extant form of the mature *Decretum* books very closely.

Ten of Ivo's seventeen books are such 'sandwich' books (namely books 1, 7, 9–15, and 17). Let us consider Ivo's first book on the sacraments of faith as an example. First, immediately behind the preface, there are two canons by Saint Augustine, the first discussing the Old and New Convenant, the other providing a definition of the Trinity (Ivo 1.1–2). In almost all manuscripts, next comes a long 'title' to the first book, followed by the Creed of Union (Ivo 1.3). The following canons are lifted from Fulgentius of Ruspe's *De fide*, attributed to Saint Augustine in the Middle Ages (Ivo 1.4–44). These forty-one canons, containing some of the most important articles of faith, have parallels in Ivo's letters, his celebrated *Prologue*, and his sermons.[212] Perhaps Ivo even had gathered them into a separate dossier of theological material beforehand which he wanted to place prominently at the very beginning of his collection, but if so, this dossier has not survived.

The rest of Ivo's first book is more 'legal' in nature, and draws on formal sources also employed for almost all other *Decretum* books. It contains Burchard's book four on baptism and related questions almost unchanged (Ivo 1.197–295); before and after this series one finds sections of non-Burchardian material. More precisely, the sections immediately before and after the Burchard block (Ivo 1.49–192 and 296–304) are taken from *Arsenal I* (Arsenal 713, fols. 117r–125v) The very last canons are taken from the *Britannica*, apparently directly (Ivo 1.308–311). Thus, although book one is

212. See Rolker, *Canon Law* 180–181 for references.

a massive work of 311 (sometimes lenghthy) canons and more than tri-
ples its Burchardian model in size, its structure is remarkably simple. The
book consists of long series of canons taken from distinct formal sources:
theological material, *Arsenal I*, Burchard, *Arsenal I* again, and finally a few
Britannica canons. The first step in the making of this book probably was
Ivo's decision to open the *Decretum* with dogmatic issues rather than the
ecclesiastical hierarchy (as other compilers had done), and in this context
Ivo probably decided to insert a creed and (Pseudo-) Augustine material
at the very beginning of his canonical collection. The second step was to
take Burchard's book four and to augment it at the beginning and the end
from *Arsenal I*, leading to the 'sandwich structure' typical of many books
in Ivo's *Decretum*. While the Burchardian material was largely copied *en
bloc* and thus did not require much labour, the main question here for Ivo
was what was lacking in Burchard's treatment of baptism; selecting and
rearranging materials to produce the respective sections of *Arsenal I* must
have been the most time-consuming part of the making of book one of
Ivo's *Decretum*. The main work, therefore, was the compilation of the *Arsenal I* collection, and annotating a copy of Pseudo-Augustine's *De fide ad
Petrum*. Only very few canons do not belong to the theological opening
section or the large 'sandwich' of Burchardian and *Arsenal I* material (i.e.
Ivo 1.45–48, 193–196, and 305–311). They come from different sources and
may have been additions made at a relatively late stage. Four of them are
from one section of the *Britannica* (Ivo 1.308–311), another one will be discussed below because of its apperance in Chartres, BM, 193 (Ivo 1.305); this
leaves only nine of 311 canons which do not come from a relatively small
set of known formal sources.

As in other books, Ivo in the first book of his *Decretum* took considerable pains to eliminate doublets. As mentioned above, Ivo and his collaborators would frequently have encountered the same canon two or
more times in the various collections they were working with. There is
good evidence that doublets that had entered the *Decretum* (often because
a Burchard canon had a parallel in at least one collection used to produce
Arsenal I) were eliminated over an extended period of time after the *Decretum* was finished. An example from book one is Ivo 1.149A (from *Arsenal I*),
dealing with priests whose Latin was so bad that they had used a bogus
formula in baptism ('Baptizo te in nomine patria et filia et spiritu scientia').[213] The canon was dropped in most *Decretum* manuscripts, as a longer

---

213. On the reception of JE 2276, see Bruce Clark Brasington, '"In nomine patria": Transmission and Reception of an Early-Medieval Papal Letter Concerning Baptism' *Codices manuscripti*
37 (2001) 1–5.

excerpt from the same letter (JE 2276) was found in Ivo 1.237, this time from Burchard. There is also evidence that already *Arsenal I* was compiled in a way that reduced overlap in the *Decretum*. After all, it was a collection meant to supplement Burchard, so the compiler had reason to avoid canons that were already found in Burchard. For example, almost all canons found in the *Tripartita*'s Leo I section are taken into the appropriate book of Ivo's *Decretum*, normally via *Arsenal I*. Among these canons is an excerpt from JK 414 on the legitimate dates for baptism (*Tripartita* A1.43.4), an important proof text for the ancient practice to baptise only on Easter and Pentecost. Nonetheless, it is one of the few Leo canons in *Tripartita* that was *not* taken into the *Decretum*. The reason for this omission apparently is that Ivo already knew a longer excerpt from the same letter from Burchard (Burchard 4.2 = Ivo 1.197); at some stage before the extant *Decretum* manuscripts were written, the doublet was dropped. Sometimes, however, it may not have been thought even desirable to avoid all overlap. For example, Ivo 1.252 (from Burchard 4.57) is an excerpt from a letter of Gelasius I (JK 636) stating that deacons should not confer baptism on their own. A longer excerpt from the same letter is found in Ivo 6.99 (from *Tripartita* A1.46.13). The overlap between these two canons of different length, even if noticed, may not have been seen as a problem; in book one it was important in the context of baptism, while in book six essentially the same canon is found among canons on the rights and duties of the lower clergy.

To return to Ivo's first book, Ivo here in only one case dropped a Burchard canon to avoid overlap; Burchard 4.23 would have duplicated Ivo 1.128 (from *Arsenal I*). This leaves only one canon from Burchard's book on baptism which Ivo did not retain—Burchard 4.1, the opening canon of the whole book. This short canon was a basic definition of baptism which Ivo may well have found unnecessary given the rather more refined theological texts he placed at the beginning of his own book.

Finally, canons were sometimes dropped by accident, and Ivo's first book is no exception. Ivo 1.122A, today preserved in *Arsenal I* and *Panormia* 1.13 but absent from all extant *Decretum* manuscripts, nonetheless must have been part of Ivo's *Decretum*.[214] While the body of the canon was dropped, the inscription was retained, resulting in the following canon being misattributed in all *Decretum* manuscripts. The *Panormia* here seems to depend on a branch of the transmission which still had the canon as it is found in *Arsenal I*; both collections contain Ivo 1.122A among the relevant

214. Brett, 'Sources' 152.

Decretum canons, strongly suggesting that this short canon too was part of an archaic version of the *Decretum*.

The *Responsa* Manuscript from Beauvais (Vat. lat. 3827)

One of the many documents Ivo helped to become more widely known was the famous *Responsa ad consulta Bulgarorum* (JE 2812; Böhmer-Herbers 822) by Pope Nicholas I, written in 866.[215] This lengthy letter-tract, traditionally divided into 106 chapters, documents the pope's replies to various questions by the Bulgarians, who at the time were about to convert to Christianity. Fragments of this letter are found in very many canonical collections from the ninth century on, but Ivo's *Decretum* introduced a significant number of passages not found in earlier collections. It therefore seems likely that Ivo had access to a fuller version of the *Responsa*, and perhaps even a complete copy of Nicholas's letter. It is even possible that the copy Ivo had at his disposal was Vat. lat. 3827, the only extant medieval manuscript of the *Responsa*. The manuscript is from Saint Peter in Beauvais, not far from where Ivo started to work on the *Decretum*. The manuscript contains no less than twenty-four Nicholas excerpts found in Ivo's *Decretum* but no earlier canon law collection.[216] In addition, excerpts from the *Responsa* were copied into a manuscript from Chartres together with other material closely linked to Ivo's *Decretum* and its sources, as will be discussed in the next paragraphs.

The Collection of Chartres, BM, 193

Chartres, BM, 193 (= 'Chartres 193' in the following) was a codex of 187 folios containing a very miscellaneous canonical collection. The manuscript was written in the eleventh century and in the Middle Ages belonged to Saint-Père-en-Vallée in Chartres. It was destroyed in 1944; for a long time, Schulte's 1868 article and the *Catalogue général* were almost the only sources to reconstruct the content of the lost manuscript.[217] Recently, however, the IRHT has digitized images of sixty-four fragments, many of them containing at least a few lines of more or less legible text.[218] Today, the fragments are preserved in Chartres, BM, liasse 352.

In the context of Ivo's *Decretum*, Chartres 193 is mainly interesting as a

215. Nicholas I, *Ep. 99* (ed. Perels, MGH Epp. 6.568–600). On the manuscript, see Jasper, 'Beginning' 114–115 (with further references).

216. Perels, 'Briefe' 108–109.

217. Johann Friedrich Schulte, 'Iter Gallicum' *Sb. Akad. Wien* 59.4 (1868) 355–496, here at 460–466 and *Catalogue général* 11 (1890) 99–100. For a bibliography, see https://www.manuscrits-de-chartres.fr/.

218. The digital images of the fragments are available online at https://bvmm.irht.cnrs.fr/. To reference individual fragments, I use the IRHT numbering.

possible formal source of the *Decretum*, and in particular as a link between the collection in Paris, BnF, lat. 13368 (= 'TC') and Ivo.[219] While the exact relation between the three works (*TC*, Chartres 193, and Ivo's *Decretum*) remains only imperfectly understood, it is clear that the Saint-Père manuscript contained rare *TC* material also used for the *Decretum*.

One of the most conspicuous parallels is found in a short series of Roman law texts taken partly from the *Pauli Sententiae* traditionally attributed to the famous Roman jurist Julius Paulus Prudentissimus, partly from the fifth-century comment (*interpretatio*) to them. As the *Sententiae* with the comment are transmitted in the *Lex Romanorum Visigothorum*, these texts were widely spread in high medieval Europe. Yet the selection of the excerpts common to *TC* and Ivo's *Decretum* is not known from any other collection.[220] Some time ago, I argued that based on older descriptions of the manuscript one could assume the presence of the same series of excerpts in Chartres 193, fol. 5r–v.[221] Thanks to the digitalization by the IRHT this hypothesis can now be tested. As it turned out, Fragment 38 (in the numbering of the IRHT) indeed contains *Decretum* 16.194–198 on what apparently was the lower half of folio 5r; the lost upper half of folio 5v can be assumed to have contained *Decretum* 16.199–205. As these texts are not found elsewhere in this combination, they constitute a strong link between *TC*, Chartres 193, and Ivo's *Decretum*. While it is impossible to establish the direction of textual dependence with any certainty for these Roman law texts, it may be significant that *TC* tends to have fuller and more correct inscriptions than Ivo's *Decretum*.[222]

Another striking parallel between the three collections is a canon on spiritual kinship (taken from JE †2003) which appears to be attributed to both a 'Pope Desiderius' and Pope Deusdedit. It may ultimately go back to Burchard's *Liber decretorum*, where it is attributed to Deusdedit; *TC*, Chartres 193, and Ivo have a shorter form which is attributed to 'Desiderius' but still contains 'Deusdedit' in the address (see Table 6).

219. Rolker, 'Genesis'; idem, *Canon Law* 115–121. While the 'TC' collection circulated relatively widely in various versions, the Roman law texts discussed in the following are only found in the *TC* version in Paris, BnF, lat. 13368.

220. *TC* cc. 2–8 = *Decretum* 16.194–205. See *Lex romana Visigothorum ad LXXVI librorum manu scriptorum fidem recognovit septem eius antiquis epitomis, quae praeter duas adhuc ineditae sunt, titulorum explanatione auxit, annotatione, appendicibus, prolegomenis*, ed. Gustav Friedrich Hänel (Leipzig 1849) 338–444.

221. Rolker, 'Genesis' 95 and idem, *Canon Law* 116–117, relying on *Catalogue général* 11 (1890) 99. On both occasions, I failed to mention the *interpretatio*.

222. The heading at the very beginning is fuller in *TC* (Paris, BnF, lat. 13368, fol. 9va): 'De lege Theodosiana sancti Pauli'; Chartres, BM, 193 omits the erroneous 'sancti' (*recte* 'sententiae'?), *Decretum* 16.194 also omits 'Pauli'. The last set of excerpts (= *PS* 1.7.10, *PS* 1.8.1–2, and the *interpretatio* ad *PS* 1.9.3) has the inscription 'Sententia Pauli de dolo, malo et vi' in *TC* (Paris, BnF, lat. 13368, fol. 9vb) while *Decretum* 16.205 has 'De lege Theodosiana'.

Table 6: JE †2003 in Burchard, TC, Chartres 193, and Ivo

Burchard 17.44 (*editio princeps*, fol. 178r)	*TC*, cc. 37–38 (Paris, BnF, lat. 13368, fol. 10r–v)	Chartres 193 (according to Schulte)	*Decretum* 1.305 (ed. Brett)
Ex decretis Deusdedit pape Gorgonio episcopo missis.	Ex decretis Desiderii pape.	Ex decretis Desiderii pape.	Ex decretis Desiderii pape.
Si mulier debeat separari a viro suo, que filium suum casu per negligentiam a fonte susceperit.*	Si mulier <s>eparari debeat a viro que filium suum negligenter de fonte suscepit [*sic*].		
Deusdedit sancte Romane et apostolice ecclesie episcopus Gordiano Hispanensis ecclesie coepiscopo et fratri dilectissimo.	Deusdedit sancte Romane ecclesie et apostolice sedis episcopus Gordiano Hispalensis <ecclesie coepiscopo et fratri dilectissimo.	Deusdedit <sancte Romane ecclesie et apostolice episcopus Gordiano Hispalensis ecclesie coepiscopo et fratri dilectissimo.	Deusdedit sancte Romane ecclesie et apostolice episcopus Gordiano Hispalensis ecclesie coepiscopo et fratri dilectissimo.
Pervenit ad nos diaconus [...] penitentiam egerit digne. Mulieres vero quum [...] et vir uxorem.	Pervenit ad nos diaconus>** [...] penitentiam egerit digne.	Pervenit ad nos diaconus [...] penitentiam egerit digne.>***	Pervenit ad nos diaconus [...] penitentiam egerit digne.
* Rubric	** Loss of two lines because of trimming.	*** Reconstructed from Schulte's description; see note 224.	

While the main text is relatively familiar,[223] the canon as found in *TC*, Chartres 193, and Ivo's *Decretum* presents several problems. First, there is no 'Pope Desiderius'. It is possible that readers around 1100 understood this as a reference to Abbot Desiderius of Montecassino, who in 1087 also was Pope Victor III. Yet the reference to 'Pope Desiderius' predates Victor's pontificate and almost certainly was due to an error, resulting perhaps from misreading 'Deusdedit' or misinterpreting an abbreviation (like 'Dd'). While the textual history of this canon remains obscure, it may well be that *TC* represents an intermediate version between some standard form of the canon, on the one hand, and the version found in

223. On JE †2003, see Jasper, 'Beginning' 94.

Chartres and Ivo on the other hand. Compared to Burchard (and many other collections), the canon as found in *TC*, Chartres 193, and Ivo's *Decretum* is significantly shorter;[224] all other collections where the canon ends with 'penitentiam egerit digne' ultimately depend on Ivo's *Decretum*. In addition, *TC* and the Ivonian collections refer to the addressee as bishop of Sevilla ('Hispalensis') instead of a Spanish bishop ('Hispanensis'). More importantly, the use of *TC* would also explain the strange double inscription of the canon in Ivo's *Decretum* (and Chartres 193), as the short passage 'Si mulier...' is easily overlooked. In Burchard, this passage clearly served as a rubric, and maybe this was the case in *TC* as well; but as the extant Paris manuscript shows, sometimes rubrics were written in the main hand, making it even easier to overlook it. Finally, as it is unlikely that the scribe of Chartres 193 and Ivo made the same mistake independently, and as Chartres 193 almost certainly predates the compilation of Ivo's *Decretum*, two possibilities remain: either Chartres 193 and Ivo depend on the same *TC* version (already lacking the passage 'Si mulier...'), or Chartres 193 is the formal source of the *Decretum* for this *TC* canon. Compared to the extant version of *TC*, the Ivonian collections have a defective address line (lacking 'sedis' in the papal title) and—by uniting what *TC* seems to treat as two texts—present a canon where the inscription contradicts the body of the canon. In any case it seems very unlikely that *TC* depends on Ivo's *Decretum*.[225]

5.5.4 Textual Manipulations by Ivo?

Ivo of Chartres introduced a great number of texts into canon law that are not found in earlier collections, and (as in the case of Burchard) some of these texts are forged, manipulated, or partisan in character; yet this has not normally provoked any suspicion that it was Ivo who was responsible for tampering with the original texts.[226] Indeed, scholarship traditionally has given Ivo the benefit of doubt in many cases where Burchard in

224. Schulte, 'Iter Gallicum' 462 only transcribed 'Ex decretis Desiderii pape. Deusdedit' and pointed to *Panormia* 6.127, which has the same version of the canon as Ivo's *Decretum*; from his account one can therefore safely deduce that Chartres 193 contained the same text as *Decretum* 1.305. The same version is also found in *Tripartita* B1.18. In contrast, Paris, Bibliothèque de l'Arsenal, 713, fol. 157v contains a different version of the canon and lacks any reference to 'Desiderius'. The Chartrain Burchard seems to have contained the standard (long) form of the canon, see Chartres, BM, 161, image no. 235 'Deusdedit sancte <ro>manae et apostolicae ecclesiae episcopus Gordi<a-no> Hispanensis ecclesiae coepiscopo et fratri <dilectis>simo: Pervenit ad nos [...].' The rubric is fairly legible, but the inscription is lost.

225. *Pace* Fowler-Magerl, 'Fine Distinctions' 181 n. 166.

226. See *Histoire* 2.80–81, followed by many scholars. For older literature, more sceptical of Ivo's fidelity to his sources, see Heinrich Geffcken, *Zur Geschichte der Ehescheidung vor Gratian* (Leipzig 1894) 81–82 and Fahrner, *Geschichte* 115.

particular would have been suspected of forgery. For example, the version of JE 2765 in *Tripartita* A and Ivo's *Decretum* is not found in earlier collections. The letter clearly is manipulated, and the way Ivo quotes from it in his letters shows he regarded it as a useful authority in his conflicts with Hugh of Lyon in particular.[227] However, despite the partisan character of the canon and the traditional view that Ivo compiled the *Tripartita*, this never seems to have led to charges of forgery against Ivo in a similar way that Burchard was suspected of having forged more or less all canons in his *Liber decretorum* of which the textual transmission was obscure.[228]

Given that Ivo introduced so many materials into 'mainstream' canon law, the question whether he interfered with his texts has far-reaching implications. On the whole, the ongoing studies of Ivo's formal sources confirm that Ivo preserved the text he found in the collections he was working with great fidelity, and the same applies to the patristic excerpts he was the first to insert in his *Decretum*. Yet at least in the law of marriage, there is evidence that Ivo was willing to select, abbbreviate, and even alter ancient laws to adopt them to what he saw as the law of the Church. The evidence for this is limited—a few lines of text, all in all—but a relatively strong case can be made that Ivo directly was responsible for these changes.

First, a passage lifted from the Justinian Code in Ivo's *Decretum* has a 'non' which was not there in Ivo's formal sources. Originally, the law confirmed the validity of marriages between first cousins; in Ivo's *Decretum* it has become another proof text against 'incest' as defined in medieval canon law.[229] Perhaps the inserted 'non' reflects the sheer disbelief of an eleventh-century scribe reading about cousin marriage being legal under Justinian, but in any case the omission can be traced to Ivo's immediate environment. As the 'non' is found in *Arsenal I* but no extant *Decretum* manuscript, it seems to have been dropped between the time *Arsenal I* was combined for the first time with the Burchardian *Decretum* material, and the making of the manuscript from which the different branches of the transmission depend. The second case concerns the delicate issue of remarriage. There was a long canon law tradition against remarriage, but there were important exceptions and borderline cases. Medieval secular legislation allowed men to remarry under certain circumstances, for ex-

---

227. On JE 2765 in Ivo's letters and in the Ivonian collections, see Rolker, *Canon Law* 195, 202, and 204 (where the manipulated version occasionally is misquoted as 'JE †2765').

228. See the end of Chapter Two 'A Forgery to End All Forgeries' (esp. note 288).

229. Cod. 1.10.2.4 was faithfully preserved in the *Britannica* (London, BL, Add. MS 8873, fol. 57v) and *Arsenal I* (Paris, Bibliothèque de l'Arsenal, 713, fol. 158r): 'Duorum autem fratrum sororumve liberi, vel fratris et sororis iungi possunt.' Only Ivo 9.1 (ed. Brett) presents a version containing a 'non' inserted before 'iungi'.

ample after repudiating an unfaithful spouse. If a marriage was dissolved on grounds of consanguinity, remarriage was also often possible; classical canon law would not count this as 'remarriage' if the first union had been declared void. Famously, Gregory II had allowed remarriage after divorce on grounds of female impotence, and Ivo retained this canon in *Decretum* 8.78 (JE 2174). Yet otherwise, many high medieval prelates sought to minimize the opportunity for remarriage, and Ivo was certainly among them.

Against this background, it is interesting to see how Ivo treated canons he found in Burchard which allowed remarriage. The *Liber decretorum* has three conciliar canons allowing remarriage (Burchard 6.40–41 and 9.54), and three times mentions remarriage in the long questionnaire in his penitential book (Burchard 19.5). While the questionnaire is absent from Ivo's *Decretum*, he largely retained Burchard's books six and nine. Indeed, Ivo in his book ten incorporates Burchard's book six almost completely, leaving the canons in their original order (Burchard 6.1–49 = Ivo 10.130–176). The only exceptions are Burchard 6.44 (found in one manuscript only), and Burchard 6.40, which is dropped. This in itself would not necessarily be significant, but it should be seen in conjunction with the fate of the other two proof texts for remarriage: Burchard 6.41 is present in Ivo's *Decretum*, but crucially, the passage allowing remarriage to the husband is lacking.[230] Likewise, Burchard 9.54 is found in Ivo's *Decretum*, but without the passage on remarriage.[231] This all strongly suggests that Ivo was responsible for omitting one canon and manipulating the other ones.[232] The only other possibility seems to assume that Ivo relied on a defective Burchard copy, but there is no evidence supporting this idea. In fact, the Chartrain Burchard copy supports the idea that Ivo knew the relevant canons in their normal form.[233] So while Ivo is rightly seen as a compiler nor-

---

230. Burchard 6.41 (*editio princeps*, fols. 105vb–106ra): 'Si qua mulier mortem viri sui cum aliis conciliata est, et ipse vir aliquem illorum se defendendo occiderit, et si hoc probare potest ille vir eam ream esse consilii (ut nobis videtur) ipsam uxorem dimittere et, si voluerit, aliam uxorem accipere. Ipsa autem insidiatrix penitentie subiecta, absque spe coniugii maneat.' Ivo 10.169 (ed. Brett) lacks the sentence 'et si voluerit aliam uxorem accipere'. It may or may not be significant that in one manuscript the canon seems to have been added: Cambridge, CCC, 19, fol. 233va.

231. Burchard 9.54 (*editio princeps*, fol. 129rb): 'Si quis necessitate inevitabili cogente, in alium ducatum seu provinciam fugerit, et uxor eius cum valet et potest amore parentum aut rerum suarum eum sequi noluerit, ipsa omni tempore, quandiu vir eius quem secuta non fuit, vivit, semper innupta permaneat. Illo vero, qui necessitate cogente in alia patria manet, si numquam in suam patriam se reversurum sperat, si se continere non potest, aliam uxorem accipiat, tamen cum poenitentia.' Ivo 8.189 (ed. Brett) lacks the last sentence.

232. See already Geffcken, *Ehescheidung* 82 and Fahrner, *Geschichte* 115.

233. Chartres, BM, 161, image no. 125: '[…] si probare potest ille vir eam ream <esse> consilii, potest, ut nobis videtur, ipsam uxorem dimittere et si voluerit al<i>am uxorem ducere; ipsa autem insidiatrix penitentie subiecta, absque spe coniugii maneat.' Earlier on the same page, parts of Burchard 6.40 are still legible.

mally preserving his proof texts without any changes (and in many cases, this can be positively tested), it would be an exaggeration to say that he never interfered with the canons found in his *Decretum*.

5.5.5 New Materials in Ivo's *Decretum*

Ivo's *Decretum* is one of the largest canonical collections of the Middle Ages, drawing on very diverse sources; in the absence of a critical edition, a full study of the formal and material sources is beyond the scope of the present study. Two observations, necessarily in summary fashion, have to be made. First and foremost, Ivo's *Decretum* is unusually rich in patristic excerpts.[234] The *Decretum* contains hundreds of excerpts from the writings of Saint Augustine alone (456 according to Munier), many of which are found in a canon law collection for the first time. There are also 152 excerpts from letters of Gregory the Great, plus more than 100 excerpts from Gregory's other writings.[235] Many of these texts would become part and parcel of Western canon law; 'Gratian the theologian' preserved many of Ivo's texts which he knew via *Tripartita* B and the *Panormia*.[236] Of course, Abelard and many other theologians likewise often worked with patristic texts ultimately going back to Ivo's *Decretum*.[237] In short, Ivo's choice of patristic texts—rather than his own opinions[238]—influenced theological and canon law discussions on the Eucharist, marriage, and many other subjects for a very long time.

While this point certainly demands further study, it is at least generally agreed in scholarship. This holds less true for the second point which needs to be addressed here. Book four of Ivo's *Decretum* according to its title deals with feasts and fasting, canonical writings, ecclesiastical customs,

234. de Ghellinck, *Mouvement* 445–455; Munier, *Sources patristiques* 28–54; Rolker, *Canon Law* 108–209

235. Own calculations, based on the inscriptions but not systematically checked against critical editions; they include a number of misattributions and forgeries, but I have ignored 'Gregorius dicit' canons taken from Burchard.

236. Giorgio G. Picasso, 'Fonti patristiche tra teologia e diritto canonico nella prima metà del secolo XII', *L'Europa dei secoli XI e XII fra novità e tradizione: sviluppi di una cultura: atti Mendola 1986* (Miscellanea 12; Milan 1989) 21–35; Peter Landau, 'Wandel und Kontinuität im kanonischen Recht bei Gratian', *Sozialer Wandel im Mittelalter. Wahrnehmungsformen, Erklärungsmuster, Regelungsmechanismen*, ed. Jürgen Miethke and Klaus Schreiner (Sigmaringen 1994) 215–233, esp. 221; Wei, *Gratian* 203 and 233–234. For Gratian's penitential theology specifically, the patristic contents of *3L* may have been even more important (ibid. 98–99).

237. Häring, 'Berengar's Definitions'; Blanche Beatrice Boyer and Richard Peter McKeon, 'The Textual Relation of Ivo and Abailard', *Peter Abailard, Sic et non: A Critical Edition*, ed. iidem (Chicago and London 1977) 617–634; Izbicki, *Eucharist* 21–24.

238. Ivo's own views seem not to have been remembered very well beyond what was found in his letters; the *sententiae* attributed to him in the sentence collections of the twelfth century (above all, the *Liber pancrisis*) only rarely are genuine, and more often than not run couner to what he had written in his letters. On this point, see Giraud and Mews, 'Liber Pancrisis' 153–159.

and the celebration of a synod. While this is all true, it does not reveal the nature of this unusual book, the largest part of which (Ivo 4.61–245) is a huge collection of miscellaneous materials that are best described as dealing with the sources of the law.[239] Filling dozens of folio (and making up seventy-two percent of the canons contained in book four), these 185 texts seem so far have largely escaped scholarly attention.

The nature of these texts is very diverse, even by the standards of pre-Gratian canon law collections, but they are at least roughtly structured according to subject matter. First, one finds canons on the biblical canon, including of course the *Decretum Gelasianum* (Ivo 4.61–65), followed by four canons on customary law (Ivo 4.66–69). Next come canons containing lists of legal sources, like Pseudo-Innocent's *De causis* (on which see the discussion on 'The Sources of the Law' in Chapter 1), or a list of sources of the law which according to Leo IV should be used in ecclesiastical courts (JE 2599),[240] interspersed with excerpts taken from Saint Augustine on the status of exegetical writing in comparison to canonical books (Ivo 4.70–74). The next series deals with the delicate issue of conflicts between synodal and papal authority (Ivo 4.75–83). What if popes did not approve of the canons of general councils? What if councils issued heretic statements? One possibility was that single canons were rejected by the pope, as in the case of Chalcedon c. 28, the first canon in this series suggests.[241] The next two canons quote a much more radical response, namely Pope John VIII abrogating the 869/870 synods of Rome and Constantinople (the synods 'against Photios') and having them 'deleted from the list of holy synods'.[242] This canon need not express Ivo's approval of John's decision, although it may be worth noting that his *Prologue* casts Photios in a positive light.[243] While Ivo seems to take a different position on the Photian affair compared to the *Tripartita* A compiler, it is important to remember that considerable confusion surrounded these synods both

239. See the short remark in Fournier, 'Collections attribuées à Yves' BEC 58.58.

240. Ivo 4.72 (ed. Brett). On JE 2599, effectively describing the contents of the *Dionysio-Hadriana*, see Herbers, *Leo IV.* 67–78 (text and transmission), Jasper, 'Beginning' 108–109 (reception), and Genka, 'Hierarchie' 109–110 (importance for Gratian in *De legibus*). This part of JE 2599 is found in no earlier collection. It appears, independently of Ivo, in *Polycarpus* 3.20.5 (ed. Erdmann and Horst 218).

241. Ivo 4.75. The material source is Gelasius I (?), JK 701 (CPL 1672), alluding to JK 490.

242. Ivo 4.76–77, taken from John VIII, JE 3273 and 3276 (Böhmer-Unger 553 and 555). For both canons, Ivo's text is that found in the Greek acts of Constantinople 879/880; see John VIII, *Ep.* 209 (ed. Caspar, MGH Epp. 7.186 lines 3–8) and 211a (ibid. 189 lines 26–29), respectively. Ivo's immediate source is unknown.

243. In his *Prologue*, Ivo quoted John VIII, JE 3271 as found in the acts of Constantinople 879/880, not the version found in the Montecassino register: John VIII, *Ep.* 207 (ed. Caspar, MGH Epp. 7.166–172). For a comparsion of both versions, see Hofmann, 'Ivo' 118–125.

in *Tripartita* A and in Ivo. It is characteristic for this confusion that in Ivo's version of *Sancta octo* the reference to 'Constantinople IV' (whether this meant the 869/870 or the 879/880 synod) was dropped, not necessarily out of opposition to the eighth synod, but more likely because of a scribal error.[244] These insecurities should also be kept in mind when looking at a second example of conflict between a general synod and the pope in Ivo's *Decretum*: Ivo quotes the account of the *Liber pontificalis* detailing Roman opposition to the Quinisextum (Ivo 4.79). Again, one should not deduce that Ivo himself was opposed to the Quinisextum; yet it is also true that despite his heavy use of *Tripartita* A, he did not take much material from this council into his *Decretum*.[245] The *Liber pontificalis* excerpt, while certainly casting Justinian II in a negative light, does not say how the conflict ended; the canon itself therefore raises the issue of papal and synodal authority, but does not solve it.

These canons, therefore, should not be reads as expressions of Ivo's personal views but rather as a collection of material on various sources of the law. Indeed, book four of Ivo's *Decretum* contains canons on virtually all legal sources—councils and decretals, but also patristic writings (Ivo 4.89–104), the *Canones Apostolorum* (Ivo 4.105–107), conciliar legislation (Ivo 4.108–139), secular law (Ivo 4.167–193), customary law (Ivo 4.194–213), and other normative material. Some of these materials describe the harmony of different sources of the law, while others highlight conflict; for example, Bede is quoted on a synod at Aquileia 'out of ignorance of the faith' not accepting the fifth synod (Ivo 4.119), and Nicaea II rejecting the 'the so-called seventh synod' of Hieria (Ivo 4.121).

Yet a large number of the texts in book four have no legal content at all, but simply relate where, when, and by which authority various canonical and legal texts were written down. For example, there is a short excerpt from John the Deacon on the register of Gregory the Great (Ivo 4.144), followed by a few lines from the *Liber pontificalis* that Hermes, inspired by an angel, wrote a book to show that Easter ought to be celebrated on Sunday (Ivo 4.145). Next come a few lines from Bede on how Theodore of Canterbury came up with his penitential book (Ivo 4.146). Later on,

---

244. Ivo 4.132 (ed. Brett): 'Sancta VIII universalia concilia, id est Nicenum, Constantinopolitanum, Ephesinum primum, Chalcedonense quintum et sextum. Item. Constantinopolitana et VII. Item Nicenum VIII quoque constanter, usque ad unum apicem immutilata servare [...] profiteor.' The reading 'constant(er)' in the *Arsenal I* collection may go back to 'Constantinopolitanum' being abbreviated in an unusual way, or the abbreviation being misunderstood. See also *Panormia* 2.103 (ed. Brett). Note that most printed editions of both Ivo and *Panormia* contain versions of *Sancta octo* adapted to Gratian but with no known basis in the manuscripts. My thanks are to Martin Brett, with whom I continue to discuss this issue; a separate study is in preparation.

245. Landau, 'Überlieferung' 220–221.

there are notes on the genesis of various lawbooks, including the Digest (Ivo 4.171) and Justinian's Novels (Ivo 4.172), the latter preserving a better reading of the text than any other manuscript (or the edition, for that matter).[246] After a note on capitularies taken from Benedictus Levita (Ivo 4.174), Ivo also quotes Bede's account how Æthelberht of Kent, 'imitating the Romans', had a law book in the vernacular language composed.[247] This passage in Bede is normally understood to refer to the lawbook of Æthelberht as extant in the *Textus Roffensis* attributed to Ernulf of Rochester.[248] It is very interesting to see that Ivo, who is known to have been in contact with Ernulf, already in the mid-1090s showed an interest in the texts that later were copied into the *Textus Roffensis*.

5.5.6 Contradicting Canons and the Unifying Principle of Charity

The *Decretum* is a monumental collection, and it would be impossible to provide a full analysis in the context of the present book. What should have become clear by the above comments is that Ivo in his *opus magnum* brought together a very rich variety of normative texts from very different sources. These materials in many cases represented not only diverse, but indeed contradicting canon law on the respective matter. While this may be true for many canonical collections, Ivo's certainly stands out in its size, the variety of its sources, and the apparent readiness to accept contradictions in canon law. As mentioned above, Ivo in book four gathered materials that addressed precisely this issue. Yet crucially, these materials are not part of any scheme to actually resolve contradictions in Ivo's own collection;[249] if anything, they add to the problem in the sense that many of them describe contradictions in canon law but do not contain any hint what to do about them.

The question of conflicting authorities is important precisely because Ivo provides his readers with many contradicting canons, and much food

---

246. Anastasius as quoted in Ivo 4.172 (ed. Brett) describes Justinian's Novels as follows: 'Removit Iustinianus Augustus contrarias leges, faciens singularem codicem, et vocans eum Novellas constitutiones'. In the edition, in contrast, one reads: 'Renovavit etiam contrarias leges [...]'. See Anastasius Bibliothecarius, 'Historia tripertita', *Theophanis Chronographia*, ed. Charles de Boos (2 vols. Leipzig 1883–1885) 2.31–346, here at 133. This was first pointed out by Conrat (Cohn), *Geschichte* 106.

247. Ivo 4.175 (ed. Brett): 'Inter cetera bona que genti sue consulendo conferebat rex Edilberht, etiam decreta illi iudiciorum, iuxta exempla Romanorum, cum consilio sapientum constituit, que conscripta Anglorum sermone hactenus habentur, et observantur ab ea.'

248. Patrick Wormald, 'Laga Eadwardi: The *Textus Roffensis* and Its Context' *Anglo-Norman Studies* 17 (1995) 244–266. For an edition, see 'Laws of Æthelberht', *The Beginnings of English Law*, ed. and tr. by Lisi Oliver (Toronto Medieval Texts and Translations; Toronto 2002) 52–116.

249. See Meyer, *Distinktionstechnik* 134 ('weitgehendes Desinteresse an dialektischen Lösungsansätzen').

for thoughts on the issue, but little if any clues how to 'solve' these contradictions—certainly not by establishing a 'hierarchy of sources'.[250] Indeed, if one takes into account Ivo's *Prologue* (and also his correspondence), it becomes clear that his point rather was that contradictions were not a problem to be 'solved' but belonged to the very nature of canon law.[251] The formula Ivo used most frequently in this context was that of God's 'mercy and justice'. Just as God was both 'just' and 'merciful', the law of the Church contained both severe and lenient regulations. Very specifically, different canons could suggest that a certain marriage was valid or not, or different penitential tariffs for one and the same sin. For Ivo, these 'contradictions' were an expression of God's will; according to his 'mercy and justice', God was willing to forgive the contrite sinner even the gravest sins, but would punish severely even secret sins. Likewise, the ecclesiastical judge and pastor in every individual case had to consider not only the nature of the sin, but also the circumstances of the case and the contrition of the sinner. Only in this way, the judge was able to find a judgement that was truly salutary for the penitent. Importantly, this did not only apply in cases where the law actually contained contradicting rules, but always. As Ivo put it in his *Prologue*:[252]

> Every ecclesiastical doctor should thus interpret or moderate ecclesiastical rules so that he may refer to the kingdom of love; nor does he err or sin here, because, concerned for the salvation of his neighbours, he endeavours to achieve the required goal in the holy institutions. Whence the blessed Augustine says when considering ecclesiastical discipline: 'Have charity and do whatever you will; if you correct, correct with charity, if you pardon, pardon with charity.'

From the perspective of later canon lawyers, such arguments, and the question of contrition may have been 'useless for the treating of cases' (as Rolan-

---

250. See Brett, 'Finding' 63 ('establishing a hierarchy of authorities rarely solved anything') and 69–70 (Ivo). As Genka argued in the case of Bernold of Konstanz, arguments on 'hierarchy of sources' were more about ecclesiology than jurisprudence: Tatsushi Genka, 'The Role of Hagiography in the Development of Canon Law in the Reform Era', *New Discourses in Medieval Canon Law Research: Challenging the Master Narrative*, ed. Christof Rolker (Medieval Law and Its Practice 28; Leiden and Boston 2019) 83–104.

251. For fuller discussion, see Brasington, *Ways of Mercy*, Rolker, *Canon Law* 165–179, idem, 'Kollisionen', and Brett, 'Finding' 70: 'The unifying principle is not in the texts themselves. In the widest sense it lies in God's purpose behind them; in the immediate context it is the application of discernment by God's ministers as confessors and shepherds of souls.'

252. Ivo, *Prologue* (ed. Brasington 116–117): 'Quicumque ergo ecclesiaticus doctor ecclesiasticas regulas ita interpretatur aut moderatur, ut ad regnum caritatis cuncta que docuerit uel exposuerit referat, nec peccat nec errat, cum saluti proximorum consulens ad finem sacris institutionibus debitum peruenire intendat. Vnde dicit beatus Augustinus de disciplina ecclesiastica tractans: Habe caritatem et fac quicquid uis, si corripis corripe cum caritate, si parcis parce cum caritate.' The translation is that of Somerville and Brasington, *Prefaces*, here at 134.

dus put it, commenting on Gratian's *De penitentia*).[253] Yet for Ivo, the concern was not only 'treating cases'; here as elsewhere, he was thinking about bishops (and other clergy) acting as teachers, preachers, judges, and confessors. More importantly, Ivo was certainly not the only one to hold such views; as already the success of his *Prologue*—which was soon attached to many collections and had a separate transmission as an independent tract[254]—suggests, this very part of his œuvre was highly valued throughout the twelfth century. Also, Ivo's exposition of 'pastoral canon law' in the *Prologue* was not only widely copied but also stimulated other prelates in their understanding of the law of Church, as the next chapter will show.

5.6 Alger of Liège on 'Mercy and Justice'

5.6.1 Biography and œuvre

Alger of Liège was born around *ca.* 1060 and spent most of his life in Liège where he became a canon, first at Saint-Bartholomew and later (around 1101) at the cathedral chapter. Having acted as schoolmaster already at Saint-Bartholomew, he became head of the prestigious cathedral school of Liège, and for some twenty years also was the secretary to bishops Olbert (1092–1119) and Frederick (1119–1121) until in 1121 he entered monastic life at Cluny.[255] Little is known about his time at Cluny (not even the date of his death), but his literary activity at Liège is well documented. According to his biographer, Alger wrote numerous letters 'on ecclesiastical affairs' and a tract defending the rights of the church of Liège. Only two of these letters have survived, both in the *Codex Udalrici*; they show that Alger was able to discuss complicated legal issues involving the ad-

---

253. *Die Summa magistri Rolandi nachmals Papstes Alexander III.* [*sic*], ed. Friedrich Thaner (Innsbruck 1874) 193 as quoted by Burden, *Crime and Sin* 1: 'Tertio quaeritur, utrum sola contritione cordis et secreta satisfactione absque oris confessione possit quis Deo satisfacere. Verum pro sui prolixitate eiusque quod ad causarum tractatum inutilitate eam ad praesens dimittimus atque sententiis inferendam et pertractandam reservamus.'

254. Brasington, *Ways of Mercy*; for a Gratian abbreviation containing Ivo's *Prologue*, see idem, 'The Abbreviatio "Exceptiones Evangelicarum": A Distinctive Regional Reception of Gratian's *Decretum*' *Codices Manuscripti* 17 (1994) 95–99.

255. Kéry 172–173. Note that Alger's *De misericordia* is not in in the 2005 version of the *Clavis* database. For recent studies, see Brett, 'Finding' esp. 64–68 (hermeneutics); Colish, *Faith* 141–145 (baptism); Wei, *Gratian*, 56 and 236–239 (Alger and Gratian); Kéry, 'Kanonessammlungen' 203–208 (overview); Ortwin Huysmans, 'The Investiture Controversy in the Diocese of Liège Reconsidered: An Inquiry into the Positions of the Abbeys of Saint-Hubert and Saint-Laurent and the Canonist Alger of Liège (1091–1106)', *Medieval Liège at the Crossroads of Europe: Monastic Society and Culture, 1000–1300*, ed. Steven Vanderputten et al. (Medieval Church Studies 37; Turnhout 2017) 183–217, here at 206–213. Much of the following is based on Robert Kretzschmar, *Alger von Lüttichs Traktat 'De misericordia et iustitia'. Ein kanonistischer Konkordanzversuch aus der Zeit des Investiturstreits: Untersuchungen und Edition* (Quellen und Forschungen zum Recht im Mittelalter 2; Sigmaringen 1985).

ministration of church property, excommunication, and procedural law.[256] The canon law quotations in both letters are clearly taken from Burchard. As for the tract on the privileges of his own church it is possible that it can be identified with an extant anonymous tract.[257] Finally, Alger composed two larger tracts, *De misericordia* (to be discussed below) and a *Liber de sacramentis*, a tract on the Eucharist. This tract, praised for example by Peter the Venerable, was widely read and copied; it is extant in twenty manuscripts plus another twelve copies of a short version.[258] As this short overview may suffice to show, Alger was an administrator, a teacher, and a scholar; his works emerged and were read in the milieu of the cathedral schools of northern Europe. Like Lanfranc of Bec, Bonizo of Sutri, and Ivo of Chartres, he dealt with 'canon law' in very different contexts—the administration of church property, ecclesiastical discipline, and the understanding of the sacraments.

5.6.2 'Mercy and Justice' in the Time of Schism

Around 1100, when Alger composed *De misericordia*, the diocese of Liège was shaken by conflicts involving the higher clergy and many lay magnates alike.[259] The main line of conflict was between bishop Otbert (1091–1119) and two monastic houses, Saint-Hubert and Saint-Laurent. Otbert's predecessor had deposed and excommunicated the abbots of both houses, but Otbert reversed this decision and deposed the new abbots. The latter prelates, who soon fled Liège, and their supporters in turn denounced the new bishop as a simonist on account of his closeness to Emperor Henry IV. Soon other parties—the cathedral chapter, monastic houses inside and outside the diocese, local nobility, the archbishop of Cologne—were drawn in the conflict; while Otbert was supported by the emperor, his opponents sought and received help from the papal curia. Shifting factions, temporary compromise, but also considerable violence marked the conflict which dragged on for more than two decades. Property was seized, prelates (including the bishop) and laypeople excommunicated, mutual accusations of simony, disobedience, and worse were raised frequently. Bishop Otbert was challenged in very his authority as bishop, while for the communities of Saint-Hubert and Saint-Laurent their 'monastic liberty' was at stake; and had the counts of Flanders inter-

---

256. *Epp.* 257 and 340 (ed. Nass, MGH Briefe dt. Kaiserzeit 10.2:427–431 and 578–583).

257. Kretzschmar, *Alger* 14 and 21–22.

258. Nikolaus M. Häring, 'A Study in the Sacramentology of Alger of Liège' MS 20 (1958) 41–78 (theology); Kretzschmar, *Alger* 15–20 (reception).

259. Kretzschmar, *Alger* 23–27; Becker, *Urban II.* 2.328–329; Somerville, *Piacenza* 14–16; Brett, 'Finding' 53–54; Huysmans, 'Controversy' 186–205.

vened with military force, as Pope Paschal II urged them to, a prolonged civil war would probably have followed.

When Alger wrote *De misericordia*—after 1095, and probably before 1106[260]—the conflict had reached its climax. As a prominent member of the powerful cathedral chapter and secretary to the bishop, Alger had first-hand knowledge of this affair, and there can be no doubt that he was thinking of this turmoil when he referred to 'various errors and schisms' in the Church in the opening lines of *De misericordia*.[261] His main theme is the distinction between 'mercy' and 'justice' (or 'rigour') in canon law; just as God was merciful and just at the same time, and both lenient and rigorous provisions were found in canon law, in practice sometimes sins had to be tolerated but sometimes the rigour of the law was to be applied. Such arguments, and the biblical language of 'mercy and justice' is well known from other sources, but most famously from the *Prologue* of Ivo of Chartres which indeed served Alger as his prime model.[262] Unlike Ivo, however, Alger not only addressed this issue in his preface, but used it to structure the whole work, therefore providing much more detailed examples of 'mercy and justice' in canon law.

While all three books of *De misericordia* deal with 'mercy and justice', the tone is clearly different in each of them. The first book focusses on 'mercy'; Alger argues extensively that there are many good reasons why 'unworthy' clergy (including perhaps married priests, as Kretzschmar suggested) should be tolerated and compromises be made.[263] He also argued at length that the sacraments conferred by 'unworthy', 'bad', and 'sinful' priests nonetheless were valid (Alger 1.47–73). Unlike Gregory VII and the Milan Patarenes, Alger held that one may well hear a 'good sermon from a bad priest' (Alger 1.50, rubric). Under certain circumstances, even baptism conferred by heretics was fully valid.[264] All in all, the first book provides many arguments why it was sometimes better to correct only discretely or even to tolerate sins in the Church.

In the second book, Alger mainly deals with procedural norms. Ac-

---

260. Gabriel Le Bras, 'Le *Liber de misericordia et justitia* d'Alger de Liège' NRHDFE 45 (1921) 80–118, here at 98, followed by Kretzschmar, *Alger* 29.

261. Alger, *Praefatio* (ed. Kretzschmar 187).

262. See, for example, Cresconius, *Preface* (ed. Zechiel-Eckes, *Concordia* 2.422) that the judge should carefully consider 'utrum ex seueritate an ex lenitate suum animum debeat moderari'. For examples from the eleventh century, see Cushing, *Papacy and Law* 24–25 (Peter Damian), Cowdrey, *Gregory VII* 417 (Gregory VII), Rolker, 'Pastoral Canon Law' (Ivo), and Robert Somerville, 'Mercy and Justice in the Early Months of Urban II's Pontificate', *Chiesa, diritto e ordinamento della «Societas Christiana» nei secoli XI e XII: atti Mendola 1983* (Miscellanea 11; Milan 1986) 138–154.

263. For this and the following, see Kretzschmar, *Alger* 39–42.

264. Alger 1.51–54 and 3.4 (ed. Kretzschmar 226–231 and 315–318); see Häring, 'Sacramentology' esp. 69–70, Kretzschmar, *Alger* 51–53, and Brett, 'Finding' 53–54 (drawing on Alger's *De sacramentis*).

cusations and even punishment, Alger explained, could well be an act of love, just as undue leniency was cruelty. In this sense, book two is about the distinction between 'apparent' and 'true' 'mercy and justice'. As for the material law, Alger's treatment of accusations of prelates deserves special attention. Canon law in Alger's time contained many provisions that made accusations against higher clergy complicated at least, and in many cases flatly forbade them. Bishops, 'the eyes of the Lord', could not be accused by their subjects and were judged by God alone according to Pseudo-Isidore.[265] Alger spent considerable effort to interpret these canons as restrictions rather than prohibitions.[266] Although he conceded certain exceptions—not all laypeople were allowed to accuse bishops under all circumstances—and insisted that procedures had to be followed, Alger's interpretation went far beyond traditional canon law and effectively allowed accusations against bishops in many cases.

Finally, in the third book the stress is definitely on 'rigour', not 'mercy', as Alger now deals with those 'outside the Church'. In this context, the distinction between mere sinners and heretics, already quoted in the *Praefatio*, is of paramount importance. Sinners sometimes had to be tolerated, if it were necessary or useful; heretics, however, could not hope for such mercy. To be more precise, is not heresy as such Alger is concerned with; he specifically deals with simony. As Alger argued at length, the buying of ecclesiastical offices is not only a crime but even an act of heresy.[267] He severely chastises Peter Damian in this respect, and unambiguously states that whoever tries to buy an ecclesiastical sinned against the Holy Spirit; the very belief that spiritual goods could be sold made him a heretic. Accordingly, Alger argued that simony should be punished severely, if need be by military force. Also, he firmly held that sacraments by simonists were invalid, directly arguing against Peter Damian who in colourful language had argued for their validity, just like 'children born out of the wedlock often are beautiful'.[268]

All three books of *De misericordia* are directly shaped by the bitter con-

---

265. For example, JK †43: 'Oves enim pastorem suum non reprehendent, plebs vero episcopum non accuset, nec vulgus eum arguet, quia non est discipulus super magistrum, neque servus super dominum. Episcopi autem a Deo sunt iudicandi, qui eos sibi oculos elegit [...].' See Wilfried Hartmann, 'Discipulus non est super magistrum (Matth. 10,24). Zur Rolle der Laien und der niederen Kleriker im Investiturstreit', *Papsttum, Kirche und Recht im Mittelalter. Festschrift für Horst Fuhrmann zum 65. Geburtstag*, ed. Hubert Mordek (Tübingen 1991) 187–200.

266. Kretzschmar, *Alger* 43. See in particular Alger 2.15–21 (ed. Kretzschmar 266–270).

267. For this and the following, see again Kretzschmar, *Alger* 39–42.

268. Alger 3.42 (ed. Kretzschmar 347), directly arguing against Peter Damian, *Ep.* 40 (ed. Reindel, MGH Briefe dt. Kaiserzeit 4.1:403) but also against the analogy Damian used later on (ibid. 447): 'Ex adulterino sepe coniugio pulchra soboles nascitur et ex obscena voluptate parentum spectabilis oritur species liberorum.' This was first spotted by Mirbt, *Publizistik* 403.

flicts of their time. Alger's tolerant position towards 'unworthy' clergy was different from many zealous reformers of his time, but his readiness to allow accusations against bishops, and the uncompromising definition of simony as an act of heresy have rightly been seen as rather 'Gregorian' positions.[269] More importantly, Alger must have been aware that his tract, despite the call for tolerance it contains, in practice must have been welcomed in particular by opponents of the bishop. From all we know, Alger himself never accused the bishop of simony, and he retained his office during Otbert's pontificate (and beyond); but he was writing his tract at the time Otbert was accused of simony by the local clergy, and Urban II had specifically excommunicated him as a simonist.[270] As in the case of *De misericordia*—which contains a number of contradictions and ambiguities—it is not easy to assess Alger's position in this conflict, but this may well be the point: amidst conflicts which seemed to force everyone to take sides, Alger quoted authorities both sides accepted as valid, presented procedural norms that helped to settle conflicts without violence, and simply refused to join with either party.

5.6.3 Material and Formal Sources

On the whole, *De misericordia* contains some 450 canon law excerpts, most of them very short; in addition, the *dicta* contain some 120 biblical quotations and allusions. The material sources are quite diverse, but there is an obvious predilection for ancient authority. The largest number of canons are from the writings of Saint Augustine, followed in this sequence by Gregory the Great, Gelasius I, Jerome, Leo I, Ambrose, and Innocent I. Conciliar decrees are almost absent (some three percent of the canons), and the most recent material are a small number of ninth-century sources, namely Hincmar of Reims and two conciliar canons.

Alger's formal sources are often difficult to establish, as he tended to quote only short passages, seems to have compared different versions of the same texts, and sometimes paraphrased rather than quoted canons or parts thereof. Fortunately, Robert Kretzschmar has very carefully analysed Alger's working method and his formal sources. A particularly interesting negative result of this study is that Alger, while evidently inspired by Ivo's *Prologue*, quoted his canon law neither from the *Prologue* itself, nor Ivo's

---

269. Kretzschmar, *Alger* 41 (tolerance, simony); Hartmann, 'Discipulus' (accusations); Mirbt, *Publizistik* 423–431 (validity of sacraments).

270. Urban II, JL 5538, to be dated after 1095 according to Somerville, *Piacenza* 14. See also ibid. 14 for this being the second time Urban II condemned Otbert, or the third, if one counts the condemnation at Piacenza too. See also Huysman, 'Controversy' 210–211 for narrative sources.

Decretum, nor any other collection this preface travelled with.[271] If Alger knew any of the Ivonian collections by the time he compiled *De misericordia*, this left no discernible trace; even where he quoted the same canon law as Ivo in his *Prologue*, Alger did not quote it from the latter.[272]

So where did Alger find the canon law he quoted in *De misericordia et iustitia*? His most important formal sources for the excerpts from papal decretals are the *Collection in 74 Titles* and the *Dionysio-Hadriana*.[273] Alger's *74T* may have been closer to the material sources than the version edited by Gilchrist, which in turn may suggest the use of an early *74T* version like the one used at Saint-Denis or for the compilation of *4L* (while *4L* itself can be excluded).[274] A handful of canons are taken from the False Decretals directly.[275] Alger also knew and used Burchard; Kretzschmar demonstrated that in several cases Alger quoted material found both in Burchard and in the *Anselmo dedicata* in a form that was closer to the latter. Whether this has to be explained by the (independend) use of both collections, by the Burchard version available at Liège, or perhaps by Alger drawing on an intermediate source that itself combined features of Burchard and *Anselmo dedicata*, remains to be studied. The *Collection in Twelve Parts*, an obvious candidate for such a 'mixed version', seems not to have been employed for *De misericordia*.[276]

In addition to these major collections, Alger also used a number of patristic florilegia, intermediate collections, and tracts.[277] This includes polemical writings by Peter Damian, Anselm of Lucca, Gebhard of Salzburg, Wenrich of Trier, and possibly others. In the case of the so-called 'error series' Kretzschmar made a strong case that Alger quoted it from Anselm's *Liber contra Wibertum* using a version similar to a manuscript from Liège.[278] Yet normally, Alger seems to have looked up the passages he wanted to quote in major collections, and quoted from these rather than the polemical literature where he came across them. This in itself suggests that Alger was well aware of the different quality of canon law

271. Kretzschmar, *Alger* 105–114, often confirming the findings of Hermann Hüffer, *Beiträge zur Geschichte der Quellen des Kirchenrechts und des Römischen Rechts im Mittelalter* (Münster 1862). See Rolker, *Canon Law* 275–276 on *De misericordia* not drawing on Ivo, and ibid. 276–277 on a link between Alger's *De sacramentis* and Ivo's *Decretum*.

272. Kretzschmar, *Alger* 116.

273. Kretzschmar, *Alger* 72–78 (55 canons from *Dionysio-Hadriana*) and 78–99 (62 canons from *74T*).

274. Alger 3.36 (ed. Kretzschmar 341) not only shares a variant with *74T* c. 136 (ed. Gilchrist 91); this also is one of the few *74T* which has no equivalent in *4L*: Gilchrist, 'Changing' 98.

275. Kretzschmar, *Alger* 99–105 (arguing for a use of class C of the False Decretals).

276. Kretzschmar, *Alger* 12 and 107–114; on *12P* see ibid. 110 n. 237.

277. Kretzschmar, *Alger* 114–140.

278. Kretzschmar, *Alger* 121–123.

Table 7: Parallels to Alger 2.58 in Other Collections

Material source	Alger (ed. Kretzschmar 306)	Burchard (*editio princeps*)	*74T* (ed. Gilchrist) / *4L* (*Clavis*)	*Sinemur.* (*Clavis*)	Ivo (ed. Brett)	*Panormia* (ed. Brett et al.)
Carthage 419 c. 19	2.58 can. a	1.160			5.270	4.106
JK 349	2.58 can. b	1.161		(1.96)**	5.271	4.105
JK †196	2.58 can. c		*74T* c. 100* = *4L* 1.13*	1.72		4.107
JK †196	2.58 can. d			1.73		
			* slightly shorter	** no overlap with Alger; see below		

quotations in the polemical literature, and perhaps also of the danger of manipulation.

To illustrate why it is so difficult to establish Alger's sources with precision, and also to test one of Kretzschmar's findings, one short passage in Alger may serve as an example. Alger 2.58 contains four canons taken from three different material sources (namely the Council of Carthage 419, a letter of Pope Boniface I, and Pseudo-Julius I). None of these texts is rare, and Alger only quotes relatively short passages from them; partly, he abbreviates his texts by paraphrasing them. Nonetheless, it is possible to find parallels to various pre-Gratian collections including Burchard, *74T* (and *4L*), the *Sinemuriensis*, Ivo, and the *Panormia* (see Table 7).

No known collection could have provided Alger with all four canons. Burchard and Ivo contain the first two canons, the *Sinemuriensis* the other two (also found in *74T* and *4L*, but slightly shorter at the end), and the *Panormia* even has three of the four canons (but not in Alger's sequence). Burchard and *74T* (or a related collection) were certainly used by Alger, while Ivo's *Decretum* and the *Panormia* in many cases where they do have parallels to *De misericordia* can be excluded as Alger's formal sources.

The parallel to the *Panormia* is particularly intriguing. Kretzschmar from other evidence showed that Alger did not know the *Panormia*, but also pointed out that it was a strange coincidence that both collections iuxtaposed the same letters. He assumed that this could be due to Alger's use of one of the *Panormia*'s formal sources. However, research on the Ivonian collections suggests otherwise. The three canons (*Panormia* 4.105–107) are taken from Ivo, while the canons both before and after seem to be taken from *4L*; thus, it was only the *Panormia* where the excerpts from JK 349 and JK †196 were combined.[279] However, it may also be worth noticing that there is a textual link between these two letters. The JK 349 excerpt as found in Burchard, Ivo, the *Panormia*, and many other collections contains a parallel to Pseudo-Julius that, for medieval readers familiar with it, must have looked like Boniface I quoting his predecessor.[280] It is therefore less surprising if two compilers independently from each other decided that the canons should be quoted next to one another. In fact, the *Sinemuriensis* compiler did something similar. Working with Burchard, he came across the Boniface letter in Burchard 1.161, but only retained a very short excerpt of three sentences, the first of which is 'Nullus dubitat', and inserted it a few pages after the Julius fragment (*Sinemuriensis* 1.96; no overlap with Alger 1.58). Neither the *Sinemuriensis* nor the *Panormia* were the formal source for Alger's excerpt from JK 349, but they show that both before and after Alger compilers noticed the relation, and indeed the overlap, between JK 349 and JK †196. The series in Alger 2.58 is probably best explained by Alger reworking quite independently at least two different formal sources, perhaps Burchard (for his canons a and b) and a *Sinemuriensis*-like collection (for canons c and d).

5.6.4 Structure

De misericordia is introduced by a preface and divided into three books; every book in turn is divided into chapters (eighty-eight, sixty-three, and eighty-six, respectively) and preceded by an individual *capitulatio*. Characteristically, every chapter is composed of a rubric, one or more *dicta* (comments) by Alger, and normally the same number of canon law quotations. Most chapters by far contain between one and five *dicta* plus an equal (or almost equal) number of canons; the most complex chapter (Alger 2.43) contains twelve canons and thirteen *dicta*. The high share of *dicta* has often been commented on; like Bonizo's *Liber de vita christiana*, Alger's *De misericordia* is a canonical collection in the form of an extended tract, only that Alger comments on almost all proof texts.

The discursive nature of the work is evident from the very structure of *De misericordia*. Every canon Alger inserted into *De misericordia* is carefully selected, often abbreviated, and placed according to its relevance for the individual points Alger wanted to demonstrate. Sometimes, Alger arranged series of chapters supporting the same, or similar, arguments,

---

279. See the apparatus to *Panormia* 4.102–111 (ed. Brett).

280. The sentence indeed is a quote, but of course not Boniface I quoting Julius I but rather Pseudo-Isidore using Boniface: Ps.-Julius, JK †196 (ed. Zechiel-Eckes, 'Blick' 73) = JK 349 (PL 67.266): 'Et nullus dubitat, quod ita iudicium nocens subterfugit quemadmodum, qui est innocens, ut absolvatur, quaerit.'

before presenting one or more chapters with arguments to the contrary. Among the many examples of (seeming) contradictions in canon law, there are several examples where papal letters contradict papal letters,[281] or one passage of Saint Ambrose contradicts another one attributed to him.[282] In any case, Alger both in his rubrics and in the *dicta* addressed these discrepancies, provided explanations how they emerged, and takes the (seeming) contradictions as a starting point for a discussion. For example, concerning the validity of ordinations conferred by heretics, Alger first quoted from Innocent I and Pseudo-Jerome to show that there were, or appeared to be, contradictions within the law.[283] Partly, the apparent contradiction could be explained by distinguishing between ordinations by heretics from those by other sinners; but above all, as Alger continued, the differences were in fact an expression of 'mercy and justice'; only if one would apply them literally and without discretion the differences would become contradictions.[284]

5.6.5 Alger on Contradictions

This habit of presenting and commenting on contradictions has attracted considerable scholarly attention, all the more as *De misericordia* was long known to belong to the formal sources of the *Decretum Gratiani*. Clearly, the question of contradictions in canon law played an important role in *De misericordia* from the very beginning. Like other early scholastic thinkers, Alger held that the apparent 'contradictions' in canon law could be understood as 'diversity'.[285] Following Ivo, he stressed, time and again, that conflicting canons actually expressed God's 'mercy and justice'. Alger linked this issue with the diverse background of decrees issued for different orders, different people, and in different places, and like Ivo stressed that both severe punishments and leniency could serve the same end.[286]

---

281. Alger 3.59–64 (ed. Kretzschmar 359–362), esp. the rubric to 6.63 (ed. Kretzschmar 361): 'Quod decretum Anastasii contrarium fuit decreto Innocentii.' Alger's interpretation of JK 744 is another quib against Peter Damian. For Innocent (JK 303) see also Alger 3.11 (ed. Kretzschmar 323).

282. Alger 1.28 dictum a (ed. Kretzschmar 208): 'Sed econtra idem Ambrosius alibi: [...]'. However, the passage quoted before is only misattributed to Ambrose.

283. Alger 3.23 (ed. Kretzschmar 330–331), esp. dictum c.: 'Sed cum Innocentius dicat [...] videtur esse contrarius Iheronimo [...].'

284. Alger 3.24 dictum (ed. Kretzschmar 332): 'Varia enim ecclesie statuta ad aliud et ad aliud relata utrobique tamen veritati et iustitie sunt consona et causarum ordini congrua. Alioquin, si inmutabiliter sine discretione tenenda sunt, maxima contraietatis confusio nascitur.'

285. Alger, *Praefatio* (ed. Kretzschmar 187–188): '[...] elaboravi, ut in canonibus adeo intentionis, utilitatis, veritatis eluceret unitas, ut nullam contrarietatis discordiam parareti aliqua eorum diversitas.'

286. Alger, *Praefatio*, dictum a (ed. Kretzschmar 187): 'Quia enim precepta canonica alia misericordie, alia sunt iustitie, adeo discrete variis ordinibus, personis et temporibus, ut nunc mi-

He also quoted the so-called Rule of Isidore,[287] but in the end he did not 'solve' contradictions by establishing a hierarchy of sources. Instead (and again like Ivo), Alger stressed that the question of whether to follow the rigour of the law or rather the spirit of forgiveness depended on the individual circumstances.[288]

Where Ivo had elaborated on these issues in his preface but explicitly left it to the reader how to apply these principles when working with the materials he gathered in his *Decretum*, Alger chose to structure his own work according to 'mercy and justice', and the opening section of the first book in particular directly continues the preface. In a programmatic rubric, Alger states that canons were issued 'at certain times, for certain people, under certain circumstances', partly because they were necessary, partly because they were useful, and sometimes to temper the rigour of the law 'out of mercy'.[289] In the following canons, Alger explains these aspects in detail and by specific examples. His example for 'necessity' is a decretal of Innocent I (JK 303) where the pope exceptionally and to avoid scandal allowed those having been ordained by heretics to keep their office after returning to the catholic faith. Alger—who himself quoted many canons prohibiting exactly this—also quoted Innocent with the important maxim that such concessions made 'out of necessity' should end *cessante necessitate*.[290]

5.6.6 Alger's Pastoral Canon Law

While such techniques may rightly be called 'legal', one should not underestimate the pastoral aspect of Alger's hermeneutics. Like Ivo, Alger mainly thinks of the ecclesiastical judge and pastor when he writes about

---

sericorida omnino remittat iustitiam, nunc iustitia omnino dissimulet misericordiam, qui per discretionem nesciunt tam diversa temperare, putant ea sibi per contraietatem discorditer obviare non attendentes hunc esse modum ecclesiastici regiminis seu indulgendo seu puniendo eamdem intentionem caritatis, eamdem operationem servare salutis ideoque canonicis regulis non canonice utentes sic precepta preceptis diverberant et impugnant, ut aliquando per indebitam gratiam suum iustitie, aliquando per intemperatam iustitiam suum gratie locum auferant.'

287. Alger, *Praefatio*, can. c (ed. Kretzschmar 189).

288. Alger, *Praefatio* (ed. Kretzschmar 188): 'suum cuique [...] pro heresi vel crimine, pro persona vel tempore.'

289. Alger 1.5, rubric (ed. Kretzschmar 196): 'Quod precepta canonica pro tempore, pro persona, pro variis rerum eventibus vel partim temperata vel omnino sunt intermissa, aliquando necessitas, aliquando utilitas, aliquando solo pietatis intuit.'

290. Alger 1.8, can. (ed. Kretzschmar 198): 'Cessante necessitate debet utique cessare pariter quod urgebat.' Both JK 303 in general and this maxim in particular were widely known; see Hincmar of Reims, *Opusculum LV capitulorum* (ed. Schieffer, MGH Conc. 4 suppl. 2.214); Bernold, *De excommunicatis vitandi* (ed. Stöckly and Jasper, MGH Fontes iuris 15.181); Deusdedit 4.376 ([157]) (ed. Wolf von Glanvell 582); Bonizo 2.63 (ed. Perels 68); Ivo 6.59–60 (ed. Brett); Ivo, *Prologue* (ed. Brasington 129). Gratian 1 in C.1 q.7 cc. 6–23 (ed. Winroth 270–273) strongly draws on JK 303, JK 636, and Alger's relevant *dicta*.

canon law. Yet for the pastor hearing confession and administering penance, the written law was only a guide in his pastoral duties; in addition to the individual circumstances, the inner disposition of the sinner was of paramount importance. Had he consented to a sinful act or not? Did he now repent the sins he confessed? If so, was the contrition real? It is no accident that the longest and most complex chapter of *De misericordia* (Alger 2.43) deals with the delicate question of 'true penance'.[291]

Alger's treatment of penance is in line with his general views on sacraments. Just like an unworthy priest may still administer sacraments, not even the most righteous priest can absolve from sin; only God's grace can.[292] This also means that an excommunication or reconciliation may well be invalid, even if there was no visible sign of this. The inner disposition of the sinner, Alger quoted Augustine, was decisive.[293] Such arguments were, of course, nothing new in medieval discourse on penance. They may be deemed as having mainly practical relevance, which they no doubt had. Nonetheless, they also are highly relevant for the rather fundamental question of what 'the law' was, and this issue became more urgent around 1100 as canon law slowly developed into an academic discipline. If many provisions could be interpreted either strictly or more leniently (or not applied at all) out of 'mercy', if only the inner disposition made a sinful act sinful, and if adequate penance depended on contrition of the ('inscrutable') heart[294]—what, then, was the relation between 'canon law' and the 'canons' as found in the collections under discussion here? In many respects, it was rather loose. As Brett put it:

> Correspondingly, authoritative guidance on the divine will in particular circumstances was not readily to be identified with any single category of text or even with any text at all. [...] To find God's law then, one might search across a boundless sea of texts, of customs or sacred narrative, yet ended in the unknowable depths of His will.[295]

The 'pastoral' aspect of canon law was, therefore, not simply the practical side of a scholarly enterprise; rather, 'the boundless sea of texts' was

---

291. Alger 2.43 (ed. Kretzschmar 289–295); see also Alger 1.74–81 (ed. Kretzschmar 244–247).

292. Alger 1.65–66 (ed. Kretzschmar 237–238).

293. Alger 1.66, can. c (ed. Kretzschmar 238): 'Quod obest homini, quod ex illa tabula vult eum rapere humana ignoratia, si de libro viventium non eum deleat iniquia conscientia?' On this point, see Brett, 'Finding' 53.

294. See, for example, Chalon 813 (quoting Ps. 50.19) as found in Burchard 19.59 (*editio princeps*, fol. 211va): 'Cor autem contritum et humiliatum Deus non despicit.' For the 'cor inscrutabile', see Jer. 17.9. For background, see Abigail A. Firey, *A Contrite Heart: Prosecution and Redemption in the Carolingian Empire* (Studies in Medieval and Reformation Traditions 145; Leiden and Boston 2009) passim.

295. Brett, 'Finding' 54–55.

only one part of God's law. Any understanding of this law, and especially so any systematic approach to it, had to consider the complex relation of (written) canons, customs, and God's will.

5.6.7 Influence

Compared to his *De sacramentis*, Alger's *De misericordia* seemed to have had a more limited circulation; only three medieval manuscripts are known. This is not to say Alger had no influence on later canon law collections. The addition of *De misericordia* excerpts to a copy of the *Panormia* may be quoted as evidence to the contrary.[296] Above all, however, it is the *Decretum Gratiani* by which Alger's thought, if indirectly, came to exercise considerable influence. Gratian 1 used *De misericordia* directly and integrated Alger's proof texts as well as his comments into his own collection, mainly so in the sections on simony and penance.[297] Gratian's discussion of the concept of *cessante necessitate* is strongly influenced by Alger.[298] The peculiar mix of often contradicting canons, on the one hand, and Alger's comment, on the other hand, may well have been among the inspirations for Gratian to structure his work the way he did. Nonetheless, the influence Alger had on Gratian's method should not be exaggerated. When it came to 'harmonizing' contradictions, Gratian employed a much wider variety of hermeneutical techniques than Alger had done.[299]

5.7 The *Panormia*: A Textbook for Generations of Lawyers

5.7.1 The *Panormia* (Overview)

The *Panormia* was compiled in the early twelfth century in northern France, perhaps at a cathedral school or at a similar place of learning, and soon became one of the most widely read canonical collections of the pre-Gratian era.[300] It seems to have been compiled around 1115, and

---

296. Brett, 'Finding' 70.

297. Kretzschmar, *Alger* 58–66 and 141–154 (general); John Wei, 'A Twelfth-Century Treatise on Charity: The Tract "Vt avtem hoc evidenter" of the Sentence Collection *Devs itaqve svmme atqve ineffabiliter bonvs*' MS 72 (2012) 1–50, here at 22–23 (direct use of Alger in *De pen.*); idem, *Gratian* 22 (simony). For Gratian's view, see Larson, *Master* ch. 1.

298. See C.1 q.7 cc.6–23 (ed. Winroth 270–273).

299. Stephan Kuttner, 'Zur Frage der theologischen Vorlagen Gratians' ZRG Kan. Abt. 54 (1934) 243–268; Kretzschmar, *Alger* 58–66 and 141–154 (followed by Meyer, *Distinktionstechnik* esp. 264 and 273); Brett, 'Finding' 71 ('wide intellectual gap'); Wei, *Gratian* 56 (different techniques). Le Bras took a different stance; expanding on Fournier's 'Tournant' article, he highlighted Alger's contribution to legal hermeneutics while downplaying the role of Gratian, whom he called a 'compilateur d'esprit médiocre'; see Le Bras, 'Alger de Liège' 117.

300. The on-going edition by Brett and his collaborators is found at https://ivo-of-chartres.github.io/ (with Brett's 'Panormia Project' introduction); for full bibliography, see Kéry 253–260

from the second quarter of the twelfth century on can be seen to have been copied, read, quoted, and reworked very frequently, especially so among the scholars of northern France, but also across the Channel. The Greek-ish title was understood as a promise that the collection contained 'all laws',[301] and indeed its about 1,200 canons, divided into eight books, cover a very broad range of issues. Most canons, however, are remarkably short, which means that the *Panormia* still fits in codices of normally 110 to 170 folios, and could be crammed on less than ninety. The sheer number of extant copies—more than one hundred—is impressive evidence of its popularity during the twelfth century and beyond. Like every successful collection, the *Panormia* could be used differently by different audiences, but it was clearly more a book for scholars and students rather than the kind of collection either a powerful bishop or an ecclesiastical judge, let alone a parish priest, would find most useful.

The *Panormia* belongs to the relatively large group of short versions of Ivo's *Decretum*, and to the even larger group of collections that normally are introduced with Ivo's celebrated preface. Mainly for this reason, the *Panormia* was long associated with Ivo of Chartres, and still is counted among the 'Ivonian' collections, even if Fournier's idea that the *Panormia* was compiled by Ivo has been proven wrong.[302] Much what has been said about the other Ivonian collections also applies to the *Panormia*; by taking Ivo's *Decretum* as his starting point, the compiler had access to a formidable library of legal texts, including a sub-collection of canons on the sources of the law (in Ivo's book four) and an elaborate introduction to the mutability, and the application, of canon law in form of Ivo's *Prologue*. This said, a general feature of the *Panormia* is that it contains a relative large number of minor errors which seem to have entered the manuscript tradition at an early stage. In particular, the inscriptions to many canons, including much material Ivo had introduced into his collection for the first time, and citing his sources with precision, are often abbreviated or confused in the *Panormia* (for examples, see the analysis of book one below). Another general feature is that the *Panormia* compiler was, as

---

and Fowler-Magerl, *Clavis* 198–202. There is no book-length study of the *Panormia*, but in addition Brett's '*Panormia* Project' see idem, '*Panormia*'. For much of the following, see also Rolker, *Canon Law* ch. 7.— All quotations from this site have been checked again in late February 2020; the revision stamp of all files used for the present studies is '2015–0923 / 898fb'.

301. See Brundage, *Medieval Origins* 95 n. 85 on the possible derivation from πανόρμος ('seaport'). The idea that the title was somehow derived from παν and νόμος is found in some medieval copies and was also quoted by Sebastian Brant in his preface (*editio princeps*, [s.p.]): 'Appellavit [Ivo, CR] autem hunc suum librum pannormiam quasi totius iusticie sive legis materiam continentem. Vel, ut alii volunt, pannormiam a norma que est regula a quibusdam dicitur.'

302. Rolker, *Canon Law* 265–289.

Ivo had been, keenly interested in patristic sources; while he dropped all penitential canons, many conciliar and papal texts, and also much of the secular law found in Ivo's *Decretum*, he was more reluctant to do so with the patristic authorities. As a result, the *Panormia* contains an even higher share of canons taken ultimately from the writings of Augustine, Gregory the Great, and other Fathers.

5.7.2 The Formal Sources of the *Panormia*

Ivo's Decretum

The *Decretum* is the main source of the *Panormia*; more than nine tenths of the material is taken from Ivo's collection. The overall structure of both collections is roughly the same, although many *Panormia* books draw on more than one book of the *Decretum*. There are some series of canons left in the sequence of the *Decretum*, but not many, and most series do not extend beyond a dozen canons or so.[303] Normally, the *Panormia* compiler not only was highly selective and abbreviated many canons, but also rearranged the *Decretum* heavily. There are marked differences between individual books. The first book of the *Panormia*, for example, is mainly based on books one and two of Ivo's *Decretum* (devoted to the sacraments). Long passages can legitimately be described as an abbreviated version of the respective *Decretum* part. *Panormia* 1.41–54, for example, on the liturgy of baptism, has no other sources than *Decretum* 1.90–116, selecting about one in two *Decretum* canons and presenting them in the very same sequence as found in this source. In contrast, other parts of the *Panormia* display a more independent position vis-à-vis Ivo's *Decretum*. Book three on the ecclesiastical hierarchy, for example, while largely constructed from *Decretum* material, adds a significant share of new material and uses the *Decretum* canons very freely. Most material of *Panormia* 3 comes from books five to seven of the *Decretum*, but single canons were also taken from Ivo's books two, three, four, eight, eleven, thirteen, and fourteen; only rarely, series of more than two or three canons are left in the same sequence as in the *Decretum*. Significantly, the opening canons of most *Decretum* books play no special role in the *Panormia*; the opening sections of books one, three, and four largely draw on materials not found in the *Decretum*,[304] and other books often begin with material Ivo has placed less prominently.

---

303. See, for example, *Panormia* 1.40–54 (lifted from Ivo 1.87–116); *Panormia* 2.142–154 (Ivo 4.168–184); *Panormia* 8.82–103 (Ivo 12.1–23).

304. *Panormia* 1.1–6, *Panormia* 3.1–3, and *Panormia* 4.2–3, 5, 9–10 are taken from sources outside Ivo's *Decretum*.

The *Collection in Four Books*

The *Collection in Four Books* (= 4L) is a version of the more famous *Collection in 74 Titles* which circulated widely in the early twelfth century. The *Panormia* compiler used an enlarged version of this collection to supplement the material he took from Ivo's *Decretum*, in particular in his third and fourth books.[305] Sometimes, the canons are still left in the sequence of 4L, and interestingly the compiler sometimes preferred 4L over Ivo's *Decretum* for certain canons, without any obvious reason in the text.[306] The use of 4L for such canons may simply be the result of the compiler first abbreviating Ivo's *Decretum* and than expanding his collection again from other collections, above all 4L. One feature that may have made 4L attractive to the *Panormia* compiler was that it contained, both in the collection itself and in the appendices found in many copies, a number of more recent texts which were relatively rare. For example, it was 4L where the *Panormia* compiler found a copy of the 1059 Papal Election Decree.[307]

The Second Arsenal Collection

As outlined above, the Arsenal 713 manuscript is an incomplete copy (in one hand) of what were at least two distinct subsets of materials: a collection compiled in direct preparation of Ivo's *Decretum* (= *Arsenal I*) mixed up with a second collection not used by Ivo (= *Arsenal II*).[308] The latter materials seem to have been used for the *Panormia*, and indeed would explain most non-Ivonian material found here, including almost all parallels between the *Panormia* and the *Britannica*. Like *Arsenal I*, the second Arsenal collection can only be reconstructed by comparing the extant manuscript to the collection drawing on it, in this case the *Panormia*. The *Panormia* canons which have a parallel in Arsenal and may have been taken from there are almost all found on fols. 129r, 131r–135v, 136v–138v, 139v–140r, and 149r–152r, often in the same sequence.[309] While *Arsenal I* was a preparatory

305. Brett, 'Urban II' 44–45 (4L); idem, 'Panormia' 209 (enlarged 4L version represented by London, BL, Arundel 713); see also the concordance table (ibid. 222–260, esp. at 235, 238, and 244).

306. For example, the series in *Panormia* 4.2–12 is taken from the very beginning of 4L, although the *Panormia* compiler could also have drawn on book five of Ivo's *Decretum* for some of these canons. *Panormia* 3.128–131 (taken from 4L, 2.131–134) is a similar case. See Brett, 'Panormia' and his edition for detail.

307. On the role of the appendices and the mutual relations of 4L with other collections, see Fowler-Magerl, 'Fine Distinctions' esp. 153–159, Jasper, *Papstwahldekret* 10–25, and idem, 'Ein Brief Papst Alexanders II. an Abt Ivo I. von Saint-Denis', *Grundlagen des Rechts. Festschrift für Peter Landau zum 65. Geburtstag*, ed. Richard H. Helmholz et al. (Rechts- und Staatswissenschaftliche Veröffentlichungen der Görres-Gesellschaft N.F. 91; Paderborn, Munich, Vienna, and Zurich 2000) 131–139, here at 131–133.

308. The following account is mainly based on Brett, 'Sources' esp. 157–160, his editions (including the concordance tables and apparatus), and Rolker, *Canon Law* 124–125.

309. Corrected from Austin, 'Arsenal' 5–6. In particular, I do not agree with her claim (ibid.

collection of non-Burchardian material specifically composed to produce Ivo's *Decretum*, the relation between *Arsenal II* and *Panormia* is much looser. The *Panormia* compiler only made a 'highly selective' use of what can be reconstructed as *Arsenal II*;[310] this also means that reconstructing *Arsenal II* is necessarily speculative to some degree.

The best evidence is available for book three of the *Panormia*, which has more parallels to the Arsenal manuscript than any other book, and crucially preserves the sequence of the Arsenal material relatively faithfully. *Panormia* 3.84–115 all have parallels in Arsenal fols. 131v–132r, 149r–151r and, in one case, 152r; the canons in another series (*Panormia* 3.133–145) all have parallels on fol. 150r–v of the extant Arsenal manuscript. This confirms the argument outlined above that both *Arsenal I* and *Arsenal II* are found largely on separate pages and folios in the extant Arsenal manuscript. In other words, while the parallels between *Panormia* 3 are scattered widely across the extant Arsenal manuscript, they are almost always found in those section which have no parallels to Ivo's *Decretum*; fol. 149v seems to draw on both *Arsenal I* and the part of *Arsenal II* that was used for book three of the *Panormia*.

Let us take a closer look at these folios (fols. 131v–132r, 149r–151r, and 152r, plus the separate series on fol. 150r–v) which contain the best starting point to reconstruct *Arsenal II*. Most *Arsenal II* canons found here have a parallel in book three of the *Panormia*, but seven have a parallel in other books (*Panormia* 2.134–135, 5.110–111, 8.3, and 77–78). Four more canons found in *Panormia* and the Arsenal manuscript (but not on the folios just mentioned) deserve attention. The first two are *Panormia* 1.106 and 7.18 which have a parallel on fols. 122r and 169r of the Arsenal manuscript. *Panormia* 1.106 is the end of a long series of canons all taken from Ivo's *Decretum*, while *Panormia* 7.18 is found in the middle of such a series. Neither the first nor the seventh book of the *Panormia* otherwise use the Arsenal collection. As Brett established, the canons found in the Arsenal manuscript and in the *Panormia* 'very probably' were also found in Ivo's *Decretum*.[311] So the *Panormia* compiler took these two texts from there, and did not use the (first) Arsenal collection for his books one and seven. The other two canons are *Panormia* 3.57 and 81, and thus part of a book known to

---

6) that fol. 125 was a section with *Arsenal II* material including *Panormia* 1.163 and perhaps other 'Arsenal II canons' (ibid. n. 16). Her account of *Panormia* 1.63 seems to be a misunderstanding of Brett, 'Sources' 158 n. 24. The text in question (LP0146 in *Clavis*) overlaps with both Ivo 6.132 and *Panormia* 6.163, but there is no reason to believe that either collection depends on Arsenal material here; rather, the canon seems to have been transmitted from Burchard 2.31 via Ivo to the *Panormia*.

310. Brett, 'Sources' 157.

311. Brett, 'Panormia' 225 n. 76 and 253 n. 130.

draw on *Arsenal II*. The former text is a short excerpt taken from Isidore's *Etymologies*; while this is a common source, the excerpt in this form before the *Panormia* seems only to be found in the Arsenal manuscript.[312] *Panormia* 3.57 is found in the middle of canons taken from Ivo's *Decretum*, but otherwise there is nothing to suggest the canon was part of a more complete *Decretum* version.[313] The case seems clearer with *Panormia* 3.81, taken from Urban II (JL 5383).[314] The *Panormia* contains seven excerpts from letters of Urban II as the most recent material, and they all are found in Arsenal. If JL 5383 was part of *Arsenal II*, the use of this collection would explain all Urban II canons in the *Panormia*, making the assumption of a direct use of the *Britannica* for this material unnecessary. (In any case, only five of the seven Urban II canons are found in the *Britannica*.) So all in all, it seems that *Panormia* 3.57 and 81 (but not *Panormia* 1.106 and 7.18) were once part of *Arsenal II*, even if they are found outside the longer series of *Arsenal II* canons in the extant manuscript. It is also remarkable that only the third book of the *Panormia* contains more than one or two canons apparently taken from *Arsenal II*.

As the use of *Panormia* to compile *Arsenal II* can be excluded,[315] these parallels help us to reconstruct one of the sources of the *Panormia*. As it is manifest in the case of *Arsenal I*, it is likely that the extant Arsenal manuscript does not preserve all *Arsenal II* material. Nonetheless, it is also clear that the relation between *Arsenal II* and *Panormia* is not as intimate as that between *Arsenal I* and Ivo's *Decretum*. More importantly, despite the Arsenal manuscript being a copy of disorganised materials, the two Arsenal collections still can be shown to have been separate works: Ivo clearly used, and indeed can be assumed to have compiled *Arsenal I*, but shows no sign of having been familiar with *Arsenal II*. Vice versa, the compiler of the *Panormia* apparently had access to *Arsenal II* but cannot be shown compellingly to have used *Arsenal I*. The compiler of the *Caesaraugustana* had access to both collections, but clearly knew them as separate collections, as will be discussed below. So the two Arsenal collections, while having been compiled independently from each other, were transmitted jointly even before the extant manuscript was made.

312. Paris, Bibliothèque de l'Arsenal, 713, fol. 171r = *Panormia* 3.57 (from where it was taken into 10P 3.19). The inscription in all three collections correctly refers to Isidore, *Etym.* 10.93 (ed. Lindsay), with 'cap. 5' referring to the section 'E'.

313. *Pace* Austin, 'Arsenal' 8 n. 26.

314. For the following, see Brett, 'Sources' 159. The transmission of JL 5383 has been subject to some controversy; like Somerville, I am not convinced by Kuttner's idea that the version in the *Britannica* depends on Ivo's *Prologue*. See Kuttner, 'Turning Point', Somerville, *Urban II* esp. 105, and Rolker, *Canon Law* esp. 95–96.

315. Brett, 'Sources' 158.

5.7.3 The *Panormia* on Baptism: Questions and Answers

The analysis of the formal sources helps us to understand in a next step how the compiler of the *Panormia* worked with his materials, which choices he made, and how he presented his materials. As will be argued in the following, despite massive overlap between the *Panormia* and Ivo's collection, the *Panormia* is a very independent work. To demonstrate this, I will focus on the first book, which mainly deals with baptism and the Eucharist. As already mentioned, the first book belongs to the more 'conservative' parts of the *Panormia* in the sense that it is mainly composed of two series drawing on the first books of the *Decretum*. The *Panormia* compiler therefore retained Ivo's decision to begin the collection with the sacraments. Most material is taken from the first two books of Ivo's *Decretum*: *Panormia* 1.7–122 are taken from Ivo's first book (with probably only two exceptions);[316] *Panormia* 1.123–162 are taken from the second (with only one exception).[317] This corresponds very roughly to a third of the canons in Ivo's first two books; but the *Panormia* tended to select shorter canons and sometimes heavily abbreviated the material, resulting in an much shorter work overall.

More importantly, the *Panormia* compiler deliberately deviated from his model, strikingly so at the beginning of his collection. While the long opening section of the *Decretum* is completely ignored,[318] most 'new' (non-Ivonian) material in the *Panormia*'s first book is placed prominently at the very beginning. The six opening canons—taken from Pseudo-Augustine— are an exposition of the Trinity and the Incarnation.[319] After this, the *Panormia* continues with the Eucharist. Here, the *Panormia* draws on Ivo's collection again; but compared to the *Decretum*, the Eucharist material is heavily abbreviated and indeed often misattributed. Interestingly, this mainly affects a number of texts which Ivo had already assembled at Saint-Quentin in a florilegium, which later became the kernel of book two of his *Decretum*. The *Panormia* compiler was apparently unaware that

316. For the role of *Panormia* in debates on 'baptism by desire' see Colish, *Faith* 29–33.

317. *Panormia* 1.13 and 106 are not found in the extant *Decretum* manuscripts but must have been part of the collection (Brett, 'Sources' 152); *Panormia* 1.19 is not found in the *Decretum* (but 4L 3.50b); and *Panormia* 1.110 is taken not from the first book of Ivo's collection, but is a short excerpt from a quotation within the very long 'canon' *Decretum* 2.9 (taken from Lanfranc's *De corpore*). *Panormia* 1.140 is not taken from the *Decretum* (nor 4L or either Arsenal collection).

318. *Decretum* 1.1–44; this material had been introduced into canon law tradition only by Ivo.

319. *Panormia* 1.1–6; the material source is Gennadius' *Liber ecclesiasticorum dogmatum* which in the Middle Ages commonly travelled under Augustine's name; see the edition by Cuthbert Turner, 'The "Liber ecclesiasticorum dogmatum" Attributed to Gennadius' *Journal of Theological Studies* 7 (1905) 78–99, here at 89–99, with additions in idem, 'The "Liber ecclesiasticorum dogmatum": Supplenda' *Journal of Theological Studies* 8 (1906) 103–114.

the material in *Decretum* 2.1–10 was taken from Lanfranc, and frequently confused Saint Augustine with Saint Ambrose (and vice versa) in his abbreviated version of Ivo's material.[320] These mistakes could in theory be explained by a defective *Decretum* copy, but the extant manuscripts suggest that is was more probably the multifarious, and sometimes perhaps chaotic, task of reworking the material into a new collection which gave rise to this confusion. In any case, the misattributions were certainly present in the earliest known stage of the *Panormia*. To judge from the quantity and the quality of errors, the *Panormia* compiler seems not to have been very familiar with the sources Ivo was working with, or with the heated debates on the Eucharist of the mid- and later eleventh century.

The sections on baptism, by contrast, are more carefully composed. Not only are there fewer mistakes of the kind just quoted, the *Panormia* compiler seems to have followed a very elaborate scheme in rearranging and updating Ivo's materials. In detail, the arrangement of canons seems to imply a certain hierarchy between the texts. There are short series of canons all dealing with highly specific aspects of baptism, often coming from different background, and equally often (seemingly) contradicting each other. Where Ivo, famously, had left it largely to his readers to deal with such complexities, the *Panormia* compiler chose to arrange the same materials in a way that highlighted some texts as more relevant than others. For example, *Panormia* 1.12 (taken from Ivo 1.120) quotes Saint Augustine on child baptism,[321] an unusual practice in the times of Saint Augustine but increasingly common in the Middle Ages. Augustine is quoted as questioning what the spiritual benefit of baptising children was, if they died soon afterwards. The rubric found in most *Panormia* manuscripts takes up this question too: 'Questio: quid prosit baptismus parvulis statim post baptismum mortuis?' The following canon, ultimately from Isidore's *De officiis*,[322] very generally affirms the utility of baptising children and other people unable to profess the faith for themselves. In most *Panormia* manuscripts, the rubric clearly marks it as the 'answer to the question' ('Solutio questionis'). This fundamentally differentiates the status of the canons; both are part of canon law, but one is marked as the question, the other as the solution. Ivo, in contrast, had quoted these and other texts with no indication which of them should be preferred over the others. To

---

320. For details, see Rolker, 'Earliest Work' and idem, *Canon Law* 271–272.

321. Augustine, *De libero arbitrio* 3.23 (ed. Green, CCL 29.314).

322. Isidore, *De ecclesiasticis officiis* 2.25 (ed. Lawson, CCL 113.105). The canon is taken from Ivo 1.122A—a canon which is not found in the extant *Decretum* manuscripts, but is found in both *Arsenal I* and the *Panormia*, and on this basis can be inferred to have been part of an archaic *Decretum*. See Brett, 'Sources' 152.

take another example, *Panormia* 1.23–34 presents different positions on the question on the baptism by lay people, women, Jews, and heretics; canon 34 (an abbreviated *Decretum* text) is not just another text but presented very much like the definitive answer to the question raised by the plethora of preceding canons.[323]

A similar tendency may be visible in the series of canons in *Panormia* 1.16–22 on the appropriate dates for baptism. Most of the canons (all taken from Ivo's *Decretum*) stress that baptism should occur only on Easter and Pentecost—ancient rules which were increasingly irrelevant as the baptism of infants became the norm in medieval societies.[324] For this reason perhaps, the *Panormia* compiler chose to turn to the *Collection in Four Books* rather than Ivo's *Decretum* for his canon 19, as this excerpt from a letter of Leo the Great (JK 414) mentioned more exceptions from this ancient rule than any canon found in Ivo's collection. In particular, Leo conceded baptism at any date if death was, or seemed, imminent. While Leo probably thought deathbed-conversions, in medieval times the argument could generally be applied, sadly without much exaggeration of the facts, to the baptism of infants. It may also be significant in this context that the *Panormia* compiler omitted that part of JK 414 in which Leo has in fact reaffirmed that Easter and Pentecost were the only legitimate dates for baptism. As a result, the canon appears almost as a comment to the preceding ones.[325] Classical canon law and provincial councils of the later Middle Ages tended to rely on the very 'exceptions' the *Panormia* compiler added to the traditional doctrine on the date of baptism.[326] Sentence collections from the school of Laon show that the same problem could also be solved differently. According to one such collection, canon law (including Leo's decretal) put parents in the awkward position of either violating canon law (unless the child was really mortally ill) or risking that their new-born would die unbaptised. Yet all canons from the ancient Church only re-

323. *Panormia* 1.34 (ed. Brett): 'Satis ostendimus ad baptismum qui verbis evangelicis consecratur non pertinere cuiusquam vel dantis vel accipientis errorem, sive de Patre sive de Filio sive de Spiritu sancto, aliter sentiat quam doctrina celestis insinuat.'

324. Janet L. Nelson, 'Parents, Children, and the Church in the Earlier Middle Ages', *The Church and Childhood*, ed. Diana Wood (Studies in Church History 31; Oxford 1994) 81–114; Joseph H. Lynch, *Christianizing Kinship: Ritual Sponsorship in Anglo-Saxon England* (Ithaca, N.Y. 1998) ch. 1.

325. *Panormia* 1.19 (ed. Brett) begins 'Porro hi qui necessitate mortis, egritudinis, obsidionis, persecutionis et naufragii urgentur, omni tempore debent baptizari.' This is in fact one of the rubrics of the letter as found in Pseudo-Isidore (ed. Hinschius 611). Immediately before, one reads in Pseudo-Isidore (but *not* in the *Panormia*): 'Hec duo tempora, Pascha videlicet et Pentecosten, ad baptizandum a Romanis pontificibus legitima sunt prefixa.' Brett in his edition points out the parallel to 74*T* c. 218 (ed. Gilchrist 138), where both rubrics of JK 414 form the canon.

326. See Richard H. Helmholz, *The Spirit of Classical Canon Law* (The Spirit of the Laws; Athens, Ga. and London 1996) esp. 205–206 (with further references).

ferred to the baptism of adult and therefore could not be applied without necessary qualifications in the present, they concluded.[327]

Given that there is very little comment—rubrics like 'Solutio questionis' are very rare—any such arguments on why the *Panormia* compiler chose to arrange his material as he did remain to some degree speculative. However, the examples just quoted suggest that the extensive rearrangement of the *Decretum* material, and the occasional use of other formal sources like *4L*, was partly motivated by the compiler's views on which parts of the tradition were more relevant than other parts, with a special view to contemporary practice (like the baptism of infants). By selecting a smaller number of mostly short canons, abbreviating many longer texts, and crucially by presenting some canons as 'solutions', the *Panormia* significantly reduces the complexity of tradition—or, to put it in a more friendly way, the compiler made it easier for a high medieval audience in northern Europe to make sense of canons reflecting the social realities of late antique Mediterranean Christianity.

5.7.4 Papal Elections and Investiture: The Case of Controversial Material in the *Panormia*

Nicholas II and Pseudo-Stephen IX on Papal Elections

The Papal Election Decree of 1059 is normally studied in the context of the early reform papacy, the polemics of the late eleventh century, and also the conflicts at the curia in the time after the death of Gregory VII. However, as the previous chapter has shown, studying the canon law collections of this time produces a negative finding—the famous decree was simply absent from all Italian collections compiled in the first 80 years after its promulgation. The *Panormia* compiler, in contrast, not only inserted the Papal Election Decree as one of his 1,200 odd canons, but indeed placed it prominently at the very beginning of book three, devoted to ecclesiastical hierarchy.[328] His immediate source was an augmented form of the *Collection in Four Books* (a derivative of the more famous *74T*).[329] Only these collections from northern France made the 1059 decree more widely known, first in north-western Europe but later also more widely, as the *Panormia* became widely disseminated.

---

327. *Sentences de l'école d'Anselme de Laon*, no. 371, ed. Odon Lottin, *Psychologie et morale aux XIIe et XIIIe siècles* (6 in 8 vols. Gembloux 1942–60), here at 5.275–276. See Marcia L. Colish, 'Another Look at the School of Laon' *Archives d'histoire doctrinale et littéraire du moyen âge* 53 (1986) 7–22, here at 13–14.

328. *Panormia* 3.1a (ed. Brett).

329. On *4L* (and the Bergamo copy in particular) see Jasper, *Papstwahldekret*. The edition in this monograph is now superseded by Jasper's own MGH edition (MGH Conc. 8.352–381).

Neither the geography nor the chronology seem to be accidental. The various versions of the Papal Election Decree had caused bitter controversies, as both the genuine and the interpolated 'imperial' version offended different groups; in fact, some conservative opponents rejected both version. The genuine version was a break with tradition that for its critics amounted to a violation of the law, as the decree curtailed traditional rights of the lower-ranking cardinals, allowed the election of non-Roman candidates, and contained an ambiguous reference to imperial intervention which could be read as confining traditional prerogatives. The interpolated version, in contrast, was seen by the curia and many supporters of the Roman church as an attempt to make papal elections dependent on royal consent, and also opposed by cardinal bishops who defended the new quasi-metropolitan rights they were collectively given in 1059. These debates, with overlapping fields of conflict, for many compilers of canon law collection must have made the decree too controversial for inclusion; other compilers, most notably Cardinal Deusdedit, actively opposed the unwelcome regulations, and integrated in their collections canons that countered the 1059 decree.[330] So it was not for lack of knowledge that the decree was omitted in the Italian collections of the decades around 1100, but an effect of its controversial nature and opposition from influential canonists.

In France, the story unfolded differently. Of course, papal elections were closely watched by secular and ecclesiastical elites. From the very beginning of his pontificate, Urban II had relied on France in his ultimately successful campaign to extend his sphere of action in regions outside southern Italy.[331] Acceptance, support, or even obedience of the French Church in the twelfth century remained crucial to decide disputed papal elections.[332] Nonetheless, the Papal Election Decree of 1059 was less central to French debates compared to Italy. Hugh of Flavigny in the 1090s quoted the decree but, significantly, did not use it when defending the election of Gregory VII.[333] In contrast, when Hugh of Fleury did quote

330. For details, see Chapter Four.

331. See Becker, *Urban II.* 2.435–437.

332. See the excellent survey by Rolf Große, 'La fille aînée de l'Église. Frankreichs Kirche und die Kurie im 12. Jahrhundert', *Römisches Zentrum und kirchliche Peripherie. Das universale Papsttum als Bezugspunkt der Kirchen von den Reformpäpsten bis zu Innozenz III.*, ed. Jochen Johrendt and Harald Müller (Abh. Akad. Göttingen N.F. 2; Berlin and New York 2008) 299–321.

333. Hugh of Flavigny, *Chronicon* a. 1059 (ed. Pertz, MGH SS 8.408–409) contains the decree, but in his apologetic account of Gregory's election Hugh does not use this text (ibid. 422–423 and 430). On Hugh's canon law sources, see Lawo, *Studien* esp. 217–237, correcting also Healy, *Chronicle*. Healy's assertions (ibid. 131–132 and 136–137) on 'authorities that he [Hugh of Flavigny, CR] took from the *Collectio Britannica*' (ibid. 136), if true, would be interesting, but like the whole section it seems not to be based on primary source evidence.

the decree, it was not to make a polemical point, but in order to find middle ground in the disputes around 1100.[334] The Papal Election Decree was relatively well known in France, but it was not itself a contentious texts as it had been for polemicsts in the Empire and around the papal curia. There is, therefore, no reason to suppose that the *Panormia* compiler inserted the text as a comment on Gregory's or any other papal election in particular. (In the 1130 schism, though, the *Panormia* would provide key players, like Bernard of Clairvaux, with the relevant canon law.[335])

Rather than disputed papal elections, it is internal evidence from the *Panormia* which helps to understand the eventual inclusion of the 1059 decree into canon law. In particular, the decree has to be seen in conjunction with the short canon with which it was combined to form the opening piece of book three of the *Panormia*. This short canon, attributed to a Pope Stephen, asserted that imperial legates had to be present at the consecration of the pope.[336] The attribution to 'Stephen' is fictitious, but the canon repeats a genuine conciliar decree of the late ninth century.[337] The provision was never quoted in canonical collections before the *Panormia*, and seems to have been unearthed only in the polemics of the 1080s. Wido of Osnabrück quoted in his pro-imperial tract of 1084/85, and attributed it to Pope Deusdedit.[338] Bonizo seems to have had this canon, or rumours about it, in mind when he rejected pro-imperial privileges attributed to 'Sergius, Stephen, and Nicholas'.[339] The attribution to Pope Stephen (IX) seems to be related to attacks on Gregory VII in

334. Hugh of Fleury, *Tractatus* (ed. Sackur, MGH Ldl 2.491–492). The decree is lifted from Hugh's *Chronicon*, as already Sackur established and Jasper confirmed (MGH Conc. 8.369).

335. Bernard Jacqueline, 'Yves de Chartres et saint Bernard', *Études d'histoire du droit canonique dédiées à Gabriel Le Bras* (2 vols. Paris 1965) 1.179–184, here at 181.

336. *Panormia* 3.1c (ed. Brett): '[…] sic electus ab omnibus presentibus legatis imperialibus consecretur […]'.

337. JE †2004a / JE †post 2542 as found in *Panormia* 3.1b (ed. Brett). As Hinschius established, the *Panormia* canon is in fact a genuine conciliar decree misattributed to a pope Stephen; it goes back to Ravenna 898 c. 10 (ed. Hartmann, MGH Conc. 5.438). See also Märtl, 'Überlieferung' 40–42, who argued convincingly that the forger probably meant to refer to Stephen IX.—The account on this canon in the third edition of the *Regesta pontificum* is quite confused and should be corrected in the light of the findings of Hinschius and Märtl. According to J³ 7365, the council in canon 10 'confirmed the papal election decree of Stephen IV', although the relevant entries for this pope do not mention such a decree. In addition, J³ †3205 wrongly reports that Ivo (i.e. the *Panormia*) attributed the canon to 'Stephen IV or VI'; this is not the case.

338. *Liber de controversia* (ed. von Heinemann, MGH Ldl 1.465–466).

339. See Bonizo's tract on investiture (ed. Berschin, *Bonizo von Sutri* 76): 'Quamvis falsissimus esse nulli dubium sit sciolo, sunt tamen qui dicunt decretis Romanorum pontificum Sergii et Stephani et Nicolai iunioris hoc regibus esse concessum.' The reference to Stephen and Nicholas fits the combination of JE †post 2542 with the genuine version (as found in *Panormia* 3.1) and even better the imperial version (Märtl, 'Überlieferung' 38–42). Yet Bonizo's reference is too vague to be certain that the forgery really existed as a text (and not only as wishful thinking from pro-imperial polemicists).

particular.[340] Whether the *Panormia* compiler (working a generation after Gregory's death) shared this attitude, is not evident; but he certainly helped to disseminate a provision calling into question the validity of the election of Gregory VII and several of his successors.

If one sees the opening canons of the third book of the *Panormia* as expressions of the ecclesiological and political views of the compiler, the evidence is therefore thoroughly mixed, indeed confusing. On the one hand, the compiler gave prominence to the (genuine) version of the Papal Election Decree, widely seen as a key document for the 'liberty' of the Roman church; at the same time, he combined this text with a forgery which asserted imperial control. However, in the light of the previsous analysis of the *Panormia*'s attitude towards conflicting authorities, another interpretation seems possible. The Papal Election Decree in early twelfth-century France was not at the centre of heated polemics; nor were French scholars mainly concerned with imperial legates present (or not) at papal elections. If, therefore, the *Panormia* combined these texts, different as they were, the reason for this is less to be sought in his desire to take a stance in the debates around these texts. Rather, the tendency observed for other parts of the *Panormia* to deliberately iuxtapose contradicting material may be a better explanation. *Panormia* 3.1 as found in almost all manuscripts may be good example of canon law in need of careful interpretation, and perhaps scholarly debate. Nineteenth- and twentieth-century German scholarship has taken special delight in devoting hundreds of pages to the correct interpretation of the few lines known as *Königsparagraph*;[341] perhaps some of this joy was also shared in the schools of northern France and Normandy, where the *Panormia* circulated widely?

Prohibitions of Investiture and False Investiture Privileges

Another set of controversial materials the *Panormia* helped to disseminate very widely are the so-called False Investiture Privileges.[342] These forgeries may have been conceived as early as the 1080s but only in the early twelfth century did supporters of Henry V make heavy use of them.[343] To indicate the most important contents, Popes Hadrian I and Leo VIII in these privileges seemed to grant Charlemagne and Otto I the title of the *patricius*, the right to nominate the pope, to invest bishops, and also

---

340. Märtl, 'Überlieferung' 40–42.

341. See the 1893 edition (ed. Weiland, MGH Const. 1.540 lines 3–6), now replaced by Jasper's edition (MGH Conc. 8.385–386).

342. JE †post 2406 (the so-called *Hadrianum*); JL †3704 (= *Privilegium minus*), †3705 (= *Privilegium maius*), and †3706 (= *Cessio donationum*), all edited by Claudia Märtl (MGH Fontes iuris 13).

343. Märtl, 'Einleitung' 72–76.

to designate their own successors; in the so-called *Cessio*, Pope Leo additionally seemed to return all imperial donations in Italy to Emperor Otto I and Adelheid. The *Panormia* contained only extracts from these elaborate forgeries (*Panormia* 8.135–136), but these canons contained all the crucial provisions, in particular on the emperor's right to invest bishops.[344]

The relevant canons are not found in all manuscripts, and their place at the end of the collection (rather than book three) makes it plausible that they were an addition, as the *Panormia* in general was often added to. Still, this addition must have been made very early and was widely accepted, as most manuscripts do contain it. Given the nature of these texts, it may also be possible that their absence in some manuscripts results from the omission of the materials. In any case the question is why the False Investiture Privileges were, for the first time, added to a major canon law collection. Were they, as I have argued in the case of canons on papal elections, seen as apt for teaching the law, debating contradictions, and musing on the precise meaning of the Latin? In the case of the False Investiture Privileges, such an explanation seems unconvincing. There was little *contrietas* to discuss on the basis of a *Panormia* containing the False Investiture Privileges. While the Papal Election Decree even in the forged version contained many ambiguities, the False Investiture Privileges are fairly blunt when it comes to imperial rights to invest bishops.[345] Furthermore, the diligent student preparing for the afternoon quodlibetal discussion ('That investiture by the emperor is lawful, and that it is not') would quickly find a straighforward 'sic', but this was not matched by any 'non' in the rest of the *Panormia*. After all, like almost all canonical collections compiled north of the Loire, the *Panormia* did not contain any of the prohibitions of investiture by Gregory VII, Urban II, or Paschal II. Therefore, the addition of the False Investiture Privileges to the *Panormia* did not create a stimulating 'sic et non' dossier on investiture; rather, it added imperial propaganda to an otherwise not very ideological collection.

There is another difference between the 1059 decree in *Panormia* 3 and the False Investiture Privileges. While the former was not at the centre of polemic debate in France around 1100, the question of imperial investiture clearly was. In fact, the polemics of the early twelfth century focussed much more on investiture than the more famous polemics of the time of Gregory VII. By that time, the French church had considerable experience

---

344. *Panormia* 8.135–136 (ed. Brett); see Märtl, 'Überlieferung'. The canons are found in the the overwhelming majority of manuscripts (ibid. 35; and see Brett's apparatus).

345. Ps.-Leo VIII, JL †3704 asserted 'ut ipsi [scil. episcopi] tamen ab eo [scil. imperatore] investituram accipiant et consecrationem recipiant'.

with dealing with the various prohibitions of investiture, and in dozens of episcopal elections the parties involved had found various, sometimes creative ways of either envoking or (more frequently) ignoring them. Nonetheless, the issue remained divisive and could cause conflict whenever royal investiture was either attacked or defendend too vigorously. This is what happened between *ca.* 1107 and 1112, and these events may have influenced the compiler of the *Panormia* directly. When Pope Paschal II visisted France in 1107, negotiations on investiture with King Philip and Emperor Henry V were high on his agenda; in the context of the *Panormia*'s stance on investiture, it may be relevant that the German bishops brought the False Investiture Privileges with them to Châlons-en-Champagne, while Paschal (after negotiations had failed) promulgated new investiture prohibitions at the Council of Troyes.[346] Prelates in northern France will also have known about the conflicts over investiture in England, and of course the high-profile case of the disputed election of Reims (1107–1109).[347] Finally, in 1111 Henry V forced Paschal II to grant him—in the form of the *pravilegium*, as it became known—the right to invest bishops with staff and ring.[348] News of these events caused an outcry, not least in France; criticism of Pope Paschal II was severe, and the danger of a French schism very real.[349] Geoffrey of Vendôme bluntly wrote to the pope that according to the canons, obedience was owed to the pope, even one of doubtful morals; but not if he deviated from the faith.[350] Even Ivo of Chartres, who himself had argued repeatedly that papal prohibitions of lay investiture should be applied with great caution—especially if the elect already had received royal investiture, or had promised to do fealty[351]—suddenly called

346. Blumenthal, *Early Councils*; Märtl, 'Einleitung' 69; Beate Schilling, 'Zur Reise Paschalis' II. nach Norditalien und Frankreich 1106/1107 (mit Itineraranhang und Karte)' *Francia* 28 (2001) 115–158, here at 134–142.

347. Foulon, *Église et réforme* 274–278. Raoul had been supported by Paschal II (against the royal candidate); after the death of his rival and also King Philip, Raoul had come to terms with Louis VI and did homage to him, a solution supported by Ivo and not commented on by the pope.

348. The literature is vast. See Tellenbach, *Church* 277–286 (general) and most recently Blumenthal '1111'.

349. Servatius, *Paschalis II.* 289–291.

350. Geoffrey, *Libellus* (ed. Sackur, MGH Ldl 2.682) 'Tolerandus quidem est pastor, ut canones dicunt, pro reprobis moribus; si vero exorbitaverit a fide, iam non est pastor, sed adversarius, a quolibet peccato tantum catholico detestandus.'

351. Ivo, *Epp.* 60 (royal investiture of Daimbert of Sens in 1097) and 190 (oath of fealty of Raoul le Vert in 1108). Even where Ivo opposed a candidate supported by the king, he chose not to quote any recent prohibitions of investiture against him; see in particular Ivo, *Ep.* 102 (Beauvais). On Ivo's flexibility of quoting, or not, relevant canon law, see Blumenthal '1111' 162–171 and John Stephens Ott, 'Clerical Networks and Canon Law: The Beauvais Election Controversy of 1100–04', *New Discourses in Medieval Canon Law Research: Challenging the Master Narrative*, ed. Christof Rolker (Medieval Law and Its Practice 28; Leiden and Boston 2019) 58–82 esp. 79–80.

those who defended lay investiture 'schismatics'.[352] Like Geoffrey, he added that there were limits to the obedience owed to the pope.[353] In the end, a French schism was avoided, and the Lateran synod of 1112 revoked the *pravilegium*; but the damage was done, and the question of investiture was at the centre of heated polemics, with the False Investiture Privileges adding even more fuel to the fire.

The *Panormia* compiler, working around 1115 in northern France, must have been aware of these events. His decision not to include the prohibitions of investiture can be assumed to have been a conscious choice; he may hav either opposed the prohibitions himself, or seen them as too controversial to be included. Whoever was responsible for adding the False Investiture Privileges to the *Panormia*, he must likewise have been aware that these materials were contentious. Apparently this did not deter him from inserting them, nor most copyists from retaining them; the result was that the *Panormia* made the False Investiture Privileges—otherwise transmitted only in a handful of manuscripts, normally together with documents relating to the events of 1107 to 1122—relatively widely known, both directly and (via Gratian) also indirectly.[354] At some point these canons became, like the curious version of the Papal Election Decree in *Panormia* 3.1, mainly cases to be discussed in classroom. Yet at the point when the *Panormia* became a collection which contained no investiture prohibition but did have the gist of the False Investiture Privileges, this was probably meant (or at least read) as a comment on contemporary church politics. With a grain of salt, the 'improved' *Panormia* version may even be called the only specimen of the 'anti-reform' canonical collections Fournier had postulated.[355] In any case it is clear from the *Panormia* that in northern France around 1115, the investiture prohibitions were still considered too devisive to be accepted as general Church law, while no such reservations seem to have existed in the case of the False Investiture Privileges.

---

352. Ivo, *Ep.* 233 (PL 162.235–236): 'De investituris Ecclesiarum quas laici faciunt, sententiam praecedentium Patrum Gregorii et Urbani, quantum in me est laudo atque confirmo. Quocunque autem nomine talis pervasio proprie vocetur, eorum sententiam qui investituras laicorum defendere volunt, schismaticam judico.' However, not much later he argued again that the prohibitions should only be enforced as far as possible: *Ep.* 236 (ed. Sackur, MGH Ldl 2.654): 'Ubi ergo sine scismate auferri non potest, cum discrete reclamatione differatur.'

353. Ivo, *Ep.* 233 (PL 162.236) 'Si vero [summi pontifices, CR] ea praecipiant quae sint contra doctrinam evangelicam vel apostolicam, ibi eis non esse obediendum exemplo docemur Pauli apostoli [...].'

354. Märtl, 'Einleitung' 96–115; Gratian, D.63 cc.22–23 (ed. Winroth 159–160; ed. Friedberg 241).

355. See *Histoire* 2.121 on collections 'parti des adversaires de la Réforme', although the label hardly fits the collection to which Fournier applied it (the *Farfensis*, on which see Chapter 3.6). For background, see Rolker, 'Fournier's Model' 22 and passim.

5.7.5 Changing the Laws of Marriage: The Case of Kin Marriage in the Twelfth Century

In the twelfth century, ecclesiastical prohibitions on kin marriage extended to the seventh degree in canonical computation, and also extended to an almost equally large number of in-laws and spiritual relatives (and spiritual relatives of in-laws). It was the most excessive set of marriage prohibitions in world history, and no doubt it caused considerable inconvenience for families, but also ecclesiastical courts. Not until 1215, however, were the prohibited degrees reduced to four (and even these still excluded all great-great-grandchildren of any of one's great-great-grandparents as legitimate partners).[356] Yet from the perspective of the twelfth century, the ban on marriages within seven degrees was established law—based on authoritative sources, found in many collections, and used (if somewhat reluctantly) by ecclesiastical courts. From early on, the 'seven degrees' worked in favour of aristocratic families seeking either to escape obligations no longer consistent with their preferences, or occasionally to challenge marriages of a third party, as in the famous Hammerstein case.[357]

The key figure in having brought about this situation was Burchard of Worms; as discussed in Chapter Two, in his *Liber decretorum* he had very carefully presented proof texts not only to make clear that marriages within seven degrees of kinship were prohibited, but that they were a horrible crime, 'incest', an 'abomination'—highly charged terminology. In the eleventh and twelfth centuries, Burchard's proof texts were not only retained but most widely disseminated. At the same time, a change of perspective becomes visible in the collections under discussion in the present chapter. One change, minute at first sight, was the addition of a short excerpt from a well-known source, namely Augustine's *City of God*. The passage first surfaces in Ivo's *Decretum*, but it is only the *Panormia* that placed it prominently at the very beginning of the canons on kin marriage. According to Augustine (as quoted in the *Panormia*), kin marriage was prohibited,[358]

---

356. The extension of the prohibitions has often been studied (see Chapter Two), their reduction less so; see my article 'The Hot and the Cold Language: Incest Discourses in the Twelfth and Thirteenth Centuries', *Proceedings Toronto 2012* MIC Subsidia 15.651–665.

357. See Ubl, *Inzestverbot* on this point in general and the Hammerstein case in particular. For French and English examples, see my 'Kings, Bishops and Incest: Extension and Subversion of the Ecclesiastical Marriage Jurisdiction Around 1100', *Discipline and Diversity: Papers Read at the 2005 Summer Meeting and the 2006 Winter Meeting of the Ecclesiastical History Society*, ed. Kate Cooper and Jeremy Gregory (Studies in Church History 43; Woodbridge 2007) 159–168. Duby, *Knight* famously had claimed that the church wanted to impose these rules on an unwilling aristocracy, but scholarship has given up this model for good reasons; see also Chapter Two (note 188).

358. *Panormia* 7.52 (from Ivo 8.39), taken ultimately from *De civitate Dei* 15.16 (ed. Dombart and Kalb, CCL 48.476–479). The translation is taken from Augustine, *The City of God Against the*

[...] not that one man should combine many relationships in his sole person, but that those relationships should be distributed among individuals, and should bind social life more effectively by involving a greater number of persons in them. Thus, 'father' and 'father-in-law' are the names of two different relationships; and so the ties of affection [*caritas*] extend to a greater number of persons when each has one man as his father and another as his father-in-law.

Of course, when writing these lines, Augustine was mainly thinking about marriage prohibitions of his own time, for example the ban on cousin marriage which was introduced (and later lifted again) in his lifetime.[359] The *Panormia* compiler, however, used the passage to comment on the wide-ranging marriage prohibitions of high medieval canon law. This combination of incest prohibitions as found in Burchard on the one hand and Augustine's comment on the other did not alter the law, but may have influenced the way it was understood. First of all, the tone was markedly different from the accumulation of highly charged terms Burchard saw fit to use in presenting the prohibitions ('abomination', 'incest'), though these still found a place in the *Panormia*. Secondly, and more importantly, while Augustine's argument could indeed be used to justify medieval marriage prohibitions, he also made clear that these prohibitions had been subject to repeated change. Specifically, a passage quoted in the *Panormia* noted that among the first humans kin marriage, even sibling marriage, had actually been 'necessary',[360] and later was prohibited on utilitarian grounds ('so the ties of affection extend to a greater number of persons'). Of course, around 1100 this could be read as justifying existing legislation—but also as stressing their mutability, as 'necessity' and 'utility' in high medieval canon law were the two reasons routinely quoted to justify legal change.[361] Indeed, this interpretation seems to have prevailed, to judge from near-contemporary *sententiae* collections which take up the Augus-

---

Pagans. Translated by Robert W. Dyson (Cambridge Texts in the History of Political Thought; Cambridge 1998), here at 664–665. For earlier uses of this passage, see Ubl, *Inzestverbot* 304–305. Gratian I placed it prominently at the beginning of his relevant *causa* on marriage prohibitions: C.35 q.1 c.1 (ed. Winroth 910–911; ed. Friedberg 1262).

359. The ban is mentioned as 'recent' legislation in *De civitate Dei* 15.16 (ed. Dombart and Kalb, CCL 48.479): 'Verum quis dubitet honestius hoc tempore etiam consobrinorum prohibita esse coniugia?' After the ban (in 385?), cousin marriage was declared legal again in 405 (Cod. 5.4.19).

360. *Panormia* 7.52 (ed. Brett): 'Cum igitur [...] opus haberet ut gignendo multiplicarent, nec essent ulli homines nisi qui ex illis duobus nati fuissent, viri coniuges sorores suas acceperunt. Quod profecto quanto est antiquius compellente necessitate, tanto postea factum est dampnabilius religione prohibente.'

361. The classical example were episcopal translations, prohibited (without exception) by Nicaea, but allowed by medieval canon law according to 'utility and necessity'; for this phrase, see for example JK †90 as quoted in Bonizo 3.66 (ed. Perels 93). For background, see Rolker, 'Kollisionen'.

tinian line of reasoning.[362] According to the *Liber pancrisis*, kin marriage was prohibited only by Church law, not by natural law.[363] Already Honorius Augustodunensis had put it in a similar way: kin marriage was a grave sin according to canon law, but no sin according to nature.[364] For the time being, these were scholarly debates, and it is significant that canon law collections provided the necessary texts but compared to sentence collections reveal less about how these patristic authorities were understood. Yet it is also clear that in the long run stressing the mutability of these rules certainly helped to reduce the excessive prohibitions, as it finally happened in 1215.[365] Peter the Chanter played an important role in this context, and he and his pupils were among those who stressed that marriage prohibitions were man-made rules that could be changed if need be.[366]

5.7.6 Conclusions

The *Panormia* is one of relatively many short versions of the *Decretum* compiled by Ivo of Chartres, but clearly stands out as the most successful of these derivative collections. Even if the Gratians had not used it, the *Panormia* would have had a lasting impact on medieval canon law in its own right, as the very large number of extant manuscripts makes clear. Several factors contributed to its wide diffusion. While the *Panormia* lacks many 'practical' materials—above all, for the administration of penance—its very brevity made it attractive to students who lacked money to copy longer books, and perhaps also the time to read them. More importantly perhaps, the brevity of *individual* canons meant that the *Panormia* presented the diversity of canon law much better than other collections of comparable length. At the same time, scholars and students in particular may

362. See *De coniugio*, ed. Franz Plazidus Bliemetzrieder, 'Paul Fournier und das literarische Werk Ivos von Chartres' AKKR 115 (1935) 53–91, here at 76; *Sententie magistri Petri Abelardi* (ed. Luscombe and Mews, CCCM 14.124); *In primis hominibus*, ed. Bernd Matecki, *Der Traktat In primis hominibus. Eine theologie- und kirchenrechtsgeschichtliche Untersuchung zu einem Ehetext der Schule von Laon aus dem 12. Jahrhundert* (Adnotationes in Ius Canonicum 20; Frankfurt and New York 2001), here at 13*–14*. Bliemetzrieder, working from Troyes, BM, 425 [not seen], claimed that *De coniugio* was part of the *Liber Pancrisis*, but this seems doubtful. For an analysis of the *Liber pancrisis*, see Giraud, *Anselme de Laon* Annexe I.

363. *Liber pancrisis*, no. 67 (ed. Lottin, *Psychologie* 5.58 lines 5–10): 'Lex enim nature non prohibet quamlibet, etiam cognatam, ducere. Lex uero institutionis prohibet. Ideo statutum in Ecclesia catholica ut parentes non commisceantur, quia magna inter eos ex ipsa natura procedit caritas.' See also the *Sententiae Atrebatenses*, no. 15 (ed. Lottin, *Psychologie* 5.436 lines 60–67) for the very same argument.

364. Honorius Augustodunensis, *Elucidarium* 2.16 (PL 176.1146): 'Discipulus: Est grave peccatum, ducere cognatam? Magister: Secundum naturam, nullum, sed secundum statutum Ecclesiae magnum.'

365. Rolker, 'Hot and Cold'.

366. John Wesley Baldwin, *Masters, Princes and Merchants: The Social Views of Peter the Chanter and His Circle* (2 vols. Princeton, N.J. 1970), here at 335–337.

have valued the high share of patristic materials and the occasional 'sic et non' elements, which helped to understand fundamental questions about canon law and its development. The case of Augustine's explanation of marriage prohibition has been quoted above to show how the *Panormia* was able to bridge the gap between practical—or, in this case, rather impractical—canon law on the one hand and theological reasoning on the other; it presented the relevant material law on the prohibited degrees, but also added excerpts from Saint Augustine, which helped readers to see the bigger picture of how these prohibitions were justified at all—and also, whether and how they could be changed. Perhaps the *Panormia* compiler indeed intended his collection as a textbook for teaching canon law; as has been argued above, the prominent presentation of contradicting and partly contentious material on papal elections are probably best understood not as expressions of the compiler's ecclesiology, but his desire to make readers aware of (apparent) inconsistencies in canon law. This is a marked difference to the Italian collections of the late eleventh and early twelfth centuries, where the inclusion or omission of canons on papal elections was often motivated by the compilers' own stance on the issue.

All in all, therefore, it seems justified to interpret the *Panormia* as a product of the schools of the early twelfth century. This does, of course, not mean the *Panormia* was only used by students and masters; any reader interested in a relatively brief, yet remarkably balanced presentation of canon law could make good use of this collection. Nonetheless, both internal evidence and the reception of the *Panormia* suggest that many readers indeed valued it as a textbook. Indeed, as late as the 1490s, a business-minded law professor had several books printed (and advertised them in the study guide he wrote himself), including the *Panormia*.[367]

5.8 The *Caesaraugustana*: The Strange Case of a Pre- and Post-Gratian Canon Law Collection

5.8.1 The *Caesaraugustana* (Overview)

The *Caesaraugustana* is a large anonymous collection from the twelfth century extant in five medieval manuscripts.[368] It takes its name from

367. The *editio princeps* is *Liber decretorum sive Panormia Ivonis* (Basel 1499) [GW M15936] by Sebastian Brant. See Barbara Halporn, 'Sebastian Brandt as an Editor of Juristic Texts' *Gutenberg-Jahrbuch* 59 (1984) 36–51.

368. Kéry 260–262; Fowler-Magerl, *Clavis* 239–244. On the contents see in particular Eloy Tejero, 'El matrimonio en la *Collectio Caesaraugustana*', *Proceedings Cambridge 1984* MIC. Subsidia 8.115–134 and idem, '"Ratio" y jerarquía de fuentes canónicas en la *Caesaraugustana*', *Hispania Christiana: estudios en honor del Prof. Dr. José Orlandis Rovira en su septuagesimo aniversario*, ed. Josep-Ignasi Saranyana and Eloy Tejero (Pamplona 1988) 303–322. The most recent accounts are

Zaragosa ('Caesaraugusta' in Latin), where the manuscript today held at Salamanca was kept when Antonio Agustín analysed the collection for the first time.[369] The *Caesaraugustana* was compiled and later reworked in Catalonia or perhaps Aquitaine; some of its content link it to the reorganisation of the Church on the Iberian Peninsula in the early twelfth century, and its reception seems to be linked to the canons of Saint-Ruf active in the western Mediterrenean.[370] The collection covers a broad range of subjects, from very fundamental questions on the sources of the law to more day-to-day business like penitential tariffs for specific sins, and is particularly rich on sacramental canon law. Partly for this reason, it contains a very large share of patristic canons; roughly one in six *Caesaraugustana* canons is taken from he works of Saint Augustine, for example.

Although the collection has been known to scholarship for a very long time, and has attracted considerable attention from both canon law and Roman law scholars, it remains only imperfectly understood. Fournier's analysis, published a century ago, remains the only study of the whole collection.[371] The present study cannot provide a full analysis of the collection, which is urgently needed; it can only make a modest contribution to facilitate such an analysis. As Blumenthal put it:[372] 'In the light of the formidable, well-known difficulties in dealing with the oldest version of the *Caesaraugustana*, even a small step forward might assist future research.'

5.8.2 'Ratio et auctoritas': The *Caesaraugustana* on the Sources of the Law

The *Caesaraugustana* in many respects is a typical 'systematic' pre-Gratian collection, with material divided into books roughly according to subject matter, and a penitential book at the very end. Clearly the most unusual

---

Uta-Renate Blumenthal, 'The *Collectio canonum Caesaraugustana* and Roman Legal Sources', *Canon Law, Religion and Politics: Liber amicorum Robert Somerville*, ed. Uta-Renate Blumenthal et al. (Washington, D.C. 2012) 15–27 and Linda Fowler-Magerl, 'Caesaraugustana', *Diccionario general de derecho canónico*, ed. Javier Otaduy et al. (7 vols. Cizur Menor 2012) 1.787–789. The three doctoral theses mentioned by Fowler-Magerl (ibid. 788) were not available to me.

369. See Antonio Agustín, *Dialogorum libri duo de emendatione Gratiani* (Paris 1607), here at 35: 'In libro Caesaraugustano Cartusianorum, qui Hieronymi Zuritae fuit [...]' and passim (as 'Caesar. lib.'). See Marcos Rodríguez, 'Tres manuscritos' 35–36 for identification with Salamanca, BU, 2644. Note that the copy he refers to as 'actualmente en la Vaticana con el n.° 535' (ibid. 36 n. 2) is in fact Barb. lat. 897, and the 'Barberini' he quotes are of course the *Ballerini* brothers, here at PL 56.352 (in the reprint). Contrary to what Rodríguez suggests, the references in Agustín, *Dialogi* 39 and 119 (on Gratian C.31 q.2 c.3 and C.25 q.1 c.5, respectively) are not specific enough to demonstrate that Agustín knew the Salamanca manuscript. In my opinion, the crucial evidence comes first from Zurita's ownership and second from the way Agústin quotes the *Caesaraugustana* by book and canon numbers; his '2.35', for example, is CA02.035 in *Clavis*.

370. Fowler-Magerl, 'Version' 273–274 (JK †446 and JE 2765), 275, and 277.

371. Paul Fournier, 'La collection canonique dite *Caesaraugustana*' NRHDFE 45 (1921) 53–79.

372. Blumenthal, 'Caesaraugustana' 15.

part of the collection are the openings sections. While the first book of many collections deals with ecclesiastical hierarchy (Burchard, Anselm), and some begin with the sacraments (Bonizo, Ivo), the *Caesaraugustana*—in all versions discussed here—begins with a series of more than 100 canons on the sources of the law.[373]

The *Caesaraugustana* was not the first collection to contain canons addressing the question of the sources of the law. Abbo of Fleury, for one, had distinguished different kinds of law—human and divine, customary and statuary, and so on—in his collection, Ivo of Chartres had assembled a great mass of relevant material too, and Gregory of San Grisogono had composed short, well-structured sections dealing with the sources of canon law. However, no collection before the *Caesaraugustana I* contained such a well-composed selection of relevant material, and none had placed it so prominently; only Gratian's tract *De legibus* is comparable to the *Caesaraugustana* in this respect.[374] As these opening sections do not contain any comment, the texts should not be read as expressions of the compiler's view on the sources of the law. Nonetheless, it is clear that the 100-odd canons at the beginning of the collection are the result of careful reading and laborious composition.

Let us therefore study this opening section in some detail. The *Caesaraugustana*, perhaps inspired by a sub-section of the *Polycarpus*,[375] begins with excerpts taken from Augustine's philosophical writings on the relation of 'reason and authority'.[376] For Augustine, this formula mainly referred to the question of human rational thinking, on the one hand, and God's revelation on the other. According to him, both eventually led to the faith, but especially in his Cassiciacum dialogues—*Contra academicos, De beata vita, De ordine,* and *Soliloquia*—he often displayed a strong belief in the special role of reason. This certainly holds for the passage that became the very first canon of the *Caesaraugustana*:[377]

373. In **S** (and only in **S**), the material is split between the first two books (= *Caes.* 1.1–64 and 2.1–54 in **S**); there is no real break in the content.

374. Jean Gaudemet, 'La doctrine des sources du droit dans le Décret de Gratien' *Revue de Droit canonique* 1 (1950) 5–31, here at 9. See also Tejero, 'Matrimonio' 124 for effects of these 'theoretical' canons on the material law, in this case marriage.

375. *Caes.* 1.1–5 = *Polycarpus* 1.27.4–6, 10, and 11 (ed. Erdmann and Horst 153–155, 159, and 160).

376. Gaudemet, 'Doctrine' 9; Roque Losada Cosme, 'La teoría de las fuentes del Derecho eclesiástico en la renascencia jurídica de principios del siglo XII' *Revista española de derecho canónico* 15 (1960) 317–372, here at 335–336; Tejero, 'Ratio y jeraquía'.

377. *Caes.* 1.1 (**R**, fol. 3r; **S**, fol. 1ra–rb): 'De ratione et auctoritate et que cui preponenda sit. Augustinus in secundo libro de ordine. Ad discendum dupliciter ducimur, auctoritate atque ratione. Tempore auctoritas, re autem ratio prior est. Aliud est enim quod in agendo [agnicio **S**] anteponitur, aliud quod in appetendo estimatur. Ita quamquam bonorum auctoritas imperite multitudini videatur esse salubrior, ratio tamen aptior [om. **S**] eruditis est [om. **S**] [...]. Quam quisque ingressus sine ulla dubitatione vite optime precepta sectatur [sectantur **S**], per que [quam **S**],

> We are necessarily led to learn in two ways, by authority and by reason. Chronologically, authority comes first; in matter, reason has priority. [...] The authority of virtuous men may be a better guide for the unlearned multitude; but for the educated, reason is more fitting. [...] Authority alone opens the door; whoever enters by it, and follows without hesitation the precepts for a life of perfection, and has been made receptive by them, then at length will learn how much reason is found in these precepts which he had followed before understanding them, and also what is reason, which he now—having left the cradle of authority, being strong and capable—both follows and understands, and finally also what intellect is, in which all things are.

Augustine had written these lines at Cassiciacum not long after his conversion in 386. Here as elsewhere, he contemplated the role of rational thinking in relation to 'authority' in a very wide sense, be it the Bible, the teaching of the Church, the example of the saints, or simply venerable Christians preaching their faith. In the context of a medieval canon law collection, the formula of 'reason and authority' must have had a different meaning for most readers. An early twelfth-century reader would probably have felt reminded of the ongoing discussion about faith, reason, and exegetical methods in the emerging discipline of theology in general, and perhaps the Eucharist debate in particular.[378] After all, the Eucharist debate started by Berengar of Tours around 1050 and continuing well into the twelfth century was an important stimulus for the emerging disciplines of theology and canon law alike, and canonical collections are an important transmission of the relevant texts. The excerpt from Augustine on 'reason and authority' may well have be an example of how 'theological' proof texts from the Berengar debate were taken into canon law. Indeed, Berengar himself was a prominent reader of the very Augustinian dialogue from which the *Caesaraugustana* took its opening canon.[379] More legally-minded readers may well have understood 'authority' as referring

---

cum docibilis factus fuerit, tum demum discet, et quanta ratione predicta [*sic*] sunt ea ipsa, que secutus est ante rationem, et que sit ipsa [ipsa sit **S**] ratio, quam post auctoritatis cunabula firmus et idoneus iam sequitur atque comprehendit, et quid intellectus, in quo universa sunt.' For the translation, I have corrected 'predicta' to 'predita' from Augustine, *De ordine* 2.9.26, ed. Therese Fuhrer in *Augustinus, Contra Academicos, De beata vita, De ordine*, ed. eadem and Simone Adam (Bibliotheca Teubneriana 2022; Berlin and Boston 2017), here at 162. The *fons formalis* is *Polycarpus* 1.27.4 (ed. Erdmann and Horst 153); this explains some of the difficulties of the Latin. **R** is clearly closer to the text of the *Polycarpus* (and Augustine) than **S**. Vat. lat. 4976, fol. 3r shares all variants with **S**, but has 'agnitione' for the corrupt 'agnicio'. The text is also found before the collection proper in **S**, fols. Iv–IIr with the very same variant readings as fol. Ir (only that it has 'sectatur' as **R**, not 'sectantur').

378. Tejero, 'Ratio y jeraquía' 307–308.

379. André Cantin, 'Bérenger, lecteur du *De ordine* de saint Augustin, ou comment se préparait, au milieu du XIe siècle, une domination de la *ratio* sur la science sacrée', *Auctoritas und ratio. Studien zu Berengar von Tours*, ed. Peter Felix Ganz et al. (Wolfenbütteler Mittelalter-Studien 2; Wiesbaden 1990) 89–107.

to the canons contained in the *Caesaraugustana*,[380] and 'reason' as the intellectual capacities needed to make sense of these inherited normative traditions. The placement at the very beginning of the collection, and also the rubric highlighting 'reason and authority', clearly made such a reading of the canon very likely, and one may indeed assume that this was why the anonymous compiler chose this text as his opening canon.

The canons that follow are also taken from the writings of Augustine (*De ordine*, *De doctrina christiana*, *De civitate Dei*, and other works); they all deal at a very abstract level with the role of human reasoning in understanding sacred scripture (*Caes.* 1.2–12). As in the case of the opening canon, twelfth-century readers of the *Caesaraugustana* may well have understood these texts as if Augustine had written on canon law rather than exegesis. For example, Augustine asserted that the authority of scripture was above that of even the most learned exegetes; the relevant excerpts in the *Caesaraugustana* could still be read this way, but the rubrics used a terminology (*canonica scriptura*) that could well be understood to refer to canon law.[381]

After this almost philosophical opening, the *Caesaraugustana* next gathers a number of canons on the role of custom; after a basic definition (*Caes.* 1.13, taken from Isidore's *Etymologies*), it brings together excerpts from decretals, patristic writings, and Roman law on the relation between custom and other sources of the law.[382] For example, as the *Caesaraugustana* quoted from the Institutes, longstanding custom could acquire force of law, provided it was not 'against reason or written law', as the next canon asserted (*Caes.* 1.25–26).[383] Also, the *Caesaraugustana* contains an assertion by Nicholas I that 'apostolic authority was above custom' (*Caes.* 1.21).[384] Nonetheless, as the *Caesaraugustana* quoted from the Digest, custom could help to understand written law.[385] These canons come from

380. For 'auctoritas' in the sense of 'canon', see prominently Gratian D.1 d.p.c.1 (ed. Winroth 1; ed. Friedberg 1), referring to the opening canon of his *Decretum*: 'Ex verbis huius auctoritatis evidenter datur intelligi, in quo differant inter se lex divina vel humana [. . .].' See also Du Cange s.v. auctoritas.

381. See the rubrics to *Caes.* I 1.6 ('Quod canonica scriptura quasi diuina sint oracula et disputationes doctorum non eis comparanda sint') and 10 ('Quod canonica dicta preualeant dictis doctorum').

382. See Peter Leisching, '*Consuetudo* und *ratio* im Dekret und in der Panormia des Bischofs Ivo von Chartres' ZRG Kan. Abt. 74 (1988) 535–542; many of Ivo's proof texts discussed by Leisching are also found in the *Caesaraugustana*.

383. See the rubrics to *Caes.* I 1.25 ('Quod diuturni mores legem imitantur') and 26 ('Pro lege habenda est que non est contra legem et rationem consuetudo').

384. *Caes.* I 1.21: 'Quod apostolica auctoritas preponenda sit consuetudini.' This rubric is only found in *Caesaraugustana*, not its formal sources (*Tripartita* A1.64.14 or Ivo 4.211). The material source is Nicholas I, JE 2691.

385. *Caes.* I 1.28 (**R**, fol. 4v): 'Quod legis interpres sit consuetudo. Si de interpretatione legis

very divergent backgrounds, use dissimilar terminology (*consuetudo, mos, usus, traditiones*), and may not necessarily form a coherent legal doctrine; however, compared to other canonical collections it is striking to see how much attention the relation between custom and other sources of the law is given in the *Caesaraugustana*. These texts may have been interesting for legal scholars, but they certainly addressed very practical problems too. After all, despite the impressive body of written canon law, medieval church life was governed more by custom than by positive law.[386] Yet urgent as this issue was, it was rarely addressed by canonical collections; the prefaces are notably silent on this issue. The *Caesaraugustana* compiler, for his part, turned to a variety of sources to extract short but useful canons which addressed a variety of possible conflicts between written and customary Church law (*Caes.*1.13–28).

Having started with 'reason', and dealt with custom as an important source of canon law, the *Caesaraugustana* compiler continued with written canon law (*Caes.* 1.29–57). While some canons stress—uncontroversially enough—the authority of papal decretals or the 'incomparable' authority of Nicaea I, many of these canons touch upon complicated, sometimes delicate questions: the partial rejection of Chalcedon by Gelasius I (*Caes.* 1.35), the bumpy reception of Nicaea II in the West (*Caes.* 1.39, 41), and Pope Sergius's opposition to the Quinisextum (*Caes.* 1.46). Interestingly, the *Caesaraugustana* has a truncated version of Bede's list of six general synods (*Caes.* 1.46), but not the *Sancta octo* list found in *Tripartita* A and Ivo. Also, there are canons from (and on) the first seven synods, but no canon is said to be taken from the eighth synod; the only reference to the eighth synod in the whole collection is the condemnation of Constantinople IV by Pope John VIII (*Caes.* 2.29). Given that the *Caesaraugustana I* compiler made intense use of the Ivonian collections which contain *Sancta octo*, canons of Constaninople IV, and other material relating to the Photian affair, this lacuna may well reflect conscious omission. Arguments from silence always are speculative to some degree, but it may indeed be the case that the *Caesaraugustana* compiler did not accept Constantinople IV as a general synod, and for this reason retained none of the documents referring to this synod, except for the letter of John VIII condemning it.

There is no clear break in the collection, but after three canons on ec-

---

quaeritur, inprimis inspiciendum est, quo iure ciuitas retro in eis modo casibus usa fuisset: optima est enim legum interpres consuetudo.' The material source is Dig. 1.3.37; the excerpt is not found in the *Britanna* or the Ivonian collections.

386. Udo Wolter, 'Die "consuetudo" im kanonischen Recht bis zum Ende des 13. Jahrhunderts', *Gewohnheitsrecht und Rechtsgewohnheit im Mittelalter* (Schriften zur Europäischen Rechts- und Verfassungsgeschichte 6; Berlin 1992) 87–116.

clesiastical law in general (*Caes.* 1.55–57) a new topic seems to govern the selection of canons, namely, the relation between imperial legislation and canon law (*Caes.* 1.58–2.2). This includes a canon which according to Blumenthal may have been a source of the *Exceptiones Petri*.[387] Like Deusdedit, the *Caesaraugustana I* compiler turned to Roman law to assert the special authority of canon law.[388] The next canons are relatively conventional material on canonical scripture in the widest sense (*Caes.* 2.3–12), including the catalogues of authorities of Pseudo-Innocent (JK †320), the *Decretum Gelasianum*, and Leo IV (JE 2599).

After this, the *Caesaraugustana* returns again to the issue of conflicting canons, and specifically the possibility of conciliar legislation being abrogated. This includes a short excerpt from the *Decretum Gelasianum* condemning the synod of Rimini 359 (*Caes.* 2.22), Gregory I rejecting Cassiodore's *Historia tripartita* (*Caes.* 2.23),[389] the 'condemnation of Ephesus I' by Chalcedon (*Caes.* 2.24), and John VIII rescinding Constantinople IV (*Caes.* 2.29). The canons, mostly taken from much longer excerpts in Ivo, clearly focus on conciliar legislation being rescinded, and the rubrics highlight this aspect too. It is less certain how much the compiler knew much about the conflicts that gave rise to the cases he quoted. Perhaps Roman opposition to Chalcedon 451 and its 'canon' 28 still (or again) was an issue in the high Middle Ages, but the sixth-century debates on the Three Chapters (Rimini 359, Cassiodore) probably were quite obscure to many twelfth-century readers. As for Constantinople IV, the John VIII fragment in the *Caesaraugustana* was difficult to understand without context. Also, as has been discussed above (in the context of *Tripartita* A2.14), there was

387. *Caes. I* 1.62, taken from Cod. 1.14.9, 'a unique passage not found in other collections' (Blumenthal, 'Caesaraugustana' 17). As already Conrat (Cohn), *Geschichte* 390 n. 11 noted, it is also contained in the *Exceptiones Petri* 1.1; possibly taken from *Caesaraugustana* (Blumenthal, 'Caesaraugustana' 17; eadem, 'Dating the Exceptiones Petri' ZRG Kan. Abt. 101 [2015] 54–85, here at 63). For an edition, see *Scritti giuridici preirneriani*, ed. Carlo Guido Mor (2 vols. Orbis Romanus. Biblioteca di testi medievali 10; Milan 1935/38) 2.47–206, here at 52. Note that in both *Caes. I* manuscripts (**R**, fol. 6v; **S**, fol. 6ra) the inscription reads '[…] ad Palladium pp', not 'ep' as found in the *Clavis* database. The abbreviation 'pp' (for 'prefecto pretorio') was later understood as 'papam' (Blumenthal, 'Dating' 63).

388. *Caes. I* 2.1a (**R**, fol. 6v; **S**, fol. 6vb): 'Canones patrum uim legum habere oportet'. The material source is *Epitome Juliani*, const. 6, cap. 1 (ed. Hänel 29). Deusdedit 4.288 (161) (ed. Wolf von Glanvell 553) is a possible formal source. In **S**, but less so in **R**, the sentence is merged with the following canon.

389. *Caes. I* 2.23 (**R**, fol. 8v; **S**, fol. 8va). Note that *Caesaraugustana* has the correct inscription 'Gregorius Eulogio episcopo Alexandrino' while the inscription in the Arsenal collection (Paris, Bibliothèque de l'Arsenal, 713, fol. 136v) does not mention Gregory: 'Eul(o)g(io) Alexandrino'. In Ivo 4.81 this became 'Fulg' Alexandrino' (Brett's manuscripts **CVP**), 'Fulgentius Alexandrino' (**B**), or even 'Fulgentius Alexandro' (**R**). Note also that the rubric in *Caesaraugustana* correctly identifies the work in question as the *Historia tripartita* where the canon only mentions Sozomen. This may indicate knowledge of the material source (Gregory I, JE 1477).

considerable confusion in Latin canon law concerning Constaninople IV. While it ultimately remains obscure to which degree the *Caesaraugustana I* compiler was able to put these canons into context, the canon on the 'condemnation of Ephesus I' at Chalcedon (as the rubric runs) strongly suggests that he was familiar neither with Ephesus I nor with Chalcedon. From his own collection he could have known that Ephesus I was counted among the general councils,[390] and neither subsequent councils nor popes had questioned the validity of its enactments. The canon in question indeed ultimately goes back to the acts of the council of Chalcedon; but the text as found in the *Caesaraugustana* gives a very distorted impression of what was going on at the council. Crucially, Chalcedon had rescinded the *second* council of Ephesus of 449—the one dubbed 'Robber Council' by Leo I (JK 475)—not the first council of Ephesus held in 431. The other events the canon alludes to—the deposition of Domnus of Antioch by Ephesus II and the acceptance of Maximus as his successor by Leo I—likewise are misrepresented in the canon as found in the *Caesaraugustana*.

Unfortunately, the textual history of the canon, as far as it is known, does not solve this puzzle. The canon found in *Caesaraugustana* is taken from Ivo's *Decretum*, which essentially has the same text; *Arsenal I* has a slightly better text.[391] Yet already in *Arsenal I* the canon seems to assert that Chalcedon rescinded Ephesus I.[392] The textual history of the canon before *Arsenal I* is obscure; it is clearly not taken from the *versio Rustici* of the acts of Chalcedon;[393] it has none of the Pseudo-Isidorian interpolations found in the *Excerptiones e concilio Chalcedonensi*.[394] As the Greek and the Latin

---

390. *Caes. I* 1.45 (CA01.045, here checked against **R**, fol. 6r; **S**, fols. 4vb–5ra; **B**, fol. 3v), ultimately taken from Bede, *De temporum ratione* (ed. Jones, CCL 123B.528) via Ivo 4.125. As Brett's edition reveals, most manuscripts of Ivo lack the reference to Ephesus I, but in two the gap is emended; one (Brett's **C**) does so by adding Bede's text in the margin, while the other (Vat. lat. 1357, fol. 63vb; Brett's **V**) inserts a different version in the main text: 'Tercia Efesina prima in qua Nestorii impietas adnullatur.' *Caes.* 1.45 has almost exactly the same text: 'Tertia prima Ephesena [Ephesina **SB**] in qua Nestorii impietas condempnatur.' The phrase almost certainly is lifted from Gregory I, JE 1092 (Ivo 4.117; *Caes.* 1.36); the parallel occurrence suggests a link between *Caesaraugustana* and Vat. lat. 1357 even if the former does not normally share the readings of the latter.

391. Ivo 1.148 (ed. Brett); Bibliothèque de l'Arsenal 713, fol. 142v. Note in particular that *Arsenal I* begins a new sentence with 'praeter ea' where the other manuscripts of Ivo's *Decretum* have 'praeterea', and also Arsenal's 'recepta est', referring to 'ordinatio', which is closer to the Greek acts than the 'recepta sunt' of the other *Decretum* manuscripts; see also the next note.

392. Bibliothèque de l'Arsenal 713, fol. 142v: 'Stephan<us> episcopus Ephesi dixit: Illa que in Ephesina sinodo prima acta sunt irrita fiant, praeter ea que contra Donnum Antiocenum facta sunt.'

393. See Chalcedon, actio X (XI), 144 and 149, *Versio Rustici* (ed. Schwartz, ACO 2.3:3, pp. 46–47); tr. Price and Gaddis, *Chalcedon* 2.303–304.

394. *Spicilegium Solesmense, complectens sanctorum patrum scriptorumque ecclesiasticorum anecdota hactenus opera, selecta e graecis orientalibusque et latinis codicibus*, ed. Jean Baptiste Pitra (4 vols. Paris 1852–58), here at 4.175–176 no. 169. See Schon, 'Exzerpte' and Zechiel-Eckes, 'Verecundus' 440.

version differ in the numbering of the sessions, it may be significant that Ivo's *Decretum* ('actio XI') gives the session number as found in the Greek acts, not the *versio antiqua* or the *versio Rustici*.[395] This is indicative of the complex transmission and reception of some of the Greek councils, and only adds to the impression that the *Caesaraugustana* compiler was perhaps not fully aware of the background of the canons he gathered into his opening section on the sources of the law. However, the way he selected and arranged his material nonetheless leaves no doubt that he followed a specific plan; he evidently was looking for proof texts on the abrogation of conciliar legislation. The fact that he inserted a canon on the 'condemnation of Ephesus I' should therefore not be read as an expression of his opposition to the council Ephesus, but rather as a sign of his interests in the possibility that conciliar legislation could be rescinded by later synods. By the same token, the rare John VIII canon revoking Constantinople IV (*Caes.* 2.29) may have been interesting as a proof text for conflicts between papal and conciliar legislation, quite independent of the actual decrees of Constantinople IV, which the compiler may have known little about.

5.8.3 Versions and Manuscripts

There are five medieval copies of the *Caesaraugustana*, plus excerpts in another medieval manuscript, and two early modern copies. In addition, the collection known as *Mare vitreum* occasionally has been referred to as a version of the *Caesaraugustana* as it draws heavily on it.[396] The accounts of the *Caesaraugustana* manuscripts in the scholarly literature can be confusing. To begin with, Roman law and canon law scholars normally have different versions of the collection in mind when they speak about the *Caesaraugustana*, simply because they used different manuscripts. Roman law scholars normally used a medieval copy of a relatively late version (Paris, BnF, lat. 3876; my **B**) as their base manuscript. Canon law scholarship, in contrast, was frequently based on an early modern copy (Barb. lat. 897) of an earlier version of the *Caesaraugustana* as found in Salamanca, BU, 2644 (my **S**). Some of the most influential accounts of the *Caesaraugustana* are based largely on the Barberini manuscript (Agustín, Ballerini, Fournier); indeed, many scholars knew the *Caesaraugustana* exclusively from this copy (Theiner, Friedberg [via Theiner], Fuhrmann, Tejero).

Some of the confusion stems from changing scholarly consensus on

---

395. For the Greek acts, see Chalcedon, actio XI, 144 and 149 (ed. Schwartz, ACO 2.3:1, p. 38 lines 6–14 and 32–37).

396. The *Mare vitreum* is extant in Napoli, BN Vittorio Emanuele III, XII. A. 27 (*male* 'XII. A. 23'; *olim* Museo Borbonico, 334. VI. 9. 36; not seen). For a brief description, see below.

the versions of the *Caesaraugustana*. Roman law scholars since the nineteenth century distinguished two versions of the collection;[397] more recent scholarship refers to two, three, or even four recensions, with considerable variation on which manuscripts are assigned to which version. Partly this represents genuine disagreement and uncertainty about the relation between the manuscripts, but partly also to the fate of individual manuscripts and an unusually high rate of misguided references in the literature. Specifically, a key manuscript of the *Caesaraugustana* (**S**) was first found in Zaragosa, copied, forgotten, rediscovered in Madrid, again forgotten, only to be discovered yet again in its present home in Salamanca.[398] To add to this confusion, both the Salamanca manuscript and an early modern copy of it—the Barberini manuscript just mentioned—were quoted more often than not by wrong shelfmarks.

To facilitate comparison of existing accounts, I therefore provide a table of the most important classifications of the *Caesaraugustana* manuscripts in chronologiccal order (Table 8) before discussing the *Caesaraugustana* versions.

As this overview helps to demonstrate, hardly any two accounts of the *Caesaraugustana* in the literature agree in all details. However, as the table also shows, some of the differences in the literature are only due to wrong shelfmarks ('BnF, lat. 3756', 'Salamanca, BU, 2664', 'Vat. lat. 535', 'Vat. lat. 3875'), the change of shelfmarks and/or relocalisation of manuscripts (Barb. lat. 897, Salamanca, BU, 2644), and the decision to include or omit early modern copies (Barb. lat. 897, Vat. lat. 4976) and fragments (Salamanca, BU, 81). The classification of Barb. lat. 897 sometimes as a manuscript of the first version, sometimes of the second—sometimes even of both!—can also be ignored; it is an early modern copy of Salamanca, BU, 2644 and should be classified accordingly.

Yet some points of difference are more substantial. First, should Paris, BnF, lat. 3875 and Salamanca, BU, 2644 be treated as representing the first version of the collection, as was the consensus in the pre-1956 literature, or as two distinct versions? Scholars taking the second position are divided over which of the two represents the earlier version; Kuttner, Brett, and Somerville have followed Gassó and Batlle in their suggestion that BnF

---

397. Conrat (Cohn), *Geschichte* 391 (**B** containing *Caesaraugustana* 'bereits in interpoliertem Zustande'); Federico Patetta, 'Per la storia del diritto romano nel medio evo: a proposito dell'opera di M. Conrat, Geschichte der Quellen und Literatur des römischen Rechts im frühen Mittelalter, 1. Band 1891' *Rivista italiana per le scienze giuridiche* 12 (1891) 307–331, here at 317 (**B** as 'rifacimento della colleczione'). This was followed e.g. by Perels, 'Briefe' 115–116 and Fournier, 'Caesaraugustana'.

398. Kuttner, 'Roman Manuscripts' 23.

Table 8: Accounts on Caesaraugustana Manuscripts

Source	First version	Second version	Third version / Comment
Friedberg LXXI	• Paris, BnF, lat. 3775 [*recte* 3875] • Paris, BnF, lat. 3876 • Barb. 286 [*recte* 2864 = Barb. lat. 897]		• [Friedberg did not distinguish different versions.]
• Schulte, *Kirchenrecht* 1.315	• Barb. 2864 [= Barb. lat. 897] • Paris, BnF, lat. 3875 • Paris, BnF, lat. 3876 • Vat. lat. 1354		[Schulte did not distinguish different versions.]
Fournier, 'Caesaraugustana' and *Histoire* 2.269–270	• Vat. lat. 535 [*recte* Barb. lat. 897] • Vat. lat. 4976 • Paris, BnF, lat. 3875 ('improved') • 'Madrid, BN' [= Salamanca, BU, 2644]	• Paris, BnF, lat. 3876 • Vat. lat. 5715	[Fournier distinguished only two versions.]
Gassó / Batlle, 'Prolegomena' XXXV–XXXIX and LXII–LXIII	• Paris, BnF, lat. 3875 ('antiquiora, forte primigenia recensio')	• Salamanca, BU, 2644 • Barcelona, ACA, San Cugat 63 ('praebet textum alterae, immo forte tertiae, recensionis')	• Paris, BnF, lat. 3876 • Vat. lat. 5715
Fowler-Magerl, 'Vier Kanonessammlungen' 144–145, followed by Gouron, 'Origins' 343	• Salamanca, BU, 2664 [*recte* 2644]	• Paris, BnF, lat. 3756 [*recte* 3876] • Vat. lat. 5715 • Barcelona, ACA, San Cugat 63	[Fowler-Magerl in 1982 distinguished only two versions.]
Kuttner / Hartmann, 'New Version' 26 n. 14 and 27–28, followed by Dolezalek / Bertram, *Catalogue*	• Paris, BnF, lat. 3875	• Salamanca, BU, 2644 • Vat. lat. 4976 • Barb. lat. 897 • Barcelona, ACA, 63: 'reorganized copy of the 3rd (or 2nd?) recension'	• Paris, BnF, lat. 3876 • Vat. lat. 5715
Beulertz, *Verbot* 10	• Barb. lat. 897 • Vat. lat. 3875 [*recte* Paris, BnF, lat. 3875]	• Paris, BnF, lat. 3876 • Vat. lat. 5715	[Beulertz distinguished only two versions.]
Martin, *Compilatio*	• Salamanca, BU, 2644	• Paris, BnF, lat. 3876	[Martin distinguished only two versions]

(*table continues*)

<table>
<tr>
<th>Source</th>
<th>First version</th>
<th>Second version</th>
<th>Third version / Comment</th>
</tr>
<tr>
<td>Brett 'Sources' 160–161</td>
<td>• Paris, BnF, lat. 3875 (Ripoll; 'may well preserve the original shape [...] most faithfully')
• Salamanca, BU, 81 ('frequently agrees with Ripoll against Paris, BN lat. 3876 and Salamanca UL 2644')</td>
<td colspan="2">'Second version' and 'later manuscripts':
• Barcelona, ACA, San Cugat 63
• Salamanca, BU, 2644
• Napoli, BN, VI. 9.36 ('described by Fowler-Magerl' [*recte* Theiner, *Disquisitiones criticae* 360–363])
• Paris, BnF, lat. 3876 ('second version')
• Vat. lat. 4976
• Barb. lat. 897
• Vat. lat. 5715 ('second version')</td>
</tr>
<tr>
<td rowspan="2">• Somerville, *Urban II* 196–197</td>
<td rowspan="2">• Paris, BnF, lat. 3875</td>
<td>• Salamanca, BU, 2644</td>
<td>• Paris, BnF, lat. 3876
• Vat. lat. 5715</td>
</tr>
<tr>
<td colspan="2">• Barcelona, ACA, San Cugat 63 ('reorganized copy')</td>
</tr>
<tr>
<td>• Kéry 260–261</td>
<td>• 'Madrid, BN' [= Salamanca, BU, 2644]
• Paris, BnF, lat. 3875
• Salamanca, BU, 81
• Vat. lat. 535 ('wrong shelfmark by Fournier [...] cf. Barb. lat. 897')
• Vat. lat. 4976</td>
<td>• Paris, BnF, lat. 3876
• Salamanca, BU, 2664 [*recte* 2644]
• Barb. lat. 897
• Vat. lat. 5715</td>
<td>• Barcelona, ACA, San Cugat 63</td>
</tr>
<tr>
<td>• Fowler-Magerl, *Clavis canonum* 240–244; eadem, 'Caesaraugustana' 788</td>
<td>• Salamanca, BU, 2664 [*recte* 2644] (her **CA**)
• Paris, BnF, lat. 3875 (her **CP**; not in database)
• Barb. lat. 897 [*sic!*] ('copía tardía de la primera versión')
• Vat. lat. 4976
• Salamanca, BU, 81</td>
<td>• Paris, BnF, lat. 3876 (her **CB**) 'y en dos copias de este manuscrito', namely
• Barb. lat. 897 and
• Vat. lat. 5715</td>
<td>• Barcelona, ACA, San Cugat 63 (her **CD**; 'third version', 'augmented version of the second version', 'tercera recensión')</td>
</tr>
<tr>
<td>• Fowler-Magerl, 'Version' 269</td>
<td>• Salamanca, BU, 2644</td>
<td>• Paris, BnF, lat. 3875</td>
<td>• Paris, BnF, lat. 3876
• Vat. lat. 5715
         • Barcelona, ACA, San Cugat 63</td>
</tr>
<tr>
<td>• Blumenthal, 'Caesaraugustana'</td>
<td>• Salamanca, BU, 2644
• Paris, BnF, lat. 3875</td>
<td>• Paris, BnF, lat. 3876
• Vat. lat. 5715</td>
<td>• Barcelona, ACA, San Cugat 63</td>
</tr>
<tr>
<td>• Schilling, 'Kanones'</td>
<td>• Salamanca, BU, 2664 [*recte* 2644]</td>
<td>• Paris, BnF, lat. 3876
• Barb. lat. 897
• Vat. lat. 5715</td>
<td>• Barcelona, ACA, San Cugat 63</td>
</tr>
</table>

lat. 3875 was the sole copy of the first version, while Fowler-Magerl held that Salamanca, BU, 2644 was more ancient. Another question concerns the status of the Barcelona copy from San Cugat, unknown to Fournier and not firmly classified as belonging to any specific version by Gassó and Batlle. It is generally accepted as a distinct version of the *Caesaraugustana*, but scholars normally hesitate to label it the 'third' (or 'fourth') version because it shares characteristics both with **S** and **B**, placing it somewhere between the versions these codices represent.[399]

Based on previous scholarship—above all the studies of Fournier, Fowler-Magerl, and Brett—and my own analysis of Paris, BnF lat. 3875 (**R**) and 3876 (**B**), Salamanca, BU, 2644 (**S**), and Vat. lat. 5715 (**V**), I propose the following model: The first version of the *Caesaraugustana* is found in **R** and **S**, with **R** clearly being closer to the lost archetype; the closely related manuscripts **B** and **V** form the second version; and the version in Barcelona, ACA, San Cugat 63 (**C**) is a separate version which I will refer to as the 'third version'. The labels for the second and third versions are mainly conventional; they are not meant to imply that the 'third' version was based on the 'second', and not even that the 'third' version emerged only after the second was completed. In fact, *Caesaraugustana II* contains more recent materials than *Caesaraugustana III* does and is extant in manuscripts which may well be later than the sole copy of the third version. The first version, however, clearly is earlier than any other version. As for the early modern copies—Barb. lat. 897 and Vat. lat. 4976—I have no reason to doubt that they are indeed copies of **S**; yet closer examination of these manuscripts may well bring about more surprises.

5.8.4 The First Version of the *Caesaraugustana*

The Manuscripts **R** and **S**

The first version of the *Caesaraugustana* is found in Paris, BnF, lat. 3875 from Ripoll (= **R**), Salamanca, BU, 2644 (= **S**), and reportedly in the excerpts in Salamanca, BU, 81 [not seen]. To begin with **R**, it seems to have been written in southern France in the twelfth century. In this manuscript, the collection it is not divided into books and lacks the material found elsewhere in books 14 and 15.[400] There are, however, faint traces of the

---

399. The only model postulating four versions is Fowler-Magerl, 'Version' 269: 'With the exception of P3876 [= **B**] and its double [= **V**], each of the medieval manuscripts [my **S**, **R**, **B**, **V**, and **C**, **CR**] represents a unique recension.' Fowler-Magerl, *Clavis* 240–244, in contrast, distinguished three versions.

400. Gassó and Batlle, 'Prolegomena' XXXV n. 27 (correcting *Histoire* 2.270).

division into books.[401] Only a few canons have rubrics, and the inscriptions are integrated in the main text. There are a number of corrections, mostly additions of single words, by the main hand. An early modern hand—probably Baluze—has added cross-references to Gratian and normally marked where a new book begins in **S**. The superior quality of **R**'s text has been established by Mommsen for the Digest,[402] by Perels for the letters of Nicholas I,[403] by Gassó and Batlle for Pelagius I,[404] by Somerville for Piacenza 1095,[405] and by Blumenthal for Roman law texts.[406] Brett confirmed this for the very substantial materials taken from the Ivonian collections.[407] The arrangement of the canons in **R** is closer to the formal sources, even compared to **S**.[408] Apart from *Caesaraugustana I*, **R** contains an *arbor iuris* and related texts at the very beginning,[409] and a few additional texts at the end.

Salamanca, BU, 2644 is a twelfth-century manuscript from Aula Dei in Zaragoza (= **S**) written in double columns.[410] It contains a *Caesaraugustana* version very similar to **R**. Compared to **R**, **S** has relatively good texts, is fuller (**S**'s books 14–15 are not found in **R**), and rearranges some of the material.[411] In **S** (and indeed only in **S**) the collection is clearly divided into fifteen books, each with a separate table of contents; the items in these *capitulationes*—but notably not the individual canons—are numbered. The first ten books in **S** are said to have titles, but they are more rubrics to individual canons.[412] Book 2 as found in **S** is less coherent than the other

---

401. **R**, fol. 39v (a large gap between the penultimate and the last canon of book five); **R**, fol. 43v and 56r (slightly larger-than-usual rubrics for the first canons of books seven and eight).

402. Theodor Mommsen, 'Digestorum excerpta quae invenitur in collectionibus canonum tribus, Ivonis Caesaraugustana Tripertita', *Digesta Iustiniani Augusti*, ed. Theodor Mommsen and Paul Krüger (2 vols. Berlin 1870) 2.41*–50*, here at 42* (**B** 'parum utilis' compared to **R**). Note that von Savigny and Krüger only used **R**, not **B**.

403. Perels, 'Briefe' 117 n. 1. Perels did not yet use **R** for his edition finished two years earlier (MGH Epp. 6).

404. For the letters of Pelagius I, **R** has clearly better text than **S**, and **S** better than **B**, let alone **V**. See, for example, the apparatus to Pelagius, *Epp.* 24 (JK 983; ed. Gassó and Batlle 75 line 30), 25 (JK 984; ibid. 79–80 lines 1 and 7), 29 (JK 988; ibid. 85 lines 7–8), and 34 (JK 993; ibid. 94–95 lines 6, 7, 14, 22, and 23).

405. Somerville, *Piacenza* 49. See, for example, Piacenza c. 6 (ibid. 92 lines 1, 5, and 6). Note that the *Caesaraugustana* (in all manuscripts) attributes the canons of Piacenza (and Melfi) to Clermont.

406. Blumenthal, 'Caesaraugustana' 17 nn. 18–19 and 20 n. 21.

407. Brett, 'Sources' 161–162 and private communication.

408. Brett, 'Sources' 161 n. 32 (correcting *Histoire* 2.273).

409. **R**, fols. 1v–2r; the *arbor* is different from that in **B**, fol. 139v.

410. Brett, 'Sources' 161; Fowler-Magerl, 'Version' 270; eadem, *Clavis* 240.

411. Brett, 'Sources' 161.

412. Printed in Fowler-Magerl, *Clavis* 240 purportedly from **S**, but her list is almost identical to that of the Ballerini who claim to have used Vat. lat. 4976 (PL 56.352). Working with a low-quality microfilm of **S** and the online digital images of Vat. lat. 4976, I have not been able to find book

books. Book 11 is a series of 34 canons on the Eucharist which in **R** are found at the very end of the collection, after canons which in **S** are found in the miscellaneous book 13.

Content and Structure

All in all, **R** and **S** are very similar, and I will refer to the collection as found in these two manuscripts as '*Caesaraugustana I*', assuming that the text of this version was as good as that of **R** but as complete as in **S**. Specifically, as **S**'s books 14 and 15 are taken from the same peculiar set of formal sources as the rest of the collection, I assume these canons too were an integral part of the first version, even if they are not found in **R**.[413] As for the structure of the first version, it seems plausible that the ancestor of **R** and **S** was divided into books, but it is less certain that this division was exactly that of **S**; books 2 and 11 may be peculiar to **S**. On the basis of these assumptions, *Caesaraugustana I* can be described as follows: the collection begins with canons on the sources of the law (book 1 and 2.1–53 in **S**); the following books contain canons on ecclesiastical hierarchy (2.54–74 and book 3), procedural law, ecclesiastical offices, and church property (books 4–7), the clergy (books 8–9), marriage (book 10), the Eucharist (book 11), baptism (book 12), sacramental theology (book 13), heresies, schism, and excommunication (book 14); the last book is a penitential.

Formal Sources

Much research remains to be done, but on the whole the treatment of the texts is conservative enough to establish the formal sources of *Caesaraugustana I* with some certainty. The compiler often abbreviated the texts he took from various formal sources, often selecting only one specific aspect from longer excerpts dealing with a multitude of issues. The inscriptions are normally taken from the formal sources, and the Roman law not taken from earlier collections is quoted with great precision. Martin claimed that the *Caesaraugustana I* more or less systematically changed inscriptions, but this is not the case.[414]

---

titles (different from the rubrics to the respective first canons) in either manuscript. Neither Marcos Rodríguez, 'Tres manuscritos' 40 nor Dolezalek and Bertram, *Catalogue III* mention book titles.

413. Brett, 'Sources' 161, especially n. 30.

414. Norbert Martin, *Die Compilatio decretorum des Kardinals Laborans. Eine Umarbeitung des Gratianischen Dekrets aus dem 12. Jahrhunderts* (2 vols. Heidelberg 1994) 1.27–28. Having quoted the case of a canon in the appendix of **B** (CC245 in the *Clavis* database; **B**, fol. 132r) where the inscription is indeed wrong, Martin suggested a pattern here (ibid. 1.28): 'Der Vorgang läuft in fast allen Fällen nach demselben Schema ab. Beim Übergang von Ivo zur Caesaraugustana finden größere

Clearly the most important formal sources of *Caesaraugustana I* are four of the Ivonian collections, namely Ivo's *Decretum*, the *Tripartita*, and both Arsenal collections.[415] No known *Decretum* manuscript stands out as being particularly close to *Caesaraugustana I*, but in one case at least the *Caesaraugustana* shares a complete sentence which in the Vatican manuscript of Ivo's collection was inserted as a correction.[416] Importantly, the first version of the *Caesaraugustana* did not yet draw on the *Panormia*, nor on the *Exceptiones Petri*, two important sources for the second version. Given the considerable overlap between the various Ivonian collections, establishing which of them specifically was used for which *Caesaraugustana I* canon can be difficult. These difficulties notwithstanding, Brett made a compelling case for the independent use of the Arsenal collections, that is, independent of Ivo's *Decretum* for which *Arsenal I* was a preparatory collection.[417] The canons on baptism may serve as an example. Book 12 of the *Caesaraugustana I* has dozens of canons also found in Ivo's first book, including very rare materials, and almost always in the same sequence as Ivo. Yet in one case at least the *Caesaraugustana* agrees with *Arsenal I* against all extant manuscripts of Ivo's *Decretum*.[418] At the same time, it is striking to see that *Caesaraugustana* 12 contains none of the approximately 100 canons Ivo took from Burchard for his book on baptism. Both phenomena can be explained easily if we assume that *Caesaraugustana* 12 did not use Ivo's *Decretum* but rather *Arsenal I*, a preparatory collection of non-Burchardian material.

Even more interesting, perhaps, are the parallels to *Arsenal II*. As Brett pointed out, the series of canons in *Caesaraugustana I* 8.46–60 has a parallel in the Arsenal collections as found on fols. 132r–151v of the extant manuscript.[419] Of the 450 canons found on these twenty folios, only 126 come

---

Textveränderungen und Verfälschungen der inscriptio statt. Mare uitreum übernimmt die falsche inscriptio und verkürzt die Kapitel [...].' He quotes six examples to support this claim, but as it turns out, five of the *Mare uitreum* canons he quotes are not found in the *Caesaraugustana*, and the last (Ivo 6.2 = *Caes. I* 8.2) does not have an inscription, neither in the first version (**R**, fol. 56r; **S**, fol. 63rb) nor the second (**B**, fol. 50v).

415. Brett, 'Sources' 161–164.

416. See above (note 390) on the striking parallel between *Caes. I* 1.45 and Ivo 4.125 as found in Vat. lat. 1357, fol. 63vb.

417. Brett, 'Sources' 163.

418. All extant *Decretum* manuscripts (and also *Panormia* 1.14) have a wrong inscription for Ivo 1.123 ('Isidore'); this inscription in fact belonged to a short canon which was dropped by accident (Ivo 1.122A). *Arsenal I*, however, has both canons with the correct inscription (Paris, Bibliothèque de l'Arsenal, 713, fol. 118v). Strikingly, *Caes.* 12.35 also retains the correct inscription for Ivo 1.122A.

419. Brett, 'Sources' 163, pointing out that among all major collections, only the Arsenal collection 'provides every one of them, largely in the same order'. The canons he refers to as '8.43–57' (according to their arrangement in **R**) are *Caes.* 8.46–60 in *Clavis* (based on **S**).

from the second Arsenal collection.[420] Nonetheless, the *Caesaraugustana* heavily draws on *Arsenal II*: Almost the complete series (*Caes.* 8.46–59) seems to be taken from the second Arsenal collection, only the last canon (*Caes.* 8.60) is not from this source.[421] This also shows that is very unlikely that the manuscript from which the *Caesaraugustana* compiler was working was similar to the extant Arsenal 713B where *Arsenal I* and *Arsenal II* are mingled.[422] For if the manuscript used by the *Caesaraugustana* compiler had combined sections from both Arsenal collections in a way comparable to the extant Arsenal 713B, it would have been difficult to select a series of canons taken from *Arsenal II* only.[423] Therefore, it seems plausible to me that the *Caesaraugustana* compiler had both Arsenal collections at his disposal, but either in the form of separate manuscripts (or quires) or, if already combined in one manuscript, in a form where both collections were kept more clearly separate than in the copy extant in Arsenal 713.

In addition to the Ivonian collections from northern France, the *Caesaraugustana I* seems to have used three Italian collections—namely Anselm, Deusdedit, and the *Polycarpus*. The strongest case for the use of Anselm's *Collectio canonum* is a series of texts taken from the Justinian Code, as already Krüger argued.[424] Indeed, the only canon which Krüger treated as an exception to the rule also seems to have come from an Anselm-related source.[425] Fournier claimed that the *Caesaraugustana* used the Barberini version of Anselm found only in Barb. lat. 535.[426] Given that

420. Paris, Bibliothèque de l'Arsenal, 713, fols. 132r–151v contains the canons numbered LP0270–725 in *Clavis*; of these, canons 356–388, 407–419, and 653–725 are part of the second Arsenal collection as defined by Austin, 'Arsenal' 6.

421. *Caes. I* 8.60 may or may not be taken from *Arsenal I*, as Paris, Bibliothèque de l'Arsenal, 713, fol. 153r–v contains a longer version of the canon. It is an excerpt (taken from Gregory I, JE 1112) which in one version or the other is found in many collections including *Tripartita* A1.55.95 and Ivo's *Decretum* where it is even found twice (Ivo 6.380 and 15.20).

422. *Pace* Rolker, *Canon Law* 285 (calling the immediate source of the *Caesaraugustana* 'very similar to the extant Arsenal manuscript'; content and structure of the individual *sections*, but not their arrangement, must have been similar to the Arsenal manuscript).

423. As Martin Brett (private communication, 4 December 2020) pointed out, it was possible that the *Caesaraugustana* compiler first went through Ivo's *Decretum* (in a version similar to the extant manuscripts) and later through the Arsenal collections; if alert enough, he could avoid *Arsenal I* material he already had taken from the *Decretum* and select only what was new to him (effectively selecting *Arsenal II* material).

424. Paul Krüger, *Kritik des Justinianischen Codex* (Berlin 1867), here at 50–51, based on **R** and Paris, BnF, lat. 12519 (= Thaner's **P**, a copy of Anselm A).

425. Cod. 8.53.1 as found in *Caes. I* 1.26 (**S**, fol. 3ra), which Krüger, *Kritik* 51 n. 3 thought to have been taken from *Anselmo dedicata*, is also contained in the Anselm-related Vatican 13L at 13.49–50 (Vat. lat. 1361, fol. 274va).

426. Fournier, 'Caesaraugustana' 62–63. Fournier probably was working with Paris, BnF, lat. 12450/12451 (not Barb. lat. 535) when comparing the *Caesaraugustana* to Anselm Bb; in the Paris copy, books 8–13 are supplemented from Vat. lat. 4983 (Anselm C), see Kéry 221.

this version ('Anselm Bb') only extends to the first seven books, while the *Caesaraugustana* seems to draw on all books of Anselm, this claim seems unlikely to begin with. Fournier rested his case on the claim that the *Caesaraugustana* contained four canons which were found in Anselm Bb but not the A version; this, however, is not the case.[427] While the precise Anselm version used for the *Caesaraugustana* remains to be studied, there is no reason to assume that it was similar to the short version in Barb. lat. 535. As for Deusdedit, the use of his collection seems to be the best explanation for rare canon law material.[428] Sometimes, the *Caesaraugustana* seems to have used a better Deusdedit version than the only extant manuscript.[429] Important evidence for the use of the *Polycarpus* comes from the sole text in he *Caesaraugustana I* taken ultimately from the *Digestum novum*.[430] The relatively large number of parallels plus this very rare text taken together strongly suggest that the *Polycarpus* was a formal source of the *Caesaraugustana*.[431] The parallels at the very beginning (*Caes.* 1.1–13) likewise support that the *Polycarpus* was a source of, and partly even a model for, the *Caesaraugustana I* compiler.

The *Caesaraugustana I* also used other materials not found in earlier collections. Again, a peculiar mix of texts otherwise known from northern France, on the one hand, and materials circulating in the western Mediterranean, on the other hand, is visible. The Roman law texts (outside the *Britannica* tradition) link *Caesaraugustana I* to collections like the *Liber Tubingensis*, the *Liber Ashburnhamensis*, and the *Exceptiones Petri* from southern France and northern Spain. They include rare texts from the Digest and an excerpt taken from the Code, which seem to have been passed on from the *Caesaraugustana I* to the *Exceptiones Petri*, as Blumenthal convincingly

427. See Fournier, 'Caesaraugustana' 62–63. Anselm Bb 5.21, 23, 25 (Barb. lat. 535, fols. 119r, 119r–119v, and 120r) = Anselm 5.20, 22, and 24 (ed. Thaner 237–238, 238–239, and 240); Anselm Bb 7.99 (Barb. lat. 535, fol. 189v) = Anselm 7.83 (ed. Thaner 399).—Note that Fournier used slightly different canon numbers; to faciliate comparison, I use those of Thaner's edition and the *Clavis* database.

428. *Caes. I* 2.1a is found partly in Deusdedit 4.288 (151) (ed. Wolf von Glanvell 553 line 14), partly in 4.165 (92) (ed. Wolf von Glanvell 477 line 24 to 478 line 1); *Caes. I* 2.18 = Deusdedit 1.187 (149) (ed. Wolf von Glanvell 115). See also the next note.

429. *Caes. I* 1.18 = Deusdedit 2.145 (119) (ed. Wolf von Glanvell 262); for this reason, Wolf von Glanvell supplemented the inscription from *Caesaraugustana* (ibid. n. 1). *Caes. I* 2.34 = Deusdedit 1.44 (36) (ed. Wolf von Glanvell 54), another rare text, likewise has no inscription in Deusdedit.

430. *Polycarpus* 6.4.69 (ed. Erdmann and Horst 1192) = *Caes. I* 10.4 (Paris, BnF, lat. 3875, fol. 72r; 'CA10.003' [*sic*] in *Clavis*). The material source is Dig. 50.17.30. The canon is also found (with the same rubric) in *3L* 3.11.68 (ed. Motta 2.132) and the San Pietro *9L* 8.1.62. It was printed from **R** by Mommsen, 'Excerpta' 43*.

431. Friedrich Carl von Savigny, *Geschichte des römischen Rechts im Mittelalter* (7 vols. Heidelberg 2nd edition 1834–51), here at 2.300 note g; Hüffer, *Beiträge* 91–92 (*Polycarpus*); Conrat (Cohn), *Geschichte* 390–391.

argued.[432] Other texts point much further north; in particular the *Visio Eucherii* is linked to Francia and Saint-Denis, not southern France.[433] Nonetheless, the *Caesaraugustana* was compiled in Aquitaine or, more likely, Catalonia. The presence of JE †446 suggests interest in the primacy claims of Arles, and a peculiar version of JE 2765 (which first surfaced in the environment of Ivo of Chartres in *Caesaraugustana I*) is quoted specifically as referring to conflicts between Narbonne and Bourges; this may be related to Bourges's claims to 'primacy in Aquitaine' in the 1120s.[434]

Date

This brings us to the date of the *Caesaraugustana I*. Its traditional label of a pre-Gratian collection goes back to the Ballerini (who thought the most recent material was from the time of Urban II) and Savigny (who held the collection was compiled before 1074).[435] Additionally, a manuscript of the second version (**B**) was erroneously treated as if providing a *terminus ante quem* for the first version. None of these arguments can be maintained, and the date has to be established by an analysis of the formal and material sources.

Most arguments were already known to Fournier, who assumed that the most recent material in the collection was a letter of Paschal II (JL 6611; dated 1099×1118) and that *Caesaraugustana I* probably used the *Polycarpus* (which he dated to 1104×1110); Fournier concluded that the collection was compiled 'shortly after 1110'.[436] Blumenthal discovered that the collection contains a canon of Paschal's council at Benevento of October 1108 (JL 6613).[437] Horst in his analysis of the *Polycarpus* argued that Gregory of San Grisogono began to work on his collection already at Lucca (before 1109) but only finished his work after 1111.[438] In particular, he pointed out that the *Polycarpus* contained canons (found in no earlier collection) and indeed a separate section on the invalidity of oaths sworn under the

432. Blumenthal, 'Caesaraugustana' 16–17 on *Caes. I* 1.62; for details, see above (note 387).

433. Fowler-Magerl, 'Version' 272–273.

434. Fowler-Magerl, 'Version' 273–274; on the textual history of JE 2765, see also Rolker, *Canon Law* 195 and 204.

435. Ballerini and Ballerini, 'De antiquis collectionibus' here at PL 56.352; von Savigny, *Geschichte* 2.145–146.

436. Fournier, 'Caesaraugustana' 58.

437. Only the transmission with the Wolfenbüttel 9L (Wolfenbüttel, HAB, Cod. Guelf. 212 Gud. lat., fol. 58v [not seen]) refers to this canon as being issued at the Council of Benevento; all *Caesaraugustana* manuscripts attribute it to Paschal II. See Max Sdralek, *Wolfenbüttler Fragmente. Analekten zur Kirchengeschichte des Mittelalters* (Kirchengeschichtliche Studien 1.2; Münster 1891), here at 138 and Blumenthal, *Early Councils* 104–105.

438. Horst, *Polycarpus* 1–6, especially 6; see above (Chapter Four) for the discussion of the date of the *Polycarpus*.

thread of force—an issue of special relevance in 1111, when Gregory was among the cardinals forced by the emperor to grant the so-called *Pravilegium*.[439] Concerning the *Caesaraugustana*, Brett concluded that any date between 1108 and *ca.* 1140 was possible.[440] Blumenthal preferred a very early date within this range, as already Fournier had done.[441] Such an early date is not impossible, but there is no evidence in favour of it either, and all new evidence that became available after Fournier's time points to a later date than he thought. Given the uncertain date of JL 6611 and the strong case Horst made for a later date of the *Polycarpus*, a compilation after 1115 to me seems likely. If the *Caesaraugustana I* compiler inserted JE †446 and JE 2765 as a comment on primacy claims in his own time, this would fit the 1120s better than the decade before. None of these arguments is cogent, but a compilation of the *Caesaraugustana I* in the 1120s or even the 1130s to me seems more likely than an earlier date.

5.8.5 The Second Version of the *Caesaraugustana*

The Manuscripts **B** and **V**

The second version of the *Caesaraugustana* is found in Paris, BnF, lat. 3876 (**B**) and Vat. lat. 5715 (**V**). The former dates from the second half of the twelfth century and strongly conveys the impression of a working manuscript; additions by several hands are found in the margins, on separate sheets, and in appendices to the collection proper. Compared to the first version, **B**'s compiler dropped a few canons, added many new texts, and rearranged the material to a considerable degree.[442] The division of the collection into books is barely visible in **B**; only larger-than-usual initial letters seem to mark the beginning of new books.[443] Such red letters of two to eight lines height mark, in this sequence, the canons corresponding to *Caesaraugustana I* 1.1, 2.71 (the *Constitutum Constantini*), the

---

439. Horst, *Polycarpus* 6. See also Blumenthal, '1111' 170–172.

440. Brett as quoted by Blumenthal, 'Caesaraugustana' 18.

441. Blumenthal, 'Caesaraugustana' 17: 'Fournier suggested a date "postérieure de peu d'années à 1110" for the *Caesaraugustana*. It is possible that he was right, as so often he was.' Fournier was indeed often right, but it is also true that he notoriously assumed that collections were compiled very soon after the *terminus post quem*, and as a result proposed dates that turned out too early (for example in the case of Burchard, the *Panormia*, and the *Polycarpus*). Blumenthal herself accepted a later date for the *Polycarpus* than Fournier did, see Blumenthal, '1111' 170 ('completed between 1111 and 1113') *pace* Fournier, 'Polycarpus' 62 (shortly after 1104).

442. The following entries in the *Clavis* database suggest that the compiler made minor changes across the whole collection: CA03.069 = CB04.091; CA08.003.01 = CB04.174, CA08.003.08 = CB04.081; CA08.004 = CB04.187, CA14.012 = CB07.042.

443. *Pace* Fowler-Magerl, *Clavis* 242–243 (who claimed that there were gaps in the text where one would expects the beginning of books 8, 10, 12, 13, 14, and 15). See also eadem, 'Vier Kanonessammlungen' 144.

first canons of books 5–10, 12, 11, 14, and 15.2.[444] Another break is found in the middle of *Caesaraugustana I* 4.72. The first part of this canon, breaking off in mid-sentence, is found on fol. 19v; the next folios contain material not found in **R** or **S**; it is taken from the *Panormia* and the *Exceptiones Petri*, beginning with the Papal Election Decree of 1059.[445] On fol. 24r, one finds the rest of *Caesaraugustana I* 4.72, and other material taken from the first into the second version. After this main part of the collection, and after an 'explicit' note (itself copied from an exemplar), **B** contains a series of 308 new canons.[446] This appendix is followed by a number of miscellaneous texts: two regnal catalogues of popes and kings of France compiled in late 1143 or early 1144, an *arbor iuris* with related texts, two liturgical comments, and excerpts from the writings of Bruno of Segni.[447] Generally, **B** contains relatively many marginal additions, most of them by the main hand. Two of them deserve special attention: one, written in the main hand, is a long quotation from Gratian;[448] the other one, on the following page, quotes from—and possibly comments on—a letter of Hadrian IV of 1154/55 (WH 533b).[449] On the whole, **B** can be described as a raw text with many signs

444. **B**, fols. 1r, 9r, 29r, 38r, 41r, 50v, 57v, 62v, 76v, 86v, 102r. The numbers for books and canons are those of the *Clavis* database (key 'CA', based on **S**). *Caes. I* 15.1 is not found in **B**.

445. **B**, fols. 19(bis)r–23v (= CB04.075–138 in *Clavis*). The numeration of folios 19 and 19bis is only due to an oversight by the modern hand foliating the codex; there is no change of hand between fols. 19 and 19bis.

446. **B**, fols. 117v–136v (= CC001–308 in *Clavis*). The 'Explicit liber ist<e>', written in the main hand, is found after *Caes. II* 15.140 (**B**, fol. 117v), followed by the appendix with no visible break or change of hand.

447. **B**, fols. 137r–139r. Innocent II and Louis VII are said to have reigned 14 and 7 years, respectively. As Innocent died in his fourteenth year as pope in September 1143, the list was likely written not much later than this date. The same list is also found in **V** and **C**. On the *arbor iuris* (**B**, fol. 139v), see Schadt, *Darstellungen* 55. For the two liturgical texts and Bruno's *De sacramentiis*, also found in **V**, see Dolezalek and Bertram, *Catalogue III*. Unlike **V**, **B** has the complete text of *De sacramentiis* and continues with excerpts from Bruno's *Life of Leo IX* on fol. 147r–v (PL 165.1110–1125), breaking off in mid-sentence at the end of the folio ('[…] et ego in eo <h>ic fert fructum multum. Si quis'). **B**, fol. 148r is empty; fols. 148v–149r begins a tract '<Q>uia quatuor elementis subsistentes Deum nocte et die offendimus' (incomplete); **B**, fol. 149v seems to be a fragment of an *Expositio divinorum officiorum* (PL 147.210).

448. **B**, fol. 56v, introduced as 'Exceptio ex decretis Gratiani'. The source is Gratian, C.16 q.1 d.p.c.41 §1 to d.p.c.45 (ed. Winroth 519–520; ed. Friedberg 774–775). See Patetta, 'Per la storia' 317 on **B**, fol. 56v and **V**, fol. 54rb–va. In the older literature the excerpts are sometimes claimed to be taken from *Quoniam egestas* rather than Gratian; see for example Peter Weimar, 'Zur Entstehung des sogenannten Tübinger Rechtsbuchs und der *Exceptiones legum Romanarum des Petrus*', *Studien zur europäischen Rechtsgeschichte. Helmut Coing zum 28. Februar 1972 von seinen Schülern und Mitarbeitern*, ed. Walter Wilhelm (Frankfurt 1972) 1–24, here at 5.

449. **B**, fol. 57r. The letter (JL –; WH 533b) is edited as no. 81 in *Decretales ineditae saeculi XII: From the Papers of Walther Holtzmann*, ed. and rev. Stanley Chodorow and Charles Duggan (MIC Corpus collectionum 4; Vatican City 1982), here at 140. See the comment (ibid. 141) for the last sentences in **B** having perhaps originated as a comment. Weimar originally thought WH 533b was written in **B**'s main hand, but later retracted: Peter Weimar, 'Die legistische Literatur der Glossatorenzeit', *Handbuch der Quellen und Literatur der neueren europäischen Privatrechtsgeschichte*,

of the collection being reworked over an extended period of time; it is a working manuscript, containing additions, corrections, and visible breaks in the text resulting from the combination of various materials.

In contrast, Vat. lat. 5715 (= **V**) is a clean manuscript written in two columns by a single hand of the late twelfth or the thirteenth century. It contains the same version of the *Caesaraugustana* as **B** and is often described as 'nearly identical' to **B**.[450] Two 'additions' reported for **V** by Patetta are in fact already present in **B**;[451] vice versa, two 'omissions' reported by Gassó and Batlle are actually found in **V**.[452] It is almost certain that **V** is a direct copy of **B**; even the use of abbreviations is strikingly similar.[453] However, the scribe of **V** added even more errors to his exemplar, some of which suggest that he struggled with the Latin of his sources. For example, as in **B**, the Vatican manuscript contains the decrees of Piacenza 1095 (and one canon from Melfi 1089) as 'Clermont', but adds even more errors to the text.[454] In addition, the initials in **V** are careless (e.g. 'Dum', 'Cum', and 'Eum' are confused), and proper names misspelled; Pope Vigilius, for example, becomes 'Pope Virgilius' (**V**, fol. 125ra). As for the division of

---

Band 1: Mittelalter (1100–1500). Die gelehrten Rechte und die Gesetzgebung, ed. Helmut Coing (Munich 1973) 129–260, here at 256 n. 2.

450. Patetta, 'Per la storia' 318 ('corrisponde perfettamente'); Weimar, 'Entstehung' 3; Brett, 'Sources' 161 ('virtually indistinguishable'); Blumenthal, 'Caesaraugustana' 16 ('twin'); Fowler-Magerl, *Clavis* 242: 'There are three nearly identical copies of a second version: Paris BN lat. 3876, Barb. lat. 897 and Vat. lat. 5715.' Her reference to the Barberini manuscript is mistaken (see above, Table 8).

451. Patetta, 'Per la storia' 317 n. 11. Both canons are also in **B**, fol. 120r.

452. Pelagius, *Epp.* 54 (ed. Gassó and Batlle 143, overlooking **V**, fol. 21ra = **B**, fol. 21r) and 55 (ed. Gassó and Batlle 144, overlooking **V**, fol. 2rb = **B**, fol. 2v), respectively. The correct folio number for the second occurrence of the same letter is **V**, fol. 7r.

453. See *Caes. II* 1.1 (**B**, fol. 1r): 'Ad disce(n)du(m) duplicit(er) ducimur, auctoritate atq(ue) r(ati)one. T(em)p(o)re auctoritas, re au(tem) ratio p(ri)or e(st).' In **V**, fol. 1ra, exactly the same abbreviations occur, only that 'disce(n)du(m)' is rendered 'discendu(m)' and 'ducimur' becomes 'ducim(ur)'.

454. **V**, fols. 16vb–17ra 'Urbanus secundus in concilio Clarimontis' = Piacenza 1095 cc. 1–7, 12 (incomplete), and 13 (ed. Somerville, *Piacenza* 90–97, without using **V**). It has the same texts, and also all omissions and variant readings Somerville reports for **B** (his **Pc2**). In addition, **V** in c. 3 (ed. Somerville 91 line 3) has 'necisse' instead of 'nescisse'; in c. 7 (ed. Somerville 93 lines 3–4) 'eiusmodo' instead of 'eiusmodi', 'debeat' instead of 'debeant', and 'optinere' instead of 'obtinere'; in c. 12 (ed. Somerville 96 lines 4–5) 'obtineant' and 'illum' instead of 'optineant' and 'illud'; c. 13 (ed. Somerville 97 line 1) begins 'Illum' instead of 'Illud'. After Piacanza c. 13 **V**, fol. 17ra continues without any break: 'Item post alia. Illum [*sic*] summopere et apostolice auctoritatis privilegio prohibentes interdicimus ut nullus in clericali ordine constitutus nullusque monachus episcopatus aut abbatie aut cuiuslibet ecclesiastice dignitatis investituram de manu laici suscipere audeat. Quod si presumpserit, depositione multetur.' This last text is Melfi 1089 c. 8 (ed. Somerville, *Urban II* 254–255), again with minor variants and one omission ('et providentes', also lacking in Somerville's **R2** = Roma, Vallicelliana, C.24, fols. 292r–294r [not seen]). See Robert Somerville, *The Councils of Urban II, Vol. 1: Decreta Claromontensia* (AHC. Supplementum 1; Amsterdam 1972) 125–126, idem, *Urban II* 197–198, and idem, *Piacenza* 49 on the conflation of Clermont/Piacenza and Melfi in *Caesaraugustana*.

books, **V** agrees with **B** against **S**; as in **B**, only larger-than-usual initials imperfectly mark the beginning of new books.[455] There is a small gap in **V** (two empty lines) where the new material taken from the *Panormia* begins in **B**.[456] The appendix found in **B** after the 'explicit' is also found in **V** with no visible break; even the 'explicit' note is copied. Two times, canons separate in **B** are merged in **V**; a loss of some 20 canons occurred later as a folio was cut out.[457] Generally, the content of **V** and **B** is almost identical. One important difference between **B** and **V** is that almost all additions in **B** are integrated into the collection proper in **V**. However, apparently because of the loss of a quire, **V** breaks off in mid-sentence in Bruno's *De sacramentis* and lacks the remaining few texts found at the end of **B**.[458] **V** also incorporates **B**'s marginal additions in the main text, including the quotations from Gratian and Hadrian IV (WH 533b), providing a secure *terminus post quem* of 1154 for **V**.[459] All in all, **V** is a clean copy written by a moderately competent scribe working almost certainly from **B** itself.

Content and Structure

The *Caesaraugustana II* as found in **B** and **V** is a distinct version of the collection clearly later than *Caesaraugustana I*. The ancestor of **B** and **V** was neither **R** nor **S**; it already had undergone some of the reworking that is also visible in **S**, but sometimes **B** preserves better readings as found in **R**.[460] As for the textual quality, it is poor in **B** and even poorer in **V**.

In both manuscripts, the division of the collection into books differs from that found in **S** and is only marked by larger-than-usual initial letters. In **B**, such letters of two to eight lines height mark, in this sequence, the canons corresponding to *Caesaraugustana I* 1.1, 2.71 (the *Constitutum Constantini*), the first canons of books 5–10, 12, 11, 14, and 15.2.[461] After this main part of the collection, and after an 'explicit' note (itself copied from an exemplar), **B** and **V** contain an appendix of 308 canons which I treat as

---

455. See, for example, **V**, fol. 8rb (three-line initial where new book begins in **B**, but not in **S**) and 9rb (no break where new book begins in **S**, but not in **B**).

456. **V**, fol. 18vb, between the canons found in **B**, fol. 19v (= *Caes. I* 4.72) and 19bis (= Papal Election Decree of 1059). See above for **B**.

457. **V**, fols. 109va–126ra; missing and merged canons (using the numbers of the *Clavis* database, key 'CC'): cc. 91–92 and 224–225 are merged (**V**, fols. 114vb and 121–122); the folio cut out after fol. 122 would have had contained cc. 267–286; **V**, fol. 126ra lacks c. 308.

458. **V**, fols. 126rb–128vb (regnal catalogue); see Dolezalek and Bertram, *Catalogue III*.

459. **V**, fol. 54rb–va (Gratian) and 54va (WH 533b).

460. Brett, 'Sources' 162.

461. **B**, fols. 1r, 9r, 29r, 38r, 41r, 50v, 57v, 62v, 76v, 86v, 102r. The numbers for books and canons are those of the *Clavis* database (key 'CA', based on **S**). Note that *Caes. I* 15.1 is not found in **B**.

part of the collection.[462] *Caesaraugustana II* therefore can be described as a collection divided into twelve books plus an appendix.

Compared to the first version (in particular **S**), some books are enlarged while others are reorganised in the second. In particular, the materials forming book two in **S** in **B** (and **V**) are united partly with book one, partly with the old books three and four plus new material. The resulting second book in *Caesaraugustana II* is by far longer than any other book of the collection, and fairly miscellaneous. The material on the Eucharist—split in books 11 and 13 in **S**—was left *en bloc* in the second version and enlarged with such new material as Berengar's 1079 oath.[463] This division of the material, while less visible than in **S**, on the whole, makes sense, sometimes more so than the division in **S** (book 1, Eucharist), sometimes less so (the new book two). The new material in book two and the appendix is not really integrated into the collection, and its addition led to some overlap.[464]

Formal Sources

While *Caesaraugustana I* is something like the last pre-Gratian collection, the second version can be described as structurally pre-Gratian but chronologically a post-Gratian collection. This sounds odd only if one believed that the availability of the *Decretum Gratiani* meant a total break in canon law history; yet collections like the *Caesaraugustana II* strongly suggest that the change was more gradual.

Apart from *Caesaraugustana I*, which materials were needed to produce the second version? For a considerable number of canons, *Caesaraugustana II* depends on the *Panormia*. This is most evident for the long series of canons taken from the *Panormia* which interrupts a canon already found in the first version.[465] The series begins with the 1059 Papal Election Decree combined with Pseudo-Stephen as found in the *Panormia*.[466]

---

462. **B**, fols. 117v–136v (= <u>CC001</u>–308 in *Clavis*). The 'Explicit liber ist<e>', written in the main hand, is found after *Caes. II* 15.140 (**B**, fol. 117v), followed by the appendix with no visible break or change of hand.

463. **B**, fol. 99r = **V**, fols. 93vb–94ra. Contrary to what the *Clavis* entry (<u>CB13.131</u>) may suggest, both manuscripts abbreviate Berengar's name ('Ego B. corde credo [...]').

464. Doublets in the second version not found in the first: <u>CA04.003</u> (retained in *Caes. II* 4.3: **B**, fol. 15r) = <u>CC060</u> (**B**, fol. 121v); <u>CA08.103</u> (**B**, fol. 56v) = <u>CC289</u> (**B**, fol. 121v); <u>CB13.153</u> (**B**, fol. 101v) = <u>CB15.034</u> (**B**, fol. 110r); <u>CB15.077</u> (**B**, fol. 113r) = <u>CC264</u> (**B**, fol. 132v [*sic*]).

465. *Caes. I* 4.72 (in **S**), split in two parts in *Caes. II* as described above. On the added material, see Fournier, 'Caesaraugustana' (reporting the series for **V**) and Fowler-Magerl, 'Vier Kanonessammlungen' 144–145 (for **B**, **V**, and **C**).

466. **B**, fol. 19(bis)r–v. See Scheffer-Boichorst, *Neuordnung* 7 and 10 (spotting the peculiar Pseudo-Stephen addition), confirmed by Jasper, *Papstwahldekret* 10–11. The following canons (=

Fowler-Magerl and Blumenthal claimed that already **S**—and hence *Caesaraugustana I*—contained the Papal Election Decree from *Panormia*, but this seems to be a misunderstanding.[467] The appendix of 308 canons found in **B** and **V** also draws heavily on the *Panormia*, and in addition contains fourteen excerpts from the *Exceptiones Petri*. Both the series beginning with the Papal Election Decree and the appendix were already found in the common ancestor of the second and third versions.

Date

Other additions to *Caesaraugustana I* which **B** and **V** do not share with **C** are partly found in the collection proper in **B**, partly in the margin; they can be used to establish the *terminus post quem* of both **B** and the *Caesaraugustana II*. The most recent of these additions in **B** are canons from Lateran II (on separate sheets), Reims 1148 (in the main text), Gratian (in the margin, but by the main hand), a letter of Hadrian IV from 1154/55 (in the margin), and a regnal catalogue compiled in 1143/44 (in the appendix, but by the main hand). In **V**, all these texts are integrated in the collection proper. While some doubts remain whether the Hadrian IV letter (WH 533b) was only a later addition, the Reims 1148 canons are an integral part of the collection as found in **B** and indeed can be used to date both the manuscript and the *Caesaraugustana* version it contains. However, this only provides a *terminus post quem* for **B** and *Caesaraugustana II*, not a precise date.[468] This needs to be stressed as **B** is often quoted in the older literature as proof that the second version of the *Caesaraugustana* existed by 1144 at the latest, which, in turn, has led to claims that **B** contained the earliest quotation from Gratian and/or allowed the dating of the *Exceptiones Petri* to be before 1144.[469] These claims, however, are not only factually

---

Panormia 3.44–45) are also good evidence for the use of the *Panormia*; note that the erroneous incipit in **V**, fol. 19v ('Dator') is also found in some *Panormia* manuscripts (**B**, fol. 19[bis]v lacks an initial).

467. Blumenthal, 'Caesaraugustana' 19 n. 17: 'The decree, albeit included in the Salamanca manuscript (CA 4.72), is not found in MS Paris, BN lat. 3875.' This is apparently based on Fowler-Magerl, *Clavis* 240 commenting on **S**: 'Space is left free after the *Constitutum Constantini* (2.71) and after the election decree of Nicholas II (4.72).' This fits **B**, fol. 19v, but not **S**. The error may go back on the slightly ambigious account in Fowler-Magerl, 'Version' 279 where the 1059 decree is mentioned in the context of **S** without saying it was found there.

468. Gassó and Batlle, 'Prolegomena' XXXVIII nn. 32–33 (correcting *Histoire* 2.270). The wrong date continues to be repeated; even Stephan Kuttner, 'Research on Gratian: Acta and Agenda', *Proceedings Cambridge 1984* MIC Subsidia 8.3–26, here at 19 n. 46 claimed **B** was 'written *c.* 1144'.

469. Namely Gouron for a long time argued that **B** was written in 1143/44 and that the *Exceptiones Petri* for this reason (!) had to be earlier. For his earlier position, see André Gouron, 'Une école ou des écoles? Sur les canonistes français (vers 1150–vers 1210)', *Proceedings Berkeley 1985* MIC Subsidia 7.223–240, here at 226; for his revised view, see the corrigenda to André Gouron, 'Le manuscrit

wrong (as **B** contains the Reims 1148 canons) but also untenable for methodological reasons: While **B** must have been written after the *Exceptiones* were available, this does not provide a *terminus ante quem* for the availability of the *Exceptiones*. In general, while there are some indications that the *Caesaraugustana II* may be older than **B** itself (the 'explicit' note in particular indicates mechanical copying), this does not provide a precise *terminus ante quem* for either **B** or *Caesaraugustana II*. The second version of the *Caesaraugustana* was compiled after 1148 but before **B** was made—perhaps still in the 1150s, perhaps only later.

5.8.6 The Third Version of the *Caesaraugustana*

The manuscript Barcelona, ACA, San Cugat 63 (my **C**; not seen) is generally thought to represent a later stage of the *Caesaraugustana*; following Fowler-Magerl, I label it the 'third version' or '*Caesaraugustana III*', even if this numbering can be misunderstood as suggesting that **C** relied on **B** or **V** (for discussion, see below). In **C**, the collection is divided into six books only, with individual *capitulationes* to books 2–5.[470] The first book in **C** comprises the contents of books 1–4 as found in **S**, the second book retains most of the material in **S**'s books 5–9, book three **S**'s books 10–12, and book four **S**'s books 13–14. Book five in **C** combines the new material which is found in **B**'s second book (beginning with the Papal Election Decree) with **B**'s appendix.[471] This includes the excerpts from the *Exceptiones Petri* and the 1143/44 regnal catalogues.[472] The sixth and last book in **C** is the penitential which is similarly the last (fifteenth) book in **S**. Some of the new books are more consistent than others; for example, book three in **C** forms a coherent book on the sacraments, but books one and five cover rather mixed subjects. At the same time, **C** abbreviates the collection; this may also have been the reason for the division into fewer books.

On account of the new material shared with **B** (and **V**), **C** may seem like a reworked version of **B**. However, there are two important argu-

---

de Prague, Metr. Knih. J. 74: à la recherche du plus ancien décrétiste à l'Ouest des Alpes' ZRG Kan. Abt. 83 (1997) 223–248 in idem, *Pionniers du droit occidental au Moyen Âge* (CSS 865; Ashgate 2006) no. I, here at 15. See also idem, '«Petrus» démasqué' *Revue historique de droit français et étranger* 82 (2004) 577–588 on the *Exceptiones* (but not *Caesaraugustana*). For **B** as establishing a *terminus ante quem* for Gratian, see Patetta, 'Per la storia' 317. Modern scholarship agrees that the earliest use of Gratian that can be dated with precision is from 1150, see Paolo Nardi, 'Fonti canoniche in una sentenza senese del 1150', *Life, Law and Letters: Historical Studies in Honour of Antonio García y García*, ed. Peter Linehan (2 vols. SG 28/29; Rome 1998) 2.661–670 and Winroth, *Making* 140–141.

470. Gassó and Batlle, 'Prolegomena' and Fowler-Magerl, *Clavis* 243, with corrections by eadem, 'Vier Kanonessammlungen' 145 and eadem, 'Version' 278.

471. Fowler-Magerl, 'Vier Kanonessammlungen' 145.

472. Fowler-Magerl, 'Vier Kanonessammlungen' 145; eadem, 'Version' 279.

ments why **C** cannot depend on either **B** or on its presumed archetype. First, **C** does not contain the material found in marginal additions in **B** (and integrated into the collection proper in **V**). Second, while **C** shares some readings with **B** (but not **V**), it sometimes agrees with **S** against **B**, indicating that the exemplar of **C** was closer to the first version than **B** is. In this sense, the 'third' version of the *Caesaraugustana* depends not simply on the second version but an archetype which shared characteristics of both the first and the second versions; the labels should not be understood as claims that the second version pre-dated the third version.

As for the extant manuscripts, **C** clearly pre-dates **V** and in my opinion also **B**. The comparison of **B** and **C** further suggests that there was an archetype with better texts than **B** already containing, or at least travelling with, the new materials found in **B**, **V**, and **C** (but not in **R** and **S**). To judge from **C**, this archetype did not yet contain the most recent elements found in **B** and **V** (Reims 1148, Gratian, and WH 533b). It is possible that the regnal catalogues found in **B**, **V**, and **C** were produced for this lost archetype, which would date it to 1143/44; this, however, is entirely speculative.

As these remarks should have made clear, the *Caesaraugustana*, and perhaps particularly the version found in **C**, still are only imperfectly understood. Only future research will establish the precise relationship between all these versions and manuscripts; until then, I retain the traditional labels but warn the reader to understand them as evidence of a linear development of the *Caesaraugustana*. The collection, like so many other collections, clearly was not only copied but inspired its readers to abbreviate, add, and reorganise the materials it contained.

5.8.7 The *Mare vitreum*: A Note on the Reception of the *Caesaraugustana*

The manuscript Biblioteca Nazionale di Napoli Vittorio Emanuele III, XII. A. 27 (*male* 'XII. A. 23'; *olim* Museo Borbonico, 334. VI. 9. 36; not seen) contains a canon law collection known as *Mare vitreum*.[473] Given the ob-

---

473. As I have not seen the Naples manuscript myself, I have to assume that the following accounts (often using different shelfmarks) all refer to the same manuscript: Theiner, *Disquitiones criticae* 360–363; Paul Hinschius, 'Nachrichten über juristische (insbesondere kanonistische) Handschriften in italienischen Bibliotheken' *Zeitschrift für Rechtsgeschichte* 1 (1861) 467–480, here at 470–471; Emil Seckel, 'Der Titel einer Canones-Sammlung in Geheimschrift' NA 41 (1919) 733–738; Fournier, 'Caesaraugustana' 75; de Ghellinck, *Mouvement* 449 n. 1; Martin, 'Mare uitreum' 52; Fowler-Magerl, *Clavis* 241. Contrary to what Brett, 'Sources' 160 n. 28 could suggest, Fowler-Magerl, 'Vier Kanonessammlungen' does not mention the Naples manuscript; the reference ('Napoli, BN, VI. 9.36 described by Fowler-Magerl') seems to conflate Theiner's account and a predecessor of Fowler-Magerl's *Clavis*.

scure character of the collection, it may seem fitting that its medieval title is encrypted.[474] According to Theiner, the manuscript was written in the thirteenth century and contained the complete *Caesaraugustana* (but no more recent material) divided into ten books, each subdivided into three to nine sections.[475] Fournier wondered whether the division of the material was inspired by Gratian, but in characteristic fashion proposed an earlier date (before 1125) as the collection did not contain, according to him, any materials postdating the pontificate of Paschal II.[476] Martin later confirmed that the collection contained almost all the material of *Caesaraugustana*, but observed that it heavily abbreviated individual canons and also took much material from other sources, with councils of Innocent II as the most recent materials.[477] According to him, the manuscript is from the last third of the twelfth century and was produced in Spain.[478] In 1985, Martin claimed that *Mare vitreum* used the first version of *Caesaraugustana*.[479] Later, he asserted the use of the *Caesaraugustana* without specifying which version was used;[480] but at least one of the canons he discussed in detail is actually from the second version.[481] Martin further pointed out that Cardinal Laborans in the late twelfth century used *Mare vitreum*, apparently for a considerable number of canons,[482] but the precise textual relations between the *Caesaraugustana* versions, *Mare vitreum*, and Laborans' *Compilatio decretorum* remain to be studied.

Nonetheless, it seems clear that *Caesaraugustana* and *Mare vitreum* overlap to a very considerable degree. In particular, the latter contains most *Caesaraugustana* material in long series, including all canons of book one and at least ninety percent of the canons of book two.[483] According to Martin, the subdivisions (called *causae*, apparently inspired by Gratian) in *Mare vitreum* are later additions, while the collection itself may or may not

---

474. It was only deciphered by Seckel, 'Titel' 735. The 'sea of glass' is an allusion to Rev. 4.6.

475. Theiner, *Disquitiones criticae* 360–363.

476. Fournier, 'Caesaraugustana' 75–76.

477. Martin, 'Mare uitreum' 54–55; idem, *Compilatio* esp. 1.28 and Appendix 3.4. His account is based on Fowler-Magerl's analysis of *Caesaraugustana I* as found in a predecessor of the *Clavis* database (Martin, 'Mare uitreum' 54 n. 16; idem, *Compilatio* 1.21 n. 13). Note that **B** and **V** also contain Lateran II canons.

478. Martin, *Compilatio* 1.22–23.

479. Martin, 'Mare uitreum' 54: '*Mare uitreum* übernimmt fast das gesamte Material der *Caesaraugustana* und zwar in der ersten Redaktion.' This was also asserted by Fowler-Magerl, *Clavis* 241 and even more positively by eadem, 'Caesaraugustana' 788.

480. Martin, *Compilatio* 1.22.

481. Martin, *Compilatio* 1.27. The canon in question (Burchard 6.49 = Ivo 10.176 = CC245 in *Clavis*) is found in **B**'s appendix (**B**, fol. 132r).

482. Martin, 'Mare uitreum' 55–59; see also his concordance tables (ibid. 58–59 and in idem, *Compilatio*, vol. 2).

483. Martin, 'Mare uitreum' 55 n. 19.

depend on Gratian.[484] The most recent material found in the *Mare vitreum* in any case are councils of Innocent II, including perhaps Lateran II.[485] In the current state of research, it is not clear whether *Mare vitreum* should be seen as an enlarged *Caesaraugustana* or as a separate collection, or how it can contribute to our understanding of earlier *Caesaraugustana* versions.

5.9 Conclusions: Ancient Authority, New Methods, and the Sacramentalisation of Canon Law

The collections discussed in this chapter emerged from the 'pre-scholastic' milieu of northern France and other regions across Europe. In some respects, these collections were quite traditional. Compared to the 'Gregorian' collections discussed in the last chapter, they contained fewer contentious texts, less recent material, and more traditional canon law. Likewise, the structure of the collections discussed in the present chapter was to considerable degree traditional; the *Collectio Lanfranci* and *Tripartita* A, for example, both resembled older versions of Pseudo-Isidore, and Ivo's *Decretum* was visibly shaped by Burchard's *Liber decretorum*. Yet 'traditional' as they are in some respects, these mostly French collections arguably changed the course of legal history more profoundly than the more experimental 'Gregorian' collections.

There are principally three areas of the law where the collections from the 'pre-scholastic' milieu of the late eleventh and early twelfth centuries had a lasting impact. The most obvious change concerns the legal texts themselves. Taken together, these collections introduced large shares of 'new' material which, on the whole, was retained for a very long time by 'mainstream' canon law. Only a small share of the 'new' material was recent legislation, which in addition was often gathered in appendices rather than integrated into the collections proper. Still, compared to collections like Burchard (where most 'recent' material is presented as if coming from more ancient sources) and *74T* (which at least appeared to contain no recent materials at all), the presence even of a growing number of recent canons was an important change. Nonetheless, on the whole, the 'new old law' was more important: canons that appeared to come, and in most cases indeed came from ancient sources. Some of this 'new' ancient material came from Pseudo-Isidorian sources, including a handful of important documents like the Donation of Constantine, which gained wide

---

484. Martin, 'Mare uitreum' 53–54; idem, *Compilatio* 1.24–25.
485. Martin, 'Mare uitreum' 55.

circulation for the first time around 1100. Another, very different source of ancient law was Roman law collections including, for the first time in centuries, the Digest. Yet the most important sources of the law for the compilers of collections discussed in the present chapters were the acts of the early councils, papal letters of the first millennium, and above all the writings of the Church Fathers like Augustine of Hippo, Ambrose of Milan, and Gregory the Great. Their names were well known, and many of their works were readily available long before the period under discussion here; but only with the Ivonian collections were they introduced into 'mainstream' canon law at a massive scale. Often, the new excerpts were not taken from some florilegia, but apparently were the result of careful reading of the patristic works in questions. This is in many cases supported by the rather precise inscriptions which indicate author, book title, and often chapter numbers—rather than only vague references like 'Gregorius dixit' one finds in earlier collections.

A look at the material sources of the *Decretum Gratiani* can help to illuminate how this development indeed changed the fabric of canon law. Not only does Gratian have massively more patristic material than any pre-1050 collection; the overlap with older collections like Burchard's *Liber decretorum* is relatively small. Most of Gratian's 1,000-odd patristic canons had only been introduced into canon law one or two generations before, with Ivo's *Decretum* ultimately contributing the largest portion.[486] The share of patristic canons was clearly rising in the century before Gratian; to take the most influential collections as an example, Burchard took less than ten percent of his material ultimately from patristic authors, but in the *Panormia* the share was already some twenty-five percent, and in Gratian roughly a third of the texts are patristic.[487] As new materials were added, other texts were dropped; Munier calculated that of Ivo's 143 patristic canons on marriage law no less than 123 were 'new' in the sense that they were not found in earlier canon law collections.[488] Unsurprisingly, the overlap between Burchard and Gratian—the collection most widely used

---

486. For the numbers, see Munier, *Sources patristiques* and Landau, 'Wandel und Kontinuität' 219–221. Landau concluded (ibid. 221): '[S]o kann man ohne Übertreibung sagen, daß im wesentlichen Ivo von Chartres und Gratian die Patristik zum Bestandteil des Kirchenrechts gemacht haben und diesem damit eine konzeptionell derart differenzierte Textgrundlage gaben, daß auf ihr sich eine wissenschaftlich selbständige Kanonistik aufbauen ließ. [. . .] [Dies war] eine geistige Leistung ersten Ranges, die man durchaus neben die Leistung der Durchdringung der Digesten durch die erste Generation der Glossatoren setzen kann.'

487. Munier, *Sources patristiques*, summarised and added to by Jean Werckmeister, 'The Reception of the Church Fathers in Canon Law', *The Reception of the Church Fathers in the West: From the Carolingians to the Maurists*, ed. Iréna Dorota Backus (2 vols. Leiden 1997) 1.51–81.

488. Munier, *Sources patristiques*.

before the Ivonian collections emerged, and the collection that became the standard textbook in the second half of the twelfth century—is very small if one only looks at the patristic material.[489]

Behind these bare numbers was a fundamental change in the sources of the law, and also the areas in which ecclesiastical law was seen as relevant. This brings us to the second point, the impact of the collections studied in this chapter on the material law. Without the massive use of patristic materials, canon law on marriage, baptism, penance, and the Eucharist could not have developed the way it did in the century or so before Gratian. At the same time, it is also true that without the extension of the Church's jurisdiction on marriage, the debates about the Eucharist, the question of the validity of sacraments of heretics and schismatics, the writings of Augustine and the other fathers would not have been searched for authoritative answers to the burning questions of this time. All collections discussed in this chapter, in different ways, were shaped by these debates, and they all in turn contributed, if only by providing more and more ancient materials, above all from patristic sources.

It is no exaggeration to say that this reception of patristic material changed the very nature of canon law. With the great influx of patristic authorities, and the more refined treatment of marriage, baptism, the Eucharist, excommunication, holy orders, and many other issues touching on the understanding of the sacraments, medieval canon law became much more 'sacramental' in character. Canon law around 1100 dealt with the sacraments in much greater detail than ever before, and contained much more sacramental theology than earlier collections had done.[490] Again the contrast between Burchard and 'Gratian the theologian' may be quoted to illustrate (not to prove) this change.[491] The new focus on the sacraments in canon law is visible in both the number and the quality of mainly patristic texts on marriage, baptism, and other 'sacramental' areas of the law, and also the fact that a considerable number of collections—the Ivonian collections, but also Bonizo, for example—placed books on the sacraments first.

Much of this 'new' material was taken from the Fathers, but charac-

---

489. Landau, 'Wandel und Kontinuität'.

490. This was rightly stressed by Peter Landau, 'Sakramentalität und Jurisdiktion', *Das Recht der Kirche, Bd. 2: Zur Geschichte des Kirchenrechts*, ed. Gerhard Rau et al. (Forschungen und Berichte der Evangelischen Studiengemeinschaft 50; Gütersloh 1995) 58–95, largely in opposition to Sohm's model of 'sacramental canon law' in the first millenium for which see Rudolph Sohm, *Das altkatholische Kirchenrecht und das Dekret Gratians. Festschrift für A. Wach* (Munich 1918).

491. See Wei, *Gratian* both on 'Gratian the theologian' and the relevant historiography. Arguments against the relevance of the 'theological' content of the *Decretum Gratiani* tend to be related to debates on Sohm's concept of 'sacramental' canon law, on which see Landau, 'Sakramentalität'.

teristically, these century-old texts were combined with much more recent texts. For example, canonical collections around 1100 came to include 'new' Augustinian material on the Eucharist, some Carolingian theology, the tracts of the Berengar controversy, and very recent conciliar acts dealing with the same debate. In other words, where Burchard mainly was content to present some canons on how to celebrate mass, scholars like Ivo of Chartres tried to integrate theological materials from the fourth, ninth, and eleventh centuries to establish a nuanced understanding of the Eucharist. Likewise, in the decades around 1100 a number of 'new' key texts on marriage were integrated into canon law; some were taken from ancient Roman law, some from papal letters of the mid-fifth century (Leo I), others from Carolingian times (Nicholas's *Responsa ad consulta Bulgarorum*). No wonder that Gratian in his treatment of marriage thought it necessary to remind his readers that the meaning of Latin terms, like *sponsa*, had changed over the centuries. Equally unsurprisingly, for the distinction of different meanings (*distinctio*) of this term, he drew on the relevant patristic literature.[492] The combination of materials from biblical times to the present in the collections made it necessary to pay more attention than ever to the background of these texts.

This brings us to the third point where the collections coming from the scholastic milieux of northern France and other parts of Europe innovated. It was one thing to search and find, relevant conciliar, papal, and patristic authorities on various aspects of canon law including the administration of the sacraments; but it was quite another to work out how to understand these proof texts. The debate on the Eucharist started (and repeatedly restarted) by Berengar of Tours served as an important reminder to pre-Gratian legal scholars that quoting the authoritative texts themselves was not enough to win a debate. Berengar may have been a 'champion of authoritative writing',[493] and likewise many of his opponents stressed time and again that their position was based on the Bible and revered patristic writings. Yet the longer the debate continued, presumably the more scholars learnt that this was not enough to convince their opponents, and in many cases not even enough to reassure their own pupils and supporters.

In short, the question of how to understand and reconcile the canons was more urgent than ever. This in itself was a reason for the new search for patristic authorities, as exegetical literature had addressed contradic-

---

492. C.27 q.2 cc.40–45 (ed. Winroth 748–751), drawing ultimately on Jerome, John Chyrsostom, Origen, Gregory the Great, etc.

493. See Holopainen, *Dialectic* 108–113 and 117 (quote).

tions in the Bible long before 'canon law' came to develop its own methods; rhetoric, secular law, and even hagiography could equally serve as models for how to distinguish different meanings and how to reconcile seeming contradictions.[494] The compilers of the collections discussed in the last two chapters approached the latter problem in different ways. Some of them addressed the issue in the prefaces, or less frequently in other forms of comment found in the collections themselves (Bonizo and Alger stand out in this respect). Yet more frequently, they used the same techniques they were familiar with for other problems. To address the issue of understanding canonical authority, they gathered excerpts on this topic taken from conciliar canons, papal letters, patristic writings, and related sources. This is true for the compiler of *Tripartita* A; when faced with the complex transmission of Greek councils and the controversies surrounding some of them, he chose to introduce the relevant sections of his collection with canons and historiographial notes on the reception of these councils (*Tripartita* A2.10A). Ivo of Chartres, in addition to his celebrated *Prologue*, in books four and five of his *Decretum* gathered canons on the authority of canons and the issue of contradictions in canon law. Gregory of San Grisogono in his *Polycarpus* did the same with fewer, very carefully selected canons on 'ratio et auctoritas' in canon law. The *Caesaraugustana*, finally, composed a complete book on this issue and placed it prominently at the beginning of the collection. All these compilers, therefore, addressed the complexities of canonical tradition by adding relevant excerpts mainly taken from the same sources, again turning mainly to patristic writings, not least Augustine's philosophical works.

All three developments—the 'rediscovery' of ancient authorities, the new emphasis on the sacraments, and the new focus on canonical authority—changed western canon law profoundly. Some of these developments directly informed the most influential canon law collection of the period, namely the *Decretum Gratiani*; for example, the Gratians were influenced very directly by the *Tripartita*, the *Panormia*, and the *Collection in Three Books* for their own choice of patristic materials. In other respects, the *Decretum Gratiani* adopted similar solutions to those sketched above without using the collections discussed here; for example, the tract *De legibus* (DD.1–20) is structurally similar to, and partly overlaps with, the first book of the *Caesaraugustana*. This in my view strengthens rather than weakens the argument that the pre-Gratian collections discussed in this chapter

---

494. See Genka, 'Hierarchie' (exegesis) and idem, 'Role of Hagiography' on hierarchies of authority in hagiographical sources; in addition, the 'distinction' of different meanings is commonplace in hagiography from early on.

made important innovations. The point is not that they helped to prepare the *Decretum Gratiani*; there is no reason to believe the *Caesaraugustana* was known in Bologna. Rather, all these collections—the *Collectio Lanfranci*, the Ivonian collections, Gratian, and so on—and likewise the works traditionally labelled 'theological' sentence collections all emerged from the same scholarly culture. Northern France played a crucial role in the emergence of this milieu of wandering scholars and growing numbers of 'schools', but as the example of the *Caesaraugustana* in particular should have made clear, this culture was not limited to any part of western Europe. Teachers and pupils travelling from place to place, scholars exchanging letters and manuscripts, canons regular building networks in northern Europe as well as in the Mediterrenean, popes and their legates travelling between Rome and various regions, synods bringing together prelates of very different background—they all directly or indirectly helped to lay the foundations of a new legal culture across large parts of Latin Europe.

6

Papal Councils, 1049–1179

Selected Topics

By Robert Somerville

6.1 Introduction

This chapter has been in the making, as has the volume in which it is printed, for a long time. In the process the chapter changed as a result of progress in research about medieval canon law in general and about the history of Church councils in particular. Better understanding of the textual traditions of many of the sources together with the perspectives of recent narrative accounts made earlier versions of the chapter in need of revision.[1] This was so especially regarding the elaborate array of footnotes which had grown up around the text. It is hoped that this newly

* Deep thanks to Robert H. Scott of the Columbia University Libraries for flawlessly transferring my old NB files into Word files, and to Yanchen Liu, now of Hong Kong University, for assistance at various points with this chapter.

1. Earlier useful works of recent decades include Odette Pontal, *Les conciles de la France capétienne jusqu'en 1215* (Paris 1995); Georg Gresser, *Die Synoden und Konzilien in der Zeit des Reformpapsttums in Deutschland und Italien von Leo IX. bis Calixt II. (1049–1123)* (Konziliengeschichte. Reihe A: Darstellungen; Paderborn, Munich, and Vienna 2006); Anne J. Duggan, 'Conciliar Law 1123–1215: The Legislation of the Four Lateran Councils', *The History of Medieval Canon Law in the Classical Period: From Gratian to the Decretals of Pope Gregory IX*, ed. Wilfried Hartmann and Kenneth Pennington (HMCL; Washington, D.C. 2008) 318–366.

revised, shorter, and less heavily documented version will be useful as a basic guide for future research on papal councils in the years between the pontificates of Leo IX and Alexander III. The topics treated were chosen from numerous possibilities for two reasons. In the first place, those issues are important for the development of the medieval Church, and secondly, they are of more than passing interest to the author.

The one hundred and thirty years between the pontificate of Leo IX (1049–54), and the end of the reign of Alexander III (1159–81), was an age of vigorous conciliar activity on the part of the bishops of Rome. The proceedings from some of those gatherings are very well known, solidly fixed in general histories of the Middle Ages, e.g., the Lateran Council of 1059, with its papal election decree; the Roman Lenten synods of 1076 and 1080, wherein Henry IV was excommunicated by Pope Gregory VII; the Council of Clermont in 1095, and its proclamation of the First Crusade; and the twelfth-century Lateran Councils of 1123, 1139, and 1179, each standing at the end of a period of particular turmoil and thus designated in a later time as 'ecumenical councils' in the Roman Catholic Church. Many important issues in medieval history cannot be understood apart from these synods[2] and their legislation, and modern works devoted to topics as diverse as lay investiture, Eucharistic theology, and even medieval rhetorical theory, have devoted serious attention to councils.[3]

The aim of this chapter, although a very short historical overview is included, is not to write 'a new history' of those assemblies or anything approaching that. There are also available in print detailed treatments of important aspects of synods such as attendance, the development of conciliar theory, and the liturgical procedures—the orders (*ordines*)—used therein.[4]

2. Medieval sources are inconsistent in using the terms 'council' and 'synod', and the words often are employed interchangeably: see Horst Fuhrmann, 'Das Ökumenische Konzil und seine historischen Grundlagen' *Geschichte in Wissenschaft und Unterricht* 12 (1961) 672–695, here at 676. They will be employed as synonyms; see also below (6.3 'General Council').

3. Rudolf Schieffer, *Die Entstehung des päpstlichen Investiturverbots für den deutschen König* (MGH Schriften 28; Stuttgart 1981); Charles M. Radding and Francis Newton, *Theology, Rhetoric, and Politics in the Eucharistic Controversy, 1078–1079: Alberic of Monte Cassino Against Berengar of Tours* (New York 2003); John O. Ward, 'Some Principles of Rhetorical Historiography in the Twelfth Century', *Classical Rhetoric and Medieval Historiography*, ed. Ernst Breisach (Studies in Medieval Culture 19; Kalamazoo, Mich. 1985) 103–165.

4. For attendance, see Georgine Tangl, *Die Teilnehmer an den allgemeinen Konzilien des Mittelalters* (Weimar 1922), with additional information in Raymonde Foreville, *Latran, I, II, III et Latran IV* (Histoire des conciles œcuméniques 6; Paris 1965). For conciliar theory, Tierney covers the canonists from Gratian into the fourteenth century: Brian Tierney, *Foundations of the Conciliar Theory: The Contribution of the Medieval Canonists from Gratian to the Great Schism* (Studies in the History of Christian Thought 92; Cambridge 1955). The essays of Sieben are useful, and some deal with the period before Gratian not dealt with by Tierney: Hermann Josef Sieben, *Die Konzilsidee des lateinischen Mittelalters (847–1378)* (Konziliengeschichte. Untersuchungen 2; Paderborn 1984). See also Schneider's exhaustive work on the transmission of the liturgical *ordines de*

A systematic discussion of the history of councils between Leo IX and Alexander III, taking account of these and other significant themes, is a desideratum on multiple fronts and especially for the study of the medieval papacy. Yet attempting to produce it is a perilous undertaking in light of questions which remain unanswered about how these gatherings worked and what they did.[5]

The starting point for those investigations is an assessment of the primary source evidence. It is not, of course, inaccurate to state that on one level the general trends and many of the acts within that history are clear, and can be found delineated and discussed in the literature. At another level, however, this history is riddled with uncertainty about important details which concern both the general picture and the activity of individual synods. The audience for this chapter includes those in early stages of historical study as well as seasoned scholars, and for both groups careful evaluation of historical sources and methods for their study is crucial. The purpose is not to cast gloom over the possibility of a general history of these synods, but rather to highlight how such a history can be made richer and especially to serve as a guide to areas where important opportunities exist for further research.

With these goals in mind the shape of the chapter can be outlined. Following this introduction, a short series of historical remarks will establish a basic chronological framework, followed in turn by two other sections: first a short essay on the often misunderstood term 'general council', as it emerged in the High Middle Ages, followed by a discussion of sources for synodal research, and in particular the conciliar canons or decrees.

6.2 Historical Overview

Many synods in the eleventh and twelfth centuries were convened across Christendom not only by popes, but also by papal legates, or by other authorities.[6] This array of conciliar history offers material for multiple chapters, and although non-papal councils obviously inform a discussion of papal assemblies in various ways (see below, 'Sources'), they will not be treated here. The papal 'general council' which emerged after the

---

celebrendo concilio: Herbert Schneider, 'Einleitung', *Die Konzilsordines des Früh- und Hochmittelalters*, ed. idem (MGH Ordines; Hanover 1996) 1–124.

5. Franz-Josef Schmale, 'Systematisches zu den Konzilien des Reformpapsttums im 12. Jahrhundert' AHC 6 (1974) 21–39 sketched a systematic framework for treating papal councils of the eleventh and twelfth centuries, in anticipation of writing a new synthesis of these gatherings. See Gresser, *Synoden und Konzilien* VII.

6. Here and at all points in this chapter recourse should be made to the material in Jasper's edition (MGH Conc. 8).

mid-eleventh century represents a new institution, whose roots are found in Roman metropolitan councils, although the influence of the Ottonian and early-Salian imperial synods cannot be discounted. The Roman provincial councils visible in the tenth and early eleventh centuries seem to be decidedly local affairs; the imperial synods were grander, where popes on occasion participated and would have had positions of authority. Even Pope Leo IX once sat in council with Emperor Henry III, at Mainz in 1049, and pope and emperor may have presided jointly over some of the proceedings. At the very poorly documented Council of Florence (1055), Henry again was on hand, this time with Pope Victor II, but leadership of the synod probably was in papal hands.

Even without the death of Henry in 1056 and the minority of his son, Henry IV, the papal Reformers' developing conciliar theory may have made repetition of Mainz or of Florence unlikely. From the time of Leo IX onward, by forceful articulation of its authority, by expanding the circle of participants to include churchmen from throughout Europe, and by treating a wide range of issues with ramifications beyond local boundaries, the papacy was able to infuse councils with broadening authority. Gérard Fransen emphasized the importance of this development by noting that even in the face of a blunt proclamation of absolute papal powers such as found in Gregory VII's *Dictatus papae*, legislation intended for the entire Church in general was set forth by the Reformers only in their synods.[7]

The replacement of earlier conciliar models by the 'general councils' of the Reform Papacy cannot be traced in great detail, either conceptually or functionally, given the fragmentary state of the evidence.[8] Towards the middle of the twelfth century, however, the maturing canonical tradition of the Latin Church systematized that development. *Distinctiones* 17 and 18 of Gratian's *Decretum* paved the way, by collecting a series of texts laying out differences between papal and non-papal synods, and subsequent commentary on Gratian sharpened and focused the discussion. The *Summa Parisiensis*, composed in the third quarter of the twelfth century, commenting in an oft-quoted passage on D.17 of the *Decretum*, put it this way:[9]

---

7. Gérard Fransen, 'L'écclésiologie des conciles médiévaux', *Le concile et les conciles: contribution à l'histoire de la vie conciliaire de l'église* ([Gembloux] 1960) 125–141, here at 132–133.

8. Sieben, *Konzilsidee* 114 laments the lack of sources for tracing conciliar theory in the Gregorian age.

9. *The Summa Parisiensis on the Decretum Gratiani*, ed. Terence P. McLaughlin (Toronto 1952), here at 17: 'Sciendum itaque quod concilium aliud generale fit praesente papa vel ejus legato vel alias ejus habita auctoritate, puta per litteras [...]. Aliud concilium est provinciale et hoc quandoque fit annuatim consuetudine, quandoque aliqua imminente necessitate fit alia vice [...].'

> It should be recognized that one type of council is general, which occurs in the presence of the pope or his legate or otherwise on the basis of his authority, for example, through letters [...]. Another type of council is provincial, and sometimes this occurs annually by custom, sometimes in another way due to some impending necessity.

The schema represented here was expressed similarly in other decretist writings, and eventually found its way into Johannes Teutonicus's *Glossa ordinaria* on Gratian. It is the culmination of intellectual traditions of conciliar theory which are at least as old as the Pseudo-Isidorian forgeries of the late Carolingian age, but which developed and moved from theory into practice during the Reforming movement of the eleventh and twelfth centuries. Church councils became both pulpits and courts. Synods proclaimed papal policies, were forums for the adjudication of disputes before the pope or his representative, and, together with the use of legates and the dispatch of briefs, constituted one of the distinctive instruments by which the Reformers labored to articulate their views to the Latin world and even beyond. Never in the history of the Church did councils under the leadership of the bishops of Rome convene as frequently as during the century from 1050 to 1150.

Yet why specifically is Leo IX's pontificate seen as a turning point in development of this process?[10] Whatever notions can be traced through the post-Carolingian period about the role of the bishop of Rome in councils, the view that the late ninth and tenth centuries were incapable, in meaningful ways, of implementing any conciliar ideas which focused on 'a Roman center' has much to commend it.[11] The mid-eleventh century, however, witnessed a change, and Leo IX's well-known letters written in 1053 to North African bishops express new views, yet views which were firmly anchored in the tradition. A 'universal council', Leo wrote, ought not to be celebrated without the approval of the bishop of Rome.[12] How Leo was using the term *universale concilium* is a debated matter, to be touched on again below in the discussion of the term 'General Council'. What is clear is the pope's emphatic statement that papal approval was determi-

---

10. E.g. Tangl, *Teilnehmer* 132; Martin Boye, 'Die Synoden Deutschlands und Reichsitaliens (922–1059). Eine kirchenverfassungsgeschichtliche Studie' ZRG Kan. Abt. 18 (1929) 131–284, here at 160; Fuhrmann, 'Ökumenisches Konzil' 681; Franz-Josef Schmale, 'Synoden Papst Alexanders II. (1061–1073). Anzahl, Termine, Entscheidungen' AHC 11 (1979) 307–338, here at 308; Johannes Laudage, *Priesterbild und Reformpapsttum im 11. Jahrhundert* (Beihefte zum Archiv für Kulturgeschichte 22; Cologne and Vienna 1984) 8; Uta-Renate Blumenthal, *The Investiture Controversy: Church and Monarchy from the Ninth to the Twelfth Century* (Philadelphia 1988) 73; Heinz Wolter, *Die Synoden im Reichsgebiet und in Reichsitalien von 916 bis 1056* (Paderborn and Munich 1988) 405–406.

11. Fuhrmann, 'Ökumenisches Konzil' 681.

12. JL 4304 and 4305.

native for a special category of synods, a category which comes to be synonymous with the 'general councils' of which the *Summa Parisiensis* will speak a century later.

What actually was new in Pope Leo's synods? The question is a fair one, although the episodic survival of information about proceedings and decisions in those assemblies does not permit as full an answer as would be hoped. Canons from Leo IX's councils apparently did not circulate widely and seem barely to be represented in canonical collections assembled in subsequent decades. It is, however, noteworthy that, even in later times Leo's pontificate and his synods, were recalled as events which set precedents. In 1075, for example, Pope Gregory VII informed a group of German dukes that the Roman Church had attacked the evils of simoniacal appointments and 'the sin of fornication' (*crimen fornicationis*) 'from the time of blessed Pope Leo often in councils'; and versions of decrees from the 1059 Lateran Synod of Pope Nicholas II, and perhaps also from a council of Alexander II, invoked Leo's 'constitution regarding chastity of the clergy'.[13]

Regulations against simony and clerical incontinence, which served as key elements of the eleventh-century Reformers' drive for purity in the Church and which did form part of Leo's synods, had been promulgated in earlier councils and as such were not new.[14] But aside from the specific formulations which Leo's decrees would have presented on those matters, his five-year reign was marked by a new zeal to resolve disputes and problems, and to travel throughout Christendom and repeatedly to celebrate synods. The papacy's function as a tribunal and as a legislative center for the whole Church was given more vivid meaning. Leo held at least eleven councils during his five-year pontificate—perhaps the number is even higher—in locations as diverse as Reims, Siponto, and Vercelli.[15] Apart from the aforementioned mutual enterprise at Mainz in 1049 with Henry III, these assemblies—some in locations far from Rome and none richly documented—seem unambiguously to have been under the pope's control.

Synods could produce dramatic moments as some anecdotal episodes illustrate. As narrated by Anselm of Saint-Rémi, who was there to see what happened, Leo's use at Reims of both his own authority and that

---

13. Gregory VII, JL 4922; Lateran 1059, JL 4404 (ed. Jasper, MGH Conc. 8.404–407); JL 4405/4406 (ibid. 402–404); Alexander II, JL 4501 (ed. Nass, MGH Briefe dt. Kaiserzeit 10.241–244 no. 155). See the questions raised by Schieffer, *Entstehung* 84–95, about the provenance of the latter text, often associated with Alexander's Easter Synod of 1063 (Schmale, 'Synoden Alexanders' 311–312) and most recently Nass (MGH Briefe dt. Kaiserzeit 10.241–242).

14. See, e.g., Blumenthal, *Investiture Controversy* 71.

15. See Jasper (MGH Conc. 8.224–250, 267–270, and 292–304) on Reims 1049, Siponte 1050, and Vercelli 1050.

of Saint-Rémi himself was masterful.[16] Eleven years later at the Council of Vienne (1060), to offer a vignette from a legatine assembly, fireworks of a different sort occurred. The presiding Cardinal Stephan of San Grisogono took in his hands and ripped to shreds a privilege which Abbot Durand of Saint-Victor was brandishing in support of his case and against a judgement of the synod.[17] Is it fanciful to connect in spirit the actions of Cardinal Stephan, who presided at Vienne, as a preamble to the canons reported, 'in place of the Lord Pope Nicholas (II)', and the recent humiliation of Berengar of Tours in Nicholas's Lateran Synod of 1059?[18] Almost a century later Eugene III's Council of Reims spent part of its time dealing with the popular preacher, Eon de Stella, a 'mental case', to quote Nicholas Häring, but who had a popular following. Eon was hauled into the assembly and before being pronounced a heretic furnished the council fathers with a bizarre set of comments which, although hardly threatening, did provide comic relief.[19]

Yet it is one thing to condemn either the Eucharistic teachings put forward by a theologian from the Loire Valley or the fantasies of a popular preacher from Brittany, but quite another to contemplate proceedings against a Roman pontiff. Although the charged atmosphere which must have surrounded the event is not accentuated in the fragmentary sources which survive, the Lenten Lateran Council of March 1112, must have convened amid intense tensions. Under the leadership of bishops and cardinals the synod may have attempted to remove Pope Paschal II, whose concessions in the previous year to Emperor Henry V about ecclesiastical elections and lay investiture were viewed by some if not by many as heretical.[20] The conciliar proceedings cannot be reconstructed in detail, but Uta-Renate Blumenthal concluded that 'the assembly must have charged Paschal with heresy and that his heresy was the main subject of discussion

16. See Anselm's text (ed. Jasper, MGH Conc. 8.213). This chapter cannot generally take account of descriptions of the councils under discussion in secondary literature, but an exception will be made for the compelling recreation and interpretation of the Council of Reims by Richard William Southern, *The Making of the Middle Ages* (London 1953), here at 125–127.

17. Robert Somerville, 'Cardinal Stephan of St. Grisogono: Some Remarks on Legates and Legatine Councils in the Eleventh Century', *Law, Church, and Society: Essays in Honor of Stephan Kuttner*, ed. Kenneth Pennington and Robert Somerville ([Philadelphia] 1977) 157–166. The Latin is 'disruptum est' (ibid. 165 n. 52).

18. For Berengar at the Lateran Council of 1059 see Detlev Jasper, '[Einleitung:] Rom Ende April–Anfang Mai 1059', *Die Konzilien Deutschlands und Reichsitaliens 1023–1059*, ed. idem (MGH Conc. 8; Hanover 2010) 352–381, here at 362–363.

19. Nikolaus M. Häring, 'Notes on the Council and the Consistory of Rheims (1148)' MS 28 (1966) 39–59, here at 45.

20. Uta-Renate Blumenthal, *The Early Councils of Pope Paschalis II 1100–1110* (PIMS Studies and Texts 43; Toronto 1978), here at 84 and 93ff.; see also Rolker's chapter on Gregory of San Grisogono in Chapter 4.7 above.

day after day'.[21] The pontiff escaped deposition, although the activities of 1111–1112 dogged the remainding five years of his reign. Notwithstanding the turmoil hidden beneath its fragmentary 'acta', however, the Lateran Synod of 1112, noted by Ian Robinson to be 'without parallel in the history of the papal synods of the late eleventh and twelfth centuries', was a temporary hiatus in the process of papal control over its councils.[22]

The pontificates of Urban II, Calixtus II, Innocent II, and Eugene III, each has been singled out for various reasons as crucial in the development of papal synodal ideas and practice. Whatever changes can be discerned in conciliar activity as the papacy traversed the years of the late-eleventh and early-twelfth centuries, e.g., shifts in legislative themes, increased authority on the part of the cardinals, increasing attendance, and even progressive lengthening of the texts of canons, it would be difficult to see papal synods after 1123 as conceived in a manner fundamentally different from those of Popes Calixtus II, or Paschal II and Urban II, or perhaps even of Gregory VII. But did papal councils convene less frequently as the twelfth century progressed? The pontificates of Calixtus II and Honorius II do reveal a fading of these assemblies from prominence in the sources, but did they actually meet less often?

The first year of Calixtus II's reign was marked by the two (relatively) well-documented papal synods of 1119, in Toulouse and Reims. No trace appears of another such gathering until the Council of Crotone, early in January, 1122.[23] Given the virtual non-existence of sources for this assembly, other councils, for which all traces now have vanished, also could have been celebrated between late 1119 and early 1122.[24] After the great Lateran Council of March, 1123, Calixtus presided over at least one additional synod, in late 1123 or early in 1124 again at the Lateran, but as with Crotone, almost nothing is known about it.[25] In November, 1127, Pope Honorius II held a council at Troia, and he seems also to have convoked a Roman synod in April of the following year.[26] Little is known about either gathering and both easily could have vanished from sight, so cau-

---

21. Blumenthal, *Early Councils* 95.

22. Ian Stuart Robinson, *The Papacy 1073–1198: Continuity and Innovation* (Cambridge Medieval Textbooks; Cambridge 1990), here at 128–131.

23. *Italia pontificia* 10.81 no. *9, referring to JL post 6941.

24. Hefele-Leclercq 5.1:608–609, saw Calixtus holding a Roman council early in January 1121, on the basis of JL 6886 (*Italia pontificia* 6.1:324 no. 7), but that text does not speak specifically of a council or synod.

25. See *Italia pontificia* 5.58 no. *192, referring to JL post 7138.

26. See *Italia pontificia* 8.34 no. *124, referring to JL ante 7294, for Troia, and JL post 7308 for Rome. For the pontificate of Calixtus II see Beate Schilling, *Guido von Vienne – Papst Calixt II.* (MGH Schriften 45; Hanover 1998).

tion is advisable in concluding that these were the only papal councils of Honorius's pontificate.

The impression is unmistakable, however, that convocation of new papal councils was a devalued activity during the third decade of the twelfth century. The reasons might be sought in several places. Andresen points to the political tensions at Rome in the 1120s to explain the inability of Honorius II to hold a Lateran Council.[27] The ratified concord between Calixtus II and Henry V on lay investiture and the concomitant slate of detailed legislation from Lateran I have been proposed to explain the subdued conciliar activity in the years immediately thereafter.[28] Yet whether or not in partial eclipse, the schism spilling from the conclave assembled in early 1130 to choose a successor for Honorius II revived papal councils on one side of the ensuing schism. Between 1130 and 1139 Pope Innocent II convened several synods (although none is documented for his papal rival Anaclete II). The legislation from these gatherings is at times strikingly repetitive, but recent work on the transmission of the decrees of Innocent II's synods provides a better basis than available up to now for evaluating these gatherings and the nuances to be found in the decrees.[29]

The Lateran Council of 1123 marked the end of a crisis for the papacy, and the same is true of Innocent II's Lateran Council of 1139. Papal councils then seem simply to vanish for almost a decade. No hint of one appears in the calendar compiled in JL for the remainder of Innocent II's pontificate, nor for the reigns of Popes Celestine II, Lucius II, and the first three years of Eugene III's pontificate. Pope Eugene did not convene a council at Trier, as has sometimes been asserted;[30] but for his Council of Reims in March, 1148, he took the severe but perhaps not unprecedented step of suspending all those who failed to obey his summons to attend.[31] This action has caused Reims to be designated by one writer as 'the first realization of the idea of papal world domination'.[32] Not world domination, however, but moral reform, and dealing with the hapless Eon de

27. Carl Andresen, 'Geschichte der abendländischen Konzile des Mittelalters', *Die ökumenischen Konzile der Christenheit*, ed. Hans Jochen Margull (Stuttgart 1961) 75–200, here at 125.

28. Robert Somerville, *Pope Alexander III and the Council of Tours (1163)* (Berkeley 1977), here at 5.

29. Martin Brett and Robert Somerville, 'The Transmission of the Councils from 1130 to 1139', *Pope Innocent II (1130–43): The World vs the City*, ed. John Doran and Damian J. Smith (CFC; Abingdon and New York 2016) 226–271.

30. Foreville, *Latran I–IV* 101; but see JL †9188 (*Germania pontificia* 4.4:242 no. †4); Häring, 'Rheims 1148' 39.

31. Häring, 'Rheims 1148' 39–41.

32. Häring, 'Rheims 1148' 58, citing Helmut Gleber, *Papst Eugen III. (1145–1153) unter besonderer Berücksichtigung seiner politischen Tätigkeit* (Beiträge zur mittelalterlichen und neueren Geschichte 6; Jena 1936) 83.

Stella, were this synod's aims,[33] although Eugene's bull of convocation sent to Salzburg was not explicit about the issues. The pontiff spoke only of the need 'for beating back many forms of wickedness which threaten, and confirming the things pleasing to God'.[34]

The decrees from Reims were similar to those of earlier synods, especially assemblies of Innocent II, and John of Salisbury lamented their redundancy.[35] John also reported a protest by German prelates against the decree banning multi-colored cloaks for the clergy (c. 2), and noted further that 'some of these [decrees] give birth to ridicule'.[36] Nicholas Häring viewed Reims generally as a badly organized venture, and wrote of the legislative program that 'the preparation for its successful launching was so poor that its message was little more than the lifeless repetition of previously promulgated canons'.[37] The urgency which Pope Eugene felt to reiterate earlier decrees is perhaps echoed by a comment of Ordericus Vitalis, who reported that the rulings from Lateran II, although circulated in all countries, were not treated seriously by the princes and the people.[38] As poorly planned and implemented as Reims might have been, however, Eugene was not totally without ideas about disseminating the canons, for a council met in Cremona four months later to promulgate those rulings in Italy.[39]

A fourteen-year hiatus seemed to have occurred between Cremona and the next known papal synod, the Council of Montpellier, celebrated in 1162 by Pope Alexander III.[40] It has been suggested that the troubles associated with Arnold of Brescia's appearance at Rome hindered Eugene III and Hadrian IV from holding a Lateran council.[41] That could be true (although Hadrian reigned until 1159, four years after Arnold's execution), yet additional factors also were at work in the mid-twelfth century to re-

33. Häring, 'Rheims 1148' 45 and 58.

34. JL 9149 (*Germania pontificia* 1.24 no. 71), where the council initially was announced for Troyes (see Häring, 'Rheims 1148' 39): '[…] pro multis, quae increverunt, enormitatibus propellendis, et confirmandis, quae Deo placitura sunt […] concilium celebrare decrevimus'.

35. *Historia pontificalis* 3, ed. and tr. Marjorie Chibnall, *The Historia Pontificalis of John of Salisbury* (Oxford Medieval Texts; Oxford and New York 1986), here at 8–9.

36. *Historia pontificalis* 3 (ed. Chibnall 8): '[…] de hiis quibusdam risus nascitur […]'.

37. Häring, 'Rheims 1148' 58.

38. *Historia ecclesiastica* 6.39, ed. and tr. Marjorie Chibnall, *The Ecclesiastical History of Orderic Vitalis* (6 vols. Oxford Medieval Texts; Oxford 1969–80), here at 6.528–531. Saint Bernard of Clairvaux later remonstrated similarly with Eugene about the 1148 canons ('You deceive yourself if you think they are observed'), and chastised him for caring more about legislating than about leadership to enforce what was decreed. Bernard of Clairvaux, *De consideratione ad Eugenium papam*, ed. in *Tractatus et opuscula*, ed. Jean Leclercq and H. M. Rochais (Sancti Bernardi Opera 3; Rome 1963) 379–493, here at 446: 'Falleris, si teneri putas.'

39. John of Salisbury, *Historia pontificalis* 21 (ed. Chibnall 50).

40. See the register in the second edition of Jaffé's *Regesta*.

41. Andresen, 'Geschichte' 128.

duce the impulse for popes to call synods. Robinson notes that the juridical function of papal synods, which previously had been an important feature, was from the time of Innocent II transferred increasingly to the meetings of pope and cardinals in consistory.[42] The twelfth-century papacy did not, of course, invent either legatine missions or papal decretal letters, but an increasingly active Roman administration found these institutions increasingly useful. Papal councils simply were becoming less essential than in decades past as a mechanism for governing the Church. Decretal letters, legates, and decisions made in other ways were supplanting the need to assemble clerics from various regions to participate in such meetings.

A crisis, however, still could demand the forum provided by a council. As Innocent II did in the 1130s, so in the early 1160s, Alexander III—away from Rome north of the Alps and facing a schism—held synods. The first, poorly documented, convened at Montpellier in May 1162, and a second, better known, met almost a year later at Tours.[43] These gatherings, together with others such as the Council of Venice in August 1177,[44] and especially the great Lateran Council of 1179, mark further stages in the development of the twelfth-century papal general council, and, to quote Georgine Tangl, are not 'something positively new'.[45] That would occur, Tangl continued, only in 1215 with Innocent III's Lateran Council and its conscious imitation of the great councils of Antiquity.

Lateran III has benefited from detailed, modern scrutiny. To select only three titles: the papers from the 'Table Ronde' convened in 1980 by the French Centre nationale de la Recherche Scientifique;[46] in 2013 a new edition of the 1179 decrees, prepared by Atria Larson and Ken Pennington, put the transmission of the canons in a new light;[47] and in 2019 Danica Summerlin published a monographic study of Lateran III, based in great part on unpublished research of Professor Walther Holtzmann of Bonn (d. 1962).[48] Ian Robinson's succinct observation that at Lateran III 'the conciliar decrees were formulated by canon lawyers' is true, and the three works

42. Robinson, *Papacy* 139 and 145.

43. Somerville, *Alexander III* 1–11.

44. JL ante 12901.

45. Tangl, *Teilnehmer* 196; and see the fine essay by Raymonde Foreville, 'La place de Latran III dans l'histoire conciliaire du XIIe siècle', *Le troisième Concile de Latran (1179): sa place dans l'histoire: communications présentées à la Table ronde du C.N.R.S., le 26 avril 1980*, ed. Jean Longère (Paris 1982) 11–17.

46. See last note.

47. COGD 2.1:115–147.

48. Danica Summerlin, *The Canons of the Third Lateran Council of 1179: Their Origins and Reception* (Life and Thought: Fourth Series 116; Cambridge 2019).

just noted offer elaboration of that fact.[49] They testify to that development, yet details of the mechanism through which this occurred, and the events behind the scenes which paved the way for the three public sessions, are difficult to discern. These factors make it feasible if not prudent to end this survey here, without attempting to encapsulate the 1179 assembly. A comparative study of Tours 1163, and Lateran III, looking at all aspects of Alexander III's two best documented synods, would be valuable and yet to be attempted. The differences and similarities would be illuminating, as the Roman Church moves from decades marked by frequent papal synods to the world in infrequent gatherings and the monarchical papacy. The decrees from Tours and Lateran III were incorporated in very great part into the *Decretales* or *Liber extra* of Pope Gregory IX (1234), thus becoming part of the Roman Catholic Church's official body of canon law.

6.3 'General Council'

The historical overview introduced a specific type of council which rose to prominence in the Church after the mid-eleventh century. The sources employ an array of terminology when speaking of these synods. Of the designations which are used, however, the words 'general' or 'universal' 'council' or 'synod' (*concilium/synodus, generale/generalis, universale/universalis*), have special interest and deserve comment.

Misunderstanding what is at issue with those terms arises for several reasons. The adjectives *generalis* and *universalis*, in the first place, occur or do not occur in what appears to be an indiscriminate manner to refer to councils of different types. They are at times employed by popes themselves, as in a well-known passage in the *Dictatus papae* of Pope Gregory VII, but the actual institution being described in such cases eludes precise characterization. A papal 'general council' in the medieval sense, moreover, can be confused with the contemporary term 'ecumenical council'. This is an understandable situation because the Lateran Synods from the years 1123, 1139, and 1179, have come to be grouped in the Roman Catholic Church, along with others both from Antiquity and also from after the twelfth century, as a special set of 'ecumenical' or 'universal' councils. The Roman Church today numbers twenty-one such assemblies, from Nicaea I in the year 325 to the Second Vatican Council of the years 1962–65. This enumeration rests on tradition, and not on papal or conciliar decree, and at different times in the late-medieval and early-modern period different synods were placed on lists of the ecumenical councils. The present rank-

---

49. Robinson, *Papacy* 141.

ing emerged at the end of the sixteenth century, but the details of how and why are beyond what can be treated here.[50]

The three twelfth-century Lateran synods could commend themselves for inclusion in such a category, however, both because of their convocation in that special location at a time when most papal councils met elsewhere, and because of the fact that each of these gatherings stood at the end of a serious controversy in the Roman Church's history: 1122–23, the conclusion of the Investiture Dispute; 1138–39, liquidation of the Anacletian Schism; 1177, peace between Pope Alexander III and Frederick Barbarossa. All three councils thus can be seen as representing turning points in the Church. For a proper understanding of the eleventh- and twelfth-century notion of 'general council', nevertheless, it is important to bear in mind that the 'universal' or 'ecumenical' status of those assemblies in the modern sense rests on determinations made about their significance long after they met. It is difficult to assess the extent to which they were viewed differently from other twelfth-century papal synods, but notwithstanding their location, as was discussed toward the end of the previous section, at least Lateran I and II probably were not conceived as strikingly dissimilar from other papal councils of the time.[51]

The definition of a general council achieved a degree of clarity in the writing of the canonists known as the Decretists, i.e., those who commented on Gratian's *Decretum*, after the middle of the twelfth century. The systematization in the *Summa Parisiensis*, which was quoted as an example above (in the 'Historical Overview') represents, it has been said, a triumph of Gregorian conciliar theory.[52] To follow the details of this development is an intricate process, and if the question is, 'What was a general council in the eleventh and twelfth centuries?' the issue is muddied and no satisfactory answer is possible because those words can be applied to many sorts are councils. Hauck's remarks from the beginning of the twentieth century, although intended for an earlier period of Church history, illustrate the way in which that designation could be used in the eleventh and twelfth centuries.

> [...] in a bishopric a diocesan synod was, in distinction from a local court (*Sendgericht*), a general synod [...]. In an archbishopric a provincial synod was, in distinction from a diocesan synod, a universal council.[53]

---

50. Fuhrmann, 'Ökumenisches Konzil' 688 n. 656, and see particularly Remigius Bäumer, 'Die Zahl der allgemeinen Konzilien in der Sicht von Theologen des 15. und 16. Jahrhunderts' AHC 1 (1969) 288–313.

51. For Lateran III see the discussion at the very end of the previous section.

52. Fuhrmann, 'Ökumenisches Konzil' 686.

53. Albert Hauck, 'Die Rezeption und Umbildung der allgemeinen Synode im Mittelalter' *Historische Vierteljahrsschrift* 10 (1907) 465–482, here at 467; Boye, 'Synoden' 191.

What did Pope Leo IX mean by the term 'universal council', when informing the African bishops in 1053 that such an assembly could not be celebrated without the approval of the bishop of Rome?[54] The two Leonine letters in question have been shown to be influenced by the ninth-century Pseudo-Isidorian forgeries,[55] and the Preface to that collection includes a statement that 'the authority of assembling synods is committed through special authorization to the apostolic see, nor do we read that any synod is legitimate which was not assembled or corroborated by its authority'.[56]

This Pseudo-Isidorian text was incorporated into his *Liber decretorum* by Burchard of Worms (Burchard 1.42), with one crucial alteration. The adjective 'generalem' was inserted before the word 'synodum': no *general* synod is legitimate which lacks papal sanction.[57] Burchard qualified the Pseudo-Isidorian dictum, perhaps because it was deemed to be too vague, or perhaps because it simply defined an impossibility. Professor Gérard Fransen pointed to the numerous texts about provincial and regional councils in the first book of Burchard's collection, and succinctly observed that as far as eleventh-century practice was concerned 'l'approbation pontificale ne fut jamais demandée'.[58] Whatever Burchard's motives might have been, however, 1.42 of his compilation appeared in several eleventh- and early twelfth-century canon law books, and also made its way into Gratian.[59]

Despite laying out this background, Leo IX's notion of a universal council remains opaque, and has been accorded different interpretations by modern scholars. Whatever such a gathering might be, however, it required papal approbation, that much is clear. The addressees of the letters in question, i.e., the Christian minority in North Africa, would seem to preclude that Leo was thinking about such an assembly from the point of view of size, or in terms of representative attendance from throughout the Christian world. Scholars instead have found Leo's meaning in an at-

---

54. See above, 'Historical Overview'.

55. Fuhrmann, 'Ökumenisches Konzil' 685; idem, *Einfluß und Verbreitung der pseudoisidorischen Fälschungen. Von ihrem Auftauchen bis in die neuere Zeit* (3 vols. MGH Schriften 24; Stuttgart 1972–74), here at 2.342–345.

56. *Praefatio* (ed. Hinschius 19): 'Synodorum vero congregandarum auctoritas apostolice sedi privata commissa est potestate, nec ullam synodum ratam esse legimus, quae eius non fuerit auctoritate congregata vel fulta.'

57. Burchard 1.42 (*editio princeps*, fol. 6ra). On Burchard, and this addition in particular, see also above, Chapter Two 'Secular Rulers and Synods' (esp. note 197).

58. Gérard Fransen, 'Papes, conciles généraux et œcuméniques', *Le istituzioni ecclesiastiche della «Societas Christiana» dei secoli XI–XII: papato, cardinalato ed episcopato: atti Mendola 1971* (Miscellanea 7; Milan 1974) 203–228, here at 207.

59. See Fuhrmann, *Einfluß und Verbreitung* 1.89, 2.484, and 3.984–985, for a list of occurrences of this passage in later collections.

tempt to offer a standard for unifying belief, morals, and law for the entire Church. However the matter is interpreted, papal approval remains at its center. Item 16 of the *Dictatus papae* was unambiguous about this point, as were canonical collections from the time of Gregory VII onward.[60] Gregory the Great's letters allowed Gregory VII to conclude that a papal legate, Bishop Syagrius of Autun, celebrated a general council in Gaul, and that even 'a certain monk named Hilary' ('monachum quendam Hylarum nomine'), who was fortified by the authority of papal letters, held a general council in Africa, although in neither instance do the texts of Gregory I contain the requisite adjective.[61] Beyond papal authority, however, Gregory VII's views about the distinguishing marks of a general council remain unclear, for the evidence does not lend itself to a detailed analysis.

The path forward from the 1070s to Gratian and the Decretists is, in one sense, clear. Yet one bit of evidence which seemingly has been overlooked in these discussions indicates, perhaps not surprisingly, that at the end of the eleventh century the notion of what a general council entailed may not have been worked out in a systematic manner, or at least not to an extent now discernible. Sometime after terminating his Council of Melfi in September 1089, Pope Urban II wrote to Bishop Pibo of Toul (JL 5409).[62] The exact date of this letter cannot be determined and Pibo did not die until 1107, but Urban must have been writing before his Council of Piacenza in March 1095.

Pibo had sent a messenger to the pontiff carrying a set of questions, among which was an inquiry, generated by the turmoil in the Church of recent years, namely, how to deal with clerics who had been ordained by excommunicated bishops. The response to Pibo is lengthy, proceeding seriatim through the questions. Urban pointed out in the first sentence that a council had formed the basis for his reply, and he was sending to Toul some chapters which had been 'confirmed by us through God's grace with the consent of a synodal council'.[63] What follows are renditions of cc. 1, 12 (partim), and 14, as commonly found in lists of decrees from Mel-

---

60. See the examples provided in Fransen, 'Papes' 218–219; see also Fuhrmann, 'Ökumenisches Konzil' 686, for the opinion of Cardinal Deusdedit.

61. JL 5081 as found in *Reg.* 6.2 (ed. Caspar, MGH Epp. sel. 2.2:392).

62. For what follows about the Council of Melfi and the letter to Bishop Pibo, see Robert Somerville (in collaboration with Stephan Kuttner), *Pope Urban II, the* Collectio Britannica, *and the Council of Melfi (1089)* (Oxford 1996), esp. 181–185. The same answer also occurs in JL 5393 (*Germania pontificia* 2.1:130–131 no. 24), sent to Bishop Gebhard of Constance, which dates from April 18, 1089, and which also is treated in Somerville, *Urban II* 134–151. For a draft edition of JL 5409 see the reference (Somerville, *Urban II.* 182 n. 32) to Rebecca Taylor, *JL 5409: A Study with Special Attention to Priests' Sons* (M.A. essay; Columbia University, New York 1990). Citations below are to the printing in Mansi.

63. Mansi 20.676.

fi, and then the statement that an opinion had not yet been fixed on the troublesome question of those ordained by bishops who were excommunicated, 'because the infection of a general illness must be burnt away by the cautery of a general synod'.[64] Urban then continued and offered a response *ad praesens*.

The issue of schismatic clergy was addressed by Urban II at the Council of Piacenza; therefore, the response to Pibo would then have been written between late September 1089, and March 1095. There is no evidence that the decrees from Melfi were repromulgated in Urban's synods at Benevento (1091) or Troia (1093), but the possibility cannot be discounted.[65] But lacking such evidence, it is not unreasonable to assume that the council cited at the beginning of JL 5409 was Melfi. Urban seemingly did not rank it as a general council (although looking forward, by implication Piacenza was).

What was the basis for Urban's assessment? Traditions can be found in the early medieval Church stipulating attendance from several provinces at a general council, but what Urban knew of them is impossible to say.[66] Such ideas, however, seem at odds both with developments on the subject from the time of Leo IX onward, and even with use of the adjective 'general' applied to councils in the writings of Urban's contemporary Bernold of Konstanz.[67]

JL 5409 does not survive in an original but only in copies, but in none of the witnesses examined do variants occur in the passages under discussion. Yet a piece of corroborating information can be brought to bear in support of the view that Urban II meant just what he wrote to Pibo about Melfi. It has long been accepted that, at Melfi, Pope Urban issued a judgment on behalf of the monastery of Cava against the bishop of Paestum-Capaccio.[68] Girgensohn edited an early twelfth-century copy of the resulting judgment found preserved in a book which he designated as the 'Chartularium parvum Salernitanum', following the lead of Hartmut Hoffmann, and which today is BAV Patetta 1621.[69] The papal decision was rendered in the Council of Melfi, but only 'in Melfino concilio', without the adjective 'generali'.

---

64. Mansi 20.676.

65. For the texts from Urban II's Councils of Benevento and Troia, see Somerville, *Urban II* 302–305.

66. See Hauck, 'Rezeption' 467 and Fuhrmann, 'Ökumenisches Konzil' 682 n. 633.

67. Sieben, *Konzilsidee* 129.

68. JL 5411, a forgery (see *Italia pontificia* 8.318 no. †6).

69. Dieter Girgensohn, *Miscellanea Italiae pontificiae. Untersuchungen und Urkunden zur mittelalterlichen Kirchengeschichte Italiens, vornehmlich Kalabriens, Siziliens und Sardiniens (zugleich Nachträge zu den Papsturkunden Italiens XI)* (Nachrichten Akad. Göttingen 1974.4; Göttingen 1974), here at 190–191 no. 2; see also ibid. 141–146 for the manuscript.

As with JL 5409, this text reveals nothing of Urban's views on general councils, but in comparison with the forged version corroborates what he wrote to Pibo about the status of the gathering at Melfi. Not every synod which could qualify as a 'general council' invariably was designated as such in the sources of the eleventh and twelfth century, but in JL 5409 the reverse occurs. A reforming pope at the end of the century seemingly denied that a synod over which he presided was a general council. It is unlikely that the issue can be clarified by limiting the inquiry to occurrences of relevant terminology derived from unambiguously authentic papal documents, given the fact that relatively few such sources are at hand for which 'contamination' can be totally disregarded (i.e., products of the papal chancery). Perhaps study of conciliar theories in the age of the Reform Papacy will someday demonstrate otherwise, but for the moment the path between the Reformers' notions of general council and those of the Decretists appears to be less direct than might be assumed.[70]

6.4 Sources

Over the last fifty years the study of medieval papal councils, 1049–1179, has benefitted from the appearance of many modern studies, both textual and interpretative.[71] These works in many instances replace Mansi and Hefele-Leclercq. Yet the sources for medieval councils are of many different varieties, e.g., canons, letters, other types of documentary and narrative sources. These appear in many places, and the process simply of amassing the information which pertains to a given council can be daunting.

In those instances in which a more modern study is not at hand, recourse should be made to Hefele-Leclercq and also the entries in the *Regesta pontificum* (JL). Much of the information available therein is rooted in the great collections of conciliar information published before the nineteenth century, of which Mansi's *Sacrorum conciliorum nova et amplissima collectio* is the last and most comprehensive. The problems in using those great tomes have been discussed often and need not be repeated

---

70. See Somerville, *Urban II* 183–185. Some Decretist commentaries include an attendance specification in defining 'general council', i.e., bishops from diverse provinces, etc.: see Fuhrmann, 'Ökumenisches Konzil' 687 n. 662 and Sieben, *Konzilsidee* 253–254. An article of the Peace of Venice, which was concluded between Pope Alexander III and Emperor Frederick Barbarossa in 1177, stated (ed. Weiland, MGH Const. 1.364 no. 25), that the pope immediately was to call a council, 'of such a sort as he can summon quickly' ('quale subito advocari poterit'), where all those who break the peace were to be excommunicated. 'Then he should do the same in a general council' ('Deinde in generali concilio idem faciat').

71. See above (note 1).

in detail here. A few words can be said, however, about the *Amplissima collectio*. This great enterprise is essentially a reprint standing at the end of a centuries-long tradition of supplemented reprints. Mansi reproduced, with additions, the *Sacrosancta concilia* of Niccolò Coleti, who in turn based his work on the collection of Philippe Labbe and Gabriel Cossart, slotting in material from the compilations of Jean Hardouin and others, and the trail of this process reaches back into the sixteenth century.[72]

A reader should be, in general, uneasy about conciliar history which is based directly on the major landmarks but without inquiring about the origin of the texts presented. The notes to this chapter, even in reduced form, provide readers with source critical studies for conciliar history. Furthermore, a group of additional points will be noted in this section to illustrate both problems and opportunities for conciliar history. This list is selective, including some things of particular interest to the author. This is hardly a very robust criterion for assembling a list of topics of interest, but in defense of the selection it would be hard to deny that these are compelling topic.

6.4.1 Chancery/Non-Chancery Texts

The councils in question are *papal* synods, but the extant sources by and large do not emanate directly from the papal chancery. There are exceptions, most conspicuous of which are the synods found registered is the Register of Gregory VII.[73] No other papal register is known to exist before Innocent III, although extracts from others, including conciliar material, can be found.[74] Papal bulls which concern some aspect of a papal synod and which survive in an original diploma also are known, but are not plentiful.[75]

Non-chancery texts will, of course, not necessarily offer distorted in-

---

72. *Sacrosancta concilia ad Regiam editionem exacta quae nunc quarta parte prodit* [...], ed. Philippe Labbe and Gabriel Cossart (17 in 18 vols. Paris 1671–72); *Sacrosancta concilia ad Regiam editionem exacta* [...] *longe locupletior et emendatior* [...], ed. Niccolò Coleti (23 vols. Venice 1728–33); *Conciliorum collectio regia maxima* [...], ed. Jean Hardouin (11 in 12 vols. Paris 1714–15). Lists of the various *Concilia* collections are conveniently listed in Hefele-Leclercq 1.1:97–114, the ACO Series secunda editions, the Konziliengeschichte volumes, and elsewhere. For Mansi and his predecessors, see the often hard-to-obtain work of Henri Quentin, *Jean-Dominique Mansi et les grandes collections conciliaires* (Paris 1900), now available online at https://archive.org/details/jeandominiquemanooquen.

73. See the information in Uta-Renate Blumenthal, 'Papal Registers in the Twelfth Century', *Proceedings Cambridge 1984* MIC Subsidia 8.137–151, here at 135.

74. See, e.g., Ivo 9.53 (ed. Brett), for a text from Urban II's Council of Troia (1093), inscribed as extracted from his register. For the Register of Paschal see Uta-Renate Blumenthal, 'Bemerkungen zum Register Paschalis II.' QF 66 (1986) 1–18, here at 14 n. 51.

75. E.g., JL 7028 (*Germania pontificia* 2.1:136, no. 49), dated March 28, 1123. Neither JL nor *Germania pontificia* noted a surviving original for this letter, but Foreville, *Latran I–IV*, facing p. 81, prints a photograph of one preserved in Karlsruhe, Generallandesarchiv, B.10.

formation about the decrees, judgments, or other facets of a synod, yet it often is difficult to be sure. There seems no reason, for example, to doubt what is said about the 1059 Lateran Council in a judgment of a dispute between Siena and Arezzo which survives in a twelfth-century copy (but as was seen in the section 6.3 above, a similar case from Melfi in 1089 has been shown to be falsified).[76] The two extensive accounts of the Council of Reims (1119), by Ordericus Vitalis and the Strasbourg cleric known as 'Hesso Scholasticus', can be used in tandem, but in other instances controlling sources is difficult.[77] Little corroborating evidence exists, for example, to ascertain whether or not Anselm of Saint-Rémi's elaborate description of Leo IX in the Council of Reims is embellished. Urban II's enemies—to cite a further example—claimed in a fiercely polemical treatise, that the canons of the synod at Piacenza (1095) 'were written down secretly and at night after the council'.[78] There is no reason to believe this, but little is known about how decrees from Urban's councils were put into circulation (see below under 'Conciliar Canons' and 'Inauthentic Texts').

A word should be said about the Papsturkunden-Pontificia projects sponsored by the Göttingen Academy and the Pius-Stiftung, aiming to collect all papal documents which survive in originals or copies which were issued before the time of Innocent III. This enterprise was organized by Paul Fridolin Kehr at the end of the nineteenth century with the goal of replacing the second edition of Jaffé's *Regesta* with a new *Regesta* organized on a country-by-country basis. Progress is painstaking but the work advances, and archival searches have uncovered hundreds of new documents whose integration with Jaffé gradually is producing a series of new, geographically organized, *Regestae*.[79] Dividends for the history of councils are, of course, unpredictable, but do occur.[80]

---

76. *Italia pontificia* 3.151, no. 25; see Detlev Jasper, *Das Papstwahldekret von 1059. Überlieferung und Textgestalt* (Beiträge zur Geschichte und Quellenkunde des Mittelalters 12; Sigmaringen 1986) 25 n. 86.

77. Ordericus Vitalis, *Historia ecclesiastica* 12.21 (ed. Chibnall 6.253–277). Hesso, *Relatio* (ed. Wattenbach, MGH Ldl 3.21–28).

78. Robert Somerville, *Pope Urban II's Council of Piacenza* (Oxford 2011) 19.

79. For this great project see the webpage of the Akademie der Wissenschaften zu Göttingen (www.papsturkunden.de), and see also the annual reports of the President of the Pius Stiftung in DA.

80. See, for example, the discussion above (under 'General Council') about the judgment issued at Urban II's Council of Melfi in a dispute between Cava and Paestum-Capaccio, and the text relevant to Tours 1163, in Dietrich Lohrmann, *Papsturkunden in Frankreich. N.F: Bd. 8,1: Diözese Paris: Urkunden und Briefsammlungen der Abteien Sainte-Geneviève und Saint-Victor* (Abh. Akad. Göttingen 3.174; Göttingen 1989) 263–265, no. 88.

6.4.2 Narrative Sources

The corpus of what can be termed narrative sources for papal synods in the eleventh and twelfth centuries is unlikely to increase significantly. It could happen, as Professors García y García and Kuttner demonstrated more than fifty years ago with their discovery of a new eye-witness account for the Fourth Lateran Council.[81] But the chief gains to be made in this area are more likely to be the appearance of better editions of known texts and deeper insight into their meaning. As noted at the beginning of this section, the process of assembling the often-scattered fragments which describe councils can be difficult, and good fortune plays a part, as the following example illustrates. The twelfth-century chronicle from the Scottish Cistercian abbey of Melrose corroborates the exclusion of the Emperor Frederick I from the condemnations issued by Alexander III at the Council of Tours in 1163.[82] This is a valuable piece of information about an obscure but important episode in the early phase of the dispute between Alexander and Frederick, and its existence in what might also be termed an 'out-of-the-way' place was fortuitous.

6.4.3 Conciliar Procedure

How papal synods operated, including a description of the liturgical proceedings, is often unclear.[83] Various conciliar *ordines* stipulate, for example, the use of a book of canons in synods. No one reference work seems to have been used for this purpose during the years under consideration, and Uta Blumenthal has shown that within one decade—i.e., 1100–1110—the councils held by Pope Paschal II may have used at least three different canonical collections (that of Cardinal Deusdedit, the *Collection in 74 Titles*, and the *Liber decretorum* of Burchard of Worms).[84]

The ways in which legislation was formulated and promulgated and what records were kept and available to participants are questions easier

81. Stephan Kuttner and Antonio García y García, 'A New Eyewitness Account of the Fourth Lateran Council' *Traditio* 20 (1964) 115–178.

82. Robert Somerville, 'The Beginning of Alexander III's Pontificate: *Aeterna et incommutabilis* and Scotland', *Miscellanea Rolando Bandinelli Papa Alessandro III*, ed. Filippo Liotta (Siena 1986) 367–368.

83. Foreville, *Latran I–IV* 136–137 (see also 195–199), uses the *Ordo Romanus qualiter concilium agatur* from the twelfth-century Roman Pontifical as a guide for Lateran III (for an edition, see *Le pontifical romain au moyen-âge 1: Le pontifical romain de XIIe siècle*, ed. Michel Andrieu [Studi e testi 86; Vatican City 1938] 255ff.) Discussion of the ordines now must be seen in light of Schneider's study and edition (MGH Ordines).

84. Blumenthal, *Early Councils* 125–27. See also the information about Calixtus II's Council of Reims in 1119 in Robert Somerville, 'Calixtus II and Canon Law', *'Panta rei': studi dedicati a Manlio Bellomo*, ed. Orazio Condorelli (5 vols. Rome 2004), 5.235–243.

to pose than to answer. Why are the acts of certain councils such as Lateran I, or especially Clermont (1095) chaotic, or why are the records for others of importance, e.g., the Lenten Synod of 1075, Bari in 1098, Innocent II's first Italian council (Piacenza in 1132), or Alexander III's first synod (Montpellier in 1162), scant or virtually non-existent?[85] What did John of Salisbury mean when he wrote concerning Reims, 1148, that to avoid prolixity he chose not to give the conciliar decrees, 'since they have been added to the canons'?[86] John seemingly wrote the *Historia* in 1164, sixteen years after Reims, so he may be recalling not what was done with the canons in the synod but what happened to them since. Even so, the remark is tantalizing. The decrees are not in Gratian, but perhaps John's allusion is to a local canonical tradition at Reims, which would have been obvious to his intended reader and 'closest friend', Peter of Celle, who was abbot of Saint-Rémi in Reims from 1162 and who may well have requested John to write the *Historia*.

Promulgation of legislation was not a uniform phenomenon across the decades from 1049 to 1179, but more material than has been collected so far can be assembled and systematized about how it happened. Non-papal synods also can provide clues and some basis for comparison, although before the thirteenth century the surviving evidence is not plentiful. The *Codex Udalrici*, for example, preserves a lengthy report on the provincial synod held at Mainz in August 1071, which concluded by noting that what was done in the synod was 'to be inserted into the ecclesiastical records and to be preserved in the archives of the Holy Church of Mainz'.[87] Anselm of Canterbury's comments about legislation from the Council at Westminster in 1102, to take a further example, show how texts could 'escape' from synods in draft form.[88] As the discussion below of 'Encyclical Letters' (under 'Conciliar Canons'), will indicate, the provincial council at Rouen in 1096 seems to be a unique witness for the circulation of some

---

85. For Lateran I, see Louis I. Hamilton and Martin Brett, 'New Evidence for the Canons of the First Lateran Council' BMCL 30 (2013) 1–20; for Clermont, Robert Somerville, *The Councils of Urban II, Vol. 1: Decreta Claromontensia* (AHC. Supplementum 1; Amsterdam 1972); for Lent 1075, idem, 'Councils of Gregory' 41–44; for Bari, *Councils and Synods with Other Documents Relating to the English Church I: AD 871–1204*, ed. Dorothy Whitelock, Martin Brett, and Christopher Nugent Lawrence Brooke (2 vols. Oxford 1981) here at 1.2:650–51; for *Piacenza*, JL post 7571, Somerville, *Piacenza* 125–27; for Montpellier, idem, *Alexander III* 54–55.

86. *Historia pontificalis* 3 (ed. Chibnall 8).

87. *Codex Udalrici* no. 147 (ed. Nass, MGH Briefe dt. Kaiserzeit 10.1:221–226, here 226 lines 9–15). See Schieffer, *Entstehung* 61 n. 58 for the unusual character of this account in eleventh-century conciliar sources.

88. See *Councils and Synods* 2.670ff, for Westminister 1102; see Brett, 'First Lateran' 25 n. 41; and also the schismatic cardinals' remarks about the rulings from Urban II's Council of Piacenza in 1095: Somerville, *Piacenza* 18–24.

type of general letter about the legislation from Urban II's Council of Clermont.

Yet it seems nearly certain that no amount of further information about how councils worked can totally clarify the questions surrounding the multiplicity of forms in which legislation from papal synods in the period under discussion circulated, nor is it likely that reasonable expectations about new evidence can explain that variety. A number of traditions exist for many of the synods between Leo IX and Alexander III from which legislation is known, and this variegated picture ranges from somewhat straightforward to chaotic.[89] The unavoidable conclusion seems to be that if papal policy to spread one slate of canons ever existed, those efforts, whatever they were, at best succeeded partially and at worst failed spectacularly. After studying both the canons of Lateran I and English synods of the same period, Martin Brett epigrammatically concluded that apparently 'the archbishop of Canterbury cared a great deal more about the canons of his councils than the pope did about his'.[90]

6.5 Conciliar Canons

6.5.1 Introduction

A council's legislation offers only one gauge of an assembly's importance, but the formulation of canons was a traditional part of synodal activity.[91] It is impossible to say that it occurred in every council, but many gatherings of the Gregorian Age and thereafter did promulgate decrees (even if only by repeating the statutes of earlier gatherings).[92] However the mechanisms to disseminate these rulings did or did not work, canon law collections dating from the late eleventh century onward had access to and incorporated decrees from many such synods. Lists of canons or citations of individual decrees also occur in chronicles, in histories on this or that topic, in papal letters, or copied on end pages and blank leaves in any manuscript where a scribe found space. Dealing with this mass of information is daunting, and an investigator will always worry that how-

---

89. This story is well known, but see for a recent assessment Robert Somerville, 'Chaos to Order: Clermont 1095 to Lateran IV, 1215', *Vergentis* 3 (2016) 267–281.

90. Brett, 'First Lateran' 28.

91. Schmale, 'Systematisches' 23; see for recitation of synodal canons at the end of the assembly the widespread *Ordo* 2, as listed in Schneider's edition (MGH Ordines.183).

92. For repetition of canons from councils of Leo IX see JL 4185, which probably should be dated later than in JL. For repetition in synods of Urban II see Robert Somerville, 'The French Councils of Urban II: Some Basic Considerations' *Archivum Historiae Pontificiae* 2 (1970) 56–65, here at 62–63; for the same in councils of Innocent II see Brett and Somerville, 'Transmission'. The examples could be multiplied for other pontificates.

ever thorough his research on the legislative traditions of a council, more information awaits discovery.

6.5.2 Content

Any summary of the content of those provisions will overlook much of importance. The synods under consideration legislated on pressing issues as well as on matters of lesser moment. Although—as stated at the beginning of this chapter—a general history is not the goal, a few remarks can be offered about the scope of the law generated in papal assemblies between Leo IX and Alexander III.

In early 1074 Gregory VII wrote to Sicard of Aquileia, inviting the patriarch to the upcoming Lenten Council. The planned gathering was to provide 'some relief and remedy, lest we see in our days the irreparable ruin and destruction of the Church'.[93] Gregory was not reticent about the troubles which the council should address: lay oppression of the Church, clerical greed, and the problems thus created for the faithful, who were devoid of guides in the path of righteousness. A century later, in his bull of convocation to clergy in Tuscany for the Lateran Council of 1179, Alexander III sounded a similar theme. He was striving, Alexander wrote, to bring together churchmen to reform what required reform, and to establish measures which seemed 'valuable for the salvation of the faithful'.[94]

Invitations to papal synods throughout the period follow no fixed format. The summonses, for example, to Bishop Lambert of Arras for Urban II's Councils of Piacenza and Clermont say little about the proposed agenda; and Calixtus II's invitation to Lateran I sent to the Archbishop of Dol and his suffragans spoke only of 'important and diverse matters of the Church'.[95] The letters from Gregory VII and Alexander III are worth citing, therefore, despite the formulaic aspect which underlies their expression of hope for reform and pastoral concern; for amidst the issues

---

93. JL 4819 (*Italia pontificia* 7.1:3, no. 63; ed. Caspar, MGH Epp. sel. 2.1:65): 'quatenus [...] aliquod solatium et remedium invenire valeamus, ne nostris temporibus inreparabilem ecclesie ruinam destructionemque videamus'.

94. JL 13097 (*Italia pontificia* 3.328, no. 44): 'que saluti fidelium visa fuerint expedire'.

95. JL 6977 (Mansi 21.255–256): 'Pro magnis et diversis Ecclesiae nogotiis [...] generale in Urbe concilium celebrare disposuimus.' For the invitations to Piacenza and Clermont see Robert Somerville, 'The Council of Clermont (1095), and Latin Christian Society' *Archivum Historiae Pontificiae* 12 (1974) 55–90, here at 57–58. In JL 5570 Urban did admonish Lambert to attend Clermont in order to take up the matter of his dispute with the church of Cambrai, and in JL *5571 Urban may have urged lay attendance at Clermont in anticipation of preaching the Crusade. The church at Arras in the time of Bishop Lambert has been the subject of two separate works: Lotte Kéry, *Die Errichtung des Bistums Arras 1093/1094* (Francia. Beihefte 33; Sigmaringen 1994) and *Le registre de Lambert, évêque d'Arras (1093–1115)*, ed. Claire Giordanengo (Sources d'histoire médiévale 34; Paris 2007).

regarding the clergy and Church politics which appear repeatedly in synods, these invitations are reminders that the laity was not to be forgotten.

Among the most famous and most frequently repeated regulations are enactments aimed at purifying the Church by enforcing clerical celibacy, canonical procedures for appointments, and especially penalties for simony in its many manifestations. Repetition of the time-honored censure against trafficking in ecclesiastical offices appears in both the earliest papal council of Leo IX (Rome 1049), and in the latest (Lateran III, 1179). A list of canons does not survive from Leo's assembly, but if reports about the event—from a *Vita* of Pope Leo, from Peter Damian, and from Bonizo of Sutri—can be believed, the synod vigorously condemned simony.[96] Were the canons themselves at hand these formulations would undoubtedly differ in various ways from those promulgated at Lateran III, but the desire to enforce the rules governing canonical appointments and to eliminate clerical venality is a constant, omnipresent in decrees in papal synods between Leo and Alexander, formulated in different ways at different times, but never absent.

Leo IX appears also to have enacted legislation at the Roman council in 1049 against priests, deacons, and subdeacons living with women.[97] Vaulting forward to 1179, the question was not ignored at Lateran III, where c. 11 forbade clerics in sacred orders to keep mistresses.[98] Between 1049 and 1179 a welter of decrees were promulgated dealing with sexuality and especially condemning clerical intimacy with women were repeatedly promulgated, in an onslaught which seemed to crest in the pontificate of Innocent II in the 1130s.[99] Nine years later, at the Council of Reims in 1148, Eugene III again issued such decrees (cc. 3 and 7), but now was ridiculed because c. 7 repeating Lateran II, c. 7.[100] Everybody knows that such marriages are illicit, John of Salisbury wrote.[101]

Together with concerns of this sort about the policies of the 'profes-

---

96. The sources are assembled and discussed in Uta-Renate Blumenthal, 'Ein neuer Text für das Reimser Konzil Leos IX. (1049)?' DA 32 (1976) 23–48, here at 39–40.

97. See Blumenthal, 'Neuer Text' 39–40. Peter Damian stated that in the synod Leo stipulated that all women at Rome who were 'priests' prostitutes' (*presbyteris prostitutae*), should henceforth be judged to be servants (*ancillae*) in the Lateran Palace: see for this text the discussion by John Joseph Ryan, *Saint Peter Damiani and His Canonical Sources: A Preliminary Study in the Antecedents of the Gregorian Reform* (PIMS Studies and Texts 2; Toronto 1956), here at 101–103, no. 197.

98. COD 217. The decree also condemns sodomy of both clerics and laity, and clerics who without proper reasons frequent nunneries. For these issues and much more see at many points in James A. Brundage, *Law, Sex and Christian Society in Medieval Europe* (Chicago and London 1987).

99. See the texts in Brett and Somerville, 'Transmission'.

100. See JL post 9197, for a summary of the provisions from the synod.

101. John of Salisbury, *Historia pontificalis* (ed. Chibnall 8): 'Quis enim hoc escit esse illicitum?'

sional' Church, conciliar canons also treat the laity, both as the oppressors of whom Gregory VII complained to Sicard of Aquileia, and as the faithful requiring guidance. Decrees against lay involvement in Church affairs and especially appointments, and condemnations of lay investiture of bishoprics and abbeys, appear in various guises from the 1070s to 1119 and are well known. The same can be said for the canons which limited warfare by means of the Truce of God, or which forbade usury.[102] But eleventh- and twelfth-century popes also formulated synodal decrees on other issues which concerned lay persons, for example, rulings on marriage,[103] on proper penance,[104] on the Crusading indulgences,[105] and, during the troubled times of the Wibertine Schism, on the complicated issue of contact with those who were excommunicated.[106] Some matters emerge with a distinctly local flavor, such as the canon from Lateran I concerned with the disposition of the property of deceased residents of the vicinity of St Peter's (c. 11),[107] or the regulation from Innocent II's Council of Pisa in 1135 (c. 6), forbidding under pain of excommunication the sale of 'any free Christian, Corsican or otherwise'.[108]

This summary is woefully incomplete. No mention has been made of the important legislation on tithes, monasticism, or the Eucharist. These councils provide regulations for the fasts of Ember Days, for safeguarding the property of those who have been shipwrecked, for dealing with non-Christians and heretics, and even for the care of lepers. Despite repetition, the range of issues which the popes considered important enough to handle in their synods between 1049 and 1179 is remarkable, and the content and development of the law embodied in those provisions can be grasped only by reading and comparing the texts.

---

102. See, e.g., Hartmut Hoffmann, *Gottesfriede und Treuga Dei* (MGH Schriften 20; Stuttgart 1964), and Terence P. McLaughlin, 'The Teaching of the Canonists on Usury (XII, XIII and XIV Centuries)' MS 1 (1939) 81–147 and 2 (1940) 1–22.

103. E.g., Reims 1049 c. 12 (ed. Jasper, MGH Conc. 8.240), here at 252; Lateran 1059 = JL 4405/4406 (ed. Jasper, MGH Conc. 8.402–406); Clermont 1095 (ed. Somerville, *Decreta Claromontensia* Appendix III, nos. 40, 53, and 55); Lateran 1123 c. 9 (COD 191); Lateran 1139 c. 17 (COD 201).

104. E.g., Lateran, Autumn 1080 c. 6. (ed. Caspar MGH Epp. sel. 2.2:404); Lateran, Lent 1080 (ibid. 481–482); Melfi 1089 c. 16 (ed. Somerville, *Urban II* 257); Lateran II c. 22 (ed. Brett and Somerville, 'Transmission' 269).

105. E.g., Clermont 1095 (see Somerville, *Decreta Claromontensia* Appendix III, no. 3); Lateran I, 1123 c. 10 (COD 191–92).

106. E.g., Lent 1078 c. 16 (ed. Caspar MGH Epp. sel. 2.2:372–373).

107. For these *Porticani* see Leonardi's note to the text in COD 192.

108. Pisa 1135 c. <6>, ed. Robert Somerville, 'The Council of Pisa, 1135: A Re-Examination of the Evidence for the Canons' *Speculum* 45 (1970) 98–114, here at 108 '[...] nullus [...] quemlibet, liberum Christianum Corsum vel alium vendere audeat [...].'

6.5.3 'Encyclical Letters'

Conciliar canons can be found cited in papal letters, although perhaps not as frequently as would be imagined.[109] Papal letters also could be formulated to provide a résumé of the legislation of a gathering. These letters, which can be called 'encyclical letters', could be addressed either generally or to specific individuals or churches, announcing what happened in a council.[110] There is not a great deal of evidence for the existence of such documents, and no such letter is known to survive in original form. How frequent a practice it was, what was and was not included, and the circumstances which engendered such documents are imponderables.

Different versions of such letters were sent out following the synod of Nicholas II in late April-early May 1059.[111] Questions about these texts, and especially about how what is summarized therein relates to the proceedings in the council itself, are complicated. A rendition of an encyclical attributed to Pope Alexander II also is known. This letter repeats verbatim long portions of the aforementioned text of Nicholas, and although referring to a council which has been identified as Alexander's Roman Synod of May 1063, is undated.[112]

Gregory VII, early in his pontificate, sent a letter to Otto of Constance in which he pointed out that since the bishop's envoys had hastened away there was no opportunity to communicate in order (*seriatim*) the decrees set forth 'in a Roman council'. It was, however, deemed necessary, Gregory continued, to send special notice about the council's ruling on simony. If the messengers had been more patient, they would have been able to bring much more information back to Constance about the synod.[113] Whether or not other bishops received letters in which the entire range of provisions was spelled out is unknown. In 1866 Wilhelm von Giesebrecht published, from among the sixteenth-century papers which today comprise Roma, Vallicelliana, C.24 (fols. 130r–131v), a text purporting to be

109. Some of Urban II's provisions from Clermont concerning relations between monks and bishops had a long history of this sort: Somerville, *Decreta Claromontensia* 139–141; Paschal II recalled a now-lost canon from the Council of Bari (1098), to Anselm (JL 5929); Celestine III reminded the abbot and monks at Kelso of c. 4 of Lateran III (Robert Somerville, *Scotia pontificia: Papal Letters to Scotland Before the Pontificate of Innocent III* [Oxford 1982]. 149–150, no. 160). Some other examples could be cited.

110. Schieffer, *Entstehung* 64ff.

111. The texts are discussed and edited by Jasper (MGH. Conc. 8.352–381 and 402–407).

112. JL 4501 is discussed and edited in Schieffer, *Entstehung* 84–95 and 213–225.

113. JL 4933 (*Germania pontificia* 2.1.127, no. 15; also ed. Cowdrey, *Epistolae vagantes* 16–18). See Robert Somerville, 'The Councils of Gregory VII' *Studi Gregoriani* 13 (1989) 33–53, here at 41–42 for a discussion of this letter and a group of related texts, none of which survives in Gregory's Register, and the problem of their date and the synod to which they refer.

an encyclical letter of Gregory VII to the clergy and people of the whole Church, conveying what was done 'in a Roman council'.[114] The document as it stands probably does not stem directly from Pope Gregory, but its existence suggests the viability for the time of this method of disseminating conciliar decisions.[115]

The Montecassino *Chronicle* declared that *exemplaria* of the proceedings of Pope Victor III's Council of Benevento (1086), were made and disseminated 'per orientem et occidentem'.[116] Writing in Normandy in the second quarter of the twelfth-century, Ordericus Vitalis reported that after the Council of Clermont in 1095, a delegation of Norman bishops left town carrying 'synodal letters' (*synodales epistolas*) to their fellow bishops.[117] The subsequent provincial synod at Rouen in 1096 'considered' (*contemplati*) the *capitula* from Clermont, and also ratified the 'papal decisions' (*apostolica scita*). What Ordericus reported as decrees from Rouen can be correlated with legislation from Clermont, but the details of the process that the monastic historian of Saint-Évroult summarizes are hazy, and the form and content of those synodal letters is a mystery. Whether or not they represented an official promulgation of legislation from Clermont, they must have had very limited circulation given the confusion which surrounds that council's surviving acts.

Further evidence possibly indicating the existence of such letters is not easily interpreted. One form of Clermont's legislation occurs as a long series of provisions, claiming in its last line to derive from a papal sermon at the council, introduced by the following words:[118]

> Urban bishop servant of the servants of God presiding in a general council at Clermont in which there were present 240 "fathers" [spoke] thus: We decree....

The ensuing farrago of stipulations is one among many summaries of what was supposedly enacted at Clermont. Whether the echo of the pro-

---

114. JL 5260: Wilhelm von Giesebrecht, 'Die Gesetzgebung der römischen Kirche zur Zeit Gregors VII.' *HJb* (1866) 91–194, here at 188–193; text printed also by Julius von Pflugk-Harttung, *Acta pontificum Romanorum inedita: Urkunden der Päpste vom Jahre 748 bis zum Jahre 1198* (3 vols. Tübingen 1881–86) 2.125–127, no. 161. See Laura Gaspari, 'Osservazioni sul codice Vallicelliano C. 24' *Studi Gregoriani* 9 (1972) 467–513.

115. See Somerville, 'The Councils of Gregory VII' 51–53.

116. MGH SS 34.455.

117. *Historia ecclesiastica* 9.2 (ed. Chibnall 5.19ff.).

118. Oxford, Bodleian, Selden Supra 90, fols. 25v–27r, printed in Somerville, *Decreta Claromontensia* 113: 'Urbanus episcopus servus servorum Dei residens apud Claru<mmontem> in concilio generali cui interfuerunt CCXL patres ut: Precipimus secundum sanctorum canonum auctoritatem [...].' The information on attendance occurs in this form in no other record for Clermont, and the designation *patres* is difficult to evaluate: see Somerville, 'Clermont and Society' 62ff.

tocol from a papal letter in the inscription (i.e., 'Urbanus episcopus servus servorum Dei'), indicates that the text stems from such a letter is unknown. Given the somewhat rambling nature of the subsequent 'canons'
this is perhaps unlikely, but cannot be discounted. Was this account to
have such a pedigree, however, it becomes even more curious for it con-
stitutes only one version of Clermont's actions, and not even the form
according to which popes from Urban through Eugene III cited those rulings in their correspondence.[119]

A papal letter underlying this text, if one ever existed, might, of course,
not have been addressed generally but sent rather to a particular recipient (cf. Gregory VII's letter to Otto of Constance). The same could be
true for the only decree known to survive from Urban II's Council of
Tours (1096).[120] Following the heading 'In concilio Turonis habito', the
words 'Urbanus servus servorum Dei' preface the canon's text. If those
four words mean that the text circulated in a papal letter, how was that
letter addressed? The set of canons from Lateran I found added to the
twelfth-century copy of Anselm of Lucca's canonical collection in Napoli,
BN, XII. A. 37, has 'Calixtus papa omnibus episcopis' as a rubric. At least
this is general, but neither for Tours nor for the Lateran Council of 1123
have hints emerged about 'synodal letters' similar to what Ordericus reported for the Council of Rouen. To see these vignettes as pale traces that
such documents once existed may be fanciful but not necessarily so.[121]

6.5.4 Canonical Collections

Perhaps the richest and least tapped source for conciliar canons of the
eleventh and twelfth centuries are the canonical collections. Canons were
both integrated into the body of these books, and sometimes added in the
margins or at the ends of sections. Decrees could even simply be copied at
the beginning or tacked onto at the end of a manuscript (a phenomenon
not unique to manuscripts of canonical collections). Locating synods in
such compilations also can help to establish how enactments circulated in

119. See Somerville, *Decreta Claromontensia* 139–141 for papal use of the rulings from Clermont, and see the Table (ibid. 142ff.), for an overview of provisions occurring in different versions. Among the omissions in the Bodleian account is the indulgence for participants on the First
Crusade.

120. Somerville, 'French Councils' 62–63, citing Metz, BM, 1212. Dr Linda Fowler-Magerl
doctae memoriae kindly has pointed out to the author another occurrence of this same text in
Erlangen, UB, MS 176.

121. See Martin Brett, 'The Canons of the First Lateran Council in English Manuscripts', *Proceedings Berkeley 1985* MIC. Subsidia 7.13–28, here at 27: 'It seems inconceivable that a whole class
of [...] letters should have sunk without a trace, yet none seem to survive for the period under
consideration, which suggests very forcefully that they were not written".

various regions. The study of the dissemination of the encyclicals from Nicholas II's Lateran Synod of 1059, for example, demonstrated how one version of one summary of the decrees (JL 4405), and the oath on the Eucharist sworn in council by Berengar of Tours, circulated in the version of the Pseudo-Isidorian False Decretals associated with Lanfranc of Bec/Canterbury (the *Collectio Lanfranci*).[122]

Access to the content of many eleventh- and twelfth-century canon law books has advanced significantly in recent years, especially through the scholarship of Linda Fowler-Magerl.[123] Note also can be made here of some work of particular significance for councils. John Gilchrist, F. Joseph Gossman, and Uta Blumenthal have published studies documenting the presence in the canonical tradition of texts of Popes Gregory VII, Urban II, and Paschal II, respectively.[124] Only three twelfth-century papal councils—Reims (1148), Tours (1163), and Lateran III (1179)—are represented in a significant manner in the late twelfth-century, post-Gratian decretal collections.[125] In addition, canons of Tours and Lateran III also appear as supplements to other twelfth-century manuscripts, as the following instances show.[126]

Some of the conciliar texts which are found in canon law collections were known to early-modern editors, and recognizing this fact through study of these collections can clarify aspects of early-modern conciliar historiography. One example will suffice. The manuscript from Aniane whence Étienne Baluze printed an important version of the canons of Clermont (1095), has been identified as a twelfth or thirteenth-century copy of the collection known as the *Polycarpus*, preserved today in Paris, BnF, lat. 3881.[127]

The use of canonical collections by early-modern editors was sporadic,

122. Schieffer, *Entstehung* 64ff.

123. See Fowler-Magerl, *Clavis* (with bibliography that lists her earlier works).

124. Francis J. Gossman, *Pope Urban II and Canon Law* (CUA Canon Law Studies 403; Washington, D.C. 1960); John T. Gilchrist, 'The Reception of Pope Gregory VII into the Canon Law (1073–1141)' ZRG Kan. Abt. 59 (1973) 35–82 and 66 (1980) 192–229; Uta-Renate Blumenthal, 'Decrees and Decretals of Pope Paschal II in Twelfth-Century Canonical Collections' BMCL 10 (1980) 15–30, with much useful information also in eadem, *Early Councils*.

125. Walther Holtzmann, *Studies in the Collections of Twelfth Century Decretals*, ed., rev., and tr. Christopher R. Cheney and Mary G. Cheney (MIC Corpus collectionum 13; Vatican City 1979), here at 335–336.

126. Somerville, *Alexander III* 44–45 and Gérard Fransen, 'Les canonistes et Latran III', *Le troisième Concile de Latran (1179): sa place dans l'histoire: communications présentées à la Table ronde du C.N.R.S., le 26 avril 1980*, ed. Jean Longère (Paris 1982) 33–40, here at 38–39.

127. Hermann Hüffer, *Beiträge zur Geschichte der Quellen des Kirchenrechts und des Römischen Rechts im Mittelalter* (Münster 1862) 79, seems to have been first to suggest that Paris, BnF, lat. 3881 was the source of Baluze's canons (although confusing the work in which Baluze printed those decrees). See Somerville, *Decreta Claromontensia* 119–121.

but valuable discoveries relating to councils still emerge from these books. Two examples will suffice.

i) The canons from Paschal II's important Lateran Council of 1110, which may have been the pope's 'final reply to Henry [V]'s military preparations and requests' prior to the onslaught of 1111, were widely disseminated.[128] As a result of a thorough study of these decrees and the realization that a prime vehicle for their transmission was early twelfth-century canonical collections, the transmission has been systematized into two groups, distinguished by the presence or the omission of c. 1, which condemns clerics who receive investiture of churches from the laity.[129]

ii) The handful of decrees which Mansi printed for Innocent II's Council of Pisa (1135), has been expanded, including a hitherto unknown text condemning the slave trade, on the basis of additions found in a manuscript of the *Panormia* from the house of Augustinian Canons at Polling in the diocese of Augsburg.[130]

These examples could be multiplied, but more important than expanding the list is noting the probability if not the certainty that not all such texts awaiting discovery have yet been found.

6.5.5 Inauthentic Texts

Evidence from the eleventh and twelfth centuries for tampering with and recasting conciliar 'acta' can be found, although the problem has yet to be treated in a systematic manner. The discovery of the authentic text of a judgment from Melfi (1089), thus exposing JL †5411, has been noted above in the discussion of the term 'general council'. A further example from about the same time is provided by Abbot Geoffrey of Vendôme, a well-known falsifier of texts who suppressed a line regarding fees owed to bishops by monasteries in a decree from Clermont in 1095.[131]

The papal election decree formulated in Nicholas II's Lateran Council of April 1059, offers a famous example of the need for careful evaluation of both the form and content of conciliar records. Two different versions of this decree survive, traditionally termed the 'papal' and the 'imperial' versions, although 'genuine' and 'false' are more appropriate.[132] In formal

---

128. Blumenthal, *Early Councils* 106 n. 121.

129. Blumenthal, *Early Councils* 109–118.

130. The texts occur in Clm 11316, fols. 113v–114v: Somerville, 'Pisa 1135' 105–108.

131. Somerville, *Decreta Claromontensia* 140 n. 149.

132. Jasper, *Papstwahldekret* 3. This important volume contains an array of information both about the 1059 synod and about councils of the period in general. See also now Jasper's edition of

terms both are identical, and present themselves as a synodal constitution whose disposition is formulated as an address from the pope himself.[133] Scholars have agreed for more than a century about which of the two was authentic and which was falsified,[134] but only recently, as a result of a new manuscript discovery, has Detlev Jasper produced a text of the genuine recension better than any hitherto known—a text containing a lengthy list of subscriptions which in all previously available transmissions of this version had been radically abbreviated.[135]

Not all 'inauthentic' conciliar texts resulted from a clear intention to deceive. A list of canons misattributed by early-modern editors to Urban II's Council of Nîmes (1096), has been unmasked as spurious through study of notes of Étienne Baluze, and of texts appended to a manuscript of Burchard of Worms's *Liber decretorum* which derives from the monastery of Saint-Aubin in Angers.[136] In all probability the mistaken attributions developed accidentally. Research on late twelfth-century decretal collection, to note an additional example, has resulted in sorting out Mansi's presentations of canons for the 1148 Council of Reims, and the 1163 Council of Tours. This is a textual mess about which Mansi himself had reservations (which he expressed not in the *Amplissima collectio*, however, but only in his edition of Baronius' *Annales*). Inter-related studies by a number of scholars have demonstrated how decrees from provincial synods at London in 1143 and Westminster in 1175 became intermingled with the papal provisions, again probably by accident.[137]

Other problematic attributions and aberrant texts remain to unravel. The puzzling ascription to Urban II in Gratian's *Decretum* of canons elsewhere attributed to Lateran I are well-known, but unexplained.[138] The mysterious *Collectio Britannica* contains a list of acts of Urban's Council of Melfi which was copied not long after the event.[139] This record is relatively lengthy although demonstrably incomplete, yet it contains information found in no other list of the legislation. Some of the account can be

---

the decrees in MGH Conc. 8.

133. See the synoptical edition of both texts in Jasper, *Papstwahldekret* 98ff.

134. Jasper, *Papstwahldekret* 1–3.

135. From the *4L* found in Bergamo, Biblioteca civica Angelo Mai, MA 244.

136. Stephan Kuttner and Robert Somerville, 'The So-Called Canons of Nîmes (1096)' *Tijdschrift voor rechtsgeschiedenis* 38 (1970) 175–189.

137. See the information summarized in Christopher Nugent Lawrence Brooke, 'The Canons of English Church Council in the Early Decretal Collections' *Traditio* 13 (1957) 471–481 and Stephan Kuttner, 'Notes on Manuscripts' *Traditio* 17 (1961) 533–542 for Reims; for Tours, see Somerville, *Alexander III* 39 n. 34 and passim. See also Brooke, 'Canons' 472–473, for assessment of the possibility that these cases of falsification were not unintentional.

138. See Hamilton and Brett, 'New Evidence' esp. 19–20.

139. See Somerville, *Urban II* 3–40 for the *Britannica*, and ibid. 175–298 for the Council of Melfi.

controlled using other sources, and where this is possible the *Britannica* is shown sometimes to give what probably is a correct reading, but at other times what just as probably is an incorrect one. The rationale is difficult to decipher, but the *Britannica*'s reputation for containing texts of dubious authenticity must be borne in mind.[140]

6.5.6 Postscript

An investigator faced only with Mansi would be unprepared to deal in an effective manner with many of the questions which have been laid out in the preceding discussion. Yet even in recent years scholars with better tools at their disposal have returned uncritically to the *Amplissima collectio* and its early-modern predecessors, more often than might be expected. To reiterate in several ways the problems and dangers of such an approach to the sources for eleventh- and twelfth-century papal councils, and to point to concomitant research opportunities, has been the prime objective of the preceding section, and indeed of the entire chapter. The bibliography and 'Index Conciliorum' to this volume will assist readers to locate modern studies of many facets of medieval conciliar history before 1215, and thus to confront directly the methodology for treating these events, and finally the challenge of creating a more accurate and a richer history of the medieval Church.

---

140. See Stephan Kuttner and Wilfried Hartmann, 'A New Version of Pope John VIII's Decree on Sacrilege (Council of Troyes, 878)', BMCL 17 (1987) 1–32, here at 26.

7

General Conclusions

The eleventh and twelfth centuries are known as a crucial period in the history of canon law, and rightly so; many scholars (not only canon law historians) have argued that the changes in legal culture of this period are central to our understanding of medieval Church and society in general. Given the broad meaning of 'canon' (discussed at the beginning of Chapter One), it should come as no surprise that the collections examined in chapters two through five, and the papal councils studied in chapter six, interacted with very different parts of society. In particular, several collections studied in the preceding chapters were employed, and in some cases specifically conceived, to calibrate the changing relations between bishops, metropolitans, the papacy, monastic houses, laypeople, and other parties. Likewise, canonical collections and councils were instrumental in the re-definition of the sacraments (especially the Eucharist), and as Chapter Five has argued, this amounted to a 'sacramentalisation of canon law' around 1100. Some of these debates concerned only a few highly educated prelates, but when it came to the validity of sacraments, lay people were also concerned, and, in some cases, they seem to have been very worried about the consequences of these debates. In our time there were many questions about simony, celibacy, the (violent) treatment of heretics and schismatics, but also about reconciliation and peace. The changing understanding of the sacraments influenced the various answers found, which in turn could have profound effects on the daily lives of many people. At the latest when it came to the regulation of marriage and sexuality, the content of the collections and sometimes even the wording of individual canons were relevant to very large sections of the population, be they lay people, clerics, or monks. The radical expansion of marriage prohibitions on grounds of consanguinity discussed in Chapter Two is perhaps the most dramatic example of legal change in this area of the law.

These are just a few examples of how the law contained in the collections had a profound impact on society as a whole. Transformation often occurred slowly and was sometimes almost invisible, but a closer look at the process of compiling the canonical collections often reveals change where on the surface there seems to be continuity. Finding (or not), retaining (or dropping), preserving (or changing) the normative texts the Latin Church had come to accept as canonical was a challenging task with potentially wide-ranging effects, and—as I have argued repeatedly in the foregoing chapters—many compilers knew very well what they were doing. This also explains why some of the collections were rather partisan in nature. Already in the eleventh century, some of them were described in military language as 'arsenals', and sometimes compilers were indeed forging intellectual weapons when assembling new collections. Yet not only partisan collections, but all collections were shaped by the needs of the environment from which they emerged, be it the household of a bishop, a monastery, or the papal curia. Just as the collections could shape society, they themselves were the product of the great changes to the fabric of society that occurred in the high Middle Ages.

Of course, canonical collections were not the only medium relevant for these debates. In many cases, however, they are the best evidence we have, if only because other primary sources were lost, or never produced in the first place. For example, of the thousands of cases heard by ecclesiastical judges, only a small number of high-profile cases—typically those involving royalty, bishops, and similarly prominent figures—can be studied in any detail from the extant sources. The same holds for marriage contracts, testaments, dispensations, and other documents which survive by the thousands from the later Middle Ages but only in exceptional cases from earlier centuries. Likewise, only from the second half of the twelfth century glosses, tracts, and lecture notes allow us to study in detail how medieval lawyers understood the canon law they were teaching in the universities; in our period, only a handful of prefaces to some collections and an even smaller number of collections containing at least some commentary can be studied in a similar way.

So to understand pre-Gratian 'canon law', we are largely left with the canonical collections, including what they (and relatively few other sources) reveal about conciliar and papal legislation in our period. As Chapter Six has made clear, papal councils in particular became increasingly important, especially towards the end of the period studied in this book. However, even for this legislation it is still true that only materials included in canonical collections had a chance to become general canon law. As has been discussed in some detail, this process was very uneven. Some materials were only received into canon law with considerable delay, in redacted versions, or in highly abbreviated form. All these qualifications apply, for example, to the 1059 Papal Election Decree which during the rest of the eleventh century was found in relatively few collections, and crucially only in an abbreviated form seriously misrepresenting what Nicholas II originally had said, before it finally found its way in the *Panormia* and the *Decretum Gratiani*. In other words, almost a century had passed before the genuine form of this famous decree was integrated into major collections and widely circulated as part of these works.

Another recurring theme was the curious blending of old and new materials in the collections. There were ancient canons that had, in one form or the other, always been part of major canon law collections since the time of Dionysius Exiguus; others, like some of the letters of Pelagius I, were more or less unknown for centuries before they entered mainstream canon law. Then there was the rather special case of the Pseudo-Isidorian collections which only in our period were fully integrated into canon law, adding a large number of both genuine and forged materials which at least looked very ancient; and finally, there was genuinely new legislation—a small number of royal capitularies, an increasing number of papal decretals, and above all the canons of very many councils—which, however unevenly, were also taken up by the compilers of canonical collections.

The resulting mix of genuine and forged, ancient and relatively recent materials of very different background is indeed characteristic of medieval canon law more generally and has often been commented upon. One can hardly exaggerate the importance of this finding. Canon law collections from the beginning of the genre (around the year 500) had a tendency to preserve ancient legislation, while at the same time more recent material was added to them; chronologically arranged collections like the *Hispana* give a vivid picture how such a collection would continue to grow decade after decade. Other collections stand out for drawing on very different genres when looking for the sources of the law; the heavy use of the Old Testament by the *Hibernensis* compiler, the large share of Roman law in the *Anselmo dedicata*, and Regino's readiness to quote from capitularies are well-known examples. As these early medieval examples also makes clear, the problem was anything but new in our period; but by the late eleventh century, both the chronological diversity and the variety of literary genres of the material sources had increased significantly. In fact, the label 'genre', if applied to traditional division of the *fontes materiales*, should not make forget the diverse background of these texts. 'Conciliar canons' included anything from the earliest councils of the Greek, African, and Gallican Churches via the diet of some Ottonian Emperor to the legatine councils of Hugh of Die. Any selection of 'decretals' could include excerpts from Pseudo-Urban I as well as Urban II, and the label 'theological literature' (as it is used in the literature) could refer to Augustine's writings on free will, Carolingian tracts on baptismal rites, and Berengar's definition of the Eucharist alike. 'Secular law' could refer to the reasoning of pre-Christian legal scholars, a rescript of Emperor Honorius, or Charlemagne's *Admonitio synodalis*, and similar examples could be drawn up for any 'genres' into which the sources of canons law are often divided. All this was 'canon law', and for many issues the range of relevant material was even more diverse than these few examples may suggest.

In short, the thousands of canons in the great collections came from a very wide range of backgrounds, from contexts far removed in time and place, and medieval readers had little chance of fully grasping this diversity. For the modern historian, it is difficult enough to find out which Pope Gregory, if any, wrote a letter from which a canon with the inscription 'Gregorius papa dixit' is taken, and to apply this knowledge to the interpretation of the canon in question. For the medieval reader, this task was almost impossible, and the increasing tendency to arrange collections thematically rather than chronologically deprived him of almost the only clue he had to the original chronology of his material.

This mixing and mingling of ancient, early medieval, and high medieval texts is fascinating for the modern historian, but what concerns us here is the effect all this had on medieval readers of these collections. Evidently, the combination of normative texts from such different traditions could pose special problems when it came to 'finding the law'.[1] While all legal texts require interpretation, the inclusive nature of many canonical collections was a peculiar challenge. High medieval readers rediscovering

---

1. Martin Brett, 'Finding the Law: The Sources of Canonical Authority Before Gratian', *Law Before Gratian: Law in Western Europe c. 500–1100*, ed. Per Andersen, Mia Münster-Swendsen, and Helle Vogt (Proceedings of the Carlsberg Academy Conference on Medieval Legal History 3; Copenhagen 2007) 51–72.

some teaching of Saint Augustine, a letter of Gelasius I, a fragment of the Digest, or a canon of the Second Council of Nicaea did not normally know much about the historical background from which all these texts had emerged, and could not rely on a continuous tradition of interpretation either. The canons culled from these sources were 'new', and so was the context in which they were read once they were integrated into canonical collections.

The problem here is not so much that ancient texts were available only from defective copies, however much this worries modern scholars trying to edit the sources in question. In fact, textual 'corruption' could sometimes mitigate problems of interpretation. When medieval scribes struggled with the Latin of their sources or what previous scribes had made of it, they would sometimes 'update' these texts, knowingly or not. The case of the Roman law provision allowing cousin marriage which was interpolated with a 'non' may well be such a case of legal change brought about by a scribe unwittingly adopting ancient law to the marriage legislation of his own time.[2] In this sense, the problem with ancient canon law was most urgent where the wording had been preserved accurately, as it was commonly the case. Famous collections like those of Pseudo-Isidore, Deusdedit, and Ivo, but also somewhat more obscure works like the *Collection in Two Books/Eight Parts*, contain surprisingly good versions of many ancient canons they provided their medieval readers with.

Yet these readers found themselves in a curious position. On the one hand, they were faced with what to the modern historian would be a wealth of primary source evidence on, for example, the legal privileges of Justiniana prima, conflicting positions in the Three Chapter Controversy, or the revocation of the 869/870 Council of Constantinople; but what were they to make of these texts if they did not know where Justiniana prima was located, what the Three Chapters were in the first place, and which of the various councils of Constantinople had issued which canons? Most medieval readers would not know this, and probably not worry too much about this, but still they tried to make sense of these texts, not as 'primary sources' but rather as legal authorities.

This situation was bound to produce much confusion, as indeed it did; it is, therefore, all the more remarkable that, from the mid-eleventh century on, there was a growing interest in ancient canon law, and an equally growing capability to give new meaning to these old texts. The writings of Saint Augustine on the use of force against the Donatists, but also the

---

2. The 'non' added to Cod. 1.10.2.4 is found in Ivo 9.1 (ed. Brett) but not yet in the *Britannica* (London, BL, Add. MS 8873, fol. 57v).

question of how to deal with heretics returning to the orthodox faith, for example, were quickly seen as being applicable in the conflicts between the followers of Gregory VII and their opponents. In other cases, ancient canon law was less directly applicable, but still provided guidance and inspiration. The lofty image of the papacy in harmonious union with pious emperors as found in the Donation of Constantine and many False Decretals, for example, must have been all the more attractive in times of bitter conflicts, when the pope excommunicated the emperor, the possessions of the Roman church were alienated, and civil war raged in large parts of Latin Europe.

In many cases, the picture is more complicated. Canon law as found in the collections normally was less lofty than the Donation of Constantine, but rarely did looking up a canon in a collection provide a straightforward answer either. Usually, a reader looking for guidance on a particular subject would encounter a mixture of canons of very different kinds, some containing moral principles, others providing clear legal arguments, and still others simply giving a penitential tariff for a specific sin. Making sense of these texts individually may have been difficult in some cases; but the real challenge for the medieval readers was to understand them all as part of canon law. To judge from the structure and content of the pre-Gratian collections, a growing number of compilers felt up to this challenge. In my understanding, the success of Burchard's *Liber decretorum* was not only due to the comprehensiveness and usability of this great collection; together with other collections, it also was an excellent model of how to compile a collection in the first place— how to select canons, how to divide materials into books, how to arrange the individual texts, and how to guide the reader in his understanding of the law. All compilers of the collections analysed in this book needed these skills, and some of them relied heavily on selecting the right material, sometimes to the point of suppressing materials they, for one reason or another, did not approve of. Atto of San Marco is unusual frank about his selection criteria, and unusually radical in their application, but not the only compiler to try to manipulate the law by deliberately ignoring certain traditions.

However, while these more partisan collections are fascinating sources for ecclesiastical history, canon law historians should be more interested in the fact that only rarely did partisan collections become very influential. (The *Collection in 74 Titles*, unique in many ways, is perhaps the only exception here.) Instead, the collections that were most influential in the long run tended to be comprehensive rather than selective. Different as they may be, Burchard of Worms, the *Tripartita* A compiler, Ivo of Chartres, and the *Panormia* compiler were all rather good at bringing together material from different backgrounds representing canon law tradition in all its complexity, not (or only rarely) imposing their own interpretation of the law on the reader. Unlike Gratian, whose *Decretum* was likewise inclusive (but outside the scope of the present study), these compilers were largely silent on how exactly the reader should deal with the complexities of tradition. One exception is Ivo's famous prologue to his *Decretum*, which discusses the question of conflicting canons at length and quotes several historical examples of legal change as well as a number of general principles. Indeed, some of the latter (including 'Love and do what you will'[3]) were so general that not all ecclesiastical judges may have found them all too helpful in imposing the proper penance for a particular sin. Nevertheless, the *Prologue* was considered useful enough to be attached to numerous collections, and even found its way into copies of abbreviated forms of the *Decretum Gratiani*.[4]

Given that the compilers are largely silent, and only rarely did other scholars address the issue—Bernold of Konstanz being the most notable exception here[5]—one is, once more, largely left with the collections themselves to understand how the problem of diversity and indeed contradictions was dealt with between the turn of the millennium and the time when the *Decretum Gratiani* became a textbook for legal scholars. Sometimes, the collections would take up canons on the interpretation of canons, and the transmission of these texts sometimes reflects the changing ideas about 'law' and its sources. In Chapter One, I have analysed the textual history of one such text—Pseudo-Innocent's *De causis*—from the early eighth to the later twelfth centuries, and as outlined in Chapter Five, collections like the *Caesaraugustana* contain a rather large number of canons which are best understood as materials teaching the reader how to understand better the material law contained in other parts of the respec-

---

3. Ivo, *Prologue* (ed. Brasington 116): 'Habe caritatem et fac quicquid uis.'

4. Bruce Clark Brasington, 'The Abbreviatio "Exceptiones Evangelicarum": A Distinctive Regional Reception of Gratian's Decretum' *Codices Manuscripti* 17 (1994) 95–99 (Gratian abbreviation) and idem, 'Studies in the Nachleben of Ivo of Chartres: The Influence of His Prologue on Several Panormia-Derivative Collections', *Proceedings Munich 1992*, MIC. Subsidia 10.63–85 (10P, *Summa Haimonis, Catalaunensis II*); Christof Rolker, *Canon Law and the Letters of Ivo of Chartres* (Life and Thought: Fourth Series 76; Cambridge 2010) 266–267 (*Tripartita, Panormia*, 10P, Vatican 13L); Martin Brett, 'Ivo, Decretum: Prefatory Note', *Ivo of Chartres: Work in Progress*, ed. idem (2015), https://ivo-of-chartres.github.io/decretum/idecforw.pdf (Harley abbreviation and other *Decretum*-derivative collections).

5. Brett, 'Finding' 59–64; Tatsushi Genka, 'The Role of Hagiography in the Development of Canon Law in the Reform Era', *New Discourses in Medieval Canon Law Research: Challenging the Master Narrative*, ed. Christof Rolker (Medieval Law and Its Practice 28; Leiden and Boston 2019) 83–104, here at 101–104.

tive collection. The main evidence, however, is the success of those collections that were inclusive not only in the sense that they included material from different sources, but indeed also representing the rich diversity of ecclesiastical tradition including the contradictions it contains. In some situations, this must have been very challenging. Yet from the success of collections like the *Panormia* one can infer that there were indeed many readers who saw this either as an adequate guide to the complexity of canon law tradition or at least as food for thought. Unlike in the *Decretum Gratiani*, these collections would not tell the reader how the 'harmony from dissonance' was achieved, but we can assume that it was not only dissonance these readers were looking for. By the time Gratian began his work, the appetite for canon law had been growing for a long time, and many scholars in many places had spent very considerable efforts to turn the mass of traditional texts into a more unified body of canon law.

Bibliography

Primary Sources: Manuscripts

Assisi, Biblioteca del Sacro Convento, 227.
Bamberg, Staatsbibliothek, Msc.Can.5.
————,————, Msc.Can.6.
————,————, Msc.Can.8.
————,————, Msc.Can.9.
Barcelona, Archivo General de la Corona de Aragón, San Cugat 63.
Bologna, Biblioteca Universitaria, 2239 (1107).
Bordeaux, Bibliothèque municipale, 11.
El Burgo del Osma, Biblioteca de la Catedral, 157.
Cambridge, Corpus Christi College, College Library, 19.
————,————, 269.
Chartres, Bibliothèque municipale [today: Médiathèque L'Apostrophe], 161.
————,————, liasse 352 (*olim* Chartres, BM, 193).
Einsiedeln, Stiftsbibliothek, Codex 193 (66).
Firenze, Biblioteca Riccardiana, 3006.
Frankfurt, Universitätsbibliothek Johann Christian Senckenberg, Ms. Barth. 7.
————,————, Ms. Barth. 50.
Freiburg, Universitätsbibliothek, Hs. 7.
Heiligenkreuz, Stiftsbibliothek, 44.
Köln, Erzbischöfliche Diözesan- und Dombibliothek, Cod. 119.
————, ————, Cod. 126.
————, Historisches Archiv, 199.
London, British Library, Add. MS 8873.
————,————, Royal MS 6 B VI.
Mantova, Biblioteca Comunale, 318.
Milano, Biblioteca Trivulziana, 601.
Montpellier, Bibliothèque interuniversitaire, Section de Médecine, H.137.
München, Bayerische Staatsbibliothek, Clm 4570.
Paris, Bibliothèque de l'Arsenal, 678.
————,————, 713.
————, Bibliothèque nationale de France, lat. 3875.
————,————, lat. 3876.
————,————, lat. 12519.
————,————, lat. 12711.
————,————, lat. 13368.
————,————, lat. 13656.
————,————, lat. 13658.
————,————, lat. 14145.
————,————, nouv. acq. lat. 326.
Parma, Biblioteca Palatina, 3777.

Praha, Národní knihovna České republiky, X.A.11.
Reims, Bibliothèque municipale, 673.
———,———, 674.
———,———, 675.
Salamanca, Biblioteca Universitaria, 2644.
Tarragona, Biblioteca Pública, 26.
Troyes, Bibliothèque municipale [today: Médiathèque de Troyes Champagne Métropole, fonds ancien], 246.
Città del Vaticano, Biblioteca Apostolica Vaticana, Barb. lat. 535.
———,———, Pal. lat. 585.
———,———, Pal. lat. 586.
———,———, Reg. lat. 973.
———,———, Vat. lat. 586.
———,———, Vat. lat. 1339.
———,———, Vat. lat. 1349.
———,———, Vat. lat. 1355.
———,———, Vat. lat. 1357.
———,———, Vat. lat. 1361.
———,———, Vat. lat. 1363.
———,———, Vat. lat. 1364.
———,———, Vat. lat. 1984.
———,———, Vat. lat. 3809.
———,———, Vat. lat. 3833.
———,———, Vat. lat. 4976.
———,———, Vat. lat. 5715.
Würzburg, Universitätsbibliothek, Mp.j.q.2.

Primary Sources: Editions, Translations, and Calendars

Editions in the great series (ACO, CCL/CCCM, CSEL, Mansi, MGH, and PL) are **not** listed here; see the list of abbreviations for these series. All online resources have been archived at www.archive.org in 2020.

Abelard. *Peter Abailard, Sic et non: A Critical Edition*, ed. Blanche Beatrice Boyer and Richard Peter McKeon (Chicago and London 1977).
Acta et scripta quae de controversiis ecclesiae Graecae et Latinae saeculo undecimo composita extant, ed. Cornelius Will (Leipzig and Marburg 1861).
Acta pontificum Romanorum inedita: Urkunden der Päpste vom Jahre 748 bis zum Jahre 1198, ed. Julius von Pflugk-Harttung (3 vols. Tübingen 1881–86).
Æthelberht. 'Laws of Æthelberht', *The Beginnings of English Law*, ed. and tr. Lisi Oliver (Toronto Medieval Texts and Translations; Toronto 2002) 52–116.
Aimo of Fleury. 'Vie d'Abbon, abbé de Fleury; Vita et passio sancti Abbonis et pièces annexes', ed. and tr. by Robert-Henri Bautier and Gilette Labory in iidem, *L'abbaye de Fleury en l'an mil* (Sources d'histoire médiévale 32; Paris 2004) 34–162.
Alger of Liège. *Liber de misericordia et iustitia*, ed. Robert Kretzschmar in idem, *Alger von Lüttichs Traktat 'De misericordia et iustitia'. Ein kanonistischer Konkordanzversuch aus der Zeit des Investiturstreits: Untersuchungen und Edition* (Quellen und Forschungen zum Recht im Mittelalter 2; Sigmaringen 1985), 187–375.
Anastasius Bibliothecarius. *Historia tripertita*, ed. Charles de Boos in idem, *Theophanis Chronographia* (2 vols. Leipzig 1883/85) 2.31–346.

Annales de Saint-Bertin, ed. Félix Grat, Jeanne Vielliard, and Suzanne Clémencet (Société de l'histoire de France 470; Paris 1964).

Anselmi episcopi Lucensis collectio canonum una cum collectione minore, ed. Friedrich Thaner (2 in 1 vols. Innsbruck 1915).

Anselmo dedicata, partly (incipit/explicit only) ed. Jean Claude Besse in idem, *Histoire des textes du droit de l'Église au Moyen-Age de Denys à Gratien: Collectio Anselmo dedicata: étude et texte* (Paris 1960).

————, partly (book 1 and preface only) ed. Jean Claude Besse in idem, 'Collectionis "Anselmo dedicata" liber primus' *Revue de Droit canonique* 9 (1959) 207–296.

————, partly (Roman law only) ed. Giuseppe Russo in idem, *Tradizione manoscritta di Leges romanae nei codici dei secoli IX e X della Biblioteca capitolare di Modena* (Modena 1980).

Atto of San Marco. *Capitulare*, ed. Angelo Mai in idem, *Scriptorum veterum nova collectio e Vaticanis codicibus edita* (10 vols. Rome 1825–38) 6.2:60–100.

Augustine. *Contra Academicos, De beata vita, De ordine*, ed. Therese Fuhrer and Simone Adam (Bibliotheca Teubneriana 2022; Berlin and Boston 2017).

————. *The City of God Against the Pagans*, tr. Robert W. Dyson (Cambridge Texts in the History of Political Thought; Cambridge 1998).

Barberiniana, ed. Mario Fornasari, 'Collectio canonum Barberiniana: textus' *Apollinaris* 36 (1963) 214–297.

Bernard of Clairvaux. *De consideratione ad Eugenium papam*, ed. Jean Leclercq and H. M. Rochais in *Tractatus et opuscula*, ed. iidem (Sancti Bernardi Opera 3; Rome 1963) 379–493.

Bonizo of Sutri. *Liber de vita christiana*, ed. Ernst Perels (Texte zur Geschichte des römischen und kanonischen Rechts im Mittelalter 1; Berlin 1930).

Bullarium diplomatum et privilegiorum sanctorum Romanorum pontificum (22 vols. Turin 1857–72).

Burchard of Worms. *Decretorum libri XX ex consiliis [sic] et orthodoxorum patrum decretis, tum etiam diversarum nationum synodis seu loci communes congesti* (Cologne 1548); reprinted as *Burchard von Worms (Burchardus Wormaciensis ecclesiae episcopus), Decretorum libri XX […]. Ergänzter Neudruck*, ed. Gérard Fransen and Theo Kölzer (Aalen 1992).

————. 'Praefacivncvla', *Burchard von Worms (Burchardus Wormaciensis ecclesiae episcopus), Decretorum libri XX […]. Ergänzter Neudruck*, ed. Gérard Fransen and Theo Kölzer (Aalen 1992), 45–49.

Capitula Angilramni, ed. Karl-Georg Schon in idem, *Die Capitula Angilramni. Eine prozessrechtliche Fälschung Pseudoisidors* (MGH Studien und Texte 39; Hanover 2006).

Catalogi bibliothecarum antiqui, ed. Gustav Becker (Bonn 1885); repr. Hildesheim 1973.

Chalcedon. *The Acts of the Council of Chalcedon*, tr. Richard Price and Michael Gaddis (3 vols. Translated Texts for Historians 45; Liverpool 2007).

Clermont. *The Councils of Urban II, Vol. 1: Decreta Claromontensia*, ed. Robert Somerville (AHC. Supplementum 1; Amsterdam 1972).

Codex Iustinianus, ed. Paul Krüger (Corpus Iuris Civilis 2; 15th edition Berlin 1970).

La colección canónica Hispana, ed. Gonzalo Martínez Díez and Félix Rodríguez (6 in 7 vols. Monumenta Hispaniae sacra. Series canonica 1–6; Madrid 1966–2002).

Collectio canonum Casinensis, ed. Roger E. Reynolds in idem, *The Collectio canonum Casinensis duodecimi seculi (Codex terscriptus). …: A Derivative of the South-Italian Collection in Five Books: An Implicit Edition with Introductory Study* (PIMS Studies and Texts 137 / Monumenta Liturgica Beneventana 3; Toronto 2001).

Collectio canonum in quinque libris: liber IV, ed. Davide Cito (Rome 1989).

Collectio canonum regesto Farfensi inserta, ed. Theo Kölzer (MIC Corpus collectionum 5; Vatican City 1982).

Collectio canonum trium librorum, ed. Giuseppe Motta (2 vols. MIC Corpus collectionum 8; Vatican City 2005–08).

Collectio Hibernensis, ed. and tr. Roy Flechner in idem, *The Hibernensis* (2 vols. SMCL 17; Washington, D.C. 2019).

———, ed. Friedrich Wilhelm Hermann Wasserschleben in idem, *Die irische Kanonensammlung* (Leipzig 1885).

Die Collectio Francofurtana: eine französische Dekretalensammlung. Analyse beruhend auf den Vorarbeiten von Walther Holtzmann (†), ed. Peter Landau and Gisela Drossbach (MIC Corpus collectionum 9; Vatican City 2007).

Collectio Toletana: A Canon Law Derivative of the South-Italian Collection in Five Books: An Implicit Edition with Introductory Study, ed. Douglas Adamson and Roger E. Reynolds (PIMS Studies and Texts 159; Toronto 2008).

Collection in 74 Titles. Ed. John T. Gilchrist as *Diuersorum patrum sententie siue Collectio in LXXIV titulos digesta* (MIC Corpus collectionum 1; Vatican City 1973).

———. *The Collection in Seventy-Four Titles: A Canon Law Manual of the Gregorian Reform*, tr. John T. Gilchrist (Mediaeval Sources in Translation 22; Toronto 1980).

Collection in Two Books/Eight Parts, ed. Jean Bernhard in idem, 'La collection en deux livres (Cod. Vat. lat. 3832): la forme primitive de la Collection en deux livres, source de la Collection en 74 titres et de la Collection d'Anselme de Lucques' *Revue de Droit canonique* 12 (1962) 9–601.

Conciliorum collectio regia maxima [...], ed. Jean Hardouin (11 in 12 vols. Paris 1714–15).

Conciliorum Oecumenicorum Decreta, ed. Giuseppe Alberigo, Péricles-Pierre Joannou, Claudio Leonardi, and Paulo Prodi (Freiburg 1962; 3rd edition Bologna 1973).

Conciliorum Oecumenicorum Generaliumque Decreta: editio critica, vol. 1: *From Nicaea I to Nicaea II (325–787)*, ed. Giuseppe Alberigo, Adolf Martin Ritter, Luise Abramowski, Ekkehard Mühlenberg, Pietro Conte, Hans-Georg Thümmel, George Nedungatt, Silvano Agrestini, Erich Lamberz, and Johannes Bernhard Uphus (CC COGD 1; Turnhout 2006); vol. 2.1: *The General Councils of Latin Christendom: From Constantinople IV to Pavia-Siena (869–1424)*, ed. Antonio García y García, Peter Gemeinhardt, Georg Gresser, Thomas M. Izbicki, Atria A. Larson, A. Melloni, Jürgen Miethke, Kenneth Pennington, B. Roberg, P. Saccenti, and P. H. Stump (CC COGD 2.1; Turnhout 2013).

Councils and Synods with Other Documents Relating to the English Church I: AD 871–1204, ed. Dorothy Whitelock, Martin Brett, and Christopher Nugent Lawrence Brooke (2 vols. Oxford 1981).

Cresconius. *Concordia canonum*, ed. Klaus Zechiel-Eckes in idem, *Die Concordia canonum des Cresconius. Studien und Edition* (2 vols. Freiburger Beiträge zur mittelalterlichen Geschichte 5; Frankfurt 1992), vol. 2.

Cummian's Letter De controversia Paschali and the De ratione conputandi, ed. and tr. Maura Walsh and Dáibhí Ó Cróinín (PIMS Studies and Texts; Toronto 1988).

Cyprian. *Saint Cyprien, Correspondence*, ed. and tr. Louis Bayard (2 vols.; Paris 1925).

De coniugio, ed. Franz Plazidus Bliemetzrieder in idem, 'Paul Fournier und das literarische Werk Ivos von Chartres' AKKR 115 (1935) 53–91.

'De iniusta vexacione Willelmi episcope primi per Willelmum regem filium Wellelmi magni Regis', ed. Hilary Sedon Offler, revised for publication by A.J. Piper and A.I. Doyle, *Chronology, Conquest and Conflict in Medieval England* (Camden Miscellany 34 / Camden Fifth Series 10; Cambridge 1997) 49–104.

Decrees of the Ecumenical Councils, ed. Norman P. Tanner (2 vols. London 1990).

Decretales ineditae saeculi XII: From the Papers of Walther Holtzmann, ed. and rev. Stanley Chodorow and Charles Duggan (MIC Corpus collectionum 4; Vatican City 1982).

Decretales Pseudo-Isidorianae et Capitula Angilramni, ed. Paul Hinschius (Leipzig 1863).

Das Decretum Gelasianum de libris recipiendis et non recipiendis, ed. Ernst von Dobschütz (Texte und Untersuchungen zur Geschichte der altchristlichen Literatur 38.4; Leipzig 1912).

Deusdedit. *Die Carmina des Kardinals Deusdedit († 1098/99)*, ed. Peter Christian Jacobsen (Editiones Heidelbergenses 31; Heidelberg 2002).

———. *Die Kanonessammlung des Kardinals Deusdedit, I. Die Kanonessammlung selbst* [all published], ed. Victor Wolf von Glanvell (Paderborn 1905).

———. *Deusdedit presbyteri cardinalis tituli apostolorum in Eudoxia collectio canonum*, ed. Pio Martinucci (Venice 1869).

Digesta, ed. Theodor Mommsen and Paul Krüger (Corpus Iuris Civilis 1; 22nd edition Berlin 1973).

du Fresne Du Cange, Charles. *Editio novissima insigniter aucta, ubi non solum e Glossario Latinitatis, sed et Graecitatis addita cuique parti supplementa, suis quaeque locis inserta sunt* (4 vols. Frankfurt 1710).

Epistolae Romanorum pontificum genuinae et quae ad eos scriptae sunt. A S. Hilaro usque ad Pelagium II., vol. I: A S. Hilario usque ad S. Hormisdam [all published], ed. Andreas Thiel (Braunsberg 1868).

Epitome Latina novellarum Iustiniani, ed. Gustav Hänel (Leipzig 1873).

Exceptiones Petri, ed. Carlo Guido Mor in idem, *Scritti giuridici preirneriani* (2 vols. Orbis Romanus. Biblioteca di testi medievali 10; Milan 1935/38) 2.47–206.

Fulbert of Chartres. *The Letters and Poems of Fulbert of Chartres*, ed. and tr. Frederick Behrends (Oxford Medieval Texts; Oxford 1976).

Gallia pontificia. Répertoire des documents concernant les relations entre la papauté et les églises et monastères en France avant 1198, vol. 3: Province ecclésiastique de Vienne, ed. Beate Schilling (3 vols. Göttingen 2006–18).

Germania pontificia sive repertorium privilegiorum et litterarum a Romanis pontificibus ante annum MCLXXXXVIII Germaniae ecclesiis monasteriis civitatibus singulisque personis concessorum, ed. Albert Brackmann et al. (Berlin [since 1978: Göttingen] 1911–) [ongoing].

Germaniae sacrae prodromus seu Collectio Monumentorum res alemannicas illustrantium, ed. Emil Ussermann (2 vols. Sankt Blasien 1792).

Grand cartulaire de La Sauve Majeure, ed. Charles Higounet, Arlette Higounet-Nadal, and Nicole de Peña (2 vols. Études et documents d'Aquitaine 8; Bordeaux 1996).

Gratian. *Decretum Gratiani: First Recension*, ed. Anders Winroth et al. (2019), www.gratian.org.

———. *The Treatise on Laws (Decretum DD. 1–20): Translated by Augustine Thompson with the Ordinary Gloss Translated by James Gordley and an Introduction by Katherine Christensen* (SMCL 2; Washington, D.C. 1993).

———. *Decretum magistri Gratiani*, ed. Emil Friedberg (Corpus iuris canonici 1; Leipzig 1879).

———. *Decretum Gratiani emendatum et notationibus illustratum una cum glossis. Gregorii XIII pontificis maximi iussu editum, ad exemplar Romanum diligenter recognitum* (Rome 1582).

———. [*Decretum Gratiani with Ordinary Gloss*] (Mainz 1472) [= GW 11353].

Gregory of Catino. *Il Chronicon Farfense di Gregorio di Catino*, ed. Ugo Balzani (2 vols. Fonti per la storia d'Italia 33/34; Rome 1903).

Gregory of San Grisogono. *Die Sammlung "Policarpus" des Kardinals Gregor von S. Griso-

gono. Angelegt und gestaltet von Carl Erdmann (†). Zum Druck vorbereitet von Uwe Horst, unter Mitarbeit von Michael Klein, herausgegeben von Horst Fuhrmann ([*ca.* 2004]), https://www.mgh.de/index.php/mgh-digital/digitale-angebote-zu-mgh-abteilungen.

————. *Prologus*, ed. Hermann Hüffer in idem, *Beiträge zur Geschichte der Quellen des Kirchenrechts und des Römischen Rechts im Mittelalter* (Münster 1862) 75–76.

Gregory VII. *The Epistolae vagantes of Pope Gregory VII*, ed. and tr. Herbert Edward John Cowdrey (Oxford Medieval Texts; Oxford 1972).

In primis hominibus, ed. Bernd Matecki in idem, *Der Traktat In primis hominibus. Eine theologie- und kirchenrechtsgeschichtliche Untersuchung zu einem Ehetext der Schule von Laon aus dem 12. Jahrhundert* (Adnotationes in Ius Canonicum 20; Frankfurt and New York 2001).

Innocent III. *Die Register Innocenz' III., 2. Band: 2. Pontifikatsjahr. Texte*, bearbeitet von Othmar Hageneder, Werner Maleczek, and Alfred A. Strnad (Publikationen des Österreichischen Kulturinstituts in Rom 2.1:2; Rome and Vienna 1979).

Institutiones, ed. Theodor Mommsen and Paul Krüger (Corpus Iuris Civilis 1; 22nd edition Berlin 1973).

Isidore of Seville. *De ecclesiasticis officiis*, tr. Thomas Louis Knoebel (Ancient Christian Writers 61; New York 2008).

————. *The Etymologies of Isidore of Seville*, tr. Stephen A. Barney, W. J. Lewis, J. A. Beach, and Oliver Berghof, with the collaboration of Muriel Hall (Cambridge 2006); repr. with corrections 2010.

————. *Isidori Hispalensis episcopi etymologiarum sive originum libri XX*, ed. Wallace M. Lindsay (2 vols. Oxford Classical Texts; Oxford 1911).

Italia pontificia sive repertorium privilegiorum et litterarum a Romanis pontificibus ante annum MCLXXXXVIII Italiae ecclesiis monasteriis civitatibus singulisque personis concessorum, ed. Paul Fridolin Kehr (8 in 10 vols. Göttingen 1906–35); vol. 9, ed. Walther Holtzmann (Berlin 1962); vol. 10, ed. Dieter Girgensohn (Zurich 1975).

Ivo of Chartres. *Decretum*, ed. Martin Brett (2015) at https://ivo-of-chartres.github.io/.

————. *Lettres d'Yves de Chartres*, ed. and tr. Geneviève Giordanengo (2017/18) at http://telma-chartes.irht.cnrs.fr/yves-de-chartres/.

————. *Prologue*, ed. Bruce Clark Brasington in idem, *Ways of Mercy. The Prologue of Ivo of Chartres: Edition and Analysis* (Vita regularis. Editionen 2; Münster 2004) 115–142.

————. *Yves de Chartres, Correspondence: tome I (1090–1098)* [all published], ed. and tr. Jean Leclercq (Les classiques de l'histoire de France au Moyen Âge 22; Paris 1949).

Ivo of Chartres (?). *Tripartita*: see below.

John of Salisbury. *The Historia Pontificalis of John of Salisbury*, ed. and tr. by Marjorie Chibnall (Oxford Medieval Texts; Oxford and New York 1986).

Paul Fridolin Kehr. *Papsturkunden in Italien. Reiseberichte zur Italia Pontificia* (6 vols. Vatican City 1977).

Lambert of Arras. *Le registre de Lambert, évêque d'Arras (1093–1115)*, ed. Claire Giordanengo (Sources d'histoire médiévale 34; Paris 2007).

Lanfranc of Canterbury. *The Letters of Lanfranc, Archbishop of Canterbury*, ed. and tr. Helen Clover and Margaret T. Gibson (Oxford Medieval Texts; Oxford 1979).

Lex romana Visigothorum ad LXXVI librorum manu scriptorum fidem recognovit septem eius antiquis epitomis, quae praeter duas adhuc ineditae sunt, titulorum explanatione auxit, annotatione, appendicibus, prolegomenis, ed. Gustav Friedrich Hänel (Leipzig 1849).

Liber canonum diuersorum sanctorum patrum siue Collectio in CLXXXIII titulos digesta, ed. Giuseppe Motta (MIC Corpus collectionum 7; Vatican City 1988).

Le Liber censuum de l'église romaine, ed. Paul Fabre and Louis Duchesne (2 vols. Bibliothèque des Écoles françaises d'Athènes et de Rome 6; Paris 1889–1910).

Liber decretorum sive Panormia Ivonis (Basel 1499).

Liber diurnus romanorum pontificum, ed. Hans Foerster (Bern 1958).

———, ed. Theodor von Sickel (Vienna 1889).

Le Liber pontificalis: texte, introduction et commentaire, ed. Louis Duchesne (2 vols. Bibliothèque des Écoles Françaises d'Athènes et de Rome, 2ᵉ série; Paris 1886/92).

Manasses of Reims. *Apologia*, ed. Mabillon in *Museum Italicum seu collectio veterum scriptorum ex bibliothecis Italicis*, ed. Jean Mabillon and Michel Germain (2 vols. Paris 1687/89) 1.2:119–127.

Mémoires pour servir de preuves à l'histoire ecclésiastique et civile de Bretagne tirés des archives de cette province, de celles de France et d'Angleterre, des recueils de plusieurs sçavans antiquaires, ed. [Pierre-]Hyacinthe Morice (3 vols. Paris 1742–46).

Nauclerus, Johannes. *Chronica succinctim compraehendentia res memorabiles seculorum omnium ac gentium ab initio mundi [...] usque ad annum presentem [...] MDXLIIII* (Cologne 1544).

Novellae, ed. Rudolf Schöll and Wilhelm Kroll (Corpus Iuris Civilis 3; 10th edition Berlin 1972).

Orderic Vitalis. *The Ecclesiastical History of Orderic Vitalis*, ed. and tr. Marjorie Chibnall (6 vols. Oxford Medieval Texts; Oxford 1969–80).

Les Ordines Romani du haut Moyen Âge, ed. Michel Andrieu (5 vols. Spicilegium sacrum Lovaniense. Études et documents 11, 23, 24, 28, and 29; Leuven 1931–61).

Panormia, ed. Martin Brett and Bruce Brasington (2015) at https://ivo-of-chartres .github.io/.

Papstregesten 844–858, bearbeitet von Klaus Herbers (J. F. Böhmer, Regesta imperii Abt. I, Band 4, Teil 2, Lieferungen 1–2; Vienna, Cologne, and Weimar 1999/2012).

Papstregesten 872–882 (Johannes VIII.), bearbeitet von Veronika Unger (J. F. Böhmer, Regesta imperii Abt. I, Band 4, Teil 3. Vienna, Cologne, and Weimar 2013).

Papstregesten 911–1024, bearbeitet von Harald Zimmermann (J. F. Böhmer, Regesta imperii Abt. II, Band 5; 2nd edition Cologne, Weimar, and Vienna 1998).

Papstregesten 1046–1058, bearbeitet von Karl Augustin Frech (J. F. Böhmer, Regesta imperii Abt. III, Band 5, Teil 1; Vienna, Cologne, and Weimar 2011).

Papsturkunden 896–1046, ed. Harald Zimmermann (3 vols. Veröffentlichungen der historischen Kommission III, 174, 177, and 178; Vienna 1984–89; 2nd edition Vienna 1988/89).

Papsturkunden in Frankreich N.F. Bd. 8: Diözese Paris I: Urkunden und Briefsammlungen der Abteien Sainte-Geneviève und Saint-Victor, ed. Dietrich Lohrmann (Abh. Akad. Göttingen 3.174; Göttingen 1989).

Papsturkunden in Frankreich N.F. Bd. 9: Diözese Paris II: Abtei Saint-Denis, ed. Rolf Große (Abh. Akad. Göttingen 3.225; Göttingen 1998).

Papsturkunden in Italien see above (Kehr).

Papsturkunden in Portugal, ed. Carl Erdmann (Abh. Akad. Göttingen 20.3; Göttingen 1928).

Patrologiae latinae cursus completus, ed. Jacques-Paul Migne (221 vols.; Paris 1844–64).

Pelagii I papae epistulae quae supersunt (556–561), ed. Pius M. Gassó and Columba Batlle (Scripta et documenta 8; Montserrat 1956).

Piacenza, ed. Robert Somerville in idem, *Pope Urban II's Council of Piacenza* (Oxford 2011).

Le pontifical romain au moyen-âge 1: Le pontifical romain de XIIe siècle, ed. Michel Andrieu (Studi e testi 86; Vatican City 1938).

Prefaces to Canon Law Books in Latin Christianity: Selected Translations, 500–1245, ed. Robert Somerville and Bruce Clark Brasington (New Haven and London 1998).

Quadripartitus. Ein englisches Rechtsbuch von 1114, ed. Felix Liebermann (Halle 1892).

Quinisextum. *Concilium Constantinopolitanum a. 691/2 in Trullo habitum (Concilium Quini-*

sextum), ed. Heinz Ohme (4 vols. ACO. Series Secunda. Concilium Universale Constantinopolitanum Tertium; Volumen III; Berlin and Boston 2013).

————. *Concilium Quinisextum / Das Konzil Quinisextum, griechisch-deutsch*, ed. and tr. Heinz Ohme (Fontes Christiani 82; Turnhout 2006).

Regesta pontificum romanorum ab condita ecclesia ad annum post Christum natum MCXCVIII, ed. Philipp Jaffé, rev. second ed. by Samuel Löwenfeld, Friedrich Kaltenbrunner, and Paul Ewald (2 vols. Leipzig 1885–88), rev. third ed. Klaus Herbers (4 vols. Göttingen 2016–19).

Regesta pontificum romanorum inde ab a. post Christum natum MCXVIII ad a. MCCCIV, ed. August Potthast (2 vols. Berlin 1874/75).

Il regesto di Farfa, ed. Ignazio Giorgi and Ugo Balzani (5 vols. Rome 1879–1914).

Regino of Prüm. *Das Sendhandbuch des Regino von Prüm*, ed. and tr. Wilfried Hartmann (FSGA 42; Darmstadt 2004).

————. *Reginonis abbatis Prumiensis libri duo de synodalibus causis et disciplinis ecclesiasticis*, ed. Friedrich Wilhelm Hermann Wasserschleben (Leipzig 1840).

Robert of Flamborough. *Liber poenitentialis*, ed. J. J. Francis Firth (PIMS Studies and Texts 18; Toronto 1971).

Rolandus. *Die Summa magistri Rolandi nachmals Papstes Alexander III.* [*sic*], ed. Friedrich Thaner (Innsbruck 1874).

Sacrosancta concilia ad Regiam editionem exacta [. . .] *longe locupletior et emendatior* [. . .], ed. Niccolò Coleti (23 vols. Venice 1728–33).

Sacrosancta concilia ad Regiam editionem exacta quae nunc quarta parte prodit [. . .], ed. Philippe Labbe and Gabriel Cossart (17 in 18 vols. Paris 1671–72).

Sanctuarium seu vitae sanctorum, ed. Boninus Mombritius (2 vols. Paris 1910).

Scotia pontificia: Papal Letters to Scotland Before the Pontificate of Innocent III, ed. Robert Somerville (Oxford 1982).

Sententie Magistri A., partly ed. Pauline Henriëtte Joanna Theresia Maas in eadem, *The Liber sententiarum Magistri A.: Its Place Amidst the Sentences Collections of the First Half of the 12th Century* (Middeleeuwse studies 11; Nijmegen 1995), 224–293.

Spicilegium Solesmense, complectens sanctorum patrum scriptorumque ecclesiasticorum anecdota hactenus opera, selecta e graecis orientalibusque et latinis codicibus, ed. Jean Baptiste Pitra (4 vols., Paris 1852–58).

The Summa Parisiensis on the Decretum Gratiani, ed. Terence P. McLaughlin (Toronto 1952).

Theodosiani libri xvi cum constitutionibus Sirmondianis, ed. Paul Krüger and Theodor Mommsen (Berlin 1905).

Thesaurus novus anecdotorum, ed. Edmond Martène and Ursin Durand (5 vols. Paris 1717).

Tripartita, ed. Martin Brett and Przemysław Nowak (2015) at https://ivo-of-chartres .github.io/.

Ulpiani liber singularis regularum / Pauli libri quinque sententiarum / Fragmenta minora, ed. Paul Krüger (Collectio librorum iuris anteiustiniani in usum scholarum 2; Berlin 1878).

Veterum scriptorum et monumentorum moralium, historicorum, dogmaticorum, ad res ecclesiasticas, monasticas et politicas illustrandas, collectio nova, ed. Edmond Martène (Rouen 1700).

Vie de Gauzlin, abbé de Fleury / Vita Gauzlini, abbatis Floriacensis monasterii, ed. and tr. Robert-Henri Bautier and Gilette Labory (Sources d'histoire médiévale 2; Paris 1969).

Secondary Literature

All online resources have been archived at www.archive.org in 2020.

Adamson, Douglas and Roger E. Reynolds. 'Introduction', *Collectio Toletana: A Canon Law Derivative of the South-Italian Collection in Five Books: An Implicit Edition with Introductory Study*, ed. iidem (PIMS Studies and Texts 159; Toronto 2008) 1–13.

Agustín, Antonio. *Dialogorum libri duo de emendatione Gratiani* (Paris 1607).

Alberigo, Giuseppe. *Cardinalato e collegialità: studi sull'ecclesiologia tra l'XI e il XIV secolo* (Testi e ricerche di scienze religiose 5; Florence 1969).

Álvarez de las Asturias, Nicolás. 'La difusión del derecho canónico "Gregoriano" en la Península Ibérica a través de las colecciones canónicas', *La reforma Gregoriana en España*, ed. José María Magaz and Nicolás Álvarez de las Asturias (Presencia y diálogo 31; Madrid 2011) 145–186.

————. *La "Collectio Lanfranci": origine e influenza di una collezione della Chiesa anglo-normanna* (Monografie giuridiche 32; Milan 2008).

Ambrosioni, Annamaria C. 'Il più antico elenco di chierici della diocesi ambrosiana ed altre aggiunte al Decretum di Burcardo in un codice della Biblioteca Ambrosiana (E 144 sup.): una voce della polemica antipatarinica?' *Aevum* 50 (1976) 274–320.

Amory, Patrick. *People and Identity in Ostrogothic Italy, 489–554* (Life and Thought: Fourth Series 33; Cambridge 1997).

Andresen, Carl. 'Geschichte der abendländischen Konzile des Mittelalters', *Die ökumenischen Konzile der Christenheit*, ed. Hans Jochen Margull (Stuttgart 1961) 75–200.

Austin, Greta. 'How the Local Council of Seligenstadt in 1023 Drew upon Books of Church Law', *The Use of Canon Law in Ecclesiastical Administration, 1000–1234*, ed. Danica Summerlin and Melodie Harris Eichbauer (Medieval Law and Its Practice 26; Leiden 2018) 159–182.

————. 'Were There Two Arsenal Collections? Arsenal 713B and the Ivonian *Panormia*', *Canon Law, Religion and Politics: Liber amicorum Robert Somerville*, ed. Uta-Renate Blumenthal, Anders Winroth, and Peter Landau (Washington, D.C. 2012) 3–14.

————. *Shaping Church Law Around the Year 1000: The Decretum of Burchard of Worms* (CFC; Farnham and Burlington 2009).

————. 'Secular Law in the *Collectio duodecim partium* and Burchard's *Decretum*', *Bishops, Texts and the Use of Canon Law Around 1100: Essays in Honour of Martin Brett*, ed. Bruce Clark Brasington and Kathleen Grace Cushing (CFC; Aldershot 2008) 28–44.

————. 'Freising and Worms in the Early Eleventh Century: Revisiting the Relationship Between the *Collectio duodecim partium* and Burchard's *Decretum*' ZRG Kan. Abt. 93 (2007) 45–108.

Autenrieth, Johanne. 'Bernold von Konstanz und die erweiterte 74-Titelsammlung' DA 14 (1958) 375–394.

————. *Die Domschule zu Konstanz zur Zeit des Investiturstreits. Die wissenschaftliche Arbeitsweise Bernolds von Konstanz und zweier Kleriker dargestellt auf Grund von Handschriftenstudien* (Forschungen zur Kirchen- und Geistesgeschichte N.F. 3; Stuttgart 1956).

van Balberghe, Émile. 'La Préface du Décret et la *Collectio XII Partium*' BMCL 3 (1973) 7–10.

Baldwin, John Wesley. *Masters, Princes and Merchants: The Social Views of Peter the Chanter and His Circle* (2 vols. Princeton, N.J. 1970).

Ballerini, Pietro and Girolamo. 'De antiquis tum editis tum ineditis collectionibus et collectoribus canonum ad Gratianum usque', *Sancti Leonis Magni Romani pontificis opera*, ed. iidem (Venice 1757) i–cccxx; repr. in PL 56.11–354.

Batiffol, Pierre. *Cathedra Petri: études d'histoire ancienne de l'Église* (Unam Sanctam 4; Paris 1938).

Bäumer, Remigius. 'Die Zahl der allgemeinen Konzilien in der Sicht von Theologen des 15. und 16. Jahrhunderts' AHC 1 (1969) 288–313.

Becker, Alfons. *Papst Urban II. (1088–1099)* (3 vols. MGH Schriften 19; Stuttgart 1964–2012).

Bellini, Roberto. 'Tra riforma e tradizione: un abrégé del Decreto di Burcardo di Worms' *Aevum* 72 (1998) 303–334.

———. 'Un abrégé del Decreto di Burcardo di Worms: la collezione canonica in 20 libri (Ms. Vat. Lat. 1350)' *Apollinaris* 69 (1996) 119–195.

Bellomo, Manlio. *The Common Legal Past of Europe, 1000–1800* (SMCL 4; Washington, D.C. 1995).

Berkhofer, Robert F. *Day of Reckoning: Power and Accountability in Medieval France* (The Middle Ages; Philadelphia 2004).

Berman, Constance H. '[Review of:] Charles Higounet and Arlette Higounet-Nadal, Eds., with Nicole De Peña, *Grand Cartulaire de la Sauve Majeure*' *Speculum* 72 (1997) 1183–1186.

Bernal Palacios, Arturo. 'La redacción breve del c. "In die surrectionis" en las colecciones canónicas pregracianas', *Proceedings Munich 1992* MIC Subsidia 10.923–952.

Berschin, Walter. 'Nachwort', *Bonizo von Sutri, Liber de vita christiana, hg. von Ernst Perels. Mit einem Nachwort zur Neuauflage*, ed. idem (Hildesheim 1998) 405–410.

———. 'Zwei neue Bonizo-Handschriften' *Scriptorium* 41 (1987) 87–90.

———. 'Herrscher, "Richter", Ritter, Frauen … Die Laienstände nach Bonizo', *Love and Marriage in the Twelfth Century*, ed. Willy van Hoecke and Andries Welkenhuysen (Mediaevalia Lovaniensia. Studia 8; Leuven 1981) 116–129.

———. *Bonizo von Sutri. Leben und Werk* (Beiträge zur Geschichte und Quellenkunde des Mittelalters 2; Berlin and New York 1972).

Bertolini, Ottorino. 'La collezione canonica Beneventana del Vat. Lat. 4939', *Collectanea Vaticana in honorem Anselmi M. Cardinalis Albareda: a Bibliotheca Apostolica edita* (2 vols. Studi e testi 219/220; Vatican City 1962) 1.119–137; repr. in idem, *Scritti scelti di storia medioevale*, ed. Ottavio Banti (2 vols. Università degli Studi di Pisa. Pubblicazioni dell'Istituto di Storia della Facoltà di Lettere 3; Livorno 1968) 2.773–789.

Besse, Jean Claude. *Histoire des textes du droit de l'Église au Moyen-Age de Denys à Gratien: Collectio Anselmo dedicata: étude et texte (extraits)* (Paris 1960).

———. 'Collectionis "Anselmo dedicata" liber primus' *Revue de Droit canonique* 9 (1959) 207–296.

Beulertz, Stefan. *Das Verbot der Laieninvestitur im Investiturstreit* (MGH Studien und Texte 2; Hanover 1991).

Bliemetzrieder, Franz Plazidus. 'Paul Fournier und das literarische Werk Ivos von Chartres' AKKR 115 (1935) 53–91.

Blumenthal, Uta-Renate. 'IIII and Canon Law in Rome' BMCL 36 (2019) 157–173.

———. 'Dating the Exceptiones Petri' ZRG Kan. Abt. 101 (2015) 54–85.

———. 'The *Collectio canonum Caesaraugustana* and Roman Legal Sources', *Canon Law, Religion and Politics: Liber amicorum Robert Somerville*, ed. Uta-Renate Blumenthal, Anders Winroth, and Peter Landau (Washington, D.C. 2012) 15–27.

———. 'Päpstliche Urkunden, Briefe und die europäische Öffentlichkeit', *Erinnerung – Niederschrift – Nutzung. Das Papsttum und die Schriftlichkeit im mittelalterlichen Westeuropa*, ed. Klaus Herbers and Ingo Fleisch (Abh. Akad. Göttingen. N.F. 11; Berlin and New York 2011) 11–30.

———. 'Poitevin Manuscripts, the Abbey of Saint-Ruf and Ecclesiastical Reform in the

Eleventh Century', *Readers, Texts and Compilers in the Earlier Middle Ages: Studies in Medieval Canon Law in Honour of Linda Fowler-Magerl*, ed. Kathleen Grace Cushing and Martin Brett (CFC; Farnham and Aldershot 2009) 87–100.

————. 'Reflections on the Influence of the *Collectio canonum* of Cardinal Deusdedit', *Mélanges en l'honneur d'Anne Lefebvre-Teillard*, ed. Bernard d'Alteroche, Florence Demoulin-Auzary, Olivier Descamps, Breandán Ó Buachalla, and Franck Roumy (Paris 2009) 135–148.

————. 'Codex 173, Biblioteca Alessandrina, Rome: The Pontifical of the Gregorian Reform?', *Procession, Performance, Liturgy, and Ritual: Essays in Honor of Bryan R. Gillingham*, ed. Nancy van Deusen (Wissenschaftliche Abhandlungen 62.8; Ottawa 2007) 65–81.

————. '*De praua consuetudine*: A Fragment of the Council of 1078?', *Grundlagen des Rechts. Festschrift für Peter Landau zum 65. Geburtstag*, ed. Richard H. Helmholz, Paul Mikat, Jörg Müller, and Michael Stolleis (Rechts- und Staatswissenschaftliche Veröffentlichungen der Görres-Gesellschaft N.F. 91; Paderborn, Munich, Vienna, and Zurich 2000) 141–154.

————. 'The Papacy and Canon Law in the Eleventh-Century Reform' CHR 84 (1998) 201–218.

————. 'Conciliar Canons and Manuscripts: The Implications of Their Transmission in the Eleventh Century', *Proceedings Munich 1992* MIC. Subsidia 10.357–379; repr. in eadem, *Papal Reform and Canon Law in the 11th and 12th Centuries* (CSS 618; Aldershot 1998) no. VII.

————. 'History and Tradition in Eleventh-Century Rome' CHR 79 (1993) 185–196; repr. in eadem, *Papal Reform and Canon Law in the 11th and 12th Centuries* (CSS 618; Aldershot 1998) no. VI.

————. 'An Episcopal Handbook from Twelfth-Century Southern Italy: Codex Rome, Bibl. Vallicelliana F. 54/III', *Studia in honorem eminentissimi Cardinalis Alphonsi M. Stickler*, ed. Rosalio J. Castillo Lara (Studia e textus historiae iuris canonici 7; Rome 1992) 13–24; repr. in eadem, *Papal Reform and Canon Law in the 11th and 12th Centuries* (CSS 618; Aldershot 1998) no. XVIII.

————. 'Rom in der Kanonistik', *Rom im hohen Mittelalter. Studien zu den Romvorstellungen und zur Rompolitik vom 10. bis zum 12. Jahrhundert. Reinhard Elze zur Vollendung seines siebzigsten Lebensjahres gewidmet*, ed. Bernhard Schimmelpfennig and Ludwig Schmugge (Sigmaringen 1992) 29–39; repr. in eadem, *Papal Reform and Canon Law in the 11th and 12th Centuries* (CSS 618; Aldershot 1998) no. V.

————. 'Papal Registers in the Twelfth Century', *Proceedings Cambridge 1984* MIC Subsidia 8.137–151; repr. in eadem, *Papal Reform and Canon Law in the 11th and 12th Centuries* (CSS 618; Aldershot 1998) no. XV.

————. 'Fälschungen bei Kanonisten der Kirchenreform des 11. Jahrhunderts', *Fälschungen im Mittelalter* (6 vols. MGH Schriften 33; Hanover 1988) 2.241–262; repr. in eadem, *Papal Reform and Canon Law in the 11th and 12th Centuries* (CSS 618; Aldershot 1998) no. IV.

————. *The Investiture Controversy: Church and Monarchy from the Ninth to the Twelfth Century* (Philadelphia 1988).

————. 'Bemerkungen zum Register Paschalis II.' QF 66 (1986) 1–18; repr. in eadem, *Papal Reform and Canon Law in the 11th and 12th Centuries* (CSS 618; Aldershot 1998) no. XIII.

————. 'Decrees and Decretals of Pope Paschal II in Twelfth-Century Canonical Collections' BMCL 10 (1980) 15–30; repr. in eadem, *Papal Reform and Canon Law in the 11th and 12th Centuries* (CSS 618; Aldershot 1998) no. XII.

————. *The Early Councils of Pope Paschalis II 1100–1110* (PIMS Studies and Texts 43; Toronto 1978).

————. 'Opposition to Pope Paschal II: Some Comments on the Lateran Council of 1112' AHC 10 (1978) 82–98; repr. in eadem, *Papal Reform and Canon Law in the 11th and 12th Centuries* (CSS 618; Aldershot 1998) no. X.

————. 'Ein neuer Text für das Reimser Konzil Leos IX. (1049)?' DA 32 (1976) 23–48; repr. in eadem, *Papal Reform and Canon Law in the 11th and 12th Centuries* (CSS 618; Aldershot 1998) no. I.

Blumenthal, Uta-Renate and Detlev Jasper. 'Licet nova consuetudo. Gregor VII. und die Liturgie', *Bishops, Texts and the Use of Canon Law Around 1100: Essays in Honour of Martin Brett*, ed. Bruce Clark Brasington and Kathleen Grace Cushing (CFC; Aldershot and Farnham 2008) 45–68.

Boye, Martin. 'Die Synoden Deutschlands und Reichsitaliens (922–1059). Eine kirchenverfassungsgeschichtliche Studie' ZRG Kan. Abt. 18 (1929) 131–284.

Boyer, Blanche Beatrice and Richard Peter McKeon. 'The Textual Relation of Ivo and Abailard', *Peter Abailard, Sic et non: A Critical Edition*, ed. iidem (Chicago and London 1977) 617–634.

Boynton, Susan. *Shaping a Monastic Identity: Liturgy and History at the Imperial Abbey of Farfa, 1000–1125* (Conjunctions of Religion and Power in the Medieval Past; Ithaca, N.Y. 2006).

Brasington, Bruce Clark. '*Crimina que episcopis inpingere dicis*: The Contribution of the *Collectio Polycarpus* to an Early *Ordo iudiciorum*', *Readers, Texts and Compilers in the Earlier Middle Ages: Studies in Medieval Canon Law in Honour of Linda Fowler-Magerl*, ed. Kathleen Grace Cushing and Martin Brett (CFC; Farnham and Aldershot 2009) 123–135.

————. '"Congrega seniores provinciae": A Note on a Hiberno-Latin Canon Concerning the Sources of Authority in Ecclesiastical Law', *Plenitude of Power: The Doctrines and Exercise of Authority in the Middle Ages: Essays in Memory of Robert Louis Benson*, ed. Robert C. Figueira (CFC; Aldershot 2006) 1–10.

————. '"In nomine patria": Transmission and Reception of an Early-Medieval Papal Letter Concerning Baptism' *Codices manuscripti* 37 (2001) 1–5.

————. 'Studies in the Nachleben of Ivo of Chartres: The Influence of His Prologue on Several Panormia-Derivative Collections', *Proceedings Munich 1992* MIC Subsidia 10.63–85.

————. 'The Abbreviatio "Exceptiones Evangelicarum": A Distinctive Regional Reception of Gratian's Decretum' *Codices Manuscripti* 17 (1994) 95–99.

————. 'Prologues to Canonical Collections as a Source for Jurisprudential Change to the Eve of the Investiture Contest' *Frühmittelalterliche Studien* 28 (1994) 226–242.

Brett, Martin. 'Ivo, Decretum: Prefatory Note', *Ivo of Chartres: Work in Progress*, ed. idem (2015), https://ivo-of-chartres.github.io/decretum/idecforw.pdf.

————. '*Panormia* Project', *Ivo of Chartres: Work in Progress*, ed. idem (2015), https://ivo-of-chartres.github.io/panormia/method.pdf.

————. 'The *De corpore et sanguine Domini* of Ernulf of Canterbury', *Canon Law, Religion and Politics: Liber amicorum Robert Somerville*, ed. Uta-Renate Blumenthal, Anders Winroth, and Peter Landau (Washington, D.C. 2012) 163–182.

————. 'English Law and Centres of Law Studies in the Later Twelfth Century', *Archbishop Eystein as Legislator: The European Connection*, ed. Tore Iversen (Trondheim 2011) 87–102.

————. 'Margin and Afterthought: The *Clavis* in Action', *Readers, Texts and Compilers in the Earlier Middle Ages: Studies in Medieval Canon Law in Honour of Linda Fowler-Magerl*, ed. Kathleen Grace Cushing and Martin Brett (CFC; Farnham and Aldershot 2009) 137–163.

———. 'Finding the Law: The Sources of Canonical Authority Before Gratian', *Law Before Gratian: Law in Western Europe c. 500–1100: Proceedings of the Third Carlsberg Academy Conference on Medieval Legal History*, ed. Per Andersen, Mia Münster-Swendsen, and Helle Vogt (Copenhagen 2007) 51–72.

———. 'Some New Letters of Popes Urban II and Paschal II' JEH 58 (2007) 75–96.

———. 'Editions, Manuscripts and Readers in Some Pre-Gratian Collections', *Ritual, Text and Law: Studies in Medieval Canon Law and Liturgy Presented to Roger E. Reynolds*, ed. Richard F. Gyug and Kathleen Grace Cushing (CFC; Aldershot 2004) 205–224.

———. 'Creeping up on the *Panormia*', *Grundlagen des Rechts. Festschrift für Peter Landau zum 65. Geburtstag*, ed. Richard H. Helmholz, Paul Mikat, Jörg Müller, and Michael Stolleis (Rechts- und Staatswissenschaftliche Veröffentlichungen der Görres-Gesellschaft N.F. 91; Paderborn, Munich, Vienna, and Zurich 2000) 205–270.

———. 'The Sources and Influence of Paris, Bibliothèque de l'Arsenal MS 713', *Proceedings Munich 1992* MIC Subsidia 10.149–167.

———. 'The English Abbeys, Their Tenants and the King (950–1150)', *Chiesa e mondo feudale nei secoli X–XII: atti Mendola 1992* (Miscellanea 40; Milan 1995) 277–302.

———. 'Gundulf and the Cathedral Communities of Canterbury and Rochester', *Canterbury and the Norman Conquest: Churches, Saints and Scholars 1066–1109*, ed. Richard G. Eales and Richard Sharpe (London and Rio Grande 1995) 15–25.

———. 'The *Collectio Lanfranci* and Its Competitors', *Intellectual Life in the Middle Ages: Essays Presented to Margaret Gibson*, ed. Lesley Janette Smith and Benedicta Ward (London 1992) 157–174.

———. 'Urban II and the Collections Attributed to Ivo of Chartres', *Proceedings San Diego 1988* MIC Subsidia 9.27–46.

———. 'The Canons of the First Lateran Council in English Manuscripts', *Proceedings Berkeley 1985* MIC Subsidia 7.13–28.

Brett, Martin and Robert Somerville. 'The Transmission of the Councils from 1130 to 1139', *Pope Innocent II (1130–43): The World vs the City*, ed. John Doran and Damian J. Smith (CFC; Abingdon and New York 2016) 226–271.

Brommer, Peter. 'Kurzformen des Dekrets Bischof Burchards von Worms' *Jahrbuch für westdeutsche Landesgeschichte* 1 (1975) 19–45.

Brooke, Zachary Nugent. *The English Church and the Papacy: From the Conquest to the Reign of John* (Cambridge 1931); repr. Cambridge 1989.

Brooke, Christopher Nugent Lawrence. 'Archbishop Lanfranc, the English Bishops and the Council of London of 1075' SG 12 (1967) 39–59.

———. 'The Canons of English Church Council in the Early Decretal Collections' *Traditio* 13 (1957) 471–481.

Brown, Virginia. *Beneventan Discoveries: Collected Manuscript Catalogues, 1978–2008*, ed. Roger E. Reynolds (Toronto 2012).

Brundage, James A. *The Medieval Origins of the Legal Profession: Canonists, Civilians, and Courts* (Chicago 2008).

———. *Law, Sex and Christian Society in Medieval Europe* (Chicago and London 1987).

Büdinger, Max. *Zu den Quellen der Geschichte Kaiser Heinrichs III.* (Vienna 1852).

Burden, John. *Between Crime and Sin: Penitential Justice in Medieval Germany, 900–1200* (Ph.D. thesis; Yale University, New Haven 2018).

Busch, Jörg W. *Der Liber de honore ecclesiae des Placidus von Nonantola. Eine kanonistische*

Problemerörterung aus dem Jahre 1111. Die Arbeitsweise ihres Autors und seine Vorlagen (Quellen und Forschungen zum Recht im Mittelalter 5; Sigmaringen 1990).

Cabaillot, Claire. 'De la theorie des trois ordres à la revue des états: Rathier de Vérone et Bonizon de Sutri' *Revue des études italiennes* 39 (1993) 35–51.

Cantin, André. 'Bérenger, lecteur du *De ordine* de saint Augustin, ou comment se préparait, au milieu du XIᵉ siècle, une domination de la *ratio* sur la science sacrée', *Auctoritas und ratio. Studien zu Berengar von Tours*, ed. Peter Felix Ganz, Robert Burchard Constantijn Huygens, and Friedrich Niewöhner (Wolfenbütteler Mittelalter-Studien 2; Wiesbaden 1990) 89–107.

Capitani, Ovidio. 'Episcopato ed ecclesiologia nell'età gregoriana', *Le istituzioni ecclesiastiche della «Societas Christiana» dei secoli XI–XII: papato, cardinalato ed episcopato: atti Mendola 1971* (Miscellanea 7; Milan 1974) 316–373; repr. in idem, *Tradizione ed interpretazione: dialettiche ecclesiologiche del secolo XI* (Storia 26; Rome 1990) 85–150.

―――. *Immunità vescovili ed ecclesiologia in età "pregregoriana" e "gregoriana": l'avvio alla "restaurazione"* (Biblioteca degli studi medievali 3; Spoleto 1966); repr. 1971.

Carloni, Chiara. 'Celle e dipendenze del monastero di Farfa in area laziale', *Teoria e pratica del lavoro nel monachesimo altomedievale: atti del Convengno internazionale di studio, Roma - Subiaco, 7–9 giugno 2013*, ed. Letizia Ermini Pani (Spoleto 2015) 163–190.

Caspar, Erich. *Geschichte des Papsttums von den Anfängen bis zur Höhe der Weltherrschaft* (2 vols. Tübingen 1930/33).

―――. 'Studien zum Register Gregors VII.' NA 38 (1913) 143–226.

―――. 'Studien zum Register Johanns VIII.' NA 36 (1911) 77–156.

Catalogue des manuscrits de la bibliothèque de la ville de Chartres (Chartres 1840).

Catalogue général des manuscrits des Bibliothèques publiques de France (116 vols., Paris 1849–1993).

Cito, Davide. *Collectio canonum in quinque libris libro IV* (Rome 1989).

Colish, Marcia L. *Faith, Fiction and Force in Medieval Baptismal Debates* (Washington, D.C. 2014).

―――. 'Another Look at the School of Laon' *Archives d'histoire doctrinale et littéraire du moyen âge* 53 (1986) 7–22.

Congar, Yves. 'Der Platz des Papsttums in der Kirchenfrömmigkeit der Reformer des 11. Jahrhunderts', *Sentire Ecclesiam. Das Bewusstsein von der Kirche als gestaltende Kraft der Frömmigkeit*, ed. Jean Daniélou and Herbert Vorgrimler (Freiburg 1961) 196–217; repr. in idem, *Église et Papauté: regards historiques* (Paris 1994) 93–115.

Conrat (Cohn), Max. *Geschichte der Quellen und Literatur des römischen Rechts im frühen Mittelalter* (Leipzig 1891).

―――. *Der Pandekten- und Institutionenauszug der brittischen Dekretalensammlung, Quelle des Ivo* (Berlin 1887).

Constable, Giles. *The Reformation of the Twelfth Century* (Cambridge 1996).

―――. 'Monastic Legislation at Cluny in the Eleventh and Twelfth Centuries', *Proceedings Toronto 1972* MIC Subsidia 5.151–161.

―――. 'The Treatise "Hortatur nos" and Accompanying Canonical Texts on the Performance of Pastoral Work by Monks', *Speculum historiale. Geschichte im Spiegel von Geschichtsschreibung und Geschichtsdeutung. Johannes Spörl aus Anlass seines 60. Geburtstages dargebracht von Weggenossen, Freunden und Schülern*, ed. Clemens Bauer, Laetitia Boehm, and Max Müller (Freiburg and Munich 1965) 567–577.

―――. *Monastic Tithes: From Their Origins to the Twelfth Century* (Life and Thought: New Series 10; Cambridge 1964).

Corbet, Patrick. *Autour de Burchard de Worms: l'église allemande et les interdits de parenté (IXᵉᵐᵉ–XIIᵉᵐᵉ siècle)* (Ius commune. Sonderhefte 142; Frankfurt 2001).

Costambeys, Marios. *Power and Patronage in Early Medieval Italy: Local Society, Italian Politics and the Abbey of Farfa, c. 700–900* (Life and Thought: Fourth Series 70; Cambridge 2007).

Cowdrey, Herbert Edward John. 'Pope Gregory VII (1073–85) and the Liturgy' *Journal of Theological Studies* 55 (2004) 55–83.

———. *Lanfranc: Scholar, Monk, and Archbishop* (Oxford 2003).

———. *Pope Gregory VII, 1073–1085* (Oxford 1998).

———. 'The Papacy and the Berengian Controversy', *Auctoritas und ratio. Studien zu Berengar von Tours*, ed. Peter Felix Ganz, Robert Burchard Constantijn Huygens, and Friedrich Niewöhner (Wolfenbütteler Mittelalter-Studien 2; Wiesbaden 1990) 109–138; repr. in idem, *Popes and Church Reform in the 11th Century* (CSS 674; Aldershot 2000) no. VI.

———. *The Cluniacs and the Gregorian Reform* (Oxford 1970).

Cramer, Peter J. 'Ernulf of Rochester and Early Anglo-Norman Canon Law' JEH 40 (1989) 483–510.

Cushing, Kathleen Grace. 'Law and Reform: The Transmission of Burchard of Worms' *Liber decretorum*', *New Discourses in Medieval Canon Law Research: Challenging the Master Narrative*, ed. Christof Rolker (Medieval Law and Its Practice 28; Leiden and Boston 2019) 33–43.

———. 'Monastic "Centres" of Law? Some Evidence from Eleventh-Century Italy', *From Learning to Love: Schools, Law and Pastoral Care in the Middle Ages: Essays in Honour of Joseph W. Goering*, ed. Tristan Sharp, Isabelle Cochelin, Greti Dinkova-Brun, Abigail A. Firey, and Giulio Silano (Papers in Mediaeval Studies 29; Toronto 2017) 315–326.

———. 'Law, Penance, and the "Gregorian" Reform: The Case of Padua, Biblioteca del Seminario Vescovile MS 529', *Canon Law, Religion and Politics: Liber amicorum Robert Somerville*, ed. Uta-Renate Blumenthal, Anders Winroth, and Peter Landau (Washington, D.C. 2012) 28–40.

———. '"Intermediate" and Minor Collections: The Case of the *Collectio canonum Barberiniana*', *Readers, Texts and Compilers in the Earlier Middle Ages: Studies in Medieval Canon Law in Honour of Linda Fowler-Magerl*, ed. Kathleen Grace Cushing and Martin Brett (CFC; Aldershot and Farnham 2009) 73–85.

———. 'Looking Behind Recension Bb of the *Collectio canonum* of Anselm of Lucca' ZRG Kan. Abt. 95 (2009) 29–47.

———. 'Polemic or Handbook? Recension Bb of Anselm of Lucca's *Collectio canonum*', *Bishops, Texts and the Use of Canon Law Around 1100: Essays in Honour of Martin Brett*, ed. Bruce Clark Brasington and Kathleen Grace Cushing (CFC; Aldershot and Farnham 2008) 69–77.

———. *Reform and the Papacy in the Eleventh Century: Spirituality and Social Change* (Manchester Medieval Studies; Manchester and New York 2005).

———. 'Anselm of Lucca and Burchard of Worms: Re-Thinking the Sources of Anselm II, *De penitentia*', *Ritual, Text and Law: Studies in Medieval Canon Law and Liturgy Presented to Roger E. Reynolds*, ed. Richard F. Gyug and Kathleen Grace Cushing (CFC; Aldershot 2004) 225–239.

———. 'Events That Led to Sainthood: Sanctity and the Reformers in the Eleventh Century', *Belief and Culture in the Middle Ages: Studies Presented to Henry Mayr-Harting*, ed. Richard Gameson and Henrietta Leyser (Oxford 2001) 187–196.

———. *Papacy and Law in the Gregorian Revolution: The Canonistic Work of Anselm of Lucca* (Oxford Historical Monographs; Oxford 1998).

———. 'Anselm of Lucca and the Doctrine of Coercion: The Legal Impact of the Schism of 1080?' CHR 81 (1995) 353–371.

d'Avray, David L. 'Lay Kinship Solidarity and Papal Law', *Law, Laity and Solidarities: Es-*

says in Honour of Susan Reynolds, ed. Pauline A. Stafford, Janet L. Nelson, and Jane Martindale (Manchester and New York 2001) 188–199.

Dachowski, Elizabeth Eileen. *First Among Abbots: The Career of Abbo of Fleury* (Washington, D.C. 2008).

Dekkers, Eligius. *Clavis patrum latinorum* (CCL; 3rd edition Steenbrugge 1995).

Delivré, Fabrice 'L'ombre de Lanfranc: l'espace canonique anglo-normand (XIᵉ–XIIᵉ siècle)', *Autour de Lanfranc (1010–2010): réforme et réformateurs dans l'Europe du Nord-Ouest (XIᵉ–XIIᵉ siècles)*, ed. Julia Barrow, Fabrice Delivré, and Véronique Gazeau (Caen 2015) 85–105.

———. 'The Foundations of Primatial Claims in the Western Church (Eleventh–Thirteenth Centuries)' JEH 59 (2008) 383–406.

Dereine, Charles. 'La prétendue Règle de Gregoire VII pour chanoines réguliers' *Revue bénédictine* 71 (1961) 108–118.

———. 'Le problème de la *cura animarum* chez Gratien' SG 2 (1954) 305–318.

———. 'Le problème de la vie commune chez les canonistes d'Anselme de Lucques à Gratien' *Studi Gregoriani* 3 (1948) 287–298.

von Dobschütz, Ernst. 'Untersuchung', *Das Decretum Gelasianum de libris recipiendis et non recipiendis*, ed. idem (Texte und Untersuchungen zur Geschichte der altchristlichen Literatur 38.4; Leipzig 1912) 135–357.

Dolcini, Carlo. 'La storia religiosa fino al secolo XI', *Storia di Cesena II,1: Il Medioevo (secoli VI–XIV)*, ed. Augusto Vasina (Storia di Cesena 2.1; Rimini 1983) 25–73.

Dolezalek, Gero Rudolf and Martin Bertram. *Catalogue of Canon and Roman Law Manuscripts in the Vatican Library, Vol. III Resuscitated [Vat. lat. 3137–11527]* (2009), https://home.uni-leipzig.de/jurarom/manuscr/VaticanCatalogue/historyvaticancatalogue.html.

von Döllinger see Janus.

Heinrich Dormeier, *Montecassino und die Laien im 11. und 12. Jahrhundert Mit einem einleitenden Beitrag: Zur Geschichte Montecassinos im 11. und 12. Jahrhundert von Hartmut Hoffmann* (MGH Schriften 27; Stuttgart 1979)

Doujat, Jean. *Histoire du droit canonique: avec l'explication des lieux qui ont donné le nom aux Conciles, ou le surnom aux Autres Ecclesiastiques et une chonologique canonique* (Paris 1680).

Duby, Georges. *The Knight, the Lady and the Priest: The Making of Modern Marriage in Medieval France* (London 1984); original: *Le chevalier, la femme et le prêtre: le mariage dans la France féodale* (Paris 1981).

Duggan, Anne J. 'Conciliar Law 1123–1215: The Legislation of the Four Lateran Councils', *The History of Medieval Canon Law in the Classical Period: From Gratian to the Decretals of Pope Gregory IX*, ed. Wilfried Hartmann and Kenneth Pennington (HMCL; Washington, D.C. 2008) 318–366.

Duggan, Charles. *Twelfth-Century Decretal Collections and Their Importance in English History* (University of London Historical Studies 12; London 1963).

Dură, Nicolae. 'The Ecumenicity of the Council in Trullo: Witnesses of the Canonical Tradition in East and West', *The Council in Trullo Revisited*, ed. George Nedungatt and Michael Featherstone (Kanonika 6; Rome 1995) 229–262.

Dusil, Stephan. *Wissensordnungen des Rechts im Wandel. Päpstlicher Jurisdiktionsprimat und Zölibat zwischen 1000 und 1215* (Mediaevalia Lovaniensia 47; Leuven 2018).

Dvornik, Francis. *The Photian Schism: History and Legend* (Cambridge 1948).

Eichbauer, Melodie Harris. 'A Desire for the Latest and the Greatest: Papal Decretals and Roman Law in the *Collectio decem partium*' BMCL 36 (2019) 195–208.

Elliot, Michael D. 'Boniface, Incest, and the Earliest Extant Version of Pope Gregory I's *Libellus responsionum* (JE 1843)' ZRG Kan. Abt. 100 (2014) 62–111.

————. *Canon Law Collections in England ca 600–1066: The Manuscript Evidence* (PhD thesis; University of Toronto, Toronto 2013).

Ewald, Paul. 'Reise nach Spanien im Winter von 1878 auf 1879' NA 6 (1881) 217–398.

————. 'Die Papstbriefe der Brittischen Sammlung' NA 5 (1880) 275–414 and 505–596.

————. 'Studien zur Ausgabe des Registers Gregors I.' NA 3 (1878) 433–625.

Fahrner, Ignaz. *Geschichte der Ehescheidung im kanonischen Recht. Teil 1: Geschichte des Unauflöslichkeitsprinzips und der vollkommenen Scheidung im kanonischen Recht* (Freiburg 1903).

Falkenstein, Ludwig. 'Zu verlorenen päpstlichen Privilegien und Schreiben: Palliumverleihungen an die Erzbischöfe von Reims (8.–12. Jahrhundert)', *Eloquentia copiosus: Festschrift für Max Kerner zum 65. Geburtstag*, ed. Lotte Kéry (Aachen 2006) 181–224.

————. 'Das Grand Cartulaire der Abtei La Sauve Majeure und seine Papsturkunden' *Francia* 26 (1999) 155–183.

————. *La papauté et les abbayes françaises aux XIᵉ et XIIᵉ siècles: exemption et protection apostolique* (Bibliothèque de l'École des hautes études: Sciences historiques et philologiques 336; Paris 1997).

————. 'Alexander III. und die Abtei Corbie. Ein Beitrag zum Gewohnheitsrecht exemter Kirchen im 12. Jahrhundert' *Archivum Historiae Pontificae* 27 (1989) 85–195.

Favreau, Robert. 'Évêques d'Angoulême et Saintes avant 1200' *Revue historique de Centre-Ouest* 9 (2010) 7–142.

Firey, Abigail A. *A Contrite Heart: Prosecution and Redemption in the Carolingian Empire* (Studies in Medieval and Reformation Traditions 145; Leiden and Boston 2009).

Fitting, Hermann Heinrich. 'Über die Stellen des römischen Rechtes in einer Streitschrift des Cardinals Deusdedit' ZRG Rom. Abt. 9 (1888) 376–381.

Flechner, Roy. *The Hibernensis* (2 vols. SMCL 17; Washington, D.C. 2019).

————. 'An Insular Tradition of Ecclesiastical Law: Fifth to Eighth Century', *Anglo-Saxon/Irish Relations Before the Vikings*, ed. James Graham-Campbell and Michael Ryan (Proceedings of the British Academy 157; Oxford 2009) 23–46.

Fletcher, Richard A. 'Magister Geraldus, Geraldus Episcopus Salamanticensis, Geraldus Scriptor: A Suggestion', *Life, Law and Letters: Historical Studies in Honour of Antonio García y García*, ed. Peter Linehan (2 vols. SG 28/29; Rome 1998) 1.249–264.

Foerster, Hans. 'Die Liber Diurnus-Fragmente in der Kanones-Sammlung des Kardinals Deusdedit', *Lebendiges Mittelalter. Festgabe für Wolfgang Stammler* (Fribourg 1958) 44–55.

Foreville, Raymonde. 'La place de Latran III dans l'histoire conciliare du XIIᵉ siècle', *Le troisième Concile de Latran (1179): sa place dans l'histoire: communications présentées à la Table ronde du C.N.R.S., le 26 avril 1980*, ed. Jean Longère (Paris 1982) 11–17.

————. *Latran, I, II, III et Latran IV* (Histoire des conciles œcuméniques 6; Paris 1965).

Fornasari, Mario. 'Introduzione', *Collectio canonum in V libris (lib. I–III)*, ed. idem (CCCM 6; Turnhout 1970) VII–XIX.

————. 'Collectio canonum Barberiniana' *Apollinaris* 36 (1963) 127–141 and 214–297.

————. 'Un manoscritto e una collezione canonica del secolo XI proveniente da Farfa' *Benedictina* 10 (1956) 199–210.

Förster, Thomas. *Bonizo von Sutri als gregorianischer Geschichtsschreiber* (MGH Studien und Texte 53; Hanover 2011).

Foulon, Jean-Hervé. *Église et réforme au Moyen Âge: papauté, milieux réformateurs et ecclésiologie dans les Pays de la Loire au tournant des XIᵉ–XIIᵉ siècles* (Bibliothèque du Moyen Âge 27; Brussels 2008).

Fournier, Paul. *Mélanges de droit canonique*, ed. Theo Kölzer (2 vols. Aalen 1983).

————. 'La collection canonique dite "Collectio XII partium": étude sur un recueil canonique allemand du XIᵉ siècle' *Revue d'Histoire de l'Eglise de France* 17 (1921) 31–62 and 229–259; repr. in idem, *Mélanges* 2.751–813.

————. 'La collection canonique dite *Caesaraugustana*' NRHDFE 45 (1921) 53–79; repr. in idem, *Mélanges* 2.815–841.

————. 'Les deux recensions de la collection canonique romaine dite le *Polycarpus*' *Mélanges d'archéologie et d'histoire de l'École française de Rome* 37 (1918) 55–101; repr. in idem, *Mélanges* 2.703–749.

————. 'Les collections canoniques romaines de l'époque de Grégoire VII' *Mémoires de l'Institut National de France, Académie des Inscriptions et Belles-Lettres* 41 (1918) 271–395; repr. in idem, *Mélanges* 2.425–550.

————. 'Les sources canonique du *Liber de vita christiana* de Bonizo' BEC 78 (1917) 117–134; repr. in idem, *Mélanges* 2.667–684.

————. 'Un tournant de l'histoire du droit 1060–1140' NRHDFE 41 (1917) 129–180; repr. in idem, *Mélanges* 2.373–424.

————. 'Un groupe de recueils canoniques italiens des Xᵉ et XIᵉ siècles' *Mémoires de l'Institut National de France, Académie des Inscriptions et Belles-Lettres* 40 (1916) 95–213; repr. in idem, *Mélanges* 2.213–331.

————. 'L'origine de la collection "Anselmo dedicata"', *Mélanges P. F. Girard: études de droit romain dédiées à Paul Frédéric Girard à l'occasion du 60e anniversaire de sa naissance (26 octobre 1912)* (Paris 1912) 475–492.

————. 'Le Décret de Burchard de Worms: ses caractères, son influence' *Revue d'histoire ecclésiastique* 12 (1911) 451–473 and 670–701; repr. in idem, *Mélanges* 1.393–447.

————. 'Études critiques sur le Décret de Burchard de Worms' NRHDFE 34 (1910) 41–112, 213–221, 289–331, and 564–584; repr. in idem, *Mélanges* 1.247–391.

————. 'De quelques collections canoniques issues du *Décret* de Burchard', *Mélanges Paul Fabre: études d'histoire du moyen âge* (Paris 1902) 189–214; repr. in idem, *Mélanges* 1.205–230.

————. 'Les collections attribuées à Yves de Chartres' BEC 57 (1896) 645–698, BEC 58 (1897), 26–77, 293–326, 410–444, and 624–676; repr. in idem, *Mélanges* 2.451–678.

————. 'Le *Liber Tarraconensis*: étude sur une collection canonique du XIᵉ siècle', *Mélanges Julien Havet: recueil de travaux d'érudition dédiés à la mémoire de Julien Havet (1853–1893)* (Paris 1895) 259–281.

————. 'La collezione canonica del regesto di Farfa' *Archivio della Società Romana di Storia Patria* 17 (1894) 285–301; repr. in idem, *Mélanges* 2.685–701.

————. 'Le premier manuel canonique de la réforme du XIᵉ siècle' *Mélanges d'archéologie et d'histoire de l'École française de Rome* 14 (1894) 147–223 and 285–290; repr. in idem, *Mélanges* 2.551–633.

Fournier, Paul and Gabriel Le Bras. *Histoire des collections canoniques en Occident, dépuis les Fausses Décrétales jusqu'au Décret de Gratien* (2 vols. Paris 1931/32).

Fowler-Magerl, Linda. 'Caesaraugustana', *Diccionario general de derecho canónico*, ed. Javier Otaduy, Antonio Viana, and Joaquin Sedano Rueda (7 vols. Cizur Menor 2012) 1.787–789.

————. *Clavis canonum: Selected Canon Law Collections Before 1140: Access with Data Processing* (MGH Hilfsmittel 21; Hanover 2005).

————. 'The Relationship Between Seemingly Unspectacular Pre-Gratian Collections in the Manuscripts Paris, Bibliothèque nationale, lat. 2858C and Florence, Biblioteca Medicea Laurenziana, Ashburnham 1554', *Scientia veritatis. Festschrift für Hubert Mordek zum 65. Geburtstag*, ed. Oliver Münsch and Thomas L. Zotz (Ostfildern 2004) 241–260.

————. 'The Version of the *Collectio Caesaraugustana* in Barcelona, Archivo de la Corona de Aragón, MS San Cugat 63', *Ritual, Text and Law: Studies in Medieval Canon Law and*

Liturgy Presented to Roger E. Reynolds, ed. Richard F. Gyug and Kathleen Grace Cushing (CFC; Aldershot 2004) 269–280.

————. 'The Use of the Letters of Pope Gregory I in Northeastern France and Lorraine Before 1100', *"Ins Wasser geworfen und Ozeane durchquert". Festschrift für Knut Wolfgang Nörr*, ed. Mario Ascheri, Friedrich Ebel, Martin Heckel, Antonio Padoa-Schioppa, Wolfgang Pöggeler, Filippo Ranieri, and Wilhelm Rütten (Cologne 2003) 237–260.

————. *Kanones. Ausgewählte Kanonessammlungen ausserhalb Italiens zwischen 1100 und 1140: Eine Aufarbeitung mittels EDV* (Piesenkofen 1998).

————. 'Fine Distinctions and the Transmission of Texts' ZRG Kan. Abt. 83 (1997) 146–186.

————. 'Vier französische und spanische vorgratianische Kanonessammlungen', *Aspekte europäischer Rechtsgeschichte. Festgabe für H. Coing zum 70. Geburtstag*, ed. Christoph Bergfeld (Ius commune. Sonderhefte 17; Frankfurt 1982) 123–146.

Frank, Hieronymus. 'Zwei Fälschungen auf den Namen Gregors des Großen und Bonifatius IV. Ein Beitrag zur Ehrenrettung Erzbischof Lanfranks von Canterbury' *Studien und Mitteilungen zur Geschichte des Benediktiner-Ordens und seiner Zweige* 55 (1937) 19–47.

Fransen, Gérard. 'Anselme de Lucques canoniste?', *Sant'Anselmo vescovo di Lucca (1073–1086) nel quadro delle trasformazioni sociali e della riforma ecclesiastica: atti del convegno internazionale di studio, Lucca 25–28 settembre 1986*, ed. Cinzio Violante (Istituto storico Italiano per il medio evo. Nuovi studi storici 13; Rome 1992) 143–155; repr. in idem, *Canones et quaestiones: évolution des doctrines et système du droit canonique*, ed. Antonio García y García (2 in 3 vols. Bibliotheca eruditorum 25; Goldbach 2002) 1.1:661*–673*.

————. 'Le Décret de Burchard', *Burchard von Worms (Burchardus Wormaciensis ecclesiae episcopus), Decretorum libri XX [...]. Ergänzter Neudruck*, ed. idem and Theo Kölzer (Aalen 1992) 25–42.

————. 'Appendix Seguntina, Liber Tarraconensis et Décret de Gratien' *Revista española de derecho canónico* 45 (1988) 31–34

————. 'L'aspect religieux du droit', *Chiesa, diritto e ordinamento della «Societas Christiana» nei secoli XI e XII: atti Mendola 1983* (Miscellanea 11; Milan 1986) 159–170.

————. 'Les canonistes et Latran III', *Le troisième Concile de Latran (1179): sa place dans l'histoire: communications présentées à la Table ronde du C.N.R.S., le 26 avril 1980*, ed. Jean Longère (Paris 1982) 33–40.

————. 'Le Décret de Burchard de Worms: valeur du texte de l'édition: essai de classement des manuscrits' ZRG Kan. Abt. 63 (1977) 1–19.

————. 'Autour de la collection en 74 titres' *Revue de Droit canonique* 25 (1975) 61–73.

————. 'Le manuscrit de Burchard de Worms conservé à la Bibliothèque municipale de Montpellier', *Mélanges Roger Aubenas* (Société d'histoire du droit et des institutions des anciens pays de droit écrit. Recueil de mémoires et travaux 9; Montpellier 1974) 301–311.

————. 'Papes, conciles généraux et œcuméniques', *Le istituzioni ecclesiastiche della «Societas Christiana» dei secoli XI–XII: papato, cardinalato ed episcopato: atti Mendola 1971* (Miscellanea 7; Milan 1974) 203–228.

————. *Les collections canoniques* (Typologie des sources du moyen âge occidental 10; Turnhout 1973).

————. 'Les sources de la Préface du Décret de Burchard de Worms' BMCL 3 (1973) 1–7; repr. in idem, *Canones et quaestiones: évolution des doctrines et système du droit canonique*, ed. Antonio García y García (2 in 3 vols. Bibliotheca eruditorum 25; Goldbach 2002) 1.1:393*–400*.

————. 'Principes d'édition des collections canoniques' *Revue d'histoire ecclésiastique* 66 (1971) 125–136.

————. 'La tradition manuscrite du Décret de Burchard de Worms: une première orientation', *Ius sacrum. Klaus Mörsdorf zum 60. Geburtstag*, ed. Audomar Scheuermann and Georg May (Munich 1969) 111–118; repr. in idem, *Canones et quaestiones: évolution des doctrines et système du droit canonique*, ed. Antonio García y García (2 in 3 vols. Bibliotheca eruditorum 25; Goldbach 2002) 1.1:197*–204*.

————. 'L'écclésiologie des conciles médiévaux', *Le concile et les conciles: contribution à l'histoire de la vie conciliaire de l'église* ([Gembloux] 1960) 125–141.

Frauenknecht, Erwin. *Die Verteidigung der Priesterehe in der Reformzeit* (MGH Studien und Texte 16; Hanover 1997).

Freeman, Ann. 'Carolingian Orthodoxy and the Fate of the *Libri Carolini*' *Viator* 16 (1985) 65–108.

Freisen, Joseph. *Geschichte des canonischen Eherechts bis zum Verfall der Glossenlitteratur* (Paderborn 1893); repr. Aalen 1963.

Freund, Stephan. *Studien zur literarischen Wirksamkeit des Petrus Damiani* (MGH Studien und Texte 13; Hanover 1995).

Friedberg, Emil. *Eine neue kritische Ausgabe des Corpus iuris canonici: I. Das Decretum Gratiani. Herrn Gustav Friedrich Hänel zur Feier seines sechzigjährigen Doctorjubiläums am 18. April 1876 überreicht von der Juristenfacultät zu Leipzig* (Leipzig 1876).

Führer, Julian. *König Ludwig VI. von Frankreich und die Kanonikerreform* (Frankfurt 2008).

Fuhrmann, Horst. 'Kurzinformation', *Die Sammlung "Policarpus" des Kardinals Gregor von S. Grisogono. Angelegt und gestaltet von Carl Erdmann (†). Zum Druck vorbereitet von Uwe Horst, unter Mitarbeit von Michael Klein, herausgegeben von Horst Fuhrmann* ([ca. 2004]), https://www.mgh.de/index.php/mgh-digital/digitale-angebote-zu-mgh-abteilungen.

————. 'Stand, Aufgaben und Perspektiven der Pseudoisidorforschung', *Fortschritt durch Fälschungen? Ursprung, Gestalt und Wirkungen der pseudoisidorischen Fälschungen. Beiträge zum gleichnamigen Symposium an der Universität Tübingen vom 27. und 28. Juli 2001*, ed. Wilfried Hartmann and Gerhard Schmitz (MGH Studien und Texte 31; Hanover 2002) 227–262.

————. 'The Pseudo-Isidorian Forgeries', *Papal Letters in the Early Middle Ages*, ed. Detlev Jasper and Horst Fuhrmann (HMCL; Washington, D.C. 2001) 135–195.

————. 'Pseudoisidor und die Bibel' *DA* 55 (1999) 183–191.

————. 'Papst Gregor VII. und das Kirchenrecht. Zum Problem des Dictatus Papae' *Studi Gregoriani* 13 (1989) 123–149; repr. in idem, *Papst Gregor VII. und das Zeitalter der Reform: Annäherungen an eine europäische Wende. Ausgewählte Aufsätze*, ed. Martina Hartmann (MGH Schriften 72; Wiesbaden 2016), 90–119.

————. 'Pseudoisidor, Otto von Ostia (Urban II.) und der Zitatenkampf von Gerstungen (1085)' *ZRG Kan. Abt.* 68 (1982) 52–69; repr. in idem, *Papst Gregor VII. und das Zeitalter der Reform: Annäherungen an eine europäische Wende. Ausgewählte Aufsätze*, ed. Martina Hartmann (MGH Schriften 72; Wiesbaden 2016) 209–225.

————. '"Quod catholicus non habeatur, qui non concordat Romanae ecclesiae". Randnotizen zum Dictatus Papae', *Festschrift für Helmut Beumann zum 65. Geburtstag*, ed. Kurt-Ulrich Jäschke and Reinhard Wenskus (Sigmaringen 1977) 263–287; repr. in idem, *Papst Gregor VII. und das Zeitalter der Reform: Annäherungen an eine europäische Wende. Ausgewählte Aufsätze*, ed. Martina Hartmann (MGH Schriften 72; Wiesbaden 2016) 59–89.

————. 'Das Reformpapsttum und die Rechtswissenschaft', *Investiturstreit und Reichsverfassung*, ed. Josef Fleckenstein (Vorträge und Forschungen 17; Sigmaringen 1973) 175–203; repr. in idem, *Papst Gregor VII. und das Zeitalter der Reform: Annäherungen an eine europäische Wende. Ausgewählte Aufsätze*, ed. Martina Hartmann (MGH Schriften 72; Wiesbaden 2016) 26–58.

————. *Einfluß und Verbreitung der pseudoisidorischen Fälschungen. Von ihrem Auftauchen bis in die neuere Zeit* (3 vols. MGH Schriften 24; Stuttgart 1972–74).

————. 'Über den Reformgeist der 74-Titel-Sammlung (Diversorum patrum sententiae)', *Festschrift für Hermann Heimpel zum 70. Geburtstag am 19. September 1971* (3 vols. Veröffentlichungen des MPI für Geschichte 36; Göttingen 1972) 2:1101–1120; repr. in idem, *Papst Gregor VII. und das Zeitalter der Reform: Annäherungen an eine europäische Wende. Ausgewählte Aufsätze*, ed. Martina Hartmann (MGH Schriften 72; Wiesbaden 2016) 398–420.

————. 'Einleitung', *Das Constitutum Constantini (Konstantinische Schenkung). Text*, ed. idem (MGH Fontes iuris 10; Hanover 1968) 7–54.

————. 'Ein Papst Ideo (zu Collectio Lipsensis [*sic*] tit. 27, 5)', *Études d'histoire du droit canonique dédiées à Gabriel Le Bras* (2 vols. Paris 1965) 1.89–98; repr. in idem, *Papst Gregor VII. und das Zeitalter der Reform: Annäherungen an eine europäische Wende. Ausgewählte Aufsätze*, ed. Martina Hartmann (MGH Schriften 72; Wiesbaden 2016) 198–208.

————. 'Das Ökumenische Konzil und seine historischen Grundlagen' *Geschichte in Wissenschaft und Unterricht* 12 (1961) 672–695; repr. in idem, *Papst Gregor VII. und das Zeitalter der Reform: Annäherungen an eine europäische Wende. Ausgewählte Aufsätze*, ed. Martina Hartmann (MGH Schriften 72; Wiesbaden 2016) 149–181.

————. 'Die Fabel von Papst Leo und Bischof Hilarius. Vom Ursprung und der Erscheinungsform einer historischen Legende' *Archiv für Kulturgeschichte* 43 (1961) 125–162; repr. in idem, *Papst Gregor VII. und das Zeitalter der Reform: Annäherungen an eine europäische Wende. Ausgewählte Aufsätze*, ed. Martina Hartmann (MGH Schriften 72; Wiesbaden 2016) 506–545.

————. 'Studien zur Geschichte mittelalterlicher Patriarchate' ZGR Kan. Abt. 39 (1953) 112–176, 40 (1954) 1–84, and 41 (1955) 95–183.

Gaastra, Adriaan H. *Between Liturgy and Canon Law: A Study of Books of Confession and Penance in Eleventh-and Twelfth-Century Italy* (PhD thesis; Universiteit Utrecht, Utrecht 2007).

————. 'Penance and the Law: The Penitential Canons of the *Collection in Nine Books*' *Early Medieval Europe* 14 (2006) 85–102.

————. 'Penitentials and Canonical Authority', *Texts and Identities in the Early Middle Ages*, ed. Richard Corradini, Rob Meens, Christina Pössel, and Philip Shaw (Forschungen zur Geschichte des Mittelalters 12; Vienna 2006) 191–204.

Galli, Michela and Christof Rolker, 'Destroyed but not Lost: A Digital Reconstruction of the Chartrain Copy of Burchard's *Liber decretorum* (Chartres BM 161)' BMCL 39 (2021) 19–58.

García y García, Antonio. 'Del derecho canonico visigotico al derecho comun medieval', *Iglesia, sociedad y derecho* (2 vols. Bibliotheca Salmanticensis: Estudios 74; Salamanca 1985/87) 1.29–43.

Gaspari, Laura. 'Osservazioni sul codice Vallicelliano C. 24' *Studi Gregoriani* 9 (1972) 467–513.

Gassó, Pius M. and Columba Batlle. 'Prolegomena', *Pelagii I papae epistulae quae supersunt (556–561)*, ed. iidem (Scripta et documenta 8; Montserrat 1956) XXI–CXIV.

Gaudemet, Jean. *Les sources du droit canonique, VIIIe–XXe siècle: repères canoniques, sources occidentales* (Paris 1993).

————. 'Le deuxième concile de Nicée (787) dans les Collections canoniques occidentales' AHC 20 (1988) 278–288; repr. in idem, *La doctrine canonique médiévale* (CSS 435; Aldershot 1994) no. VII.

————. 'Le droit romain dans la *Collectio Canonum* du Cardinal Deusdedit', *Etudes d'histoire du droit medieval en souvenir de Josette Metman* (Mémoires de la Société pour l'Histoire du Droit et des Institutions des anciens pays bourguignons, comtois et romands 45; Dijon 1988) 155–165; repr. in idem, *La doctrine canonique médiévale* (CSS 435; Aldershot 1994) no. IV; also in idem, *Formation du droit canonique et gouvernement de l'Église de l'Antiquité à l'âge classique: recueil d'articles* (Société, droit et religion; Strasbourg 2008) no. 7.

———. *Le mariage en Occident: les mœurs et le droit* (Paris 1987).

———. 'Recherche sur les origines historiques de la faculté de rompre le mariage non consommé', *Proceedings Salamanca 1980* MIC Subsidia 6.309–331; repr. in idem, *Sociétés et mariage* (Recherches institutionnelles 4; Strasbourg 1980) 210–229.

———. 'La doctrine des sources du droit dans le Décret de Gratien' *Revue de Droit canonique* 1 (1950) 5–31; repr. in idem, *La formation du droit canonique médiévale* (CSS 111; London 1980) no. VIII.

Geffcken, Heinrich. *Zur Geschichte der Ehescheidung vor Gratian* (Leipzig 1894).

Gelting, Michael H. 'Marriage, Peace and the Canonical Incest Prohibitions: Making Sense of an Absurdity?', *Nordic Perspectives on Medieval Canon Law*, ed. Mia Korpiola (Publications of Matthias Calonius Society 2; Saarijärvi 1999) 93–124.

Genka, Tatsushi. 'The Role of Hagiography in the Development of Canon Law in the Reform Era', *New Discourses in Medieval Canon Law Research: Challenging the Master Narrative*, ed. Christof Rolker (Medieval Law and Its Practice 28; Leiden and Boston 2019) 83–104.

———. 'Hierarchie der Texte, Hierarchie der Autoritäten. Zur Hierarchie der Rechtsquellen bei Gratian' ZRG Kan. Abt. 95 (2009) 101–127.

Gesamtkatalog der Wiegendrucke (Berlin 1925– [ongoing]).

Gfrörer, August-Friedrich. *Allgemeine Kirchengeschichte* (4 in 7 vols. Stuttgart 1846).

de Ghellinck, Joseph. *Le mouvement théologique du XIIᵉ siècle: sa préparation lointaine avant et autour de Pierre Lombard, ses rapports avec les initiatives des canonistes: études, recherches et documents* (Museum Lessianum. Section historique 10; 2nd edition Bruges 1948); repr. Brussels 1969.

von Giesebrecht, Wilhelm. 'Die Gesetzgebung der römischen Kirche zur Zeit Gregors VII.' *Historisches Jahrbuch* (1866) 91–194.

Gilchrist, John T. 'The *Collectio canonum* of Bishop Anselm II of Lucca (d. 1086): Recension B of Berlin Staatsbibliothek Preussischer Kulturbesitz Cod. 597', *Cristianità ed Europa: miscellanea di studi in onore di Luigi Prosdocimi*, ed. Cesare Alzati (2 in 3 vols. Rome 1994–2000) 1.2:377–403.

———. 'Introduction', *Canon Law in the Age of Reform, 11th–12th Centuries* (CSS 406; Aldershot 1993) xi–xix.

———. 'Changing the Structure of a Canonical Collection: The Collection in Seventy-Four Titles, Four Books, and the Pseudo-Isidorian Decretals', *In iure veritas: Studies in Canon Law in Memory of Schafer Williams*, ed. Steven B. Bowman and Blanche E. Cody (Cincinnati 1991) 93–117.

———. 'The Influence of the Monastic Forgeries Attributed to Pope Gregory I (JE †1951) and Boniface IV (JE †1996)', *Fälschungen im Mittelalter* (6 vols. MGH Schriften 33; Hanover 1988) 2.263–287.

———. 'Die Epistola Widonis oder Pseudo-Paschalis. Der erweiterte Text' DA 37 (1981) 576–604.

———. 'Introduction', *The Collection in Seventy-Four Titles: A Canon Law Manual of the Gregorian Reform* (Mediaeval Sources in Translation 22; Toronto 1980) 1–48.

———. 'Prolegomena', *Diuersorum patrum sententie siue Collectio in LXXIV titulos digesta*, ed. idem (MIC Corpus collectionum 1; Vatican City 1973) xvii–cxxv.

———. 'The Reception of Pope Gregory VII into the Canon Law (1073–1141)' ZRG Kan. Abt. 59 (1973) 35–82 and 66 (1980) 192–229; repr. in idem, *Canon Law in the Age of Reform, 11th–12th Centuries* (CSS 406; Aldershot 1993) nos. VIII and IX.

———. 'Review of Berschin, *Bonizo von Sutri*' ZRG Kan. Abt. 59 (1973) 427–432.

———. 'Was There a Gregorian Reform Movement in the Eleventh Century?' *Study Sessions of the Canadian Catholic Historical Association* 37 (1970) 1–10; repr. in idem, *Canon Law in the Age of Reform, 11th–12th Centuries* (CSS 406; Aldershot 1993) no. VII.

———. '*Simoniaca haeresis* and the Problem of Orders from Leo IX to Gratian', *Proceedings Boston 1963* MIC Subsidia 1.209–235; repr. in idem, *Canon Law in the Age of Reform, 11th–12th Centuries* (CSS 406; Aldershot 1993) no. IV.

———. 'Canon Law Aspects of the Eleventh-Century Gregorian Reform Programme' JEH 13 (1962) 21–38; repr. in idem, *Canon Law in the Age of Reform, 11th–12th Centuries* (CSS 406; Aldershot 1993) no. III.

Giordanengo, Gérard. 'La Collectio canonum d'Abbon de Fleury', *Autour de Gerbert d'Aurillac, le pape de l'an Mil: album de documents commentés*, ed. Olivier Guyotjeannin and Emmanuel Poulle (Matériaux pour l'histoire publiés par l'École des chartes 1; Paris 1996) 157–163.

Giorgi, Ignazio. 'Prefazione', *Il regesto di Farfa*, ed. idem and Ugo Balzani (5 vols. Rome 1879–1914) 1.XXXIX–XLVII.

Giraud, Cédric. *"Per verba magistri": Anselme de Laon et son école au XIIe siècle* (Bibliothèque d'histoire culturelle du Moyen Âge 8; Turnhout 2010).

Giraud, Cédric and Constant J. Mews. 'Le *Liber pancrisis*, un florilège des Pères et des maitres modernes du XIIe siècle' *Bulletin du Cange* 64 (2006) 145–191.

Girgensohn, Dieter. *Miscellanea Italiae pontificiae. Untersuchungen und Urkunden zur mittelalterlichen Kirchengeschichte Italiens, vornehmlich Kalabriens, Siziliens und Sardiniens (zugleich Nachträge zu den Papsturkunden Italiens XI)* (Nachrichten Akad. Göttingen 1974.4; Göttingen 1974).

Gleber, Helmut. *Papst Eugen III. (1145–1153) unter besonderer Berücksichtigung seiner politischen Tätigkeit* (Beiträge zur mittelalterlichen und neueren Geschichte 6; Jena 1936).

Glenn, Jason. *Politics and History in the Tenth Century: The Work and World of Richer of Reims* (Life and Thought: Fourth Series 60; Cambridge 2004).

Goering, Joseph. 'Bishops, Law, and Reform in Aragon, 1076–1126, and the Liber Tarraconensis' ZRG Kan. Abt. 95 (2009) 1–28.

———. 'The Internal Forum and the Literature of Penance and Confession', *The History of Medieval Canon Law in the Classical Period, 1140–1234: From Gratian to the Decretals of Pope Gregory IX*, ed. Wilfried Hartmann and Kenneth Pennington (HMCL; Washington, D.C. 2008) 379–425.

Goody, Jack. *The Development of the Family and Marriage in Europe* (Cambridge and New York 1983).

Gossman, Francis J. *Pope Urban II and Canon Law* (CUA Canon Law Studies 403; Washington, D.C. 1960).

Gotter, Rebekka. *Das Breviar Attos von San Marco* (MA thesis; Rheinische Friedrich-Wilhelms-Universität, Bonn 2018).

Gouron, André. '«Petrus» démasqué' *Revue historique de droit français et étranger* 82 (2004) 577–588.

———. 'Le manuscrit de Prague, Metr. Knih. J. 74: à la recherche du plus ancien décrétiste à l'Ouest des Alpes' ZRG Kan. Abt. 83 (1997) 223–248; repr. with corrections in idem, *Pionniers du droit occidental au Moyen Âge* (CSS 865; Aldershot 2006) no. I.

———. 'Une école ou des écoles? Sur les canonistes français (vers 1150–vers 1210)', *Pro-*

ceedings Berkeley 1985 MIC Subsidia 7.223–240; repr. in idem, *Droit et coutume en France aux XIIe et XIIIe siècles* (CSS 422; Aldershot 1993) no. VIII.

Grant, Lindy. 'Suger and the Anglo-Norman World' *Anglo-Norman Studies* 19 (1996) 51–68.

Gresser, Georg. *Die Synoden und Konzilien in der Zeit des Reformpapsttums in Deutschland und Italien von Leo IX. bis Calixt II. (1049–1123)* (Konziliengeschichte. Reihe A: Darstellungen; Paderborn, Munich, and Vienna 2006).

Große, Rolf. 'La fille aînée de l'Église. Frankreichs Kirche und die Kurie im 12. Jahrhundert', *Römisches Zentrum und kirchliche Peripherie. Das universale Papsttum als Bezugspunkt der Kirchen von den Reformpäpsten bis zu Innozenz III.*, ed. Jochen Johrendt and Harald Müller (Abh. Akad. Göttingen N.F. 2; Berlin and New York 2008) 299–321.

———. 'Frühe Papsturkunden und Exemtion des Klosters Saint-Denis (7.–12. Jh.)', *Hundert Jahre Papsturkundenforschung. Bilanz – Methoden – Perspektiven, Akten eines Kolloquiums zum hundertjährigen Bestehen der Regesta Pontificum Romanorum vom 9.–11. Oktober 1996 in Göttingen*, ed. Rudolf Hiestand (Abh. Akad. Göttingen. 3. Folge 261; Göttingen 2003) 167–188.

———. *Saint-Denis zwischen Adel und König. Die Zeit vor Suger (1053–1122)* (Francia. Beihefte 57; Stuttgart 2002).

Guerreau-Jalabert, Anita. 'Sur la structure de parenté dans l'Europe médiévale' *Annales ESC* 36 (1981) 1028–1049.

Guillot, Olivier. 'Un exemple de la méthode suivie par Abbon de Fleury pour recueillir et ordonner les textes à partir des lettres de Grégoire le Grand incluses dans l'*Epistola XIV*', *Le istituzioni ecclesiastiche della «Societas Christiana» dei secoli XI–XII: diocesi, pievi e parrocchie: atti della sesta Settimana internazionale di studio, Milano, 1–7 settembre 1974* (Miscellanea 8; Milan 1977) 399–405.

Gujer, Regula. *Concordia discordantium codicum manuscriptorum? Die Textentwicklung von 18 Handschriften anhand der D. 16 des Decretum Gratiani* (Forschungen zur kirchlichen Rechtsgeschichte und zum Kirchenrecht 23; Cologne, Weimar, and Vienna 2004).

Gullick, Michael. 'Lanfranc and the Oldest Manuscript of the *Collectio Lanfranci*', *Bishops, Texts and the Use of Canon Law Around 1100: Essays in Honour of Martin Brett*, ed. Bruce Clark Brasington and Kathleen Grace Cushing (CFC; Aldershot and Farnham 2008) 79–89.

Günther, Otto. *Avellana-Studien* (Vienna 1896).

Gyug, Richard F. 'The List of Authorities in the Illustrations of the *Collection in 5 Books* (MS Vat. lat. 1339)', *Ritual, Text and Law: Studies in Medieval Canon Law and Liturgy Presented to Roger E. Reynolds*, ed. Richard F. Gyug and Kathleen Grace Cushing (CFC; Aldershot 2004) 241–254.

Haarländer, Stephanie. 'Die Vita Burchardi im Rahmen der Bischofsviten seiner Zeit', *Bischof Burchard von Worms, 1000–1025*, ed. Wilfried Hartmann (Quellen und Abhandlungen zur mittelrheinischen Kirchengeschichte 100; Mainz 2000) 129–160.

Hageneder, Othmar. 'Die Häresie des Ungehorsams und das Entstehen des hierokratischen Papsttums' *Römische historische Mitteilungen* 20 (1978) 29–47.

———. 'Papstregister und Dekretalenrecht', *Recht und Schrift im Mittelalter*, ed. Peter Classen (Vorträge und Forschungen 23; Sigmaringen 1977) 319–347.

Halporn, Barbara. 'Sebastian Brandt as an Editor of Juristic Texts' *Gutenberg-Jahrbuch* 59 (1984) 36–51.

Hamilton, Louis I. and Martin Brett. 'New Evidence for the Canons of the First Lateran Council,' BMCL 30 (2013) 1–20.

Harder, Clara. *Pseudoisidor und das Papsttum. Funktion und Bedeutung des apostolischen Stuhls in den pseudoisidorischen Fälschungen* (Papsttum im mittelalterlichen Europa 2; Cologne, Weimar, and Vienna 2014).

Häring, Nikolaus M. 'Notes on the Council and the Consistory of Rheims (1148)' MS 28 (1966) 39–59.

———. 'A Study in the Sacramentology of Alger of Liège' MS 20 (1958) 41–78.

———. 'Berengar's Definitions of *Sacramentum* and Their Influence on Medieval Sacramentology' MS 10 (1948) 109–146.

Hartmann, Wilfried. *Kirche und Kirchenrecht um 900. Die Bedeutung der spätkarolingischen Zeit für Tradition und Innovation im kirchlichen Recht* (MGH Schriften 58; Hanover 2008).

———. 'Capita incerta im Sendhandbuch Reginos von Prüm', *Scientia veritatis. Festschrift für Hubert Mordek zum 65. Geburtstag*, ed. Oliver Münsch and Thomas L. Zotz (Ostfildern 2004) 207–226.

———. 'Einleitung. Regino von Prüm und sein Sendhandbuch', *Das Sendhandbuch des Regino von Prüm*, ed. and tr. idem (FSGA 42; Darmstadt 2004) 3–9.

———. 'Burchards Dekret. Stand der Forschung und offene Fragen', *Bischof Burchard von Worms, 1000–1025*, ed. idem (Quellen und Abhandlungen zur mittelrheinischen Kirchengeschichte 100; Mainz 2000) 161–166.

———. 'Bemerkungen zum Eherecht nach Burchard von Worms', *Bischof Burchard von Worms, 1000–1025*, ed. idem (Quellen und Abhandlungen zur mittelrheinischen Kirchengeschichte 100; Mainz 2000) 227–250.

———. 'Discipulus non est super magistrum (Matth. 10,24). Zur Rolle der Laien und der niederen Kleriker im Investiturstreit', *Papsttum, Kirche und Recht im Mittelalter. Festschrift für Horst Fuhrmann zum 65. Geburtstag*, ed. Hubert Mordek (Tübingen 1991) 187–200.

———. 'Autoritäten im Kirchenrecht und Autorität des Kirchenrechts in der Salierzeit', *Gesellschaftlicher und ideengeschichtlicher Wandel im Reich der Salier*, ed. Stefan Weinfurter and Hubertus Seibert (Die Salier und das Reich 3; Sigmaringen 1991) 425–446.

Harttung, Julius. 'Beiträge zur Geschichte Heinrichs II. Die Synode von Seligenstadt und Burchards Decretum' *Forschungen zur deutschen Geschichte* 16 (1876) 587–598.

Hauck, Albert. 'Die Rezeption und Umbildung der allgemeinen Synode im Mittelalter' *Historische Vierteljahrsschrift* 10 (1907) 465–482.

———. 'Ueber den liber decretorum Burchard's von Worms' *Sb. Leipzig* 46 (1894) 65–86.

———. *Kirchengeschichte Deutschlands* (5 in 6 vols. Berlin 1887–1920; 8th ed. Leipzig 1954).

Head, Thomas. *Hagiography and the Cult of Saints: The Diocese of Orléans, 800–1200* (Life and Thought: Fourth Series 14; Cambridge 1990).

Healy, Patrick. *The Chronicle of Hugh of Flavigny: Reform and the Investiture Contest in the Late Eleventh Century* (CFC; Aldershot and Burlington 2006).

Hefele, Charles Joseph [i.e. Karl Joseph von Hefele and Henri Leclercq], *Histoire des conciles d'après les documents originaux: nouvelle traduction française faite sur la deuxième édition allemande corrigée et augmentée* [...] (11 in 22 vols. Paris 1907–49).

Hehl, Ernst-Dieter. 'Vorbemerkung zum zweiten Teil (962–1001)', *Die Konzilien Deutschlands und Reichsitaliens 916–1001, Teil 2: 962–1001*, ed. idem (MGH Conc. 6.2; Hanover 2007) XI–XIV.

———. 'Willigis von Mainz. Päpstlicher Vikar, Metropolit und Reichspolitiker', *Bischof Burchard von Worms, 1000–1025*, ed. Wilfried Hartmann (Quellen und Abhandlungen zur mittelrheinischen Kirchengeschichte 100; Mainz 2000) 51–77.

———. 'Der widerspenstige Bischof. Bischöfliche Zustimmung und bischöflicher Protest in der ottonischen Reichskirche', *Herrschaftsrepräsentation im ottonischen Sachsen*, ed. Gerd Althoff and Ernst Schubert (Vorträge und Forschungen 46; Sigmaringen 1998) 295–344.

———. 'Herrscher, Kirche und Kirchenrecht im spätottonischen Reich', *Otto III. – Heinrich*

II. Eine Wende, ed. Bernd Schneidmüller and Stefan Weinfurter (Mittelalter-Forschungen 1; Sigmaringen 1997) 169–203.

———. 'Hohenaltheim', *Die Konzilien Deutschlands und Reichsitaliens 916–1001, Teil 1: 916–961*, ed. idem (MGH Conc. 6.1; Hanover 1987) 1–40.

Heinzelmann, Karl. *Die Farfenser Streitschriften. Ein Beitrag zur Geschichte des Investiturstreites* (diss. phil.; Kaiser-Wilhelm-Universität, Strasbourg 1904).

Helmholz, Richard H. *The Canon Law and Ecclesiastical Jurisdiction from 597 to the 1640s* (The Oxford History of the Laws of England 1; Oxford 2004).

———. *The Spirit of Classical Canon Law* (The Spirit of the Laws; Athens, Ga. and London 1996).

Herbers, Klaus. 'Einleitung', *Papstregesten 844–858*, ed. idem (Regesta imperii Abt. I, Band 4, Teil 2, Lieferung 1; Cologne, Weimar, and Vienna 1999) VII–XIV.

———. *Leo IV. und das Papsttum in der Mitte des 9. Jahrhunderts. Möglichkeiten und Grenzen päpstlicher Herrschaft in der späten Karolingerzeit* (Päpste und Papsttum 27; Stuttgart 1996).

Hergenröther, Joseph. *Photius, Patriarch von Constantinopel. Sein Leben, seine Schriften und das griechische Schisma* (3 vols. Regensburg 1867–69).

Hiestand, Rudolf. 'Les légats pontificaux en France du milieu du XIe à la fin du XIIe siècle', *L'Église de France et la papauté (X^e–XIIIe siècle) / Die französische Kirche und das Papsttum (10.–13. Jahrhundert): actes du XXVIe Colloque franco-allemand organisé en coopération avec l'École nationale des chartes par l'Institut historique allemand de Paris (Paris, 17–19 octobre 1990)*, ed. Rolf Große (Studien und Dokumente zur Gallia Pontificia 1; Bonn 1993) 54–80.

Hinschius, Paul. 'De collectione decretalium et canonum Isidori Mercatoris', *Decretales Pseudo-Isidorianae et Capitula Angilramni*, ed. idem (Leipzig 1863) xi–ccxxxviii.

———. 'Nachrichten über juristische (insbesondere kanonistische) Handschriften in italienischen Bibliotheken' *Zeitschrift für Rechtsgeschichte* 1 (1861) 467–480

Hirsch, Ernst. 'Die rechtliche Stellung der römischen Kirche und des Papstes nach Kardinal Deusdedit' AKKR 88 (1908) 595–624.

Hoffmann, Hartmut. *Bamberger Handschriften des 10. und des 11. Jahrhunderts* (MGH Schriften 39; Hanover 1995).

———. *Buchkunst und Königtum im ottonischen und frühsalischen Reich* (2 vols. Stuttgart 1986).

———. 'Der Kalender des Leo Marsicanus' DA 21 (1965) 82–149.

———. *Gottesfriede und Treuga Dei* (MGH Schriften 20; Stuttgart 1964).

Hoffmann, Hartmut and Rudolf Pokorny. *Das Dekret des Bischofs Burchard von Worms. Textstufen – Frühe Verbreitung – Vorlagen* (MGH Hilfsmittel 12; Munich 1991).

Hofmann, Georg. 'Ivo von Chartres über Photios' *Orientalia Christiana Periodica* 14 (1948) 105–137.

Hofmeister, Philipp. *Die christlichen Eidesformen. Eine liturgie- und rechtsgeschichtliche Untersuchung* (Munich 1957).

Holopainen, Toivo J. *Dialectic and Theology in the Eleventh Century* (Studien und Texte zur Geistesgeschichte des Mittelalters 54; Leiden 1996).

Holtzmann, Walther. *Studies in the Collections of Twelfth Century Decretals*, ed., rev., and tr. Christopher R. Cheney and Mary G. Cheney (MIC Corpus collectionum 13; Vatican City 1979).

———. 'Kardinal Deusdedit als Dichter' *Historisches Jahrbuch* 57 (1937) 217–232.

Horn, Michael. 'Der Streit um die Primatswürde der Erzbischöfe von Toledo. Ein Beitrag zur Geschichte der älteren Papstregister' *Archivum Historiae Pontificiae* 29 (1991) 259–280.

Horst, Uwe. *Die Kanonessammlung Polycarpus des Gregor von S. Grisogono. Quellen und Tendenzen* (MGH Hilfsmittel 5; Munich 1980).

Howe, John. *Before the Gregorian Reform: The Latin Church at the Turn of the First Millennium* (Ithaca, N.Y. and London 2016).

———. 'Monasteria semper libera: Cluniac-Type Monastic Liberties in Some Eleventh-Century Central Italian Monasteries' CHR 78 (1992) 19–34.

Hüffer, Hermann. *Beiträge zur Geschichte der Quellen des Kirchenrechts und des Römischen Rechts im Mittelalter* (Münster 1862).

Hüls, Rudolf. *Kardinäle, Klerus und Kirchen Roms 1049–1130* (Bibliothek des Deutschen Historischen Instituts in Rom 48; Tübingen 1977).

Huschner, Wolfgang. 'Benevent, Magdeburg, Salerno. Das Papsttum und die neuen Erzbistümer in ottonischer Zeit', *Das Papsttum und das vielgestaltige Italien. Hundert Jahre Italia Pontificia*, ed. Klaus Herbers and Jochen Johrendt (Abh. Akad. Göttingen N.F. 5; Berlin 2009) 87–108.

Huygens, R. B. C. 'Bérenger de Tours, Lanfranc et Bernold de Constance' *Sacris erudiri* 16 (1965) 355–403.

Huysmans, Ortwin. 'The Investiture Controversy in the Diocese of Liège Reconsidered: An Inquiry into the Positions of the Abbeys of Saint-Hubert and Saint-Laurent and the Canonist Alger of Liège (1091–1106)', *Medieval Liège at the Crossroads of Europe: Monastic Society and Culture, 1000–1300*, ed. Steven Vanderputten, Tjamke Snijders, and Jay Diehl (Medieval Church Studies 37; Turnhout 2017) 183–217.

Izbicki, Thomas M. *The Eucharist in Medieval Canon Law* (Cambridge 2015).

Jacqueline, Bernard. 'Yves de Chartres et saint Bernard', *Etudes d'histoire du droit canonique dédiées à Gabriel Le Bras* (2 vols. Paris 1965) 1.179–184.

Jakobs, Hermann. 'Spätottonische Klosterfreiheit. Die Privilegien "Creditae speculationis" Johannes' XIII. und Benedikts VII. für Thankmarsfelde/Nienburg, Aisleben und Arneburg', *Papsturkundenforschung und Historie: Aus der Germania Pontificia Halberstadt und Lüttich*, ed. Hermann Jakobs and Wolfgang Petke (Studien und Vorarbeiten zur Germania Pontificia 9; Cologne, Weimar, and Vienna 2008) 1–128.

Janus [= Johann Joseph Ignaz von Döllinger]. *Der Papst und das Concil* (Leipzig 1869).

Jasper, Detlev. 'The Deposition and Excommunication of Emperors and Kings: A Collection of Historical Examples from the Investiture Conflict', *Canon Law, Religion and Politics: Liber amicorum Robert Somerville*, ed. Uta-Renate Blumenthal, Anders Winroth, and Peter Landau (Washington, D.C. 2012) 199–214.

———. '[Einleitung:] Rom Ende April–Anfang Mai 1059', *Die Konzilien Deutschlands und Reichsitaliens 1023–1059*, ed. idem (MGH. Concilia 8; Hanover 2010) 352–381.

———. 'The Beginning of the Decretal Tradition: Papal Letters from the Origin of the Genre Through the Pontificate of Stephen V', *Papal Letters in the Early Middle Ages*, ed. idem and Horst Fuhrmann (HMCL; Washington, D.C. 2001) 3–133.

———. 'Burchards Dekret in der Sicht der Gregorianer', *Bischof Burchard von Worms, 1000–1025*, ed. Wilfried Hartmann (Quellen und Abhandlungen zur mittelrheinischen Kirchengeschichte 100; Mainz 2000) 167–198.

———. 'Ein Brief Papst Alexanders II. an Abt Ivo I. von Saint-Denis', *Grundlagen des Rechts. Festschrift für Peter Landau zum 65. Geburtstag*, ed. Richard H. Helmholz, Paul Mikat, Jörg Müller, and Michael Stolleis (Rechts- und Staatswissenschaftliche Veröffentlichungen der Görres-Gesellschaft N.F. 91; Paderborn, Munich, Vienna, and Zurich 2000) 131–139.

———. 'Inveni in canonibus apostolorum. Zu einer mittelalterlichen Fälschung auf Papst Clemens I.', *Papsttum, Kirche und Recht im Mittelalter. Festschrift für Horst Fuhrmann zum 65. Geburtstag*, ed. Hubert Mordek (Tübingen 1991) 201–213.

———. *Das Papstwahldekret von 1059. Überlieferung und Textgestalt* (Beiträge zur Geschichte und Quellenkunde des Mittelalters 12; Sigmaringen 1986).

Johrendt, Jochen. 'Die Reisen der frühen Reformpäpste. Ihre Ursachen und Funktionen' *Römische Quartalschrift für christliche Altertumskunde und Kirchengeschichte* 96 (2001) 57–94.

Jones, Anna Trumbore. *Noble Lord, Good Shepherd: Episcopal Power and Piety in Aquitaine, 877–1050* (Brill's Series on the Early Middle Ages 17; Leiden and Boston, Ma. 2009).

de Jong, Mayke. 'To the Limits of Kinship: Anti-Incest Legislation in the Early Medieval West (500–900)', *From Sappho to De Sade: Moments in the History of Sexuality*, ed. Jan N. Bremmer (London 1989) 36–59.

Jordan, Karl. 'Zur päpstlichen Finanzgeschichte im 11. und 12. Jahrhundert' QF 25 (1933/34) 61–104.

Judic, Bruno. 'La production et la diffusion du registre des lettres de Grégoire le Grand', *Les échanges culturels au moyen âge: XXXIIe congrès de la SHMES (Université du Littoral Côte d'Opale, juin 2001)*, ed. Patrick Boucheron (Publications de la Sorbonne. Série Histoire ancienne et médiévale 70; Paris 2002) 71–87.

Jussen, Bernhard. *Patenschaft und Adoption im frühen Mittelalter. Künstliche Verwandtschaft als soziale Praxis* (Veröffentlichungen des MPI für Geschichte 98; Göttingen 1991).

Kaiser, Wolfgang. 'Verkürzt und wiederaufgefüllt?' *Rechtsgeschichte* 11 (2007) 182–185.

———. *Die Epitome Iuliani. Beiträge zum römischen Recht im frühen Mittelalter und zum byzantinischen Rechtsunterricht* (Ius commune Sonderhefte 175; Frankfurt 2004).

Kantorowicz, Ernst Hartwig. *Laudes regiae: A Study in Liturgical Acclamations and Mediaeval Ruler Worship* (Berkeley and Los Angeles 1958).

Keller, Hagen. 'Le origini sociali et famigliari del vescovo Anselmo', *Sant'Anselmo vescovo di Lucca (1073–1086) nel quadro delle trasformazioni sociali e della riforma ecclesiastica: atti del convegno internazionale di studio, Lucca 25–28 settembre 1986*, ed. Cinzio Violante (Istituto storico Italiano per il medio evo. Nuovi studi storici 13; Rome 1992) 27–50.

Kerff, Franz. 'Das Paenitentiale Pseudo-Gregorii III. Eine kritische Edition', *Aus Archiven und Bibliotheken. Festschrift für Raymund Kottje zum 65. Geburtstag*, ed. Hubert Mordek (Freiburger Beiträge zur mittelalterlichen Geschichte. Studien und Texte 3; Frankfurt 1992) 161–188

———. *Der Quadripartitus. Ein Handbuch der karolingischen Kirchenreform. Überlieferung, Quellen und Rezeption* (Quellen und Forschungen zum Recht im Mittelalter 1; Sigmaringen 1982).

Kern, Anton. *Die Handschriften der Universitätsbibliothek Graz: Band 1* (Leipzig 1942).

Kerner, Max, Franz Kerff, Rudolf Pokorny, Karl Georg Schon, and Hubert Tills. 'Textidentifikation und Provenienzanalyse im Decretum Burchardi' SG 20 [= *Mélanges G. Fransen 2*] (1976) 19–63.

Kéry, Lotte. 'Kanonessammlungen aus dem lotharingischen Raum', *Lotharingien und das Papsttum im Früh- und Hochmittelalter. Wechselwirkungen im Grenzraum zwischen Germania und Gallia*, ed. Klaus Herbers and Harald Müller (Abh. Akad. Göttingen N.F. 45; Berlin and Boston 2017) 189–212.

———. 'Recht im Dienst der Reform. Kanonistische Sammlungen der Reformzeit und ihre "Adressaten"', *Brief und Kommunikation im Wandel. Medien, Autoren und Kontexte in den Debatten des Investiturstreits*, ed. Florian Hartmann (Papsttum im mittelalterlichen Europa 5; Cologne, Weimar, and Vienna 2016) 335–380.

———. 'Klosterfreiheit und päpstliche Organisationsgewalt. Exemtion als Herrschaftsinstrument des Papsttums?', *Rom und die Regionen. Studien zur Homogenisierung der lateinischen Kirche im Hochmittelalter*, ed. Jochen Johrendt and Harald Müller (Abh. Akad. Göttingen N.F. 19; Berlin and Boston 2012) 83–144.

———. 'Kanonessammlungen als Fundorte für päpstliche Schreiben', *Das Papsttum und das vielgestaltige Italien. Hundert Jahre Italia Pontificia*, ed. Klaus Herbers and Jochen Johrendt (Abh. Akad. Göttingen N.F. 5; Berlin and Boston 2009) 275–298.

———. *Canonical Collections of the Early Middle Ages (ca. 400–1140): A Bibliographical Guide to the Manuscripts and Literature* (HMCL; Washington, D.C. 1999).

———. *Die Errichtung des Bistums Arras 1093/1094* (Francia. Beihefte 33; Sigmaringen 1994).

Klemm, Elisabeth. *Die ottonischen und frühromanischen Handschriften der Bayerischen Staatsbibliothek* (2 vols. Katalog der illuminierten Handschriften der Bayerischen Staatsbibliothek in München 2; Wiesbaden 2004).

Klewitz, Hans-Walter. 'Die Entstehung des Kardinalkollegiums' ZRG Kan. Abt. 25 (1936) 115–221; repr. in idem, *Reformpapsttum und Kardinalkolleg* (Darmstadt 1957) 9–134.

Knibbs, Eric. 'Pseudo-Isidore at the Field of Lies: *Divinis praeceptis* (JE †2579) as an Authentic Decretal' BMCL 29 (2012) 1–34.

Koal, Valeska. *Studien zur Nachwirkung der Kapitularien in den Kanonessammlungen des Frühmittelalters* (Freiburger Beiträge zur mittelalterlichen Geschichte 13; Frankfurt 2001).

———. 'Zur Überlieferungsgeschichte der Fünf-Bücher-Sammlung', *Quellen, Kritik, Interpretation. Festgabe zum 60. Geburtstag von Hubert Mordek*, ed. Thomas Martin Buck and Julia Herrmann (Frankfurt 1999) 127–134.

Koeniger, Albert Michael. *Burchard I. von Worms und die deutsche Kirche seiner Zeit (1000–1025). Ein kirchen- und sittengeschichtliches Zeitbild* (Veröffentlichungen aus dem kirchenhistorischen Seminar München 2.6; Munich 1905).

Kölzer, Theo. 'Burchard I., Bischof von Worms (1000–1025)', *Burchard von Worms (Burchardus Wormaciensis ecclesiae episcopus), Decretorum libri XX [...]. Ergänzter Neudruck*, ed. Gérard Fransen and Theo Kölzer (Aalen 1992) 7–23.

———. 'Mönchtum und Außenwelt – Norm und Realität', *Proceedings San Diego 1988* MIC Subsidia 9.265–283.

———. 'Codex Libertatis: Überlegungen zur Funktion des "Regestum Farfense" und anderer Klosterchartulare', *Il ducato di Spoleto: atti del IX congresso internazionale di studi sull'alto medioevo* (2 vols. Spoleto 1983) 2.609–653.

———. 'Mönchtum und Kirchenrecht. Bemerkungen zu monastischen Kanonessammlungen der vorgratianischen Zeit' ZRG Kan. Abt. 69 (1983) 121–142.

———. 'Prolegomena', *Collectio canonum Regesto Farfensi inserta*, ed. idem (MIC Corpus collectionum 5; Vatican City 1982) 1–123.

Körntgen, Ludger. 'Canon Law and the Practice of Penance: Burchard of Worms's Penitential' *Early Medieval Europe* 14 (2006) 103–117.

———. 'Fortschreibung frühmittelalterlicher Bußpraxis. Burchards "Liber corrector" und seine Quellen', *Bischof Burchard von Worms, 1000–1025*, ed. Wilfried Hartmann (Quellen und Abhandlungen zur mittelrheinischen Kirchengeschichte 100; Mainz 2000) 199–226.

Kortüm, Hans-Henning. 'Necessitas temporis. Zur historischen Bedingtheit des Rechts im früheren Mittelalter' ZRG Kan. Abt. 79 (1993) 34–55.

Kouamé, Thierry. '*Monachus non doctoris, sed plangentis habet officium*: l'autorité de Jérôme dans le débat sur l'enseignement des moines aux XIe et XIIe siècles' *Cahiers de recherches médiévales et humanistes* 18 (2009) 9–38.

Krause, Hans-Georg. *Das Papstwahldekret von 1059 und seine Rolle im Investiturstreit* (Studi Gregoriani 7; Rome 1960).

Krause, Victor. 'Die Münchener Handschriften 3851 [und] 3853 mit einer Compilation von 181 Wormser Schlüssen' NA 19 (1893) 85–139.

Kretzschmar, Robert. *Alger von Lüttichs Traktat 'De misericordia et iustitia'. Ein kanonis-*

tischer Konkordanzversuch aus der Zeit des Investiturstreits: Untersuchungen und Edition (Quellen und Forschungen zum Recht im Mittelalter 2; Sigmaringen 1985).

Krüger, Paul. *Kritik des Justinianischen Codex* (Berlin 1867).

Kurze, Wilhelm. 'Notizen zu den Päpsten Johannes VII., Gregor III. und Benedikt III. in der Kanonessammlung des Kardinals Deusdedit' QF (1990) 23–45.

Kuttner, Stephan. 'Research on Gratian: Acta and Agenda', *Proceedings Cambridge 1984* MIC Subsidia 8.3–26; repr. in idem, *Studies in the History of Medieval Canon Law* (CSS 325; Aldershot 1990) no. V.

———. 'Universal Pope or Servant of God's Servants: The Canonists, Papal Titles, and Innocent III' *Revue de Droit canonique* 32 (1981) 109–149; repr. in idem, *Studies in the History of Medieval Canon Law* (CSS 325; Aldershot 1990) no. VIII.

———. 'Urban II and the Doctrine of Interpretation: A Turning Point?' SG 15 (1972) 55–86; repr. in idem, *The History of Ideas and Doctrines of Canon Law in the Middle Ages* (CSS 113; Aldershot 1980, 2nd edition 1992) no. IV.

———. 'Some Roman Manuscripts of Canonical Collections' BMCL 1 (1971) 7–29; repr. in idem, *Medieval Councils, Decretals, and Collections of Canon Law: Selected Essays* (CSS 126; Aldershot 1980, 2nd edition 1992) no. II.

———. 'Notes on Manuscripts' *Traditio* 17 (1961) 533–542.

———. *Harmony from Dissonance: An Interpretation of Medieval Canon Law* (The Wimmer Lecture 10; Latrobe, Penn. 1960); repr. in idem, *The History of Ideas and Doctrines of Canon Law in the Middle Ages* (CSS 113; Aldershot 1980, 2nd edition 1992) no. I.

———. '*Liber canonicus*: A Note on the "Dictatus papae" c. 17' *Studi Gregoriani* 2 (1947) 387–401; repr. in idem, *The History of Ideas and Doctrines of Canon Law in the Middle Ages* (CSS 113; Aldershot 1980, 2nd edition 1992) no. II.

———. 'Cardinalis: The History of a Canonical Concept' *Traditio* 3 (1945) 129–214; repr. in idem, *The History of Ideas and Doctrines of Canon Law in the Middle Ages* (CSS 113; Aldershot 1980, 2nd edition 1992) no. IX.

———. 'The Father of the Science of Canon Law' *The Jurist* 1 (1941) 2–19.

———. 'Zur Frage der theologischen Vorlagen Gratians' ZRG Kan. Abt. 54 (1934) 243–268; repr. in idem, *Gratian and the Schools of Law, 1140–1234* (CSS 185; Aldershot 1983, 2nd edition 2018) no. III.

Kuttner, Stephan and Reinhard Elze. *A Catalogue of Canon and Roman Law Manuscripts in the Vatican Library, vol. 1: Codices Vaticani Latini 541–2299* (Studi e testi 322; Vatican City 1986).

Kuttner, Stephan and Antonio García y García, 'A New Eyewitness Account of the Fourth Lateran Council' *Traditio* 20 (1964) 115–178; repr. in Stephan Kuttner, *Medieval Councils, Decretals, and Collections of Canon Law: Selected Essays* (CSS 126; Aldershot 1980, 2nd edition 1992) no. IX; also in Antonio García y García, *Iglesia, sociedad y derecho* (2 vols. Bibliotheca Salmanticensis: Estudios 74; Salamanca 1985) 2.61–121.

Kuttner, Stephan and Wilfried Hartmann. 'A New Version of Pope John VIII's Decree on Sacrilege (Council of Troyes, 878)' BMCL 17 (1987) 1–32.

Kuttner, Stephan and Robert Somerville. 'The So-Called Canons of Nîmes (1096)' *Tijdschrift voor rechtsgeschiedenis* 38 (1970) 175–189; repr. in Stephan Kuttner, *Medieval Councils, Decretals, and Collections of Canon Law: Selected Essays* (CSS 126; Aldershot 1980, 2nd edition 1992) no. III; also in Robert Somerville, *Papacy, Councils and Canon Law in the 11th–12th Centuries* (CSS 312; Aldershot 1990) no. IX.

Lamberz, Erich. 'Einleitung', *Concilium Universale Nicaenum Secundum 1*, ed. idem (ACO. Series Secunda: Concilium Universale Constantinopolitanum Tertium. Volumen III. Pars 1; Berlin and Boston 2008) VII–LXX.

———. 'Die Überlieferung und Rezeption des VII. Ökumenischen Konzils (787) in Rom und im lateinischen Westen', *Roma fra Oriente e Occidente: 19–24 aprile 2001* (2 vols. Settimane 49; Spoleto 2002) 2.1053–1099.

———. 'Studien zur Überlieferung der Akten des VII. ökumenischen Konzils: Der Brief Hadrians I. an Konstantin VI. und Irene (JE 2448)' DA 53 (1997) 1–43.

Landau, Peter. 'Gratian and the *Decretum Gratiani*', *The History of Medieval Canon Law in the Classical Period, 1140–1234: From Gratian to the Decretals of Pope Gregory IX*, ed. Wilfried Hartmann and Kenneth Pennington (HMCL; Washington, D.C. 2008) 22–54.

———. 'Die Quellen der mittelitalienischen Kanonessammlung in sieben Büchern (MS Vat. Lat. 1346)', *Ritual, Text and Law: Studies in Medieval Canon Law and Liturgy Presented to Roger E. Reynolds*, ed. Richard F. Gyug and Kathleen Grace Cushing (CFC; Aldershot 2004) 255–268.

———. 'Seelsorge in den Kanonessammlungen von der Zeit der gregorianischen Reformen bis zu Gratian', *La pastorale della Chiesa in Occidente dall'età ottoniana al Concilio lateranense IV: atti Mendola 2001* (Ricerche: Storia 26; Milan 2004) 93–123.

———. 'Burchard de Worms et Gratien: à propos des sources immédiates de Gratien' *Revue de Droit canonique* 48 (1998) 233–245.

———. 'Sakramentalität und Jurisdiktion', *Das Recht der Kirche. Bd. 2: Zur Geschichte des Kirchenrechts*, ed. Gerhard Rau, Hans-Richard Reuter, and Klaus Schlaich (Forschungen und Berichte der Evangelischen Studiengemeinschaft 50; Gütersloh 1995) 58–95.

———. 'Überlieferung und Bedeutung der Kanones des Trullanischen Konzils im westlichen kanonischen Recht', *The Council in Trullo Revisited*, ed. George Nedungatt and Michael Featherstone (Kanonika 6; Rome 1995) 215–227.

———. 'Wandel und Kontinuität im kanonischen Recht bei Gratian', *Sozialer Wandel im Mittelalter. Wahrnehmungsformen, Erklärungsmuster, Regelungsmechanismen*, ed. Jürgen Miethke and Klaus Schreiner (Sigmaringen 1994) 215–233.

———. 'Vorgratianische Kanonessammlungen bei den Dekretisten und in frühen Dekretalensammlungen', *Proceedings San Diego 1988* MIC Subsidia 9.93–116.

———. 'Die "duae leges" im kanonischen Recht des 12. Jahrhunderts', *Officium und Libertas christiana* (Sb. Akad. München 1991.3; Munich 1991) 55–96.

———. 'Kanonessammlungen in der Lombardei im frühen und hohen Mittelalter', *Atti dell'undecimo congresso internazionale di studi sull'alto medioevo: Milano, 26–30 ottobre 1987* (2 vols. Spoleto 1989) 1.425–457; repr. in idem, *Kanones und Dekretalen. Beiträge zur Geschichte der Quellen des kanonischen Rechts* (Bibliotheca Eruditorum 2; Goldbach 1997) 437*–469*.

———. 'Gefälschtes Recht in den Rechtssammlungen bis Gratian', *Fälschungen im Mittelalter* (6 vols. MGH Schriften 33; Hanover 1988) 2.11–49; repr. in idem, *Kanones und Dekretalen. Beiträge zur Geschichte der Quellen des kanonischen Rechts* (Bibliotheca Eruditorum 2; Goldbach 1997) 3*–41*.

———. 'Erweiterte Fassungen der Kanonessammlung des Anselm von Lucca aus dem 12. Jahrhundert', *Sant'Anselmo, Mantova e la lotta per le investiture: atti di convegno internazionale di studi (Mantova 23–24–25 maggio 1986)*, ed. Paolo Golinelli (Bologna 1987) 323–337; repr. in idem, *Kanones und Dekretalen. Beiträge zur Geschichte der Quellen des kanonischen Rechts* (Bibliotheca Eruditorum 2; Goldbach 1997) 81*–96*.

———. 'Die Rezension C der Sammlung des Anselm von Lucca' BMCL 16 (1986) 17–54; repr. in idem, *Kanones und Dekretalen. Beiträge zur Geschichte der Quellen des kanonischen Rechts* (Bibliotheca Eruditorum 2; Goldbach 1997) 43*–80*.

Larson, Atria Ann. *Master of Penance: Gratian and the Development of Penitential Thought and Law in the Twelfth Century* (SMCL 11; Washington, D.C. 2014).

Laudage, Johannes. *Priesterbild und Reformpapsttum im 11. Jahrhundert* (Beihefte zum Archiv für Kulturgeschichte 22; Cologne and Vienna 1984).

Lawo, Matthias. *Studien zu Hugo von Flavigny* (MGH Schriften 61; Hanover 2010).

Le Bras, Gabriel. 'L'activité canonique à Poitiers pendant la réforme grégorienne (1049–1099)', *Mélanges offerts à René Crozet: à l'occasion de son soixante-dixième anniversaire*, ed. Pierre Gallais (2 vols. Poitiers 1966) 1.237–239.

———. 'Note sur la vie commune des clercs dans les collections canoniques', *La vita comune del clero nei secoli XI e XII: atti Mendola 1959* (2 vols. Miscellanea 3; Milan 1962) 1.16–18.

———. 'Le *Liber de misericordia et justitia* d'Alger de Liège' NRHDFE 45 (1921) 80–118.

Leclercq, Jean. *The Love of Learning of the Desire of God: A Study of Monastic Culture* (New York 1982); original: *L'amour des lettres et le désir de Dieu* (Paris 1957).

———. *Monks on Marriage: A Twelfth-Century-View* (New York 1982).

———. 'Y at-il une culture monastique?', *Il monachesimo nell'alto Medioevo e la formazione della civiltà occidentale, 8–14 aprile 1956* (Settimane 4; Spoleto 1957) 339–356.

Leisching, Peter. '*Consuetudo* und *ratio* im Dekret und in der Panormia des Bischofs Ivo von Chartres' ZRG Kan. Abt. 74 (1988) 535–542.

Lemarignier, Jean-François. 'Political and Monastic Structures in France at the End of the Tenth and the Beginning of the Eleventh Century', *Lordship and Community in Medieval Europe: Selected Readings*, ed. F. L. Cheyette (New York 1968) 100–127.

———. 'Les institutions ecclésiastiques en France de la fin du Xe au milieu du XIIe siècle', *Histoire des institutions françaises au Moyen Âge*, ed. Jean-François Lemarignier, Jean Gaudemet, and Michel Mollat (3 vols. Histoire du droit et des institutions de l'Eglise en Occident 3; Paris 1962) 1–139.

———. 'L'exemption monastique et les origines de la réforme grégorienne', *À Cluny: congrès scientifique: fêtes et cérémonies liturgiques en l'honneur des saints Abbés Odon et Odilon, 9–11 juillet 1949* (Dijon 1950) 288–340; repr. in idem, *Structures politiques et religieuses dans la France du haut Moyen Âge: recueil d'articles rassemblés par ses disciples*, ed. Dominique Barthélemy (Publications de l'Université de Rouen 206. Rouen 1995) 285–337.

Lenherr, Titus. 'Die "Glossa ordinaria" zur Bibel als Quelle von Gratians Dekret' BMCL 24 (2000) 97–129.

———. 'Zur Überlieferung des Kapitels *Duae sunt*' AKKR 168 (1999) 369–374.

———. *Die Exkommunikations- und Depositionsgewalt der Häretiker bei Gratian und den Dekretisten bis zur "Glossa Ordinaria" des Johannes Teutonicus* (Münchener theologische Studien, Kanonistische Abteilung 42; Sankt Ottilien 1987).

de León, Enrique. *La «cognatio spiritualis» según Graciano* (Pontificio Ateneo delle Santa Croce. Monografie giuridiche 11; Milan 1996).

Levillain, Léon. 'Études sur l'abbaye de Saint-Denis à l'époque mérovingienne. III. Privilegium et immunitates ou Saint-Denis dans l'église et dan l'état' BEC 87 (1926) 20–97 and 245–346.

Lewald, Ursula. *An der Schwelle der Scholastik. Bonizo von Sutri und das Kirchenrecht seiner Tage* (Weimar 1938).

———. 'Das Eherecht in Bonizos von Sutri *Liber de Vita Christiana*' ZRG Kan. Abt. 27 (1938) 560–598.

Liebermann, Felix. Über das englische Rechtsbuch Leges Henrici (Halle 1901).

———. *Quadripartitus. Ein englisches Rechtsbuch von 1114* (Halle 1892).

Lohmer, Christian. 'Pseudoepigraphica of Peter Damian: Truly and Falsely Attributed Works of a Church Reformer', *Proceedings Washington 2004* MIC Subsidia 13.108–126.

Lohrmann, Dietrich. *Das Register Papst Johannes' VIII. (872–882). Neue Studien zur Abschrift Reg. Vat. I, zum verlorenen Originalregister und zum Diktat der Briefe* (Bibliothek des Deutschen Historischen Instituts in Rom 30; Tübingen 1968).

Losada Cosme, Roque. 'La teoría de las fuentes del Derecho eclesiástico en la renascencia jurídica de principios del siglo XII' *Revista española de derecho canónico* 15 (1960) 317–372.

Lottin, Odon. *Psychologie et morale aux XIIe et XIIIe siècles* (6 in 8 vols. Gembloux 1942–60).

Loud, Graham A. *The Age of Robert Guiscard: Southern Italy and the Northern Conquest* (London and New York 2014).

Löwenfeld, Samuel. 'Die Canonsammlung des Cardinals Deusdedit und das Register Gregors VII.' NA 10 (1885) 309–329.

Lugge, Margret. *"Gallia" und "Francia" im Mittelalter. Untersuchungen über den Zusammenhang zwischen geographisch-historischer Terminologie und politischem Denken vom 6.–15. Jahrhundert* (Bonner historische Forschungen 15; Bonn 1960).

Lynch, Joseph H. *Christianizing Kinship: Ritual Sponsorship in Anglo-Saxon England* (Ithaca, N.Y. 1998).

Maas, Pauline Henriëtte Joanna Theresia. *The* Liber sententiarum Magistri A.: *Its Place Amidst the Sentences Collections of the First Half of the 12th Century* (Middeleeuwse studies 11; Nijmegen 1995).

Maassen, Friedrich. *Geschichte der Quellen und der Literatur des canonischen Rechts im Abendlande bis zum Ausgange des Mittelalters. Vol. 1: Die Rechtssammlungen bis zur Mitte des 9. Jahrhunderts* [all published] (Graz 1870).

Marcos Rodríguez, Florencio. 'Tres manuscritos del siglo XII con colecciones canónicas' *Analecta sacra Tarraconensia* 32 (1959) 35–54.

Markus, R. A. 'Carthage-Prima Justiniana-Ravenna: An Aspect of Justinian's Kirchenpolitik' *Byzantion* 49 (1979) 277–302.

Martin, Norbert. *Die Compilatio decretorum des Kardinals Laborans. Eine Umarbeitung des Gratianischen Dekrets aus dem 12. Jahrhunderts* (2 vols. Heidelberg 1994)

———. '"Mare uitreum" (Neapel, Bibl.naz.MS XII A 27). Eine Quelle der "Compilatio decretorum" des Kardinals Laborans' BMCL 15 (1985) 51–59.

Märtl, Claudia. 'Die kanonistische Überlieferung der falschen Investiturprivilegien (Ivo, Panormia 8.135 und 136; D. 63 c. 22 und 23)' BMCL 17 (1987) 33–44.

———. 'Einleitung', *Die falschen Investiturprivilegien*, ed. eadem (MGH Fontes iuris 13; Hanover 1986) 7–124.

———. 'Zur Überlieferung des *Liber contra Wibertum* Anselms von Lucca' DA 41 (1985) 192–202.

———. 'Ein angeblicher Text zum Bußgang von Canossa' DA 38 (1982) 555–563.

Matecki, Bernd. *Der Traktat In primis hominibus. Eine theologie- und kirchenrechtsgeschichtliche Untersuchung zu einem Ehetext der Schule von Laon aus dem 12. Jahrhundert* (Adnotationes in Ius Canonicum 20; Frankfurt and New York 2001).

McClendon, Charles B. *The Imperial Abbey of Farfa: Architectural Currents of the Early Middle Ages* (Yale Publications in the History of Art 36; New Haven and London 1987).

McLaughlin, Terence P. 'The Teaching of the Canonists on Usury (XII, XIII and XIV Centuries)' MS 1 (1939) 81–147 and 2 (1940) 1–22.

Meens, Rob. *Penance in Medieval Europe, 600–1200* (Cambridge 2014).

———. 'The Historiography of Early Medieval Penance', *A New History of Penance*, ed. Abigail A. Firey (Brill's Companions to the Christian Tradition 14; Leiden and Boston 2008) 73–96.

———. 'Die Bußbücher und das Recht im 9. und 10. Jahrhundert. Kontinuität und Wandel', *Recht und Gericht in Kirche und Welt um 900*, ed. Annette Grabowsky and Wilfried Hartmann (Schriften des Historischen Kollegs. Kolloquien 69; Munich 2007) 217–234.

Meijns, Brigitte. 'Opposition to Clerical Continence and the Gregorian Celibacy Legislation in the Diocese of Thérouanne: *Tractatus pro clericorum conubio* (c. 1077–1078)' *Sacris erudiri* 47 (2008) 223–290.

Melloni, Alberto. 'Essence, Concept, or History: What Is at Stake in a Dispute over the COGD' CHR 101 (2015) 578–587.

Melville, Gert. 'Regeln – Consuetudines-Texte – Statuten. Positionen für eine Typologie des normativen Schrifttums religiöser Gemeinschaften im Mittelalter', *Regulae – Consuetudines – Statuta: studi sulle fonti normative degli ordini religioni nei secoli centrali del Medioevo: atti del I e del II Seminario internazionale di studio del Centro italo-tedesco di storia comparata degli ordini religiosi (Bari/Noci/Lecce, 26–27 ottobre 2002 / Castiglione delle Stiviere, 23–24 maggio 2003)*, ed. Cristina Andenna and Gert Melville (Vita regularis 25; Münster 2005) 5–37.

Meulenberg, Leo. *Der Primat der römischen Kirche im Denken und Handeln Gregors VII.* (Mededelingen van het Nederlands Historisch Instituut te Rome 33.2; The Hague 1965).

Meyer, Christoph H. F. *Die Distinktionstechnik in der Kanonistik des 12. Jahrhunderts. Ein Beitrag zur Wissenschaftsgeschichte des Hochmittelalters* (Mediaevalia Lovaniensia. Studia 29; Leuven 2000).

Meyer, Otto. 'Überlieferung und Verbreitung des Dekrets des Bischofs Burchard von Worms' ZRG Kan. Abt. 24 (1935) 141–183.

Meyvaert, Paul. 'Le *Libellus responsionum* à Augustin de Cantorbéry: une œuvre authentique de Saint Grégoire le Grand', *Grégoire le Grand*, ed. Jacques Fontaine, Robert Gillet, and Stan M. Pellistrandi (Colloques internationaux de Centre national de la recherche scientifique; Paris 1986) 543–550.

Miccoli, Giovanni. 'Un florilegio sulla dignità e i diritti del monachesimo: Cod. Pis. S. Cat. 59, ff. 1–16', *Volume in onore del Prof. Ottorino Bertolini* (Livorno 1967) 117–129.

———. 'Un nuovo manoscritto del *Liber de vita christiana* di Bonizone di Sutri' *Studi medievali, serie terza* 7 (1966) 371–398.

Michel, Anton. *Humbert und Kerullarios: Studien* (2 vols. Paderborn 1924/30).

Mirbt, Carl. *Die Publizistik im Zeitalter Gregors VII.* (Leipzig 1894).

Mitrofanov, Andrey. *L'ecclésiologie d'Anselme de Lucques (1036–1086) au service de Grégoire VII: genèse, contenu et impact de sa «Collection canonique»* (Instrumenta patristica et mediaevalia 69; Turnhout 2015).

Mommsen, Theodor. 'Digestorum excerpta quae invenitur in collectionibus canonum tribus, Ivonis Caesaraugustana Tripertita', *Digesta Iustiniani Augusti*, ed. Theodor Mommsen and Paul Krüger (2 vols. Berlin 1870) 2.41*–50*.

Mor, Carlo Guido. 'Il Digesto nell'età preirneriana e la formazione della *Vulgata*', *Per il xiv centenario delle Pandette e del Codice di Giustiniano* (Pavia 1934) 559–697; repr. in idem, *Scritti di storia giuridica altomedievale* (Pisa 1977) 83–234.

Mordek, Hubert. *Studien zur fränkischen Herrschergesetzgebung. Aufsätze über Kapitularien und Kapitulariensammlungen – ausgewählt zum 60. Geburtstag* (Frankfurt 2000).

———. *Bibliotheca capitularium regum Francorum manuscripta. Überlieferung und Traditionszusammenhang der fränkischen Herrschererlasse* (MGH Hilfsmittel 15; Munich 1995).

———. 'Kanonistik und Gregorianische Reform. Marginalien zu einem nicht-marginalen Thema', *Reich und Kirche vor dem Investiturstreit. Vorträge beim wissenschaftlichen Kolloquium aus Anlaß des 80. Geburtstags von Gerd Tellenbach*, ed. Karl Schmid (Sigmaringen 1985) 65–82.

———. *Kirchenrecht und Reform im Frankenreich. Die Collectio Vetus Gallica, die älteste systematische Kanonessammlung des fränkischen Gallien: Studien und Edition* (Beiträge zur Geschichte und Quellenkunde des Mittelalters 1; Berlin and New York 1975).

———. 'Die historische Wirkung der *Collectio Herovalliana*' *Zeitschrift für Kirchengeschichte* 81 (1970) 220–243.

Moreau, Dominic. 'Non impar conciliorum extat auctoritas: l'origine de l'introduction des lettres pontificales dans le droit canonique', *L'étude des correspondances dans le monde romain de l'Antiquité classique à l'Antiquité tardive: permanences et mutations*, ed. Janine Desmulliez, Christine Hoët-van Cauwenberghe, and Jean-Christophe Jolivet (Travaux et recherches 3; Lille 2010) 487–509.

Morelle, Laurent. 'Par delà le vrai et le faux: trois études critiques sur les premiers privilèges pontificaux reçus par l'abbaye de Saint-Bertin (1057–1107)', *L'acte pontifical et sa critique*, ed. Rolf Große (Studien und Dokumente zur Gallia Pontificia 5; Bonn 2007) 51–86.

———. 'Moines de Corbie sous influence sandionysienne? Les préparatifs corbéiens du synode romain de 1065', *L'Église de France et la papauté (Xe–XIIIe siècle) / Die französische Kirche und das Papsttum (10.–13. Jahrhundert): actes du XXVIe Colloque franco-allemand organisé en coopération avec l'École nationale des chartes par l'Institut historique allemand de Paris (Paris, 17–19 octobre 1990)*, ed. Rolf Große (Studien und Dokumente zur Gallia Pontificia 1; Bonn 1993) 197–218.

Mostert, Marco. *The Library of Fleury: A Provisional List of Manuscripts* (Middeleeuwse studies en bronnen 3; Hilversum 1989).

———. 'Die Urkundenfälschungen Abbos von Fleury', *Fälschungen im Mittelalter* (6 vols. MGH Schriften 33; Munich 1988) 4.287–318.

———. *The Political Theology of Abbo of Fleury: A Study of the Ideas About Society and Law of the 10th-Century Monastic Reform Movement* (Middeleeuwse studies en bronnen 2; Hilversum 1987).

Motta, Giuseppe. 'Una silloge canonistica del sec. XII tra Deusdedit ed Anselmo di Lucca (Torino, Biblioteca Nazionale E.V.44)', *De iure canonico medii aevi. Festschrift für Rudolf Weigand*, ed. Peter Landau (SG 27; Rome 1996) 413–442

———. 'La redazione A "aucta" della *Collectio Anselmi episcopi Lucensis*', *Studia in honorem eminentissimi Cardinalis Alphonsi M. Stickler*, ed. Rosalio J. Castillo Lara (Studia e textus historiae iuris canonici 7; Rome 1992) 375–449.

———. 'Introduzione', *Liber canonum diuersorum sanctorum patrum sive Collectio in CLXXXIII titulos digesta*, ed. idem (MIC Corpus collectionum 7; Vatican City 1988) xvii–lxviii.

Moynihan, James M. *Papal Immunity and Liability in the Writings of the Medieval Canonists* (Analecta Gregoriana 120; Rome 1961).

Müller, Jörg. 'Die Überlieferung der Briefe Papst Gregors I. im Rahmen der CDP', *Licet preter solitum. Ludwig Falkenstein zum 65. Geburtstag*, ed. Lotte Kéry, Dietrich Lohrmann, and Harald Müller (Aachen 1998) 17–31.

———. *Die Collectio duodecim partium und ihr Freisinger Umfeld* (1995), https://epub.ub.uni-muenchen.de/13882/.

———. *Untersuchungen zur Collectio Duodecim Partium* (Abhandlungen zur rechtswissenschaftlichen Grundlagenforschung 73; Ebelsbach 1989).

Munier, Charles. *Les sources patristiques du droit de l'église du VIIIe au XIIIe siècle* (Mulhouse 1957).

Münsch, Oliver. 'Ein Streitschriftenfragment zur Simonie' DA (2006) 619–629.

———. 'Die Orthodoxa defensio imperialis. Ein Beitrag zur Publizistik des Investiturstreits', *Quellen, Kritik, Interpretation. Festgabe zum 60. Geburtstag von Hubert Mordek*, ed. Thomas Martin Buck and Julia Herrmann (Frankfurt 1999) 135–154.

Nardi, Paolo. 'Fonti canoniche in una sentenza senese del 1150', *Life, Law and Letters: Historical Studies in Honour of Antonio García y García*, ed. Peter Linehan (2 vols. SG 28/29; Rome 1998) 2.661–670.

Nelson, Janet L. 'Law and Its Applications', *Early Medieval Christianities, c.600–c.1100*, ed. Thomas F. X. Noble and Julia M. H. Smith (The Cambridge History of Christianity 3; Cambridge 2008) 299–326.

————. 'Parents, Children, and the Church in the Earlier Middle Ages', *The Church and Childhood*, ed. Diana Wood (Studies in Church History 31; Oxford 1994) 81–114.

Nitzsch, Karl Wilhelm. *Ministerialität und Bürgerthum im 11. und 12. Jahrhundert* (Leipzig 1859).

North, William L. 'Bonizo of Sutri, the *Dicta Bonizonis* and the Development of the Jurisprudence of Canon Law Before Gratian', *The Use of Canon Law in Ecclesiastical Administration, 1000–1234*, ed. Danica Summerlin and Melodie Harris Eichbauer (Medieval Law and Its Practice 26; Leiden 2018) 159–182.

Nortier, Geneviève. *Les bibliothèques médiévales des abbayes bénédictines de Normandie: Fécamp, Le Bec, Le Mont Saint-Michel, Saint-Évroul, Lyre, Jumièges, Saint-Wandrille, Saint-Ouen* (Bibliothèque d'histoire et d'archéologie chretiennes 9; Paris 1971).

Nowak, Przemysław. 'A Legation of Galo, Bishop-Elect of Beauvais, to Poland in 1104 and the Collectio Tripartita', *Proceedings Paris 2016* MIC Subsidia 16.347–355.

————. 'Recent Work on the *Dagome Iudex* in the *Collectio canonum* of Cardinal Deusdedit', *Sacri canones editandi: Studies on Medieval Canon Law in Memory of Jiří Kejř*, ed. Pavel Otmar Krafl (2nd edition Nitra 2020) 25–39.

————. '*Dagome iudex* w *Zbiorze kanonów* kardynała Deusdedita' *Studia Źródłoznawcze - Commentationes* 51 (2013) 75–94.

————. 'Das Papsttum und Ostmitteleuropa (Böhmen-Mähren, Polen, Ungarn) vom ausgehenden 10. bis zum Beginn des 13. Jahrhunderts. Mit einer Neuedition von JL 9067', *Rom und die Regionen. Studien zur Homogenisierung der lateinischen Kirche im Hochmittelalter*, ed. Jochen Johrendt and Harald Müller (Abh. Akad. Göttingen N.F. 19; Berlin and Boston 2012) 331–369.

————. 'The Manuscripts of the *Collectio Tripartita* in Poland', *Bishops, Texts and the Use of Canon Law Around 1100: Essays in Honour of Martin Brett*, ed. Bruce Clark Brasington and Kathleen Grace Cushing (CFC; Aldershot and Farnham 2008) 91–109.

Oberste, Jörg. '*Contra prelatos qui gravant loca et personas ordinis*: Bischöfe und Cluniazenser im Zeitalter von Krisen und Reformen (12./13. Jahrhundert)', *Die Cluniazenser in ihrem politisch-sozialen Umfeld*, ed. Giles Constable, Gert Melville, and Jörg Oberste (Vita regularis 7; Münster 1998) 349–392.

Ohme, Heinz. 'Einleitung', *Concilium Constantinopolitanum a. 691/2 in Trullo habitum (Concilium Quinisextum)*, ed. idem (ACO. Series Secunda. Concilium Universale Constantinopolitanum Tertium; Volumen III. Pars 4; Berlin and Boston 2013) VII–CIX.

————. 'Sources of the Greek Canon Law to the Quinisext Council (691/2): Councils and Church Fathers', *The History of Byzantine and Eastern Canon Law to 1500*, ed. Wilfried Hartmann and Kenneth Pennington (HMCL; Washington, D.C. 2012) 24–114.

————. *Kanon ekklesiastikos. Die Bedeutung des altkirchlichen Kanonbegriffs* (Berlin 1998).

————. 'Die sogenannten "antirömischen Kanones" des Concilium Quinisextum (692) – Vereinheitlichung als Gefahr für die Einheit der Kirche', *The Council in Trullo Revisited*, ed. George Nedungatt and Michael Featherstone (Kanonika 6; Rome 1995) 307–321.

————. *Das Concilium Quinisextum und seine Bischofsliste. Studien zum Konstantinopeler Konzil von 692* (Arbeiten zur Kirchengeschichte 56; Berlin and New York 1990).

Ott, John Stephens. 'Clerical Networks and Canon Law: The Beauvais Election Controversy of 1100–04', *New Discourses in Medieval Canon Law Research: Challenging the Master Narrative*, ed. Christof Rolker (Medieval Law and Its Practice 28; Leiden and Boston 2019) 58–82.

————. *Bishops, Authority and Community in Northwestern Europe, c. 1050–1150* (Life and Thought: Fourth Series 102; Cambridge 2015).

————. '"Reims and Rome Are Equals": Archbishop Manasses I (c. 1069–1080), Pope Gregory VII, and the Fortunes of Historical Exceptionalism', *Envisioning the Bishop:*

Images and the Episcopacy in the Middle Ages, ed. Sigrid Danielson and Evan A. Gatti (Medieval Church Studies 29; Turnhout 2014) 275–302.

Ott, John Stephens and Anna Trumbore Jones. 'Introduction: The Bishop Reformed', *The Bishop Reformed: Studies of Episcopal Power and Culture in the Central Middle Ages*, ed. iidem (CFC; Aldershot 2007) 1–20.

Pásztor, Edith. 'Lotta per le investiture e "ius belli": la posizione di Anselmo di Lucca', *Sant'Anselmo, Mantova e la lotta per le investiture: atti di convegno internazionale di studi (Mantova 23–24–25 maggio 1986)*, ed. Paolo Golinelli (Bologna 1987) 375–421.

Patetta, Federico. 'Per la storia del diritto romano nel medio evo: a proposito dell'opera di M. Conrat, Geschichte der Quellen und Literatur des römischen Rechts im frühen Mittelalter, 1. Band 1891' *Rivista italiana per le scienze giuridiche* 12 (1891) 307–331; repr. in idem, *Studi sulle fonti giuridiche medievali* (Turin 1967) 161–185.

Paxton, Frederick S. 'Abbas and Rex: Power and Authority in the Literature of Fleury, 987–1044', *The Experience of Power in Medieval Europe, 950–1350: Essays in Honor of Thomas N. Bisson*, ed. Robert F. Berkhofer, Alan Cooper, and Adam J. Kosto (London 2005) 197–212.

Payer, Pierre J. *Sex and the Penitentials: The Development of a Sexual Code, 550–1150* (Toronto, Buffalo, and London 1984).

Peitz, Wilhelm Maria. *Das Register Gregors I.: Beiträge zur Kenntnis des päpstlichen Kanzlei- und Registerwesens bis auf Gregor VII.* (Stimmen der Zeit 2; Freiburg 1917).

———. *Das Originalregister Gregors VII. im vatikanischen Archiv (Reg. Vat. 2) nebst Beiträgen zur Kenntnis der Originalregister Innozenz' III. und Honorius' III. (Reg. Vat. 4–11)* (Sb. Akad. Wien 165.5; Vienna 1911).

Pelster, Friedrich. 'Das Dekret Burkhards von Worms in einer Redaktion aus dem Beginn der gregorianischen Reform (Cod. Vat. Lat. 3809 und Cod. Monacen. Lat. 4570)' *Studi Gregoriani* 1 (1947) 321–351.

Peltzer, Jörg. *Canon Law, Careers and Conquest: Episcopal Elections in Normandy and Greater Anjou, c. 1140–c. 1230* (Life and Thought: Fourth Series 71; Cambridge 2008).

Perels, Ernst. 'Einleitung', *Bonizo von Sutri, Liber de vita christiana*, ed. idem (Texte zur Geschichte des römischen und kanonischen Rechts im Mittelalter 1; Berlin 1930) IX–LXXIX.

———. 'Die Briefe Papst Nikolaus' I. Die kanonistische Überlieferung' NA 39 (1914) 43–153.

Petersmann, Johanna. 'Die kanonistische Überlieferung des Constitutum Constantini bis zum Dekret Gratians. Untersuchung und Edition' DA 30 (1974) 356–449.

Philpott, Mark. 'The *De iniusta vexacione Willelmi episcopi primi* and Canon Law in Anglo-Norman Durham', *Anglo-Norman Durham, 1093–1193*, ed. David W. Rollason, Margaret M. Harvey, and Michael C. Prestwich (Woodbridge 1994) 125–137.

Picasso, Giorgio G. '"Quam sit necessarium monasteriorum quieti prospicere" (Reg. Epist. 8.17): sulla fortuna di un canone gregoriano', *Cristianità ed Europa: miscellanea di studi in onore di Luigi Prosdocimi*, ed. Cesare Alzati (2 in 3 vols. Rome 1994–2000) 2.95–105.

———. 'Ancora un florilegio patristico sulle prerogative dei monaci (Firenze, Riccardiana 3006, ff. 203r–205v)', *Nobiltà e chiese nel Medioevo e altri saggi: scritti in onore di Gerd G. Tellenbach*, ed. Cinzio Violante (Pubblicazioni del dipartimento di medievistica dell'Università di Pisa 3; Rome 1993) 223–232; repr. in idem, «Sacri canones et monastica regula»: disciplina canonica e vita monastica nella società medievale (Bibliotheca erudita. Studi e documenti di storia e filologia 27; Milan 2006) 205–217.

———. 'Fonti patristiche tra teologia e diritto canonico nella prima metà del secolo XII', *L'Europa dei secoli XI e XII fra novità e tradizione: sviluppi di una cultura: atti Mendola 1986*

(Miscellanea 12; Milan 1989) 21–35; repr. in idem, «Sacri canones et monastica regula»: disciplina canonica e vita monastica nella società medievale (Bibliotheca erudita. Studi e documenti di storia e filologia 27; Milan 2006) 85–102.

———. 'Monachesimo e canoniche nelle sillogi canonistiche e nei concili particolari', *Istituzioni monastiche e istituzioni canonicali in Occidente (1123–1215): atti Mendola 1977* (Miscellanea 9; Milan 1980) 133–158; repr. in idem, «Sacri canones et monastica regula»: disciplina canonica e vita monastica nella società medievale (Bibliotheca erudita. Studi e documenti di storia e filologia 27; Milan 2006) 161–190.

———. *Collezioni canoniche milanesi del secolo XII* (Pubblicazioni dell'Università cattolica del S. Cuore. Saggi e ricerche. Scienze storiche 2; Milan 1969).

Pokorny, Rudolf. 'Reichsbischof, Kirchenrecht und Diözesanverwaltung um das Jahr 1000', *Bernward von Hildesheim und das Zeitalter der Ottonen. Katalog der Ausstellung Hildesheim 1993*, ed. Michael Brandt and Arne Eggebrecht (2 vols. Hildesheim and Mainz 1993) 1.113–122.

Pokorny, Rudolf and Hans Jakob Schuffels. 'Kirchenrechtliche Materialsammlung (233-Kapitel-Sammlung)', *Bernward von Hildesheim und das Zeitalter der Ottonen. Katalog der Ausstellung Hildesheim 1993*, ed. Michael Brandt and Arne Eggebrecht (2 vols. Hildesheim and Mainz 1993) 2.486–489.

Pontal, Odette. *Les conciles de la France capétienne jusqu'en 1215* (Paris 1995).

Quentin, Henri. *Jean-Dominique Mansi et les grandes collections conciliaires* (Paris 1900).

Radding, Charles M. and Antonio Ciaralli. *The Corpus Iuris Civilis in the Middle Ages: Manuscripts and Transmission from the Sixth Century to the Juristic Revival* (Brill's Studies in Intellectual History 147; Turnhout 2007).

Radding, Charles M. and Francis Newton. *Theology, Rhetoric, and Politics in the Eucharistic Controversy, 1078–1079: Alberic of Monte Cassino Against Berengar of Tours* (New York 2003).

Ramseyer, Valerie. *The Transformation of a Religious Landscape: Medieval Southern Italy 850–1150* (Conjunctions of Religion and Power in the Medieval Past; Ithaca, N.Y. 2006).

Rathsack, Mogens. *Die Fuldaer Fälschungen. Eine rechtshistorische Analyse der päpstlichen Privilegien des Klosters Fulda von 751 bis ca. 1158* (2 vols. Päpste und Papsttum 24; Stuttgart 1989); original: *Fuldaforfalskningerne. En retshistorisk analyse af klostret Fuldas pavelige privilegier 751 – ca. 1158* (Copenhagen 1980).

Rau, Reinhold. 'Einleitung', *Briefe des Bonifatius. Willibalds Leben des Bonifatius*, ed. and tr. idem (FSGA 4B; Darmstadt 1968) 3–15.

Remensnyder, Amy G. 'Pollution, Purity and Peace: An Aspect of Social Reform Between the Late Tenth Century and 1076', *The Peace of God: Social Violence and Religious Response in France Around the Year 1000*, ed. Thomas Head and Richard Landes (Ithaca, N.Y. 1992) 280–307.

Rennie, Kriston R. *The Collectio Burdegalensis: A Study and Register of an Eleventh-Century Canon Law Collection* (Medieval Law and Theology 6; Toronto 2013).

———. 'The Turin Collection Revisited' ZRG Kan. Abt. 98 (2012) 46–63.

———. 'Poitevine Collections: Looking Behind the Manuscript Evidence' ZRG Kan. Abt. 97 (2011) 59–75.

Reuter, Timothy. 'A Europe of Bishops: The Age of Wulfstan of York and Burchard of Worms', *Strukturen bischöflicher Herrschaftsgewalt im westlichen Europa des 10. und 11. Jahrhunderts / Patterns of Episcopal Power: Bishops in Tenth and Eleventh Century Western Europe*, ed. Ludger Körntgen and Dominik Wassenhoven (Prinz-Albert-Forschungen 6; Berlin and Boston 2011) 17–38; original: 'Ein Europa der Bischöfe. Das Zeitalter Burchards von Worms', *Bischof Burchard von Worms, 1000–1025*, ed. Wilfried Hartmann

(Quellen und Abhandlungen zur mittelrheinischen Kirchengeschichte 100; Mainz 2000) 1–28.

Reynolds, Philip L. *How Marriage Became One of the Sacraments: The Sacramental Theology of Marriage from Its Medieval Origins to the Council of Trent* (Cambridge Studies in Law and Christianity; Cambridge 2016).

Reynolds, Roger E. 'The Influence of Eastern Patristic Fathers on the Canonical Collections of South Italy in the Eleventh and Early Twelfth Centuries', *Canon Law, Religion and Politics: Liber amicorum Robert Somerville*, ed. Uta-Renate Blumenthal, Anders Winroth, and Peter Landau (Washington, D.C. 2012) 75–106.

————. *Studies on Medieval Liturgical and Legal Manuscripts from Spain and Italy* (CSS 927; Aldershot 2009).

————. 'The *Collectio Angelica*: A Canon Law Derivative of the South Italian *Collection in Five Books*', *Bishops, Texts and the Use of Canon Law Around 1100: Essays in Honour of Martin Brett*, ed. Bruce Clark Brasington and Kathleen Grace Cushing (CFC; Aldershot and Farnham 2008) 7–28.

————. 'Penitentials in South and Central Italian Canon Law Manuscripts of the Tenth and Eleventh Centuries' *Early Medieval Europe* 14 (2006) 65–84.

————. 'Further Evidence for the Influence of the *Hibernensis* in Southern Italy: An Early Eleventh-Century Canonistic Florilegium at Montecassino' *Peritia* 19 (2005) 119–135.

————. *The Collectio canonum Casinensis duodecimi seculi (Codex terscriptus)….: A Derivative of the South-Italian Collection in Five Books: An Implicit Edition with Introductory Study* (PIMS Studies and Texts 137 / Monumenta Liturgica Beneventana 3; Toronto 2001).

————. 'The South Italian *Collection in Five Books* and Its Derivatives: A South Italian Appendix to the Collection in Seventy-Four Titles' MS 63 (2001) 353–365. Quoted as 'Five Books [2001]'.

————. 'The Transmission of the *Hibernensis* in Italy: Tenth to the Twelfth Century' *Peritia* 14 (2000) 20–50.

————. 'Canonistica Beneventiana', *Proceedings Munich 1992* MIC Subsidia 10.21–40.

————. The South Italian *Collection in Five Books* and Its Derivates: Maastricht Excerpta' MS 58 (1996) 273–284. Quoted as 'Five Books [1996]'.

————. 'The Organisation, Law and Liturgy of the Western Church, 700–900', *The New Cambridge Medieval History* (7 vols. Cambridge 1995–2005) 2.587–621.

————. 'The South-Italian *Collection in Five Books* and Its Derivates: The Collection of Vallicelliana Tome XXI', *Proceedings San Diego 1988* MIC Subsidia 9.77–91; repr. in idem, *Law and Liturgy in the Latin Church, 5th–12th Centuries* (CSS 457; Aldershot 1994) no. XVI. Quoted as 'Five Books [1992]'.

————. 'The South-Italian Canon Law *Collection in Five Books* and Its Derivates: New Evidence on Its Origins, Diffusion and Use' MS 52 (1990) 278–295; repr. in idem, *Law and Liturgy in the Latin Church, 5th–12th Centuries* (CSS 457; Aldershot 1994) no. XIV. Quoted as 'Five Books [1990]'.

————. 'Rites and Signs of Conciliar Decisions in the Early Middle Ages', *Segni e riti nella chiesa altomedievale occidentale, 11–17 aprile 1985* (2 vols. Settimane 33; Spoleto 1987) 1.207–247; repr. in idem, *Clerics in the Early Middle Ages* (CSS 669; Aldershot 1999) no. IX.

————. 'Review of Schaafer William, *Codices Pseudo-Isidoriani*' *Speculum* 47 (1972) 821.

————. 'The *Turin Collection in Seven Books*: A Poitevin Canonical Collection' *Traditio* 25 (1969) 508–514; repr. in idem, *Law and Liturgy in the Latin Church, 5th–12th Centuries* (CSS 457; Aldershot 1994) no. XVII.

Riché, Pierre. *Abbon de Fleury: un moine savant et combatif (vers 950–1004)* (Turnhout 2004).

Richter, Joachim. 'Stufen pseudo-isidorischer Verfälschung. Untersuchungen zum Konzilsteil der pseudoisidorischen Dekretalen' ZRG Kan. Abt. 64 (1978) 1–72.

Ring, Richard R. 'Review of Stroll, The Medieval Abbey of Farfa' *The Medieval Review* (1999) https://scholarworks.iu.edu/journals/index.php/tmr/article/view/14704.

Robinson, Ian Stuart. 'Introduction', *The Papal Reform of the Eleventh Century: Lives of Pope Leo IX and Pope Gregory VII*, ed. idem (Manchester Medieval Sources; Manchester 2004) 1–95.

———. *The Papacy, 1073–1198: Continuity and Innovation* (Cambridge Medieval Textbooks; Cambridge 1990).

———. *Authority and Resistance in the Investiture Contest: The Polemical Literature of the Late Eleventh Century* (Manchester 1978).

———. 'Periculosus homo: Pope Gregory VII and Episcopal Authority' *Viator* 9 (1978) 103–131.

Röckelein, Hedwig. 'Die Auswirkung der Kanonikerreform des 12. Jahrhunderts auf Kanonissen, Augustinerchorfrauen und Benediktinerinnen', *Institution und Charisma. Festschrift für Gert Melville zum 65. Geburtstag*, ed. Franz J. Felten, Annette Kehnel, and Stefan Weinfurter (Cologne and Vienna 2009) 55–72.

Rolker, Christof. 'Kollisionen und Interferenzen in den Sammlungen des kanonischen Rechts (8.–12. Jahrhundert)', *Kollision und Interferenz normativer Ordnungen im frühen und hohen Mittelalter*, ed. Stefan Esders and Karl Ubl (Vorträge und Forschungen; Ostfildern) [forthcoming].

———. 'The *Collectio Anselmo dedicata*: A Monster in Canon Law History?', *The History of Western Canon Law to 1000*, ed. Wilfried Hartmann and Kenneth Pennington (History of Medieval Canon Law; Washington, D.C.) [forthcoming].

———. 'The *Collectio Britannica* and its Sources: Reviewing the Trustworthiness of a Key Witness of Medieval Papal Letters' ZRG Kan. Abt. 108 (2022) 111–169.

———. 'Bonizo von Sutri, die "Sammlung in zwei Büchern/acht Teilen" und das Gespenst der gregorianischen Zwischensammlung' BMCL 37 (2020) 55–105.

———. 'Monastic Canon Law in the Tenth, Eleventh, and Twelfth Centuries', *The Cambridge History of Medieval Monasticism in the Latin West, Volume 1: Origins to the Eleventh Century*, ed. Alison I. Beach and Isabelle Cochelin (Cambridge 2020) 618–630.

———. 'Die Briefe Papst Pelagius' I.: Handschriften, Editionen und Regesten. Kritische Notiz zur dritten Auflage der Regesta pontificum' DA 75 (2019) 415–447.

———. 'Fournier's Model and Its Merits', *New Discourses in Medieval Canon Law Research: Challenging the Master Narrative*, ed. idem (Medieval Law and Its Practice 28; Leiden and Boston 2019) 4–32.

———. 'The Hot and the Cold Language: Incest Discourses in the Twelfth and Thirteenth Centuries', *Proceedings Toronto 2012* MIC Subsidia 15.651–665.

———. 'Two Models of Incest: Conflict and Confusion in High Medieval Discourse on Kinship and Marriage', *Law and Marriage in Medieval and Early Modern Times: Proceedings of the Eighth Carlsberg Academy Conference on Medieval Legal History*, ed. Peer Andersen, Mia Münster-Swendsen, and Helle Vogt (Copenhagen 2012) 139–159.

———. *Canon Law and the Letters of Ivo of Chartres* (Life and Thought: Fourth Series 76; Cambridge 2010).

———. 'The *Collection in Seventy-Four Titles*: A Monastic Canon Law Collection from Eleventh-Century France', *Readers, Texts and Compilers in the Earlier Middle Ages: Studies in Medieval Canon Law in Honour of Linda Fowler-Magerl*, ed. Kathleen Grace Cushing and Martin Brett (CFC; Aldershot and Farnham 2009) 59–72.

———. 'History and Canon Law in the *Collectio Britannica*: A New Date for London, BL

Add. 8873', *Bishops, Texts and the Use of Canon Law Around 1100: Essays in Honour of Martin Brett*, ed. Bruce Clark Brasington and Kathleen Grace Cushing (CFC; Aldershot and Farnham 2008) 141–152.

———. 'The Earliest Work of Ivo of Chartres: The Case of Ivo's Eucharist Florilegium and the Canon Law Collections Attributed to Him' ZRG Kan. Abt. 93 (2007) 109–127.

———. 'Kings, Bishops and Incest: Extension and Subversion of the Ecclesiastical Marriage Jurisdiction Around 1100', *Discipline and Diversity: Papers Read at the 2005 Summer Meeting and the 2006 Winter Meeting of the Ecclesiastical History Society*, ed. Kate Cooper and Jeremy Gregory (Studies in Church History 43; Woodbridge 2007) 159–168.

———. 'Ivo of Chartres' Pastoral Canon Law' BMCL 25 (2006) 114–145.

———. 'Genesis and Influence of the Canon Law Collection in BN lat. 13368' ZRG Kan. Abt. 91 (2005) 74–105.

Rolker, Christof and Marcel Schawe. 'Das Gutachten Ivos von Chartres zur Krönung Ludwigs VI. Quellenstudium und Edition von ep. 189' *Francia* 34 (2007) 147–157.

Rosenwein, Barbara H., Thomas Head, and Sharon Farmer. 'Monks and Their Enemies: A Comparative Approach' *Speculum* 66 (1991) 764–796.

Roumy, Franck. 'Remarques sur l'œuvre canonique d'Abbon de Fleury', *Abbon, un abbé de l'an mil*, ed. Anne Dufour and Gilette Labory (Bibliothèque d'histoire culturelle du Moyen Âge 6; Turnhout 2008) 311–342.

Russo, Giuseppe. *Tradizione manoscritta di Leges romanae nei codici dei secoli IX e X della Biblioteca capitolare di Modena* (Deputazione di storia patria per le antiche provincie Modenesi: Biblioteca Nova Series 56; Modena 1980).

Ryan, John Joseph. 'Observations on the Pre-Gratian Canonical Collections: Some Recent Work and Present Problems', *Congrès de droit canonique médiéval: Louvain et Bruxelles 22–26 Juillet 1958*, ed. Stephan Kuttner, Henri Wagnon, and Gérard Fransen (Bibliothèque de la revue d'histoire ecclésiastique 33; Leuven 1959) 88–103.

———. *Saint Peter Damiani and His Canonical Sources: A Preliminary Study in the Antecedents of the Gregorian Reform* (PIMS Studies and Texts 2; Toronto 1956).

Sackur, Ernst. 'Der *Dictatus papae* und die Canonsammlung des Deusdedit' NA 18 (1893) 137–153.

———. *Die Cluniacenser in ihrer kirchlichen und allgemeingeschichtlichen Wirksamkeit: bis zur Mitte des elften Jahrhunderts* (2 vols. Halle 1892/94).

———. 'Zu den Streitschriften des Deusdedit und Hugo von Fleury' NA 16 (1891) 347–386.

von Savigny, Friedrich Carl. *Geschichte des römischen Rechts im Mittelalter* (7 vols.; 2nd edition Heidelberg 1834–51); repr. Darmstadt 1961.

Scaravelli, Irene. 'La collezione canonica "Anselmo dedicata": lo status quaestionis nella prospettiva di un edizione critica', *Le storie e la memoria: in onore di Arnold Esch*, ed. Roberto delle Donne and Andrea Zorzi (Florence 2002) 33–52.

Schadt, Hermann. *Die Darstellungen der Arbores consanguinitatis und der Arbores affinitatis. Bildschemata in juristischen Handschriften* (Tübingen 1982).

Scheffer-Boichorst, Paul. *Die Neuordnung der Papstwahl durch Nikolaus II. Texte und Forschungen zur Geschichte des Papstthums im 11. Jahrhundert* (Strasbourg 1879).

Schieffer, Rudolf. 'Die päpstlichen Register vor 1198', *Das Papsttum und das vielgestaltige Italien. Hundert Jahre Italia Pontificia*, ed. Klaus Herbers and Jochen Johrendt (Abh. Akad. Göttingen N.F. 5; Berlin and Boston 2009) 259–274.

———. 'Motu proprio. Über die papstgeschichtliche Wende im 11. Jahrhundert' *Historisches Jahrbuch* 122 (2002) 27–41.

———. 'Burchard von Worms. Ein Reichsbischof und das Königtum', *Bischof Burchard von Worms, 1000–1025*, ed. Wilfried Hartmann (Quellen und Abhandlungen zur mittel-rheinischen Kirchengeschichte 100; Mainz 2000) 29–49.

————. *Die Entstehung des päpstlichen Investiturverbots für den deutschen König* (MGH Schriften 28; Stuttgart 1981).

————. 'Das V. ökumenische Konzil in kanonistischer Überlieferung' ZRG Kan. Abt. 59 (1973) 1–34.

————. 'Spirituales latrones. Zu den Hintergründen der Simonieprozesse in Deutschland zwischen 1069 und 1075' *Historisches Jahrbuch* 92 (1972) 19–60.

————. 'Tomus Gregorii papae. Bemerkungen zur Diskussion um das Register Gregors VII.' *Archiv für Diplomatik* 17 (1971) 169–184.

Schieffer, Theodor. *Die päpstlichen Legaten in Frankreich vom Vertrage von Meersen (870) bis zum Schisma von 1130* (Historische Studien 263; Berlin 1935).

Schilling, Beate. 'Die Kanones des Konzils von Poitiers (1078) (mit Textedition). Ein Versuch' ZRG Kan. Abt. 103 (2017) 70–130.

————. 'Zur Reise Paschalis' II. nach Norditalien und Frankreich 1106 / 1107 (mit Itinerar-anhang und Karte)' *Francia* 28 (2001) 115–158.

————. *Guido von Vienne – Papst Calixt II.* (MGH Schriften 45; Hanover 1998).

Schludi, Ulrich. *Die Entstehung des Kardinalkollegiums. Funktion, Selbstverständnis, Entwicklungsstufen* (Mittelalter-Forschungen 24; Ostfildern 2014).

Schmale, Franz-Josef. 'Synoden Papst Alexanders II. (1061–1073). Anzahl, Termine, Entscheidungen' AHC 11 (1979) 307–338.

————. 'Systematisches zu den Konzilien des Reformpapsttums im 12. Jahrhundert' AHC 6 (1974) 21–39.

Schmidt, Tilmann. *Alexander II. (1061–1073) und die römische Reformgruppe seiner Zeit* (Päpste und Papsttum 11; Stuttgart 1977).

Schmitz, Hermann Joseph. *Die Bussbücher und die Bussdisciplin der Kirche. Nach handschriftlichen Quellen dargestellt* (2 vols; Mainz 1883 and Dusseldorf 1898); repr. Graz 1958.

Schmugge, Ludwig. 'Leo IX, JL 4269: An Attempt at an Edition', *The Two Laws: Studies in Medieval Legal History Dedicated to Stephen Kuttner*, ed. Laurent Mayali and Stephanie A. J. Tibbetts (SMCL 1; Washington, D.C. 1990) 31–39.

————. 'Die Dekretale Papst Leos IX. "Relatum est auribus nostris" (JL 4269) in der kanonistischen Tradition (1052–1234)' ZRG Kan. Abt. 73 (1987) 41–69.

Schneider, Herbert. 'New Wine in Old Skins? Remarks on the *Collectio Burdegalensis*', *Canon Law, Religion and Politics: Liber amicorum Robert Somerville*, ed. Uta-Renate Blumenthal, Anders Winroth, and Peter Landau (Washington, D.C. 2012) 41–55.

————. 'Einleitung', *Die Konzilsordines des Früh- und Hochmittelalters*, ed. idem (MGH Ordines; Hanover 1996) 1–124.

Schneidmüller, Bernd. '"Tausend Jahre sind für dich wie der Tag, der gestern vergangen ist". Die Gründung des Bistums Bamberg 1007', *Das Bistum Bamberg in der Welt des Mittelalters. Vorträge der Ringvorlesung des Zentrums für Mittelalterstudien der Otto-Friedrich-Universität Bamberg im Sommersemester 2007*, ed. Christine van Eickels und Klaus van Eickels (Bamberger interdisziplinäre Mittelalterstudien. Vorträge und Vorlesungen 1; Bamberg 2007) 15–32.

Schoenig, Steven A. 'An Erased Canon and Roman Law in the *Collectio Britannica*', *The Making and Influence of Canon Law in the Long Twelfth Century (c. 1073–1234)*, ed. Travis Baker [forthcoming].

————. *Bonds of Wool: The Pallium and Papal Power in the Middle Ages* (SMCL 15; Washington, D.C. 2016).

Scholz, Bernhard W. 'Two Forged Charters from the Abbey of Westminster and Their Relationship with St. Denis' *English Historical Review* 76 (1961) 466–478.

Scholz, Sebastian. *Transmigration und Translation. Studien zum Bistumswechsel der Bischöfe von der Spätantike bis zum Hohen Mittelalter* (Kölner historische Abhandlungen 37; Cologne, Weimar, and Vienna 1992).

Schon, Karl Georg. *Rezeptionstabelle* ([ca. 2006]), http://www.pseudoisidor.mgh.de/pdf/000_Rezeptionstabelle.pdf.

———. *Die Capitula Angilramni. Eine prozessrechtliche Fälschung Pseudoisidors* (MGH Studien und Texte 39; Hanover 2006).

———. 'Eine Redaktion der pseudoisidorischen Dekretalen aus der Zeit der Fälschung' DA 34 (1978) 500–511

———. 'Exzerpte aus den Akten von Chalkedon bei Pseudoisidor und in der 74-Titel-Sammlung' DA 32 (1976) 546–557.

Schramm, Percy Ernst. *Kaiser, Rom und Renovatio. Studien zur Geschichte des römischen Erneuersgedankens vom Ende des karolingischen Reiches bis zum Investiturstreit* (2 vols. Studien der Bibliothek Warburg 17; Leipzig 1929).

Schreiber, Georg. *Kurie und Kloster im 12. Jahrhundert. Studien zur Privilegierung, Verfassung und besonders zum Eigenkirchenwesen der Vorfranziskanischen Orden vornehmlich auf Grund der Papsturkunden von Paschalis II. bis auf Lucius III. (1099–1181)* (2 vols. Kirchenrechtliche Abhandlungen 65–68; Stuttgart 1910); repr. Amsterdam 1965.

Schreiner, Klaus. 'Observantia regularis. Normbildung, Normkontrolle und Normwandel im Mönchtum des hohen und späten Mittelalters', *Prozesse der Normbildung und Normveränderung im mittelalterlichen Europa*, ed. Doris Ruhe, Karl-Heinz Spieß, and Ralf-Gunnar Werlich (Stuttgart 2000) 275–313.

Schrör, Matthias. *Metropolitangewalt und papstgeschichtliche Wende* (Historische Studien 494; Husum 2009).

Schulte, Johann Friedrich. 'Iter Gallicum' Sb. Akad. Wien 59.4 (1868) 355–496.

———. *Das katholische Kirchenrecht* (2 vols. Giessen 1856–60).

Sdralek, Max. *Wolfenbüttler Fragmente. Analekten zur Kirchengeschichte des Mittelalters* (Kirchengeschichtliche Studien 1.2; Münster 1891).

Seckel, Emil. *Die erste Zeile Pseudoisidors, die Hadriana-Rezension In nomine domini incipit praefatio libri huius und die Geschichte der Invokationen in den Rechtsquellen. Aus dem Nachlaß mit Ergänzungen hrsg. von Horst Fuhrmann* (Sb. Akad. Berlin 1959.4; Berlin 1959).

———. 'Studien zu Benedictus Levita VIII (Studie VIII, Schlußteil V), ergänzt und aus dem Nachlass herausgegeben von Josef Juncker' ZRG Kan. Abt. 24 (1935) 1–112

———. 'Der Titel einer Canones-Sammlung in Geheimschrift' NA 41 (1919) 733–738.

———. 'Pseudoisidor', *Real-Encyklopädie für protestantische Theologie und Kirche* (24 vols. Leipzig 1896–1913) 16.265–307.

———. 'Zu den Acten der Triburer Synode von 895' NA 18 (1893) 367–408.

Sedano Rueda, Joaquin. 'The Manuscript Tradition of the Collection in Ten Parts', *Proceedings Esztergom 2008* MIC Subsidia 14.261–272.

———. *La colección canónica en 10 partes* (diss. iur. can.; Pontificia universitas Sanctae Crucis, Rome 2008).

Seibert, Hubertus. *Abtserhebungen zwischen Rechtsnorm und Rechtswirklichkeit. Formen der Nachfolgeregelung in lothringischen und schwäbischen Klöstern der Salierzeit (1024–1125)* (Quellen und Abhandlungen zur mittelrheinischen Kirchengeschichte 78; Mainz 1995).

———. 'Eine unbekannte Überlieferung der 74-Titel-Sammlung aus Rheinau', *Deus qui mutat tempora. Menschen und Institutionen im Wandel des Mittelalters. Festschrift für Alfons Becker zu seinem fünfundsechzigsten Geburtstag*, ed. Ernst-Dieter Hehl, Hubertus Seibert, and Franz Staab (Sigmaringen 1987) 87–100.

Servatius, Carlo. *Paschalis II. (1099–1118). Studien zu seiner Person und seiner Politik* (Päpste und Papsttum 14; Stuttgart 1979).

Sharpe, Richard. 'The Dating of the Quadripartitus Again', *English Law Before Magna Carta: Felix Liebermann and Die Gesetze der Angelsachsen*, ed. Stefan Jurasinski, Lisi Oliver, and Andrew Rabin (Medieval Law and Its Practice 8; Leiden and Boston 2010) 81–93.

Sickel, Theodor. *Das Privilegium Otto I. für die römische Kirche vom Jahre 962* (Innsbruck 1883).

Sieben, Hermann Josef. *Studien zum ökumenischen Konzil. Definitionen und Begriffe, Tagebücher und Augustinus-Rezeption* (Konziliengeschichte. Untersuchungen; Paderborn 2010).

⸻. *Die Konzilsidee des lateinischen Mittelalters (847–1378)* (Konziliengeschichte. Untersuchungen 2; Paderborn 1984).

Smalley, Beryl. 'Ecclesiastical Attitudes to Novelty *c.* 1100–*c.* 1250', *Church, Society and Politics*, ed. Derek Baker (Studies in Church History 12; Oxford 1975) 113–131; repr. in eadem, *Studies in Medieval Thought and Learning: From Abelard to Wycliff* (History Series 6; London 1981) 97–115.

de Smet, Joseph Marie. *De heilige Jan van Waasten en de Gregoriaansche hervorming in het bisdom Terwaan* (Mémoire de licence; Université catholique de Louvain, Leuven 1943).

Smith, Julia M. H. *Province and Empire: Brittany and the Carolingians* (Life and Thought: Fourth Series 18; Cambridge and New York 1992).

Sohm, Rudolph. *Das altkatholische Kirchenrecht und das Dekret Gratians. Festschrift für A. Wach* (Munich 1918).

Somerville, Robert. 'Chaos to Order: Clermont 1095 to Lateran IV, 1215', *Vergentis* 3 (2016) 267–281

⸻. *Pope Urban II's Council of Piacenza* (Oxford 2011).

⸻. 'Calixtus II and Canon Law', *'Panta rei': studi dedicati a Manlio Bellomo*, ed. Orazio Condorelli (5 vols. Rome 2004), 5.235–243.

⸻. 'Cardinal Deusdedit's *Collectio canonum* at Benevento', *Ritual, Text and Law: Studies in Medieval Canon Law and Liturgy Presented to Roger E. Reynolds*, ed. Richard F. Gyug and Kathleen Grace Cushing (CFC; Aldershot 2004) 281–292.

⸻. 'Canon Law, Inspired Law, and Papal Authority', *Neṭi'ot le-David: Jubilee Volume for David Weiss Halivni* (Jerusalem 2004) 119–134.

⸻. 'Papal Excerpts in Arsenal MS 713B: Alexander II and Urban II', *Proceedings Munich 1992* MIC Subsidia 10.169–184.

⸻. 'Pope Nicholas I and John Scottus Eriugena: JE 2833' ZRG Kan. Abt. 83 (1997) 67–85.

⸻ (in collaboration with Stephan Kuttner). *Pope Urban II, the* Collectio Britannica, *and the Council of Melfi (1089)* (Oxford 1996).

⸻. 'The Councils of Gregory VII' *Studi Gregoriani* 13 (1989) 33–53.

⸻. 'The Beginning of Alexander III's Pontificate: *Aeterna et incommutabilis* and Scotland', *Miscellanea Rolando Bandinelli Papa Alessandro III*, ed. Filippo Liotta (Siena 1986) 367–368; repr. in idem, *Papacy, Councils and Canon Law in the 11th–12th Centuries* (CSS 312; Aldershot 1990) no. XVIII.

⸻. 'Mercy and Justice in the Early Months of Urban II's Pontificate', *Chiesa, diritto e ordinamento della «Societas Christiana» nei secoli XI e XII: atti Mendola 1983* (Miscellanea 11; Milan 1986) 138–154; repr. in idem, *Papacy, Councils and Canon Law in the 11th–12th Centuries* (CSS 312; Aldershot 1990) no. IV.

⸻. 'The Councils of Pope Calixtus II and the *Collection in Ten Parts*' BMCL 11 (1981) 80–86; repr. in idem, *Papacy, Councils and Canon Law in the 11th–12th Centuries* (CSS 312; Aldershot 1990) no. XI.

————. 'Anselm of Lucca and Wibert of Ravenna' BMCL 10 (1980) 1–13; repr. in idem, *Papacy, Councils and Canon Law in the 11th–12th Centuries* (CSS 312; Aldershot 1990) no. III.

————. 'Cardinal Stephan of St. Grisogono: Some Remarks on Legates and Legatine Councils in the Eleventh Century', *Law, Church, and Society: Essays in Honor of Stephan Kuttner*, ed. Kenneth Pennington and Robert Somerville ([Philadelphia] 1977) 157–166; repr. in idem, *Papacy, Councils and Canon Law in the 11th–12th Centuries* (CSS 312; Aldershot 1990) no. II.

————. *Pope Alexander III and the Council of Tours (1163)* (Berkeley 1977).

————. 'Pope Innocent II and the Study of Roman Law' *Revue des études islamiques* 44 (1976) 105–114; repr. in idem, *Papacy, Councils and Canon Law in the 11th–12th Centuries* (CSS 312; Aldershot 1990) no. XIV.

————. 'The Council of Clermont (1095), and Latin Christian Society' *Archivum Historiae Pontificiae* 12 (1974) 55–90; repr. in idem, *Papacy, Councils and Canon Law in the 11th–12th Centuries* (CSS 312; Aldershot 1990) no. VII.

————. 'The Case Against Berengar of Tours: A New Text' *Studi Gregoriani* 9 (1972) 55–75; repr. in idem, *Papacy, Councils and Canon Law in the 11th–12th Centuries* (CSS 312; Aldershot 1990) no. I.

————. *The Councils of Urban II, vol. 1: Decreta Claromontensia* (AHC. Supplementum 1; Amsterdam 1972).

————. 'Prolegomena' ibid. 3–41; repr. in idem, *Papacy, Councils and Canon Law in the 11th–12th Centuries* (CSS 312; Aldershot 1990) no. VI.

————. 'The Council of Pisa, 1135: A Re-Examination of the Evidence for the Canons' *Speculum* 45 (1970) 98–114.

————. 'The French Councils of Urban II: Some Basic Considerations' *Archivum Historiae Pontificiae* 2 (1970) 56–65; repr. in idem, *Papacy, Councils and Canon Law in the 11th–12th Centuries* (Variorum Collected Studies Series 312; Aldershot 1990) no. VII.

Somerville, Robert and Bruce Clark Brasington. *Prefaces to Canon Law Books in Latin Christianity: Selected Translations, 500–1245* (New Haven and London 1998).

Somerville, Robert and Hartmut Zapp, 'An "Eighth Book" of the Collection in Seven Books', *Grundlagen des Rechts. Festschrift für Peter Landau zum 65. Geburtstag*, ed. Richard H. Helmholz, Paul Mikat, Jörg Müller, and Michael Stolleis (Rechts- und Staatswissenschaftliche Veröffentlichungen der Görres-Gesellschaft N.F. 91; Paderborn, Munich, Vienna, and Zurich 2000) 163–177.

Southern, Richard William. *The Making of the Middle Ages* (London 1953); repr. 1968.

Sprandel, Rolf. *Ivo von Chartres und seine Stellung in der Kirchengeschichte* (Pariser historische Studien 1; Stuttgart 1962).

Steckel, Sita. *Kulturen des Lehrens im Früh- und Hochmittelalter. Autorität, Wissenskonzepte und Netzwerke von Gelehrten* (Norm und Struktur 39; Cologne, Weimar, and Vienna 2011).

Stiernon, Daniel. *Constantinople IV* (Histoire des conciles œcuméniques 5; Paris 1967).

Stadelmaier, Michael. *Die Collectio Sangermanensis XXI titulorum. Eine systematische Kanonessammlung der frühen Karolingerzeit: Studien und Edition* (Frankfurt 2004)

Stöckly, Doris and Detlev Jasper. 'Einleitung', *De excommunicatis vitandis, de reconciliatione lapsorum et de fontibus iuris ecclesiastici (libellus X)*, ed. iidem (MGH Fontes iuris 15; Hanover 2000) 1–69.

Stoller, Michael E. *Schism in the Reform Papacy: The Documents and Councils of the Antipopes, 1061–1121* (PhD thesis; Columbia University, New York 1985).

Stratmann, Martina. 'Zur Wirkungsgeschichte Hinkmars von Reims' *Francia* 22.1 (1995) 1–43.

Strupp, Sabine. *Die kanonistischen Quellen des 'Liber de unitate ecclesia conservanda'. Zu den*

Vorlagen und der Arbeitsweise eines hochmittelalterlichen Traktatverfassers (Magisterarbeit; Johann Wolfgang Goethe-Universität, Frankfurt 2014).

Suckale-Redlefsen, Gude. *Die Handschriften des 8. bis 11. Jahrhunderts der Staatsbibliothek Bamberg* (2 vols. Katalog der illuminierten Handschriften der Staatsbibliothek Bamberg 1–2; Wiesbaden 2004).

Summerlin, Danica. 'Using the "Old Law" in Twelfth-Century Decretal Collections', *New Discourses in Medieval Canon Law Research: Challenging the Master Narrative*, ed. Christof Rolker (Medieval Law and Its Practice 28; Leiden and Boston 2019) 145–169.

———. *The Canons of the Third Lateran Council of 1179: Their Origins and Reception* (Life and Thought: Fourth Series 116; Cambridge 2019).

Sydow, Jürgen. 'Untersuchungen zur kurialen Verwaltungsgeschichte im Zeitalter des Reformpapsttums' DA 11 (1954/55) 18–73.

Szabó-Bechstein, Brigitte. *Libertas ecclesiae. Ein Schlüsselbegriff des Investiturstreits und seine Vorgeschichte. 4.–11. Jahrhundert* (Studi Gregoriani 12; Rome 1985).

Szuromi, Szabolcs Anzelm. *Anselm of Lucca as a Canonist* (Adnotationes in ius canonicum 34; Frankfurt 2006).

Tangl, Georgine. *Die Teilnehmer an den allgemeinen Konzilien des Mittelalters* (Weimar 1922).

Tangl, Michael. 'Studien zur Neuausgabe der Bonifatius-Briefe' NA 40 (1916) 639–790 and 41 (1919) 23–101; repr. in idem, *Das Mittelalter in Quellenkunde und Diplomatik. Ausgewählte Schriften* (2 vols. Graz 1966) 1.60–240.

Tardif, Adolphe. 'Une collection canonique poitevine' NRHDFE 21 (1897) 149–216.

Taylor, Rebecca. *JL 5409: A Study with Special Attention to Priests' Sons* (M.A. essay; Columbia University, New York 1990).

Tejero, Eloy. '"Ratio" y jerarquía de fuentes canónicas en la *Caesaraugustana*', *Hispania Christiana: estudios en honor del Prof. Dr. José Orlandis Rovira en su septuagesimo aniversario*, ed. Josep-Ignasi Saranyana and Eloy Tejero (Pamplona 1988) 303–322.

———. 'El matrimonio en la *Collectio Caesaraugustana*', *Proceedings Cambridge 1984* MIC. Subsidia 8.115–134.

Tellenbach, Gerd. *The Church in Western Europe from the Tenth to the Early Twelfth Century* (Cambridge Medieval Textbooks; Cambridge 1993); original: *Die westliche Kirche vom 10. bis zum frühen 12. Jahrhundert* (Die Kirche in ihrer Geschichte 2.1; Göttingen 1988).

———. '"Gregorianische Reform". Kritische Besinnungen', *Reich und Kirche vor dem Investiturstreit. Vorträge beim wissenschaftlichen Kolloquium aus Anlaß des 80. Geburtstags von Gerd Tellenbach*, ed. Karl Schmid (Sigmaringen 1985) 99–113.

Theiner, Augustin. *Disquisitiones criticae in praecipuas canonum et decretalium collectiones: seu syllogus Gallandianae dissertationum de vetustis canonum collectionibus continuatio* (Rome 1836).

Thier, Andreas. *Hierarchie und Autonomie. Regelungstraditionen der Bischofsbestellung in der Geschichte des kirchlichen Wahlrechts bis 1140* (Recht im ersten Jahrtausend 1; Frankfurt 2011).

Thurn, Hans. *Bestand bis zur Säkularisierung. Erwerbungen und Zugänge bis 1803* (Die Handschriften der Universitätsbibliothek Würzburg 5; Wiesbaden 1994).

Tierney, Brian. *Foundations of the Conciliar Theory: The Contribution of the Medieval Canonists from Gratian to the Great Schism* (Studies in the History of Christian Thought 92; Cambridge 1955); repr. London 1968.

Tosti, Luigi. *Storia della Badia di Montecassino divisa in libri nove, ed illustrata di note e documenti* (3 vols. Naples 1842–43).

Toubert, Pierre. *Les structures du Latium médiéval: le Latium méridional et la Sabine du IXe siècle à la fin du XIIe siècle* (2 vols. Bibliothèque des Écoles françaises d'Athènes et de Rome 221; Rome 1973).

Truhlář, Josef. *Catalogus codicum manu scriptorum latinorum qui in C. R. Bibliotheca publica atque Universitatis pragensis asservantur* (2 vols. Prague 1905/06).

Turner, Cuthbert. 'The "Liber ecclesiasticorum dogmatum": Supplenda' *Journal of Theological Studies* 8 (1906) 103–114.

———. 'The "Liber ecclesiasticorum dogmatum" Attributed to Gennadius' *Journal of Theological Studies* 7 (1905) 78–99.

Ubl, Karl. *Inzestverbot und Gesetzgebung. Die Konstruktion eines Verbrechens (300–1100)* (Millenium-Studien 20; Berlin and New York 2008).

Ullmann, Walter. *Gelasius I. (492–496). Das Papsttum an der Wende der Spätantike zum Mittelalter* (Päpste und Papsttum 18; Stuttgart 1981).

———. '"Nos si aliquid incompetenter …":' Some Observations on the Register Fragments of Leo IV in the Collectio Britannica' *Ephemerides iuris canonici* 9 (1953) 3–11; repr. in idem, *The Church and the Law in the Earlier Middle Ages: Selected Essays* (CSS 38; London 1975) no. VII.

Unger, Veronika. 'Einleitung' *Papstregesten 872–882 (Johannes VIII.)* (J. F. Böhmer, Regesta imperii Abt. I, Band 4, Teil 3; Vienna, Cologne, and Weimar 2013) VII–XVI.

Vacca, Salvatore. *Prima sedes a nemine iudicatur: genesi e sviluppo storico dell'assioma fino al Decreto di Graziano* (Miscellanea historiae pontificiae 61; Rome 1993).

Vones, Ludwig. 'Legation und Konzilien. Der päpstliche Legat Richard von Marseille und die konziliare Tätigkeit auf der Iberischen Halbinsel', *Das begrenzte Papsttum. Spielräume päpstlichen Handelns. Legaten – "delegierte Richter" – Grenzen*, ed. Klaus Herbers, Fernando López Alsina, and Frank Engel (Abh. Akad. Göttingen N.F. 25; Berlin 2013) 213–236.

———. 'Kardinal Rainer von San Clemente als päpstlicher Legat in Katalonien und Südwestfrankreich. Politische und diplomatische Aspekte', *Aspects diplomatiques des voyages pontificaux*, ed. Bernard Barbiche and Rolf Große (Studien und Dokumente zur Gallia Pontificia 6; Bonn 2009) 203–218.

———. *Die "Historia Compostellana" und die Kirchenpolitik des nordwestspanischen Raumes 1070–1130. Ein Beitrag zur Geschichte der Beziehungen zwischen Spanien und dem Papsttum zu Beginn des 12. Jahrhunderts* (Kölner historische Abhandlungen 29; Cologne 1980).

Waelkens, Laurent and Dirk van den Auweele. 'La collection de Thérouanne en IX livres à l'abbaye de Saint-Pierre-au-Mont-Blandin: le Codex Gandavensis 235' *Sacris erudiri* 24 (1980) 115–153.

Waldman, Thomas G. 'Charters and Influences from Saint-Denis, c. 1000–1070', *Bury St Edmunds and the Norman Conquest*, ed. Tom Licence (Woodbridge 2014) 22–30.

Ward, John O. 'Some Principles of Rhetorical Historiography in the Twelfth Century', *Classical Rhetoric and Medieval Historiography*, ed. Ernst Breisach (Studies in Medieval Culture 19; Kalamazoo, Mich. 1985) 103–165.

Wasner, Francisco. 'De consecratione inthronizatione coronatione summi pontificis' *Apollinaris* 8 (1935) 86–125, 249–299, and 428–439.

Wasserschleben, Friedrich Wilhelm Hermann. *Beiträge zur Geschichte der vorgratianischen Kirchenrechtsquellen* (Leipzig 1839).

Wei, John. 'Of Scholasticism and Canon Law: Narratives Old and New', *New Discourses in Medieval Canon Law Research: Challenging the Master Narrative*, ed. Christof Rolker (Medieval Law and Its Practice 28; Leiden and Boston 2019) 105–126.

———. *Gratian the Theologian* (SMCL 13; Washington, D.C. 2016).

———. 'A Twelfth-Century Treatise on Charity: The Tract "Vt avtem hoc evidenter" of the Sentence Collection *Devs itaqve svmme atqve ineffabiliter bonvs*' *MS* 72 (2012) 1–50.

———. 'Gratian and the School of Laon' *Traditio* 64 (2009) 279–322.

Weigand, Rudolf. 'Mittelalterliche Texte. Gregor I., Burchard und Gratian' ZRG Kan. Abt. 84 (1998) 330–344.

———. 'Burchardauszüge in Dekrethandschriften und ihre Verwendung bei Rufin als Paleae im Dekret Gratians' AKKR 158 (1989) 429–451.

Weimar, Peter. 'Die legistische Literatur der Glossatorenzeit', *Handbuch der Quellen und Literatur der neueren europäischen Privatrechtsgeschichte, Band 1: Mittelalter (1100–1500). Die gelehrten Rechte und die Gesetzgebung*, ed. Helmut Coing (Munich 1973) 129–260.

———. 'Zur Entstehung des sogenannten Tübinger Rechtsbuchs und der *Exceptiones legum Romanarum des Petrus*', *Studien zur europäischen Rechtsgeschichte. Helmut Coing zum 28. Februar 1972 von seinen Schülern und Mitarbeitern*, ed. Walter Wilhelm (Frankfurt 1972) 1–24.

Werckmeister, Jean. 'The Reception of the Church Fathers in Canon Law', *The Reception of the Church Fathers in the West: From the Carolingians to the Maurists*, ed. Iréna Dorota Backus (2 vols. Leiden 1997) 1.51–81.

West, Charles. 'Pope Leo of Bourges, Clerical Immunity and the Early Medieval Secular' *Early Medieval Europe* 29 (2021) 86–108.

Wetzstein, Thomas. 'Noverca omnium ecclesiarum. Der römische Universalepiskopat des Hochmittelalters im Spiegel der päpstlichen Finanzgeschichte', *Rom und die Regionen. Studien zur Homogenisierung der lateinischen Kirche im Hochmittelalter*, ed. Jochen Johrendt and Harald Müller (Abh. Akad. Göttingen N.F. 19; Berlin 2012) 13–62.

Williams, Schafer. *Codices Pseudo-Isidoriani: A Paleographico-Historical Study* (MIC Subsidia 3; New York 1971).

Winroth, Anders. 'Where Gratian Slept: The Life and Death of the Father of Canon Law' ZRG Kan. Abt. 99 (2013) 105–128.

———. *The Making of Gratian's Decretum* (Life and Thought: Fourth Series 49; Cambridge 2000).

Wojtowytsch, Myron. 'Die Kanones *Henrici regis*. Bemerkungen zur römischen Synode vom Februar 1014', *Papsttum, Kirche und Recht im Mittelalter. Festschrift für Horst Fuhrmann zum 65. Geburtstag*, ed. Hubert Mordek (Tübingen 1991) 155–168.

Wolf von Glanvell, Victor. 'Einleitung', *Die Kanonessammlung des Kardinals Deusdedit, I. Die Kanonessammlung selbst*, ed. idem (Paderborn 1905) IX–LIV.

Wolter, Heinz. *Die Synoden im Reichsgebiet und in Reichsitalien von 916 bis 1056* (Paderborn and Munich 1988).

Wolter, Udo. 'Die "consuetudo" im kanonischen Recht bis zum Ende des 13. Jahrhunderts', *Gewohnheitsrecht und Rechtsgewohnheit im Mittelalter* (Schriften zur Europäischen Rechts- und Verfassungsgeschichte 6; Berlin 1992) 87–116.

Wood, Susan. *The Proprietary Church in the Medieval West* (Oxford 2006).

Wormald, Patrick. 'Laga Eadwardi: The Textus Roffensis and Its Context' *Anglo-Norman Studies* 17 (1995) 244–266; repr. (with corrections) in idem, *Legal Culture in the Early Medieval West: Law as Text, Image and Experience* (London 1999) 115–138.

Zafarana, Zelina. 'Ricerche sul *Liber de unitate ecclesiae conservanda*' *Studi medievali, serie terza* 7 (1966) 617–700.

———. 'Sul *conventus* del clero romano nel maggio 1082' *Studi medievali, serie terza* 7 (1966) 399–403.

Zechiel-Eckes, Klaus. *Die erste Dekretale. Der Brief Papst Siricius' an Bischof Himerius von Tarragona vom Jahr 385 (JK 255). Aus dem Nachlass herausgegeben von Detlev Jasper* (MGH Studien und Texte 55; Hanover 2013).

———. 'Quellenkritische Anmerkungen zur *Collectio Anselmo dedicata*', *Recht und Gericht in Kirche und Welt um 900*, ed. Annette Grabowsky and Wilfried Hartmann (Schriften des Historischen Kollegs. Kolloquien 69; Munich 2007) 49–65.

———. 'Der "unbeugsame" Exterminator? Isidorus Mercator und der Kampf gegen den Chorepiskopat', *Scientia veritatis. Festschrift für Hubert Mordek zum 65. Geburtstag*, ed. Oliver Münsch and Thomas L. Zotz (Ostfildern 2004) 175–190.

———. 'Ein Blick in Pseudoisidors Werkstatt. Studien zum Entstehungsprozeß der falschen Dekretalen. Mit einem exemplarischen editorischen Anhang (Pseudo-Julius an die orientalischen Bischöfe, JK †196)' *Francia* 28/1 (2001) 37–90.

———. 'Verecundus oder Pseudoisidor? Zur Genese der Excerptiones de gestis Chalcedonensis concilii' DA 56 (2000) 413–446.

———. 'Eine Mailänder Redaktion des Kirchenrechtssammlung Bischof Anselms II. von Lucca (1073–1086)' ZRG Kan. Abt. 81 (1995) 130–147.

———. *Die Concordia canonum des Cresconius. Studien und Edition* (2 vols. Freiburger Beiträge zur mittelalterlichen Geschichte 5; Frankfurt 1992).

Zey, Claudia. 'Entstehung und erste Konsolidierung. Das Kardinalskollegium zwischen 1049 und 1143', *Geschichte des Kardinalats im Mittelalter*, ed. Jürgen Dendorfer and Ralf Lützelschwab (Päpste und Papsttum 39; Stuttgart 2011) 63–94.

———. 'Die Augen des Papstes. Zu Eigenschaften und Vollmachten päpstlicher Legaten', *Römisches Zentrum und kirchliche Peripherie. Das universale Papsttum als Bezugspunkt der Kirchen von den Reformpäpsten bis zu Innozenz III.*, ed. Jochen Johrendt and Harald Müller (Abh. Akad. Göttingen N.F. 2; Berlin 2008) 77–108.

Zimmermann, Harald. *Papstabsetzungen des Mittelalters* (Graz, Vienna, and Cologne 1968).

Indices

Canonical Collections

Collections known by the numbers of chapters, titles, or books they are composed of, are found under their conventional sigla here. For all collections, but above all those preserved in only one manuscript, see also the manuscript index.

2L/8P = Collection in Two Books / Eight Parts, 203n85, 232–33, 457; and Anselm, 206–7, 230, 232–33; and *Avellana?*, 233n267; and Bonizo, 206, 233; and Burchard, 80n285; and Deusdedit, 206–7, 233; and Pseudo-Isidore, 206

3L = Collection in Three Books, 58n182, 238n287, 280–81, 404n430, 419; and Anselm, 238; and Deusdedit, 218n188, 225; and Gratian, 73, 352n236, 419; and Gregory VII, 190n19; on ecclesiastical titles, 57n175; on excommunication, 203n85; on papal elections, 225; patristic content, 352n236

4L = Collection in Four Books, 125n176, 127, 159n319, 169, 179, 226n425, 283n487, 288, 362, 363, 371, 377, 451n135; and *74T*, 123n168, 127, 138n224, 159n319, 183, 362n274; and Alger, 363; and *Panormia*, 222n207, 363–64, 371, 374n317

5L = Collection in Five Books, 104–21; and (Vatican) *9L*, 109–10, 114; and *74T*, 117–19; and Burchard, 27, 111–17, 117–18; and Cresconius, 105n78, 110; derivatives of, 105–6, 117–19; diagrams in, 111, 113; glossed, 106; Henry II and, 27; prefaces (several), 106

7L (Turin) = Turin Collection in Seven Books, 256–67; and *74T*, 134, 173n377; and Deusdedit, 224, 235n273; and Gregory VII, 190–91; on monks and penance, 173n377

7L (Vienna) = Vienna Collection in Seven Books, 54n162, 218n188, 237n280; additions to, 251; and Bonizo, 251; and Burchard, 80n285; and *Polycarpus*, 280; on monks and penance, 173n377

9L (San Pietro) = San Pietro Collection in Nine Books, 54n162, 57n175, 204n85, 225n225, 280, 404n430; on investiture, 283n487; and Gregory VII, 190n19

9L (Vatican) = Vatican Collection in Nine Books, 57n175, 67n224, 109, 113–14, 183; and *5L*, 109–10, 114; and *Herovalliana*, 109; and Montecassino dossier, 119–20; Greek Fathers in, 16n64

9L (Wolfenbüttel) = Wolfenbüttel Collection in Nine Books, 178, 284, 405n437; and *Atrebatensis*, 177n394, 266–67; and *10P*, 178–79; on investiture, 266–67

10P = Collection in Ten Parts, 167n349, 177–82, 183, 285, 288, 373n312; on investiture, 180, 266–67

10P (Cologne) = Cologne Collection in Ten Parts, 313n100

12P = Collection in Twelve Parts, 44–72, 82, 188n11; and *Anselmo dedicata*, 38–39, 42, 45–52, 52–60, 70; and Bernold of Konstanz, 44; and *Dacheriana*, 38n88, 39n94, 40; and *Hibernensis*, 40, 45; and Pseudo-Isidore, 38, 52–59; and Regino, 39–40; opening canons, 42, 53–58, 59; versions of, 36–37, 39, 41–44, 68n234, 69

13L (Berlin) = Berlin Collection in Thirteen Books, 176n393, 256–67; and Gregory VII, 190n19, 191; on investiture, 283n487; on monks and penance, 173n377, 173n379

13L (Vatican) = Vatican Collection in Thirteen Books, 173–76, 229n239, 237n280; and *13L* (Berlin), 250n390; and *Ambrosiana II*, 179n405; and Anselm, 229n239, 237, 240–41; and *Polycarpus*, 280; on papal elections, 240–41

17L = Collection in Seventeen Books, 169–73, 257, 258n390, 260

20L = Collection in Twenty Books, 168–69

22C = Collection in 22 Chapters, 28n36

72C = Collection in 72 Chapters (Vallicelliana T. XVIII), 109–10

Councils

Manuscripts

Papal Letters

The numbers are those of the second edition of Jaffé's *Regesta pontificum*. Letters and fragments not calendared here are referred to by numbers of the *Gallia pontificia*, *Italia pontificia*, Böhmer-Zimmermann, the Walter-Holtzmann-Kartei (WH), Potthast's *Regesta*, or the third edition of Jaffé's *Regesta pontificum*. For texts found in none of these works, the incipit is provided; for more famous works like the *Decretum Gelasianum*, conventional titles are added.

General Index

Persons of the same name are sorted in this sequence: biblical figures, popes, cardinals, archbishops, bishops, other clergy, emperors, kings, other laypeople. Eponymous kings, emperors, and popes are arranged chronologically. In the case of religious houses, all forms of 'Saint' are ignored (Saint-Denis is found after 'Decretum Gelasianum', 'Sankt Emmeran' just before 'emperor', and so on).

61, 150; and metropolitans, 20–22, 24–26, 96–98, 308, 329–30; and monastic houses, 92, 95–99, 103, 141–45, 161–62, 182–83, 358–59, 436; depositions of, 95–97, 265; elections of, 191–92, 226–27, 247, 329, 381–82. *See also* investiture; metropolitans; primacy

Bishops, in canon law, 19, 20–24, 33, 52–59, 84, 86; accusations against, 21–22, 50, 62, 86, 131, 330, 333, 360–61; and *chorepiscopi*, 48, 132; and ecclesiastical property, 86, 130, 161, 267–68; and kings / emperors, 21, 23, 59–62, 81, 150; and metropolitans, 20, 22, 45–51, 293; and monks, 33, 86, 91–92, 96, 98–99, 130, 151, 161, 172; and pope, 20–32, 228; 'anti-episcopal' collections?, 48–52, 122, 128n193, 163; as 'the eyes of the Lord', 131; 'bishops of the first see', 48, 52, 56–59, 80; canonical collections for bishops, 14, 32–33; consecration of, 258–62; depositions of, 22, 218, 273–74; elections of, 21, 54n161, 101, 160, 176, 236, 240 (Anselm), 255 (Bonizo), 270, 273 (Polycarpus), 325 (Tripartita), 333–34 (Ivo); 'episcopal arrogance', 91, 100–1; episcopal capitularies, 3, 10, 30, 31n51; episcopal character of canon law, 21–24; ordination of, 106, 172, 228, 238, 250, 255 258, 259t4, 260–62, 270, 288, 365; translations of, 93n36, 102, 110, 273, 276, 385n361

Bobbio, monastery, 263–64

Boniface, saint: in *Britannica*, 296, 302–3, 312–13

Bonizo of Sutri, bishop, 190–91, 235–36, 246–47, 253–55; individual works of (apart from *De vita*): *De parentela*, 249n338, 251n344; *Liber ad amicum*, 247, 249n338, 250, 252, 254; *Liber in Ugonem*, 247; *Paradisus*, 252; tract on investiture, 247. *See also the index to canonical collections*

Boso, cardinal, 251

Bourges, church, 144, 265, 405; primacy claims, 263, 405

Brandt, Sebastian, 387

Brett, Martin, x, xi, 35n72, 193n33, 196n48, 246n313, 309, 311, 313, 341–42, 400, 402–3

Breviary of Alaric, *see* Roman law

Brittany, *see* Dol; Tours

Burchard of Worms, 24, 28, 33; and Egilbert of Freising, 27n28, 37; and Olbert, 84; and Willigis of Mainz, 24. *See also the index to canonical collections*

Caesarius of Arles, 110

Calixtus II, pope (Guido of Vienne), 281, 428–29, 443, 448

Cambrai and Arras, *see* Arras

Canon law, 1–19; and theology, 3, 172, 181, 249–51, 287–89, 327, 386–87, 389–91, 401, 416–20, 456; contradictions in, 11–12, 64, 71–72, 93, 132, 255–57, 278, 288, 317, 330, 355–61, 365–66, 368, 374–77, 380–81, 387, 392–95, 418–19, 457–60; dispensation, 67, 251, 271, 275–76, 331, 352–54, 326, 454; legal change, 80–83, 93, 101–2, 248–49, 376–77, 384–85, 459; 'mercy and justice' in, 12, 251, 256–57, 356–61, 365–66

Canon law, meaning of individual terms: *agiographa*, 4–6; *auctoritas*, 2, 4–6, 49n142, 50n150, 391, 12n45, 388–95, 418, 424n9; *canon* (and κανών), 2, 3–8; *caritas*, 355–57, 385, 459; *causa*, 4, 5n15, 415; *concilium*, 432; *decretalia*, 18n72; *distinctio*, 418; *generalis* (of councils), 317–18, 424–25, 432–37, 443; *incestum*, 63–64, 65, 67–68; *infula*, 269; kinship terminology, 112, 114, 137n115, 277, 385; *misericordia*, 357–58, 358–61; *necessitas*, 99, 102, 275–76, 366, 385–86; *provincia*, 7, 8; *ratio*, 388–95, 419; *senior*, 5n15, 6n20, 7n28; *sponsa*, 418; *synodus*, 432; *tomus*, 96n45, 205, 216n174; *universalis* (of councils), 222, 425–26, 432–37; *universalis* (of pope), 212–13, 221–22

Canon law, sources of, 3–8, 18–19, 275–76, 316–17, 388–95, 416–20, 455–57; Bede on, 319–320, 392, 394n390; Burchard on, 435; *Caesaraugustana* on, 388–95; Deusdedit on, 207, 221–222, 282; Gregory VII on, 221, 432, 435; hierarchy of sources, 3–8, 12, 255–56, 356, 366; in prefaces, 8–12, 99, 389; Ivo on, 352–55, 388–95, 402; Leo IX on, 425–26, 434–35; *Polycarpus* on, 275–76; *Sancta octo* list of, 175, 317–18, 354, 392; *Tripartita A* on, 316–27. *See also* Bible, Church Fathers; councils; custom; decretals; Roman law

Canonical collections, different kinds of: 'anti-episcopal', 48–52, 122, 128n193, 163; 'anti-reform', 163, 383; 'farraginous', 19, 110, 336; Gregorian, 186–91, 235–36, 281–86; intermediate, 30–31, 40–41, 192–93, 197–98, 205–7, 216–17, 230, 224, 232–34, 234, 216, 253, 278–79, 282, 362; 'Poitevin', 256–66; pre- / post-Gratian, 1–2, 17–18, 180–83, 405–6, 410, 449; 'pro-episcopal', 21–22, 33, 52–59, 84, 86, 122, 290, 293, 334; 'reform collections', 88–89, 188n11, 190, 281–82, 300

Canonical collections, elements of, *see* appendices; *capitulationes*; comments; cross-references; glosses; opening canons; prefaces; rubrics